nes, Trails and Roads 1886

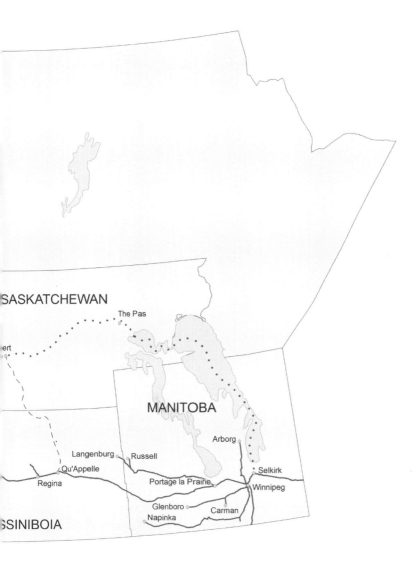

SASKATCHEWAN

The Pas

ert

MANITOBA

Arborg

Langenburg · Russell

Qu'Appelle

Regina

Selkirk

Portage la Prairie

Winnipeg

Glenboro · Carman

Napinka

SSINIBOIA

1:9,500,000

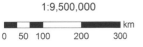
km
0   50 100   200   300

By: Anne Krahnen, CPRC, Nov. 2007.
Sources: Department of Natural Resources Canada. All rights reserved.
The Canadian Prairies: A History (Toronto: University of
Toronto Press, 1987), Map 9.

Immigration and Settlement, 1870–1939

edited by Gregory P. Marchildon

2009

UNIVERSITY OF
REGINA

CPRC PRESS

Canadian Plains Research Center
University of Regina
Regina, Saskatchewan S4S 0A2
Canada
Tel: (306) 585-4758/Fax: (306) 585-4699
e-mail: canadian.plains@uregina.ca
http://www.cprc.uregina.ca

Library and Archives Canada Cataloguing in Publication
Immigration and settlement, 1870–1939/edited by Gregory P. Marchildon.

(History of the Prairie West series ; 2)
Includes bibliographical references and index.
ISBN 978-0-88977-230-4

1. Prairie Provinces—Emigration and immigration. 2. Frontier and pioneer life—Prairie Provinces. 3. Prairie Provinces—History.
I. Marchildon, Gregory P., 1956- II. University of Regina. Canadian Plains Research Center III. Series: History of the Prairie West series ; 2

FC3242.9.I4I55 2009   971.2'02   C2009-901446-7
Cover design: The Noblet Design Group, Regina
Cover illustration,
Index prepared by Patricia Furdek (pafurdek@yahoo.com)
Printed and bound in Altona, Manitoba, Canada by Friesens.

Publisher's Note:
We acknowledge the financial support of the Government of Canada through the Book Publishing Industry Development Program (BPDIP) for our publishing activities. We also acknowledge the support of the Canada Council for the Arts for our publishing program.

Contents

Preface

Since its inception in 1975, *Prairie Forum* has been a major repository of articles on the history of the northern Great Plains, in particular the region encompassed within the current political boundaries of the three Prairie Provinces of Manitoba, Saskatchewan and Alberta. The purpose of the *History of the Prairie West* series is to make available the very best of *Prairie Forum* to as broad an audience as possible. Each volume in this series is devoted to a single, focused theme. Accompanied by dozens of new illustrations and maps as well as a searchable index, these volumes are intended to be of interest to the general reader as well as the professional historian.

The editor of the *History of the Prairie West* series is Gregory P. Marchildon, Canada Research Chair in Public Policy and Economic History at the Johnson-Shoyama Graduate School of Public Policy at the University of Regina campus. In addition to selecting and organizing the articles based upon their quality and thematic connections to the volumes, he has chosen a cover painting for each volume which reflects the essence of each period and theme.

Acknowledgements

The editor of the "History of the Prairie West" series wishes to thank the Canadian Plains Research Center for its support in making this publication possible. In particular, he wishes to thank David McLennan, CPRC Editorial Assistant, for the many hours he spent researching and selecting the additional images which were used to enhance the original articles included in this volume.

Introduction to *Immigration and Settlement, 1870–1939*

Gregory P. Marchildon

This volume of essays focuses on the nature and patterns of settlement in the Prairie West. The "opening" of the vast prairies for agricultural settlement is a key element in Canada's national narrative including the completion of the first transcontinental railway linking the provinces and territories of a vast country, immortalized in Pierre Berton's *The Last Spike*, and the pioneers from afar who settled on homestead quarter sections of land to eke a living out of the prairie soils. It is also the separate narratives of dozens of immigrant groups, whether English, German, Norwegian, Russian, Ukrainian, Hungarian, Chinese, or religious minorities such as the Doukhobours and Mennonites seeking basic freedoms, or First Nations who were moved onto reserves in order to open prairie lands for Euro-Canadian agricultural settlement. This land was intended to become the breadbasket of the world and make the 20th century belong to Canada.

Before this, there was a high degree of caution, if not scepticism, about the economic potential of the Prairie West. Responsible for conducting an investigation of the region for the British government in the late 1850s, Captain John Palliser concluded that the southern portion of the Canadian prairies was unsuitable for agriculture. His judgment was shared by Henry Youle Hind who explored the same region at roughly the same time but on behalf of the United Province of Canada. Both were visiting during a prolonged drought. Palliser viewed this region as an extension of the Great American Desert and it was his name that would identify this semi-arid zone as the Palliser Triangle. But the rains eventually returned, and a later explorer, John Macoun, concluded that most of the region was in fact good agricultural land.[1]

Following the one-chapter overview of the long-term patterns of immigration and settlement, subsequent chapters have been organized into four historical themes: the initial "opening" of the Prairie West by Euro-

Canadians; the policy of containing First Nations through the reserve system; the patterns of immigration and settlement including the establishment of de facto ethnic blocks as well as colonies based on religion, culture and language; and finally, relations among the varied ethnic groups in the Prairie West and the creation of a new identity in Western Canada.

Overview

Even if the notion of "geography as destiny" is a gross exaggeration of the impact of landscape on human settlement and culture, it is nonetheless the case that the natural environment in which people live exerts a profound influence on the way in which they live and see the world. Of course, it is the nature of human beings to change and reshape their landscapes so the influence really flows both ways. In their major overview, historical geographers John Lehr, John Everitt and Simon Evans present a sweeping view of the evolving prairie landscape from the first European contact with the Indigenous inhabitants of the region to the 1930s by which time all the most important features were in place. These features include agricultural settlement on the square homestead pattern set by the Government of Canada's legal survey system and the Dominion Lands Act, as well as the ethnic and religious settlement patterns shaped by the federal government. In large part because the Prairie Provinces were unique among provinces in the country in not having constitutional control over their public lands until the 1930 natural resource transfer agreements, the reshaped landscapes of Manitoba, Saskatchewan and Alberta would share much in common.

The "Opening" of the Prairie West

The building of the Canadian Pacific Railway (CPR) was a critical first step in facilitating settlement of the Prairie West. However, as historian Bill Waiser notes, the selection of the main line of the CPR was one of the "more controversial" decisions in Western Canadian history. Why the main line was ultimately located on the southern grasslands—straight through the heart of the Palliser Triangle—rather than the more northerly route through the fertile belt is the subject of Waiser's essay. While Macoun had done much to overturn Palliser's conclusion that the Palliser Triangle was a semi-arid desert unfit for cultivation, the real reason was to ensure that the CPR, rather than the American Northern Pacific Railroad, transported settlers moving into the southern portion of the Canadian Plains.

P.L. McCormick gives us a closer look at the logistical challenges faced by settlers wanting to move to the Prairie West. Before the railway, settlement was limited to the few who were willing and able to travel thousands of kilometres by horse-drawn or ox-drawn wagons to reach their homsteads. Even after the CPR mainline was up and running, however, homesteaders depended on prairie trails—generally the old trails used to provision the fur trade—to reach their new farms from the rail line. In other words, except for the very few families lucky enough to homestead a very short distance from the CPR mainline, rail plus prairie trail were both used by settlers. Indeed, the closer to the main rail line, the more likely were settlers to specialize in grain farming for export, and the further from the main line, the more likely were families to engage in mixed farming to ensure an indigenous source of food throughout the year. In McCormick's memorable words, the "aggressive frontier" of the southern grain farmer near the CPR line was a world apart from the "quiet frontier" of the mixed farmer. Eventually a spider's web of branch lines would spread throughout the west, reducing (though never completely eliminating) this dichotomy between the aggressive and the quiet frontier.[2]

Canada's other main continental railway was the Canadian National Railway (CNR)—Canadian Northern before it became a public company and absorbed the Grand Trunk, the Grand Trunk Pacific and the Intercolonial railway companies between 1919 and 1923. As Osborne and Wurtele point out in their chapter, the CNR's Department of Colonization and Agriculture played a key role in immigrant settlement in the interwar years and its corporate interest in maximizing immigration may have (at least eventually) influenced government policy to move in the direction of a more open and cosmopolitan policy and away from a highly discriminatory policy clearly favouring certain classes of Northern Europeans.

The so-called "opening of the West" was accompanied by an influx of single young men seeking railway, construction and farm labouring jobs. The bunkhouses and barracks where they lived bore witness to their bleak existences. Not surprisingly, alcohol and prostitution were common features in frontier life, and the latter in particular was tolerated by the North-West Mounted Police (NWMP). In Horrall's essay on the treatment of prostitution by the NWMP (later to be renamed the Royal Canadian Mounted Police), we find colourful characters right out of Hollywood—or perhaps more accurately, Deadwood—with stage names such as Diamond Dolly and Pearl Rogers. The relationship between the police and prostitutes would eventually change as the frontier gave way to established communities.[3]

A few of the established communities grew into larger, urban centres that influenced the economic, social and cultural development of the hinterlands around them. From the beginning, these centres vied to become the most influential cities in the region. Binnema's essay explores the extent to which these new cities operated within a hierarchy where one city could pay tribute to a larger centre yet still be the metropolis within a hinterland of its own. For decades, the metropolitan centre of the Prairie West was Winnipeg, a position that would not be forfeited until well after World War II. Other secondary cities such as Brandon, Regina, Saskatoon, Edmonton and Calgary emerged as major centres exerting their own, limited, influence on the people and towns around them.

First Nations and the Policy of Containment

Before settlers could stream into the prairies, the government had to get First Nations to surrender their control of enormous territories. This was done through eleven numbered treaties negotiated between the Crown acting on behalf of the Dominion of Canada and the First Nations then inhabiting what are now the Prairie Provinces, Northern Ontario, the Peace River district of British Columbia and the northern territories. The Indians of the northern plains agreed to move onto reserves in return for guarantees concerning education and medicine as well as agricultural equipment and training so that they could begin farming. From the perspective of First Nations, the purpose of the treaties was to gain self-sufficiency with the Crown providing assistance in the event of famine or disease. From the Canadian government's perspective, however, these same First Nations were now wards of the state whose interests were very secondary to ensuring rapid "white" agrarian settlement of the West, a point made clear in D.J. Hall's essay on the Canadian government's Indian administration. Clifford Sifton, the Minister of the Interior and Superintendent General of Indian Affairs in the Laurier government from 1896 until 1905, left Indian policy in the hands of an "Indian Affairs" bureaucracy with little sympathy for the aspirations of First Nations.[4] This laid the groundwork for the Canadian government's policy of re-taking lands reserved for Indians through the surrender of some 725,000 acres, contrary to both the spirit and the letter of the treaties. In addition, at the time of treaty, bands were told they could select their reserve lands at a later date, but the controversy concerning location and amount of land that would be actually allocated under this understanding continued until the latter part of the 20th century. From a First Nations' perspective, it seemed they "could have any land they wanted, as long as nobody else wanted it."[5]

Laurie Barron's chapter on the Indian pass system was designed to keep First Nations in their respective reserves and away from white communities. This system ensured the segregation of "Indians" from the new settler population in order to minimize friction with the Euro-Canadian majority but ran counter to treaty promises of no restrictions on movement. This policy

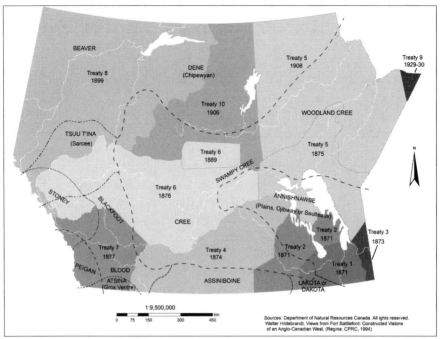

Plains Indians boundaries, ca. 1850, with later Treaty areas superimposed (courtesy of the Canadian Plains Research Center.

combined with a lack of investment on reserve, especially marked in terms of medical care and perhaps most disastrously through the church-based administration of residential schools, almost guaranteed second-class citizenship status for First Nations' peoples throughout the Prairie West.[6]

At the same time, Canadian Indian administrators encouraged farming on the reserves as a solution to what they termed the "Indian problem."[7] Farm colonies on reserves, such as the File Hills Farm Colony, were used to showcase the success of Canadian native policy. The author of a book on the experience of prairie reserve farmers, Sarah Carter describes the Potemkin village aspect of the File Hills colony relative to more typical reserve farms in Western Canada.[8] She also illustrates the connection between the farm colonies and their schools—industrial and residential—with their denigration of Aboriginal languages and their emphasis on farming knowledge and technologies.

Patterns of Settlement

The chapters in "Patterns of Settlement" give us a sampling of the types of immigrants and the manner in which they chose, or were directed, to settle in the Prairie West. Although the Canadian government, through its policies and its actions, preferred settlers from the United States, Great Britain and northern Europe, particularly Germany, Belgium, Holland and the Scandinavian countries, there were not enough immigrants from these countries to fill the prairies fast enough. As a consequence, settlers from Eastern Europe and the Russian Empire were eventually encouraged to take up homesteads in the Canadian West. The mass immigration of Ukrainians, for example did not begin until 1897.

John Lehr challenges the accepted historical view that Ukrainians were continually funnelled to inferior land in the prairies. While Canadian immigration agents exercised some coercion, it was actually Ukrainians who preferred to be settled in large ethnic blocks for cultural and linguistic reasons. More individualistic settlers from Great Britain, northwestern Europe, central Canada, and the United States, were more focused on economic factors in their selection of homestead lands.[9]

As Randy Widdis points out in his detailed account, American immigration to Canada is a misnomer in the sense that so many of the settlers who came from the United States were actually European-born or Canadian-born migrants.[10] He argues in favour of a view that the Canadian prairies were an extension of the American agrarian frontier. Of course, once the American Great Plains of the United States filled with settlers, this pushed both existing and new settlers into the "Last Best West" of the Canadian Great Plains.[11]

Jason Kovacs presents the fascinating story of Count Paul O. d'Esterhazy and the Hungarian colonies he promoted at Huns Valley in southwestern Manitoba and at Esterhaz (now Esterhazy) in what is now southeastern Saskatchewan. Contrary to the view that Esterhazy was a land speculator who fraudulently convinced his countrymen to move to the prairies, Kovacs argues that Count Esterhazy was motivated by more noble sentiments. Esterhazy tried his best to get the Canadian government to make an exception to its Dominion Lands Act settlement policy of dispersing land between settlers and the railways—a policy that actually encouraged dispersion and assimilation—in order to keep the settlements more spatially and culturally bound together.

Howard and Tamara Palmer trace the history of Dutch immigration to Alberta. The fifth largest ethnic group in that province, the Dutch made only a limited cultural impact because of their dispersed settlement patterns, their cultural affinity to Anglo-Canadian norms, and their rapid linguistic assimilation. Wayne Davies provides a very fine grained study of Welsh immigration to the Wood River area of Alberta. The Welsh were the least visible—culturally, religiously and linguistically—of the four nationalities of the British Isles. Despite their tiny numbers and their rapid assimilation through marriage, fragments of Welsh culture lived on for decades in at least some Wood River communities.

Since historians have not studied the history of immigration and settlement during the interwar years as intensely as the earlier era, Grant Grams' chapter on interwar immigration and return migration of German nationals is of great interest. Of all the Prairie Provinces, Saskatchewan had the largest German communities by the end of World War I, and therefore appeared to offer the best prospects for German immigrants to retain their culture and language. As a consequence, the province attracted a significant number of German immigrants after World War I. With the arrival of prolonged drought and the Great Depression, however, immigration slowed to a trickle. In contrast to the Canadian economy, the German economy improved with the stimulus of the Nazi remilitarization. As a consequence, a sizeable number of German immigrants, facilitated by the German government and its effective propaganda machine, chose to return to Germany during the 1930s.

Ethnic Relations and Identity in the New West

National and ethnic identities varied considerably across the Prairie West and the differences were most marked during the first phase of immigration during the great Laurier boom between 1896 and World War I. Cultural, religious and linguistic differences often produced divisions among the various ethnic groups. Since the Canadian business and political elite (outside Quebec) was British-Canadian, English-speaking and Protestant in religion, these were the values that were "instilled" in newcomers. But as David Smith also points out, "British" needs to be understood as made up of the English, Scottish, Welsh and two warring groups of Irish, while Protestant did not automatically mean the Church of England. Indeed, Presbyterians (mainly of Scottish heritage) were the single largest group in the Prairie Provinces by 1911 and, at least in Saskatchewan and Alberta, there were more Roman Catholics as well as Methodists than Anglicans. Thus, even the British-Canadian identity was far from homogenous.

It is misleading to look at other groups only in terms of their relationship with the British-Canadian establishment or norm, the typical way in which the "Sheepskin People" (the term applied to immigrants from Eastern Europe) were perceived by Clifford Sifton and his government officials. Beyond this, each group should also be analysed in terms of their relationship with neighbouring groups. Fred Stambrook and Stella Hryniuk do precisely this in their case study of the Jews, Poles and Ukrainians who settled and lived together in Manitoba during the first phase of homestead settlement. They discover that the members of these three groups were more diverse within their own communities, and more collaborative and harmonious across communities, at least before World War I, than previously thought.

This is not to say that Eastern Europeans did not encounter difficulties in this new society. The opposite is true—they faced enormous discrimination.[12] However, with the possible exception of the racism endured by Aboriginal residents, the group that suffered the greatest challenge from the bigotry of (Western) Euro-Canadian settlers, were African-Americans. Bruce Shepard tells the story of black immigration from Oklahoma to Saskatchewan and Alberta and the systematic discrimination, both from the Canadian government and their white neighbours. It is was not unusual for the men to be accused of rape without evidence. As a settlement group, they were often petitioned by their neighbours to return to the United States. In 1911, the federal Cabinet actually passed an order prohibiting any further "Negro" immigration for a time on the basis that their "race is deemed unsuitable to the climate and requirements of Canada."[13]

In some cases, ancient ethnic and religious antagonisms travelled with the new immigrants. One case in point was the sharp division between Irish Protestants with their British identity and Irish Catholics with their indigenous Irish identity. Michael Cottrell's essay explores the antagonistic relationship between the Orange Order and the Roman Catholic Church in Saskatchewan. The Orange Order with its hundreds of lodges, and its ideological anti-Catholicism, reached the pinnacle of its influence in the Prairie Provinces by the late 1920s and early 1930s. Irish Catholics responded to the Orange Order with their own society, the Knights of Columbus, while French-speaking Roman Catholics created their own secret society—La Patente—to fight British-Protestant discrimination.[14]

Not all was prejudice and division in the Prairie West. John Lehr illustrated how the geographical and ethnic mix of the region actually produced greater collaboration, by encouraging the unification of three distinct churches with their distinct followers. The establishment of the United Church of Canada through the merger of the Presbyterian, Methodist and Congregationalist churches was spurred by the need to cooperate in the settlement of the West. Of course, this co-operation was limited to congregations that shared language and an Anglo-Scots heritage. Moreover, one of the main motives behind union was to establish a more effective organization in order to better promote British-Protestant values and religions in the East European block settlements.

Notes

1. See Irene M. Spry, *The Palliser Expedition: An Account of John Palliser's British North American Expedition, 1857–1860* (Toronto: Macmillan, 1963); Doug Owram, *The Promise of Eden: The Canadian Expansionist Movement and the Idea of the West, 1856–1900* (Toronto: University of Toronto Press, 1989); and Donald Lemmen and Lisa Dale-Burnett, "The Palliser Triangle," in Ka-iu Fung (ed.), *Atlas of Saskatchewan: Second Edition* (Saskatoon: University of Saskatchewan, 1999), 41.

2. See, for example, John A. Eagle, *The Canadian Pacific Railway and the Development of Western Canada* (Montreal and Kingston: McGill-Queen's University Press, 1989).

3. On the NWMP transition to the RCMP, see Steve Hewitt, *Riding to the Rescue: The Transformation of the RCMP in Alberta and Saskatchewan, 1914–1939* (Toronto: University of Toronto Press, 2006).

4. See D.J. Hall's two-volume biography of Sifton: *Clifford Sifton: The Young Napoleon, 1861–1900* (Vancouver: University of British Columbia Press, 1981); and *Clifford Sifton: A Lonely Eminence, 1901–1929* (Vancouver: University of British Columbia Press, 1985).

5. See, for example, James M. Pitsula, "The Blakeney Government and the Settlement of Treaty Indian Land Entitlements in Saskatchewan, 1975–1982," *Historical Papers* 24, no. 1 (1989): 201.

6. On health, see James B. Waldram, D. Ann Herring, and T. Kue Young, *Aboriginal Health in Canada: Historical, Cultural, and Epidemiological Perspectives* (Toronto: University of Toronto Press, 1995), and on residential schools, see J.R. Miller, *Shingwauk's Vision: A History of Native Residential Schools* (Toronto: University of Toronto Press, 1996).

7. On the historical failure of this policy, see Helen Buckley, *From Wooden Ploughs to Welfare: Why Indian Policy Failed in the Prairie Provinces* (Montreal and Kingston: McGill-Queen's University Press, 1993).

8. Sarah Carter, *Lost Harvests: Prairie Indian Reserve Farmers and Government Policy* (Montreal and Kingston: McGill-Queen's University Press, 1990). Also see Sarah Carter, *Aboriginal People and Colonizers of Western Canada to 1900* (Toronto: University of Toronto Press, 1999).

9. On Ukrainian settlement from Russia (as opposed to the Austro-Hungarian Empire), see Vadim Kukushkin, *From Peasants to Labourers: Ukrainian and Belarusan Immigration from the Russian Empire to Canada* (Montreal and Kingston: McGill-Queen's University Press, 2007).

10. Also see Randy Widdis, *With Scarcely a Ripple: Anglo-Canadian Migration into the United States and Western Canada, 1880–1920* (Montreal and Kingston: McGill-Queen's University Press, 1998).

11. Jean Bruce, *The Last Best West* (Toronto: Fitzhenry & Whiteside, 1976).

12. See, for example, Frances Swyripa, "Negotiating Sex and Gender in the Ukrainian Bloc Settlement: East-Central Alberta between the Wars," *Prairie Forum* 20, no. 2 (1995): 149–74.

13. As quoted in R. Bruce Shepard, "Plain Racism: The Reaction against Oklahoma Black Immigration to the Canadian Plains," *Prairie Forum* 10, no. 2 (1985): 365–82.

14. See Brian E. Rainey, "The Fransaskois and the Irish Catholics: An Uneasy Relationship," *Prairie Forum* 24, no. 2 (1999): 211–17.

Overview

1.   The Making of the Prairie Landscape

John C. Lehr, John Everitt and Simon Evans

Most people who have never visited the Canadian west have images of vast wheat fields extending to a forever retreating horizon. It is a powerful image of a region where topographical uniformity is matched by social homogeneity, a land scenically and socially bereft, the empty space between the shield of Ontario and the mountains of British Columbia. The image may in part be the legacy of imperialistic propaganda, which at the turn of the century promoted the flat fertile lands of the prairie as the "Last Best West" awaiting exploitation by the sons of the British Empire, or it may have sprung from the efforts of writers who strove to capture something of the harsh haunting magnificence of what Rees so aptly called a "New and Naked Land."[1] This search for an overarching image which can capture the essence of the prairies yet still embrace their geographical extent, can unwittingly lead to a simplification of the region's rich topographical variety and a dismissal of its diverse social mosaic, which

"The Last Best West." A promotional poster produced by the federal Department of Agriculture, typical of the idealized promotional material used to draw immigrants to Western Canada (Courtesy of Library and Archives Canada/C83564).

together create some of the most intriguing and impressive rural landscapes in Canada.

In fact there is considerable variation in the physical geography of the prairies. The continental scale of the region often obscures this diversity as it is seldom evident at a local regional level. An appreciation of this variety can be gleaned from a consideration of prairie landscapes in southern Manitoba alone: the Red River bottomlands, the Carberry Sandhills, the Manitoba escarpment, the Tiger Hills, the Pembina Valley and the Grand Valley of the Assiniboine, and the rugged bush country of the Interlake district. Even on the prairies railways were not pushed over the land with bland disregard for topography. As elsewhere in Canada, terrain had a strong influence on line routing. For instance, tracks often followed the sides of the glacial spillways and river valleys to avoid excessive grades. At Minnedosa, despite the best efforts of engineers and surveyors, the track rose 264 feet in 4.5 miles, making an auxiliary pusher engine necessary for trains to make the westward grade.[2]

The Frenchman River Valley in southwestern Saskatchewan. To avoid excessive grades, the Canadian Pacific Railway constructed its line along this glacial meltwater channel between Eastend and Ravenscrag (Courtesy of David McLennan/University of Regina).

Many have struggled to come to terms with the prairies. Their size and lack of a clear cultural impress overwhelmed many early European visitors and immigrants. Rupert Brooke eloquently expressed the European's sense of anomie in this vast new land when he wrote "one can at a pinch do without gods ... but one misses the dead."[3] To Brooke, and to many newcomers, the prairies were too new, too vast, perhaps too raw and harsh, for them to understand. For the first generation of Europeans, in contrast to the Indigenous peoples, there was no sense of the sacred. As Brooke was clearly aware, it takes generations for a people to feel at home in a new land. It requires meanings to be carved into the landscape, icons to be created and recognized, and myths of place developed. The culture must be moulded by the place and place moulded by the culture.

The Ukrainian Greek Orthodox Church of St. Elia, built in 1953, is a long-recognized landmark in east-central Saskatchewan. Located in Wroxton, approximately 40 km east of Yorkton, the church's traditional onion-domed design clearly reflects the ethnicity of the community (Courtesy of David McLennan/University of Regina).

Even today the prairies defy easy description for the immensely varied ecological niches, and the diversity of European settlement in rural areas has produced a bewildering array of cultural landscapes.[4] Ranching landscapes, dry-farming landscapes, irrigated landscapes, and mixed farming landscapes may also carry the varied signatures of European settlement. Scattered among them are Indian Reserves, National and Provincial Parks, and other federally and provincially managed lands each of which have their own characteristics.

Before European colonization the picture was perhaps less cluttered.

Variety was found in ecological diversity. For the Aboriginal peoples these "new" lands—the prairies—were home. Places had meaning and deep connection with the lives of the people and the societies of which they were a part. Their feet trod lightly on the land and even the first Europeans to enter the region viewed evidence of their occupation as episodic and ephemeral. The anthropogenic nature of a fire-induced or fire-extended grassland would not have been immediately apparent to most observers. Their nomadic wanderings in pursuit of the bison and other game were marked only by transitory camps along water courses and by buffalo jumps. Before the first Europeans penetrated into the area in the mid-18th century, the cultural landscapes of the native peoples blended easily into the sweeping grandeur of the prairies.

In the 18th century competition for control of the fur trade between the Hudson's Bay Company (HBC), operating out of its Bay-side forts, and the Northwest Company, dispatching its voyageurs out of Montreal, drew the fur traders ever deeper into the western interior.[5] Leapfrogging each other in a desperate quest to intercept the choicest furs as the Native middlemen freighted them towards the European buyers, the companies established a network of posts along the rivers which were the lifelines of the trade. While the posts themselves were merely specks in the wilderness, the demands they created for supplies played a crucial role in opening the prairies to agricultural settlement.

Lord Selkirk's wish to provide a haven for his impoverished countrymen came to fruition only because the HBC saw the establishment of a farming community to be in its best interests. For decades the Company had regarded agriculture as antithetical to the efficient prosecution of the fur trade, but by 1812 had reluctantly come to see the creation of a farm settlement at the junction of the Red and Assiniboine as a useful source of supplies and a convenient bastion against the expansion of its rival. Although the settlement did not fulfil either role effectively, it did mark the first settlement of Europeans in the Canadian west and eventually it did demonstrate the viability of agriculture in what was then still a largely unknown or misunderstood region.[6]

For the Selkirk settlers the most pressing problem was survival in a new and unfamiliar environment. Miles Macdonell, Lord Selkirk's agent charged with allocating land for the settlers, used the river lot as the basic unit of land subdivision, perhaps copying from the Seigniorial system of Quebec, or perhaps simply adopting a pragmatic solution to the problem of securing an equitable division of the resource base. Along the Red River, Macdonell deviated from the Quebec example, widening the lots to accommodate settlers' needs on the inhospitable prairie and running the lots out on the grasslands for a distance of two miles.[7]

The long lot was adopted by the HBC as the only vehicle for settlement in the prairie environment. It was used by its Métis servants who assisted in its spread more than fifty miles westward along the banks of the Assiniboine and south along the Red River, virtually to what would become the United States border. Its practicability for technologically unsophisticated peoples led the Métis to take it with them when they moved westwards under the pressures of an encroaching civilization. Thus the river lot survey appeared at Fish Creek and Batoche in Saskatchewan, on the Seine River in Manitoba, and at the Victoria settlement on the North Saskatchewan in Alberta. Nevertheless, in terms of area the river lots were relatively minor scratchings in the topography of the west, although they were later to play a crucial role in shaping the street patterns of Winnipeg and other centres which arose decades later on the banks of the Red.

When the HBC formally ceded its vast territory of Rupert's Land to Canada in 1870 it was clear to the government of Canada that a number of things had to be set in place: the establishment of law and order, the building of a transcontinental rail link, the confinement of the Native peoples to their reserves, and the survey of the land.

A series of treaties was quickly concluded with the various nations native to the west (the Cree, Ojibway, Saulteaux, Chippawayan, Assiniboines, Dakota, Blackfoot, Blood, Piegan, and Sarcees), by which bewildered and powerless Natives were restricted to a fraction of the land across which they had wandered, on to reserves described by one Métis as "prisons of grass."[8]

The transcontinental rail link was not effected with the same dispatch but the survey had its framework cast by the Dominion Lands Act of 1872.[9] Its intent was clear and its effects indelible on the prairie landscape: land was to be occupied only by *bona fide* settlers, it was to be allocated in the most straightforward and administratively simple fashion, and the needs of corporations which were involved in the process were to be accommodated. To effect this mandate the government elected to use a version of the survey system used across the American west. Disregarding all topographical obstacles, and excepting only Indian reserves and the rare river lot surveys the land was subdivided into townships six miles square, each further subdivided into mile square sections which in turn were quartered into the 160 acres then thought to be the optimum size of a farm for a pioneer farmer.[10] To facilitate the building of schools two sections (11 and 29) were set aside as school lands, one and three-quarter sections were ceded to the HBC, and over vast areas of the west all odd-numbered sections were deeded to a variety of railway companies as payment in kind for building the track that was to open up and develop the west. Many of these lands were later acquired by the Canadian Pacific Railway (CPR) and the Canadian National Railway (CNR) when other lines were leased or bought.[11]

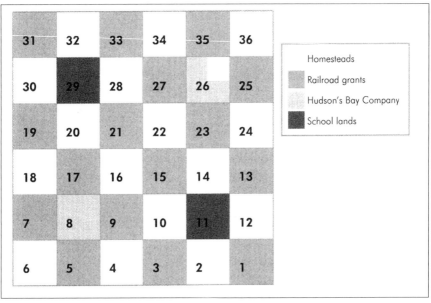

Township land appropriations (Courtesy of the Canadian Plains Research Center/adapted from *Understanding Western Canada's Dominion Land Survey System*).

The result was a framework which established the pattern of settlement over the greater part of the Canadian west. The requirements for the granting of homestead lands to prospective settlers—that they reside on the specific quarter section they were claiming for a period of at least three years, erect substantial buildings and make other improvements, and clear and break 30 or more acres of land—ensured the dispersal of settlers on individual homesteads, isolated and separated from the social benefits of close congregation. It did much to set the look of the landscape over almost all of the prairies until the present day, and certainly deepened the sense of isolation and alienation experienced by many immigrants carving out homesteads on the vast sweep of the prairies.

The survey itself was mechanistic. Its lines cut across the land with mathematical precision, oblivious to the demands of topography or vegetation. Survey lines and the roads which later followed in their train traversed swamps or muskeg with the same disregard with which they bisected sloughs, lakes, and rivers, cut through aspen groves and slashed through the boreal forest. Only the curvature of the earth, and the impossibility of reconciling plane and spherical geometry, extracted grudging adjustment of the grid and some deviation from its rigid symmetry. In its scope and inflexibility it was almost inhuman, but its lines of imperial measure determined the size of prairie farms and the placement of the road transportation network. As a framework which was antithetical to the congregation of people it sometimes did much to determine the failure of settlements established by groups bent on perpetuating a particular religious philosophy for whom close contact was a necessary element in maintaining group cohesion and religious enthusiasm.

Significant settlement of the west was closely tied to the building of the railways. Until the completion of the CPR transcontinental line across the Prairies in the early 1880s, almost all settlers, who still lacked the technological sophistication to launch out on to the open grasslands, were tied to the watercourses, hostage to the need for wood, water, and meadowland. In consequence, movement out on to the prairie was tentative and halting, clinging to the security of the aspen parkland. Even after the CPR was built, for some time settlement on the open prairie was strongly influenced by access to the lifeline of railway communications.

There were exceptions. Patterns of settlement of the Aboriginal peoples were not controlled by the Dominion Lands Act. Indian Reserve lands were held in trust by the federal government, so individuals had no legal basis for owning land within a reserve and band members could locate wherever they wished within the confines of the reserve. This gave the Native communities a distinctive and unstructured appearance heightened by the cultural contrasts in definition and use of family territory around residences which differentiated reserve lands from the surrounding agricultural landscapes. It would be naive, however, to believe that the reserve landscape was immune from governmental influence as the federal government determined many aspects of reserve life under the auspices of the Indian Act. Indeed, the very location and size of the reserves themselves was ultimately determined by the government. It has also been suggested that in some instances church workers may have influenced the location of reserves since they wished to see Aboriginal peoples concentrated around their missions.[12]

In southern Manitoba, as another example, in 1874 Mennonite settlers had located on a special reserve of land in the bush country east of the Red, which the government had set aside for their exclusive settlement. Dissatisfied with the quality of this land they began to drift across to the open grasslands west of the river in 1875, causing the government to allocate a second reserve of land of 19 townships for exclusive settlement by Mennonites.[13] In these two areas these settlers created one of the most distinctive cultural landscapes of western Canada. They were able to move on to the prairie only because they had adaptive strategies and a system of settlement which freed them from dependence upon easy access to wood for fuel, building, and fencing. Their open-field landscape reflected this. Granted exemption from the obligation to settle on a specific homestead and thus able to create villages, the Mennonites laid out their strassendorf villages along creeks as with Reinland and Altbergthal, or aligned them to the cardinal points of the compass as with Hochfeld and Schoenwiese. Land was pooled and divided into strips allocated by lot after the fashion of the medieval open field system. Stock was herded on village lands thereby eliminating the need for the fencing of fields.[14]

After a few years of settlement, soundly built log houses, built in the traditional Mennonite house-barn style and oriented at right angles to the street, replaced Semlins, the earth-covered dug-outs that provided shelter in the early days. Cottonwoods planted along the length of the village street eventually matured into the shade trees that became emblematic of the Mennonite villages. The unpainted houses and barns, or the choice of plain white and subdued green or blue trim where paint was used, reflected a philosophical aversion to ostentatious display, as did their austere church buildings, at first glance almost indistinguishable from the houses in the village.

Over 90 villages were established on the east and west reserves.[15] Many were short-lived, victims of the government's refusal to permit the Mennonite villages to hold land in common. As each village farmer then held title to a specific quarter section of land he had the option of withdrawing his land from the village system and establishing his farm on his own quarter section. Quarrels between neighbours, religious differences, or the dissatisfaction of progressive farmers with the slow rate of agricultural innovation, could prompt a decision to withdraw from the open field system and pursue farming on the quarter section to which legal title had been granted. When this occurred it meant not merely the loss of one member but the dissolution of the village open field system and, more often than not, the decline of the village. By the 1930s the open field system was dead, a victim of 20th-century agricultural technology and the legal restrictions of the Dominion Lands Act. Today scarcely more than a dozen villages, all on the West Reserve, are readily recognizable as Mennonite *strassendorfer*.[16] The Mennonite landscape, like that of most other ethnic groups who settled on the prairies, has never been static but is in constant flux. It has evolved, changed with advances in technology and shifts in social mores, eventually, and only grudgingly, adjusting to the pressures of assimilation and acculturation.

Many settlers who were enticed to settle in the Canadian West before the completion of the transcontinental railway did so in the face of the attractions of the American West: free homesteads, better communications, and a climate generally regarded as less severe south of the border. But the American West held less attraction for those groups who sought to maintain religious and

---

FREE FARMS

FOR MILLIONS.

.⊁ .⊁ .⊁

200 MILLION ACRES

Wheat and Grazing Lands for Settlement in Manitoba and the Canadian North-West.

.⊁ .⊁ .⊁

Deep soil, well watered, wooded, and the richest in the world, easily reached by railways. Wheat : Average 30 bushels to the acre, with fair farming. The Great Fertile Belt: Red River Valley, Saskatchewan Valley, Peace River Valley, and the Great Fertile Plains. Vast areas, suitable for grains and grasses, largest (yet unoccupied) in the world. Vast mineral riches: Gold, silver, iron, copper, salt, petroleum, etc., etc. Immense Coal Fields. Illimitable supply of cheap fuel.

The Canadian Government gives FREE FARMS of 160 ACRES to every male adult of 18 years, and to every female who is head of a family, on condition of living on it, offering undependencies for life to everyone with little means, but having sufficient energy to settle. Climate healthiest in the world.

For information, not afforded by this publication, address:

THE SECRETARY,

Department of the Interior, Ottawa, Canada.

[Mark envelope " Immigration Branch."]

THE COMMISSIONER OF IMMIGRATION,

WINNIPEG, MANITOBA.

Or to the Agent whose name and address are stamped on the cover of this publication.

Immigration Halls are maintained by the Government at Halifax, Quebec, Winnipeg, Lake Dauphin, Brandon, Prince Albert, Calgary, Red Deer and Edmonton, in which shelter is afforded to newly arrived Immigrants and their families, and every attention is paid to their comfort, FREE OF CHARGE.

"Free Farms for Millions." Advertisement in the *Nor'-West Farmer*, June 1897 (Courtesy of the Archives of Manitoba/N11695).

social integrity, since the Canadian government, in a desperate attempt to attract and keep such settlers, offered special exemptions and privileges to discrete social groups who were deemed to be settlers of superior potential, peoples such as the Mennonites in 1874–76, Icelanders in 1875, Mormons in 1887, and Doukhobors in 1899.[17] In contrast, agricultural groups that came later when the frontier was closed received no special treatment from government. The Hutterites, who first arrived in 1918, in order to establish their colonies were obliged to buy land from earlier settlers and in fact, in some cases had restrictions placed upon their land purchases.[18]

The degree to which patterns of settlement were transferred from the area of origin depended upon the social cohesion of the group and the extent to which the morphology of settlement was linked to the perpetuation of a particular way of life. Whereas Mennonites, Mormons, and later, Doukhobors, who saw nucleated settlement as vital to a continuation of religious zeal, transferred their distinctive village formations into the Canadian West, the Icelanders, to whom village settlement meant little in religious or philosophical terms, easily accepted dispersed settlement and made no attempt to circumvent the requirements of the Dominion Lands Act.[19]

Considering that the Dominion Lands Act had been framed with the family farmer in mind, it is ironic that it was the corporate cattlemen and not

Mormon pioneers of Cardston, Alberta, 1887 (Courtesy of the Glenbow Archives/NA-114-15).

Texas Longhorns. To the north of Vanguard, Saskatchewan, toward Hallonquist, lies the Turkey Track Ranch, once one of southern Saskatchewan's most massive ranching operations. The Turkey Track brand was registered in Texas in 1840, and A.J. (Tony) Day began using the brand in southern Texas around the end of the American Civil War in 1865. As the open range in the United States began to become filled with homesteads, the Turkey Track began moving northwards, entering Canada from South Dakota in 1902 with 600 horses and 25,000 head of cattle. An additional 8,000 yearlings and two-year-old steers were purchased in Manitoba and rebranded with the Turkey Track brand, augmenting the already enormous herd. The range extended form the CPR main line to the Canada-United States border, and from the Wood Mountain Plateau to the Whitemud (Frenchman) River Valley. After the loss of 10,000 head including 600 herd bulls during the catastrophic winter of 1906-07, and the opening of ranch lands to homesteaders, a significantly downsized Turkey Track operation was sold. In 1917, Percy Ostrander purchased the ranch and it remains in the Ostrander family to this day (Courtesy of David McLennan/University of Regina).

the homesteading wheat farmers who were among the first to benefit from its provisions. Large-scale ranching was promoted by the federal government as a plank in its National Policy,[20] which sought to develop the resources of the West and the manufactures of central Canada. A comprehensive legislative package was introduced in 1881 which enabled individuals or companies to lease up to 100,000 acres of grazing land for 21 years at an annual rent of 1¢ per year. The response was immediate and overwhelming. In 1882 alone, 154 applications for leases were received and 75 leases were authorized, covering a total of more than four million acres. The estimated number of stock on the range rose from 9,000 to 100,000 head in the five years between 1881 and 1886. These early leases formed a compact block of townships reaching northward from the international boundary to the Bow River. The line of the Whoop-Up Trail ran through the middle of this block and there was little penetration of the grasslands for more than 20 miles east of this axis. Indeed, Mormon homesteaders seeking land in Alberta close to the international boundary line almost despaired of finding suitable land for settlement, it "all being taken up under grazing leases." In 1887 they were very fortunate to find a cancelled lease which was then open for homesteading, which enabled them to establish the village of Cardston which became a bridgehead for later Mormon settlement in the area.[21]

This creation of a "Big Man's Frontier" in the West, promoted by Senator Cochrane and his colleagues, was potentially a dangerous political departure. Sir John A. Macdonald was undoubtedly swayed by a host of pragmatic considerations. At the time the possibilities for developing arable farming in the region were uncertain and obscured by lingering images of the Great American Desert. Furthermore, the price of wheat remained low and despite the government's best efforts the anticipated influx of settlers remained a dream.[22] On the one hand there was overwhelming evidence that stock-raising could be pursued successfully. Some Canadian ranch cattle were being used to meet treaty obligations but the bulk of contracts for feeding the North-West Mounted Police (NWMP) and the Indians were still being filled by Montana-based trading companies. This was uneconomic and politically unacceptable.

On the other hand, what would appear more statesmanlike than to encourage those who had already proved themselves as stockmen in the Eastern Townships of Quebec to establish large ranches on the underused grasslands of the North-West? In the short term, ranching would provide meat for local markets; in the longer term it would provide valuable freight for the trans-continental railway, and promised to further the flourishing trade in live cattle which had developed between eastern Canada and Great Britain.

Thus the growth of the range cattle industry in western Canada took place within a legal framework and was regulated on the spot by agents of the federal government.[23] Holders of grazing leases could rely on the support of the NWMP against the depredations of poachers and the incursions of "nesters." At the same time the Department of Agriculture actively promoted the sale of cattle to Great Britain and established regulatory controls to ensure that steers arrived in Liverpool and London in top condition. This comprehensive involvement of the Dominion government in regulating and promoting the cattle industry was in stark contrast to the situation in the United States where the cattle boom took place outside of any legal or regulatory framework, and where illegal fencing, fraudulent land acquisition, and range wars were spawned from the prescriptive right to "accustomed range."

Nevertheless, the government's unqualified support for the Cattle Kingdom was short lived. By the mid 1880s the infrastructure for development was in place and the cattle trade on a solid footing. As homesteads flourished in and around the grazing country, the political costs of supporting the cattlemen rose. After inspecting the ranching district, the Deputy Minister of the Interior remarked that "there can be no doubt that when the actual settler desires land for the purpose of making his house on it, it would be impossible, even if it were expedient, to keep him out..."[24] As tension between incoming settlers and ranchers threatened to erupt into violence the government's unequivocal support of the cattle compact weakened.

The contrasts between the carefully managed lease system in Canada and the "Free land" ethos espoused by those who occupied the high plains of the American West was paralleled by far-reaching social differences. Even before the lease legislation was passed, the scattering of small ranchers in southern Alberta were hardly typical frontiersmen. Many were former members of the NWMP, recruited from middle-class backgrounds in eastern Canada. The presence of Englishmen "of good family" was often mentioned by visitors, and the affectations of the English "remittance men" attracted the scorn of egalitarian humorists such as Bob Edwards of the *Calgary Eye-Opener*.[25]

The social landscape of the Canadian ranching frontier was thus radically different from the homesteading—or farming—frontier. Ranching required a larger initial investment than did farming and depended upon the work of hired hands, few, if any, of whom had the means to launch out into similar endeavours. Thus there was a division between the owner and employees which could not be replicated on the farming frontier where operations were smaller in scale and where the opportunities for independent farming made it virtually impossible to retain a stable team of farm labourers. Expatriate English gentry tried to replicate the rural squire–tenant relationship on the farming frontier, at Cannington Manor in Saskatchewan, for example, but were foiled by an inability to secure settlers willing to work for others when they could farm for themselves. Only ranchers under the umbrella of economic success and political power achieved by a handful of major cattle companies could attain a leisured lifestyle. Southern Alberta became the "land of the second son."[26]

Far from seeking release from the restraints of traditional ways, this society sought to recreate and preserve the kind of community in which they

An artist's conception of the village of Cannington Manor, drawn in part from an old photograph. Centre: riders have gathered to follow the Cannington pack of hounds in a fox hunt. The group of buildings to the right, from front to rear, are the Moose Mountain Trading Co., a store, R. Bird's house, the Mitre Hotel, a blacksmith's shop, and the wheelwright's house and shop. All Saints Anglican Church, left, built in 1884, still stands. Not shown in the sketch is the flour mill which stood to the west of the church (Courtesy of the Saskatchewan Archives Board/R-A8519-1).

had been nurtured, but which was fast disappearing in Britain. Professor L.G. Thomas, himself the son of an English-born rancher, observed: "Perhaps no pioneer community devoted so much time to amusement."[27] Horse racing and polo were pursued with vigour, while "shooting, fishing, and hunting, just the things which would bring you to the verge of bank-ruptcy at home, you can enjoy here for practically nothing."[28] Although the owners and managers of foothills ranches were vociferous in their hostility to incoming farm settlers, they welcomed young men and women who had good connections in eastern Canada or Great Britain. "Social contiguity" based upon common origins and shared educational advantages, and fostered by similar political and religious beliefs, meant that established ranch-ers tolerated newcomers of "the right sort" and even helped them to get started in stock rearing.

The flow of privileged male immigrants to southern Alberta was paral-leled by an influx of women who came west to look after their brothers, or to act as governesses, housekeepers, and companions.[29] Mrs. Agnes Bedingfeld, although a truly remarkable woman, was by no means atypical. The widow of a colonel in the Indian Army, she saw that there was little opportunity for a single woman of limited means in England, so she brought her son Frank to Alberta in 1886. She went to work for Fred Stimson at the Bar U Ranch on

Pekisko Creek as housekeeper. Frank quickly learned the essentials of ranching, and, when he turned 18, mother and son took out adjacent homesteads along the creek from the big ranch.

Over the next 30 years the Bedingfelds put down deep roots in Alberta. At first Frank continued to work for the Bar U, but gradually he acquired some cattle of his own which he ran with the main herd. The original log cabin was transformed into a comfortable eight-room ranch house, flanked with an attractive veranda and surrounded by a rough lawn and some native shrubs. Upstairs was a dormitory-like "bachelors' hall" to which the Bedingfelds welcomed young men from the neighbourhood. They would drift in from their cramped quarters to enjoy the amenities of a civilized home, some well-cooked meals off fine china, and music, cards, and an opportunity to share the news from around the district and from home. By the turn of the century the Bedingfelds owned 1,440 acres, and controlled a further 40,000 acres through leases. But their ties with England remained very strong: when Frank finally got married, his mother retired to Hertfordshire. Similarly, when war broke out in 1914, Frank pulled every string imaginable to get into uniform. In spite of the fact that he was 47 years old, and that the ranch was producing valuable mounts for the army, he was accepted as an ambulance driver. He served for two years in Belgium and France, and returned to Alberta in poor health in 1919. The family then sold their ranch and moved back to England. Frank Bedingfeld's story is all too typical, for the foundations of the privileged

The Bedingfeld ranch house at Pekisko, Alberta, 1911. The ranch was later bought by Edward, Prince of Wales (Courtesy of the Glenbow Archives/NA-2467-4).

ranching society were tragically shaken by World War I. Young men returned to the United Kingdom to rejoin their regiments, and the foothills communities sent a disproportionate number to the slaughter of the Western Front.

Both the collective "folk memory" of early ranchers, preserved in letters, diaries, and unpublished memoirs, and the scholarly treatment of this material by Thomas and Breen stresses the continuity and preservation in the Canadian west of many of the attributes of life enjoyed in the "shires" of Victorian Britain. Perhaps it was necessary to draw a stark contrast between the genteel ranching frontier of the Alberta foothills and the "Wild West" of Montana and Wyoming, in order to rectify an important omission in Canadian historiography. Many privileged immigrants quickly learned new skills and adapted to new ways. Adjustments had to be made to a life virtually without servants. Hard and sometimes dangerous manual labour, day in and day out, made the social and sporting occasions, so fondly recalled, all the sweeter. Women might relish "A flannel shirt and liberty," but they had to cope with a lack of inside plumbing, never-ending chores, and the loneliness which greater distances and a sparse population imposed. Although it would never have occurred to the members of the Anglo-Canadian ranching elite to think of themselves as an "ethnic group," they did possess distinct cultural traits, and these traits were no more immune to acculturation than were those of other groups. They underwent profound changes with every year they remained in Alberta.

This process was encouraged by the presence among them of men from all over the North American West. Frank Bedingfeld was taught his business by cowboys from south of the line like Herb Miller, Jim Minesinger, and the famous black cowboy, John Ware. Many of these men established ranches of their own and merged without difficulty into foothills society. Some, like George Lane, rose to become leaders of the Canadian cattle industry. Indeed, Lane's career seems almost too much of a romantic stereotype to be real. He was born in Des Moines, Iowa, in 1856, and followed his father northward to the Montana gold fields as a teenager. He worked as cowboy, teamster, and Indian scout during the 1870s, and, on the recommendation of the Montana Stock Growers' Association, Lane became foreman of the Bar U in 1884. Nearly 20 years later he was in a position to purchase a whole spread in one of the biggest land deals ever witnessed in the region. He went on to become a prime mover in the Western Stock Growers' Association, and, in 1919, he established The Cattlemen's Protective Association of Western Canada. As his political stature rose, so too did his position in the emerging new Canadian society of the foothills. He was the man chosen to host the

Edward, Prince of Wales (left, and later Edward VIII), inspecting cattle on his ranch in typical foothills country at Pekisko, Alberta (Courtesy of the Saskatchewan Archives Board/R-A352).

young Prince of Wales on his cross-Canada tour in 1919, and the rancher and the Prince remained friends until Lane's death in 1925.

This unique socio-economic milieu did not produce an equally distinct landscape. Indeed, evidence of human occupation in the foothills and grasslands of southern Alberta during the open range period was extremely limited. The legal boundaries of leases were unmarked and herds were separated according to their brands at the annual fall round-up. Only along the edges of streams, often masked by cottonwood and willow, were signs of occupation obvious. Long low ranch houses were surrounded by an assemblage of barns, corrals, and outbuildings. Few, if any, of these homes have survived, although many of the original ranch sites have been continuously occupied. From the 1890s onwards, the original log structures were replaced by more fashionable frame structures.[30]

Virtually the only other landscape elements associated with the ranching period were the shipping points from which the grass-fed cattle started on their long journey east, first to Point Levis on the St. Lawrence, then across the Atlantic to the British markets.[31] These shipping points were the Canadian equivalent of the roaring cow towns of the American Great Plains such as Abilene and Dodge City, and they too enjoyed brief periods of exuberant life before the extension of the railways or changes in shipping patterns left them high and dry. The tiny village of Cayley in the 1890s was briefly the biggest shipping point in the North-West Territories. Four or five corrals covered a considerable area, and could hold 1,000 head of cattle.[32] From these the steers were loaded up four chutes into waiting boxcars. After the fall round-up herds from the foothills ranches were driven to the railhead at Cayley where combined herds of up to 10,000 head were held along Mosquito Creek awaiting their turn to load. Each ranch outfit camped around its chuckwagon, with the annual get-together being the high point on the social calendar, especially after the Cayley hotel opened in 1903.[33]

The Cayley Hotel, circa 1903 (Courtesy of the Glenbow Archives/NA-1306-2).

The open range endured so long as the Canadian government failed to attract sufficient immigrants to effect the agricultural settlement of the West. Until the completion of the rail link between St. Paul, Minnesota, and Winnipeg in 1878 there was no easy access into the West and no access to eastern markets for western produce. The completion of the transcontinental railway in 1885 opened an all-Canadian route to the West but the expected rush of settlers did not materialize, and those who did arrive clung to the base of the parkland crescent—areas where wood, water and hay were readily available—to those districts which were easily accessible by rail or which had good prospects for the imminent development of rail communications.

Many of the homestead entries made between 1883 and 1890 in Manitoba and adjoining parts of the North-West Territories were made by speculators who made little contribution to the development or the settlement of the country. From 1874 until 1896 homestead entries averaged under 3,000 a year. In some years there were as many cancellations as there were new entries partly because of the provision for relocation if the initial homestead proved disappointing. At the same time the vacant lands of the Dakotas were being settled, in large part by emigrant Canadians. The *Winnipeg Times* lamented that the "trails from Manitoba to the [United] States were worn bare and barren by the footprints of departing [Canadian] settlers."[34]

The inability of the Canadian West to attract and hold its own country-men was a severe disappointment and a source of real concern. There was little that the government could do to change the environmental and economic deterrents to settlement in the West. To many prospective settlers the memory of the grasshopper plagues of the 1870s was still fresh and the uncertainty of cereal production was beginning to diminish only with the introduction of Red Fife wheat in 1885. Furthermore, transportation costs were high, manufactured goods expensive, wheat prices on the newly accessible world market were low, the cost of credit was high, and dry farming techniques were slow to be adopted. The government did little to overcome these restrictions when, in a quest for loyal, English speaking, Protestant, or easily assimilated immigrants, it directed its somewhat lacklustre immigration campaigns to the British Isles, north-western Europe, and the United States, areas which had already been thoroughly scoured for potential agricultural immigrants. The Department of the Interior was described, a little unfairly, by Clifford Sifton as "a department of delay, a department of circumlocution, a department in which people could not get business done, a department which tired men to death who undertook to get any business transacted with it."[35]

The CPR was also involved in the promotion of immigration and western settlement, for its road to financial stability lay in the agricultural settlement of the districts where it had selected lands granted to it for building tracks in the West, the sale of those lands, and the development of traffic from those areas. Despite an apparently energetic and imaginative campaign it had little success before 1896, probably because it also directed its efforts towards the northwestern European market in a time of general economic malaise. These immigration policies were geographically expressed in the rate and character of settlement in the west. Firstly, it meant that large areas of the West remained largely unsettled until the mid-1890s. Secondly, it was English-speaking settlers who predominated in the settled areas in the base of the parkland crescent and along the axis of the Canadian Pacific Railway, firmly establishing the social and linguistic character of early western agricultural society.

It is difficult, if not impossible, to separate the building of the railways from the building of the Canadian West. The railways—the CPR, Canadian Northern, the Grand Trunk Pacific and their subsidiaries—built tracks across the prairies in a frenzied determination to secure economic advantage. The result was an overbuilding of track, which was to become apparent in later years when uneconomic branch lines and spur lines were gradually abandoned.[36]

Paradoxically, the railways may well have served to impede the progress of settlement in the late 1880s and early 1890s. To encourage railway companies to build trackage in the West the federal government made grants of land for each mile of track laid. The CPR, for example, received 12,000 acres per mile for the first 900 miles of the transcontinental railway, 16.666 acres for 450 miles and 9.615 acres for 640 miles. In its own name alone the CPR acquired and retained 19,816,009 acres of Dominion lands; through its subsidiaries it acquired a further 6,239,453 acres for a total of 26,055,462 acres out of the 31,783,654 acres of railway land grants.

These lands were to be selected from areas "fairly fit for settlement" along the route of the transcontinental line and in areas far distant from it, as far north as Edmonton, Alberta, and Dauphin, Manitoba. To reduce their taxation obligations railway companies delayed selection of these lands for as long as possible, locking up from settlement huge tracts of territory until they had completed their selection. By 1896 only two million acres of a possible 28.5 million acres had been selected, hence much of the west was effectively removed from settlement by uncertainty over the exact status of areas where the railways reserved their right to choose land. The CPR, moreover, concentrated its land promotion efforts on its lands in the south. In the northern areas it delayed selection and occupation until "the cultivation and development of government land brought about a sharp appreciation in the value of railway sections."[37] The effect of Railway land policy was to concentrate attention on those lands which could be settled only by settlers with considerable capital and experience, the most elusive type of settler in the 1880s and 1890s.

The CPR had other effects upon the landscape and society of the West. Few westerners viewed the company in a benevolent light and it was hated for its policies by many. The apocryphal story of the farmer whose wheat crop was hailed out shaking his fist at the heavens and cursing the CPR illustrates well the relationship between the struggling farmer and the company upon which he was dependent. To many settlers the CPR appeared to be mercenary and merciless. Station halts, town sites and rights of way were planned to favour the best interests of the company rather than those of the districts being served. Town sites were placed on CPR-owned land even when existing town sites could easily have served the purpose. Nelsonville, at one time the third largest town in Manitoba, with a full range of social and administrative services, became a ghost town when the CPR terminated its branch line some four miles short of the settlement.[38] A small station halt at the head of rail at Dead Horse Creek, on a CPR section, eventually grew into the thriving regional centre of Morden. Similarly, in Alberta, the town of Vegreville, bypassed by the railway, had to move to the railway line or face extinction. Buildings were skidded across the prairie and the town reassembled. Such examples were legion. One settler boasted of burying his father three times: first in the riverbank for expediency, afterwards moving him to the local settlement's cemetery, then moving and reinterring him when the settlement relocated on to the railway.[39]

The power of the railway corporations was demonstrated by the lack of success of the HBC in establishing settlements on the properties which it had been granted. Unable to influence the routing of lines or the placement of halts, its attempts to create settlements were mostly failures.[40] In Manitoba, for example, on the west bank of the Red River at the international boundary, the HBC surveyed the townsite of West Lynne. The CPR ran its line down the east bank and established its own settlement at Emerson opposite West Lynne, effectively blocking the HBC's endeavour.

A change of government in 1896 and the appointment of Clifford Sifton as Minister of the Interior in 1897 was a turning point in western settlement. Laurier's Liberal administration was undeniably fortunate that its assumption of power coincided with a world-wide economic upswing, but there can be no doubt that the vigorous policies implemented by Sifton accelerated the rate of western settlement and, more importantly, changed the nature and social composition of the immigration into the West.

Sifton pursued agricultural immigrants with a single-minded determination, redirecting recruitment efforts towards the non-Protestant European peasant heartland. At the same time he still actively sought Canadian and American farmers who he thought to be "of the finest quality and the most desirable settlers."[41] He consistently opposed recruitment of artisans from the cities and towns of Europe, whether British or not, because of their ambivalence towards farm work and their tendency to give up on farming and drift into the towns and swell the ranks of the unemployed.[42] Speculation was discouraged and land was opened for settlement by Sifton's decision to cancel time sales. By forcing the railway companies to complete their selection of land he opened vast new areas to homestead settlement within three years.[43] During his tenure as Minister (1897–1905) the map of the social geography of the prairie West was redrawn as peasants from multi-ethnic Austria-Hungary joined the stream of immigrants to Canada. A polyglot crowd of Ukrainians, Poles, Finns, Magyars, Scandinavians, ethnic Germans, Belgians, French, Jews and others, mingled with the North Americans and British seeking free lands across the West.

A Bukovinian mother and child in Sheho, Saskatchewan, circa 1907 (Courtesy of the Archives of Manitoba/N9621).

With only rare exceptions they settled within the framework of the Dominion Lands Act, each family residing upon its own homestead, scattered and isolated from each other.

From an administrative perspective the European occupation of land in western Canada may appear to have been highly structured and exceptionally orderly. For the most part it was, at least in the view of those charged with the task of accomplishing the process. All immigrants, regardless of their nationality, were eligible to select land wherever they wished, provided that they chose land which had been declared open for settlement, that is, land not set aside for any special purpose by the government whether as a railway land grant, Indian Reserve, Timber Reserve or the like. Officials of the Department of the Interior were stationed throughout the West to facilitate the land selection process and to channel specific ethnic groups into districts where the government thought the physical environment would be to their liking, and perhaps more importantly, the nature of the land was such as would permit cash-poor settlers to survive without assistance from the government.

Even English-speaking settlers with capital found homesteading in the West a stressful process. Without experience of prairie farming and often without significant agricultural experience at all, many settlers chose their homesteads on emotional rather than on rational grounds, picking a homestead because the topography was reminiscent of "home" or because of the proximity of friends or relatives.[44] The prairie environment was new, strange and unexpectedly severe, and it often spawned what appeared to be bizarre decision-making behaviour. One westerner recalled that "One of the strangest land seeking phenomena was the way in which experienced farmers, after trailing over innumerable townships in which there was nothing to offend the plough, would choose some stony lot which, compared to what they might have had, was too poor to raise a disturbance on it."[45]

Many such decisions in settlement were, in fact, not at all irrational. Any settler who was not well endowed with capital had to evaluate land from the perspective of its potential to sustain a family in the short term rather than to offer the promise of economic gain in the long term. Cash-poor settlers sought out land which offered a wide resource base for subsistence agriculture. Wood, water, and meadow were eagerly sought out. Wood was vital for building, fencing and fuel. Settlers from Eastern Europe had often had to pay exorbitant prices for wood in their homeland and were anxious to ensure that their homesteads offered a plentiful supply. This obsession with wood seemed strange even to experienced immigration officials. In 1897 Immigration Commissioner William McCreary confided to the Deputy Minister of the Interior that "The Galicians are a peculiar people; they will not accept as a gift 160 acres of what we should consider the best land in Manitoba, that is first class wheat growing prairie land; what they want is wood, and they care but little whether the land is heavy soil or light gravel; but each man must have some wood on his place."[46]

Even features of the environment ignored or shunned by settlers intent upon an immediate entry into the market economy were highly prized. Marshland provided slough grass, useful for thatching or for fodder, water for cattle and a habitat for game birds. Scrub or bush, in addition to small and occasionally large game, provided fruits, nuts, and berries, as well as the chance to gather mushrooms, giving dietary variety and easily

Using what was readily available, Joe Wacha and his wife construct their home four miles north of Vita, Manitoba in 1916 Courtesy of the Archives of Manitoba/N9631).

preserved and highly regarded culinary items. In the Interlake district of Manitoba, for example, Ukrainian and Polish settlers gathered three types of mushroom, wild raspberries, strawberries, Saskatoon berries, chokecherries, wild plums, and hazel nuts.[47]

Other facets of the environment which did not concern the wealthier settler greatly interested the peasant immigrant. Heavy clay, sand, stone and the presence of willow and juniper were all useful for construction of houses in the traditional style and enhanced the desirability of a homestead in the eyes of such settlers.[48] In his study of Finnish settlement in Canada Van Cleef remarked that "a little muskeg now and then is not unwelcome to a Finn,"[49] but he might well have included all peasant immigrants in his comment.

Environmental preferences, or the lack of financial reserves, were important in steering Ukrainian, Polish, and Romanian settlement to the bush country of the aspen parkland belt, where they established bloc settlements running in a discontinuous arc from southeastern Manitoba, through Saskatchewan, into central Alberta.

For foreign settlers, especially the peasants from Eastern Europe, the entire process of immigration and settlement must have been bewildering and chaotic. Without an understanding of English, often illiterate, or literate only in the Cyrillic script, unfamiliar with the social mores and institutions of the host country, most "foreign" settlers clung to the security of the familiar. With dogged determination they sought out the company of their friends, kin, and countrymen who had preceded them: people who appraised land as they did and who by their very survival and progress had affirmed the validity of their shared perceptions.

Within the ethnic blocs that emerged as a result of chain migration there was surprising geographical diversity based on the grouping of immigrants according to family loyalties, their village, district, and province of origin. Within the Ukrainian settlements, for example, immigrants from the province of Galicia generally settled apart from those from the province of Bukovyna, if indeed they settled together in the same bloc.[50] This preference for those of like background, who shared adherence to the same church, spoke the same language or dialect, practised the same customs, and who held the same weltanschauung, eventually led to a replication in microcosm of the basic social geography of their homeland within many of the "foreign" districts.

In view of the social and economic insecurity of most land seekers it is hardly surprising that there were very few primary decision makers. Analyses of the settlement process of Ukrainians, Icelanders, Mennonites, and Belgians as well as the memoirs of pioneers reveal the intense magnetism of the known and familiar upon newly arrived immigrants who chose destinations on the basis of the presence of relatives or acquaintances. Many were content to remain ignorant of, or shunned, alternative opportunities. In 1898, for example, Cyril Genik, himself a Ukrainian immigrant, then working as an interpreter for the Department of the Interior, made passionate but unsuccessful attempts to persuade his arriving countrymen not to blindly follow their relatives into Manitoba's Interlake, one of the worst districts then open for homesteading. Peasant immigrants, especially, tended to rank social factors above physical ones when evaluating locations for settlement. Colonisation Officers working in the field were frustrated by their inability to persuade many Slavic immigrants to look after their own economic best interests and cut away their cultural ties. Immigration Commissioner William McCreary wrote of the Ukrainians:

> They are apparently an obstreperous, obstinate, rebellious
> lot. I am just about sick of these people. They are worse than
> cattle to handle. You cannot get them, by persuasion or
> argument to go to a new colony except by force. They all
> want to go where the others have gone...[51]

This tendency to hive together, by no means confined to the Ukrainians, led to the geographic clustering of immigrants of various ethnic groups in specific localities. Together with the special reserves set aside for cohesive groups such as the Mennonites and Doukhobors a mosaic of ethnically derived landscapes emerged from the frontier of settlement. The geography of this mosaic was complex, shaped by a multiplicity of forces which defy easy description. Nevertheless, some broad formative factors may be identified: chain migration, ethnic stereotyping and the attempts of the federal government to steer immigrants of certain ethnic origins towards specific land types thought to be best suited to their needs, political concerns to prevent the growth of large solid blocks of "foreign" settlement which would be resistant to assimilation, and the environmental preferences of the immigrants themselves.

Within these bloc settlements pioneer settlers created landscapes in the image of those they left behind in their homelands. The design, arrangement, decoration and orientation of dwellings and farm buildings, religious architecture, fence types, agricultural practices, and some crops, were all transferred to the new land. In many of the ethnic bloc settlements the cultural landscape was more reminiscent of that of eastern Europe or Russia than that of Ontario or Great Britain. Writing of her visit to the Ukrainian district of Lamont, Alberta, in 1911 an Ontario journalist observed that:

> When less than five miles of our journey [from the village of Lamont] were covered we entered a district as typically Russian as though we had dropped into Russia itself. Here and there beside the winding trail loomed up groups of buildings, low browed, and heavily thatched. These always faced south. The houses were all of rough logs, rough hewed and chinked with a mortar made of clay and straw. Some were plastered on the exterior, and almost all had been lime washed to a dazzling whiteness.[52]

Survival of folk customs and the material culture of the "foreign" immigrants was fostered by the size of the blocs of ethnic settlement, the degree to which they were isolated from assimilative influences, and the heterogeneous character of many of them. In most, if not all, Ukrainian settlements, the cultural landscape was not merely Slavic or Ukrainian, although it may have been categorized as such by Anglo-Canadian observers. To the pioneers who produced the landscapes, nuances of house design or decor bespoke ethnographic and regional geographic origins just as surely as the design and symbols of their Byzantine domed churches announced their religious affiliation.[53]

The peasant settlers from central Europe played no role in establishing the nascent urban centres of the West. That role was the preserve of the powerful—the railway companies who decided on the routings of tracks and the points where station halts would be made. In some districts it was only after several years or more of settlement that the railway passed through. By that time some tiny small "crossroad" settlements of four farms, one of which may have had a small store or the local post office, may have emerged but seldom anything more. The railway quickly transformed the situation. In the Ukrainian district of Stuartburn in southeastern Manitoba, for example, the railway pushed through in 1906 and a series of halts were established at regular distances along the line. None corresponded in any way with the shadowy economic and social geography that was beginning to emerge from pioneer society at the time. Halts were named by surveyors and construction bosses: Gardenton, Vita, Caliento, Sundown, Menisino, names which eclipsed the toponyms bestowed by those who first settled the area: Sirko, Shevchenko, and Arbakka.[54] Although not Ukrainian in name, these station halts, and others like them in other bloc settlements through-out the West, became socially Ukrainian, as they attracted people from the surrounding area and assumed the role of local service centres.

A woman working in a field near the Bukovinian (Bukovynian) church near the hamlet of Gardenton, Manitoba, c. 1915 (Courtesy of the Archives of Manitoba/N9614).

In the hamlet of Gardenton the *lingua franca* was Ukrainian as spoken in the Kitsman, Zastavna, and Chernowitz districts of northern Bukovyna; the women favoured the traditional Bukovynian costume with an embroidered blouse, long wrapped skirt and ornate head-dress or kerchief (babuska), and the social round was governed as much by the placement of holy days and festivals according to the Julian calendar used by the Orthodox Churches as it was by the timetables and calendars of the Protestant Canadian elite. Within the hamlet domestic architecture bore few clues as to the prevailing culture. The settlement's main street, fronting on to the single line of the

Canadian Northern Railway, boasted half a dozen false-fronted wood frame buildings and a standard design Canadian Northern station. Behind the Main Street lay a cluster of nondescript frame dwellings, most with a distinctive tall *zhuravel'*—well sweep—in the yard alongside stacks of cordwood for winter use. Until 1935 Gardenton had no church. In 1899, only three years after arrival, the settlers in the district had built a log church some three miles west of the point where the railway chose to locate their station. Almost all of those who helped to build this church were Boykos from the villages of Onut and Bridok in the Zastavna district of northern Bukovyna, hence they built their church in the traditional three-chambered Boyko style. The poor state of the roads, which were virtually impassable during the spring thaw, hastened the reorientation of much social activity to points served by the railway, thus the initial site of the "Onutska" church, as it was known, increasingly became less convenient. A new wood frame church, once again built in the Ukrainian style, although larger and showing traces of the incorporation of alien influences, was built in the centre of Gardenton in 1935. It was, and still is, the largest and most imposing building in the settlement, for Gardenton, unlike most settlements in the prairies, never received enough grain to warrant the construction of an elevator.

In the surrounding countryside the landscape for many years was a rough, crude, unpolished transplanted version of the landscape of Bukovyna and Galicia.[55] Hacking a farm out of the rough bush country was a painstakingly slow process for peasant settlers who generally lacked capital and were obliged to devote precious time to "working out" or cutting cordwood for sale in order to generate enough cash to buy basic supplies so as to ensure survival through the winter months. Small clearings were scratched out of the woods with tremendous effort: stones had to be moved, broken into movable pieces, or buried; trees felled, the stumps dug out and hauled away; and roots grubbed out by hand, before ploughing could begin. Even with the entire family involved in the work it was difficult to clear and break more than a few acres each year.

Typical, perhaps, of thousands of Ukrainian, Polish, and Romanian immigrants who took up homesteads in the aspen parkland belt was Iwan Mihaychuk who homesteaded in the Arbakka district of Manitoba in the early years of the century. In 1900, faced with a depressing future for his children, Iwan sold his three-hectare farm in Bridok, Bukovyna, and immigrated to Canada. He was lured by the promise of a $10-homestead and enthusiastic reports of opportunity in Manitoba received by friends and relatives who had kin already settled in southeastern Manitoba.

During the long journey across Canada, Wesley Speers and Kyrillo

Genik, the Crown agents who accompanied the Mihaychuk's party, attempted to convince Iwan to head out to Yorkton, Saskatchewan, where good land was available for homesteading. In southern Manitoba, they cautioned, all the better lands had been taken. All lands left were of inferior quality. The attraction of friends and kin was a powerful one, however, and on arrival in Winnipeg the Mihaychuks headed south to the Stuartburn district of southeastern Manitoba, where some of their former neighbours and his wife's relatives had homesteaded. There, while searching for a vacant homestead, he rented a cabin and subsisted by digging and selling snakeroot (seneca root), picking nuts and berries and harvesting some vegetables grown in their garden. In 1901 Iwan selected and applied for a homestead, built a small house on it, then abandoned his claim when he realized that the quarter was "stony and low swamp land" which, with only two hectares of dry land, he could not hope to farm successfully.

After spending a winter with relatives the Mihaychuks trekked eastwards and squatted on a quarter section in a township not officially open for settlement. With his wife and eldest children Iwan cleared and broke just under a hectare of land which was planted in vegetables, wheat and barley. To obtain cash to buy oxen Iwan "worked out," cut cordwood on his quarter, and with his sons, picked snakeroot to trade for supplies at the local store.

In 1903 his land was officially opened to settlement and along with a number of other squatters, some of whom were relatives who had come out to join him, Iwan quickly made his entry legal.[56] Although the family now had some degree of security, living conditions were still harsh. Furniture in the small cabin was hand made and minimal. As other Ukrainians entered the district seeking homesteads the Mihaychuks found themselves accommodating them until they could erect their own shelters. Up to 30 people all crowded together on the floor of the small two-room cabin, with hay as a mattress, their own clothes for covers and the Mihaychuk's calf wandering loose among them.

Clearing and breaking a few hectares of land each year the Mihaychuk family were able to obtain the patent to their homestead in 1907. By that time they had fenced their quarter with a three rail wood fence, had 15 hectares under cultivation, mostly in wheat and barley with some vegetables, and had effected improvements valued at $531, including a house, barn, granary, pig house and a well.[57]

As the settlers became better established cropping patterns shifted. Increased acreage of oats denoted the replacement of the ox, the predominant draught animal in the pioneer phase, by horses. Hemp, grown widely in the early years for its fibre and oil-bearing seeds, diminished in importance as store-bought cloth replaced hand-woven material and commercial cooking oil displaced homemade hemp oil in settlers' homes. Sickles and scythes, employed in the first years by some, became impracticable and gave way to ox- or horse-drawn machinery as the area under cultivation expanded. Even before World War I steam-powered equipment made an appearance followed shortly thereafter by gasoline tractors. In the more prosperous districts, but not in Gardenton or Arbakka, wheat became sufficiently important in the local economy to warrant the building of an elevator, an emblem of the integration of the local pioneer economy with the wider regional market.

By 1914 the Mihaychuk family was sufficiently well established to build a large, two-storey wood-frame house on their property. It bore no hint of the Ukrainian background of its builder and marked the beginning of the erosion of the Ukrainian pioneer landscape in the Arbakka district.

Between the southern margins of the bush country of the aspen parkland belt, where mixed farming prevailed, and the northern limits of the ranching country on the short-grass prairie of southwestern Saskatchewan and southern Alberta, lay the prairie landscapes which fascinated scores of writers who, with varying degrees of success, have striven to capture its haunting magnificence. Sinclair Ross, Robert Stead, and W.O. Mitchell have portrayed a land devoid of trees, open, windswept and forbidding, a land which could shatter dreams and break the hardiest of souls. Yet despite the dramatic physical contrasts between the open prairie and the parkland there are many similarities in the cultural landscapes, the process and the chronology of settlement.

Whereas in the parkland mixed farming prevailed, on the open prairie wheat was king. The rapid expansion of homestead settlement onto the open grasslands was dependent upon railway linkages to import the necessities of life and to haul grain to the lakeshore and oceanfront terminals. Barbed wire, the chilled steel plough and the wind pump all played crucial roles in the European expansion onto the short-grass prairie which eventually brought the ranching era to an end.

In the parkland it was possible for a peasant settler bent on subsistence agriculture to begin farming armed with little more than an axe, hoe, spade, scythe and perhaps $20 or $30 in cash. Needs and costs were greater on the prairie. Estimates of the costs of prairie settlement vary considerably, but the capital needed in the late 1880s for a man with a wife and four children to start farming was placed by pioneers in southwestern Manitoba at a low of 90 to a maximum of $1,000.[58] Settlers on the grasslands, like their counterparts in the parkland "worked out" to generate capital to effect improvements on their farms. Prairie settlers, in a less physically diverse environment than their parkland counterparts, lacked a similar range of options for generating capital. Consequently, even if initially better provided with capital, they were obliged to seek off-farm work equally frequently, if not more so. Nevertheless, progress was generally more rapid for the grassland settlers. They entered the market economy quickly and did not face the same difficulties of clearing land before it could be broken.

Few settlers on the northern margins of the parkland belt could have hoped to match the progress of settlers from Ontario who settled in the Abernethy district of Saskatchewan. With the critical advantage of having arrived first and with choice of the best lands, they were also favoured by the liberal provisions of the Dominion Lands Act then in force. Until 1884 settlers were allowed to make a pre-emption on a second quarter for $2.50 an acre after receiving the patent to their first homestead, after which they were permitted to make an entry for a second homestead. For some settlers the total cash outlay to acquire three quarters of prime farmland was only $420. Some of the more aggressive settlers in this district used these exceptional circumstances to acquire large holdings and to thereby secure a springboard to launch into large-scale farming within an unusually short period after settlement. W.R. Motherwell from Lanark, Ontario, who settled in the Abernethy district in 1882, was representative of this type of settler.

First taking out a homestead in the Pheasant Hills district, Motherwell first built a modest log house, hauling in the timber from nearby woods. Others, further away, built sod houses, obtaining the building material simply by ploughing the prairie turf. By 1890 Motherwell had broken 100 acres and in the following year he pre-empted a neighbouring quarter.[59] Years of collecting field stones enabled him to have a stonemason erect a stable in 1896 and a large fieldstone house in the following year. He also began a program of tree-planting on his farmstead in order to provide some shade, shelter from the wind and soil conservation. As a consequence, the Motherwell farm, like those of other Ontario settlers, became "an oasis-like haven in an otherwise barren prairie landscape … a concrete example of the Ontarian attempt to transplant a whole system of values, institutions, and even physical environments to the prairie."[60]

Like most successful farmers on the prairie Motherwell diversified his operation so as to be less dependent upon wheat as the primary crop, a crop for which the price was notoriously unstable, and which was subject to the vagaries of the prairie climate. A bushel of No. 1 Northern, for example, brought 89¢ in 1914, $2.24 in 1918 and $1.07 in 1923.[61] In 1888, Motherwell's frozen wheat crop yielded a paltry 300 bushels, but he was able to cover expenses by selling $200 worth of pork. In 1893, when wheat prices plummeted, he expanded his herd of cattle to 50 head.

By 1912 Motherwell's farm had grown to six quarter-sections, one of the largest farms in the district. The "handsome" stone house was set in "impressively landscaped grounds" which included a lawn tennis court, ornamental flower beds and cropped hedges. In contrast Motherwell's son, who was given a half-section by his father in 1913 ran a more modest holding with a stucco farm house in sharp contrast to his father's ostentatious home just a mile down the road. Unable to acquire land with the ease of his father he concentrated instead upon supplying dairy milk to the local village population. He reflected the reduced ambitions of those who entered farming in the time of decreasing opportunity.

"Lanark Place." This was the name W.R. Motherwell gave to his farm, now known as the Motherwell Homestead National Historic site, which is located 4 kilometres south of present-day Abernethy, Saskatchewan. He chose the name to remember his Ontario birthplace. Over the years Motherwell had collected fieldstone from his fields and the nearby Pheasant Creek coulee, and in 1896 he hired a local stone mason, Adam Cantelon, to build a stone stable. In 1897, Cantelon constructed Motherwell's large Italianate-style house, which replaced an earlier home made of logs. The massive superstructure of the red, Ontario-style barn in the left of the photograph was erected upon the stone stable in 1907 (Courtesy of David McLennan/University of Regina).

Nevertheless, even at a time of reduced opportunity, literate and English-speaking farmers still had an edge through their adoption of new farming techniques. In the Abernethy area farmers who were successful showed a capacity to adjust to the exigencies of dry-farming by adopting the practise of summer fallowing and other new approaches advocated by the Dominion

Experimental Farm, established at Indian Head in 1887. Motherwell's progress was not matched by German settlers who settled the nearby Neudorf district after 1889. By then the liberal homestead regulations had changed and the better lands in the area had been taken by Ontario settlers. In many cases lands entered then abandoned by Ontarians were reoccupied by Germans who also realized their inferior nature after a few years and abandoned them in their turn. The penalties of late arrival, the encounter with more strict regulations, and the diminished choice of homestead land, were compounded by the Germans' unfamiliarity with English and ignorance of the complexities of the Dominion Lands Act.

Given their economic and social handicaps, it is not surprising that Motherwell's German neighbours did not emulate his rapid rise to economic security and political influence. Even English-speaking settlers less advantaged than Motherwell had a tough time of it. The 1890s were particularly hard years for newcomers who had not had a chance to become financially able to withstand the effects of crop failures and depressed wheat prices. In 1895, according to an account in the *Qu'Appelle Progress*, one area bachelor farmer lost his yoke of oxen, suffered the strangulation of his mare and experienced a complete failure of his grain crop. He was forced to survive on a diet of bread and tea.[62]

The agricultural progress of the west was dependent upon the integration of the region's economy with the international wheat economy. The "grain trade of the western provinces [had] made its first hesitant step" in 1876 with the export of 857.17 bushels of wheat,[63] but was soon to dominate the local and regional landscapes with "King Wheat" building his kingdom and becoming a critical element of Canada's National Policy. Growth of the prairie settlement was fuelled, in part, by the burgeoning demand for wheat and flour in the industrialised nations of the North Atlantic world. The largest market was Great Britain where the food deficit rose consistently through the 19th century until, by 1900, domestic suppliers could furnish only one sixth of total demand. Agricultural progress in the west was thus dependent upon the integration of the region's economy with the international wheat economy. Corporate influence came to bear strongly on the prairie landscape in wheat-growing areas, particularly in the 500 or so small towns and villages which were "the mainstay of prairie farm society."[64] Thus within them a "strong degree of sameness" prevailed, reflective of the penetration of corporate organization into the establishment and management of the prairie urban network. Prairie townscapes were dominated by the railways, which standardized their townsites through the division of land, the layout of streets and the placement of the railway station in relation to the main street. Interlocking directorships and monopolies, between railways, banks, flour milling and grain elevator and lumber companies, together with the dominance of a small number of social institutions—the Women's Institute, the Women's Christian Temperance Union, the Masons, Foresters, Oddfellows or Loyal Orange Lodge—injected a degree of uniformity into settlements throughout the wheat belt. In a similar vein, small-scale flour mills, creameries, and other local enterprises also heightened the sense of small-town uniformity. Many of these enterprises, and particularly the flour mills, were lured to settlements by the promise of a fiscal bonus provided the community.[65] Designs for bank branches were often identical, elevators showed little variation in design, the office of the local lumber yard was likely to be one of a growing number of line yards that dominated the retail lumber business on behalf of manufacturers. Agricultural implement agents, Eaton's mail-order catalogue outlets and, in later years, the branches of gasoline stations, all contributed to the corporate uniformity of prairie towns. Within this general uniformity there were differences from place to place as at various times each railway company had its own model of station intended for different town sizes,[66] and the ubiquitous grain elevators were owned by a multitude of proprietors, and were built in somewhat different styles.

The intertwining of corporate interests is well illustrated by the activities of Toronto investors William Mackenzie and Donald Mann and their Canadian Northern Railway. Along many of the railway's branch lines their company's bank, the Toronto-based Canadian Bank of Commerce, was the only bank in town. Mackenzie and Mann and other CNR directors purchased a British Columbia sawmill, renamed it the Canadian Western Lumber Company, then developed line yards connected with Western Canada Flour Mills, another company which they promoted and which had 96 elevators in 1920–21 and 85 elevators in 84 communities by 1928.[67] They also acquired or established Security Lumber in Saskatchewan, Coast Lumber based in Winnipeg, and Crown Lumber in Alberta. By 1912 Crown Lumber alone controlled 175 lumber yards on the prairies. In Alberta representatives of Western Canada Flour Mills and the Canadian Bank of Commerce were allowed to drive the surveyed routes of proposed branch lines and to have first selection of lots at each town site.[68] These entrepreneurs composed such an efficient cartel that in at least one instance an elevator was built and ready for harvest before the necessary branch line reached it!

The Canadian Bank of Commerce developed what it saw as a prairie bank style. Along the CNR branch lines the company initially erected small prefabricated wooden "temple" banks but quickly sought to consolidate its

The Watson and District Heritage Museum is located in the town's immaculately preserved 1906 Canadian Bank of Commerce building. A prefabricated structure designed by notable Toronto architects Darling and Pearson (who incidentally were among the seven competitors seeking the contract for Saskatchewan's Legislative Building in 1907), the Watson bank was declared in 1977 by the Historic Sites and Monuments Board of Canada to be representative of a classical bank design which became a familiar western Canadian landmark (Courtesy of David McLennan/University of Regina).

position, and image, by replacing them with more imposing buildings designed by the bank's Toronto architects. These were prefabricated wooden versions of the stone or brick bank buildings found in the larger settlements which provided staff quarters upstairs and ample banking space.[69]

Prairie settlements were thus points of convergence for a plethora of more or less interrelated extra-regional interests whose signatures became clearly written in townsite layouts, styles of commercial and domestic architecture, and regional toponymy. Nevertheless, Anglo-Canadian corporations did not achieve complete homogeny. Even the grain distribution system which arose to serve prairie agriculture was no corporate monolith—although many farmers who saw the Grain Exchange as "The house with the closed shutters" believed that the grain trade was a monopoly, that the companies controlling the trade were "the syndicate of syndicates," and worse still were in cahoots with the CPR. In reality, however, the grain trade was a complex mesh of corporate linkages interspersed with the holdings of many individual entrepreneurs, the aim of which was to integrate the prairies into the "world system"—and make money for those who controlled it.[70] Many of the grain traders succeeded in both these aims, and consequently the Richardsons, the Patersons, the Parrishes, the Heimbeckers, the Bawlfs, and other elevator-owning giants built their mansions along Wellington Crescent in Winnipeg, took their places among society's leaders, and propelled the prairies into the world of commercial agriculture.

Whereas its clientele was multi-ethnic the grain trade was multi-enterprise, and like ranching there was a strong influence from the United States—where the elevator itself had been invented. In 1911, for example, there were 1860 elevators on the prairies owned by some 275 different companies—many of which were owned by men of American origin, such as the Searles, the McCabes, and the Peavey family. Of these numbers, there were over 700 elevators in Manitoba, operated by about 100 different companies such as the Atlas Elevator Co. and the Imperial Elevator and Lumber Co., mostly centred in Winnipeg, the Grain Trade "capital." In many ways Minnesotan William Bettingen symbolized the dominant American presence of the early 1900s. He had operated a line of grain elevators and lumberyards in the northern United States before selling out in 1903 and coming to Canada to organize, along with his German-immigrant brother-in-law, William Leistikow, the Imperial Elevator and Lumber Company. He made this move as he "believed that the greatest opportunity for the grain trade lay in the Canadian west" and certainly for Bettingen and his family this proved to be the case. In 1906, he was to become vice president of both the Winnipeg Grain and Produce Exchange, and the Retail Lumber Dealers' Association. He became the first American-born president of the Winnipeg Grain and Produce Exchange in 1907.

Although Ogilvie Flour Mills (a company once as despised by the farmers as was the CPR) owned over 100 of the prairie elevators in 1911, and other operators (such as the Canadian Elevator Co. with 110 "houses") also had some significant lines, there were many more elevator owners such as the "Ethelburt Business Men Grain Buyers Association," Klassen Brothers and Schellenberg, and "The C.K. Wing and Co." that had only single "houses." The picture in Saskatchewan was equally complex. On the CPR line alone there were 586 elevators out of a provincial total of 904, owned by 103 companies. These ranged in size from the Canadian Elevator Company with 45 elevators, to 63 companies such as "Hogg and Lytle" and "Fred Karlenzig" which owned only one.[71]

Alberta was still relatively underdeveloped in 1911. It had only 260 elevators but reflected a similar picture. The CPR was home to 208 elevators owned by 61 companies, ranging from the Alberta Pacific Grain Company with 71 to 37 companies with only one "house." Alberta Pacific grew to be one of the largest privately owned companies on the Prairies, boosted to a great extent by its takeover in 1912 by Sir Max Aitken and R.B. Bennett, KC, MP, along with "a number of English Associates."[72]

In many cases these companies added a distinct spatial element by confining their operations to specific regions or rail company lines. The State Elevator Company (owned by English-based interests), for example, restricted its operations to central and southwest Saskatchewan; Gillespie Grain operated within the Edmonton area; and Young Grain was confined to southwest Manitoba. Both the Gillespie and Security companies were owned by families from "south of the border." Similarly the Security Elevator Company operated along the Grand Trunk Pacific's lines, the McCabe Elevator Company owned all but one elevator along the Great Northern-held Brandon, Saskatchewan and Hudson's Bay Railway, and Ogilvie and Lake of the Woods Milling Company elevators were principally confined to Canadian Pacific trackage.[73] Even by 1933 when there had been a major shake out in the prairie grain trade there were still 37 major companies operating in the trade. A further 54 operators still held elevators in the prairie provinces. Clearly diversity rather than uniformity was the hallmark of the prairie grain trade for the first several decades of operation.

Within a surprisingly short period prairie farmers of all nationalities began to organize their own endeavours so as to reduce dependency on commercial institutions perceived to be either unresponsive to farmers' needs or downright exploitive. In 1917, for example, a number of Ukrainian farmer—entrepreneurs established "The Ruthenian Farmer's Elevator Company" which by 1923 operated 14 elevators, mostly in Ukrainian districts.[74] Lack of management experience caused difficulties and their number of elevators gradually declined. In 1928 the business operated eight, but by 1932 all had been disposed of to other companies. A similar story could be told for the Doukhobor-owned Christian Community of Universal Brotherhood Company once head-officed in Veregin, Saskatchewan. Indeed, this was not atypical of many farmer elevator companies, and it soon became evident that only a company centralized in Winnipeg could compete effectively with the more powerful line companies which frequently had control of, or were controlled by, companies in the export field, operating terminal elevators and maintaining commission departments.

Farmer ownership of grain elevators began in the 19th century, often reflecting the spread of social movements such as The Patrons of Industry. It was numerically relatively unimportant, however, and few locally owned farmers' elevators survived the first decade of the 20th century. However, government-funded experiments such as the Manitoba Elevator

Commission ensured the survival of the concept of farmer-ownership and led to the rise of the Grain Growers' Grain Company as an elevator-operating enterprise. The United Grain Growers (UGG), the company that resulted from a 1917 amalgamation of The Grain Growers' Grain Company and the Alberta Farmers' Cooperative Elevator Company, controlled only 8% of the total number of elevators in the early 1920s—but they exerted considerable influence on the prosecution of the trade nonetheless. By the end of the decade the three provincial pools and the UGG had triggered off a round of amalgamations (and some bankruptcies) in the private trade as line elevator companies had to meet their prices and business procedures. However, although this consolidation trend has continued to characterize the industry to the present day, direct farmer-ownership has almost disappeared.

At the end of the 19th century and well into the 20th the infrastructural symbol of the grain trade, and probably of the region as a whole, was the small wooden "crib" line elevator. Today the grain elevator is most likely to be a huge concrete one belonging to one of the six companies that now control over 80% of them. Nevertheless, the grain elevator still has arguably retained its significance as a regional icon.

The heady success of the rapid settlement and development of the prairies experienced in the years prior to the outbreak of war in 1914 could not last forever. A harbinger of things to come was the collapse of the real estate market in Winnipeg in 1913 that saw the ruin of many who envisaged

Elevator row in Limerick, Saskatchewan, circa 1930s (Courtesy of Garrett Wilson, Regina, Saskatchewan).

unending riches flowing from the west. The tide of optimism that fuelled so much western development was seen in the still undeveloped lots of unneeded subdivisions in countless small prairie towns such as Rapid City, Manitoba. The full extent of the overdevelopment of the prairies by competing companies and by overly sanguine agriculturalists was not fully revealed until the economic and ecological trauma of the "Dirty Thirties." The dramatic retreat of agriculture from marginal dry land environments was achieved at a terrible human cost as "dried out" wheat farmers hauled their families northwards in their "Bennett buggies" to the last frontier in the Peace River country. This was the era that spawned so much of the imagery of the prairies, where a vertical man confronts a horizontal landscape, where a forbidding economic outlook complements a socially sterile society set in a harsh unyielding land. Significantly, these rather depressing literary images found in the fiction of prairie writers such as Sinclair Ross, Robert Stead and Frederick Philip Grove are absent from the visual art of William Kuralek whose subjects were the Ukrainian families of the less prosperous parklands. Less integrated into the market economy of the region, the foreign settlers on marginal homesteads were better able to survive the lean years by retrenching into the semi-subsistence economy that many of them were still struggling to escape when the economic downturn put their aspirations out of reach.

It is ironic and unfortunate that the prevailing images of the prairies held by those outside of the region are so often at odds with the reality of prairie history and geography. Ecologically diverse, the prairies were settled by an amazing variety of peoples pursuing a wide range of agricultural options. The corporate and institutional frameworks that moulded this emerging economy and society were similarly varied. In a few decades before the World War I this unusual mix of peoples, institutions, and environments, came together to create a complex mosaic of cultural landscapes, most of which survived until the 1930s, and many of which survive today. More importantly, new mythologies of place were developed and a vibrant regional identity added to the national fabric. In a way that Rupert Brooke could not have foreseen, this vast land acquired the qualities of home for thousands of European agriculturalists and their descendants.

Notes

This article first appeared in *Prairie Forum* 33, no. 1 (2008): 1–38.

1. Ronald Rees, *New and Naked Land* (Saskatoon: Western Producer Prairie Books, 1988). See also, Aubrey Fullerton, "The Lure of the Better West," *The Canadian Magazine* 26 (1905): 126–32; Klaus Peter Stich, "Canada's Century: The Rhetoric of Propaganda," *Prairie Forum* 1 (1976): 19–29.

2. Lawrence A. Stuckey, *Prairie Cinders; Railway Recollections* (Sudbury: Nickel Belt Rails, 1993).

3. Sandra Martin and Roger Mall (eds.), *Rupert Brooke in Canada* (Toronto: Peter Martin Associates Ltd., 1978), 125–26.

4. W.A. Mackintosh and W.L.G. Joerg (eds.), *Canadian Frontiers of Settlement*, 9 vols. (Macmillan Company of Canada, 1934). See vol. 1, W.A. Mackintosh, *Prairie Settlement*, and vol. 7, C.A. Dawson, *Group Settlement: Ethnic Communities in Western Canada*.

5. See Cole Harris (ed.), *Historical Atlas of Canada* vol. 1 (Toronto: University of Toronto Press, 1987), Plates 57 and 62.

6. William J. Carlyle, "Rural change in the Prairies," in Guy M. Robinson (ed.), *A Social Geography of Canada* (Toronto and Oxford: Dundurn Press, 1991), 330–31.

7. John Warkentin, "Manitoba Settlement Patterns," in Robert M. Irving (ed.), *Readings in Canadian Geography* (Toronto: Holt Rinehart and Winston of Canada Ltd., 1968), 57–58.

8. Howard Adams, *Prison of Grass: Canada from a Native Point of View* (Saskatoon: Fifth House Publishers, 1989).

9. Chester Martin, *Dominion Lands Policy*, edited by Lewis H. Thomas, The Carlton Library No. 69 (Toronto: McClelland and Stewart, 1973); also James M. Richtik, "The Policy Framework for Settling the Canadian West 1870–1880," *Agricultural History* 49 (1975): 613–28.

10. Martin, *Dominion Lands Policy*, 141–42. A series of exotic railway company names graced the prairies during the early years of settlement, including the Manitoba and SouthWestern Colonization Railway, the Great North West Central Railway, and the Brandon, Saskatchewan and Hudson's Bay [sic] Railway. The names were often, if not usually, related to myth rather than reality. The latter line, for instance, did reach (and terminate at) Brandon, but never operated in Saskatchewan, and was hundreds of miles away from Hudson Bay.

11. Ibid., 38–80.

12. Claudia Notzke "The Past and the Present: Spatial and Land Use Change on Two Indian Reserves" in L.A. Rosenvall and S.M. Evans (eds.), *Essays on the Historical Geography of the Canadian West: Regional Perspectives on the Settlement Process* (Calgary: University of Calgary Press, 1987), 100–01.

13. Frank H. Epp, *Mennonites in Canada 1786–1920* (Toronto: MacMillan Company of Canada, 1974), 209–23; and John Warkentin, "Mennonite Agricultural Settlements of Southern Manitoba," *Geographical Review* 49 (1959): 342–68.

14. Epp, *Mennonites in Canada*, 214; Warkentin, "Manitoba Settlement," 66.

15. Epp, *Mennonites in Canada*, 212.

16. According to Epp, *Mennonites in Canada*, 227, by 1900 there were not more than 18 complete villages in the West Reserve and less than 25 in the East Reserve. Today there are less than 20 recognizable Mennonite villages, all of which are in the West Reserve. David K. Butterfield and Edward M. Ledohowski, *Architectural Heritage: The MSTW Planning District* (Winnipeg: Historic Resources Branch, Department of Culture Heritage and Recreation, 1984), 15; also Warkentin, "Manitoba Settlement," 64.

17. Under the terms of the Dominion Lands Act the Minister of the Interior was empowered "in the case of settlements being formed of immigrants in communities" (such as those of Mennonites or Icelanders) to waive the requirements of residence and cultivation on each quarter section and could permit settlers to reside in a hamlet or village so as to facilitate the establishment of schools, churches etc. See Kirk N. Lambrecht, *The Administration of Dominion Lands 1870–1930* (Regina: Canadian Plains Research Center, 1991), 112–13.

18. John Everitt, "Social Space and Group Life-Styles in Rural Manitoba," *The Canadian Geographer* 24, no. 3 (1980): 237–54; Simon Evans "The Hutterites in Alberta: Past and Present Settlement Patterns" in L.A. Rosenvall and S.M. Evans (eds.), *Essays on the Historical Geography of the Canadian West: Regional Perspectives on the Settlement Process* (Calgary: University of Calgary Press, 1987), 145–71; Victor Peters, *All Things Common: The Hutterian Way of Life* (Minneapolis: University of Minnesota Press, 1965), 51–71.

19. B.G. Vanderkill and D.E. Christensen, "The Settlement of New Iceland," *Annals of the Association of American Geographers* 53 (1963): 350–63.

20. For a discussion of this claim, see Simon M. Evans, "Some Spatial Aspects of the Cattle Kingdom: The First Decade 1882-1892," in A.W. Rasporich and H.C. Klassen (eds.), *Frontier Calgary* (Calgary: McClelland and Stewart West, 1975).

21. Donald G. Godfrey and Brigham Y. Card, *The Diary of Charles Ora Card: The Canadian Years 1886–1903* (Salt Lake City: University of Utah Press, 1993), 51–53, and John C. Lehr, "The Sequence of Mormon Settlement in Alberta," *Alberta Geographer* 10 (1974): 20–29.

22. Brian W. Blouet and Merlin P. Lawson (eds.), *Images of the Plains* (Lincoln: University of Nebraska Press, 1975); and Gary S. Dunbar, "Isotherms and Politics: Perception of the North West in the 1880s," in A.W. Rasporich, *Prairie Perspectives* 2 (Toronto: Holt, Rinehart and Winston, 1973).

23. Simon M. Evans, "The Origins of Ranching in Western Canada," in L.A. Rosenvall and S.M. Evans (eds.), *Essays on the Historical Geography of the Canadian West* (Calgary: Department of Geography, University of Calgary, 1987).

24. D.H. Breen, *The Canadian Prairie West and Ranching Frontier, 1874–1924* (Toronto: University of Toronto Press, 1983), 56.

25. Hugh Dempsey (ed.), *The Best of Bob Edwards* (Edmonton: Hurtig Publishers, 1975), 135–57.

26. Patrick A. Dunae, *Gentlemen Emigrants* (Vancouver: Douglas and McIntyre, 1981). For an assessment of attitudes and perceptions, see R. Douglas Francis, *Images of the West* (Saskatoon: Western Producer Prairie Books, 1989).

27. Lewis G. Thomas, "The Ranching Tradition and the Life of Ranchers," in Patrick A. Dunae (ed.), *Rancher's Legacy* (Edmonton: University of Alberta Press, 1986), 33; and Sheilagh Jameson, "The Social Elite of the Rancher's Community and Calgary" in Rasporich and Klassen, *Frontier Calgary*.

28. Moira O'Neill, "A Lady's Life on a Ranch," *Blackwood's Edinburgh Magazine* (January 1898): 7.

29. Susan Jackel, *A Flannel Shirt and Liberty* (Vancouver: University of British Columbia Press, 1982); and Sheilagh Jameson, "Women in the Southern Alberta Ranch Community," in H.C. Klassen (ed.), *The Canadian West* (Calgary: ComPrint, 1977).

30. Lewis G. Thomas, "Ranch Houses of the Alberta Foothills" in Dunae, *Rancher's Legacy*.

31. H.S. Arkill, "The Cattle Industry" in Henry J. Boam (ed.), *Twentieth Century Impressions of Canada* (Montreal: Sells, 1914); and Simon M. Evans, "Canadian Beef for Victorian Britain," *Agricultural History* 53, no. 4 (1979): 748–62.

32. For the changing patterns of major shipping points, see, "Prairie Agriculture," Plate 18, in Donald Kerr and Deryck W. Holdsworth (eds.), *Historical Atlas of Canada* vol. 3: *Addressing the Twentieth Century* (Toronto: University of Toronto Press, 1990).

33. Iris Keller, "Biggest Shipping Point in N.W.T.," *Canadian Cattlemen* (July 1955): 13 ff.

34. *Winnipeg Times* quoted in John W. Dafoe, *Clifford Sifton in Relation to His Times* (Freeport, NY: Books for Libraries Press, 1971), 103–04.

35. Joseph Schnell, *Laurier* (Toronto: Macmillan Company of Canada, 1967), 336; on

Sifton's policies see David J. Hall, *Clifford Sifton: The Young Napoleon* (Vancouver: UBC Press, 1981), 122–58.

36. John Everitt, Roberta Kempthorne and Charles Schafer, "Controlled Aggression: James J. Hill and The Brandon, Saskatchewan and Hudson's Bay Railway" *North Dakota History* 56, no. 2 (Spring 1989): 3–19; Allison Williams and John Everitt, "An Analysis of Settlement Development in Southwest Manitoba: The Lenore Extension 1902–1982" in H. John Selwood and John C. Lehr (eds.), *Prairie and Northern Perspectives: Geographical Essays* (Winnipeg: University of Winnipeg, 1989), 87–105.

37. James B. Hedges, *The Federal Railway Land Subsidy Policy of Canada* (Cambridge: Harvard University Press, 1934), 48.

38. James M. Richtik, "Manitoba Settlement 1870–1886" (PhD dissertation, University of Minnesota, 1971), 446–47.

39. Personal comment, Vera Pybus, Winnipeg, June 20, 1992.

40. H. John Selwood and Evelyn Baril "The Hudson's Bay Company and Prairie Town Development, 1870–1888," in A.F.J. Artibise (ed.), *Town and City: Aspects of Western Canadian Urban Development* (Regina: Canadian Plains Research Center, 1981), 61–94; and H. John Selwood, "The Hudson's Bay Company at Riding Mountain House (Elphinstone)" in Selwood and Lehr (eds.), *Prairie and Northern Perspectives*, 78–85.

41. Clifford Sifton, "The Immigrants Canada Wants," *Maclean's Magazine* (April 1, 1922): 16.

42. Ibid., 16, 33. For further insights into Sifton's attitudes to immigration and immigrants see, Peter H. Bryce, *The Value to Canada of the Continental Immigrant* (n.p.: 1928), 8–10.

43. Canada, House of Commons, *Debates*, February 16, 1898, c 668–669; and D.J. Hall, "The Political Career of Clifford Sifton 1896-1905" (PhD dissertation, University of Toronto, 1973), 171–73.

44. See, for example, Vladimir J. Kaye, *Early Ukrainian Settlements in Canada 1895–1900* (Toronto: University of Toronto Press for the Ukrainian-Canadian Research Foundation, 1964), 203; and Michael Ewanchuk, *Pioneer Settlers: Ukrainians in the Dauphin Area 1896–1926* (published by the author, 1988), 23–29.

45. Beecham Trotter, *A Horseman and the West* (Toronto: Macmillan Company of Canada, 1925), 40.

46. Library and Archives Canada (LAC) RG 76, Vol. 144, File 34214, pt. 1, William F. McCreary, Winnipeg, to James A. Smart, Ottawa, May 14, 1897.

47. John C. Lehr, "Peopling the Prairies with Ukrainians" in Lubomyr Luciuk and Stella Hryniuk (eds.), *Canada's Ukrainians: Negotiating an Identity* (Toronto: University of Toronto Press, 1991), 30–52.

48. John C. Lehr, "The Process and Pattern of Ukrainian Rural Settlement in Western Canada 1891–1914" (PhD dissertation, University of Manitoba, 1978), 151–52.

49. Eugene Van Cleef, "Finnish Settlement in Canada," *Geographical Review* 42 (Spring 1952): 253.

50. John C. Lehr, "Kinship and Society in the Ukrainian Pioneer Settlement of the Canadian West," *Canadian Geographer* 29, no. 3 (1985): 207–19.

51. LAC, RG 76, Vol. 144, file 34214, pt. 2, William F. McCreary, Winnipeg, to James A. Smart, Ottawa, May 20, 1898.

52. Miriam Elston, "The Russian in Our Midst," *Westminister* (1915): 532.

53. For a comprehensive review of the landscape of Ukrainian settlement see, James W. Darlington, "The Ukrainian Impress on the Canadian West," in Luciuk and Hryniuk (eds.), *Canada's Ukrainians*, 53–80. On the specifics of the religious landscape see, Basil

Rotoff, Roman Yereniuk and Stella Hryniuk, *Monuments to Faith: Ukrainian Churches in Manitoba* (Winnipeg: University of Manitoba Press, 1990); and Victor Deneka, "Ukrainian Church Architecture of Canada: Yesterday, Today and Tomorrow," in Oleh W. Gerus and Alexander Baran (eds.), *Millennium of Christianity in Ukraine 988—1988* (Winnipeg: Ukrainian Academy of Arts and Sciences in Canada, 1989), 275–92. For a review of Ukrainian vernacular architecture in Canada see, John C. Lehr, "Ukrainians," in Allan Noble (ed.), *To Build in a New Land* (Baltimore: Johns Hopkins Press, 1992), 309–30.

54. J.B. Rudnyckyj, *Manitoba Mosaic of Place Names* (Winnipeg: Canadian Institute of Onomastic Sciences, 1970), 13–14; and Penny Ham, *Place Names of Manitoba* (Saskatoon: Western Producer Prairie Books, 1980).

55. John C. Lehr, "The Landscape of Ukrainian Settlement in the Canadian West," *Great Plains Quarterly* 2, no. 2 (1982): 96–99.

56. Application for Entry, SE 20 1-8E, March 3, 1903. Manitoba Records of Homestead Entry.

57. John C. Lehr, "One Family's Frontier: Life History and the Process of Ukrainian Settlement in the Stuartburn District of Southeastern Manitoba," *Canadian Geographer* 40, no. 2 (1996): 98–108.

58. *The Nor'West Farmer and Manitoba Miller* 4 (July 1885): 153; 7 (March, 1888), 70—71; 7 (May 1888): 125; and 7 (June, 1888): 156.

59. Lyle Dick, *Farmers "Making Good": The Development of Abernethy District, Saskatchewan 1880–1920* (Ottawa: Environment Canada, 1989), 43–46.

60. *Motherwell Homestead National Historic Site Management Plan* (Ottawa: Parks Canada, 1981), 12.

61. Kerr and Holdsworth, *Historical Atlas of Canada* vol. 3, plate 19.

62. Dick, *Farmers "Making Good,"* 79.

63. R.T. Naylor, *The Banks and Finance Capital* vol. 1 of *The History of Canadian Business, 1867–1914* (Toronto: J. Lorimer, 1975), 15.

64. Gerald Friesen, *The Canadian Prairies: A History* (Toronto: University of Toronto Press, 1984), 13, 321.

65. John Everitt and Roberta Kempthorne "Prairie 'Custom' Flour Mills," in Selwood and Lehr (eds.), *Reflections from the Prairies*, 41–60; John Everitt and Roberta Kempthorne "Flour Mills in Manitoba," *Manitoba History* 26 (Autumn 1993): 2–14.

66. Deryck Holdsworth and John Everitt, "Bank Branches and Elevators: Experiences of Big Corporations in Small Prairie Towns," *Prairie Forum* 13, no. 2 (1988): 173–90. Charles Bohi, *Canadian National's Western Depots: The Country Stations in Western Canada* (Toronto: Railfare Enterprises, 1977); Charles Bohi and Leslie S. Kozma, *Canadian Pacific's Western Depots: The Country Stations in Western Canada* (David City, NE: South Platte Press, 1993); J. Edward Martin, *Railway Stations of Western Canada* (White Rock, BC: Studio E, 1980); and David Butterfield, *Railway Stations of Manitoba* (Winnipeg: Historic Resources Branch, Manitoba Culture, Heritage and Recreation, 1984).

67. John Everitt, "The Early Development of the Flour Milling Industry on the Prairies," *The Journal of Historical Geography* 19, no. 3 (1993): 278–98.

68. Glenbow Archives, Calgary, H.F. Chritchley Papers, Letter from H.F. Chritchley to T.A. Fraser, June 2, 1965. The (American) Piper Douglas consortium had also at one time toured Canadian Northern lines with the expectation of receiving the choicest locations for what became Canadian Elevator Company "houses." Clearly opportunities were not equal for everybody.

69. Holdsworth and Everitt, "Bank Branches," 177–78.

70. Peter Hugill and John Everitt "Macro Landscapes: The Cultural Landscape Revised by World System Theory," in S.T. Wong (ed.), *Person, Place and Thing: Interpretive and Empirical Essays in Cultural Geography, Geoscience and Man Series,* volume 31 (Baton Rouge: Louisiana State University, 1992), 177–94.

71. John Everitt and Roberta Kempthorne, "Flour Mills in Manitoba," *Manitoba History* 26 (Autumn 1993): 2–14.

72. John Everitt, "The Line Elevator in Alberta (Part One)," *Alberta History* 40, no. 4 (Autumn 1992): 16–22; *List of Licensed Elevators and Warehouses in the Manitoba Grain Inspection Division 1911–12* (Ottawa: Department of Trade and Commerce, 1912), various pages; *Winnipeg Free Press* (September 2, 1911–2): 1.

73. John Everitt, "The Line Elevator in Alberta (Part Two)" *Alberta History* 41, no. 1 (Winter 1993): 20–26; John Everitt, "The Line Elevator in Saskatchewan," *Saskatchewan History* 44, no. 2 (Spring 1992): 41–58; *List of Grain Elevators in the Western and Eastern Divisions License Year 1933–34* (Ottawa: King's Printer, 1934), various pages.

74. *List of Licensed Elevators and Warehouses in the Western Grain Inspection Division, License Year 1923–24* (Ottawa: King's Printer, 1924), various pages.

The "Opening" of the Prairie West

2.   A Willing Scapegoat:
John Macoun and the Route of the CPR

W.A. Waiser

One of the more controversial decisions in Western Canadian history was the routing of the Canadian Pacific Railway main line through the southern prairie district, rather than along the North Saskatchewan. Throughout the 1870s, the federal government had contemplated two possible northern routes for the transcontinental railroad: the Yellowhead-Burrard Inlet route and the Pine River-Bute Inlet route. By February 17, 1881, however, when the newly formed CPR Syndicate, officially assumed control of the project, it was practically a foregone conclusion that the rail line would pass via the so-called fertile belt to Edmonton, from there through the Yellowhead Pass, and thence down the Fraser River to Burrard Inlet on the Pacific; a Conservative Order-in-Council, dated October 14, 1879, had recommended this route. The Syndicate's announcement in the spring of 1881 that it would build directly westward from Winnipeg, across the prairie grasslands and through a more southerly mountain pass was therefore a great surprise. This decision focussed activity in the nearly, empty prairie, region for the next twenty years, and away from the established settlements of the fertile belt. As one historian has observed, it meant "that the Canadian Pacific Railway did not have anything like the effect it might have had on the northward advance of Canada's frontiers... The 'Northwest,' for practical purposes, became replaced by the 'West'."[1]

Several reasons have been advanced to explain this last minute abandonment of the more popular and more certain Yellowhead route.[2] Many commentators agree that Professor John Macoun's enthusiastic endorsement of the agricultural potential of the prairie grasslands in 1879–80 was a contributing factor, if not the major reason, in the decision to bring the CPR main line south. For example, in *Men Against the Desert*, James Gray argues that, "It was Macoun's report which helped guide the CPR through the southern Prairies and led to the settlement of Saskatchewan."[3] Pierre Berton is more explicit, indirectly blaming Macoun for the ecological problems of the 1930s:

> It was he, perhaps more than anyone else, who eventually convinced the Government, the public at large, and finally, the men who built the Canadian Pacific Railway, that Hind and Palliser were wrong—the land to the south of the Saskatchewan River was not an arid belt but a fertile plain. In doing so he helped change the course of the railway and thus, for better or for worse, the very shape of Canada. It is possible that the South Saskatchewan farmers, eking out an existence along the drought-stricken right of way during the 1930s, might have cursed his memory, had they been aware of it.[4]

Even recent historical scholarship implicates Macoun. "It is no exaggeration to conclude that he influenced decisions that shifted the whole axis of development in the North West," writes Doug Owram in *Promise of Eden*. "Had the original assumption still existed that the southern prairie was desert, however, the Canadian Pacific would not have been constructed through it."[5]

Despite these assertions, John Macoun's revelations about the agricultural potential of the prairie region were a minor factor in selecting the CPR main line route. Rather, the decision to locate the railway through the southern grasslands was based on the determination of the Syndicate to meet the threat posed by the American Northern Pacific Railroad and to secure the traffic of the Canadian West for its own line.[6] The CPR builders thought primarily in terms of national strategy and not local settlement; they would have built across the prairies even if the area had been poorly regarded, relying on branch lines north into the fertile belt. If anything, Macoun's

John Macoun (1831–1920) (Courtesy of the Saskatchewan Archives Board/R-A4897).

Sir Sandford Fleming (1827–1915) (Courtesy of the Saskatchewan Archives Board/R-B11,485).

part in the building of the transcontinental railway was limited to the idea that the western interior had great potential. His work provided the agricultural justification for a route that had been selected for essentially other reasons.

John Macoun became involved in the debate over the best route for the CPR by accident. Professor of Natural History at Albert College, Belleville, Ontario, he was on one of his annual botanical excursions to Northern Ontario in July 1872 when he encountered the Canadian surveyor, Sandford Fleming. It was a fortuitous meeting. When the Canadian government decided to build a transcontinental railway to British Columbia and to open the vast prairie interior to agricultural colonization, Fleming was appointed engineer-in-chief and was given the crucial task of determining the most suitable route. The new chief engineer realized that locating the rail line across the western interior was not a simple matter of noting and overcoming any engineering problems; the line had to be directed through or near those regions best suited for immediate settlement. It was for this reason that Fleming was going west in 1872 to acquaint himself with the country and its resources. This concern was also reflected in his initial choice of route for the railroad. Aware that the Palliser and Hind expeditions of the late 1850s had extolled the merits of the wooded fertile belt of the North Saskatchewan country over those of the arid southern grasslands, Fleming thought that the rail line should pass through this region to Edmonton and then through the Yellowhead Pass[7]—the same route he now proposed to travel. Because a man with Macoun's practical field experience would prove invaluable to Fleming's purpose, he invited the plant geographer to join the expedition and to assess the agricultural prospects of various interior tracts.

From the outset, Macoun carried out his assignment with vigorous enthusiasm. He was continually collecting specimens:

The sight of a perpendicular face of rock, either dry or dripping with moisture, drew him like a magnet, and, with yells of triumph, he would summon the others to come and behold the trifle he had lit upon. Scrambling, panting, rubbing their shins against rocks, and half breaking their necks, they trailed painfully after him only to find him on his knees before some "thing of beauty" that seemed to us little different from what we had passed with indifference thousands of times.[8]

On reaching Thunder Bay, Macoun combined this search for new species with a careful inspection of the overall vegetation. For him, the natural flora of a district indicated the area's agricultural capabilities:

the botanist [can] determine, by inspection of plants from a certain locality, the character of the soil and of the climate, and the consequent adaptability of the district for the growth of certain varieties of cultivated plants ... this botanical test was the only true criterion by which the agricultural status of any district should be judged.[9]

This procedure in examining the land was not peculiar to Macoun. Both the Palliser and Hind expeditions had appraised the agricultural prospects of the western interior on the basis of vegetation. It was also an accepted practice among members of the Geological Survey of Canada. Yet, because of Macoun's training as a geographical botanist, his dependence upon such a simple general test was much greater; it effectively determined the line of thought he pursued. Daring assumptions and bold generalizations were the outcome.

From Thunder Bay, the party worked its way along the land and water links of the Dawson Road to Fort Garry (Winnipeg), then explored northwestward to Edmonton, covering the 900 miles in a record 25 days. Here, Fleming dispatched Macoun and the expedition's outfitter, Charles Horetzky, on a reconnaissance survey of the Peace River district, while the rest of the expedition continued westward through the Yellowhead Pass to the Pacific coast. As the two men passed through the prairie parkland bordering the mighty Peace River, Macoun lauded the country as being ahead of anything he had yet seen in terms of beauty and fertility. "I would prefer risking wheat," he recorded in his notebook on October 4, 1872, "on any part of the prairie passed over today than either in the neighbourhood of Victoria or Edmonton. Nothing in either soil, plants or climate would cause me to hesitate in giving this opinion."[10] By the time the pair reached Fort St. John, the survey had degenerated into a quarrelsome venture. The seasoned Horetzky had decided that the botanist was a burden and wanted to ascend the Pine River alone in search of a previously unknown pass reported by the local Indians. Macoun flatly refused to turn back. Determined to push on even if it meant leaving his bones in the mountains, he travelled as far as Fort St. James with Horetzky and then fled south with two Indian companions over the snow-laden Telegraph Trail to Victoria.

At Fleming's request, on his return home in the new year Macoun prepared a summary of his activities for the 1874 railway report.[11] Throughout the course of his historic trek from Fort Garry to Edmonton, then up the Peace River through the mountains to the coast, his floral studies had indicated a regional uniformity in vegetation, suggesting that the Canadian West was a complete geographical entity. "The hill-top, the plain, the marsh, the aspen copse, the willow thicket," he reported, "each had its own flora throughout the region, never varying and scarcely ever becoming intermixed."[12] These findings, combined with a reading of Lorin Blodget's provocative *The Climatology of North America* (Philadephia, 1857), convinced him of the northward expansion of summer isotherms into the region and the irrelevance of winter temperatures.[13] He suggested that grazing would be profitable in the North-West wherever conditions were not suitable for grain production. In fact, Macoun strongly favoured the agricultural potential of the Peace River Country above all other regions he had observed, including the North Saskatchewan country.[14]

After Dr. A.R.C. Selwyn, Director of the Geological Survey of Canada, read the proof sheets of this report during a visit to Ottawa, he invited Macoun to return with him to the Peace River district in the summer of 1875. Although the new Liberal government of Alexander Mackenzie had adopted Fleming's Yellowhead route, there was a growing interest in the Peace River country. Charles Horetzky was also convinced of the advantages of the region for settlement and he projected the rail line through the yet undiscovered Pine River Pass in his *Canada on the Pacific*.[15] A further voice was added to the cause by Captain William F. Butler, renowned author of *The Great Lone Land*. In the account of his journey up the Peace River in the spring of 1872, he also argued in favour of a northern pass for the railway.[16] The Selwyn expedition, therefore, was dispatched to ascertain these recent claims about the character of the region, as well as to survey the Peace and Pine River Passes. Macoun was responsible for making notes on the region's flora, climate and agricultural potential.

The first part of the Selwyn expedition was essentially a retracing of the route followed by the botanist three years earlier. From Quesnel, on the

Fraser River, they headed overland by pack train to Fort Macleod in the northern British Columbian wilderness and then, continuing by water, descended the Peace River to Fort St. John. There were few incidents along the way—a halt always found Macoun drying, packing and labelling some of the 20,000 plant specimens which eventually formed his collection[17]—and the party arrived safely at the post. At Fort St. John, Macoun left the expedition and continued 700 miles downriver to Fort Chipewyan in a cottonwood dugout, accompanied a Hudson's Bay Company clerk. During this descent of the Peace, he not only found plant species common in the prairies and central Canada but came across prolific grain and vegetable crops at each of the fur trade posts along the way. Macoun reflected on these findings at Fort Chipewyan:

> the soil wherever tried throughout the whole extent of this vast region gives enormous returns for little labour, giving promise of the day when the land will be filled with a busy multitude who, instead of living by the chase will cultivate the rich soil and develop the unbounded resources of this wonderful land.[18]

He eventually reached home late that fall, having travelled 8,000 miles in eight months.

The Selwyn expedition greatly strengthened Macoun's belief in the northland's agricultural potential. In his report for the Geological Survey, he declared the Peace River district better suited for settlement than the land around Edmonton and he advocated a northern pass for the rail line.[19] He made similar claims about the region before the House of Commons Select Committee on Agricultural and Colonization in March 1876,[20] as well as in the special assessment of western lands that he prepared at the Prime Minister's request for the 1877 railway report.[21] Mackenzie was not pleased. At the outset, he had characteristically cautioned the botanist not to draw upon his imagination. He consequently dismissed Macoun's statements as exaggerations and remained committed to sending the railway through the Yellowhead Pass, then down the Fraser Valley to Burrard Inlet, near New Westminster.

Mackenzie became even more determined to take the rail line this way, thanks largely to the actions of Marcus Smith, former engineer-in-chief of the British Columbia section of the CPR, who became acting chief engineer during Fleming's absence in England. Following their electoral defeat in 1874, the Conservatives had come to advocate Bute Inlet as the Pacific Terminus for the railway, by way of a more northerly pass through the Rockies. In an effort to enhance his future prospects when and if Macdonald resumed office, the wily Smith did everything in his power to assist this position, including the secret dispatch of CPR engineer Joseph Hunter in the spring of 1877 to locate and survey the elusive Pine Pass.[22] When Prime Minister Mackenzie learned of Smith's behind-the-scene intrigues, the acting chief engineer was removed from his position of authority. Fleming was summoned back to Canada and, after reviewing the recent survey work, confirmed the desirability of the Yellowhead–Burrard route.[23] There the matter rested when the Conservative Party, under the banner of its "National Policy," romped back into office in the 1878 autumn federal election.

Even though the new Macdonald administration favoured the Pine River-Bute Inlet route, Fleming remained firm in his resolve that the rail line would best serve the interests of the country if it followed the Yellowhead-Burrard route. The Conservatives, however, could not reverse their position without giving the impression that the former Liberal government had been right all along. Sir Charles Tupper, the new Minister of Railways and Canals, therefore decided to have the merits of the two routes investigated one more time, and field parties were assembled for the 1879 field season.[24] Macoun was approached to head one of the field parties. The chance to become involved again in official field work was an attractive proposition, but Macoun hesitated to accept because the work was seasonal. Consequently, he refused his services unless he was to be offered a permanent postion. Tupper acquiesced. In the spring of 1879, Macoun was made the Canadian government's explorer in the North-West Territories, an informal arrangement to be in effect as long as the Conservatives remained in power.[25]

Macoun's first assignment was an exploration of the prairie district south of the projected railway line and north of the 51st parallel. The only person commissioned to explore the southern prairie territory that year, Macoun had evidently been sent to refute Palliser and Hind's conclusions about the aridity of the district.[26] Several weeks after the botanist had left for the field, Tupper began to emphasize the overall fertility of the lands of the western interior. "We have vast regions only partially explored which are not second to any lands in the West," he told the House on May 10. "We believe that we have there the garden of the world."[27] Such extravagant claims were made necessary by the Conservative scheme to attract railway builders by the offer of a large grant; the promise of wonderfully fertile lands would greatly facilitate this task. This is probably why Macoun was dispatched to the prairie district. Two years earlier, before he had even seen the region, he had called into doubt the existence of an interior desert.[28] Now, he was being called upon the confirm this assessment and thereby demonstrate that the potential profit from railroad construction was very great.

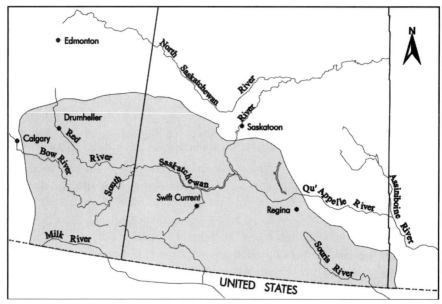

The Palliser Triangle. In his 1862 report to the British government, Captain John Palliser argued that a triangular portion of what is now the southern prairie provinces was a northern extension of the arid, central desert of the United States: "This central desert extends, however, but a short way into the British territory, forming a triangle, having for its base the 49th parallel from longitude 100° to 114° W, with its apex reaching to the 52nd parallel of latitude." Palliser described this triangular region as "desert, or semi-desert in character, which can never be expected to become occupied by settlers." The boundary of the Palliser Triangle is not fixed like a political boundary; rather, it fluctuates depending on climatic cycles (Courtesy Canadian Plains Research Center Mapping Division).

On October 2, 1879, with Fleming in attendance, the cabinet reviewed the results of the past summer's surveys and officially endorsed the Yellowhead-Burrard route for the railway. That the matter was finally settled was evidenced by the subsequent calling of tenders for the Burrard Inlet line.[29] Macoun, in the meantime, had not disappointed Tupper. On the basis of his findings between Battleford and Calgary, he had concluded that the great plain's apparent aridity was a simple matter of the nature of the surface cover, not the climate. "I am quite safe in saying," he declared in his report, "that 80 per cent of the whole country is suited for the raising of grain and cattle, and would not be the least surprised if future explorers formed a more favourable estimate."[30] Converted into acreage figures, there were at least 150 million acres of land suitable for agriculture and stockraising between the international border and the 57th parallel.

That winter, the Liberals continued to question the reliability of Macoun's estimates. One of Mackenzie's speeches so incensed Macoun that he apparently called out to the Opposition Leader from the visitors' gallery.

Even Prime Minister Macdonald "scarcely allowed himself to accept as fact that which was so ardently desired."[31] Tupper, on the other hand, entertained no such doubts. Before the final report of the 1879 field parties was released, he reported on March 3, 1880:

> I believe that information will be found to be of a very satisfactory and assuring character. It will be found that, instead of having overrated the character of the country, the most sanguine views in relation to the fertility of the Great North-West will be more than borne out by the positive information we will be able to lay before the House on the subject.[32]

A month later, when the report was tabled before the House, Tupper first underlined the need for favourable views about the western country for the success of the railway venture. He then confidently quoted Macoun's 1879 figures to back up his earlier assertions, giving the impression that the these findings were irrefutable.[33] Privately, however, the reliability of Macoun's estimates seems to have been secondary to the fact that they coincided with Tupper's contentions. Although the minister did briefly question Macoun before making his April speech, he also "encouraged [him] to do [his] duty and stick to what [he] conceived to be the truth."[34] It was thus not so much Macoun's findings as it was Tupper's use of them that made the botanist such a central figure in the railway debates.

Tupper was so determined to demonstrate the potential value of a railway land grant in the North-west that Macoun returned to the southern prairie district in the 1880 field season. This time, he was given a zig-zag itinerary of all the areas south of the Qu'Appelle and South Saskatchewan Rivers poorly regarded in previous reports. Starting from Brandon, the five-man party proceeded westward by cart over the almost perfectly level short grass prairie of the Great Souris Plain. But beyond Moose Mountain, as they drew near the Missouri Coteau or third prairie steppe, they came upon a badlands country with baked clay outcrops, dried-up streams and stunted vegetation. In some places, Macoun reported that the surface was so rough that "our carts were nearly shaken to pieces and patches of skin were jerked off the necks of our horses by the twisting caused by the hummocks and hollows."[35] Any sobering influence that this experience might have had on the botanist's enthusiasm, however, was quickly nullified by his findings at a homestead located 30 miles northwest of the Cypress Hills on a branch of Maple Creek. An unassuming farmer had sown the seemingly worthless Cretaceous till in late May and, despite a long June drought, the results were astounding. Wheat and potatoes flourished in the same field with the cacti

Badlands just east of Avonlea, Saskatchewan, exhibiting natural land forms of 70 million-year-old rock, Cretaceous shales characteristic of what is known as the Bearpaw Formation, sedimentary remnants of north-western North America's Western Interior Seaway. The Missouri Coteau rises in the distance (Courtesy of David McLennan/University of Regina).

and sagebrush. Writing from Fort Walsh, Macoun excitedly related his new finding to Sandford Fleming: "I confess that this latest discovery has again unsettled my views regarding this country and I am now prepared to take even *higher flights* than I have taken before."[36] In his report to the government that autumn, he extolled the virtues of the treeless plain for large scale agricultural colonization.[37] This message was spread in a series of highly entertaining lectures that he delivered to crowded halls throughout Ontario. In a Hamilton speech, he proclaimed, "There [is] no such thing as the fertile belt. It [is] all equally good."[38]

These new findings were subsequently used by Tupper to justify certain features of the railway contract that the Canadian government finally signed, on October 21, 1880 with the Canadian promoters of the highly successful St. Paul, Minneapolis and Manitoba Railway. Under the terms of the contract, the Syndicate agreed to build within 10 years an all-Canadian transcontinental line for among other things, 25 million acres of land "fairly fit for settlement." During debate on the proposed contract, Sir Charles drew particular attention to Macoun's recent exploration to allay opposition concerns that much of the best land in the North-West would fall into the Syndicate's hands; only a small portion of the fertile lands would be absorbed by the railway land grant. "Now we find that Professor Macoun," the Minister advised the House,

> found that that great Missouri section of barren country which was supposed to extend into Canada in the Northwest, was in great measure valuable and fertile land. He found that the idea that it was a desert was an entire delusion and that instead of that a great portion of these lands … are largely fit for settlement, and they are included in the contract in the lands "fairly fit for settlement."[39]

Macoun's field work also seemed to have figured in the wording of the Railway Act, passed into law February 17, 1881. According to the legislation, the railway land grant was to be secured within the fertile belt, "that is to say the land lying between parallels 49 and 57 degrees north latitude."[40] The boundaries of this enlarged fertile belt just happened to correspond with those in Macoun's 1879 report.

There is also widespread belief that Macoun's revelations figured in the location of the CPR across the prairies. When the Syndicate officially assumed control of the project, one of its first acts was the re-routing of the main line some 200 miles to the south of Fleming's Yellowhead route; the chief engineer's 10 years of surveys, at a cost of $4,166,187, had been for naught. Macoun is credited with influencing this decision, in light of his enthusiastic endorsement of the agricultural potential of the prairie region. There is also the matter of his meeting with three members of the CPR Syndicate, J.J. Hill, George Stephen and Robert Angus, in St. Paul, Minnesota, in the late spring of 1881, around the time the route change was announced.[41] This meeting, however, raises more questions than it answers about the locating of the main line.

In the first place, there is reason to doubt whether this crucial gathering actually took place. A faithful recorder of his activities in the field, Macoun makes no mention of it in his 1881 field notebook, his 1881 diary, or his correspondence for that year. Nor does he say anything about it in his massive *Manitoba in the Great North-West* (1882), a compilation of his activities in Western Canada over the previous 10 years. The James J. Hill papers, moreover, do not contain any reference to the meeting or to Macoun in 1881.[42] The only recorded account of the meeting appears in Macoun's *Autobiography*, written nearly 40 years after the event took place. One is forced to conclude that the meeting probably took place either at another time in another location or, perhaps, it went unrecorded at the time.

The nature of the meeting's conversation is also curious. Macoun, for his part, had apparently been summoned to St. Paul because of his field work in southern Alberta in 1879 and he was quizzed on the suitability of the Bow River or Kicking Horse Pass for a rail line. The agricultural potential of the southern grasslands was not even discussed. It could be argued that Macoun's opinions on the capabilities of the southern grasslands were already well known and the purpose of the meeting was to discuss engineering problems. It does seem strange, however, that the Syndicate did not take advantage of Macoun's presence to ask him some detailed questions about his field work; the re-routing of the CPR main line would have great consequence for the development of Western Canada. At the very least, he could have been called upon to reinforce their decision to bring the line south. Then again, the question of the agricultural potential of the prairies may have been of secondary importance to other Syndicate concerns about the route location.

Finally, many observers have argued that the decision to send the railway across the southern plains was made at this meeting. Pierre Berton, for example, places considerable emphasis on the gathering in *The Last Spike*, entitling a chapter subsection, "How John Macoun Altered the Map."[43] Yet John Macoun did not convince the Syndicate that a more southern line was practicable for the simple reason that the route change had already been determined. When he arrived at Hill's St. Paul office, the men were evidently debating whether the rail line could proceed westward from Moose Jaw or turn northward to Battleford and proceed through the Yellowhead Pass: they had brought the rail line south without being certain of a suitable pass through the mountains. That the route change was already being considered before this date is confirmed by Hill's decision in December 1880 to send Major A.B. Rogers in search of a pass through the Selkirk Range the following spring.[44] The Conservative government also seemed to be aware that the Syndicate was toying with the idea of a more southerly route through the Rockies at this time. In April 1881 J.S. Dennis, Deputy Minister of the Interior, arranged with Dr. Selwyn to have geologist George Mercer Dawson conduct a special survey of the resources "of the country on the east slope of the mountains northerly from the boundary."[45] As a general rule, such surveys tended to be restricted to those regions where immediate development was anticipated.[46]

In explaining the Syndicate's actions, it would be ridiculous to suggest that it was not aware of Macoun's highly favourable 1879 and 1880 reports; Charles Tupper's speeches in Parliament had seen to that. That Macoun's assessment had been the key factor in influencing the Syndicate to adopt a more southerly route as early as the autumn of 1880 is another matter entirely. There is very little reference to the botanist or his work in correspondence between Syndicate members. On the other hand, there is a great deal about rivalry with other lines and competitive positions. Herein lies the key to the CPR strategy.[47]

The task of locating the route that the CPR main line would follow across western Canada fell to the General Manager of the St. Paul, Minneapolis and Manitoba Railway, James Hill. A Canadian by birth, Hill was a veteran of American railway development, as well as a shrewd businessman. It was Hill who had convinced George Stephen, President of the Bank of Montreal, that the Manitoba road had great potential. From the beginning, Hill was thoroughly opposed to the Superior section of the CPR and tried to see whether this aspect of the contract could be changed before an agreement was reached. "After the [Superior] line is completed," he argued to fellow Syndicate member, Robert Angus, in July 1880, "I cannot see that it would have any local business whatever for some time and the through traffic would not afford it enough money to meet the payrolls and fuel, saying nothing of repairs and renewals."[48] Far from being concerned with the profitability of the Superior segment, Hill was more interested in the general welfare of the St. Paul, Minneapolis and Manitoba Railway. He saw the railroad serving as an American middle link between eastern and western Canada.[49] A more southerly route across the prairies would thus best accommodate this scheme.[50]

Even after it became clear that the Canadian government would accept nothing less than an all-Canadian route for the line, Hill still agreed to enter the Syndicate, albeit reluctantly. This decision was prompted by his fear of the activities of the Northern Pacific Railway. The St. Paul, Minneapolis and Manitoba Railway had an uneasy relationship with this rival American line, as both companies vied for the lucrative grain traffic of the upper Red River Valley. Thomas Oakes of the Northern Pacific attested to this situation several years later:

> I want to say in reference to the early days of the Northern Pacific management, that the board of directors, almost without an exception, felt very sore over the fact that the Great Northern road, then known as the St. Paul, Minneapolis & Manitoba, had taken possession of the Red River Valley and had built lines in all directions... They always felt that they had rights in the Red River valley, and that it was to be part of the policy of the Northern Pacific to build into the Red River country and develop the grain traffic there and become a factor in the matter. That view of the case logically lent strength to the idea that they [N.P.] would have to extend such a line into Manitoba.[51]

Sir George Stephen (1829–1921), president of the Canadian Pacific Railway 1881–88, photographed 1890 (Courtesy of the Glenbow Archives/NA-1375-4).

Now, just as the CPR Syndicate was being formed, the Northern Pacific decided to build a through line across the continent from Bismark to Spokane and Portland. This thrust to the Pacific threatened the future survival of the local Manitoba road. Hill consequently had little choice but to enter the Syndicate in the hope that the Superior section would in the end prove unfeasible; the alternative was to turn the St. Paul, Minneapolis and Manitoba Railway into a transcontinental line as well.[52] A more southerly route for the CPR, meanwhile, assumed even greater importance to Hill. It would effectively "close the way for other ambitious parties who could come after us."[53]

George Stephen, CPR president, shared Hill's concerns about the intentions of the Northern Pacific and his belief in the desirability of a more southerly route. He greatly feared that the rival company, under the indomitable Henry Villard, would invade Canadian territory at some point along the international boundary, or gain controlling interest in a line in Manitoba; either action would be potentially disastrous to the CPR.[54] Stephen therefore encouraged Hill in 1881 to make "an earnest effort" to settle all outstanding differences with the Northern Pacific.[55] Yet, he did not delude himself about the chances of an equitable agreement. "But as matters stand, while a man of the egotistic stamp of Villard is in control," he warned Hill, "it will not be easy to arrive at any reasonable and permanent agreement. Villard's vanity will be apt to lead him to reject any treaty of peace that does not seem to gratify his vain desire to obtain a triumph." Stephen's own position did not make such a settlement any easier. He was determined not "to sacrifice any of the substantial advantages of the position to which we are justly entitled."

This suspicion of the Northern Pacific's intentions had been a major factor in Stephen's negotiations with the Conservative government. "Now what do you think would be the position of the CPR or of the men bound to own or operate it," he asked Prime Minister Macdonald in October 1880, if it were tapped at Winnipeg or at any other point west of it by a line or lines running towards the U.S. boundary. What would, in such a case, be the value of the CPR line from Winnipeg to Ottawa? No sane man would give one dollar for the whole line east of Winn. I need not say more on this point as it must be clear to you that any and every line south of the line of the CPR running towards the boundary line must be owned and controlled by the CPR. Otherwise the CPR would be strangled.[56]

Stephen's preferred solution to this problem called for part of the CPR land grant to be composed of a 12-mile wide belt of land along the 49th parallel from Manitoba to the Rocky Mountains; even the ever-enthusiastic Macoun had few kind words about the capabilities of the land along the boundary.[57] The government, however, balked at this suggestion and agreed instead to grant the Syndicate a 20-year monopoly over western traffic.[58] This much-criticized monopoly clause certainly went a long way in easing the Syndicate's concerns, but it was still not enough. Realizing that the main line could serve or control only a limited area, it decided to crowd the boundary as closely as possible in order to restrict the territory of the rival Northern Pacific. Originally, the Syndicate had wanted to build the line through the Crow's Nest Pass. The Conservatives, however, for security reasons preferred that the road be built 100 miles north of the international border. Roger's Pass offered a compromise between the two positions.[59] It is questionable whether the CPR main line would have turned north from Moose Jaw if this pass had not been discovered.

This attempt to prevent American inroads into the Canadian West was further necessitated because the CPR was intended to be an all-Canadian line running through the wilderness north of Lake Superior. Stephen had initially regarded such an undertaking as great folly. Once he accepted the challenge, however, he realized that a more southerly route was necessary if the CPR was to secure as much western traffic as possible for this otherwise "useless" section north of the Great Lakes. Stephen lectured Macdonald:

How do you suppose the line north of Lake Superior can be maintained and operated if the N.P. succeeds in getting control of the traffic of Manitoba or what is practically the same thing forcing down the rates to a point which leaves no profit? The N.P. have no line north of L. Superior to sustain, and as I have always told you without a through line north of Lake Superior there would be no CPR. The line north of

>Lake Superior cannot be operated unless it can get the traf-
>fic, and reasonably fair rates.[60]

This concern for the welfare of the Superior segment also figured in Stephen's 1888 purchase of the Minneapolis, St. Paul and Sault Ste. Marie rail line, the so-called "Soo line" that ran south of Superior. By such a move, he hoped to prevent the line from falling into the hands of the CPR's rivals and being used against the Superior section. "In securing this position," Stephen explained to Macdonald, "I think I have done more to secure the traffic of the Canadian North West to the CPR for all time to come, than anything I have yet done for it."[61] His overriding concern was nothing less than "the maintenance of the power and independence of the national highway."

The construction of the CPR main line above Superior eventually forced Hill to withdraw from the Syndicate in May 1883. He realized that if he was to secure a through line to the Pacific for the Manitoba road he would have to construct it himself at some future date. His three-year membership in the Syndicate, however, had had its benefits, in that the St. Paul line had carried most of the construction materials for the CPR's prairie section. Even after Hill's departure, relations between the two lines remained relatively cordial, since it was in their best interests to continue to co-operate in the North-West against rival lines. Stephen emphasized this point in a letter to Hill in November 1883: "The interest of the two roads, properly understood, is to work together, each respecting the interests and rights of the other standing shoulder to shoulder against all intruders."[62] Such a strategic position would not have been possible had the CPR main line followed Fleming's Yellowhead route. Indeed, reflecting on the recent completion of the project, Christmas Day 1885, Stephen was more than ever convinced of the wisdom of the decision to build across the prairie grasslands. "To have taken the northern route would have been a *fatal* mistake in every way," he confided to Hill, "Whatever other mistakes have been made there may be no error in the location of the route."[63]

The rerouting of the CPR main line was thus not based on John Macoun's explorations in the prairie region in 1879 and 1880. The decision nonetheless did have great implications for his work. Before the route change had been made, Macoun was one of the most vocal advocates of the agricultural potential of the southern grasslands. When the Syndicate subsequently built where they did, it was a genuine coincidence, but one that suggested that Macoun's field work had been responsible for the change in route. People connected with the railway locational question in the 1870s, including Sandford Fleming, were astonished at the abandonment of the Yellowhead route. Searching for an explanation, they fell upon Macoun's pronouncements

The task accomplished. Less than five years after the company was incorporated, the Canadian Pacific Railway completed its Montreal-Vancouver railway with the driving of the last spike, pictured here, at Craigellachie in Eagle Pass of the Gold Range, Rocky Mountains, at 9:30 a.m., November 7, 1885. Contrary to popular belief, the spike was *not* a gold one. It was an ordinary iron spike "just as good" said Sir William Van Horne, general manager of the CPR, "as any of the other iron spikes which have been used to build this railway." Through rail service commenced the following July (Courtesy of the Saskatchewan Archives Board/R-B4291).

which had been given government support by Tupper and now happened to provide the agricultural justification for the route.[64] The Syndicate, in defending the quality of the land along the main line, also seemed to suggest that Macoun's work had been a factor.[65] Somewhat ironically, however, Tupper made no mention of Macoun's work during the debate on the bill to authorize the route change. He simply argued that the Kicking Horse Pass offered a shorter route.[66] This other reason for the route change has also tended to obscure the real issues upon which the Syndicate based its decision. The Kicking Horse route may have been shorter but it resulted in significantly higher grades than those of the Yellowhead.[67] Today, a television actor portraying Donald Smith announces that the CPR will build an extensive tunnel network to avoid the grade problems of the mountain pass.

Macoun himself did much to foster the belief that his field work had accounted for the main line location-a belief that he held personally. Following the route relocation, he tried to help the CPR cause by popularizing the southern plains at the expense of the fertile belt. In *Manitoba and the*

Great North-West, he suggested that the North Saskatchewan country was not as well suited for agriculture because of early frosts and wet harvests.[68] This distinction between regions was totally out of character. Before the route change, Macoun had tended to emphasize the merits of each region, whether it was the Peace River district or the third prairie steppe. He had been more concerned with extending fertility over the entire North-West and he was convinced that the physical disabilities of any region could be overcome or simply dismissed. His reports could have been used to justify any route. Now, however, he heralded the prairie grasslands as embracing the best farmlands. "Want either present or future is not to be feared," he prophesied, "and man living in a healthy and soul invigorating atmosphere will attain his highest development, and a nation will yet arise on these great plains that will have no superior on the American continent."[69] Macoun also portrayed himself, particularly in his autobiography, as the discoverer of the real truths about the character of the Western Interior.[70] He believed that the Syndicate had rerouted the CPR main line because his resource research had demonstrated that the southern plains were not an irreclaimable desert but actually the garden of the North-west. If, as many commentators have suggested, the building of the CPR main line across the sub-humid prairie district was a serious error, John Macoun was a willing scapegoat.

Notes

This article first appeared in *Prairie Forum* 10, no. 1 (1985): 65–82.

The research for this paper was funded by a grant from the Dean's Discretionary Fund, College of Arts and Science, University of Saskatchewan.

1. Morris Zaslow, *The Opening of the Canadian North, 1870–1914* (Toronto: McClelland and Stewart, 1971), 28–29.

2. See F.G. Roe, "An Unresolved Problem of Canadian History," *Canadian Historical Association Annual Report* (1936), 65–77; Pierre Berton, *The Last Spike* (Toronto: McClelland and Stewart, 1971), 11–23.

3. James Gray, *Men Against the Desert* (Saskatoon: Western Producer Prairie Books, 1967), 7.

4. Pierre Berton, *The National Dream* (Toronto: McClelland and Stewart, 1970), 45.

5. Doug Owram, *Promise of Eden. The Canadian Expansionist Movement and the Idea of the West 1856–1900* (Toronto: University of Toronto Press; 1980), 161–62.

6. This idea that the route was changed to meet the threat of possible American competition is not new. See V.C. Fowke, *The National Policy and the Wheat Economy* (Toronto: University of Toronto Press, 1957), 52; H.A. Innis, *A History of the Canadian Pacific Railway* (Toronto: University of Toronto Press, 1923), 102–03; J.L. McDougall, *Canadian Pacific* (Montreal: McGill University Press, 1968), 51–52; P.B. Waite, *Canada 1874–1896: Arduous Destiny. Canada 1874–1896* (Toronto: McClelland and Stewart, 1971), 127. The recently opened J.J. Hill papers in St. Paul, Minnesota and newly discovered Macoun manuscript materials, however, tend to confirm this interpretation.

7. John Warkentin, "Steppe, Prairie and Empire" in A.W. Rasporich and H.C. Klassen (eds.), *Prairie Perspectives 2* (Toronto: Holt, Rhinehart and Winston of Canada, 1973), 124.

8. G.M. Grant, *Ocean to Ocean* (Toronto: James Campbell and Son, 1873), 23.

9. John Macoun, "The Capabilities of the Prairie Lands of the Great North-West, as Shown by Their Fauna and Flora," *Ottawa Field-Naturalists' Club Transactions* 3, no. 2 (1881): 37–38.

10. Library and Archives Canada (hereafter LAC), Manuscript Division. John Macoun Papers, 1872 field notebook, October 4, 1872.

11. John Macoun, "Botanical Report, Lake Superior to Pacific Ocean" in S. Fleming (ed.), *Canadian Pacific Railway Report of Progress on the Explorations and Surveys up to January, 1874* (Ottawa: Maclean, Roger and Company, 1874), Appendix C, 56–98.

12. Ibid., 65.

13. John Macoun, *Autobiography of John Macoun* (Ottawa: Ottawa Field-Naturalists' Club, 1922), 88.

14. Macoun, "Botanical Report, Lake Superior to Pacific Ocean," 94.

15. C. Horetzky, *Canada on the Pacific* (Montreal: Dawson Brothers, 1874), 198–99.

16. W.F. Butler, *The Wild North Land* (London: Low Marston, Low and Searle, 1873), 353–56.

17. Royal Kew Gardens. British North America Letters, v. 195, John Macoun to J.D. Hooker, September 5, 1876.

18. Macoun Papers, 1875 field notebook, Geological Notes on Peace River.

19. John Macoun, "Report on the Botanical Features of the Country Traversed from Vancouver to Carlton on the Saskatchewan," *Geological Survey of Canada Report of Progress for 1875–1876* (Montreal: Dawson Brothers, 1877), 110–232, Even Dr. Selwyn, who had lauded the fertility of the North Saskatchewan country only two years earlier, stated in his report that the Peace River district was a magnificent agricultural country, deserving of thorough examination.

20. Canada. House of Commons. *Journals*, v. 10, 1876, "Report of the Select Standing Committee on Agriculture and Colonization," Appendix 8, 20–43 (Macoun testimony).

21. John Macoun, "Sketch of that Portion of Canada Between Lake Superior and the Rocky Mountains, with Special Reference to its Agricultural Capabilities," in S. Fleming (ed.), *Report on Surveys and Preliminary Operations on the Canadian Pacific Railway up to January, 1877* (Ottawa: Maclean, Roger and Company, 1877), Appendix 10, 313–36.

22. Horetzky had been unable to secure either guides or boats for his planned ascent of the Pine River in 1872. Dr. Selwyn tried twice to find the pass in 1875 but failed both times.

23. A. Wilson, "Fleming and Tupper: The Fall of the Siamese Twins, 1880," in J.S. Moir (ed.), *Character and Circumstance* (Toronto: Macmillan, 1970), 109–13.

24. Ibid., 115–16.

25. Macoun, *Autobiography*, 135.

26. Fleming, in the 1880 railway report, simply stated that the prairie region required further exploration. S. Fleming (ed.), *Report and Documents in Reference to the Canadian Pacific Railway, 1880* (Ottawa: Maclean, Roger and Company, 1800), 13.

27. Canada. House of Commons. *Debates*, May 10, 1879, p. 1893.

28. Macoun, "Sketch of that Portion of Canada Between Lake Superior and the Rocky Mountains," 64.

29. Wilson, "Fleming and Tupper," 119–20.

30. John Macoun, "General Remarks on the Land, Wood and Water of the North-West Territories, from the 102nd to 115th meridian, and between the 51st and 53rd parallels

of latitude," in Fleming (ed.), *Report and Documents in Reference to the Canadian Pacific Railway, 1880*, Appendix 14, 240.

31. John Macoun, *Manitoba and the Great North-West* (Guelph: World Publishing Company, 1882), 612.

32. Canada. House of Commons. *Debates*, March 3, 1880, p. 391.

33. Ibid., April 15, 1880, 1407–09.

34. Macoun, *Manitoba and the Great North-West*, 612.

35. John Macoun, "Extract from a Report of Exploration in the North-West Territories" in Canada. *Sessional Papers*, 1881, n. 3, Report of the Department of the Interior for 1880, part 1, p. 10,

36. LAC, Sandford Fleming Papers, J. Macoun to S. Fleming, August 14, 1880.

37. Macoun, "Extract from a Report of Exploration," 22.

38. Quoted in Manitoba *Free Press*, April 7, 1881.

39. Canada. House of Commons. *Debates*, December 14, 880, p. 73.

40. *Statutes of Canada*, 44 Vic. 1880, C. 1, 11.

41. Macoun, *Autobiography*, 184–85.

42. Personal communication, W.T. White to W.A. Waiser, February 18, 1982.

43. See note 2.

44. The James Jerome Hill Reference Library, J.J. Hill Papers, J.J. Hill to R. Angus, December 17, 1880. Quoted in Albro Martin, *James J. Hill and the Opening of the Northwest* (New York: Oxford University Press, 1976), 246.

45. LAC, J.A. Macdonald Papers, v. 209, 88954–56, J.S. Dennis to J.A. Macdonald, April 22, 1881.

46. A.A. den Otter, *Civilizing the West, the Galts and the Development of Western Canada* (Edmonton: University of Alberta Press, 1982), 77.

47. I am indebted to Dr. T.D. Regehr for sharing his vast knowledge of Western Canadian railway history with me. He guided me to several important letters dealing with the CPR route selection.

48. Hill Papers, J.J. Hill to R. Angus, July 8, 1880. Quoted in Martin, *Hill and the Opening of the Northwest*, 247.

49. Ibid., 239.

50. Albro Martin suggests that Macoun's field work was one of the factors that convinced Hill to bring the main line south. Martin's source of reference, however, is Macoun's own *Manitoba and the Great North-West*, personal communication, A. Martin to W.A. Waiser, January 25, 1982.

51. Baker Library, Harvard University, H. Villard papers, "Northern Pacific and Manitoba Railway Company Testimony" folder, Thomas Oakes testimony, June 14, 1894.

52. "The only reason for going into the scheme was for the purpose of benefitting the St. P.M.&M. Ry.," J.J. Hill to R. Angus, October 18, 1880. Quoted in Martin, *Hill and the Opening of the Northwest*, 247.

53. J.J. Hill to R. Angus, December 17, 1880. Quoted in ibid., 246.

54. Heather Gilbert, *Awakening Continent* (Aberdeen: Aberdeen University Press, 1965), 75, 85.

55. LAC, Hill Papers, G. Stephen to J.J. Hill, December 19, 1881.

56. LAC, Macdonald Papers, v. 268, 121836–38, G. Stephen to J. A. Macdonald, October 18, 1880.

57. Macoun, "Extract from a Report of Exploration…," 17–18.

58. Gilbert, *Awakening Continent*, 74.

59. "Were it not for the objections raised by the Government of that day, the Canadian Pacific Railway would originally have been built through the Crow's Nest Pass. It was thought by the Government, however, that it brought the Transcontinental line too close to the international frontier, and as a consequence the present pass known as 'Kicking Horse' was utilized…" LAC, Shaughnessy letterbook, n. 51, p. 785, Thomas Shaughnessy to Sir Oliver Mowat, April 14, 1897. "When the Canadian Pacific Company entered upon its undertaking in 1881 its intention was to survey the Crow's Nest Pass with a view to carrying the line that way, but the Government would not consent to this because it would bring it so near the International Boundary that in the event of war with the United States the line could be easily cut, and it was with difficulty that the Government could be induced to the building of the line as far south as the Kicking Horse." LAC, Van Horne letterbook, n. 52, p. 118, Van Horne to J.P. Edgar, October 2, 1896.

60. LAC, Macdonald Papers, v. 271, 124120–25, G. Stephen to J.A. Macdonald, November 19, 1888.

61. Ibid., v. 271, 123911–14, G. Stephen to J.A. Macdonald, April 22, 1888.

62. LAC, Hill Papers, G. Stephen to J.J. Hill, November 14, 1883.

63. Ibid., December 25, 1885.

64. Macoun, *Autobiography*, 185.

65. See, for example, G. Stephen to Editor, Toronto *Globe*, September 10, 1883. Quoted in Gilbert, *Awakening Continent*, Appendix 2.

66. Canada. House of Commons. *Debates*, April 17, 1882, p. 953; April 19, 1882, p. 1030.

67. Roe, "An Unresolved Problem…" 71–72. For a dicussion of the Rogers Pass situation, see Alan Brown, "CPR Tackling Rogers Pass… Again!," *Canadian Geographer* 103, no. 4 (September 1983): 34–40.

68. Macoun, *Manitoba and the Great North-West*, 119.

69. Ibid., 264.

70. Macoun, *Autobiography*, 162.

3.   Transportation and Settlement: Problems in the
      Expansion of the Frontier of Saskatchewan and
      Assiniboia in 1904

P.L. McCormick

The period 1901–11 has been referred to as the "boom decade" in
Canadian economic history.[1] Certainly it was an era of unprecedented
expansion, and the focus for most of its energy and activity was the western
interior of Canada. There the atmosphere of growth and optimism appeared
to have few restraints, political, economic or social. This fundamental confidence in the future of the Canadian west was constantly reinforced, moreover, by an impressive list of tangible accomplishments. The accelerating
production and export of wheat spurred the whole Canadian economy to
expand and diversify; two additional transcontinental railways were under
construction; and almost a million migrants sought a better life on the
Canadian prairies. During this decade, settlers, politicians and entrepreneurs alike successfully internalized the values of change, development and
progress so familiar and essential to the opening of a frontier area.

Transportation routes were vitally important in prompting the rapid
transformation and settlement of the Northwest. During this period, the
railways provided the new immigrant with access to the interior of Canada
and, along with the prairie trails, with access to his farmland. The railways
also furnished contact with the eastern and foreign markets which the new
settlers needed in order to participate in the grain-marketing economy.
Moreover, the growth of railway lines was the story of the growth of service
centres along their routes. In short, one major concern of prairie life was the
need for more and better transportation routes.

After the turn of the century, a dense network of railway lines was built
up across the plains. The pace of railway building and the pace of settlement
during this period, however, did not always coincide. In 1904, a year of high
immigration, railway construction badly lagged behind settlement in the

Immigrants arrive at the Canadian Pacific Railway station in Winnipeg, Manitoba (Courtesy of the Archives of Manitoba/N2066).

Districts of Saskatchewan and Assiniboia. The demand for more railway lines was strident and persistent, but the settlers in the new districts had to accommodate their needs for transportation by using the old prairie trails or by blazing new trails as the need arose.

Trails in Assiniboia and Saskatchewan

Many of the trails used in 1904 (Figure 1) had their origins in the fur trade and in the early years of the North-West Mounted Police (NWMP).[2] In the District of Saskatchewan most of these historic trails converged on Fort Carleton and Batoche; in Assiniboia they met at Fort Qu'Appelle. These trails were well trodden and usually surveyed.

Just as survey lines tended to persist through time, so did the prairie trail.[3] Long after Fort Carleton had lost its economic and strategic position, the trails linking it to other abandoned forts, such as Fort a la Corne and Fort Touchwood, continued to be used by settlers and traders. However, the lines of communication had shifted some-what and, in 1904, many major trails joined the numerous NWMP Stations in the Districts.[4]

New trails were broken as the need arose. By 1904 there were many areas where the trails criss-crossed like filigree. Along the main line of the Canadian Pacific Railway (CPR), from the Manitoba border to Regina, an area of older settlement, the trails formed a particularly dense network. There were also many surveyed and informal trails in the Rosthern, Duck Lake and Prince Albert district.

The trails seldom followed the survey lines. The settlers, who were naturally concerned with economy of energy, whether their own or their animals, chose the shortest and driest route between two points, and so they ignored the road allowances provided in the survey. The trails, then, were

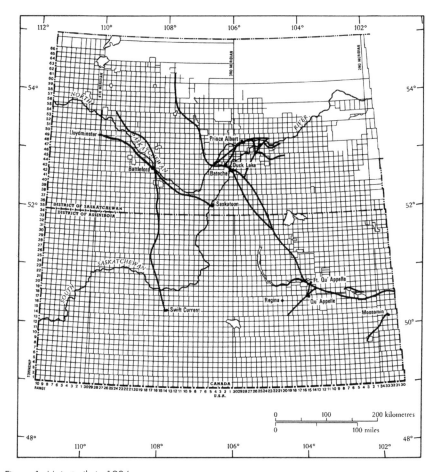

Figure 1. Main trails in 1904.
Source: Canada, *Map Showing Mounted Police Stations in the North-West Territories, 1904.* LAC, V3/700, 1904.

made for the purposes of accessibility and convenience. In fact, they were one of the few cultural features on the prairie landscape which did not conform to a strict north-south or east-west orientation. The radial pattern, formed by the convergence of trails at Fort Carleton or Fort Qu'Appelle, presented a disarming exception to the imposition of the survey grid on the plains.

The density of trails tended to increase as settlement advanced, but the breaking of more and more land for cultivation was beginning to threaten their existence. By 1904, some farmers had started to fence their property and to forbid access to other settlers and traders:

> The closing of some of the trails gives a good deal of inconvenience to the traveller and stranger and should be properly advertised, not only in the local papers, but in public places.[5]

The trails were often impassable in the spring, when snowmelt and spring rains turned low spots into quagmires. Summer thunderstorms could also transform the hard clay surface into a muddy morass. When harvesting was completed in the fall, the prudent farmer usually waited until the autumn frosts had penetrated the surface of the trails before hauling his grain to the railway.[6]

Some trails, however, were kept in better condition than others, no matter what the season. As gravel was scarce, any improvements to the trails were expensive, and only the major trails were maintained. The *Phenix* reported that the trail from Saskatoon to Lloydminster was well beaten and "always passable."[7] The trail from Lloydminster to Edmonton, on the other hand, was "nothing but a series of swamps and muskegs, through which it was impossible to haul an empty wagon, much less a heavily-laden one."[8] The Saskatoon-Battleford Trail had an additional advantage:

> The Saskatoon route is very much different this year. Travellers are hardly out of sight of houses and in no case is the distance between stopping houses further than 12 miles.[9]

The trails were much more important in the settlement of the west than they appeared from their modest form and light tracings on the landscape. Before the railways could carry new settlers to their destinations, the trails acted as the main transportation route to the homesteads.[10] The Saskatoon-Battleford Trail and the Eagle Creek Trail which ran west of Saskatoon channelled much of the new settlement along their margins. In Assiniboia, the trails radiating from Fort Touchwood were important pathways.

When I arrived at Fort Qu'Appelle in 1904 I found that owing to the extremely high snowfall of the previous winter the Qu'Appelle River had overflowed its banks so that the grade approach to the old wooden bridge had been under several feet of water. Several hundred homesteaders going to the File Hills, Loon Creek, and Last Mountain Valley had to stay in their tents for about two weeks... . The only road going north was up the old Telegraph Hill which was just a prairie trail up a winding steep coulee. From there I followed the old Touchwood Trail, which at that time was a dozen or so deep ruts which meandered in a generally northerly direction to Kutawa. Upon arriving at a point where a halfbreed family lived, whose name was Sangre, I turned off in a north-westerly direction to my homestead. This Sangre ran a stopping place for homesteaders.[11]

Access to a good trail, therefore, was almost as important as access to a railway line. And just as settlement tended to proceed outward from the railway lines, so too did settlement spread outward from the trails. In 1904, for

Lumsden, North-West Territories, 1904. The flooding of the Qu'Appelle River causes one of the worst floods in the community's history. The railway tracks through the Qu'Appelle Valley between Regina and Saskatoon were washed out, causing delays and other difficulties for settlers travelling north (Courtesy Saskatchewan Archives Board R-A9646).

example, an agent of the Department of the Interior reported that many new Ontario immigrants had settled in the area south of Battleford, which was not yet serviced by a railway. These settlers used the Saskatoon-Battleford Trail or the Eagle Hills Trail to gain access to their homesteads.[12]

Railways

Homestead land was the lure held out by the federal government to attract prospective immigrants, but the railways were needed to get them there. The distribution of railway lines and their projected extensions had a profound effect on settlement patterns in the Great Plains. As Isaiah Bowman

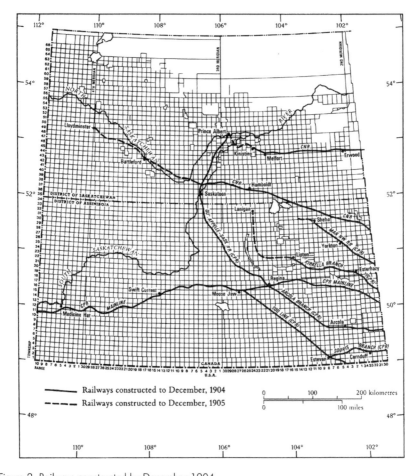

Figure 2. Railways constructed by December 1904.
Source: Canada, *Map Showing Mounted Police Stations in the North-West Territories, 1904*. LAC, V3/700, 1904, corrected for railway extensions by *Map of Railway Steel laid in Saskatchewan, prior to January 1, 1908*. Saskatchewan Archives Board A25/3.

succinctly remarked: "the railroad is the forerunner of development, the pre-pioneer, the base line of agriculture."[13] People not only settled along all existing lines, but they also tried to anticipate future railway routes. As Warkentin noted in his study of the Canadian North-West in 1886: "Transportation facilities, of course, had guided the flow of settlers, so that areas having similar natural environments did not necessarily have corresponding levels of development."[14]

In the grain belt of the Canadian prairies access to a railway line was imperative if a settler were to move out of a subsistence economy and to start selling his wheat in the export market.[15] Although instances of hauling grain 50–60 miles to the nearest railway station frequently occurred, the farmer was unlikely to transport his grain economically by horse and wagon more than 10 miles.[16] Accordingly, towns and villages were strung out 7–8 miles apart along the numerous railway branch lines, and homesteads were located as close as possible to them.

Homestead land was thus in greatest demand near existing railway lines, or in areas where railway lines were projected. The Battleford agent of the Department of the Interior, for example, reported in 1904 that the patience of settlers in the area was finally about to be rewarded:

> As there is still no means of profitable transportation, no farm products are intended for export. But in view of the probable completion early next spring of the line of the Canadian Northern Railway, preparations are now being made by the farmers here for more extensive seeding operations next spring. It is expected that there will be 15,000 acres under crop next year, whereas the present area is scarcely 9,000 acres.[17]

But the problem of outguessing the railway surveyors and bosses, by correctly anticipating the future route of a railway, was still a difficult one.[18] According to a map published in 1904, the projected route of the Kirkella branch of the CPR was to travel in a north-westerly direction from Lipton to Saskatoon.[19] In 1905, when the branch was extended past Lipton, it was built amost due west to Bulyea, and then northward along the eastern shore of Last Mountain lake to Lanigan.

By the end of 1904, construction had added several hundred miles of railway lines in Saskatchewan and Assiniboia (Figure 2).[20] Between January and December 1904, the main line of the Canadian Northern Railway was extended from the Manitoba border to the "elbow" of the North Saskatchewan River northwest of Saskatoon, and grading was almost completed to Battleford.[21] The Arcola branch of the CPR reached its terminus at

Regina.[22] The Kirkella branch of the same company had steel laid as far as Lipton, and grading had advanced as far as Strassburg.[23] The Canadian Northern Erwood branch had reached Kinistino and was graded to within 18 miles of Prince Albert.[24] The Manitoba and North Western Railway, leased to the CPR, on the other hand, had made little headway. The line had been extended from Yorkton to Sheho, a mere 43 miles.[25]

The distribution of railway lines in Saskatchewan and Assiniboia by the end of 1904 was quite irregular. Only the CPR main line traversed the area in an east-west direction. All the other lines, except for the Soo Line and the Qu'Appelle, Long Lake and Saskatchewan Railway, originated in Manitoba and for the most part were still operational only in the eastern half of the two Districts. The Canadian Northern main line did reach Lloydminster by the end of 1905, but that still does not alter the fact that the western half of the Districts, the frontier areas where much of the immigration was flowing, badly needed railway lines to service it. In 1904, most settlers were being forced to seek land at less economic distances from the railways, as homestead land near the railways had almost all been taken up.[26]

The growth of railway lines in Assiniboia and Saskatchewan was also the story of the growth of service centres along their routes.[27] As W.L. Morton remarked, the first requirement for a service centre was the railroad:

> The development of homestead site, indeed, the mere anticipation of it, brought about the rise of centres of distribution. The competition for distributive sites was even keener than that for homestead sites, for the potential gains, both from the speculation and operation, were greater. Distributive site was a function of transport, credit and the agricultural hinterland.[28]

The emergence of prairie villages, dominated by grain elevators and dotted along the railway lines, was a direct result of the control of the limits of the grain haul to the railway on settlement. And if the railway did not come to a pre-existing settlement, the villagers often picked up their buildings and moved to the railway.

A village situation on the railway in the midst of a settled area was virtually assured of rapid growth in 1904. Belle Plaine, a village east of Moose Jaw on the CPR main line, had only one store and two elevators in 1902; in 1904 it boasted one church, two stores, three elevators, two livery stables, coal sheds, lumber yard, a flour and feed store and a blacksmith's shop.[29] Moreover there were always opportunities for the enterprising businessman. The editor of the new Craik newspaper was a farmer from Wolseley who came up here last spring, invested in town lots and built a business block 16 X 24 X 14 for the accommodation of his different branches of business, which include general merchandise, a restaurant, hardware and butcher shop. He is also the proprietor of the skating rink, and a manufacturer of lime.[30]

Settlement in 1904: Homestead Land

In choosing land to settle, the new immigrant in Saskatchewan and Assiniboia faced basically three alternatives. He/she could homestead 160 acres of raw prairie; could purchase new or improved land from the railway companies, the Hudson's Bay Company or from one of the many land companies; or could opt for a combination of homestead and purchased land.

A Ukrainian family in front of their home at Malonton, Manitoba, circa 1915 (Courtesy of the Archives of Manitoba/N11632).

The option which the new settler chose depended mainly on his economic status, and, to a lesser extent, on his cultural needs. Many of the European immigrants had little or no capital to start farming even on a modest scale and, after they had filed for homestead entry, they were forced to seek outside work in order to buy stock and equipment. The Ukrainians, Doukhobors and Hungarians all suffered from these economic constraints. In addition, most European immigrants wished to pursue mixed farming and so they preferred to settle in the park belt where there were plentiful supplies of water, wood and meadows. Moreover, they often sought homesteads located near those of their compatriots. As J.C. Lehr has pointed out, many Ukrainians were willing to farm marginal agricultural land simply to live in close proximity to relatives or friends from the same village or from the same area of the Ukraine.[31]

Other immigrants from eastern Canada, Britain and the United States, of course, entered for homestead land in great numbers, but they were more individualistic, and they had little reason to be preoccupied with the maintenance of an ethnic identity. The Americans, in particular, were in an antithetical position to that of the eastern European immigrants. Most of the American settlers were mid-western farmers who were able to transport much of their machinery, stock and accumulated capital north of the border. The Americans also had experience with dry-land farming techniques, and they therefore preferred to settle on the easily cleared grasslands and to go into wheat farming immediately. If homestead land near an existing railway line was not available, then the alternative of acquiring land by purchase still existed. Except for very special groups like the German-Catholic St. Joseph's colonists, who deliberately chose an isolated area near the present town of Kerrobert to maintain their ethnic cohesion, the Americans were willing to subordinate their cultural or social needs to economic goals.

There arose, then, a dichotomy between the American or Canadian settlers and the European immigrants. Not only did they separate out spatially during this period, but they also tended to pursue quite different economic and cultural ends.

In the Districts of Saskatchewan and Assiniboia, homestead entries for the fiscal year 1904 totalled 15,707, or the equivalent of 2,513,120 acres.[32] This was a decrease of over 4,000 entries from the previous year, and officials of the Department of the Interior were at pains to rationalize the drop in the number of immigrants.[33] In their opinion, the wet spring and the floods, "making the prairies one vast slough," undoubtedly deterred many American settlers from travelling into the west that year.[34] And 1903 clearly had been an exceptional year. Land companies, like the Saskatchewan Valley

Land Company, were especially active, and the Doukhobors had followed Peter Verigin's advice to file for their land that year.

By far the most active agency in 1904 was Yorkton, with 3,918 entries, followed by Regina (2,297) and the Saskatoon sub-agency (1,237).[35] Although overall homestead entries for the year showed a decrease, several agencies showed quite dramatic increases. Broadly speaking, most of the increases took place in areas (Figure 3) where settlement was burgeoning, the frontier fringe of 1904, and, significantly, where the railways had not yet built lines. The Lloydminster and Battleford sub-agencies (Figure 4) experienced a rush of entries from settlers in the area south of the North Saskatchewan River but located at an uneconomic distance from the projected Canadian

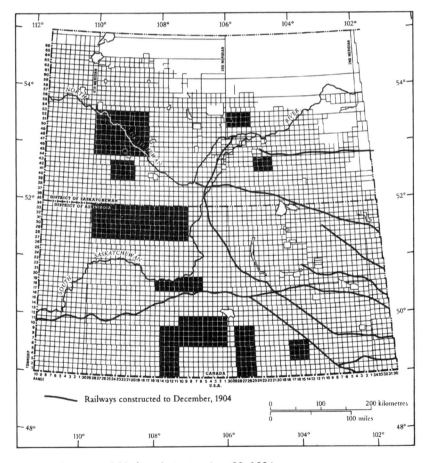

Figure 3. New districts available for colonization, June 30, 1904.
Source: Canada, *Sessional Papers*, 4–5 Ed. VII (1905),no. 25, part II, pp. 90–91.

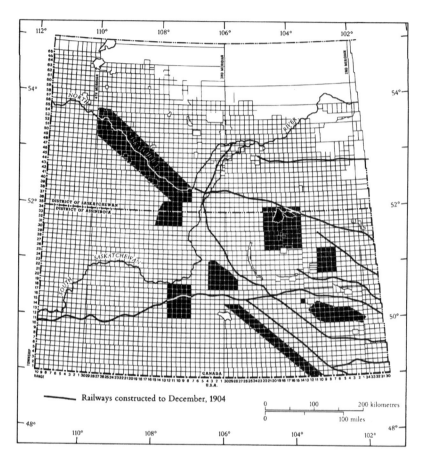

Figure 4. Areas to which land guides were to direct settlement.
Source: Memo, James Smart to W.D. Scott, December 21, 1904. LAC, RG 76, vol. 78, file 6382, part 2.

Northern line.[36] Another region of new settlement was the triangle formed by Foam Lake, the Touchwood Hills and Grenfell, an area to be serviced, somewhere, by the Grand Trunk Pacific.[37] And lastly, settlement was moving south, east and north of the Swift Current-Moose Jaw line.

In the Alameda agency, the Regina area and the Rosthern-Duck Lake district, on the other hand, much of the homestead land accessible to railways had been taken up, and this fact was reflected in the drop in the number of entries in 1904. The demand for good land in these areas, however, still existed, and it could only be satisfied either by purchasing land or by seeking cancellation of a homestead entry. Applications for cancellation of homestead entry, then, increased as the availability of good homestead land decreased. The Regina and Alameda Agencies had the highest number of applications for cancellation (1,911 and 1,011).[38] As the Dundurn correspondent reported in the *Phenix*:

> It is stated that fully fifty homesteads within a small radius back of the hill might be cancelled, owing to the negligence of those who hold them. The farmers there threaten to cancel all the home-steads that are not attended to. There are land seekers through here every day who would settle at once, if they were not prevented by these nominal claimants.[39]

The Yorkton agent, James Pleaker, also received many applications for cancellation, and, one suspects, it was land in the Doukhobor reserves that many settlers coveted.[40]

According to the Patents Branch of the Department of the Interior, most of the cancellations which were eventually granted were of entries originally made only a year or two years before (Table 1). In other words, entries made in 1902 and 1903 were those most frequently cancelled in 1904.[41] The ratio of cancellations to patents in 1904 is rather unsettling (Table 2). In Saskatchewan and Assiniboia agents approved 4,994 cancellations; at the same time they received only 1,640 applications for letters patent.[42] The toll of homesteading, in human terms, must have been high.

Table 1. Cancellations of Homestead Entries in 1904 (fiscal year)

Year of Entry	No. of Cancellations
1904	279
1903	4,125
1902	3,340
1901	426
1900	158
pre-1900	374
Total:	8,702

Source: CSP, 4–5 Ed. VII (1905), no. 25, part 1, p. 80.

Table 2. Homestead Entries, Applications for Patent, Entries Cancelled: 1904 (fiscal year)

	Entries	Applications for Patent	Entries Cancelled
Alameda	1,682	418	1,098
Battleford	1,774	4	314
Prince Albert	1,637	272	660
Regina	6,622	603	1,911
Yorkton	3,992	343	1,011
Totals:	15,707	1,640	4,994

Source: CSP, 4–5 Ed. VII (1905), no. 25, part 1, p. 6.

Railway Land

Land grants to railway companies were an important adjunct to the "Dominion Lands" policy of the federal government. In effect, public lands were used to finance the railway companies. The land grants were specifically designed to encourage the railways to build their lines quickly, thereby earning their subsidy, and to prod the railways into initiating an active immigration policy to fill up both homestead and railway lands in the west.

The railway companies received a specified number of acres for each mile of railway line constructed.[43] In this way, they acquired the odd-numbered sections in townships deemed, in their opinion, "fairly fit for settlement." The "fairly fit for settlement" clause was applied with varying degrees of rigour by the railway companies, and they usually showed little haste in selecting their lands. As a result, vast railway reserves were set up and held for the railways until they had completed their obligations and made their land selection. One direct consequence of the railway reserves, then, was to take out of circulation temporarily lands which would ultimately be made available for homesteading. By 1904 selections from the railway reserves were still taking place, although the large CPR main line grant had been settled with the establishment of the Irrigation Block in southern Alberta in August, 1903.[44]

The Canadian Pacific Railway Company, "the largest private owner of land in Canada," pursued the most aggressive immigration policy of all the railway companies.[45] It was particularly active in promoting immigration from eastern Canada (which, for political reasons, the Department of the Interior was forbidden to do), Britain and, after 1900, the United States. The main line grant was the focus for their promotional activities. By 1896, much of the homestead land along the main line east of Moose Jaw had been taken up.[46] The CPR then concentrated on selling its railway land in that area, and encouraging homesteaders to file entries on the land south of the line. By 1904, the CPR had sold most of its best land east of Moose Jaw and south of the main line for $3–$6 an acre.[47] Moreover, in that year, the Arcola branch was completed and it then supplemented the Soo Line and the CPR main line in servicing most of eastern Assiniboia.

Although the CPR was conscientious and enterprising in its efforts to bring new settlers into Assiniboia, it did not expend such energies in promoting settlement in the District of Saskatchewan. The Canadian Northern serviced that region by the end of 1904. As Hedges noted:

> The zeal which the company displayed in the work of settling the south was largely absent in the north, where ordinary business sense dictated a policy of waiting for the

> enjoyment of the unearned increment resulting from the
> labor and capital expended by others.[48]

In this area, known as the Battleford Block, it nonetheless sold land as the demand occurred. From June 1902 to June 1904, the CPR sold 630,818 acres in the Battleford area, and, as the government agent at Battleford remarked, "These lands were selected by the company many years ago, but there was practically no market for them until recent times."[49]

The CPR preferred to sell to actual settlers, but with the boom in settlement, especially after 1902, it quickly resorted to bulk sales to large and small land companies and speculators.[50] The largest of these companies was the North-West Colonization Company. In 1902, it acquired 986,949 acres on either side of the Soo Line from the CPR and the Canadian North-West Land Company. Sales were brisk in 1903 and 1904, and by the spring of 1905, all the land had been sold, mainly to Americans.[51]

In handling its land grants, the Canadian Northern Railway pursued a quiet different policy from that of the CPR. Mackenzie and Mann, the Canadian Northern's two principals, were astute businessmen, and they were very fussy in choosing their land subsidy. Not only did they wheel and deal with the government—by 1907 they had selected, with the government's consent, 712,901 acres from the reserve of the Qu'Appelle, Long Lake, and Saskatchewan Railway—but they also used their network of cruisers, and, in particular, station agents to choose the land.[52] The agents knew their districts intimately, and could make judicious choices of railway land for the company. And as they also served as land agents, the company saved money by their agents' performing a dual function.[53]

The other so-called colonization railway companies did not fare as well as the Canadian Pacific or Canadian Northern, nor did they feel under any obligation to promote settlement in the Northwest. By 1904 most of the land grants of the smaller companies either had been transferred to the CPR or the Canadian Northern through the purchase of the smaller lines, or had passed undocumented through the hands of large or small speculators.

Not only did the existence of railway land subsidies and reserves limit the amount of homestead land available to new settlers, therefore, but it also had a strong impact on the density of settlement. The presence of empty railway land adjacent to occupied homestead land was often an irritant and a source of grievance to the new immigrants in the frontier areas. It caused a greater dispersal of settlement at the very time when the homesteaders needed the social advantages of fairly dense or even nucleated settlement. And unless their own railway line ran through the land grant area, the railway companies were reluctant to sell their lands until a good price could be obtained. In addition, the railways were often disinclined even to choose their lands, let alone to sell them, as they would then have to pay taxes on them. In the early years of settlement, then, it was the homesteader who suffered from the government's lenient policy with the railways.

However, the presence of railway land on odd-numbered sections did have advantages for some settlers. These advantages tended to vary temporally and spatially. In the frontier areas of Saskatchewan and in the mixed farming region of the parkbelt, the farmers felt little need to increase their holdings by the purchase of adjoining railway land. In most cases they had neither the cash nor the inclination to farm a larger area.

But the situation was quite different in the grain belt. There the extensive cultivation of wheat and other grains prompted a general movement to larger, more economic holdings. In the older settlements of Assiniboia, the purchase of railway land was a common occurrence. As the Milestone agent reported in 1904: "Many homesteaders now having their entire quarter-section under crop ... are buying adjoining land. In some cases a whole square mile is under cultivation."[54] Even in the few frontier areas left in Assiniboia, the influx of Americans with substantial amounts of capital resulted in some families acquiring large blocks of land composed of homestead and contiguous railway lands. A description of the type of settler who was in a position to purchase land is given in a report by the St. Paul agent in July 1904.

> The average farmer takes in with him a car load of farm stock and implements and from $1,500 up in cash; one of them took with him over $38,000 in stock, cash and implements. It is not uncommon [for us] to send a settler with from $5,000 to $7,000 in cash.[55]

Railway land grants, therefore, were necessary for the financing of the railway lines which, in turn, served as the main transportation routes for the settlers and the wheat they exported. But the land subsidies were a mixed blessing to many settlers. To the homesteader of meagre means, they imposed heavy social and, at times, economic costs. In 1904 these substantial costs were still acutely felt in many of the frontier regions of Saskatchewan and Assiniboia. To the immigrant with capital, however, the availability of railway land speeded the transition from pioneer to large-scale grain farmer.

Conclusion

Two myths of the western Canadian frontier at the turn of the century are thus challenged. The first is the conventional belief that the railways preceded settlement into a new district and that, in fact, the railways were essential for the opening up of a frontier area. The second is the myth that rapid economic advancement was possible for the enterprising homesteader in the grain belt, even if he possessed little capital to begin with, and that he could achieve this mobility through dint of hard work and frugal living.

There exists, of course, some truth in both statements. But it is obvious that in 1904, a year of very rapid settlement in Saskatchewan and Assiniboia, there was only a modicum of truth in either. They formed, in fact, the exceptions to the rule.

Because of sluggish railway construction, pre-existing transportation routes played a significant part in directing settlement along their flanks. In this way the surveyed and well-beaten trails which linked the older settlements were still the highways of the incoming settlers. But with the rush of immigrants in 1904, new trails needed to be broken for access to choice farming areas; and in the more settled districts, complexes of new trails were built up as communications between settlers increased. In this way the trails were still the forerunners of development, to use Bowman's phrase, not the railways, especially in the raw frontier areas.

Despite their importance, the trails were to be an ephemeral feature on the landscape. With increased cultivation came the rapid obliteration of the trails by the plough. The private desire for maximum profits and easy cultivation superseded the public need for pathways. In 1904 the transition from the meandering trail to the rigid grid road system was just beginning.

Railways, because of the capital outlay involved in their construction and their vital economic role in the wheat economy, were a more permanent feature on the landscape. Settlement both followed the railway lines and anticipated their future routes. The railway was a necessary condition for the settler to rise above the subsistence level in agriculture. This applied most obviously to the grain farmer. In fact, the railway was a strong influence on the type of livelihood the pioneer pursued. The rancher lived furthest from the railway and drove his herds long distances to a railhead. The small mixed farmer, who consumed most of his produce himself or sold it to the local market, was able to survive at a greater distance from the railway. But the grain farmer had to be within economic hauling distance of an elevator. Consequently there was almost constant agitation for new railway lines to service the grain-belt farmers.

Access to railway lines improved in 1904, as new tracks were laid in both districts. But there was still a great need for more north-south links and railway lines west of the third meridian, where the thrust of new settlement was greatest. With the railways falling behind settlement, new immigrants had to buy rather than homestead land if they wished to enter into the grain-marketing economy. This is where both the economic and cultural differences, inherent in the ethnic background of the settlers, became apparent. Although there were exceptions, the European settlers were largely content to homestead a quarter-section in the parkbelt, to seek outside work to obtain capital and then to go into mixed farming, remaining at the subsistence level if necessary until a railway came through the district. Their preference, then, was for the wooded parkbelt, and their peasant expectations about wealth and land holdings made them self-sufficient, hard-working mixed farmers.

American settlers on their way to Alberta (Courtesy of the Archives of Manitoba/N7933).

The Americans, on the other hand, were a different breed. Most were second or third-generation immigrants from Europe who had farmed successfully in the US but had found it difficult to maintain their ethnicity. They wanted land near a railway line, and they usually wanted more than a quarter-section. They also wanted land that was easily cleared and suitable for grain farming. The short supply of homestead land which satisfied these requirements presented few problems to many American immigrants. In most cases they possessed enough capital to buy land outright from a railway, land company or the Hudson's Bay Company. With their machinery, farming experience and knowledge of dryland farming, they were able to go into extensive grain farming almost immediately. In contrast to the European immigrants, then, the American settlers with capital had high expectations for economic advancement, and they were impatient to achieve their ambitions. The American or Canadian settler who possessed little capital, however, was placed in roughly the same position as that of the European immigrant, but with none of the cultural support which came from belonging to a cohesive ethnic group.

Thus there appeared a disjunction between the quiet frontier of the mixed farmer and the more aggressive frontier of the grain farmer. This disjunction pointed out the differences in expectations and opportunities between the settlers with means and those possessing little capital. The popular belief that the frontier was open to all of strong limb and spirit was correct. But the myth that rapid economic gain was accessible to all was incorrect. In 1904 the settler who could expect great social and economic mobility was the settler who possessed capital to begin with.

Notes

This article first appeared in *Prairie Forum* 5, no. 1 (1980): 1–18. It is an expanded version of a paper presented at the meeting of the Canadian Association of Geographers in Victoria, May 1979.

1. W.T. Easterbrook and H.G.J. Aitken, *Canadian Economic History* (Toronto: Macmillan, 1958), 482.

2. See the map of historic trails in J.H. Richards and K.I. Fung (eds.), *The Atlas of Saskatchewan* (Saskatoon: University of Saskatchewan, 1969), 11.

3. See Norman Thrower's book, *Original Survey and Land Subdivision: A Comparative Study of the Form and Effect of Contrasting Cadastral Systems*, Monograph Series of the AAG (Chicago: n.p., 1966), 1. It is interesting to note that there is little correspondence between the major trails and the present highways in Saskatchewan. It would seem that the railway influenced the location of most highways, which merely provided an alternate transportation mode for the townspeople living along the railway lines.

4. Library and Archives Canada (LAC), *Map Showing Mounted Police Stations in the North-West Territories, 1904*, V3/700, 1904.

5. *Saskatoon Phenix*, June 17, 1904.

6. James Mavor, *Report to the Board of Trade on the North-West of Canada with Special Reference to Wheat Production for Export* (London: King's Printer, 1905), 92.

7. *Saskatoon Phenix*, March 18, 1904.

8. Ibid., March 18, 1904. There was a great debate in the *Phenix* over the merits of sending 3,000 British immigrants by trail from Saskatoon to Lloydminster or by rail to Edmonton and thence by trail or scow to Lloydminster.

9. *Saskatchewan Herald*, March 30, 1904.

10. John Friesen's observation on the function of the trails in Manitoba is similar: "The settlers found their way to their homesteads on the plains by following trails which were in use right up to the time the railways superseded them." "Expansion of Settlement in Manitoba, 1870–1900," in D. Swainson (ed.), *Historical Essays on the Prairie Provinces* (Toronto: McClelland and Stewart, 1970), 124.

11. G.F.W. Bruce, "Questionnaire Notes" (Saskatchewan Archives Questionnaire: Pioneer Farming Experiences), *Saskatchewan History* 8, no. 2 (Spring 1955): 55.

12. Canada. *Sessional Papers*, 4–5 Ed. VII (1905), no. 25, part II, p. 13. (Hereafter cited as CSP).

13. Isaiah Bowman, *The Pioneer Fringe* (New York: American Geographical Society, Special Publication No. 13, 1931), 74.

14. J. Warkentin, "Western Canada in 1886," in R. Louis Gentilcore (ed.), *Canada's Changing Geography* (Englewood Cliffs: Prentice-Hall, 1967), 77.

15. The railways, apparently, were just as eager for settlers to start producing grain for export. In an interview, Mr. Mann of the Canadian Northern reported: "Settlers ... are still pouring into the North West. To the ordinary observer this would mean that the railways were making money, but such is not the case. When a railway is built into a

new district where settlers are rapidly taking up land, it will be three to five years before much product is shipped out. If there is a surplus of wheat or other grain this is required by the new settlers for food, feed and seed, and it is not until their wants in these respects are satisfied and they themselves are raising crops that the railway does much business." *Saskatoon Phenix*, January 27, 1904.

16. Mavor, in his *Report to the Board of Trade*, mentioned the consequences of the time-distance factor in hauling grain for two types of farmer. The farmer with capital and a large holding near the railway could haul his grain immediately after harvesting it and secure payment. In this way, he, and other prosperous farmers like him, could, in a good crop year, effectively "block" the local elevator. He also had the option of shipping the grain himself under the conditions of the Manitoba Grain Act (63 and 64 Vict. C. 39, s. 58) if he thought the elevator price seemed too low.

On the other hand, the farmer with little capital and a small holding at some distance from the railway usually had to choose between ploughing his land or hauling his grain to the elevator after the harvest. There was seldom time for both activities. He therefore had to store his grain at his own cost, face deductions from the price of grain once he got it to the elevator, or even have his wheat rejected by the elevator manager for lack of storage space. Unless he had a box-car load of grain (1,000 bushels), he could not ship the grain himself.

The elevator managers stopped buying wheat at summer rates on October 20. In 1904, they discounted the price of wheat paid to the farmer after that date by 8¢-10¢ a bushel. Mavor, *Report to the Board of Trade*, 102–05.

17. *CSP*, 4–5 Ed. VII (1905), no. 25, p. 25.

18. As Bowman noted, those who anticipated the future route of a railway line got the best land and achieved the greatest margin between the original cost and later value. Bowman, *The Pioneer Fringe*, 70. "The end of the railway in a region of active pioneering is an area of wild speculation. The rails may be extended now or later, a town will spring up here or not there, and every settler feels that his choice of a location is in the path of progress. This means so rapid an increase of capital value, if he is right, that he is willing to endure all manner of hardship for a time and rest his case upon the hazard of his guess." Ibid., 64–65.

19. LAC, *Map Showing Mounted Police Stations, 1904*.

20. Approximately 500 miles of railway track was laid in 1904. The Canadian Northern main line advanced 200 miles; its Erwood line 110 miles; the Manitoba and North Western 45 miles; and the CPR's Kirkella branch 130 miles.

21. *Saskatoon Phenix*, November 11, 1904.

22. Report of Supt. Wilson of Regina, December 1903, NWMP Reports, *CSP* 3–4 Ed. VII (1904), No. 28, Part I, p. 95. The Arcola branch was nearing completion when Wilson made his report.

23. *Saskatoon Phenix*, November 18, 1904.

24. Report of Supt. Morris of Prince Albert, NWMP Reports, *CSP* 45 Ed. VII (1905), no. 28, part I, p. 63.

25. Ibid.

26. Settlers in the Outlook and Eagle Creek areas were badly in need of railway lines in 1904–05.

27. "A railway built through unsettled country exercises a profound influence not only on rural development but also on the growth of towns; it becomes, in fact, the chief promoter of town-sites." James Hedges, *Building the Canadian West: The Land and Colonization Policies of the Canadian Pacific Railway* (New York: Macmillan), 84.

28. W.L. Morton, "The Significance of Site in the Settlement of the American and Canadian Wests," *Agricultural History* 25, no. 3 (July 1951): 101.

29. *Moose Jaw Times*, January 14, 1904.

30. *Saskatoon Phenix*, February 12, 1904.

31. J.C. Lehr, "The Spatial Structure of Ukrainian Block Settlement in Western Canada," a paper presented to the Annual Meeting of the Canadian Association of Geographers in Victoria, May 1979.

32. *CSP*, 4–5 Ed. VII (1905), no. 25, p. xxiv.

33. *CSP*, 3–4 Ed. VII (1904), no. 25, p. xxiii.

34. *CSP*, 4–5 Ed. VII (1905), no. 25, part I, p. 76.

35. Ibid., pp. 6–7.

36. The Vermilion River sub-agent reported that 10 months before there had been only two other persons within 30 miles of his homestead, but since then 200 new settlers, mostly American and Canadian, had made entry. He stated that there were good homesteads still available 2 to 3 miles from the projected Canadian Northern line. *CSP*, 4–5 Ed. VII (1905), no. 25, part II, p. 76.

37. "The extension of the north-western branch of the Canadian Pacific from Yorkton to Sheho has filled every available quarter-section in the vicinity of the last-named town." *CSP*, 4–5 Ed. VII (1905), no. 25, part I, p. 60.
The Foam Lake Land Guide reported a continuous stream of immigrants into that area. Ibid., Part II, p. 85.

38. Ibid., p. 80.

39. *Saskatoon Phenix*, June 3, 1904.

40. "Needless to say these cancellations affect land close to railways, being closely watched by settlers with regard to the performance of homestead duties." *CSP*, 4–5 Ed. VII (1905), no. 25, part I, p. 30.

41. Ibid., p. 80.

42. Ibid., p. 6.

43. The Manitoba and North Western Railway Company and the Calgary and Edmonton Company received 6,400 acres for each mile of railway built. According to Hedges, the CPR land grant worked out to approximately 13,000 acres per mile of railway. Hedges, *Building the Canadian West*, 138.

44. All earned subsidies were located and patented by 1907.

45. For the CPR land grant in Saskatchewan and Assiniboia, see the map in Hedges, *Building the Canadian West*, 138.

46. Ibid., 156.

47. Ibid., 159 and 166. The *Saskatoon Phenix* (November 25, 1904) reported that in the month of October, 1904, the CPR sold 23,802 acres in the North-West at an average price of $4.50 an acre, the highest on record.

48. Ibid., 46.

49. *CSP*, 4–5 Ed. VII (1905), no. 25, part I, p. 12. Mr. Graviston of s. 25, 40-11-W3, bought a farm in 1901 from the CPR. By 1904, he had broken 130 acres and built a log house and granary. He then sold the farm to "an eastern capitalist" from Ontario for $5,000. *Saskatoon Phenix*, July 8, 1904.

50. Hedges reported that much of the CPR land sold to speculators was considered marginal in quality. Hedges, *Building the Canadian West*, 160. The speculators had to pay for their land within 6 years; settlers were given 10 years to pay. Between December 1901 and July 1906, the CPR sold 2,300,000 acres (in parcels of 40,000 acres each) to 13 land

companies. There were also many sales of smaller parcels. (less than 1,000 acres) to individual speculators. Ibid.

51. Ibid., 162–63.

52. Hedges, *The Federal Railway Land Subsidy Policy of Canada*, Harvard Historical Monographs III (Cambridge: Harvard University Press, 1934), 1 I1.

53. Board of Arbitration, Canadian Northern Railway, *Evidence*, 1918, vol. 4, pp. 2135–36.

54. *CSP*, 4–5 Ed. VII (1905), no. 25, part II, p. 82.

55. Ibid., p. 39. Each railway car of settlers' effects or stock was worth approximately $1,000. *Saskatoon Phenix*, November 11, 1904.

4. The Other Railway: Canadian National's Department of Colonization and Agriculture

Brian S. Osborne Susan E. Wurtele

The Canadian Pacific Railway (CPR) occupies a central position in the metanarrative of the settlement and development of Canada, and in particular of the Canadian West. It performed a grand role as part of the 19th-century *realpolitik* of nation building. Furthermore, it provided a more pragmatic service as dispenser of lands, carrier of goods and people, and as an active agent in the development of Canada's socioeconomic infrastructure. In each of these regards the CPR has received considerable attention.[1] With its colourful history and its position as Canada's first transcontinental railway, the CPR has captured the historical imagination of Canadians.[2]

But the CPR was not alone in these nation-building activities. From the close of the 19th century, it was joined by other railway ventures, notably the Canadian Northern Railway and the Grand Trunk Pacific.[3] The financial collapse of these ventures, and federal government intervention to pick up the pieces, resulted in the appearance of a new actor, the Canadian National Railways (CNR).[4]

The attention directed to the CPR's various roles has been further limited by the tendency to focus on the pre-1914 period: the dramatic period of western expansion and immigration associated with the Laurier–Sifton years. However, both the CPR and CNR were much involved in the significant immigration and settlement that continued during the 1918–61 period. During these years, some four million persons entered Canada and the two railways were active, not only as carriers of immigrants from eastern ports, but also as proponents of pro-immigration policies. Indeed, during the years of the "Railways-Government Agreement" (hereafter Railways Agreement) from 1925–30, and in modified form from 1947–61, they were closely integrated into federal immigration policy and practice.[5]

But if this period has received little attention, the role of the CNR as an active agency of national and regional development has also been neglected. To this end, this article will direct attention to the CNR's principal agency for promoting the colonization, settlement, and economic development of the regions tributary to its rail network: the Department of Colonization and Agriculture.

Organizing Colonization: The First Steps

Between 1919 and 1923, the Canadian National Railways system assembled and integrated a number of railway corporations including the Canadian Northern, the Grand Trunk, the Grand Trunk Pacific, and the Intercolonial. The origins of the CNR's colonization and settlement activities are to be found in the somewhat similar organizations developed by these predecessors. Thus, the Canadian Northern's promotional department was the model for the CNR's Industrial and Resources Department (IRD) established in 1919. Initially concerned with shepherding Canadian and American prospective settlers to unoccupied lands tributary to its western lines, in 1920 the IRD undertook the responsibility for colonization work in the Grand Trunk Pacific's lands in Manitoba and Saskatchewan, and expanded its operation out of the sales of land and into agricultural development. The first annual report for the IRD's operations in 1919 expressed the optimism of the new organization:

> Never in the history of the West has there been such a land settlement movement as that which has taken place along the Canadian National Railways lines this year; that is as to bona fide farmers going on the land with the intention of establishing permanent homes and working their farms. There has been little or no speculation. The class of settlers coming in, especially from the United States, has been of a fine and highly desirable type. Pessimists have fled from the country and every person engaged in the land business today, is anticipating a big business in 1920.[6]

While this boosterish tone continued into the next year, a note of caution identified a concern with assimilation and absorption of newcomers that was to become a common refrain in subsequent years:

> it is not advisable to rush people in faster than the country can take care of them, and especially now that it is most desirable that all immigrants should go on the land and be of a class likely to make good there. With indiscriminate immigration a large percentage of immigrants would soon drift into the cities and towns, already too crowded in

comparison with rural settlement, and become a burden on the public, and still worse, enter into unfair competition with our native sons, so many of whom train for town work and who have been brought up to higher standards than have many of the immigrants of the class that is likely to drift to the cities and into the hands of the welfare and charitable organizations.[7]

Peasant woman and children, Higgins Avenue, Winnipeg, circa 1907 (Courtesy of the Archives of Manitoba/N7935).

The very language of favoured "class," "indiscriminate" immigration, public "burden," "unfair competition," and "native sons" highlighted contemporary concerns. Nativism, which Palmer has described as an "amalgam of ethnic prejudice and nationalism," is clearly evident in the language of the report, as is a growing emphasis on issues of social reform.[8] The social reform movement, frequently associated with J.S. Woodsworth and the All People's Mission in Winnipeg, paid particular attention to the perceived problems associated with immigrants in modern urban conditions.[9] The IRD's rhetoric reflects the tendency towards applying principles of social engineering as appropriate means for dealing with such "problems." Finally, the IRD's comments demonstrate an emerging sensitivity, on the part of the "government's railway," to current Dominion immigration priorities. This is particularly evident in the efforts to minimize the drift of agricultural immigrants from rural to urban areas, which, it was believed, contributed to the negative public image of immigration in general.

In 1923, Sir Henry Thornton assumed the post of president of the CNR and brought with him a dynamic view of immigration, colonization and agricultural development. Thornton was anxious to see settlement on the vacant lands throughout the 22,000 miles of the CNR system. Such settlement would, he hoped, increase the economic productivity of those lands, and thus increase the volume and revenue of passenger and freight traffic. As noted in a corporate assessment of Thornton's vision of the task before him,

> one of the first conclusions he reached was that if the problem were ever to be solved there must be a larger population to provide patronage for the vast railway mileage of the Dominion, and hence a revival of the immigration which characterized the years immediately preceding the war.[10]

The facts supported Thornton's view of "the problem." In 1921, some 191,183 vacant homesteads amounting to 30,589,280 acres were still available along the northern edge of the Prairies, albeit in remote districts. Of these, 100,000 were in the Athabasca, Grande Prairie, and Peace River districts of Alberta; 40,000 in the northern fringe of the Saskatchewan parklands; and 34,000 in northwest Manitoba and the Interlake region.[11] In addition, there were also thousands of farms lying unoccupied and under-developed after being abandoned because of poor quality land, personal failure, or opportunities elsewhere. Contemporary theory argued that rail systems needed 400 persons per mile of track to be economically viable. Canadian railways had only about 300 persons per mile, with this figure dropping to a mere 100 persons per mile in the Prairies. Clearly, colonization, settlement, and development had to be a top corporate priority if the new railway was to be a commercially successful operation.[12]

Moreover, Thornton was very aware of the competition facing the CNR:

> Much was said in those days about the need of making the C.N.R. known, both in Great Britain and the Continent; railway stations and other public places had for years been placarded with Canadian Pacific posters depicting the grain fields of the West and the many opportunities which the Dominion offered prospective settlers; Canada and the C.P.R. were synonymous in the public mind of the old lands. A determined effort was to be made to remedy this situation.[13]

Accordingly, Thornton was an energetic promoter of the image of the CNR, working to increase public awareness of the railway's arrival on the Canadian corporate landscape. In 1923, he took steps toward creating an organization "to influence the largest possible rail movement and settlement to Canadian National lines."[14] The CNR's Department of Colonization and Development was established under the direction of the vice-president, W.D. Robb, with C. Price-Green as commissioner of Colonization and Development in the Montreal headquarters, and Dr. W.J. Black as European commissioner with headquarters in London, England.

Thornton was a firm believer in the professionalization of the railway's upper management. As the case of Dr. Black illustrates, Thornton hired trained and experienced men who were widely regarded as experts in their fields. Prior to joining the railway, Black had been president of the Manitoba Agricultural College from 1906 to 1914, deputy minister of Agriculture in Manitoba, chairman of the Soldier Settlement Board, and the federal deputy minister of Immigration.[15] He was clearly well qualified for the job. Indeed, in 1924, he was promoted from the London office to the position of head of the entire Department of Colonization and Development.

The new department was provided with a set of principles that underscored the fit between corporate and government priorities:

1. To influence the immigration and satisfactory settlement in Canada of the largest possible number of people of productive capacity which the country can absorb and assimilate;

2. to contribute to the dissemination of information concerning the vast and extensive natural resources of the Dominion and the widespread opportunities for industrial development so that capital may be attracted from other countries;

3. to promote the land settlement of new Canadians under conditions that will ensure the maximum success in their farming operations and enable them to enjoy such social and religious institutions as are necessary to individual happiness and contentment;

4. to encourage improvement in agriculture so that more diversified methods may be used in farming, and that crop, livestock and dairy production may be increased in accordance with market demands and prospects;

5. to assist by organized effort in the immigration of young people of desirable type and character, especially from

Great Britain, and in their placement in respectable rural homes, where they may become qualified to participate in constructive activities and acquire citizenship of distinct value to Canada;

6. to aid in the development of new opportunities for service and to facilitate every effective means of selecting immigrants physically fit and anxious for work;

7. to co-operate with the federal and provincial governments and business organizations throughout the Dominion in promoting all measures calculated to contribute toward an increase in immigration of adaptable people and in their settlement under the most favourable conditions possible.[16]

While intended as a corporate mission statement, the policy is replete with patriotic and progressive rhetoric. No reference is made to the CNR or to its corporate agenda and vested interests in the project; but much attention is paid to the social and economic development of the Dominion which would be achieved through the attraction of "people of productive capacity," young people of "desirable type and character, especially from Great Britain," and those "physically fit and anxious to work." The lack of reference to the railway's own agenda sends an implicit message that CNR development and success were considered to be synonymous with Canadian development and success. Clearly, the CNR did not wish to transgress Canada's current immigration policies aimed at admitting only those who could be absorbed by the agriculture-natural resource sector and assimilated into an essentially Franco-British model of Canadian identity.[17]

CNR and the Railways Agreement

In the years following World War I, both the CPR and CNR were anxious for the federal government to return to its prewar pro-immigration posture. Corporate interests would be advanced by large influxes of immigrants moving west by rail, and railway traffic would be stimulated by the settlement and development of lands throughout their respective territories. Indeed, in 1925, the companies pressed Mackenzie King's Liberal government to allow them a more aggressive role in the processing and movement of immigrants. Their efforts met with a positive reception and the Railways Agreement was signed on September 1, 1925. Henceforth, the CPR and CNR would be delegated a principal role in the immigration process because of their vested interest in colonization and because "their transportation facilities by land and sea are specially qualified to procure, select, and settle immigrants of the classes mentioned, and have the necessary organizations for that purpose."[18] Charged with the responsibility for processing and transporting "continental" immigrants, the government went out of its way to emphasize particular restrictions. The railways could only bring to Canada those categories of immigrants allowed by the current federal immigration policy; the definition of these categories was to be a constant bone of contention between the corporations and the government. Moreover, the railway companies were to be responsible for repatriating to their home countries all those who became "public charges" within a year of entry into Canada. Clearly, the Railways Agreement was a clever political ploy: it capitulated to the powerful corporate interests arguing for increased immigration, and at the same time used those corporations as a buffer between government and public opinion with regard to the sensitive matter of "continental" immigration. This contemporary sensitivity is central to any understanding of the policy and practice of Canadian immigration during the interwar years.

The records of the federal Department of Immigration and Colonization reveal a profound tension concerning the matter of who the railways were allowed to bring to Canada.[19] The federal officials carefully monitored the railways' recruitment of immigrants.[20] The railways were warned particularly to select, transport, and locate only those who were "mentally, morally, physically and industrially fit and of a type suitable for permanent settlement in the Dominion."[21] The current regulations only allowed entry to those judged to be agriculturalists, agricultural workers, or domestic servants from a restricted list of continental European countries.

The countries were further classified into the insidious categories of "preferred" and "non-preferred."[22] These descriptions emanated from a conflation of racialist, eugenic, and geographic determinist theories of the day. Thus, Section 38, Chapter (c), of the Immigration Act of 1910 had excluded "immigrants belonging to any race deemed unsuitable to the climatic requirements of Canada, or immigrants of any specified class, occupation or character."[23] Xenophobia and political paranoia gripped Canada following World War I; the Soviet Revolution and the Winnipeg General Strike of 1919 exacerbated this tension. Accordingly, in 1919, Section 38, Chapter (c) was beefed up to exclude those

> deemed undesirable owing to their peculiar customs, habits, modes of life and methods of holding property, and because of their probable inability to become readily assimilated or to assume the duties and responsibilities of Canadian citizenship within a reasonable time after their entry.[24]

Table 1. CNR's 1929 Guidelines Under the "Continental Family Settlement Programme"			
Scheme	Minimum Capital Requirements	Nationalities Included	Restrictions
X	$1,000	G, U, P, H, L	• arrival between March 15 and October 31
A	$500	G, U, P, H	• arrival between April 15 and 1 September 1 • parents of mature age, with no more than 2 children under 6 years old
B	$250	G, U, P	• arrival between May 1 and August 1 • parents of mature age, with no more than 3 children under 12 years old, and no children under 6 years old • parents advised they would be placed in outlying districts, under pioneer conditions, would probably have to erect their own buildings, and "work out" for a number of years
C	$100	G, U, P	• arrival between March 15 and May 15, preferably in April • "agriculturalists" without previous residence in Canada or the U.S. accustomed to manual labour • parents advised they would be placed in outlying districts, under pioneer conditions, would probably have to erect their own buildings, and "work out" for a number of years • required to sign agreement (written in their own language) to accept farm employment under the CNR's direction on arrival
J	$100	G, U, P	• same as for Scheme "C" • parents between 21 and 40 years old, with no more than 3 children under 15 years old, and no children under 3 years old • parents must be prepared to take separate employment if necessary
Nationalities: G - German-speaking; U - Ukrainian; P - Polish; H - Hungarian; L - Lithuanian			
Source: NA, RG 30, vol. 8400, "Continental Family Settlement, Western Canada, 1929."			

Subsequent orders-in-council prohibited the entry of nationals from Germany, Austria-Hungary, Bulgaria and Turkey, as well as Doukhobors, Hutterites and Mennonites. While the latter were revoked by the newly elected Liberal government of Mackenzie King in 1922, the overall tenor of the legislation remained.[25]

Explicit criteria were applied to the selection process. Those who were "preferred" were British, French, Americans, and immigrants from the northwestern European nations of Norway, Sweden, Denmark, Iceland, Belgium, Holland, and Switzerland. Ironically, despite their initial exclusion, people of German background - whatever their current location - were constantly singled out as being desirable colonists.[26] Persons from Central Europe including Poland, Hungary, Czechoslovakia, Austria, and Yugoslavia were classified as "non-preferred" and were only admitted according to quotas determined annually for agriculturalists, farm labourers, and domestics.[27] Finally, a long alphabetized list stretching from Albanians, through Hebrews, to Turks were classified as "others" and were to be excluded; their admission would only be considered for special cases by the federal immigration authorities.

Furthermore, the need to ensure that prospective "continental" (read "non-preferred") immigrants met the socioeconomic priorities of the day resulted in a blending of ethnic, national, and economic criteria. Thus, the "Continental Family Settlement Programme" broke down colonists into "X," "A," "B," "C," and "J" groups according to amounts of capital, marriage status and family size, and national origins (Table 1).[28] Quotas were also assigned to more refined categories such as "L" and "M" for German Lutherans, "T" for German Baptists, and "P" and "K" for German Catholics. Finally, as is illustrated in Table 1, the colonization of each group was carefully directed by department policy: specific arrival periods were assigned; intending immigrants were advised as to whether they could select their own locations or whether they would be directed to "outlying districts, [to settle] under pioneer conditions"; certain groups were required "to erect their own buildings and work out for a number of years"; while others were warned that the family unit would be disrupted and parents required to take separate employment.

Predictably, both the CPR and CNR entered into the Railways Agreement enthusiastically as a means of harnessing national policy to their respective corporate interests. In anticipation of its new role, the CNR restructured its colonization arm in 1924, appointing Dr. Black as director, and renaming it the Department of Colonization, Agriculture, and Natural Resources (DCANR). Its new corporate policy principles were aligned to the objectives of the Railways Agreement:

> 1. To arrange for the settlement and development of vacant farm lands adjacent to Canadian National lines, with a view to producing new freight traffic to and from such lands. This represents the whole basis of our colonization and immigration work.
>
> 2. To promote the settlement on the land of the largest number possible of our own Canadian people, either

resident in urban centres or so situated in rural districts as to require settlement elsewhere.

3. To encourage, insofar as conditions justify, the emigration of agricultural settlers from the British Isles, United States and other countries, who have sufficient capital to establish themselves on land, and who are liable to succeed.

4. To co-operate with our allied steamship lines in the general development of all immigrant traffic, operating as their colonization agents in Canada with a view to the enlargement of their goodwill and securing through them the maximum of freight and passenger traffic to and from overseas.

5. To encourage and direct for settlement on the land only those settlers who have a reasonable prospect of succeeding.

6. To encourage in every way possible the development of mixed farming and better farming methods, and to use our influence in having the various schemes of the Federal and Provincial Governments for agricultural development directed as much as possible to districts on our lines from the standpoint of increasing farm revenues.

7. To assist farmers in securing suitable farm help and thus encourage increased production in our territory.

8. In every way possible to interpret and make known the interests of the Railway to our farming population and, in like manner, the view-point of the farming interests to the railway management.[29]

While many of the original 1923 objectives remained, the tenor of the 1924 statement had changed. Whereas in 1923 no mention was made of the railway as a corporate entity in and of itself, the 1924 restructuring placed a strong emphasis on ensuring the economic viability of the railway, and on protecting its interests.

The organizational structure developed for DCANR reflected its role as determined by CNR corporate interests within the mandate of the Railways Agreement (see Figure 1).[30] The European office, located at 17 Cockspur Street, London, England, was responsible for contacting, evaluating, and forwarding "suitable" immigrants to Canada. It also administered branch offices in Liverpool, Belfast, and Glasgow. London also controlled the CNR's business on the Continent. Originally, there were four district offices: Oslo, Gothenburg, Copenhagen, and Rotterdam. Following 1925 and the Railways Agreement, the CNR established "certificate issuing officers" (CIOs) in

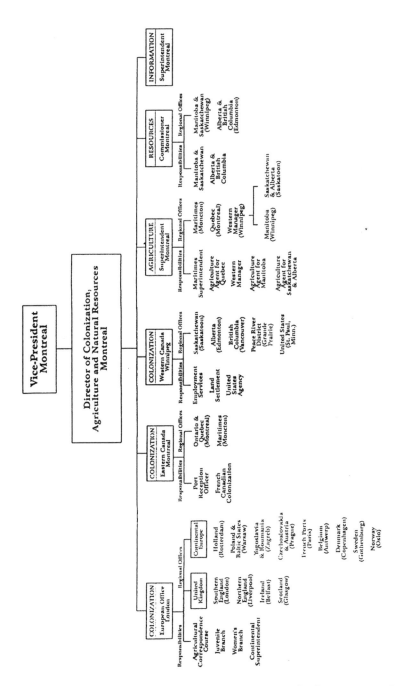

Figure 1. Regional and organizational structure of the CNR's Department of Colonization, Agriculture and Natural Resources, 1925.

Warsaw, Prague, and Zagreb (that is, in "non-preferred" countries), and part-time officers in Paris, Antwerp, and Rotterdam. As the railways were not allowed to effect promotional activities in the "non-preferred" countries, the CIOs examined only those immigration prospects who came to them from steamship agents. This situation made the railway's relationship with the steamship lines particularly important.

In Canada, the CNR's colonization activity was divided into Eastern and Western Divisions. The Eastern Division was controlled by headquarters in Montreal, with sub-offices at Moncton and Toronto and a "port reception officer" at Halifax. The Western Division was administered from "Room 100" in the CNR's Winnipeg station. Saskatoon and Edmonton were regional sub-offices, while the Vancouver office was concerned more with resource development than with agricultural colonization. For a few years, the CNR also operated offices in the United States at Boston, St. Paul, and Seattle.

This was the organizational structure that advanced the CNR's promotional program, attracted immigrants, and "moved settlers forward." Information was disseminated by means of advertisements in the press, public lectures, radio, widely circulated promotional brochures, and films; advisors were in place to assist prospective settlers; and prospective farmers were trained by mail-order courses and CNR experimental farms. Considerable effort was directed to the compilation of dossiers that detailed the origins, arrival, location, and progress of the various categories of "continental" immigrants forwarded by the CNR (see Figure 2). These collections

Head of Family:	Jan Klopot-Makarczuk	Sergiej Klopot-Makarcxuk
European Address:	O.P. Bugryn, Wies Bin	O.P. Burgyn, Wies Ilin
	Pow. Rowno, Wolyn	Pow. Rowno, Wolyn
	Poland.	Poland.
Nationality:	Ukrainian Orthodox	Ukrainian Orthodox
Arrived Canada:	April 20, 1929, ex.s.s.	May 11, 1929, ex.s.s.
	FREDERICK VIII	HELLIG OLAV
Steamship Line:	Scandinavian American	Scandinavian American
Present Address:	Stenen, Sask.	Stenen, Sask.
Land Location:	NW¼ 16-35-3-W /2nd	NW¼ 16-35-3-W /2nd
	(Scheme A - 2229-160)	(Scheme A - 2229-371)

These two families upon their arrival in Canada were directed by the Canadian National Railways to the Stenen district in Saskatchewan where they purchased in partnership a partially improved 160 acre farm for $1200.00, paying $300.00 cash. They now have 4 horses, a colt, 3 cows and calves, poultry and machinery. In the above photograph the wives are shown beside their new home. When visited recently both men were out working earning good wages.

Figure 2. Example of a CNR dossier detailing central European immigrants settled by the railway. Source: LAC, RG 30, vol. 5893.

served a number of purposes. First, they were a signal demonstration of the corporation's diligence in monitoring and regulating its immigration activities under the terms of the Railways Agreement. Secondly, suitably packaged selections of immigrants' dossiers appear to have been used to provide prospective settlers with knowledge of the conditions and opportunities associated with a particular region. If the DCANR system is to be appreciated in full, however, attention should also be directed to three other associated operations: the Canadian National Land Settlement Association (CNLSA), the shipping companies, and the colonization system.

Canadian National Land Settlement Association
As part of the departmental restructuring leading to the Railways Agreement, the DCANR organized and incorporated an ancillary organization, the CNLSA.[31] Intended to be operated as a land settlement division of the CNR's colonization department, the CNLSA had two objectives: to receive and hold the money that all settlers were required to place on deposit as surety of their commitment to establish themselves on the land and to act as liaison with land agents who were encouraged to locate settlers on lands adjacent to CNR lines. The motivating assumption was that if the DCANR was to pursue these objectives itself, there was the danger of misunderstanding or even legal liability. Accordingly, to avoid the impression of conflicting interests, the CNLSA was set up to act as a land settlement service for CNR settlers. However, the fact that Messrs. Black, England, Kirkwood, Devlin, McGowan, all key members of the DCANR, were included among the officers of CNLSA, clearly demonstrated that, although legally and administratively removed, the Association was not operating far from CNR control.[32]

In practice, the CNLSA found, listed, and handled the purchases of farms, especially those in CNR territory. In this capacity, it intervened between settlers and property owners, negotiated appropriate conditions, assisted in the purchase of stock and equipment, and provided guidance in bringing lands into production. The principal concern was to get settlers on the land with as little financial obligation as possible in order to maximize chances for success, productivity, and further interaction with the CNR's traffic department.

CNR's "Friendly" Shipping Allies
Also central to the CNR colonization operation was its well-developed contacts with an array of "friendly" shipping companies. Trans-Atlantic carriers also had a vested interest in maintaining an active flow of immigrants from Europe to Canada. The restrictions on promotion of emigration opportunities which existed in many "non-preferred" countries made close cooperation

between the railways and the steamship agents essential. Accordingly, the shipping companies' networks of offices and staff were co-opted by the DCANR to promote Canada and establish preliminary contacts with prospective immigrants who would then be interviewed by the department's field operatives (CIOs) in Europe. For their part, the shipping lines profited from the traffic generated, and their agents were compensated on a commission base for the number of prospective passengers-cum-immigrants they directed to the CNR offices. It was a well-orchestrated concert of interest.

Unlike the CPR's reliance upon its own carrier—the Canadian Pacific Steamships—Canadian National did not develop its own fleet of passenger carriers. Rather, it relied upon a cosmopolitan fleet that was divided into two groups: the "British Lines" and the "National Lines."[33] In 1927, and for much of the interwar years, the CNR passenger traffic was organized into two systems. The St. Lawrence ports of Quebec City and Montreal were served by only CPS and the British Lines (Anchor Donaldson, Cunard, White Star Line); as these ports only operated during the summer season, traffic shifted to Halifax during the winter months. Several "Continental" or "National" lines used Halifax year-round as the Canadian terminus for landing CNR immigrants, before continuing on to New York. The principal carriers were Baltic American, Hamburg American, Holland America, North German Lloyd, Norwegian American, Swedish American, United American; occasional service was provided by the Mediterranean Lines of Fabre Line, Lloyd Sabaudo, Navigazione General Italiana, and Trans-Atlantic Italiana.[34] Others were added over the years, and this list of the CNR's most active partners—the "Allied Steamship Companies"—reads like an inventory of carriers during the peak period of the age of trans-Atlantic navigation.

However refined the linkages with the "friendly" companies were, the CNR recognized that it still operated at a disadvantage with its main competitor as "we cannot attain the advantage possessed by the Canadian Pacific whose rail and ocean services are of one single control."[35] Nevertheless, the CNR persevered with its "friendly lines." By allying itself with this considerable array of national carriers, it was able to tap into well-established systems of traffic agents and field operatives. These contacts were able to direct potential immigrants to the CIOs representing the CNR system. It would appear, therefore, that the CNR was not handicapped by not having its own steamships. Rather, collaborations with these independent carriers, if anything, gave the CNR an advantage over its competitor in the interwar years because of its range of recruitment contacts in both Europe and Canada.

Leaving Liverpool for Canada, 1925 (Courtesy of the Saskatchewan Archives Board/R-B9804-2).

CNR's Colonization System

In the field of colonization, the CNR's activities differed again from those of its primary competitor. Unlike the CPR system, the DCANR did not rely upon clubs, boards, associations, or private firms specializing in attracting immigrants.[36] Rather, the DCANR and CNLSA developed a centrally controlled system of some 400 part-time field operatives who surveyed settlement possibilities, met immigrants, and assisted in locating them. Moreover, the DCANR availed itself of the services of 2,221 railway station agents throughout Canada (700 in the Prairies) who also participated in the colonization effort by acting as contact points for new settlers.[37] Finally, the DCANR nurtured close contacts with a variety of organizations that were motivated by diverse philanthropic, cultural, and self-serving concerns, and that sustained contacts on both sides of the Atlantic. Several should be noted here: British Immigration and Colonial Society, British Dominions' Emigration Society, Polish Catholic Immigration Society, Norwegian Lutheran Church, Mennonite Board, Verein Deutschen, Canadischen Katholiken, German Lutheran Immigration Board, Canadian Lutheran Immigration Aid Society, German Catholic Immigrant Aid Society, German Baptist Society, and several Ukrainian organizations.[38] These and other agencies were essential to the immigration and colonization enterprise as they facilitated and

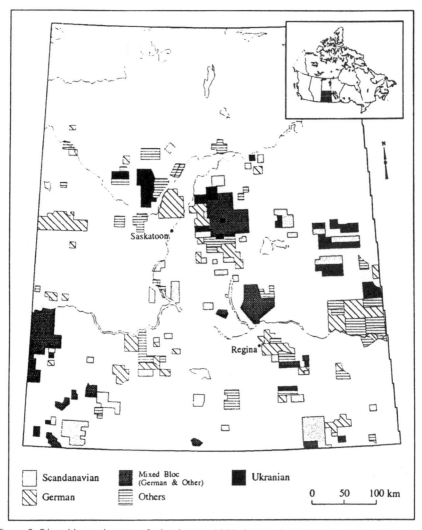

Figure 3. Ethnic bloc settlement in Saskatchewan, 1929. Source: Susan E. Wurtele, "Nation-Building from the Ground Up: Assimilation Through Domestic and Community Transformation in Inter-War Saskatchewan" (PhD dissertation, Queen's University, 1993).

orchestrated the contacts, connections and sponsorship that were increasingly required by Canada's new immigration policy.

In this way the DCANR drew on a prairie-wide system of local community agents. This large network of independent agents working on commission was in charge of the distribution of farm help, nurturing contacts with steamship representatives, and assisting in settlement work.[39] They also maintained close links with ethnic and religious groups, especially with the

Continental Europeans who dominated the large bloc settlements through-out the northern Prairies served by CNR's lines (see Figure 3). Accordingly, the DCANR's colonization efforts focussed particularly on Polish, Ukrainian and various German-speaking groups.

The process developed by CNR's field operatives capitalized upon the extensive network of social contacts they had developed within their respective communities. Typically, an agent would approach prominent businessmen, farmers, and traders and induce them to agree to sponsor settlers. If successful, the agent would survey the community, estimating the number of farm workers or domestics that could be distributed to employers, and the amount of vacant land and its cost for intending immigrant farm families. These statistics were consolidated by the Winnipeg office which then estimated the number of immigrants that could be received. Based on the information collected by the field agents, the Winnipeg office calculated how many immigrants could be accommodated in each of the above-mentioned categories (see Table 1). These estimates were directed to the CNR's London office, to allow it to establish recruiting targets. Once recruit-ed and processed by European field agents, prospective immigrants were transported to Canada, and then forwarded to Winnipeg. From there they were dispersed and put in the hands of the local colonization agent nearest to their intended destination.

Ideally, it was a reciprocating process: information flowed from the com-munity, to the agent, to the Winnipeg office, to Europe, to the CIOs, and to the intended immigrant; immigrants flowed from their communities, to the CIOs, to ports of departure, to the port of arrival, to Winnipeg, and to their destination community in western Canada.[40] Those with resources were directed by the CNLSA to improved farms that were available for sale. But as these were out of the reach of most continental immigrants, poorer fami-lies were directed to homesteads and partially improved lands throughout the more remote northerly sections of the CNR railway network. But immi-grants wanted to settle near established communities of their countrymen. Recognizing this "group settlement psychology," the CNR often grouped new settlers by nationality, placing them together in remote areas.[41] This practice was aimed at overcoming the perceived isolation, and further, it was hoped that by establishing these ethnic nuclei, subsequent immigrants of the same ethnic background would be attracted, thus helping to settle these areas.

Clearly, during the peak immigration years of 1925–30, CNR's DCANR and CNLSA developed a sophisticated and comprehensive system of immi-gration, colonization, and development. While the operation was often

Ukrainian women at Stenen, Saskatchewan, 1929. Large numbers of Ukrainians settled in the area, and today a notable village landmark is St. Demetrious Ukrainian Orthodox Church, built in the mid-1950s (Courtesy of the Saskatchewan Archives Board/R-A32763).

represented in philanthropic and patriotic terms, its corporate mission was quite prosaic:

> These and many other varied activities enable this depart-
> ment to promote the development of farming and the good-
> will of farming people along C.N. lines and at the same time
> increase immediate traffic for the Company. While every
> effort is made to secure immediate traffic, nevertheless the
> general policy is one of development directed to the future
> with a view to promoting better living and more profitable
> farming in order to secure a greater permanency of our rail-
> way operations.[42]

Justification for the CNR's involvement in colonization could be sought in the account books: in 1927, for an operating budget of a mere $170,000, the Colonization Department recouped direct receipts of $160,000 in rail fares and a share of ship passage. When consideration is also made of the future indirect benefits to be derived from the traffic generated by the settlers, the financial justification for the department's operations is made even clearer.[43] Indeed, the CNR's annual report for 1927 predicted an extra $1 million rev-enue because of future freight from the additional lands brought into pro-duction by the breaking and improving of both homesteads and vacant lands that had been accomplished in that year.[44] Such sanguine promotional rhetoric failed to take into consideration the ramifications of a deepening global depression and falling grain prices. These developments eroded the confidence of those expected to participate in the railways' grandiose plans of continued settlement expansion, and government intervention effectively closed the doors to new immigration.

Retrenchment

By 1930, a combination of economic crisis and growing nativist pressures generated profound anti-immigration sentiments across the country.[45] After campaigning on an anti-immigration platform, Bennett's newly elected Conservative government moved immediately to revoke the Railways Agreement and restrict continental immigration. Whereas postwar immigration had peaked in 1928 at 166,783, it collapsed to a mere 20,591 in 1932, and hit a post-Confederation low of 11,277 in 1935.[46] Between 1925 and 1930, the DCANR had recruited and settled some 203,740 immigrants, including 11,070 families, on 2,017,067 acres of land.[47] It was recognized, however, that falling immigration rates necessitated new initiatives to replace the lost immigrant traffic and land-settlement business.

In the face of these pressures, the CNR reorganized its colonization department yet again. Natural Resources was transferred from the DCANR to the Industrial Department, leaving behind the rump unit, Colonization and Agriculture (DCA). Moreover, the new circumstances required a shift in operational emphasis. Rather than attracting, transporting, and settling foreign immigrants, the DCA directed its efforts to "internal" colonization work. Henceforth, the primary focus was on increasing the productivity of, and traffic from, those lands already settled, and on participating in the relocation of settlers, educational programs, and infrastructure development.[48] Accordingly, in cooperation with the federal, provincial, and various metropolitan administrations, the CNR became involved in the Dominion-Provincial Land Settlement Scheme, the Dominion-Provincial Training Farms Plan, and the "Back-to-the-Land Movement."[49] Motivated by the need to rehabilitate marginal lands, keep rural families out of cities, and even return others from cities to farms, the logistics of these exercises in rural planning, social engineering, and redistributions of settlers also provided the railways with much needed passenger and cargo traffic.

But while CNR's willing participation in such initiatives in regional development fitted its corporate agenda, it must also be noted that the DCA had long been advocating and practicing principles of planned settlement and development that were becoming increasingly in vogue. As early as 1917, Thomas Adams of the Canadian Commission of Conservation had proposed a more regularized and holistic approach to rural settlement and development:

> Whatever maybe said as to the success of the system of land
> settlement in Canada ... the time has come to abandon care-
> less methods of placing people on the land without proper
> organization and careful planning. If the farmer is to be
> kept on the land he must have the kind of organization and
> facilities provided for him to enable him to make profitable
> use of the land.[50]

The benefits of a more scientific approach to settlement were of considerable interest to CNR's Department of Colonization and Agriculture which
was officered by several people (Black, McGowan, Devlin) who had had formal agricultural science backgrounds. Moreover, the CNR cooperated closely with Isaiah Bowman, director of the American Geographical Society and
advocate of the "science of settlement," who was actively promoting the
"Canadian Frontiers of Settlement Project."[51] It was in this context that
Robert England, superintendant of the DCA's Western Department, complained that "[p]ioneer communities develop their agriculture largely by
trial and error experiment and imitation stimulated or driven by economic
demand, without much regard to research, scientific managment or
method," and argued for educational programs and support that would
"reduce for the pioneer the hazards of the supreme gamble of his life and
capital against the forces of nature... ."[52]

During the 1930s, the CNR was also sensitive to the fact that the newly
imposed reduction in immigration was a political response to prevailing
social attitudes. Given the flexibility that was built into Canada's immigration laws at this time, negative public opinion toward immigrants could be
translated, almost instantly, into "closed doors."[53] Accordingly, both of the
national railways became advocates of a pluralist view of Canadian national identity and established programs that promoted positive images of
immigrants. The railways hoped that fostering broad-based appreciation of
immigrant culture might be translated into support for, or at least tolerance
of, a post-Depression return to high levels of immigration.

The CNR's initiatives in nurturing a Canadian sensitivity to the richness
of the nation's cultural pluralism can be noted in several areas. Commenc-
ing in 1929, CNR's own radio station broadcast concerts including Montreal's Balalaika Orchestra, poetry readings by W.J. Drummond and Pauline
Johnson, and an historical drama series, "The Romance of Canada," to
"encourage Canadian national consciousness" among listeners in general,
and new Canadians in particular.[54] A more grass-roots initiative in nation
building was the DCA's sponsorship of the "Community Progress Competitions!"[55] Between 1930 and 1933, this program encouraged Canadianization

SCORE CARD

A. Education (275 Points)

1. Percentage School Attendance... 25
2. Percentage attending High Schools, Secondary Schools, Agricultural Colleges, Collegiate Institutes or Universities 50
3. School efficiency—quality of teaching, progress of pupils, efficiency of school boards 75
4. School Grounds, library, equipment, layout, condition of gardens, premises and outhouses, sanitation. 100
5. General 25
   —— 275

B. Agricultural Development (275 Points)

1. General plan and appearance of farms, buildings, gardens, water supply, etc. 100
2. Crops—purity of crops, freedom from weeds, practise of approved crop rotations 75
3. Livestock (Horses, Cattle, Swine, Sheep, Poultry):
   (a) Number of head per farm..20
   (b) Quality, feeding, management, etc. 25
   (c) Quality and use of purebred sires 30
   75
4. General 25
   —— 275

C. Citizenship, Co-operation, Social Welfare (300 Points)

Public Health

1. Evidence of interest in public health (sanitation, immunization and preventive work, hospitalization, education in health)........ 100

Community Effort and Respect of Law

2. Interest in community enterprises and general development (good roads, public buildings, community recreation centres, etc.) and observance of law and order....... 30
3. Interest of farmers in co-operative activities..................... 60
4. Percentage of farmers who are members of organizations such as agricultural societies, school fairs, etc........................... 25

Boys and Girls

5. Percge of membership in Swine, Calf, Sheep, Grain, Poultry, Bee, Potato, Canning and Dressmaking Clubs, or other boys' and girls community activities of a constructive character 35
6. Interest shown in school or agricultural fairs 25
7. General 25
   —— 300

D. Arts, Handicraft and Domestic Economy (150 Points)

1. Handicraft (Embroidery, Weaving, Rug-making, Knitting, Basketry, Toy-making, Painting, Pottery, Vegetable dyes, etc.) 60
   (a) Useful—clothing and foods. 30
   (b) Decorative—clothing and house.................. 30
   60
2. Home manufacturing (carpentering, blacksmithing, leather work, rope-making, etc.)................. 30
3. Interest in cultural activities (dramatic, musical, social, athletic, folk dancing, etc.).................. 45
4. General 15
   —— 150

GRAND TOTAL 1000

WINNERS 1931 COMPETITIONS

In Alberta

FIRST PRIZE—Lloyd George (Scandinavian)
SECOND PRIZE—Montgomery (Scandinavian-German)
THIRD PRIZE—Eagle (Ukrainian-Roumanian)
HIGHLY COMMENDED—Liberty (Ukrainian-German-Scandinavian)
COMMENDED—The Pines (Ukrainian)
COMMENDED—Beaver Lake (Ukrainian-Scandinavian)

In Saskatchewan

FIRST PRIZE—Laird (Mennonite)
SECOND PRIZE—Redberry (Ukrainian)
THIRD PRIZE—St. Peter (German)
HIGHLY COMMENDED—Warman (Mennonite)
COMMENDED—Round Lake (Scandinavian)
COMMENDED—Bekevar (Hungarian)

In Manitoba

FIRST PRIZE—Rhineland (Mennonite)
SECOND PRIZE—Stuartburn (Ukrainian)
THIRD PRIZE—Hanover (Mennonite)
HIGHLY COMMENDED—Sifton (Ukrainian)
COMMENDED—Ethelbert (Ukrainian)

Figure 4. Community Progress Competition Score Card.
Source: LAC, RG 30, vol. 5934.

and community improvements by manipulating group consciousness through intercommunity competition and peer and social pressure.[56] "Progress" was measured in a variety of fields including education, agriculture and citizenship (see Figure 4). Overtly committed to the Canadianization of new and established immigrants, the mission of the Community Progress Competition fitted the prevailing political and social climate and at the same time attempted to counter the anti-immigration sentiments that threatened corporate balance sheets.

The deepening economic depression prematurely ended the Community Progress Competitions and a dramatic curtailment of DCA's operations in general. The department was "down" but not yet "out." By increasing its flexibility and cutting back its operations, the DCA was able to survive throughout the 1930s. It continued with its involvement in resettlement schemes such as "Back-to-the-Land" programs, and participated in the joint CNR-CPR development of the Peace River District.[57] All of these Depression-era operations, however, were focussed on colonization work directed at improving the conditions of those already in Canada, with little revenue being generated from the transportation, location, and settlement of foreign immigrants.

Postwar Decline and Closure

The decline in immigration continued from 1930 until the end of World War II. Following the war, both of the national railways were called back into service to handle returning troops, a considerable flow of refugees, and a gradually increasing intake of immigrants that peaked at 282,164 in 1957.[58] The old "colonist cars" were recalled into service for moving immigrants from Halifax to points west. But three significant changes reshaped the socioeconomic climate within which the department operated: the erosion of rural settlement and the growth of industry and urbanization challenged DCA's old priorities; post-World War II political alignments throughout Europe disrupted the DCA's well-established connections with traditional immigrant recruiting areas; and, finally, the burgeoning of trans-Atlantic air traffic cut into the former system of ship-rail movement of immigrants. While the distribution of some agricultural and resource labourers continued, and while the development of the Abitibi colonization schemes burgeoned, DCA's European recruitment infrastructure had been destroyed and the original rationale of agricultural colonization had been rendered redundant. A much changed, but still vibrant, department managed to survive until it was eliminated in the overall corporate restructuring of CNR in the early 1960s.

On December 31, 1961, the federal government finally terminated its immigration-related cooperation with the railways, and the CNR's Department of Colonization was left to close its doors and clean out its records. One of the final members of the Department to retire or be relocated was Tommy Devlin, head of western operations. The headquarters of CNR's immigration reception in Winnipeg—"Room 100"—was closed in the spring of 1964 and on May 22 of that year, Devlin wrote a long, rambling letter to his former colleague, Robert England. Full of nostalgic references to personnel with whom he had interacted over the previous 40 years of "Colonization and Agriculture," Devlin commented on the forthcoming events:

> When I retire that will be the end of the old Department of Colonization and Agriculture. … The old Department made a real contribution to the development of Western Canada, but like everything else, change is inevitable. The Department of Citizenship and Immigration now feels able to handle all immigration and settlement work themselves. The CPR also has eliminated their Department of Colonization and Immigration, and retired a considerable number of their staff who were 60 or over. We are busy cleaning out what remains of Room 100. It is an awful job and much has been thrown out which we dislike seeing going into the discard.59

To be sure, "Colonization and Agriculture" did make a "real contribution to the development of Western Canada" - and to the rest of Canada too. A 1958 report summarized some of the salient facts: the transportation of 1,190,800 immigrants from eastern Canadian ports of arrival to inland destinations (out of a total of 2,326,252 arrivals to Canada), the settlement of 71,500 farm families, 232,000 farm placements in agricultural employment, and the settlement of 10,785,265 acres of newly broken and some cultivated land.[60] One detailed analysis of DCA's settlement of 61,995 farm families on 9 million acres between 1930 and 1955 came up with a cost-benefit analysis. Noting various estimates of settler-generated traffic revenues of $1,000 for the American Great Northern line, $746 for CPR, and $417 for the CNR, the analysis applied an average of $700 per annum for DCA settlers. It was concluded that new settlement by DCA had contributed new revenues amounting to $1.75 million per annum, and that each settler "may be regarded as a small industry located on our lines and from which we shall secure traffic for an indefinite period of time."[61]

However, it may be argued that the legacy of the CNR's Department of Colonization and Agriculture was more than economic. The corporation's several initiatives in immigration, colonization, and development did much to influence subsequent thinking in several important areas: selective immigration; regional development; and an advocacy of a Canada that was pluralistic and cosmopolitan rather than one that was nominally bicultural, ideally liberal, but essentially xenophobic. To be sure, such views were motivated more by the vested interests of corporate capitalism than by any grand designs of nation building. Nonetheless, spokespersons such as CPR's John

Murray Gibbon and CNR's Robert England argued for a more diverse Canada and cultivated the ground for others who would propose an even more radical model of multiculturalism.

Notes

This article first appeared in *Prairie Forum* 20, no. 2 (1995): 231–54.

1. See for example, H.A. Innis, *A History of the Canadian Pacific Railway* (Toronto: University of Toronto Press, 1923, 1971); James B. Hedges, *The Federal Railway Land Subsidy Policy of Canada* (Cambridge: Harvard University Press, 1934); G.P. Glazebrook, *A History of Transportation in Canada, Volume 2, National Economy, 1867–1936* (Toronto: McClelland and Stewart Ltd, 1964); Robert Chodos, *The CPR: A Century of Corporate Welfare* (Toronto: James Lewis and Samuel, Publishers, 1973); W. Kaye Lamb, *History of the Canadian Pacific Railway* (New York: Macmillan Publishing Co., 1977); John A. Eagle, *The Canadian Pacific Railway and the Development of Western Canada, 1896–1914* (Montreal/Kingston: McGill-Queen's University Press, 1989).

2. There are several examples of this: Pierre Berton, *The National Dream: The Great Railway, 1871–1881* (Toronto: McClelland and Stewart, 1970), and *The Last Spike: The Great Railway, 1881–1885* (Toronto: McClelland and Stewart, 1971); David Cruise and Alison Griffiths, *Lords of the Line: The Men Who Built the CPR* (Markham: Viking, 1988).

3. The most notable treatment of these ventures is the work of T.D. Regehr, *The Canadian Northern Railway: Pioneer Road of the Northern Prairies, 1895–1918* (Toronto: Macmillan, 1976); and the corporately sponsored: G.R. Stevens, *Canadian National Railways, Volume 1: Sixty Years of Trial and Error, 1836–1896* and *Volume 2: Towards the Inevitable, 1896–1922* (Toronto: Clarke, Irwin and Company Limited, 1960 and 1962).

4. The most recent work on the CNR is Donald MacKay, *The People's Railway: A History of Canadian National* (Vancouver: Douglas and McIntyre, 1992).

5. Jane Brooks, "Immigration Policy and the Railways: The Formation of the Railway Agreement" (MA thesis, Concordia University, 1977).

6. Library and Archives of Canada (LAC), RG 30, vol. 5567, "First Annual Report: Industrial & Resources Department, Winnipeg," November 1919.

7. Ibid., "Second Annual Report: Industrial & Resources Department, Winnipeg," January 1921.

8. Howard Palmer, *Patterns of Prejudice: A History of Nativism in Alberta* (Toronto: McClelland and Stewart, 1982), 6.

9. J.S. Woodsworth, *Strangers Within Our Gates* (Toronto: University of Toronto Press, 1972).

10. LAC, RG 30, Miscellaneous file, W.H. Hobbs, "Report on the Department of Colonization and Agriculture," March 5, 1934.

11. Ibid., "Third Annual Report: Industrial & Resources Department, Winnipeg," January 1922.

12. Canada, Minutes of the Federal-Provincial Conference on Immigration, Ottawa, November 14–15, 1923, p. 171.

13. LAC, RG 30, Miscellaneous file, W.H. Hobbs, "Report on the Department of Colonization and Agriculture," March 5, 1934.

14. Ibid.

15. Susan E. Wurtele, "Nation-Building from the Ground Up: Assimilation Through Domestic and Community Transformation in Inter-War Saskatchewan" (PhD dissertation, Queen's University, 1993).

16. LAC, RG 30, Annual Reports, "Annual Report of the Canadian National System," 1923.

17. Palmer, *Patterns of Prejudice*; and Brian S. Osborne, "'Non-Preferred' People: Inter-war Ukrainian Immigration to Canada," in Lubomyr Luciuk and Stella Hryniuk (eds.), *Canada's Ukrainians: Negotiating an Identity* (Toronto: University of Toronto Press, 1991).

18. "Agreement between the Minister of Immigration and the CNR and CPR," in Brooks, "Immigration Policy and the Railways," 110.

19. LAC, RG 76, vol. 263, various memos and letters, Federal Department of Immigration and Colonization.

20. Valerie Knowles, *Strangers at Our Gates: Canadian Immigration and Immigration Policy, 1540–1990* (Toronto: Dundum Press, 1992); Donald Avery, *"Dangerous Foreigners": European Immigrant Workers and Labour Radicalism in Canada, 1896–1932* (Toronto: McClelland and Stewart, 1979).

21. Brooks, "Immigration Policy and the Railways," 110.

22. Palmer, *Patterns of Prejudice*; Osborne, "'Non-Preferred' People"; and Avery, *"Dangerous Foreigners."*

23. Canada, Immigration Act, 1910, Section 38, Chapter (c).

24. Ibid.

25. Knowles, *Strangers at Our Gates.*

26. Osborne, "'Non-Preferred' People."

27. LAC, RG 76, vol. 263, various memos and letters, Federal Department of Immigration and Colonization.

28. LAC, RG 30, vol. 8400, "Continental Family Settlement, Western Canada, 1929."

29. Quoted in LAC, RG 30, (Misc. file), "Department of Colonization and Agriculture, CNR, Historical Synopsis," 1958.

30. Brooks, "Immigration Policy and the Railways," 106–09.

31. LAC, RG 30, W.H. Hobbs, Miscellaneous file, "Report on the Department of Colonization and Agriculture, Exhibit 2," March 5, 1934.

32. Brooks, "Immigration Policy and the Railways," 108–09.

33. LAC, RG 30, vol. 3081, F. 600, "Committee on Transatlantic Steamship Services," September 1927.

34. Ibid., vol. 5570, "CNLSA Annual Report, Winnipeg," 1927.

35. Ibid.

36. For information on the CPR's colonization activities see J.B. Hedges, *Building the Canadian West: The Land and Colonization Policies of the Canadian Pacific Railway* (New York: Russell and Russell, 1939).

37. Brooks, "Immigration Policy and Railways," 108.

38. LAC, RG 30, Miscellaneous file, "Survey of the Operations of the Department of Colonization & Agriculture," April 4, 1955.

39. Myron Gulka-Tiechko, "Inter-War Ukrainian Immigration to Canada, 1919–1939" (MA thesis, University of Manitoba, 1983), 82–84.

40. For more details, see the excellent account in Gulka-Tiechko, "Inter-War Ukrainian Immigration."

41. Robert England, *The Colonization of Western Canada: A Study of Contemporary Land Settlement (1896–1934)* (London: P.S. King and Son, 1936).

42. LAC, RG 30, vol. 5571, "Colonization and Agriculture Department, Annual Report, Montreal," 1934.

43. Ibid., vol. 5570, F.J. Freer to J.S. McGowan, 6 November, 1928.

44. Ibid.

45. Palmer, *Patterns of Prejudice*.

46. Freda Hawkins, *Canada and Immigration: Public Policy and Public Concern*, 2nd ed. (Montreal/Kingston: McGill-Queen's University Press, 1988), 402.

47. LAC, RG 30, F.B. Kirkwood, Miscellaneous file, "History of the Department of Colonization and Agriculture," n.d., p. 20.

48. England, *Colonization of Western Canada*, 107.

49. Ibid.

50. Thomas Adams, *Rural Planning and Development: A Study of Rural Conditions and Problems in Canada* (Ottawa: Commission of Conservation Canada, 1917), 11.

51. Isaiah Bowman, *The Pioneer Fringe* (New York: American Geographical Society, 1931) and *Limits of Land Settlement: A Report on Present-Day Possibilities* (New York: Council on Foreign Relations, 1937).

52. England, *Colonization of Western Canada*, 165.

53. As was discussed earlier, Canada's Immigration Act of 1919 was very vaguely worded. Interpretation of the law was made through ministerial orders-in-council, which did not require Parliamentary approval. As a result, new interpretations could be, and indeed were, translated into policy and action very quickly.

54. Maria Tippett, *Making Culture: English-Canadian Institutions and the Arts Before the Massey Commission* (Toronto: University of Toronto Press, 1990), 50.

55. Susan E. Wurtele, "'Apostles of Canadian Citizenship': Robert England, the CNR and Prairie Settlement," in H. John Selwood and John C. Lehr (eds.), *Reflections from the Prairies: Geographical Essays* (Winnipeg: Department of Geography, University of Winnipeg, 1992); and Wurtele "Nation-Building from the Ground Up."

56. England, *Colonization of Western Canada*.

57. Ineke J. Dijks, "Rails to 'The Great Inland Empire': The Canadian National Railway, Colonization and Settlement in Alberta, 1925–1930, with Special Reference to the Peace River Region" (MA thesis, Queen's University, 1994).

58. Hawkins, *Canada and Immigration*, 402.

59. LAC, MG 30, C 181, vol. 1, Devlin to Robert England, May 22, 1964.

60. LAC, RG 30, "Report: Department of Colonization and Agriculture, Montreal," March 11, 1958.

61. Ibid., "Survey of the Operations of the Department of Colonization & Agriculture," April 4, 1955.

5.   The (Royal) North-West Mounted Police and Prostitution on the Canadian Prairies

S.W. Horrall

Prostitution was not the oldest profession to be practiced on the Canadian prairies, but it was a part of the vanguard of settlement. Calgary has the dubious honour of having the first brothel to be closed by the Mounted Police. In March 1884 Inspector S.B. Steele, JP, found Nina Dow and Nellie Swift guilty of keeping a "house of ill-fame." Steele gave them a choice of sentence—six months imprisonment, or leave town on the next train. They chose the train.[1]

Prostitution had arrived in the North-West Territories a year or so earlier. As in the American West, the demimondaines were a part of the retinue of the railway construction crews. They flourished wherever there was a large body of unattached males. Their presence accompanied the laying of the track of the Canadian Pacific Railway, advancing westward with each new construction camp from Winnipeg, where they had existed as early as 1875.[2] Only a few months after the line reached Regina, a local newspaper complained of the number of brothels in the town north of the tracks.[3] After Nellie Swift was forced out of Calgary, she did what many of her colleagues would do. She moved on to the next construction camp at Laggan, where four months later she was convicted by Steele again and fined $50.[4] From the rail lines the women moved to the mining camps that followed, and they finally settled in the red light districts of the new urban communities. Prostitution was part of the process of settling and developing the Canadian West.

As the principal law enforcement agency in what is now Alberta and Saskatchewan, from the 1870s until the outbreak of World War I in 1914, the (R) NWMP became deeply involved in the policing and control of prostitution. During the early years the "social evil" presented little difficulty for police. With few settlers and fewer social institutions, the ascendant position of the Mounted Police enabled them to act in what they believed were the community's best interests. The course of action adopted by the Mounted Police to regulate prostitution was well-defined in a 1904 investigation into charges that Medicine Hat was threatened by a syphilis epidemic. Eventually, however, the dominant position of the Mounted Police was challenged as settlement increased and urban centres developed. Municipal councils, reform groups, the establishment of local police forces and the appearance of provincial governments created a more complex milieu in which the Mounted Police had to function. As with other forms of crime, the new conditions forced them reluctantly to change or modify their behaviour regarding prostitution.

From the time of their arrival on the prairies until World War I, officers of the Mounted Police, with no important exceptions, looked upon prostitution as a necessary evil which, given the basic urges of human nature, would never be eradicated.[5] In fact, they saw a positive benefit in allowing it to exist. Prostitution provided an outlet for those men who were unable to control themselves, and made them less likely to prey upon the respectable women in society. In other words, the prostitute's existence helped to protect their own wives and daughters. They did not favour its legalization, however.

The legalization of prostitution was fiercely debated from time to time during the latter part of the 19th century in both Europe and North America. In most European states it did attain a legal status, usually under the supervision of the local police. One of the few exceptions was Britain. In 1864 the British Parliament adopted a measure which gave prostitution a quasi-legal status, but public reaction resulted in the measure's repeal in 1886. The British stuck to the Victorian double standard. Prostitution might be necessary and it might be impossible to suppress, but it would not be legalized. Canada and the United States followed the British pattern. An attempt in the 1870s to have it legitimized by Congress failed. Instead, respectable society and the legislative authorities of both countries turned a blind eye to the presence of prostitutes, leaving the police to devise some *modus operandi* for the control of their illegal but desirable activities.

At the annual meeting of the International Association of Chiefs of Police in 1907, Chief Kohler of the Cleveland Police Department outlined the three options open to law enforcement agencies.[6] The first was official acceptance. This, he stated, could not be the policy of any police administration whose avowed function was the maintenance of public decency. Another serious drawback for the police was that prostitution was usually accompanied by graft and official corruption. Official acceptance nevertheless was police practice in some parts of the United States. In 1897 New Orleans passed a law permitting prostitution in a part of the old French Quarter known as Storyville, the so-called "Storyville Option." The chief described the second course open to police as "suppression by crusade," which usually came as part of a "reform wave." When that method failed, as it invariably did, he continued, the police are blamed for being unsympathetic. Instead of rooting prostitution out, it scattered it throughout the community making control more difficult. The third method, he explained, was the one most calculated "to produce the best possible results from a moral and police standpoint." The solution was the orderly supervision of prostitution by the police, who would suppress it as individual cases or circumstances warranted.

Few police chiefs in the United States or Canada, the officers of the Mounted Police included, would have disagreed with the principles laid down by Kohler. On the prairies the police took a pragmatic approach to the problem of control. The best means to assure prostitution's orderly supervision was to confine its activities to one area of the community, a place where prostitutes would not intrude on the life of the respectable classes. By segregation, the Mounted Police could easily maintain surveillance and keep the operators in line by occasional raids and fines. The majesty of the law would be upheld and the prostitutes would be reminded who was in control. Provided the police acted efficiently, there would be no public complaint.

Under Canadian criminal law it was an indictable offence to operate, to frequent or to be an inmate of a house of ill-fame. Upon conviction an offender was liable to a sentence of up to one year in prison.[7] The Mounted Police, however, usually treated these offences as misdemeanors and proceeded under the less severe provisions of Sections 238–239 of the Criminal Code relating to vagrancy.[8] These provisions defined as a vagrant anyone who:

(a) being a common prostitute wanders in the fields, public streets or highways and does not give a satisfactory account of herself;

(b) is a keeper or inmate of a bawdy house or house of ill-fame;

(c) is in the habit of frequenting such houses;

(d) supports himself by the avails of prostitution.

Upon conviction for vagrancy an offender was liable to a fine of up to $50, or imprisonment for up to six months, or both. There was no substantial change in the laws relating to prostitution until the Criminal Code was amended just prior to World War I in an effort to stiffen the penalties, particularly against procuring.

A house of ill-fame was defined as any "house, room, set of rooms or place of any kind kept for the purposes of prostitution or the practice of acts of indecency."[9] To convict keepers and inmates it was not necessary for the police to show that money changed hands, or that sexual acts actually took place. The law required only evidence that the house was resorted to by men and lewd conduct took place.[10] Likewise, the common prostitute, or street walker, was guilty if she was unable to give a satisfactory account of herself. Interestingly enough, it was quite common during this period for the police to charge the frequenters or customers. In part, this was due to the attitudes of the time. For a considerable section of society, no stigma was attached to visiting a brothel. Men did so openly in broad daylight, rather than furtively in the dark of night.

The construction of railways across the prairies required many men, such as these pictured here in southern Saskatchewan in the early 1900s. Prostitution flourished wherever there was such a large body of unattached males (Courtesy of the Saskatchewan Archives Board/R-B375).

Until the early 1890s prostitution received little attention from the police. The records show only 12 convictions of inmates or keepers from 1874 until 1890, mostly associated with the railway construction camps.[11] In the male-dominated frontier settlements prostitution appears to have been openly tolerated. The Mounted Police records reveal no complaints about its existence, and the police seem to have been concerned only that it did not become too unruly in its operation. The rank and file of the force were themselves some of the prostitutes' best customers, although the prostitutes were off limits to commissioned officers, who were clearly expected to identify with the respectable class in society and to act like gentlemen. With tongue in cheek the *Regina Leader* reported that the

> red-coat of the Mounted Policeman is seen flashing in and
> out from these dens at all hours. As no arrests have been
> made the character of these visits may easily be surmised.[12]

The newspaper went on to report that those in authority in the force considered the houses a necessary evil. The paper did not criticize. Nicholas Flood Davin, the publisher, would probably have agreed with Kipling that "Single men in barracks don't grow into plaster saints."

The rank and file of the force was made up almost entirely of young single men under the age of 30. There had been reports of them frequenting brothels as early as 1875.[13] Such activity was not considered a disciplinary offence, at least not a serious one. Commissioner Herchmer, nevertheless, was concerned about the venereal disease contracted by the men. A fervent guardian of the public purse, he felt that it was downright unreasonable that men should be off duty sick and receiving medical attention at government expense because of their own indiscretions.[14] As a result, a regulation was sanctioned that authorized deductions from the pay of such constables would cover the cost of their hospitalization.[15] Making men pay for treatment they needed because of their immoral behaviour was not a new idea. It had been tried as a deterrent by the British Army. There was one drawback—the men tended to hide their condition and instead of obtaining qualified medical attention, they sought instead unprofessional remedies. No instances of this problem, however, have come to light in the Mounted Police records.

Sometimes things did go a little too far. On the evening of October 24, 1888, three constables being transferred to Calgary the next day came into Edmonton to celebrate. On their way into the settlement of some six hundred souls, one of them dropped off at Nellie Webb's establishment, while the other two set out to paint the town red. Sometime later, quite drunk, these two also headed for Nellie's house. Nellie refused to let them in. According to her testimony later, they threatened to wreck the house and to kill her. Drunken customers were one of the hazards of being a prostitute, but Nellie Webb knew how to take care of herself. She got the .38 revolver she kept in the house and warned them that if they tried to break in, she would use it. When they started kicking the door down, she fired through the broken panels hitting Constable Cairney in the thigh, breaking his hip.[16]

Nellie claimed she fired in self-defence. Nonetheless, Sergeant Davidson of the town detachment arrested her. She was charged with malicious shooting and released on $2,000 bail. The Mounted Police were not anxious to keep her in the cells as she was also the local midwife and her services were required at any moment.

The case against her never came to court. The most likely reason was that the constables were too drunk to testify reliably as to what happened. Instead, Nellie was convicted of keeping a house of ill-fame and fined $20 and costs.[17] Edmonton was too hot for her then, and like "The Outcasts of Poker Flat" she was forced to move on. She went south to Calgary and set up business again. Constable Cairney spent several weeks recovering in the barracks' hospital at Fort Saskatchewan; then he was dismissed.

The residents of Edmonton were used to drunkenness and brawling but the Nellie Webb incident went too far. Frank Oliver, the editor of the local newspaper, described it as "one of the most disgraceful affairs that has ever happened in Edmonton, through a set of men that are supposed to protect the citizens and their property."[18] He went on to place the real fault at the feet of those in charge of the Mounted Police. It was one sign that westerners were beginning to demand better moral standards from those who policed them.

About 1890 the Mounted Police started to develop a more systematic approach to the handling of prostitution. Behind the change was pressure from moral reformers, usually Protestant clergy. They were often the same groups or individuals who pressed for prohibition. If prostitution was illegal, they argued, it should not be allowed to exist. Apart from being immoral, it ruined innocent girls and it was the cause of disease and crime. The police themselves should set an example by not patronizing the houses. There were citizen groups, too, who objected to the presence of the brothels, perhaps because these houses affected property values and were a deterrent to settlement.

Conditions varied from place to place, but the NWMP evolved a fairly standard procedure for handling the matter. Once a complaint was made the house was raided and the women charged. Often they were given the alternative of a suspended sentence instead of a fine, if they promised to leave town. If they stayed and remained in business, the Mounted Police would raid them again from time to time and impose further fines. This system of licence by fine, which was common elsewhere, was from time to time pacticed in most districts.

In response to public criticism, the police also established more control over the operation of the brothel and the lives of their inmates. The movements of the women were restricted. They were prevented from flaunting their profession in the face of the town's respectable women. In some cases they were also required to undergo periodic medical examinations. As for the houses, the police usually required them to be segregated to some area where they were out of sight and sound of the rest of the town. Under Herchmer disciplinary steps were also taken to make it clear that consorting with prostitutes was not acceptable behaviour for a member of the NWMP. In January 1891 Constable G.T. Emigh received fourteen days hard labour for walking the streets of Macleod with a prostitute after being repeatedly warned not to do so.[19]

Mounted Police officers, however, did consider prostitution a necessary evil and, for a time, they were able to resist pressures to have it completely suppressed. Even when they closed houses and told the women to leave, they knew that the former residents would soon be replaced by another party of "soiled doves." In July 1889 the Mayor of Regina asked the Mounted Police to close a house on Lorne Street run by a Mrs. Turner.[20] (The territorial capital still had no police force of its own.) The house was closed. The following year the police gave another group of the demimonde 24 hours to leave town. The *Regina Leader* reported that they went bag and baggage.[21] Within a few weeks another contingent had arrived.[22] A group of citizens complained to the mayor. Once again he called upon the sergeant at the town station. The women were arrested but later were released when they promised to leave Regina. No doubt further replacements soon followed.

With a population of almost four thousand in 1891, Calgary was the largest settlement in the territories. It was also rapidly becoming its prostitution capital. Early that year, the Mounted Police stepped up enforcement against the numerous houses which had been established just outside the town limits. The *Calgary Herald* applauded the Colonel's (Supt. J.H. McIllree) efforts to punish the "strumpets."[23] During that year, about 30 convictions were obtained against keepers and inmates.[24] Often the same women were charged every few months. For the first offence the fines were usually $20 for keeping a house of ill-fame and $5 for being an inmate. The alternative was imprisonment for a few days. Three men found guilty of being frequenters had to pay $1 and spend one day in jail. All those convicted in Calgary that year paid a fine.

One Calgary madam was a thorn in the side of the NWMP for some time, undermining morale and proving difficult to dislodge. Her name was Lottie

NWMP "Town Station" in Regina, North-West Territories, 1895 (Courtesy of the Saskatchewan Archives Board/E.B. Williams Album, P. 22, No. 4).

Carkeek, alias Dutch Lottie, alias Lottie Diamond. Prostitutes frequently changed their names and seemed to prefer diminutive first names like Tilley, Trixie, Georgie, Lulu and Allie that had a friendly ring of familiarity. Occasionally they adopted a more ribald sobriquet; the two women who once functioned in the Empress Hotel in Moose Jaw were known as "Knockout Duffy" and "Pussy Jake."[25] In their tussle with Lottie Diamond, the Mounted Police ran into a problem they would find elsewhere—conflict with the local police.

Lottie first established a house of ill-fame in Calgary in 1888. She soon struck up an affair with Sergeant Sargent, the son of a Church of England missionary and a member of the local NWMP post. The liaison resulted in Sargent being disciplined and reduced to the rank of constable. A short time later he obtained his discharge and married Lottie. The newlyweds moved to Vancouver, but Lottie must have tired of respectable life because in 1891 she returned to Calgary and started a business on the bank of the Elbow River, a short walk from the Mounted Police barracks.[26]

In spite of being "old and withered in appearance," Lottie proved to have some unusual quality that NCOs of the Mounted Police could not resist.

Within a few months one sergeant-major, two staff-sergeants and one sergeant had been reduced in rank for being intimately involved with her. In June 1892 Commissioner Herchmer was forced to order her house declared out of bounds to members of the NWMP.[27] The clandestine visits continued, however, and the Sergeants' Mess became bitterly divided between the "friends" of Lottie and those who wanted to see her closed down.

The personnel problem was solved by transferring a number of men to other districts, but moving Lottie was not so easy. In trying to do so the Mounted Police stepped on the toes of the Chief of the Calgary Police. Lottie's house was within the town limits. It lay, therefore, within the jurisdiction of the town force, although it would probably not have been illegal for the Mounted Police to act.

In June 1892 Inspector A.R. Cuthbert, who had replaced McIllree in command of the Calgary District, wrote to the mayor asking him to take action against Lottie. The mayor was sympathetic but Chief of Police English seemed slow to move. Cuthbert believed that he was protecting Lottie. The most likely explanation is that English was tolerating prostitution as the Mounted Police did.[28] In any event, Cuthbert threatened to raid her house every night until she was driven out. This brought some action on the part of the town police, but not the results that Cuthbert hoped for. Lottie was charged with keeping a house of ill-fame and fined $50. By this time relations between the two police forces had soured, and Chief English was threatening a civil suit against Cuthbert for suggesting that he was protecting a prostitute.[29]

Prostitution also flourished in Lethbridge during the 1890s. The hundreds of men who worked in the nearby coal mines flocked into town on Saturday nights to enjoy themselves, thus providing a lure to prostitutes. The town was incorporated in 1891 and its first council quickly passed a bylaw aimed at closing the brothels. It was an abortive attempt, however. The newly appointed town constable proved to be ineffective and the bylaw was considered *ultra vires*.[30] Nevertheless, two dedicated guardians of the town's morals kept prodding local authorities to act. Getting no response, one of them, the Reverend Charles McKillop, a Presbyterian minister, finally wrote to Herchmer asking him to remove the houses from the town.[31] McKillop, who was known locally as the "Fighting Parson," claimed that there had been 26 prostitutes in the community since he moved there in 1886.

He received no satisfaction from the Mounted Police, who had just taken over the policing of the town under an arrangement with the council. Deane, the commanding officer in Lethbridge, told Herchmer that McKillop and the Methodist minister, the Reverend Bates, had publically addressed the town council on the matter but got no satisfaction and "retired covered with ridicule."[32] Deane had no sympathy with their cause. He was a strong believer in tolerating prostitution under the strict control of the police.[33] According to Deane, the two clergymen would have done better to pay more attention to the juvenile depravity among their own congregations as two of their respectable young ladies had recently been involved in love affairs with married men. The "professional ladies," said Deane, are "orderly, clean, and on the whole not bad looking."[34]

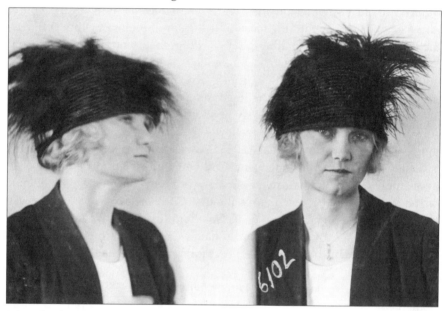

Police identification photograph of Pauline Sylvia Fair, age 23. Fined as a keeper of a "disorderly house"; later fined for vagrancy as Irene Walker. Listed as Danish from the United States and a prostitute (Courtesy of the Glenbow Archives/NA-625-16).

A few years later, at Macleod, Deane successfully thwarted another attempt to disturb the control of the police over prostitution. The Macleod Town Council asked him to close the establishments in the municipality. Deane knew that this action would result in the prostitutes scattering throughout the district, which would make supervision more difficult. He artfully responded, therefore, by telling the town fathers that if the houses in Macleod, were closed they would not be allowed to open elsewhere. In other words, he gave the councillors a choice of prostitution in the town under the eye of the police, or no prostitution at all. Under this threat, another council meeting was quickly called and it was decided to leave the matter to the discretion of the Mounted Police.[35]

One of the frequent accusations of those who wished to close brothels was that they were a major cause of the spread of venereal disease. In April 1904 the deputy Attorney General in Regina received an anonymous letter which claimed that over 100 new cases of syphilis had been treated by a doctor in Medicine Hat in the previous two months.[36] The cause of this epidemic, the letter claimed, was the local sporting houses. The Mounted Police investigation that followed revealed a good deal about their supervision of prostitution. It also raised the question of confidentiality in the relationship between medical practitioners and their patients.

Syphilis was first diagnosed among French soldiers in Naples in 1495. It was initially dubbed *morbus gallicus*, or the French disease. The name syphilis originated from an Italian poem of 1530 in which the gods inflict the disease upon a shepherd named Syphilis as a punishment. The origin of the great pox, as it was also called, is still in dispute.[37] Some claim that it existed in Europe before 1495, but was not identified. Others give Asia or Central America as its source. The French said that their troops contracted it in Naples from Spaniards who had been in contact with Columbus's crews. Clearly, nobody wanted the stigma of being associated with its spread. Its name, therefore, varied. The English and the Italians called it the French Pox. The French called it the Neapolitan Pox. The Turks called it the Christian Pox and the Chinese labelled it the Portuguese Pox.

Its spread in Europe in the 16th century resulted in a reaction against prostitution. Brothels in London and Paris were closed and their business was driven underground. Another consequence of the appearance of syphilis at this time was the development of the first sheaths or condoms as a means of preventing infection. It would not be until the vulcanization of rubber in the 19th century, however, that these would be widely used.

There was no reliable medical cure for syphilis until 1910 when the German Nobel prize winner Paul Ehrlich developed an arsenical preparation known as salvarsan. The most common treatment in North American prior to this was the use of salts of mercury taken orally or by injection.[38] There was no guarantee that this provided a cure, however, as there was no dependable means of diagnosing the disease until Wasserman's development of the blood test in 1906. All the patient could do was wait and hope that the usually fatal tertiary stage of its progress, which could take years, did not appear.

The deputy Attorney General forwarded the anonymous letter to Perry and asked him to investigate the claims. The Commissioner sent it on to the indomitable Deane who, by now, was in command of the Maple Creek District, which included Medicine Hat. Deane referred to Maple Creek as that "funny little Methodist-ridden place."[39] Perry told him to observe the usual practice. If the houses of ill-fame had become a nuisance, close them. Deane's initial reaction was that he did not believe there was any truth in the accusations. The only case he had heard of was that of one of the hotel clerks who was infected by an entirely unprofessional source.[40]

The NWMP maintained a four-man detachment in Medicine Hat in 1904. The town, with a population of about 2,000, was a busy divisional depot for the CPR. It was also close to the branch line to the Lethbridge coal mines. As a result, there were railway workers residing there, as well as miners and other travellers passing through the town. Deane called upon the officer in charge at Medicine Hat, Inspector C. Starnes, to carry out the investigations.

Starnes's first thought was that the letter was probably written by the Reverend Nicholl, a Church of England clergyman. Nicholl had complained earlier about a house and had asked that it be closed. Starnes had taken no action, however, as the house was in a quiet spot about two and one half miles from town and no one else seemed to support the minister. Given the nature of the new charge, the inspector began his investigation by interviewing the town's three doctors. They were co-operative to a point, and proved to be Starnes's main source of information. Dr. Smyth reported that he had treated only six cases of syphilis in Medicine Hat in the last year. He had traced three of these to the brothels. Dr. C.F. Smith informed Starnes that he had been practicing in the town for nine years and in all that time he had diagnosed only ten cases of syphilis. He believed that two of these originated from the houses. He had treated many cases of gonorrhea, but the sources in most cases were non-professional. Smith also stated that he was called to the house run by Stella Hattley quite frequently as she was very particular about the health of her inmates.

Dr. J.G. Calder's assessment varied from those of the other two medical men. He told Starnes that he had treated 50 cases in the last six months, more than he had seen in the previous 16 years. He claimed to have traced the majority of cases back to the prostitutes. According to Calder, the inmates did not use proper antiseptic precautions. He accused the madams of allowing their women to get drunk and to neglect themselves. He had been asked to examine the prostitutes, he stated, but he had refused because many of them were either drunk or addicted to cocaine and morphia. All three doctors steadfastly refused to reveal the names of their patients, claiming that such information was privileged.[41] Deane grumbled that the police could hardly be expected to do their job if vital information was held from them. But the Mounted Police did not challenge this claim to confidentiality, although the claim had no basis in law.

South Railway Street, Medicine Hat, 1904 (Courtesy of the Glenbow Archives/NA-567-7).

Meanwhile, two of the town's justices of the peace, Benson and Crosskill, had also written to the Attorney General's office complaining that the brothels were running wide open and that over 100 cases of syphilis were at that moment being treated in Medicine Hat. Starnes spoke with Benson, who admitted writing the first anonymous letter. He told the inspector that his source of information was one of the town's doctors. Starnes had no doubt that the doctor in question was Calder. Starnes had the two houses raided and fined two keepers and 10 inmates, as well as two Chinese cooks, and 12 customers.[42]

The epidemic clearly had been deliberately exaggerated, probably with the intent of closing the houses. Nevertheless, to what extent were the prostitutes of Medicine Hat a source of disease? Deane instructed Starnes to obtain a medical certificate for each girl, informing him that if any was diseased, she was to be told that she could not stay in business. The two madams, Stella Hattley and Marjorie Dale, were summoned to the police detachment. Starnes told them that they must have all their girls medically examined and that they should return next day with certified health statements for each one. He also got the madams to agree that the inmates would no longer be seen in the town. Instead, the madams would come to town once weekly to purchase necessities. In return, Starnes promised to do something about the drunken men who broke into their houses and damaged that their possessions.[43] The next day the two women dutifully returned. Each had a certificate signed by Dr. Smith which asserted, in effect, that every prostitute was free from contagious disease. It was safer to pay in Medicine Hat than play around. The accusation that the local prostitutes were the source of a venereal disease epidemic appeared to be false, although it should be remembered that medical diagnosis at the time was not entirely dependable.

By June, Deane was able to tell the Commissioner that life in Medicine Hat had returned to normal. The prostitutes had been punished to remind them that their illegal activities would be tolerated only as long as they behaved themselves. Everyone was happy with the situation again, reported Deane, even the "kickers."[44] In Regina, the deputy Attorney General expressed his satisfaction with the outcome, although he was concerned about the difficulty of enforcing the liquor laws in Medicine Hat, a politically more sensitive issue.

The reports of venereal disease were not the only reason that the presence of prostitution in the community was no longer accepted by some citizens. The attempt to close the brothels was also sparked by the relaxation of police control over prostitution. The women had got out of hand. They had been allowed to visit the town where they were noisy, gaudily dressed, and flaunted their profession in the faces of "respectable" citizens. At the root of the problem was a serious staffing problem. With a constable's basic pay at sixty cents daily, the NWMP was experiencing considerable difficulty in recruiting enough men of good character and steady habits.[45] In 1904 alone just over 10% of the rank and file either were dismissed for serious breaches of discipline or they deserted. Of those who remained, the majority would not re-enlist when their period of service was complete because wages were low and there were few opportunities for advancement. As a result, most of the men on strength in these years were young and of short service.

The corporal and two constables at Medicine Hat who made up Inspector Starnes's detachment were unmarried, inexperienced men in their early 20s. The corporal had only three years' service, while the constables had just a few months. As Deane said, they easily "succumbed to the temptations of the place," and discipline deteriorated. In March 1904 one of the constables was dismissed for theft. Early the following month, his replacement and the other constable deserted after becoming involved in some unpoliceman-like activity. They stole two horses and headed for the United States border. The corporal, meanwhile, had been drinking heavily and had struck up a liaison with one of the sporting women. When Deane heard that this woman had visited the barracks, he recalled the corporal to Maple Creek. Rather than face Deane's wrath, however, the corporal decided to join his comrades in Montana. His replacement, an experienced sergeant, soon straightened things out. As Deane reported later, the women had been permitted to come and go as they please, "but they are seldom seen in town now. When they do go, they dress and behave quietly. It is easy to keep them in order, if the non-commissioned officer is firm."[46]

After the inauguration of the provinces, the enforcement of the laws against prostitution by the NWMP entered a new phase. In 1906 an agreement between federal and provincial authorities placed the Mounted Police under the direction of the attorneys general of the new governments as far as the administration of criminal justice was concerned. During the colonial period, the police had a freer hand in determining their activities and, consequently, they dragged their heels with their new masters. Gradually, however, more and more control was exerted over the police.

The change saw a more determined movement for moral reform. This first appeared in 1904 in Winnipeg, where a long and vigorous campaign to remove social evil was to be fought. The Reverend C.W. Gordon (Ralph Connor), author of one of the early novels about the Mounted Police, denounced immorality amongst women from his pulpit in the city. Gordon and his reformers were not entirely successful, but they would try again, and what happened in Winnipeg would be repeated in many Alberta and Saskatchewan communities in the next decade.

Rapid urban growth also complicated the handling of prostitution for the Mounted Police. The force was relieved not only of responsibility for law enforcement in many settlements as they were transformed into incorporated municipalities, but existing towns and cities also expanded their police departments. As a result, the matter of jurisdiction became complicated and differences occurred over enforcement. In addition, there was a reaction among the prostitutes to the movement to put them out of business permanently. Some were neither willing to pay fines or to pack their bags and move on. Instead they fought back in the courts.

For a time the Mounted Police tried to follow their former practices with regard to prostitution, but it was soon evident that new influences were at work. In June 1904 the Calgary City Police closed three of the city's brothels. The former occupants moved across the Bow River into the village of Riverside and started to build new establishments. The residents of Riverside did not welcome them as three houses were operating in the village already. A petition was drawn up and sent to Superintendent Sanders, the officer commanding the Calgary District, asking him to close all the brothels. Sanders later told the Commissioner that at night it was not safe to cross the Langevin Bridge, which connected the village with Calgary,

Calgary City Police identification photograph of Jenny Lebousky, alias Jennie Johnson, alias Babe Johnson, age 23 (Courtesy of the Glenbow Archives/NA-625-11).

because numerous teams carrying customers travelled over it at breakneck speed. As a result of this danger and the petition, he closed the brothels and told the women to leave. Perry approved this action because local citizens had protested.[47]

In the spring of 1906 the Moose Jaw Council passed a resolution calling upon the Mounted Police to close the two houses of ill-fame just outside the city. The task was delegated to South African-born Corporal R.B.C. Mundy, who was later to become one of the force's outstanding detectives. Mundy was unable to find sufficient evidence to lay charges so he gave the prostitutes 48 hours to leave. He allowed the two madams to remain, however, as one owned the house she was using and the other had hers leased until the end of the month.[48] Later that year the possibility of conflict with the Edmonton City Police arose after its members raided houses of ill-fame outside the city limits. Inspector Worsley was concerned that a serious dispute might result between his men and those of the Edmonton force. He wanted to raise the matter with the chief of police but Commissioner Perry cautioned him against it.[49]

Venereal disease remained a problem. In Calgary, in February 1907, it was reported to Perry that diseased Japanese women were in business in houses on Nose Creek, a red light district across the river from Calgary and outside the city limits. The district was by now under the command of Superintendent R.B. Deane, a firm believer in the segregation and supervision of prostitution. Deane told his superior that, in addition to white women operating on Nose Creek, there were four Japanese houses with a total of 12 inmates. These, he informed the Commissioner, were medically examined every nine days, and all but one were free of disease. With regard to suppression, he continued, there is a "very pronounced body of opinion" that believed that the prostitutes were a necessary evil. If the houses were closed, the inmates would scatter all over the city, as they had done in Winnipeg, and there would be no control whatever.[50] When Deane's report reached Edmonton the deputy Attorney General there was shocked to find that the mounted policeman had not closed the brothels. He wrote directly to Deane instructing him that "if such houses are known to exist, they exist contrary to the law of the land and this should not be permitted."[51] It was a sign of the provincial authorities' changing attitude towards prostitution. Deane, however, seems to have quietly ignored this directive from his nominal superior. One can hear him muttering to himself and saying that he had been keeping law and order on the prairies for over 25 years and no jumped-up official in Edmonton was going to tell him how to go about it. In any case, Calgary citizens were happy with the arrangement, at least for the present.

The forces of change were growing, however. The fury of their attack would be concentrated in the larger urban centres where gambling, prostitution and illegal drinking appeared to be flourishing under the protection of the authorities. The municipal police forces and local police commissions would feel the brunt of this campaign. Accusations would be followed by public enquiries and police chiefs would be forced to resign. The Mounted Police were not to escape. The reformers were also active in the construction camp towns along the new rail lines and on the fringe of the municipalities where the Force still had jurisdiction.

In Calgary a Citizens' League was organized in autumn 1907. It brought charges against the police chief that the city's houses of ill-fame were being protected. Exerting pressure upon the Attorney General, the League succeeded in getting a judicial enquiry established to look into the accusations. Lawyers for the Citizens' League asked the Mounted Police to assist them in obtaining evidence against the chief by raiding the houses.[52] Deane balked at the suggestion. Relations between the two forces had not been good in the past. He did not now wish to be the means of its exposure. He fell back on an old excuse. He told the lawyers that the Mounted Police had no jurisdiction within the city limits. The representatives of the Citizens' League were not to be diverted from their objective, however. The Attorney General was contacted and he instructed Deane to raid the houses. It would be a familiar story in Alberta. When local police forces were under investigation or suspicion, the Mounted Police, or the provincial detectives in the Attorney General's department, would conduct enquiries.

Two years later, the Calgary reformers turned their attention to the brothels outside the city. The Presbyterian and Methodist ministers in the city's east end complained to Deane that the colony of sporting women on Nose Creek "was prejudicially affecting the morals and welfare of the community."[53] In company with his sergeant-major, Deane visited all the houses and told its madames that they must find another locality for their establishments. The houses were soon re-occupied by new prostitutes. Deane found that they were paying from $100 to $150 rent monthly. He suggested that the most effective way to deal with the trouble would be to make it unlawful for a person to rent a house for the purposes of prostitution.

Entwistle, Alberta, made the newspaper headlines as a place of vice and debauchery in May 1909. The source of the story was the Reverend J.J. Wright, the local Methodist minister. In letters to the Edmonton newspapers Wright claimed that Entwistle was a wide-open town where gross immorality was rampant and that the Mounted Police did nothing about this state of affairs.[54] Another Methodist minister came to his support and, far away in Toronto, the editor of the *Globe* thundered against the inaction of the North West Mounted Police. Wright also complained directly to the Attorney General.

Entwistle was a centre for the construction camps on the Grand Trunk Pacific Railway. At weekends hundreds of men descended on the town looking for one diversion or another. They brought money and business profited. The citizens of Entwistle did not take kindly to the clergyman's public statements. In fact, they were very angry and a public indignation meeting was held to denounce Wright and to express support for the Mounted Police. A petition also was circulated and this was then sent to the Methodist Council calling for the removal of the clergyman from the town.

The Attorney General reacted by dispatching a Provincial Detective to Entwistle to crack down on the unlicensed liquor vendors and any other irregularities. Among other items, he unearthed a prostitute who was selling photographs of herself having sexual intercourse with an Irish prize-fighter named Kelly. Kelly managed to elude the police, but the prostitute was sentenced to six months' imprisonment. "Dirty pictures" do not appear to have been common on the prairies at this time.

The NWMP reacted quickly too. The officer commanding the district ordered the NCO at Entwistle, Sergeant V.J. MacGillicuddy, to close all the brothels. Perry, meanwhile, arranged for Deane to hold an enquiry in the town concerning the accusations. Deane heard the testimony of a number of witnesses. A.J. Gayfer, chief engineer for the GTP testified that:

> compared with many other railway towns Entwistle has been a quiet town... I have never known a construction town where prostitution, gambling and illegal selling of liquor did not go on.

MacGillicuddy stated that the prostitutes conducted themselves well and as "I considered that it was a necessary evil where there [sic] so many men passing through and as there were no complaints about it I let it run." Deane discovered that Wright, the Methodist minister, had formerly been a private detective. Apparently, he had gathered the evidence for his charges by sneaking around the town at night and peering in windows. Deane made it clear that he considered Wright a troublemaker who was upsetting the entire community using religion as a guise for his real intentions. Most of Entwhistle's citizens would probably have agreed with Deane, who concluded his enquiry by finding that no blame could be attached to the Mounted Police.[55] There had been several brothels in the town but these had been raided periodically and the prostitutes had been charged. In coming down in favour of the old order Deane was refusing to accept the reformers' view that prostitution could no longer be controlled by a practice of raids and fines.

Even the intransigent Deane was eventually forced to accept that the pendulum was beginning to swing in another direction. In Calgary, reformers maintained pressure on him to take action on Nose Creek. Deane began replacing fines with mandatory prison sentences in a number of cases where prostitutes were convicted. This reduced the number of brothels, but it also brought more determined resistance from the women.

One of the most intransigent was Diamond Dolly, a familiar figure in Calgary and one of the most notorious brothel operators of the period. Deane was determined to close her Nose Creek establishment. One reason was that this brothel had become an attraction for some of his own constables. During the early hours of July 12, 1910, the Sergeant Major had led a surprise raid on one of the houses where he found ten who had broken out of barracks. Two weeks later plans were laid to raid Diamond Dolly's house. A search warrant was obtained and at 5:00 A.M. on July 26, 1910, Corporal Denis Ryan and Constable Rosenkrantz (later Baron Rosenkrantz of Orumgaard, Denmark) raided the brothel. The keeper, Ray Mason, admitted them without any trouble. They found a woman in bed alone in one room

Houses of "ill repute" located in the Nose Creek district, north of the railway bridge over the Bow River, just outside of Calgary's city limits, 1911 (Courtesy of the Glenbow Archives/NA-673-9).

and a man and woman in bed together in another room. The man claimed that the woman was sick and he was nursing her.

Subsequently, the keeper and the two women inmates were charged and convicted by Superintendent Deane and Inspector Duffus, JPs. All three were given prison sentences. To Deane's surprise however, an appeal was launched in the case of Mason, the keeper. To his even greater amazement, a few weeks later the District Court quashed the conviction, ruling that there was insufficient evidence. With typical sarcasm Deane warned the Moral Reform League that it was going to be difficult to suppress the social evil if, in future, unmarried men and women could go to bed together providing one was sick and the other a nurse.[56] Perry drew the case to the Attorney General's attention, complaining of his men's difficulty, and of the unreasonable demands of the moral reformers.[57]

Not everyone was prepared to knuckle down to the moral minority. In October 1911 a pimp named Joe Kelly set up a house with three girls north of Hardisty, Alberta. The CPR was building a branch line close by and, as a result, there were large numbers of construction workers about the town. Constable S.L. Warrior of Hardisty Detachment, who had already closed one brothel a month earlier, reported to his commanding officer with respect to the latest establishment that:

> the general opinion of this town is strongly in favour of a house of this kind owing to there being such a big bunch of railroaders here, but there are a few who will not stand for it and two complaints have come to me today.[58]

Before taking any action, Warrior requested that a plainclothesman be sent there to try and find what was going on. This task was given to D/Sgt. Tucker. He learned that Kelly had actually bought the house from the local JP, who had at one time considered going into partnership with the pimp. He also discovered that Kelly owed money to several merchants for furnishings and other items. The businessmen of Hardisty had no personal liking for Kelly, but they did have a vested interest in seeing that his brothel was not closed.

Nevertheless, the Mounted Police decided to close the house. A complaint had been made about it to the attorney general's office. Burbridge, the local JP, obviously could not be trusted, so arrangements were made for Inspector Worsley to come from Edmonton to hear the case. Once the townspeople knew what was afoot they drew up a petition calling on Worsley to give the brothelkeeper a fine instead of a prison sentence. Kelly couldn't pay his bills while he was in jail. The petition was signed by thirty residents, mostly merchants. Worsley, however, was not to be moved. He gave Kelly thirty days hard labour and a $50 fine. Warrior considered that "the moral standard of the majority of the residents of Hardisty was so low that they would sign a petition for the release of such a man as Kelly."[59]

On February 20, 1909, the Regina *Morning Leader* carried an article by a prominent United States district attorney exposing the growth of the white slave traffic in that country.[60] The crusade against white slavery was one more nail in the coffin of the toleration of prostitution by the Mounted Police. This expose was printed at the request of the Moral and Social Reform Council of Canada who wished to alert Canadians to the danger of this vicious trade and to encourage them to agitate for tougher penalties against those responsible. The attack on white slavery was the latest crusade to sweep northwards across the border. The struggle to suppress the trade had started in Europe about two decades earlier, during the I880s, the London *Pall Mall Gazette* had waged a vigorous campaign to expose the traffic in English girls being lured to Belgium, the principal centre for white slavery on the continent. In 1902 representatives of 16 countries met in Paris to draft an international agreement for the suppression of the *traite de blanches*. The campaign in the United States started shortly after, and quickly gained ground there; in 1910 Congress passed the Mann Act which made it a criminal offence to transport women across state lines for immoral purposes. Three years later the Borden government reacted to Canadian public pressure to suppress white slavery by increasing the Criminal Code penalty for procuring.

The traffic in women for immoral purpose gave a new edge to the campaign against prostitution. It became difficult to argue for its toleration when, as reformers asserted, many of the women were tricked, drugged or lured into becoming prostitutes against their will. The view that some women freely chose to be prostitutes was not accepted. The inflammatory and exaggerated claims regarding the extent of the traffic captured public attention. A speaker at a WCTU Conference in Sherbrooke in 1911 said that 1,500 Canadian girls disappeared every year, most of them ending up in the Chicago brothels.[61] The previous year there had been shocking allegations of the traffic in several Canadian cities. What really caught the public's attention, however, was the claim in November 1910 by the Reverend Dr. J.G. Shearer, National Secretary of the Temperance and Moral Reform Council, that Winnipeg was the most vice ridden city in the country.[62] Writing in the Toronto *Globe*, Shearer accused Winnipeg's civic and police authorities of allowing some 50 brothels to operate in the city in a segregated area. Winnipeg, he charged, was a market place for white slavery. The Synod of the Presbyterian Church in Manitoba agreed with him. The outcry forced the provincial government to hold a judicial enquiry into prostitution in the city.

The police fraternity was sceptical of the reformers' claims. At the 1913 annual meeting of the Canadian Association of Chiefs of Police in Halifax, the country's top police expressed the view that the issue of white slavery had been exaggerated in the public mind. They went on to say that reports of thousands of Canadian girls being lured annually to the United States were misleading and unreliable.[63] White slavery was certainly not a subject which occupied the attention of the Mounted Police in Saskatchewan and Alberta. They received a few reports of its existence but, with one exception, they proved to be unfounded. The Mounted Police, however, did not escape some of the criticism of the reformers. It was no longer possible to defend prostitution as a necessary evil. The uncompromising crusaders would not listen to that argument. They wanted the brothels closed, even if the police had no evidence to do so. Under increasing pressure themselves, the attorneys general responded to the latest waves of reform.

One prostitute whose spirits had not been dampened by the ardour of the reformers was Renée Costa. She stormed into Perry's Regina office one day in July 1912 to make a bitter complaint. According to her, the Mounted Police at Swift Current had discriminated against her, and had prevented her from continuing to make a living. The substance of her complaint was that they had allowed two other prostitutes to build a house just outside the town, but had refused to let her do so. The response of the former gentleman cadet of the Royal Military College is not recorded. Orders quickly went to Swift Current Detachment, however, to close all brothels in the area.[64]

In November 1912 Shearer aimed his guns at Superintendent J.O. Wilson who was in charge of Lethbridge District. While on a tour of the west, Shearer had come across three houses of ill-fame outside Medicine Hat. He spoke to Wilson about closing them. Wilson objected, pointing out that he had no legal right to order the prostitutes out of their houses and that it was difficult to get evidence if they decided to fight conviction. Shearer, however, was not interested in legalities. He took the case to the Attorney General and the houses were subsequently closed on his orders.[65]

Dr. A.T. Moore, General Secretary of the Temperance and Moral Reform Department of the Methodist Church, was active in seeing that the police carried out their duties. Hearing of gambling and prostitution in the Macleod District, he fired off a letter from his Toronto office to Superintendent Primrose, complaining of his inaction. Primrose, something of a martinet, was not one to take criticism lightly. In reply, he told the eastern busybody that the reports were exaggerated. He also informed him that he "was firmly of the opinion that the laws are just as well enforced in Southern Alberta as they are in Toronto."[66] Actually, most of the places mentioned by Moore were incorporated towns where the Mounted Police had no jurisdiction. The reformers often neither understood the question of police jurisdiction nor considered it relevant. Moore continued to make charges of irregularities against the RNWMP.

As with the temperance movement, the crusade against prostitution reached its peak in 1913. Thereafter the pressure from moral reformers tapered. The economic dislocation and the outbreak of war that followed deflected attention to other issues. They also brought new and more urgent duties for the Mounted Police that occupied more and more of its time. The end of an era in the policing of the Canadian prairies came in 1916. At the end of that year the federal-provincial contracts for the services of the RNWMP were terminated, and the enforcement of the Criminal Code in Alberta and Saskatchewan was taken over by provincial police forces.

The published reports of the Mounted Police annually record the number of convictions obtained against the keepers of houses of ill-fame and their inmates.[67] Starting in the 1880s the rate rises steadily, reaches a peak in the years 1906–13, and then begins to decline. Lack of other data, however, make it impossible to derive any meaningful conclusions from these figures. For example, they cannot be reliably related to the number of prostitutes who were active, or to the operations of other police forces. As the population of the prairies grew substantially during these years, it would be reasonable to assume that the number of prostitutes also grew, and that, consequently, there were more convictions. Unfortunately, this is too simple. First, the growing population was not matched by a substantial increase in police. The amount of work and the duties grew, but the number of men remained much the same. Second, after 1900 the incorporation of numerous towns and cities resulted in the establishment of local police forces who took over from the Mounted Police in those areas where prostitutes were most likely to be active. A more likely explanation for the rise in convictions, particularly after 1900, is that they represent an increase in activity by the Mounted Police against a diminishing or fairly static number of prostitutes within their jurisdiction, in response to pressures from various social and political forces.

Mounted Police reports also reveal something about the prostitutes themselves and the nature of their business. They do not show clearly, however, to what extent the women were victims of socio-economic conditions or marital circumstances. More about their personal lives will be known when the 1891 and subsequent census returns are made public. No evidence links prostitution to organized crime. The Hardisty case was the only one uncovered where the brothel was operated by a male. According to Mounted Police records, pimps had a very small role in prostitution on the prairies. The basic economic unit appears to have been an independent. group of women who occupied a house owned or rented by one to whom the rest paid a rent or percentage of their income for accommodation. The madam acted as manager or overseer. The establishment might also include a Chinese cook or houseboy. The price of service ranged from $3 to $10. It probably varied according to what they could induce from the customer. Leona Stanley, an inmate of Pearl Rogers's house on Wood Street in Lethbridge, complained because the police burst in upon her and a patron before she had time to collect her $3. She was fined $5.[68] Of the scores of cases documented in police files, not one was found where a prostitute was unable to pay her fine.

In Macleod, one brothel was run by two sisters named Jean and Addie Hughes, who led double lives. When they closed their Macleod business they returned to respectability on a fruit farm they owned in California. There they were known as Mrs. Herring and Mrs. Boyes. Prostitution, it seems, was a seasonable occupation.[69] It is difficult to imagine that the two fruit farmers were forced by dire economic need to operate a brothel in Alberta. Perhaps prostitution had been the means of their entering the respectable property-owning class.

There was another side to the prostitute's life. The possibility of becoming pregnant or contracting venereal disease was a constant hazard. Police files reveal nothing regarding birth control methods. There were also the problems of alcohol and drugs. One Japanese woman whom Deane noted as

Police identification photograph of Audrey Mauda, age 28, born in Norway. Charged with keeping a "disorderly house" (Courtesy of the Glenbow Archives/NA-625-17).

being diseased with syphilis was a particularly unfortunate case. She had only been in Calgary a few days when the Mounted Police discovered her condition. She had a small child with her and no money. Deane tried to get her admitted to Holy Cross Hospital, but the hospital would not take her. Deane asked CPR officials to pay her fare back to her home in California. The company was prepared to pay half of it, but no more. He then turned to the attorney general's office in Edmonton, enquiring as to whether she would qualify for deportation. In reply, the Deputy Attorney General instructed him to charge her under the Criminal Code and deport her, if convicted. What finally happened the records do not say.[70]

Police records clearly identify prostitutes as belonging to a morally inferior class. It should be remembered, however, that the officers who wrote most of the reports considered themselves morally superior. They would have included many other westerners in the same class as prostitutes, including most of their own men. As for these men, their relationships with prostitutes could go beyond sexual contact. One who was familiar with the prostitutes of Macleod just after the turn of the century remembered them with admiration, noting that they came into town on Thursdays to shop and on those occasions you saw better dressed and more attractive women than on the other days of the week. The women, he continued, were constantly changing and most were American.[71] They sometimes assisted the police by passing on information about their customers. It was a tip from a prostitute that enabled the Mounted Police to solve the brutal murder of Tucker Peach in 1910. The police reports put the prostitute in her place, but their tone was still tolerant. They expressed disapproval, but not condemnation. They contain none of the abhorrence reserved for the male homosexual, who for the mounted policemen was the unspeakable social pariah of western society. After all, Nellie Webb was also Edmonton's midwife. From what we know of her, she fits the typical image of the dance hall girl of the western movies, with a tough exterior covering a heart of gold.

The Mounted Police took a realistic approach to the problem of policing prostitution, based upon their own experience. They believed that society could no more outlaw illicit sex than the consumption of alcohol. To control prostitution they adopted methods that were widely used throughout North America. Their action was based upon standards of behaviour that communities would accept. This was a familiar role for the Mounted Police who, as a colonizing instrument of the federal government, had considerable discretionary power in carrying out their duties. In their own field they became something of a ruling elite. As the example of Medicine Hat shows, their methods worked quite well, until moral reformers and others muddied the waters for their own narrow interests. Reluctantly, the Mounted Police bowed to the changing order. But their experience with prostitution was one more reason why the management of the force became disenchanted with the prospect of continuing to police the increasingly industrialized and urbanized self-governing provinces. The halcyon days were over. As Commissioner Perry was fond of saying, the Mounted Police is a "Frontier" police not a "Civil" police. He looked forward to the termination of the contracts for its services and a return to its original role in the new frontiers of the Yukon and the Arctic.

Notes

This article first appeared in *Prairie Forum* 10, no. 1 (1985): 105–28.

1. Canada. *Sessional Papers, 1884*, no. 15, "Report of the Commissioner of the NWMP," (hereafter referred to as the *(R)NWMP Annual Report*), 54.

2. *A Chronicle of the Canadian West; NWMP Annual Report, 1875* (Calgary: Historical Society of Alberta, 1975), 24.

3. *Regina Leader*, May 17, 1883.

4. *(R)NWMP Report, 1884*, 58.

5. The prostitution of Indian women, which the Mounted Police regarded in quite a different light, is not examined here.

6. D.C. Dilworth (ed.), *The Blue and the Brass* (Gaithersburg, MD: International Association of Chiefs of Police, 1976), 135.

7. Canada. Criminal Code, 1892, 55–56 Vic., C.29, ss. 228–229.

8. Ibid., ss. 238–239.

9. Ibid., s. 225.

10. *Canadian Criminal Cases* (abridgement 1892–1925) (Toronto: Carswell, 1926), 172.

11. *(R)NWMP Annual Reports, 1874–1890.*

12. *Regina Leader*, May 17, 1883.

13. *A Chronicle of the Canadian West*, 24.

14. Library and Archives Canada (LAC), Royal Canadian Mounted Police Records, RG 18, vol. 1065, Herchmer to White, September 30, 1887.

15. Ibid., vol. 2328, General order 384, August 1886.

16. *Edmonton Bulletin*, October 27 and November 3, 1888.

17. Ibid., November 10, 1888.

18. Ibid., November 3, 1888.

19. LAC, Royal Canadian Mounted Police Records, RG 18, vol. 1217.

20. Ibid., vol. 1160, Mayor of Regina to Herchmer, July 22, 1889.

21. *Regina Leader*, September 30, 1890.

22. Ibid., October 21, 1890.

23. *Calgary Herald*, January 22, 1891.

24. *(R)NWMP Annual Report, 1891*, 156–60.

25. LAC, Royal Canadian Mounted Police Records, RG 18, vol. 1786, file 170.

26. Ibid., vol. 86, file 659–93.

27. Ibid., vol. 3339, file 878.

28. Chief English remained head of the Calgary Police Department until 1909 when he fell victim to a crusade for moral reform.

29. LAC, Royal Canadian Mounted Police Records, RG 18, vol. 69, file 616.

30. J.H. Carpenter, *The Badge and the Blotter* (Lethbridge: Historical Society of Alberta, 1975), 12.

31. LAC, Royal Canadian Mounted Police Records, RG 18, vol. 1269, file 220, McKillop to Herchmer, June 12, 1894.

32. Ibid., vol. 91, file 148, Monthly Report "K" Division, July 1894.

33. *(R)NWMP Annual Report, 1890*, 51.

34. LAC, Royal Canadian Mounted Police Records, RG 18, vol. 91, file 148, Monthly Report "K" Division, July 1894.

35. Ibid., vol. 1416, file 120, Monthly Report "D" Division, September 1898.

36. Ibid., vol. 1533, file 7, Perry to C.O. "A" Division, April 26, 1904.

37. Vern L. Bullough, *The History of Prostitution* (New York: University Books, 1964), 132.

38. W.A.R. Thomson, *Black's Medical Dictionary* (London: Black, 1965), 867.

39. R. Burton Deane, *Mounted Police Life in Canada* (Toronto: Coles Publishing, 1973), 97.

40. LAC, Royal Canadian Mounted Police Records, RG 18, vol. 1533, file 7, Deane to Perry, April 28, 1904.

41. Ibid., Starnes to Deane, April 30, 1904. (Anyone who knowingly did not take steps to prevent the spread of a contagious disease could have been subject to charges under the Public Health Ordinances.) The Canadian Medical Association code of ethics of 1868 included a provision for confidentiality between patient and doctor based upon historic tradition. See C.D. Naylor, "The Canadian Medical Association's First Code of Ethics" in *Journal of Canadian Studies* 17, no. 4 (1982).

42. Ibid., Starnes to Deane, May 9, 1904.

43. Ibid., Starnes to Deane, May 4, 1904.

44. Ibid., Deane to Perry, June 16, 1904.

45. *(R)NWMP Annual Report, 1904*, 11.

46. Loc. cit.

47. LAC, Royal Canadian Mounted Police Records, RG 18, vol. 1546, file 133, Sanders to Perry, June 7, 1904.

48. Ibid., vol. 1580, file 133, Mundy to C.O. "B" Division, May 5, 1906.

49. Ibid., Perry to Worsley, October 1906.

50. Ibid., vol. 1605, file 133, Deane to Perry, February 27, 1907.

51. Ibid., D.A.G., Alberta to Deane, March 13, 1907.

52. Provincial Archives of Alberta (PAA), Records of the Attorney General's Department, box 17, file 282.

53. *(R)NWMP Annual Report, 1909*, 31.

54. LAC, Royal Canadian Mounted Police Records, RG 18, vol. 376, file 386.

55. Ibid.

56. *(R)NWMP Annual Report, 1910*, 33.

57. PAA, Records of the Attorney General's Department, box 16, file 531.

58. LAC, Royal Canadian Mounted Police Records, RG 18, vol. 415, file 1911, Warrior to C.O. "G" Division, October 30, 1911.

59. Ibid., Warrior to C.O. "G" Division, December 13, 1911.

60. Regina *Morning Leader*, February 20, 1909.

61. *Canadian Annual Review of Public Affairs* (Toronto: Copp Clark, 1911), 366.

62. Ibid. (1910), 569.

63. Regina *Morning Leader*, July 9, 1913.

64. LAC, Royal Canadian Mounted Police Records, RG 18, vol. 1683, file 74.

65. Ibid., vol. 444, file 507.

66. Ibid.

67. (R)NWMP Annual Reports, 1874–1916.

68. Carpenter, *The Badge and the Blotter*, 29.

69. LAC, Royal Canadian Mounted Police Records, RG 18, vol. 409, file 212.

70. Ibid., vol. 1605, file 133, D.A.G., Alberta to Deane, March 13, 1907.

71. Ex-S/Sgt. G.E. Blake, interview by S.W. Horrall, Calgary, January 13, 1969.

6. "A Feudal Chain of Vassalage": Limited Identities in the Prairie West, 1870–1896

Theodore Binnema

The University of Toronto historian J.M.S. Careless has long been associated with the metropolitan approach and the idea of "limited identities" in Canada. Careless has been almost alone, however, in consistently and explicitly linking these two ideas together.[1] In his 1954 article "Frontierism, Metropolitanism and Canadian History," Professor Careless first suggested that Canadian historians should give greater attention to the role of metropolitan centres in Canadian history.[2] While some have interpreted this article as Careless's obituary for frontierism, it is critical to understand that Careless was merely promoting the idea of metropolitanism as "the other side of the coin to frontier expansion."[3] Careless emphasized the influence of metropolitan centres on their hinterlands but he did not deny the two-way nature of the relationship. The Laurentian School, associated with historians such as D.G. Creighton and economist H.A. Innis, embodied an essentially metropolitan perspective that focussed on the impact of large national and international metropolitan centres on Canadian development. Careless endorsed a more subtle metropolitan idea. According to Careless, a metropolitan approach that recognizes "a chain, almost a feudal chain of vassalage, wherein one city may stand tributary to a bigger centre and yet be the metropolis of a sizable region of its own," and that acknowledges that metropolitan power has been more important in Canadian history than in United States history "may do more to explain the course of Canadian history than concepts of frontierism borrowed from the United States."[4]

In December 1967, as Canada's Centennial year drew to a close, Professor Careless presented his well-known paper on limited identities in Canada, a response to the nation-building school of historical interpretation.[5] Careless argued that in seeking to trace the development of nationalism in Canada the nation-building approach "neglects and obscures even while it explains and illuminates."[6] Historians, Careless suggested, ought to pay greater attention to the role played in the history of the Canadian community by the limited identities associated with region, ethnicity, and class. Tying the idea of limited identities to the metropolitan approach, Careless suggested that the rise of dominant metropolitan centres had served to reinforce regional identities in Canada.[7] Thus, according to Careless, the nation-building school was neglecting the importance of regional identities and the role of regional metropolitan centres in Canadian history.

Canadian historiography has undergone a dramatic transformation since 1967. If historians could be accused of overlooking the limited identities of region, class, ethnicity, and gender before 1967, the same could not be said of historians in subsequent years. Indeed, social historians have ensured that the term "limited identities" would find a prominent place in the Canadian historiographical lexicon. Strangely, however, although Canadian scholars have made use of metropolitan interpretations in regional studies, they have rarely acknowledged the complexity of the "feudal chain of vassalage" among Canadian metropolitan centres.[8] Perhaps this helps explain why, only a decade after his "Limited Identities" article was published, Careless himself felt dismayed with the regional interpretations that had emerged in the intervening ten years. In 1980 he appeared to retreat from his argument in "Limited Identities" when he urged historians to balance their regional interpretations with a wider national perspective.[9]

By contrast, Careless has defended his metropolitan idea against all critics. The most persuasive critic of metropolitanism, Donald F. Davis, has suggested that metropolitan interpretations, like the frontier interpretations, had ceased to offer innovative insight into Canadian history.[10] Careless's response to Davis is remarkable because, in arguing that both the frontier and metropolitan approaches "considered together, still have much to offer," Careless alluded to his 1967 "Limited Identities" paper. Developing his assertion that the metropolitan approach assumed the existence of "almost a feudal chain of vassalage," Careless wrote: "clearly, small local communities hold their own limited identities; to a large extent delimited and defined in spatial terms."[11] Careless has not retreated from the "limited identities" idea because, for him, it was an adjunct to his metropolitan approach.

In the same way that the nation-building approaches had earlier obscured important regional aspects of the Canadian experience, many approaches to regional history have neglected important intraregional factors. For example, historians have emphasized the development of a prairie regional identity in the early settlement era but have given little attention to

"Prosperity Follows Settlement in Western Canada" – cover of a pamphlet produced by the federal Department of the Interior (Courtesy of the Saskatchewan Archives Board/G86.3).

the even more limited local identities. Prairie promotional literature reveals that, between 1870 and 1896, the development of prairie regionalism was accompanied, among the business elite in any case, by various "limited identities" that can be understood adequately only by employing a metropolitan approach.

Pamphlets promoting a particular city, district, or region as a field for immigration or investment have generally been treated dismissively by historians. Civic boosters may have played an important part in deciding the fortunes of some cities *vis-à-vis* their nearby rivals, but most historians agree that neither the promotional literature produced by the federal government nor by local boosters attracted many settlers to western Canada in general or to any particular city in the period from 1870 to 1896. Despite the efforts of the Canadian government and prairie boosters, immigrants trickled into the Canadian West only slowly. Similarly, promotional literature appears to have had little to do with the flood of immigrants after 1896.[12] Furthermore, historians often remind us that the claims made in promotional literature often had much more to do with the overly optimistic views of boosters than with objective reality.[13] Nevertheless, this promotional literature merits careful consideration. The vast number of pamphlets published by the Canadian government, the Canadian Pacific Railway (CPR), the provinces and territories, and by municipalities, reveal the amount of intellectual energy spent on this endeavour.[14] More important, promotional literature offers considerable insight into how local elites perceived the West and the potential of particular places to achieve metropolitan dominance.[15]

The goal of promotional literature was simple: the attraction of immigrants and investment to a particular location. Boosters, however, viewed another location's gain as their loss. Naturally then, boosters promoted their city and its *perceived* hinterland by comparing their region with other regions that they *perceived* were in competition with their city. The implications of this fact deserve closer examination than they have received. Alan F.J. Artibise, the most prolific historian of prairie boosterism, has described the apparently unvarying metropolitan ambitions of prairie cities:

> while all prairie boosters wanted the region to grow rapidly, they were especially concerned with the growth of their own communities. Despite the early prominence of Winnipeg, the boosters of the other four cities [Regina, Calgary, Saskatoon and Edmonton] optimistically envisioned their centre becoming the pre-eminent metropolis of the area... Each centre zealously competed with the others for economic advantage and prestige.[16]

A superficial examination of promotional literature would suggest that Artibise is correct. Boosters of each city or district would inevitably describe their soil, climate, resources, and community as the best in the entire Canadian North-West. A more careful examination of prairie promotional literature produced before 1896, however, reveals that the elite in most cities produced promotional literature that reflects a much more modest assessment of their cities' potential. Local boosters carefully identified the area with which they believed their own economic prospects were tied. They judged areas outside this hinterland to be in direct competition for immigrants and investment. These areas were as prominent in promotional literature as the area being championed, for boosters were convinced that prospective immigrants and investors needed to be persuaded that their own area was equal, if not superior, to these other regions in its agricultural and economic potential. Thus, even if each city's boosters made bold claims that their city would eventually emerge as the preeminent western metropolis, they tailored their promotional literature to fit more moderate assessments of their city's prospects. The "sameness" of promotional literature is superficial: each city or district advertised that it enjoyed the greatest economic potential in the entire Canadian North-West. The critical differences in the promotional literature become evident when the researcher notes the extent of the area being promoted by the boosters of each city or region, and the *specific* areas with which that city or region is compared. In noting these aspects of the literature, the researcher can appreciate the very different metropolitan ambitions of the elites of various cities and regions.

Promotional literature produced by the federal government illustrates this salient point. The acquisition of the North-West was the result of an expansionist movement centred primarily in what is now Ontario. This expansionist movement was not propelled by popular sentiment in the North-West, although some Ontario residents may have believed that most of the inhabitants of the North-West sought annexation.[17] Neither was the expansionist movement driven primarily by a desire to extend the benefits of British civilization to the people of the territory. Put simply, the Ontario elite viewed annexation of the territory as essential to the survival of Canada in the face of potential confinement by an expanding United States.[18] Once Canada acquired the North-West, federal policy toward the territory reflected this belief.[19] Thus the federal government's promotional literature not only vigorously promoted the climate, soil, and organization of the Canadian Prairies, but also explicitly and favourably compared the Canadian Prairies to the northern Plains states.[20] With the northern Plains states consistently attracting far greater numbers of settlers (including settlers from Canada) than the Canadian Prairies, the Canadian government obviously aimed to convince prospective settlers of the superior economic potential of the Canadian Prairies. Even if many western settlers originated in Ontario, they were not considered lost to that province if they settled on the adjacent Prairies. These settlers could supply central Canada with important agricultural products while providing a market for central Canadian manufactured goods. Clearly, it was not by historical accident that the West became a hinterland of central Canada; it was intentionally developed as such.

The same metropolitan perspective can be applied within the prairie region. In the western "hinterland," the elite of every city estimated the position their city could attain in the hierarchy of prairie cities. In 1870 these assessments were made in the context of the conclusions provided by the expeditions of Captain John Palliser and Henry Youle Hind between 1857 and 1860. These expeditions replaced an earlier belief that the entire North-West lacked agricultural potential with the view that certain regions of the northern Plains, running in a crescent from the Red River Valley northwest along the Saskatchewan River and then south along the foothills of the Rocky Mountains, embodied a "fertile belt" on the northern rim of the "Great American Desert." In 1870 the nonindigenous population of the newly acquired territory was small, but by historical accident the bulk of this non-Native population was centred in small settlements within this "fertile belt."[21] These small communities including Winnipeg, Prince Albert, Battleford, and Edmonton, seemed destined to form the nucleus of future settlement. When the federal government promised to build a trans-continental railway, its projected route ran northwest from the Red River Valley to Edmonton and toward the Yellowhead Pass.[22]

If there was reason for optimism, nowhere was this more true than in Manitoba. The province, created in 1870, was the centre of the largest non-Native population on the Prairies. Manitoba boosters immediately assumed that the entire western region, as far west as the Rocky Mountains, would become their hinterland. The 1871 report of a Manitoba government committee on agriculture, immigration, and colonization, betrays this belief. The committee reported not only on the agricultural potential of Manitoba, but of the North-West Territories as well. Repeated references to "Manitoba and the North-West Territories" reveal no attempt to compare the advantages of any part of the Canadian Prairies with any other. Instead, the committee recommended that the government adopt the aim of "diminishing the current of emigration to the United States."[23] The committee recommended that to realize this goal "we must of necessity hold out to the emigrant advantages fully equal at least to those which he finds amongst our neighbors [sic] in Minnesota."[24] This is the strategy that the Manitoba government followed not only in the early years of settlement, but even after settlements in the North-West Territories had announced their own competing metropolitan ambitions.

An 1889 provincial government pamphlet provides an example of the nature of Manitoba advertising. While the pamphlet includes such general claims as "Manitoba is beyond all doubt the most attractive and important part of the Canadian North-West," it includes no disparaging remarks about any specific area on the Canadian Prairies.[25] In fact, it occasionally promotes the entire region. For example, after arguing that the American wheat fields were becoming exhausted, it asserts that "Informed Americans admit without hesitation that the supply of WHEAT MUST COME FROM NORTH OF THE INTERNATIONAL BOUNDARY."[26] On the other hand, the pamphlet makes repeated comparisons with specific western states and territories, and eastern Canadian provinces. For example, it claims that:

> The almost universal verdict [of those who have lived in the country for several years] is that the CLIMATE OF MANITOBA IS MORE AGREEABLE THAN THAT OF ANY PART OF ONTARIO, QUEBEC OR THE EASTERN PROVINCES. … It is decidedly preferable to Dakota, Minnesota, Montana, Kansas, Nebraska, Illinois, California or any other State in the Union.[27]

Other comparisons of Manitoba with Canada's eastern provinces and specific states appear in passages dealing with scenery, soils, laws and society, frequency of storms, and quality of pasture land.[28] Naturally, in each case, Manitoba appears equal or better than its competition. Conspicuously absent throughout this pamphlet are disparaging references to regions within Manitoba's hinterland. Lack of such references is general to Manitoba promotional literature produced in this era.[29]

Within the West, Winnipeg was ideally located to become the metropolis of the entire prairie region. Alan Artibise has argued that Winnipeg's emergence as the preeminent city of western Canada was brought about by its particularly dynamic business community and "was the result of neither geographical locational or initial advantage."[30] While Artibise has clearly shown that Winnipeg's specific physical site had important drawbacks, especially in comparison with the neighbouring town of Selkirk, geographer A.F. Burghardt has also proven that Winnipeg was ideally located to assume the role as the gateway city for the Canadian West.[31] Not only was Winnipeg in 1870 the largest settlement on the Prairies, but established as it was on the eastern edge of the Prairies, it enjoyed significant locational advantages over other centres. Winnipeg boosters may not have been alone in boasting that their city was destined to become the metropolitan centre of the Canadian North-West, but the promotional literature produced before 1896 indicates that only Winnipeg boosters viewed the entire Canadian prairie region as tributary to their city. Winnipeg was the only prairie city that consistently promoted the entire Canadian North-West between 1870 and 1896. While some have credited the Winnipeg elite with having the broadest western vision, Winnipeg's broad vision and other cities' "parochialism" maybe more a reflection of the relative metropolitan potential of the various cities than of the attributes of city leaders.[32]

Unlike any other city, Winnipeg's economic, political, and social influence was intimately tied to the prospects of the entire West. Thus, when John Macoun announced in 1880 that the agricultural potential of lands outside the "fertile belt" identified by Palliser's expedition in 1860 had been greatly underestimated, Winnipeg residents, unlike the residents in other areas within the fertile belt, showed no disappointment. In fact, the Winnipeg elite, like the federal government, quickly abandoned earlier views and adopted Macoun's dogma. An 1886 Winnipeg pamphlet boasted that "What are known as the 'American desert' and as the 'bad lands' to the south disappear almost entirely when the Canadian border has been crossed."[33] Manitoba and Winnipeg boosters viewed the entire West as their hinterland just as central Canadian boosters did. Not surprisingly then, Manitoba and

Winnipeg promotional literature bears much closer resemblance to the Canadian government literature than to the promotional literature produced elsewhere in the West.

In 1871 few westerners doubted that the preeminent city on the Canadian Prairies would emerge along the Red River Valley. Winnipeg's only real rivals for this position were its nearest neighbours. The most important of these pretenders, Selkirk, was situated only 20 miles north of Winnipeg. In 1874 Winnipeggers learned that the federal government planned to build the main line of the transcontinental railway through Selkirk rather than Winnipeg.[34] Winnipeggers understood what the stakes were. They knew that one of these two cities, the one that would secure the main line of the transcontinental railway, would evolve into the metropolitan centre of the entire West; the other would never rise above the level of a local centre. Winnipeg's civic boosters understood that this rivalry could not be won with printer's ink, for Winnipeg's promotional literature of the time does not mention Selkirk.[35] The Winnipeg elite continued to promote the entire Canadian North-West as Winnipeg's hinterland. A pamphlet produced in 1874, when the route of the main line seemed destined to go to Selkirk, included a map of the Canadian North-West "Shewing [sic] the Convergence of the North Western System of Navigable Water Towards Fort Garry."[36] Five years later, before the issue of the transcontinental railway had been settled, two Winnipeg businessmen confidently asserted: "That Winnipeg is destined to be the great distributing and railway centre of the vast North-West is now no empty figure of speech."[37]

After the route of the CPR was confirmed in 1881, so was Winnipeg's position as dominant city. Although the city boasted a permanent population of only 9,000 in 1881, it laid claim to a hinterland that extended to the Rocky Mountains. Winnipeg boosters consistently advertised the entire prairie region. An 1882 Winnipeg pamphlet did not promote merely the Winnipeg environs but the entire area between Lake Superior and the Rocky Mountains. Its writers did not feel it irrelevant to predict that settlers would soon be taking up homes in the shadow of the Rocky Mountains.[38] Even after the railway was completed and other prairie cities proclaimed their own metropolitan ambitions, frequently by denigrating Winnipeg, the Winnipeg elite continued to promote the entire Canadian West. A pamphlet issued by Winnipeg's Board of Trade in 1883 advertised the advantageous effects of the chinook winds on the climate of the eastern slopes of the Rocky Mountains and assured readers that the climate of the Canadian North-West was as favourable as that of Dakota and Minnesota.[39] An 1886 pamphlet printed by the Winnipeg *Commercial* boldly predicted that "a few years

Main Street, Winnipeg, in the summer of 1882 (Courtesy of the Glenbow Archives/NA-118-23).

hence will see the preponderance of population, production and political power west of Lake Superior" and that Winnipeg had been destined by geography and the "inevitable laws of supply and demand" to become the metropolis of the North-West:

> Winnipeg becomes by its very position the natural middle-man between the east and the west. Whatever, then, the immense region embraced in Manitoba, Assiniboia, Alberta, Saskatchewan and Athabaska [*sic*], may in the future, become, aggregating the greater part of the area of the Dominion, Winnipeg will be its chief mart and metropolis.[40]

In the ensuing years Winnipeg pamphlets continued to praise the agricultural potential of lands as far west as the Rocky Mountains, to refer to specific coal resources as far west as Lethbridge and Banff, and to extol the quality of grazing lands as far away as southern Alberta.[41]

Clearly, promotional literature produced by Manitoba and Winnipeg boosters in the early years of settlement does not conform neatly to generalizations of prairie boosterism. Despite the competing metropolitan claims of other cities on the Prairies, Winnipeg promotional literature made no disparaging references to other prairie cities. Paul Rutherford's survey of the western press suggests that the Winnipeg press displayed a similar confidence. The Winnipeg press appears to have promoted the entire Canadian West, and did not instigate acrimonious exchanges with the press of other cities.[42] Winnipeg's boosters behaved this way because they understood that Winnipeg enjoyed the greatest metropolitan potential of any city in the West, not because of their unique vision. They knew that in casting aspersions on any area of the Canadian West, they would be calling into question the potential of their own hinterland.

If Winnipeg's rate of growth failed to meet expectations of optimistic boosters who compared it with Chicago, developments did seem continually to confirm its position as the dominant city of the West. In 1881 the future seemed only somewhat less promising for the isolated settlements of Battleford, Prince Albert, and Edmonton. Steamers had begun plying the Saskatchewan River system in the 1870s. Construction of a telegraph line between Winnipeg and Edmonton along the route of the projected transcontinental railway began in 1875, and Battleford was chosen as the capital city of the North-West Territories in 1876. Most important, the proposed route of the transcontinental railway passed through these settlements. Prospects for the Saskatchewan River settlements changed radically, however, after 1880 when botanist John Macoun dismissed the earlier assessments that suggested that the "Great American Desert" extended into the southwestern Canadian Prairies.[44] The implications of Macoun's report were made tangible in 1882 when the CPR received the government's permission to build its main line through the heart of "Palliser's Triangle" rather than through the "fertile belt." Soon after this decision, the capital of the North-West Territories, and the headquarters of the North-West Mounted Police were moved from Battleford to Regina. Investment and settlement were also diverted from the Saskatchewan River settlements to the southern prairies.[45]

While Winnipeg boosters welcomed Macoun's announcement, those in the Saskatchewan River settlements were dismayed. The case of Charles Mair is instructive. As founding member of the nationalist organization, Canada First, and later as settler at Red River, Mair had vigorously promoted the North-West. Having relocated to Prince Albert in 1877, however, his vision had become somewhat more narrow by 1880. According to Doug Owram, Mair, resisting the notion that the entire Canadian North-West was a fertile belt, "retained the use of the term 'fertile belt' in its original and more restrictive sense.[46] The term "fertile belt" also survives in the title of an 1893 pamphlet promoting the Kinistino district near Prince Albert.[47] More pointedly, Battleford newspaper editor Patrick Gammie Laurie complained

Capital Lost. The seat of government for the North-West Territories from 1877–1882 was at Battleford. More than two-thirds of Canada's geographical land mass was administered from Battleford's Government House, pictured here circa 1877. The Territorial capital was moved to Regina in 1883 (Courtesy of the Fort Battleford National Historic Park Library).

that Battleford had lost its status as capital city because it had been the victim of "every variety of misrepresentation and falsification."[48] A similar hint of bitterness was expressed by Prince Albert promoter, Henry Thomas McPhillips, in 1888. Perhaps because of the recent North-West Rebellion, McPhillips felt constrained to assure his readers that "we are Canadians, and hold national paramount to provincial interests"; otherwise, he continued, "we might not scruple to complain of its [the decision to build the railway through the southern prairies] having turned the tide of immigration away from us."[49] Although residents along the North Saskatchewan River remained optimistic in the early 1880s, the mood gradually became gloomier as the economic depression of the mid-1880s delayed the construction of branch lines to the Saskatchewan River settlements.[50] Branch lines to the Prince Albert and Edmonton districts were not completed until 1890 and 1891 respectively. Even after they were built, the railways allowed the northern settlements to carve out only very modest prairie hinterlands. Growth of these centres remained very slow throughout the period before 1896.[51]

Without an east-west rail connection Edmonton could expect to dominate only a very small district to the south, east, or west. Early on, then,

Edmonton boosters consoled themselves with an extensive northern hinterland. The improvement of a cart road from Edmonton to Athabasca Landing in the early 1880s, and the establishment of steamboat navigation on the Athabasca and Mackenzie Rivers between 1883 and 1887, made Edmonton the metropolitan centre of a vast albeit sparsely populated region of northern Canada.[52] In 1883 the *Edmonton Bulletin* produced a promotional pamphlet predicting that

> [t]he timbered regions of the Athabasca, the farming lands
> of the Peace river, the gold bearing Liard, the fur country of
> the Mackenzie, the salt deposits of the Great Slave or lower
> Peace river, the petroleum beds of the lower Athabasca, the
> fisheries of the mighty lakes all will have to seek some point
> on the Saskatchewan as their outlet and market. To possess
> the trade of such a country, when developed, must build up
> a great city, and what place more likely to possess that trade
> than Edmonton?[53]

While the North is presented as Canada's El Dorado, Edmontonians would have to wait several decades before they derived significant benefit from it. Meanwhile Edmonton needed to attract settlers. Edmonton's boosters understood that if settlers were to be attracted to the Edmonton district, they would have to be convinced not only to bypass the northern states, but also Manitoba and southern prairie regions. Promotional material reflected this concern. An Edmonton pamphlet produced in 1892 argues that Edmonton farmers enjoyed higher prices for their wheat than Winnipeg farmers, greater proximity to markets, and less exposure to troublesome diseases. It also advised that Edmonton winters were warmer than Manitoba winters, while its climate was less windy and dry than that of southern Alberta.[54] For its main argument, however, this pamphlet alluded to the traditional belief that treeless lands were unsuitable for farming: "Forest growth tends to distribute the rainfall evenly, to equalize the temperature, reduce the force of the winds, and to prevent undue evaporation. In other words it prevents destructive rainstorms, and equally destructive summer drouths [sic] as well as summer frosts and cyclones and winter blizzards."[55] Finally, the pamphlet assured readers that gophers, troublesome pests throughout the prairies, were almost unknown in Edmonton.[56] Regarding the decision to build the CPR through the southern prairies, the pamphlet admits that this had instilled a belief that the "north country" was inferior to the southern prairies, but it asserts that construction of "[t]he Calgary and Edmonton Railway reversed this argument, and the inference was at once established that there must be something worth building for."[57]

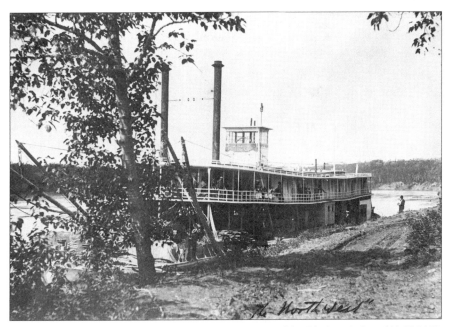

Steamboat *The Northwest* at Edmonton, circa 1890s (Courtesy of the Glenbow Archives/NA-1244-2).

Superficially at least, boosters in the District of Saskatchewan continued to express confidence during the early 1880s. The *Prince Albert Times* of November 15, 1882, for example, predicted that Prince Albert would "ere long be one of the most important cities in the Dominion of Canada."[58] Like Edmonton boosters, however, Prince Albert citizens faced the unenviable challenge of convincing settlers and investors that ideal conditions existed in an isolated location. In their efforts, Prince Albert promoters used similar arguments to those used by Edmontonians. Blizzards which affected the prairies, a Prince Albert pamphlet assured, "pass harmlessly over the wood-ed Saskatchewan country," and the grasshoppers and gophers that were so destructive on the prairies were not a problem along the Saskatchewan.[59] In 1888 the *Prince Albert Times* undertook to promote the northern regions after damning the south with faint praise:

> We have nothing to say in depreciation of the Canadian prairies. They are as rich as any in existence, and will in a few years be covered with prosperous communities. But the pioneer—especially the pioneer with limited means—finds near the rivers advantages he cannot find on the open prairies. On the latter he has no lumber for his house, no water till he digs a well; and frequently fuel is scarce. Along

the rivers he finds good water in abundance, logs for the
walls of his house, and so soon as a demand for sawn
lumber is established there it is certain that sawmills will
quickly spring up.[60]

Like Edmontonians, the residents of Prince Albert saw the north as their
extensive hinterland: "Prince Albert will be to the Great Peace River Valley
in process of settlement what Winnipeg was and still is to the Valley of the
Saskatchewan, THE BASE OF SUPPLIES."[61] Clearly, the promotional literature of the Saskatchewan River settlements reflects the very limited expectations of local residents. While its residents may have firmly believed in the
superiority of their district, they readily recognized that the rerouting of the
CPR had sealed their fate. The restraint and the occasional hints of bitterness
evident among the elite of the Saskatchewan River settlements contrast
sharply with Winnipeg's ebullience.

While the northern prairie centres may have faced stagnation and frustration, new centres such as Brandon, Regina, Moose Jaw, Medicine Hat, and
Calgary sprang up along the CPR between 1881 and 1883. Tiny by modern
standards, these new towns quickly eclipsed older settlements along the
North Saskatchewan River in both size and influence. The relocation of the
capital of the North-West Territories from Battleford to Regina in 1883
reflected and reenforced this southward shift in influence.

Even northern economic development worked as much in favour of
southern centres as the Saskatchewan River settlements. By 1883, even
before railways had reached Edmonton and Prince Albert, the CPR had
usurped steamboat transportation on the Saskatchewan River. Goods or
people destined for or originating in Edmonton or Prince Albert were carried via cart roads to Calgary, Regina, or Qu'Appelle; businesses benefited
from the increased trade.[62] Northern settlements remained entirely in the
orbit of southern metropolitan centres.

Residents of these new southern cities quickly recognized their metropolitan potential and promoted the development of their hinterlands in
comparison with competing cities. Perhaps all of these cities made grandi-
ose claims as the future metropolis of the West, but their promotional strategies reflect modest expectations. Pamphlets produced in Brandon, for example, reveal that, despite its lofty claims, the Brandon elite understood that
their city had only a limited metropolitan potential. While Winnipeg promotional literature never mentions Brandon either in a positive or negative
light, Brandon's literature includes frequent negative remarks regarding
Winnipeg. A pamphlet produced in 1882 takes aim at Winnipeg and its surroundings, dismissing the idea that the bulk of the best land in the North-

West was in the Red River Valley. The same pamphlet extols the virtues of Brandon's surroundings, including Turtle Mountain, the Souris Valley, and the Qu'Appelle Valley.[63] Seven years later, little had changed. Again, a pamphlet written for the Brandon Board of Trade targeted Winnipeg: "While it is true that Winnipeg, by being the capital of the Province must always command a certain prestige, yet the locality and surroundings of Brandon are such that it must be the distributing centre for the entire business of the west." The pamphlet suggested that a day would come when Winnipeg and Brandon would be compared in the same way as one compares Fredericton and St. John's [*sic*], or Quebec City and Montreal.[64] Curiously, a map entitled "Brandon's Railway System" shows, not the entire West, but only branch lines in Brandon's environs. Similarly, the pamphlet promotes the agricultural potential of only a small region surrounding the city of Brandon. None of the expansiveness of Winnipeg literature appears in the Brandon literature. According to Paul Rutherford, Brandon newspapers also exhibited these limited ambitions.[65]

Regina's boosters behaved much like Brandon's. Promotional literature produced by the Regina Board of Trade in 1889 advises immigrants "don't be persuaded to get off the cars in Manitoba by Manitoba agents. Come right through to Regina."[66] The Regina Board of Trade promoted an area including the Qu'Appelle Valley and the Moose Jaw region. After explaining that the Qu'Appelle Valley was as good ranching country as Alberta, an 1891 pamphlet continues: "We mention this to show that the territories tributary to Regina both north and south, are as well suited to accommodate the prospective rancher as any other portion of these territories."[67] Thus, Regina promotional literature not only takes aim at Winnipeg and other centres to the east, but also disparages Alberta. This suggests that Regina boosters understood that no city between Vancouver and Winnipeg had greater metropolitan potential than Calgary. Clearly the Regina boosters, like other cities' boosters, did not recklessly malign every other city in the West, but determined which areas to promote or degrade based on their place in the metropolitan hierarchy. For Regina before 1896, this meant promoting Moose Jaw, Battleford, and Prince Albert.

Calgary, like Winnipeg, was situated on the edge of the prairies. Once served by the railway, this village formerly supplied from distant Fort Benton, Montana, was suddenly poised to serve as an important gateway city. Nevertheless, Calgary boosters recognized the limits of their hinterland. Only 20 days after the first train arrived in Calgary, the inaugural edition of the *Calgary Herald* conceded Calgary's place in the prairie urban hierarchy by suggesting that Calgary, in becoming the supply centre for

"The Canadian Denver." Calgary grew rapidly from its inception: this photograph of Stephen Avenue (now 8th Avenue) was taken in April, 1890. Calgary was incorporated as a town in 1884; in 1894 the community attained city status with a population of 3,900 (Courtesy of the Glenbow Archives/NA-205-1).

Edmonton, Peace River, Slave Lake, and Macleod was to "become the greatest distributing point west of Winnipeg."[68] The Calgary District Agricultural Society, like the *Herald*, was convinced that Calgary would dominate the provisional district of Alberta. Its promotional literature proclaimed Alberta as the banner district of the four provisional districts of the North-West Territories.[69] The same pamphlet ends by claiming that Calgary "is the embryo from which the future metropolis of the far North-west is to develop into commercial greatness."[70] An 1884 pamphlet assures prospective settlers that "after being carried over that monotonously level stretch of prairie that extends from east of Winnipeg to the western boundary of Assiniboia, [the traveller] finds himself suddenly ushered into a district where the scenery is of remarkable beauty."[71] Referring to the agricultural potential of these lands, the Herald added that "On all sides of [Calgary] the soil is not only as rich as the soil in the Red River Valley, but produces grasses possessing nutriment for stock surpassing infinitely anything of the kind to the east of it. The land running away to the north and south is a belt of the most fertile character."[72] An 1885 pamphlet that advertises Calgary as the "Canadian Denver" also explicitly promotes the Macleod region as a rich grazing country blessed with particularly warm winters. Chinooks, the pamphlet cautions, are "not experienced except rarely in Saskatchewan, Central or eastern Assiniboia, and in Manitoba they are unknown."[73] Most interesting, the pamphlet not only promotes the Red Deer River region as a rich resource area, but even promotes Edmonton as "the centre of a rich farming district" surrounded by valuable forests.[74] In 1893 the *Herald* attempted to quell rumours that the Edmonton region had poor farming land. Citing a former farmer from Edmonton, the *Herald* declared "the high lands in the Edmonton District equal to any to be found anywhere for grain raising, any low lands there were being well adapted for grazing and much of them for farming also."[75]

Notwithstanding its overblown claims, and notwithstanding its doubtful efficacy, prairie promotional literature is a more useful historical source than has been assumed. Prairie promotional literature clearly reveals that the business elite of the Canadian Prairies quickly developed a shared mental image of the Canadian West. According to this image, Winnipeg would inevitably dominate the region between the Lakehead and the Rocky Mountains. Once the CPR was built, other settlements along the railway seemed destined to possess considerable hinterlands within Winnipeg's expansive hinterland. Lower-order settlements would dominate small or sparsely settled regions. It could hardly be considered a startling revelation if this mental image conformed to actual patterns of economic dominance, but promotional literature clearly cannot prove that it did. Rather, what promotional literature reveals is the hitherto unacknowledged fact that many prairie residents, even in the formative early years of settlement, *perceived* the prairies in terms of a hierarchy of cities and hinterlands. Because boosters obviously planned their promotional campaigns in the context of thoughtful assessments of their city's locational and geographical advantages, the literature they produced reflects the changing historical circumstances. For example, booster literature reveals that promoters altered their strategies after the CPR was built through the southern prairies. One can predict, then, that promotional literature changed again when the Canadian Northern Railway was completed from Winnipeg to the Yellowhead Pass via the North Saskatchewan River settlements in 1905. The emergence of new centres of political power in 1905 would also have complicated the image.

Promotional literature also sheds light on an embryonic sense of regionalism on the Prairies. Since the late 1960s, the phenomenon of regionalism has spawned considerable scholarly discussion in Canada, not only among historians, but also among geographers, political scientists, and sociologists. While a sense of loyalty to a certain area is a defining characteristic of regionalism, this loyalty is often accompanied by a sense of alienation from outside centres of power and influence. Much of the literature on regionalism was produced during years of intense regional discontent.[76] Gerald

Friesen has gone so far as to assert "Regionalism implies protest. It speaks of injustice, of neglect, perhaps even of one community's alleged superiority or power over another."[77] In this context, there has been discussion over whether regionalism is the inevitable product of the physical environment, the consequence of historical relationships between and among communities, or the result of a human response to an environment.[78] Evidence from prairie promotional literature supports the conclusion of Professor Careless (regarding Atlantic Canada) that "much of what is often called regionalism may be better expressed in terms of metropolitan relations and activities."[79] Regionalism on the Canadian Prairies is not merely the product of a distinct physical environment, but of human perceptions of that physical environment and of the resulting judgements of the proper place of a particular community within a broader community.

Prairie boosters, however, have left evidence, not primarily of a broad regional identity, but of more limited identities. They have left evidence of an almost feudal chain of local and regional loyalties and grievances. In order to shed light on contemporary circumstances many scholars have focussed their work on the development of prairie regionalism, but a contextualist approach, an approach that attempts to understand the past in the context of its own circumstances, would require that greater attention be paid to these limited identities. Before 1896, the business elite (and perhaps many other residents) of each city clearly identified their interests with a particular settlement and its hinterland. Thus, the apparently broad vision of the Winnipeg elite and the more narrow vision of the elite of other cities can be readily understood. Furthermore, while an incipient western regionalism may have been forming during the early settlement era, many migrants to the prairie West also quickly identified with a particular part of the region. It would not be surprising if scholars should find other evidence of such identities. During the formative years many settlements remained small and isolated, with transportation and communication among them difficult. These circumstances would have tended to encourage localism.[80]

If regionalism implies protest, perhaps local identities were accompanied with local grievances. Dissatisfaction on the part of the "hinterlanders" with those in remote metropolitan centres who appear either to misunderstand or to exploit them, is perhaps the essence of "frontierism." A metropolitan approach which views hinterland protest as the other side of the coin of metropolitan dominance may clarify our understanding of local and regional grievances as much as it illuminates local and regional loyalties. Local grievances appear to have coexisted with regional grievances. For example, Paul Rutherford suggests that residents of small settlements such as Lethbridge and Macleod reserved some of their hostility for Calgarians.[81] Together with Calgarians and other westerners, however, they also chafed at the freight rate concessions and other privileges secured by Winnipeg merchants. Lethbridgians, Calgarians, and all other westerners, in turn, could join Winnipeggers in their opposition to the CPR, the Canadian government, and many other "eastern" institutions. Until further research is completed, it will be impossible to judge whether these intraregional grievances might have stifled regional unity in the early years of settlement. Promotional literature suggests that even the shared western grievances against the Canadian government and the CPR would have had local variants. Manitoba's loss of disputed territory to Ontario and the Canadian government's disallowance of railways and its inaction on improvements to the St. Andrews Rapids on the Red River annoyed Winnipeggers, but government policy toward big ranching companies was more important to Calgarians. Those in Battleford would have been particularly rankled by the routing of the CPR and the relocation of the capital of the North-West Territories.

Plainly, then, a subtle metropolitan approach as proposed by J.M.S. Careless remains useful, not only insofar as it helps understand economic, political, and cultural development and interaction, but also insofar as it allows historians to understand the minds of the historical actors. Such a contextual approach would help to recover the past in all its complexity. In the end, historians maybe led to the conclusion that prairie regionalism and discontent are not primarily the product of a particularly visionary (or malignant) elite in Winnipeg, Ottawa, or Toronto, but primarily a result of that innate human tendency to assert, as circumstances allow, self-interest even at the expense of others.

Notes

This article first appeared in Prairie Forum 20, no. 1 (1995): 1–18. It is derived from a paper prepared for a graduate seminar at the University of Alberta. The author wishes to acknowledge the advice and encouragement of Professor David J. Hall, the instructor. As always, errors that may remain are the sole responsibility of the author.

1. The connection is implied in Paul Voisey, *Vulcan: The Making of a Prairie Community* (Toronto: University of Toronto Press, 1988), especially 5–6.
2. J.M.S. Careless, "Frontierism, Metropolitanism and Canadian History, " reprinted in Carl Berger (ed.), *Approaches to Canadian History* (Toronto: University of Toronto Press, 1967), 63–83.
3. Donald F. Davis, "The 'Metropolitan Thesis' and the Writing of Canadian Urban History," *Urban History Review* 14 (1985): 95; Kenneth McNaught, "'Us Old-Type Relativist Historians': The Historical Scholarship of J.M.S. Careless," in David Keane and Colin Read (eds.), *Old Ontario: Essays in Honour of J.M.S. Careless* (Toronto: Dundum Press, 1990), 38; Careless, "Frontierism," 80.
4. Careless, "Frontierism," 79, 82.

5. Careless presented his paper at the meeting of the American Historical Association in Toronto, December 1967. A later version was published as "'Limited Identities' in Canada," *Canadian Historical Review* 50 (1969): 1–10. Careless derived the term "limited identities" from Ramsay Cook, "Canadian Centennial Cerebrations," *International Journal* 22 (1967): 659–63.

6. Careless, "'Limited Identities'," 2.

7. Ibid., 6.

8. In this respect Paul Voisey's *Vulcan*, the case study of a small southern Alberta town, is a notable exception.

9. J.M.S. Careless, "Limited Identities—Ten Years Later," *Manitoba History* 1 (1980): 3–9.

10. Davis, "The 'Metropolitan Thesis'," 113. L.D. McCann also attacked the metropolitan approach in "The Myth of the Metropolis," *Urban History Review* 9, no. 3 (February 1981): 52–58.

11. Careless, "Frontierism," 79; Careless, "The View From Ontario: Further Thoughts on Metropolitanism in Canada," in *Careless At Work: Selected Historical Studies* (Toronto: Dundurn Press, 1990), 177. Careless has not developed this idea of the hierarchy among western cities beyond a rudimentary level: see Careless, *Frontier and Metropolis: Regions, Cities, and Identities Before 1914* (Toronto: University of Toronto Press, 1989), 11, 86–87.

12. Kenneth H. Norrie has argued persuasively that exogenous factors determined the timing of prairie settlement. Neither promotional efforts, nor the national policy, he argued, had more than a minor impact: see "The National Policy and the Rate of Prairie Settlement: A Review," in R. Douglas Francis and Howard Palmer (eds.), *The Prairie West: Historical Readings* (Edmonton: Pica Pica Press, 1985), 246, 249–50.

13. For example, in 1886 Winnipeg boosters optimistically suggested that the port of Churchill, when reached by railway, would have a 12-month shipping season: "The City of Winnipeg, The Capital of Manitoba and the Commercial, Railway and Financial Metropolis of the Northwest: Past and Present Development and Future Prospects" (Winnipeg, 1886), 72.

14. An essay contest advertised in the *Prince Albert Times* of November 1, 1882 suggests that all residents of the West were invited to participate in promotional efforts.

15. Thus, while metropolitanism is usually used to explain the dominant economic, political, and cultural position attained by certain centres, this study focusses on the *perceptions* of cities' elite regarding the *potential* of their cities to achieve economic dominance.

16. Alan F. J. Artibise, "Boosterism and the Development of Prairie Cities, 1871-1913," in Francis and Palmer (eds.), *The Prairie West*, 411. Paul Rutherford makes a similar statement: see "The Western Press and Regionalism, 1870–96," *Canadian Historical Review* 52 (1971): 289.

17. Doug Owram, *Promise of Eden: The Canadian Expansionist Movement and the Idea of the West, 1856–1900* (Toronto: University of Toronto Press, 1980), 84.

18. Ibid., 3, 38–78.

19. See Lewis H. Thomas, *The Struggle For Responsible Government in the North-West Territories* (Toronto: University of Toronto Press, 1978), 12–16.

20. A fine discussion of the federal government's promotional literature can be found in Owram, *Promise of Eden*, 105–18.

21. Ibid., 59–78. The non-Native population of the region had concentrated in this region because of factors arising from the fur trade, long before these expeditions had released their findings.

22. Ibid., 114.

23. *Report of the Joint Committee of Both Houses, on Agriculture, Immigration, and Colonization, During the First Session of the First Legislature of Manitoba* (Winnipeg: Queen's Printer, 1871), 3.

24. Ibid., 18.

25. [Manitoba] Provincial Government, *Manitoba the Home for Agriculturalists, Stock Raisers, Dairymen, and all who Desire Comfort and Prosperity* (Brandon, 1889), 3.

26. Ibid., 7, 9. Emphasis in the original text.

27. Ibid., 6. Emphasis in the original text.

28. Ibid., 4, 10, 12, 17.

29. See [Manitoba] Minister of Agriculture and Immigration (Thomas Greenway), *Fruitful Manitoba: Homes for Millions: The Best Wheat Land and the Richest Grazing Country Under the Sun* (Toronto: ca. 1891).

30. Alan F. J. Artibise, "Winnipeg, 1874–1914," *Urban History Review* 1 (June 1975): 43. This same argument is expressed in *Winnipeg: A Social History of Urban Growth 1874–1914* (Montreal/Kingston: McGill-Queen's University Press, 1975).

31. A.F. Burghardt, "A Hypothesis about Gateway Cities," *Annals of the Association of American Geographers* 61 (1971): 269–85.

32. Artibise, *Winnipeg*, 13–15. Also see Rutherford, "Western Press," 288, 289.

33. See "The City of Winnipeg," 73; Owram, *Promise of Eden*, 162.

34. For an account of Winnipeg's rivalry with neighbouring cities, including a discussion of how Winnipeg civic leaders succeeded in wresting the CPR main line from nearby Selkirk see Artibise, *Winnipeg*, 64–73.

35. Winnipeg's battle was won largely after Winnipeg built a bridge over the Red River; see ibid., 64–68.

36. George Babington Elliot, *Winnipeg As It Is in 1874, and As It Was in 1860* (Ottawa: 1875).

37. Alexander Begg and Walter R. Nursery, *Ten Years in Winnipeg: A Narrative of the Principal Events in the History of the City of Winnipeg From the Year A.D., 1870, To the Year A.D., 1879, Inclusive* (Winnipeg: Times Printing and Publishing House, 1879), 226.

38. *Winnipeg, Manitoba, and Her Industries* (Winnipeg: Steen and Boyce, 1882).

39. *Circular From the Board of Trade, Winnipeg* (Winnipeg: 1883), 2.

40. *The City of Winnipeg*, 61, 62. The argument of this passage is similar to Burghardt's argument concerning Winnipeg's locational advantage.

41. See *Winnipeg, Manitoba and her Industries*, 2; *Winnipeg Daily Tribune*, "Winnipeg, Manitoba: The Prairie City, Its Wonderful History and Future Prospects: A General Historical, Statistical and Descriptive Review of the Railroad Centre of the Northwest" (1891); *The City of Winnipeg*, 73, 81, 83–85. Indeed, Winnipeg businessmen played a part in the development of western coal fields, Ruben Bellan, *Winnipeg First Century: An Economic History* (Winnipeg: Queenston House, 1978), 11.

42. See Rutherford, "Western Press," 289, 291.

43. See ibid., 291.

44. Owram, *Promise of Eden*, 149–67.

45. See Morris Zaslow, *The Opening of the Canadian North: 1870–1914* (Toronto: McClelland and Stewart, 1971), 28–29.

46. Owram, *Promise of Eden*, 163.

47. *Facts About Grain Growing, Stock Raising and Dairying in the Midst of the Great Fertile Belt: the District of Kinistino, Saskatchewan, Northwest Territories of Canada* (Winnipeg:1893).

48. As quoted in Owram, *Promise of Eden*, 163.

49. Henry Thomas McPhillips, *McPhillips' Alphabetical and Business Directory of the District of Saskatchewan, N.W.T. Together With Brief Historical Sketches of Prince Albert, Battleford and Other Settlements in the District* (Qu'Appelle: 1888), 16.

50. Gary William David Abrams, "A History of Prince Albert, Saskatchewan to 1914" (MA thesis, Department of History, University of Saskatchewan, 1965), 69–76.

51. Thomas, *Struggle for Responsible Government*, 104.

52. Zaslow, *Opening of the Canadian North*, 56.

53. *Edmonton Bulletin*, March 10, 1883 as quoted in Zaslow, *Opening of the Canadian North*, 89. The full-page promotion was printed in the *Bulletin* as well as separately for more general distribution.

54. Edmonton Town Council, *A Few Plain Facts About the Edmonton District of Northern Alberta, North-West Territories of Canada as a Field for Settlement* (Winnipeg: Acton Burrows, 1892), 2, 4, 5–6.

55. Ibid., 2.

56. Ibid., 3.

57. Ibid., 5.

58. Also see Abrams, "History of Prince Albert," 74.

59. McPhillips, *McPhillips' Alphabetical and Business Directory*, 19.

60. *Prince Albert Times*, January 13, 1888.

61. Ibid., May 30, 1883.

62. Zaslow, *Opening of the Canadian North*, 56.

63. *Brandon, Manitoba and Her Industries* (Winnipeg: Steen and Boyce, 1882).

64. Brandon Board of Trade, *A Handbook of the County of Brandon the Garden of the Province and the City of Brandon the Metropolis of the West* (Brandon: 1889).

65. Rutherford, "Western Press," 290.

66. Regina Board of Trade, *A Few Facts Respecting the Regina District in the Great Grain Growing and Stock Raising Province of Assiniboia, North-West Territories, Canada* (Regina: 1889), 4.

67. Ibid., 11–12. See also, Regina Board of Trade, *An Unvarnished Tale of Regina and its Agricultural and Ranching District, in the Great Province of Assiniboia, N.W.T., Canada* (Regina: 1891).

68. *Calgary Herald*, August 31, 1883.

69. *Calgary, Alberta, Canada: Her Industries and Resources* (Calgary: Burns and Elliot, 1885).

70. Ibid.,15.

71. Calgary District Agricultural Society, "Dominion of Canada: District of Alberta, NWT," 1884.

72. *Calgary Herald*, January 2, 1884.

73. "Calgary, Alberta, Canada," 6.

74. Ibid., 11.

75. *Calgary Herald*, May 17, 1893.

76. Scholarly expressions of regional discontent reached their high water mark in David Jay Bercuson (ed.), *Canada and the Burden of Unity* (Toronto: Macmillan, 1977), but remain fully in evidence in George Melnyk (ed.), *Riel to Reform: A History of Protest in Western Canada* (Saskatoon: Fifth House, 1992).

77. Gerald Friesen, "The Prairies as Region: The Contemporary Meaning of an Old Idea, " in James N. McCrorie and Martha L. MacDonald (eds.), *The Constitutional Future of the Prairie and Atlantic Regions of Canada* (Regina: Canadian Plains Research Center, 1992), 6.

78. See ibid., 2–5 for a discussion of the formal, relational, and imagined approaches to regionalism. Janine Brodie, *The Political Economy of Canadian Regionalism* (Toronto: Harcourt Brace Jovanovich, 1990), includes a fine discussion of various approaches and an excellent interdisciplinary bibliography of regionalism.

79. J.M.S. Careless, "Aspects of Metropolitanism in Atlantic Canada," in Mason Wade (ed.), *Regionalism in the Canadian Community 1867–1967* (Toronto: University of Toronto Press, 1969), 117.

80. The literature on localism in the prairie West is small, but Lewis H. Thomas has suggested that local issues often overshadowed national or regional issues in the minds of westerners. For example, he argued that "restrictions on municipal and school district organization caused, perhaps, more discontent in the Territories than the lack of popular representation in the Council": Thomas, *Struggle for Responsible Government*, 89. Abrams's history of Prince Albert includes discussions of local, regional, and national issues in Prince Albert. The existence of local identities, of course, did not inevitably undermine a regional identity any more than a regional identity inevitably threatened loyalty to the country. Thus Paul Rutherford may have overstated his case when he argued that "metropolitan rivalries throughout the prairies naturally undermined regional unity": Rutherford, "Western Press," 290. Rutherford himself asserted that regional identities are not necessarily anti-Canadian, see ibid., 292.

81. The Lethbridge and Macleod press appear to have targeted Calgary; see Rutherford, "Western Press," 290. This raises the obvious question of how many links existed in this chain. Jean Burnet's sociological study of the Hanna district suggests that the town of Hanna (2,000 people in 1951) was "regarded by the rural communities around as a distinct, and at times hostile social entity," see *Next Year Country: A Study of Rural Social Organization in Alberta* (Toronto: University of Toronto Press, 1951), 75. She found no such town-country hostility in the case of Oyen (population 400 in 1951). Using Burnet's findings and his own research on Vulcan (a town of 800 in 1831), Paul Voisey has argued that smaller towns such as Oyen and Vulcan maintained such close ties with their rural communities that town-country harmony was encouraged, see Voisey, *Vulcan*, 234–35.

First Nations and the
Policy of Containment

7. Clifford Sifton and Canadian Indian Administration, 1896–1905

D.J. Hall

In December 1896 Clifford Sifton observed that, "the Indians were the wards of the government and when he settled down to work he would see that we either had more Indians to look after or less officials, for at present there were nearly as many officials as Indians."[1] Undoubtedly an appreciative ripple of applause and laughter flowed through his attentive audience of Liberal supporters. Sifton recently had been appointed Minister of the Interior and Superintendent General of Indian Affairs in the Laurier government, and was on a speaking tour of the West before assuming his duties in Ottawa. That Sifton's remarks merely reflected conventional wisdom among Liberals is scarcely surprising, for his main concern was with the Interior department, and with western development generally.

There appears to be little evidence that Sifton ever had anything but the most casual interest in Indian affairs before being called to Ottawa. He did recall the events of 1885 when, as a member of the home guard in Brandon, he had paraded "the street with a six shooter and a shot gun four or five evenings in succession,"[2] but he did not seem to have been profoundly affected by the Indian and Métis uprising. In 1882, aged only 21, he had begun to practice law in Brandon, and was elected to the provincial legislature in 1888. In 1891 he entered the Greenway government as Attorney General where he gained provincial and national notoriety as the able defender of Manitoba's "national" school system. Sifton's great talents as an organizer, administrator and politician were very evident by 1896 when Laurier made him the youngest member of his cabinet and placed him in charge of western development.

Indian Affairs had long been closely associated with the Department of the Interior, which was the principal instrument through which the federal government attempted to implement its developmental policies for the prairie West. The Dominion authorities were charged with responsibility for all of Canada's Indians, but it was the prairie Indians who created the greatest problems for the government, and to whom the government had the most obligations. Indian Affairs was still a branch of the Department of the Interior when most of the numbered treaties were signed in the 1870s. Although created a separate department in 1880, it thereafter normally retained its association with the Department of the Interior by coming under the aegis of the Minister of the Interior until 1936. Thus the Indians were viewed always in the context of western development; their interests, while not ignored, only rarely commanded the full attention of the responsible minister.

Sifton illustrates these problems well. There is plenty of evidence of his desire to serve what he believed to be the best interests of the Indians. Yet he shared some pretty conventional prejudices and misconceptions about them, was heavily influenced by his officials and always had an eye on the political repercussions of his policies. He further obscured the already hazy separate identity of Indian Affairs by placing it and the Interior department under a single deputy minister. During Sifton's tenure, furthermore, the national budget more than doubled, the Department of the Interior budget nearly quintupled, but that of Indian Affairs increased by less than 30%.[3] The fact was that the government—and, indeed, Parliament—had an unvaryingly parsimonious attitude toward the Indians.

By 1896 the western Indians had for some years been settled on reserves which, it was hoped, would serve both to protect and ultimately to acculturate them. The general philosophy of the department, which Sifton shared, seemed to be that the Indians should be quietly maintained on reserves, where they should create as little political difficulty as possible. There they should be prepared for assimilation to white society, or at least become willing and able to achieve a state of economic independence. In the meantime, the government would act as a sort of guardian to prevent exploitation of the Indian, while the various leading Christian denominations were aided in the task of giving him a moral and general education. "Great progress" had been made in this direction, Sifton assured the House of Commons in 1901:

> In the organized portion of the country there is no Indian population that may be considered dangerous so far as the peace of the country is concerned. The Indians are becoming rapidly a peaceful population and self-sustaining. The expenditure we are making is very large, but it is made in the pursuance of a policy favoured by parliament for many years based upon a belief that it is better—aside from the

justice of the question—to bring the Indians into a state of civilization or comparative civilization, than to take any chance of their becoming a disturbing factor in the community. Generally the results have been satisfactory.[4]

Upon arriving at Ottawa late in 1896 Sifton plunged into departmental reorganization. Indian Affairs had for years been a splendid source of patronage and sinecures for the Conservative party faithful, and Sifton was determined that Liberals would now share the spoils of power. Beyond that, the government was under much pressure to slash budgets because for years the Liberals had denounced the lavish spending of the Tories.[5] Sifton applied the knife to Indian Affairs

Clifford Sifton (1861–1929), Laurier's Minister of the Interior and Superintendent General of Indian Affairs (Courtesy of the Saskatchewan Archives Board/R-1863).

as thoroughly as it was used on any department. Personnel were dropped, the western agencies reorganized, and salaries generally reduced.

The first and most serious battle which Sifton fought in order to bring about a thorough reorganization was to remove the deputies of the Interior and Indian Affairs departments, A.M. Burgess and Hayter Reed respectively, and to place both departments under a single deputy of his own choosing. Firing of deputies by an incoming minister was not accepted practice. Sifton was the only Liberal minister to do so and had to overcome opposition from within the Cabinet and from the Governor General.[6]

Placed over the two departments was a political ally from Brandon, James A. Smart. Like Sifton a former Ontarian who had moved west, Smart had operated a hardware business in Brandon, and served as Minister of Public Works and Provincial Secretary in the early years of the Greenway administration in Manitoba. He certainly left his mark on the Department of the Interior, where he served until the end of 1904, but it is questionable how much influence he had on Indian Affairs. Under Reed even the trivial matters of the daily operation of the office were dealt with by the Deputy; under Smart, almost all letters went out over the signature of the departmental secretary, J.D. McLean.[7] Smart in fact dealt with only the more politically sensitive matters of general policy or patronage.

Of the Indian Affairs officials, Sifton worked most closely with James Andrew Joseph McKenna, a second-class clerk who was promoted to be the Minister's private secretary for the department.[8] In reality this was a highly political position. Through McKenna, Sifton probably had more input into departmental policy-making than is apparent from the written record, where he appears to have confined himself largely to making recommendations to the Governor General in Council, usually based on the advice of his officials. Furthermore, McKenna had Sifton's ear, and was placed in charge of some delicate and important activities, ranging from investigation of local squabbles over patronage, to treaty and halfbreed scrip commissions, to negotiations with the British Columbia government. From July 1, 1901, McKenna was Assistant Indian Commissioner and Chief Inspector for Manitoba and the North-West Territories.

Sifton did not institute these changes in order to effect any drastic new Indian policy. He was interested in efficiency and economy of operation, and in political considerations. Yet the changes were a wrench with the past, and prepared the way for more drastic changes in the future. Not only was Indian Affairs placed in a position inferior to the Interior Department, but the traditional policy-making structure was thoroughly shaken up. The new men had had little direct contact with the Indians, and most were relatively unsympathetic, if not "hard-line," in their attitudes.[9] Smart knew nothing of the Indians. Prior to going to Ottawa he was directed to familiarize himself with the western operations of the Department of the Interior; almost incidentally Sifton suggested that he also tour all the Indian schools in Manitoba.[10] McLean, thoroughly experienced in the operations at Ottawa, seems to have had little or no direct experience in the outside service. Despite his later fame in Indian Affairs, the chief accountant, poet D.C. Scott, had the outlook of an economizing bookkeeper, expressing concern for cutting costs, living within budgets, and demonstrating absolutely no sympathy for the realities of administration at the reserve level. Finally, as will be seen, McKenna had an uncompromising attitude which clearly found favour with the Minister.

Only in Manitoba and the North-West Territories could Sifton hope to effect significant savings. While perhaps less than one-quarter of Canada's Indians lived in this region, about three-quarters of the Indian Affairs budget was expended there.[11] This was mainly because of government obligations contracted when the treaties were signed, to provide assistance in education and agricultural instruction, food for the destitute, annuities, and medical services. During the 1880s most Indians were settled on reserves, agents assigned to supervise and assist them, farm instructors and schools established to instil new ways and ideas.[12]

Necessarily the service had been somewhat decentralized in early years when communications were poor. The Commissioner of Indian Affairs, located at Regina and the chief administrative officer in the West, had been empowered to make many vital decisions on the spot.

Shortly after his arrival in Ottawa, Sifton received from A.E. Forget, then Commissioner of Indian Affairs, a recommendation for a drastic restructuring of the western administration. It called for centralization of the administration at Ottawa, the removal of the Commissioner's office from Regina to Winnipeg, reduction of the Commissioner's staff from fourteen to three, the creation of six inspectorates (three in the Territories and three in Manitoba), and the closing down of several agencies.[13] Such a course had been suggested within the department as early as 1888, and again by the Royal Commission on the Civil Service of 1892, but had been rejected by the government.[14] The new Superintendent General, however, had little hesitation in approving the proposed changes with only slight modifications.[15] The basic effect was to change the Commissioner's office "very largely from a transmitting office to … an inspectoral one."[16] That is, until 1897 the Commissioner's office was occupied principally with checking accounts and reports, a procedure which was repeated in Ottawa, and also was the instrument through which western operations were carried out. Such duplication of effort was henceforth to be substantially reduced, and the Commissioner was expected to occupy himself with overseeing the inspection of western agencies and schools, making recommendations and helping in the preparation of estimates for western operations. The agencies and schools were now to receive their directions mainly from Ottawa.

One of the expected benefits of this change was reduced manpower. The changes were drastic. When Sifton took over the department there were 144 employees; within two years some 57 had been dismissed or resigned from the North-West service alone.[17] Naturally there was not a proportionate decrease in the service because Liberals were appointed to many of the vacancies. In 1897–98 the department budgeted for 115 officers, and by 1904–05 it had increased to 133.[18] Still the reorganization, which resulted initially in dropping 29 officials, could be said to have been successful in effecting a reduction in the size of the department.

Closely associated with this was Sifton's decision to institute widespread reductions in salaries for many of those fortunate enough to retain their positions. In 1896–97 the average annual salary was $712.33; in 1897–98 this became $683.32, or a drop of about 4%. The salaries of Indian agents had ranged up to $1400; all were to be cut to $1000 or $900. The salaries of departmental clerks were reduced, none to exceed $600. Farm instructors, who had drawn up to $600, were reduced to a range of $300 to $480.[19] Some in this way found their salaries reduced as much as $300, or 25%.[20] Undoubtedly these drastic reductions encouraged some employees to resign or seek superannuation; and it is unlikely that departmental morale was much improved. The department claimed a saving in salaries of $27,189 in the reorganization of the North-West service, but there was a gradual recovery in rates of pay, so that by 1904–05 the average was $725.67.[21]

Whatever the political benefits of a $27,000 saving in salaries, and of a flurry of dismissals and resignations, the Indian department budget continued to grow steadily.[22] The changes were instituted in the name of greater efficiency, which of course meant speed in bringing the Indians to self-sufficiency and ultimately assimilation.[23]

One change which did not last long, however, was the attempt to combine two departments under one deputy. The rapid expansion of immigration and settlement made the combined responsibility too heavy, and in 1902 the Indian department was again given its own Deputy Superintendent General. Sifton appointed Frank Pedley, a Toronto lawyer who had become Superintendent of Immigration in 1897. Although he had had no experience in Indian Affairs, Pedley had proven himself to be an excellent administrator, and would remain at his new post until 1913.[24]

The effectiveness of these administrative changes was debated rather heatedly within the department in 1904.[25] The evidence which emerged suggested they were probably justified, but that they had never been as effective as they should have been because of incredibly lax inspection procedures. Most agencies were inspected less than once a year, and several were well over two years between inspections. The inspectors were responsible for schools as well. Some had been overburdened, while others simply had not been doing their job.[26] With an average of four or five agencies and a few schools per instructor, there seems to be little reason why the inspections could not have been done at least once a year, if not every six months as recommended. But hard work was rarely demanded of most officials, whether in the outside service or at Ottawa.[27]

The administrative changes, in sum, did result in a slightly smaller staff and a lower cost in salaries. As an economy measure the effect was not marked, because most departmental expenditures were on items over which Sifton had little or no control: schools, annuities, feeding the destitute, and so forth. As an attempt at improving administrative efficiency the effect was marginal. But by centralizing control in the hands of the Ottawa bureaucrats, who were much more concerned with ledger books than difficulties on the reserves, the potential for a much more rigorous prosecution of departmental goals was created.

"Next to the solution of the problem of immigration to the North-west, there is nothing that will add greater lustre to Mr. Sifton's administration than the solving of the problem of teaching the North-west Indians to live like human beings."[28] Such was the opinion of the *Manitoba Free Press*, which claimed that an effective method of educating the Indians had yet to be devised. Few problems claimed as much time or money from the Department of Indian Affairs.

Once the last treaties were signed and the Indians largely settled on the reserves, the federal government faced the problem of how to fulfil its obligations to provide education to the Indians.[29] In 1879 Nicholas Flood Davin produced a report for the government which recommended continuation of existing mission schools and establishment of denominational industrial boarding schools on the American model.[30] The government, however, did not begin its experiment with industrial schools until 1884, and ignored Davin's strictures about the need for high salaries to attract good teachers and the dangers of allowing religious denominations a free hand. It established the principle of sharing the costs with various denominations (Roman Catholic, Anglican, Presbyterian, Methodist) which shouldered the major burden of running the schools. The result of parsimony, low standards, poor enforcement and inadequate inspection was both white and Indian discontent with the system.[31] Plainly it was substantially a failure.

Rigorous inspections and higher expenditures might have done something to salvage the situation. Neither was undertaken. As a result of the departmental administrative reorganization the position of school inspector was abolished, for a time at least, and the duties handed over to agency inspectors. Sifton was unequivocal that increases in education costs could not be contemplated: "the expenditure upon Indians, and particularly upon Indian education, has reached the high water mark, and we must now look to reducing rather than increasing it in any way."[32]

"The object of Indian education," he explained, was "to try and get them to take care of themselves as rapidly as possible." The difficulty was greatest among the Indians of Manitoba and the North-West Territories, which were "the hardest Indians in Canada to deal with, because of the fact that they are the farthest removed from the ordinary type of the workingman. They are the hardest to get settled down to work."[33] Indians educated for years seemed to revert quickly to the old ways once back on the reserves, and the sentiment was wide-spread that attempting to educate the Indians was a hopeless cause. Frank Oliver, the aggressive independent Liberal from Alberta, and Sifton's eventual successor, argued that educating Indians in industrial schools was self-defeating: "we are educating these Indians to compete industrially with our own people, which seems to me a very undesirable use of public money, or else we are not able to educate them to compete, in which case our money is thrown away."[34] Sifton scarcely disagreed. He believed that a highly specialized education was generally a waste of time. "I have no hesitation in saying-we may as well be frank-that the Indian cannot go out from school, making his own way and compete with the white man… He has not the physical, mental or moral get-up to enable him to compete. He cannot do it."[35]

When Sifton first came into office, he seems to have believed that the goal of making the Indians "self-supporting citizens" could be achieved only "by persistent and patient effort along the lines followed in the past." The system which had evolved contained basically three kinds of schools. The first was the day school, the oldest and most widespread, but probably least effective, where poorly paid and usually underqualified teachers laboured with Indian children on or near reserves.[36] The second type was the boarding school, also on or near reserves, but where Indian children were more removed from the tribal atmosphere and given "a general and moral education." The third type was the industrial school, which was well removed from the reservations, and gave the most varied and specialized curriculum. The day schools were poorest in Sifton's view because "the Indian children are not removed from the surroundings which tend to keep them in a state of more or less degradation." The industrial school, by contrast, removed the child from the reservation and tried to make him competitive with whites, which the Indian was incapable of becoming. Besides, the cost of these schools was very high. The best solution, he concluded, would be to expand the number of boarding schools, "which would give not so great an amount of education, but a reasonable education, to a much larger number of Indian children, [and] the result would be better on the whole for the Indian population."[37]

That he believed he had made important changes in the system was the burden of Sifton's remarks to the House of Commons in 1904:

> My own belief is that the system of industrial schools as I
> found it in operation when I took office, is not the best, or

A staged photograph of a young Aboriginal boy before (left) and after (right) admission to the Regina Indian Industrial School in 1897 (Courtesy of the Saskatchewan Archives Board/R-A8223-1 & R-A8223-2 respectively).

the most effective, or the most economic way of improving the condition of the Indians. I thought the system adopted was an artificial system. I found that Indian boys and girls were being kept in these schools in some cases until they were 23, 24 and 25 years of age. The Dominion of Canada is not under any obligation to conduct a system of education for an Indian tribe, under which the education of each child becomes so expensive and so artificial. I put in force a rule that children were not to remain in the schools after the age of eighteen. ... We have substituted a less elaborate system; a system of what we call boarding schools where a larger number of children can for a shorter time be educated more economically and generally more effectively. What we desire to do is not to give a highly specialized education to half a dozen out of a large band of Indians, but if possible to distribute over the whole band a moderate amount of education and intelligence, so that the general status of the band would be raised.[38]

During Sifton's term as Superintendent General there was no serious attempt either to reform the school system or to enforce attendance regulations. The number of Indian children registered in the schools grew slightly from 9,700 in 1896 to 10,000 in 1905, the average attendance rising over 7%.[39] He refused, however, to offer any inducements to Indian parents to send their children to school.[40] And he told the House of Commons that much of his time in the Indian Department was spent resisting demands for more money for schools. "Our position with reference to the Indians is this," he said: "We have them with us, and we have to deal with them as wards of the country. There is no question that the method we have adopted of spending money to educate them is the best possible method of bringing these people to an improved state." To those who objected that little progress was being made, Sifton countered with emphatic denial. He added that the schools were perhaps less efficient than white ones, because "you cannot press the Indian children as you can the children of white people, you cannot require so much from them." He also admitted the difficulty of getting competent teachers. In theory they were required to have a third-class certificate, but "when you pay $300 a year and send a young woman, or a young man, out to a lonesome place where there are no social advantages it is very difficult to get a competent teacher under those circumstances."[41] That $300 was less than half what teachers could expect to make in the city must have been known to most members of Parliament. Yet the chief criticism directed at Sifton concerned the rising cost of Indian education, not whether better salaries might secure better teachers.[42]

There was indeed a strong tendency within the department to blame the churches for the weaknesses and failures of the system. Wrote Inspector Martin Benson in 1903,

> The Indians do not appreciate the instruction in religion and manners their children receive at these schools. What would impress them would be a practical education that would fit them to earn their own living and assist them to better their condition. That they do not receive such an education is generally admitted.[43]

Religious and moral instruction was naturally of central importance to the churches. The government, on the other hand, wanted the Indians to receive a straightforward practical education leading to self-sufficiency. Departmental officials upbraided the churches for not taking greater responsibility for placing graduates of the schools in jobs, for not securing fully qualified teachers, for teaching too much religion and not enough practical training for an agricultural life on the reserves. But churches then, as always, had limited funds and depended upon the government. The government, in its turn, refused to take the full responsibility.[44] The objective of Indian education was to change completely the moral and spiritual values of the primitive societies, a function widely regarded as properly the province of the churches.[45] Thus a continuing role in Indian education for the churches simply was not disputed.

If standards were not improved, nor attendance regulations enforced, the government still had made some important decisions. The industrial school was considerably diminished in importance. Some pressure was exerted to make Indian education more practical and relevant to life on the reservation. But, as will be seen, this was not always to be done through formal educational institutions; the schools had not been a great success, and the way was opened to consider alternatives.

The policy of the Department of Indian Affairs, wrote Deputy Minister Frank Pedley in 1904, was "to bring the Indians as near the status of the white man as can be and make them a moral, industrious and self supporting class."[46] This was a comprehensive purpose of which formal education could fulfil only a part.

Certain attitudes, however, tended to hamper the desired development. Rarely was the opinion of an Indian taken seriously unless corroborated by some white man. To one correspondent who was inquiring about Indian protests over a medical officer, Sifton replied that the Department found considerable difficulty in arriving at facts where the Indians were concerned. "That difficulty," he wrote, "is such that it is almost impossible for a person who has not had experience with the Indians to understand! It is possible for persons to get the Indians to sign almost any kind of statements, if a little excitement and agitation be got up beforehand, and we are unable therefore to rely to any extent upon written statements that come in signed by Indians."[47] This attitude was reflected time and again in departmental dealings with correspondence from local chiefs and petitions from Indian bands.

A similar attitude prevailed with respect to band funds. Theoretically interest from Indian trust funds was to be distributed to the tribes to promote a sense of responsibility and self-government. In practice the department was reluctant to release the money, and did so only for projects of which it approved. The reason, explained Hayter Reed, was that "the money distributed as interest is a positive deterrent to individual improvement amongst the Indians; they learn to depend too largely upon these payments, and frequently they squander them..." Department policy forced the Indians to rely "upon their own resources," which "cannot fail to promote self-reliance."[48]

The government attitude was forcibly demonstrated when the government dismissed for political partisanship a doctor attending the Mohawk Indians of the Bay of Quinte Reservation. The gentleman in question not only was popular with the Indians, but had been paid entirely out of band funds. When the dismissal was protested by the Indians, they appealed first to the Department and then to the Queen. Governor General Lord Minto attempted to use his influence to correct what he viewed as an injustice, but was firmly rebuffed by Sifton:

> [I]t is quite clear that the officials who are paid out of Indian funds are regarded as officials of the Department of Indian Affairs and are fully responsible to the Department in the same way as any other departmental officers and while the views of the Indians are properly considered whenever possible the right of the Indians to control the action of the Department is not under any circumstances recognized... .
> It is as Your Excellency remarks quite correct that the Indians have always looked upon Her Majesty as a final Court of appeal for any complaint which they may wish to make. As a matter of practice however the actual discharge of such functions has for many years been confined to recommending the representations which may be made by the Indians, to the careful attention of the advisers of the Crown.[49]

The paternal grip of the department was in no way to be relaxed. It was felt in innumerable ways, from everyday administrative trivia to issues of band politics. For years the department had assumed the power to depose chiefs who "retarded progress" on the reserves, and there seems to have been little hesitation in using it. One such headman, described as "Tom, alias Kah-pah-pah-mah-am-wa-ko-we-ko-chin" of Moose Mountain Agency, was said to have brought up his children "to think that anything in the way of work at farming, cattle keeping or schools is not good for Indians," and his example therefore hindered progress on the reserve.[50]

It was indeed the hope of the Canadian government to change within a generation or two a nomadic hunting society into independent self-supporting agriculturalists. The reasons for the difficulty in making the transition were complex. Departmental planning was often poorly related to the realities of the local conditions and tribal attitudes. Not all farm instructors were either competent or conscientious. Tribal customs were deeply entrenched; and the point must never be forgotten that to change a society from a hunting to a settled agricultural existence meant fundamental adjustments in values and outlook. These could not be altered overnight.

At times the department seemed very far removed from the practical difficulties encountered upon the prairie reserves. It was proposed at one point to impose sheep raising upon the Indians, despite objections from Agents, farm instructors and Indians. But the deputy was convinced it would be good for the Indians, particularly the women: "In connection with this industry will be carding, spinning, and weaving of this wool, for there is no reason why the women, who are greatly in need of constant and useful employment, should not make all the cloth required by the Indians for wear."[51] It was an industry which understandably never seems to have succeeded.

Under Sifton the Indians encountered much greater pressure to farm for themselves. "I may say," wrote J.A.J. McKenna, "that I am convinced that the Indians can only be advanced through labour [that is, being taught, and even virtually forced, to grow grain and raise cattle] and that I propose doing what I can to hasten the day when ration houses shall cease to exist and the Indians be self-supporting. That day will never come if officers continue the system of handling Indians through bribing them with food."[52] The Indians were gradually taught principles of cattle breeding, were discouraged from concentrating on ponies, and were taught also the value of growing grain for profit. This paternalism, Sifton pointed out, was likely to be required for some time. But he did want the Indians to receive a practical agricultural education, and both Indians and farm instructors who were successful were encouraged by the department.

One of the farm instructors, for example, was being supported in an experiment in which several young Indian couples, graduates of the schools, were settled away from their tribes and urged to produce beyond their immediate needs, not sharing with the tribe, and keeping the profits for themselves. "As a matter of practice," stated Sifton, "one of the most serious difficulties in improving an Indian band is that just as soon as an Indian couple show an inclination to thrift and gather a little property around them, all their Indian relations think it is not necessary for them to work just in proportion as this couple is prosperous. Their relations take their supplies, and consequently they have no encouragement to accumulate property." He hoped more and more to see Indian school graduates settled separately, "where they can have [a] much higher type of civilized life than they could if they settled amongst the other Indians."[53]

The department's efforts did have some effect, nonetheless, and it could demonstrate some impressive figures showing agricultural progress amongst the Indians of the Territories. In later years Sifton believed that the system which he had initiated was working out very well.[54]

The department had also been engaged in breaking down tribal customs and structures in other ways. Particularly important was the question of tribal ceremonies and dances, crucial for the maintenance and survival of the tribal entity. Shortly after Sifton assumed his duties at Ottawa, the British Columbia government appealed against the prohibition of the potlatch.[55] After investigation Sifton concluded that the prohibition was justified. The potlatch, he argued, had a demoralizing effect upon the Indians, and the consensus of those working amongst the Indians was that judicious or prudent enforcement of the law would cause no difficulty. A younger generation was rising to power, and was opposed to the customs. Finally, "the repeal of the law now ... would be viewed by the Indians as an evidence on the part of the Government of weakness and vacillation and would produce disrespect and want of confidence in the source from which it emanates."[56]

The traditional discouragement of the sun dance among prairie tribes was also maintained. Although the dance was not proscribed by law, except where torture, mutilation or giving away of property was involved, the department opposed it because it meant that the Indians abandoned their farm work, left the livestock to starve, and so forth. The department was willing to allow dances involving no torture, no compulsion to attend, where children were not withdrawn from school, which had a fixed time limit, and on occasion provided that tribes or bands from other reserves did not attend. Of course all these qualifications precisely undermined the social and spiritual meaning of the dance to the Indian collectively.[57]

In 1902 Lord Minto toured the West and decided to take up the issue of the sun dance, which he believed was unreasonably prohibited.[58] The Governor General might have considered the dance to be harmless, but unfortunately the Indians for whom he was so concerned happened to be in the Qu'Appelle Agency under Indian Agent Graham, who ran a model agency from the point of view of the department. His methods, while firm, had made the Indians much more "progressive." Defending his prohibition of the sun dance at some length, Graham argued that the dances were one of the most important mechanisms of reinforcing tribal authority and of undoing all the work of years in the schools to "civilize" the Indians.[59] Once again Minto's appeal had fallen upon deaf ears.[60]

Apart from prohibiting or strongly discouraging a few such activities, the department took only limited action in the area of Indian morality. Revisions of the Indian Act in 1898 included some controls on immorality, particularly with respect to delinquent parents and parents of illegitimate children,

Participants in a Blackfoot Sun Dance ceremony, date unknown (Courtesy of the Saskatchewan Archives Board/R-A3963).

who would no longer be eligible to receive the government allowances for their children.[61] The sale of liquor to Indians on reserves was stringently forbidden by the Indian Act, but the fact that only $500 was voted by the government to enforce the law in central and eastern Canada reflected a very limited concern with the problem. "It is hopeless," wrote J.D. McLean, "to expect that this traffic with the Indians can be entirely suppressed."[62] Naturally drunkenness on the part of civil servants working with the Indians was not long tolerated.[63] On the reserves, however, the Indian Agent had considerable powers as prosecutor and judge in dealing with the alcohol problem. McLean commented,

> There are many reasons why it is often best to let the Agent
> exercise the powers conferred upon him by the Indian Act,
> to hear and determine such cases-as for instance the desire
> to avoid unnecessary trouble and expense, the fact that he is
> probably in the best position to weigh the value of Indians'
> evidence, and to judge as to the nature of the punishment
> likely to have the best effect upon individual culprits, and
> because the meting out of justice by the Agent direct, tends
> to instil proper respect for his authority.[64]

Sifton himself did not favour strong government initiatives, for he believed that the power of the law in enforcing morals was very limited. The government could discourage, but not prohibit, Indian camp meetings, he told one correspondent, and when they were held it could only "take all possible steps to preserve order and decorum." Before he introduced his amendments to the Indian Act of 1898 he commented, "The question of immorality among Indian women on reserves is one that the Department has made efforts to cope with, but it finds it very difficult to adopt any method that will wipe out the evil. The Department has gone to great lengths in procuring legislation with this end in view ... but I fear that statutory enactments will be slow in effecting reform, and that we must place our hope mainly on Christianising agencies."[65]

Such complacency extended also to an area of vital concern to the Indians, that of medical attendance. Most of the western treaties included provision for such attendance as required by the Indians, a government responsibility which was extended in varying degrees to Indians across the country. It was beyond question that the standard of these services was poor. When Sifton took office the decline in the general Indian population was continuing, though it levelled off and began a slow recovery early in the 20th century. Reports from Agents and others constantly made reference to the poor state of health of the Indians, a situation largely taken for granted by the government. For example, one of the problems which exercised the department was the high mortality rate among graduates of the industrial schools. The concern, however, was not with improving conditions, but with selecting healthier students so that the investment in their education would not be wasted.[66] In a scathing attack on conditions in the Territories a doctor from Macleod observed that the mortality rate among the Bloods and Piegans was "over ninety per thousand."[67]

The doctor's suggestions for reform were not followed up, because as always the members of Parliament were most concerned with reducing costs.[68] Sifton hoped to minimize costs by instituting a policy of paying a fixed stipend, rather than fees for actual attendance.[69] He claimed that it was a continual struggle to effect economy in medical expenses: "When an Indian gets medicine one day, he imagines he cannot get along unless he gets more the next, and there are bound to be increases from time to time, but we are doing the best we can to keep down the expenditure."[70] "You never can satisfy Indians that they are being properly attended to medically," he declared. "The more medical attendance that is provided the more they want."[71]

Mounting criticism was such that in 1904 Sifton appointed a "medical inspector of the Department of the Interior and Indian Affairs," Dr. P.H. Bryce. His duties would be to supervise the medical attendance of immigrants and Indians, and in this capacity Bryce conducted the first systematic survey of the health of Canadian Indian tribes.[72]

Ungenerous and inadequate as this policy appears in retrospect, it must be admitted that the government believed that the Indians receiving free medical attendance were obtaining services denied to the average Canadian. The very fact that the Indians were wards of the government tended, in Sifton's view, to render them more dependent unless a firm line were taken pressing them to independence.

The government was at great pains to prove that there was progress in this direction. Tables prepared for Sifton demonstrated a decline in the amount of government rations to Indians, a decline which according to Frank Pedley, was "in a large measure, due to the growing ability of the individual Indians to support themselves."[73] It was departmental policy, he added, "not to pauperize the Indian but to make him furnish as near as possible an equivalent in labour for the assistance rendered." The intent of the department was to make "a strenuous effort in all directions … to make all Indians self-sustaining."[74]

The administration of Indian lands was one of the least understood functions of the department.[75] To many speculators, businessmen and settlers the situation seemed quite clear. The Indians were sitting on valuable land which could be used more profitably by whites; accordingly the Indians should give way or be removed. Others conceded the Indians' right to some land, but contended that the reserves, originally based on calculation of a certain number of acres per capita or head of family, were unrealistically large when the number of Indians had been dwindling steadily. As the prairies began to fill with white settlers, pressure on the government to obtain some or all of these lands for efficient exploitation increased. Such attitudes had been present almost since the treaties were signed-indeed in one form or another since the very arrival of Europeans in North America— and had if anything hardened in wake of the 1885 rebellion.[76] It was the influx of settlers in the 20th century, however, which would help to generate very different policies, particularly when Frank Oliver came to office in 1905. The Indians would thenceforth come under every inducement and pressure to sell their lands and become assimilated.

Publicly, at least, Sifton refused to accede to these pressures and was thus the last Superintendent General who operated even superficially on the basis of the old philosophy. His was not a whole-hearted commitment to the Indian cause, but to pleas that he open up Indian lands, whether for agricultural, timber or mineral exploitation, he made the same dogged response throughout his term of office. The government acted as trustee for the Indians. "The law," he told Frank Oliver, "is very specific and clear." The Alberta member wanted a reserve at Stony Plain thrown open for settlement.

He was firmly informed that "in no case in which the Indians are in posses-sion of a reserve can the same be taken from them without their consent and the money placed to the general credit of all the Indians in the country... . This system makes it ... impossible to throw land held by the Indians open for settlement immediately on a proposition to that effect being made, even in cases in which it is clear to the Department that it is in the general inter-est as well as in the interest of any particular band themselves that such land should be thrown open."[77] Annually Sifton had to explain to Parliament that very little could be done without the consent of the tribes concerned, and that sometimes that was difficult to obtain. "Whatever may be deemed desirable or otherwise," he told A.A.C. LaRivière, MP, "the fact of the mat-ter is that the Indians own these lands just as much as my hon. friend (Mr. LaRivière) owns any piece of land for which he has a title in fee simple. The faith of the government of Canada is pledged to the maintenance of the title of these Indians in that land." The government would seek Indian consent to exploitation of their lands, "when we think it will not interfere with the means of livelihood of the Indians."[78]

The problems, and Sifton's approaches to them, are best illustrated with specific examples. The Dokis Indians' refusal to accede to the exploitation of pine timber on their reserve in Ontario particularly exercised departmental officials. The forest was mature, and if it was not lost to fire, it would soon begin to rot and lose its value. Even taking only those trees over nine inch-es at the base, it was calculated that some 45 million board feet of timber could be harvested. In this case Sifton had the power and was quite pre-pared to legislate to impose an arrangement whereby the band, consisting of 80 people, would receive some $250,000 cash bonus, and a royalty of $1 per 1000 board feet. That the deal was perfectly logical and advantageous for the Indians seemed obvious to the department. But there was some impatience with the attitude of the aged chief Dokis who was unimpressed with the prospect of monetary gain; he believed he had a moral or spiritual obliga-tion to preserve the forest intact for his successors.[79]

In another case, the Canadian Northern Railway promoters, Mackenzie and Mann, wished in 1904 to obtain a townsite for a divisional point, to be located on the Cote Reserve in north-east Assiniboia. It was, they claimed, the best site in twenty miles. The Indians were willing to surrender the land because of the high cash value, and they were supported by the local Agent. But Sifton believed that the town (Kamsack), being located on the reserve, would create serious social problems. Only reluctantly did he agree to the sale, after ensuring that the Indians would profit from the arrangement as would any ordinary landowner. Unhappily the adverse effects foreseen by Sifton were realized in the future.[80]

A different problem faced the department at the Roseau River Reserve in the early 1890s, located on first-class agricultural land. By 1898 the population had declined to 261 and much of the land was not being used. There was pressure from the surrounding areas and from Indian Department officials to obtain a surrender of at least part of the lands. By 1900 the population was reduced to 244, and by 1902 to 209. The Indians simply were making no progress; as the districts around the reserve were settled the Indians seemed unwilling to work and were tempted to drift into nearby settlements. Their numbers depleted by disease and their spirit sapped, the agent believed that the only hope was to obtain a surrender and use the money to purchase a more isolated reserve where they could be relocated. This was done, after some difficulty in persuading the Indians, in 1903.[81]

In southern Alberta the Blackfoot Indians refused all methods of persuasion by the ranching community to obtain grazing leases on the reserve. There was nothing the department could do in face of such intransigence.[82] On the other hand, the Blackfoot tribe could only have been reinforced in their position by observing the nearby Blood Reserve, where the chiefs had agreed to a lease. When a group of the tribe protested to Ottawa, they claimed that the chiefs had not been representative of the tribe and that each man should have been consulted in a tribal vote, that the leaseholders had not taken up their leases promptly as prescribed in the leases, and that promises of money and free trips to Ottawa for the chiefs (obviously not in the lease) had not been fulfilled. In this case Sifton flatly rejected the tribal contentions.[83] Unquestionably he saw the issue simply in terms of a legal contract, the obligations of which the Indians must fulfill.

The most extended case involving Indian lands in these years concerned the Songhees Reserve which was located precisely where the city of Victoria, BC, wished to expand. In British Columbia the province had reversionary rights to any Indian lands sold, or funds arising therefrom. The local government viewed the land as a potential source of public money, insisting that the Indians were only entitled to the original value of the land, not the tremendous increment to its value caused by its being in an urban setting. The provincial government hoped through this subterfuge to buy the land for a song, and then parcel it out at high prices to various urban interests. It also wanted the federal government to assume the costs of obtaining a new reserve and removing the Indians. Sifton absolutely refused such terms. He was as desirous as anyone to remove the Indians from the "contaminating influences of city life with the worst and most demoralizing features of which they are constantly brought in contact."[84] But the Indians must, he insisted, obtain the full value of the lands.[85]

Land surrenders and leases could serve many purposes. They could be a source of funds to repay tribal debts, or to provide capital for new equipment or enterprises. Timber, grazing or mineral leases in particular were designed to produce income, and sometimes work, for Indians over a number of years. On occasion it was desirable, at least to the department, to remove the Indians from demoralizing urban influences. Similary when a reserve declined in population Indians began to drift to other reserves, and the lands could be sold and the money put to use for the benefit of the other bands.[86] Undeniably the department was sometimes wrong in its judgment, and also induced some Indians in questionable ways to give up their lands. There seemed to be a belief that the Indian population would continue to dwindle, so that large tracts of land on some reserves simply would never be required; why not sell the land, or lease it, when the monetary benefits seemed so obvious? The government also made the assumption that all Indians could and should become agricultural, even in some unsuitable districts, influencing its attitude to non-agricultural lands.[87]

Indian land surrenders were by no means new when Sifton came to office.[88] It is not clear how much land was surrendered during Sifton's term of office, but Frank Oliver claimed that 724,517 acres of Indian lands were sold between July 1, 1896 and March 31, 1909.[89] Generally speaking this was seen positively by the white community. Any criticism was directed at the government's failure to obtain more land from the Indians; the Indians, it was said, must not be allowed to stand in the way of progress, and the Indians' general well-being.[90] But no serious attempt was made to change the law to facilitate the appropriation of Indian lands by whites.[91] As to what the Indians themselves thought, the department tended to be impatient. Old Indian concepts of land and ownership were considered simply vestiges of a passing culture which was of itself inferior and inevitably giving way to "civilization" and "progress." The government quite sincerely believed that this was in the best interest of the Indians.

Clifford Sifton's tenure as Superintendent General of Indian Affairs did not occasion dramatic changes in Canadian Indian policy. He had almost no creative new ideas to offer, and most of his policy statements and administrative reforms appear to have been generated substantially within the department. It is arguable that his administrative reforms made the service more efficient, more highly centralized, and that he made a fairly steady effort to minimize the number of incompetent officials. He left his stamp on the department in many of the leading personnel, and indeed in the drastic upheaval at all levels of the staff. The changes tended to bring to power men who were if anything less sympathetic to the Indians, and to place expenditure under the control of a cost-conscious bureaucracy.

Disillusionment with the reserve system was already present in the department when Sifton came to office, and before long would become more widespread. "Experience does not favour the view that the system makes for the advancement of the Indians," McKenna told Sifton in 1898.[92] The education system in particular was much slower in breaking down old customs than had been hoped. Yet there was no movement toward fundamental change, and Sifton tried to alter the existing reserve administration and the method of education to make them more efficient. Assimilation of individual Indians came to be regarded as the longer-term goal because of the difficulty of educating Indians to compete with whites or to make their way individually off the reserves. In the short run the emphasis was to be on a practical, limited education for entire bands, to make the Indian self-sufficient agriculturalists on the reserves, and to "wean" them from dependence upon the government. With this end in view the department also encouraged examples of progress among the Indians by special attention to successful Indians and agents.

In these years the Indians seemed at long last to be making the adjustment to reserve life; the decline in population was arrested and, perhaps with the aid of a program of vaccination for all Indian children, slight increases in population began to be noticed early in the 20th century. Government officials could point to some improvements in agricultural progress on the reserves. Although Sifton accepted the widespread belief that Indians could not compete in white society and would require continued government assistance, he resisted complete acceptance of the policy of paternalism. He endeavoured to reduce Indian dependence upon the government. In the long run he hoped to see the Indians self-supporting, civilized, and accepting the competitive and individualistic values of his own society. But continued parsimony in the administration reflected his view that Indians were not a major priority. They were a responsibility to be lived with, not likely to contribute significantly to the progress of the country.

This is to state the obvious: how else did men of Sifton's day regard Indians? Even Lord Minto, no admirer of Sifton and critical of certain details in the Indian administration, concluded by the time he left the country in 1904 that "Canada's management of her Indians has been excellent and something to be proud of for it's a very difficult question, or rather has been, for it is practically worked out now."[93]

Not all of Minto's contemporaries would have agreed. With Sifton's successor, Frank Oliver, and a new Indian Act in 1906, a different era of greater firmness and of serious efforts to assimilate the Indians and obtain their lands was ushered in. By comparison Sifton's term of office appears to be but a mild transition from the practices of early administration, an effort to make past policies more efficient. But in a sense it was also a period which helped to make possible the more drastic change realized under his successors.

Notes

This article first appeared in Prairie Forum 2, no. 2 (1977): 127–52.

1. *Winnipeg Daily Tribune*, December 12, 1896.

2. Library and Archives of Canada (LAC), Sir Clifford Sifton Papers, vol. 242, pp. 231–32, Sifton to Walter Scott, MP, March 5, 1901.

3. Canada. House of Commons, *Sessional Papers*, 1898, #1 (Auditor General's Report for 1896–97), pt. A, p. 4; pt. G, pp. 2–3; pt. H, p. 2; 1906, #1 (Auditor General's Report for 1904–05), pt. C, p. 5; pt. J, p. 2, pt. L, p. 2. The national budget increased from $43,174,000 in 1896–97 to $88,584,111 in 1904–05; the Department of the Interior budget from $817,394 to $4,175,000; and the Department of Indian Affairs from $962,977 to $1,248,000.

4. Canada. House of Commons, *Debates*, 1901, col. 2763, April 10, 1901.

5. *Winnipeg Daily Tribune*, April 12, 1897. Even by Liberal calculations the total saving in government estimates for 1897 was only about $1.5 million, despite claims while in opposition that savings of $3 million or $4 million could be effected.

6. For greater detail on this issue, see D.J. Hall, "The Political Career of Clifford Sifton, 1896–1905" (PhD dissertation, University of Toronto, 1973), 140–42. Hayter Reed was a former militia officer who had entered the Interior service in 1881 and became an Indian Agent and then Assistant Indian Commissioner for the North-West Territories in 1884. In 1893 he was promoted to the post of Deputy Superintendent General in Ottawa. See H.J. Morgan, *The Canadian Men and Women of the Time*, 2nd ed. (Toronto: William Briggs, 1912), 931; John Frederick Lewis Prince, "The Education and Acculturation of the Western Canadian Indian 1880-1970, with Reference to Hayter Reed" (MA thesis, Bishop's University, 1974), esp. 38ff.

7. Sifton must have realized that this would be the case; see *Debates*, 1897, cols. 1709–21, May 4, 1897. McLean was promoted from head of the Land and Timber Branch to become Secretary and Chief Clerk. Sifton had a high regard for his ability; but a perusal of McLean's correspondence suggested a man of short temper, concerned with picayune detail in day-to-day matters, and very impressed with his own importance. On more than one occasion he complained to the Deputy that he was not being treated with due deference by other employees. When Sifton took over the department McLean sent him a long screed complaining of gross inefficiency in the Department (LAC, Sifton Papers, vol. 7, 3880–4025, December 31, 1896, and encl.). McLean, grandson of a Liberal MP at the time of Alexander Mackenzie, one John Farris, had been appointed to the department in October 1876, rising to the position of first class clerk by 1896 (see memo in ibid., 3973–87).

8. The appointment was effective February 1, 1897. McKenna was an Irish Catholic, born in Prince Edward Island in 1862. He had been Private Secretary to the Superintendent General in 1887–88, and a clerk thereafter. LAC, Department of Indian Affairs (DIA) Records, vol. 3853, file 77144; H.J. Morgan, *Canadian Men and Women of the Time*, 775.

9. In fairness it must be conceded that a hard line was not new. Certainly Reed, and sometimes his predecessor as Deputy, L. Vankoughnet, could be inflexible and unwilling to consider the Indian viewpoint. Reed, nevertheless, had had at least two years' experience as an Indian agent. On his attitudes, see Prince, "Education and Acculturation," 64, 66, 74, 85. He admitted in 1895 that he was "necessarily out of touch, to a great extent, with the Indians."

10. LAC, Sifton Papers, vol. 214, pp. 6924, Sifton to Smart, December 28, 1896; see also vol. 33, file "Smart, J.A. 1897."

11.

Years	Total	Manitoba and North-West Territories
1896–97	$962,977.25	$701,503.83
1897–98	$1,001,304.93	$734,919.82
1898–99	$1,037,531.04	$776,192.92
1899–1900	$1,093,429.01	$823,951.34
1900–01	$1,075,849.22	$798,908.30
1901–02	$1,115,271.94	$822,444.00
1902–03	$1,141,099.08	$818,576.54
1903–04	$1,159,712.24	$804,098.55
1904–05	$1,248,305.00	$869,980.95

Source: *Sessional Papers*, 1898–1906, Auditor General's Reports. British Columbia Indians accounted for about one-tenth of the budget, and Ottawa office expenditure for about 6% or 7%, which obviously did not leave much for Indians in the rest of the country.

12. See J.B.D. Larmour, "Edgar Dewdney, Commissioner of Indian Affairs and Lieutenant Governor of the North-West Territories" (MA thesis, University of Saskatchewan, Regina, 1969), 276–77. On the earlier period, see H.D. Kemp, "The Department of the Interior in the West 1873–1883: An Examination of Some Hitherto Neglected Aspects of the Work of the Outside Service" (MA thesis, University of Manitoba, 1950) 12–32.

13. LAC, Sifton Papers, vol. 19, 12029–40, Forget to Sifton, January 20, 1897. The figures were those of Forget; in fact the reduction was from 19 employees to 6 in the Commissioner's office. The agencies abolished were Clandeboye, Portage la Prairie, Rat Portage, and Savanne. DIA Records, vol. 3877, file 91839-1.

14. Ibid.; and DIA Records, vol. 3635, file 6567, D. C. Scott to the Deputy Superintendent General of Indian Affairs, March 3, 1904.

15. Ibid., vol. 19, 12059–60, Sifton to Forget, May 21, 1897; DIA Records, vol. 3877, file 91839-1. It should be noted that when Reed was Deputy Minister the administration had been centralized in practice in Ottawa, as he had been unwilling to delegate any authority. Seen in this light, Sifton's changes simply gave legal sanction to a situation which already existed; but it also permitted a reduction in manpower which redounded to the political credit of the Liberals. I am grateful to Dr. John Tobias of Red Deer College for pointing this out.

16. Ibid., vol. 3635, file 6567, Frank Pedley (Deputy Superintendent General) to Sifton, March 24, 1904; Sifton Papers, vol. 221, pp. 346–47, Sifton to J. W. Smith, July 10, 1897.

17. DIA Records, vol. 3984, file 168921, James A. Smart, Return to the House of Commons concerning dismissals, June 1896 to April 25, 1898; vol. 3635, file 6567, D. C. Scott to the Deputy Superintendent General, March 3, 1904, pp. 17–18. Apart from those who resigned, twelve found their positions abolished and were not rehired, eight were removed for political partisanship, and eleven were removed for incompetence, disobedience, insubordination, drunkenness and related problems. (See also ibid., vol. 3877, file 91839-1.) Those dismissed received gratuities on the following schedule: up to 5 years' service, 1 month's salary; 5 to 7 years' service, 2 months' salary; over 7 years' service, 3 months' salary. (Ibid., Sifton to Forget, July 6, 1897.) To one correspondent who complained of the treatment meted out to civil servants, Sifton replied, "I can assure you that it has been no pleasure to me to dispense with the services of officials in

the West, but in the public interest it was absolutely necessary to bring the expenditure on the Indian service within reasonable bounds, and this could not be done without dismissing some of the staff. Every effort was made in the reorganization to provide for as many of the old hands as possible..." LAC, Sifton Papers, vol. 220, pp. 619–20, Sifton to Dr. Hardy, May 29, 1897.

18. LAC, DIA Records, vol. 3635, file 6567, D. C. Scott to the Deputy Superintendent General, March 3, 1904, pp. 17–18.

19. LAC, Sifton Papers, vol. 278, file 12; vol. 279, file 13; vol. 280, 18576–77.

20. LAC, DIA Records, vol. 1120, p. 467, Sifton to Governor General in Council, July 7, 1897. One group of 11 employees had their salaries cut an aggregate of $2,200.

21. LAC, Sifton Papers, loc. cit.; DIA Records, vol. 3635, file 6567, D. C. Scott to the Deputy Superintendent General, March 3, 1904, p. 18.

22. See above, fn. 11.

23. See Sifton's explanation of the changes in *Debates*, 1899, cols. 5722–25, June 22, 1899. There were also changes in administrative structure at Ottawa, though less change in personnel. Sifton consolidated some seven branches of the department (Land and Timber, Accountant's, Correspondence, Registry, Technical, Statistics and Supply, and School) into three branches (Secretarial, Accountants, Land and Timber).

24. H.J. Morgan, *The Canadian Men and Women of the Time*, 893; *Debates*, 1902, cols. 3035–37, April 8, 1902; *Sessional Papers*, 1904, #27, p. xvii. It should be added that petty rivalries among the leading officials in the Indian Affairs department were perhaps an important factor in Sifton's decision to appoint someone from outside.

25. LAC, DIA Records, vol. 3635, file 6567, J.A.J. McKenna to The Superintendent General, January 12, 1904; and passim.

26. Ibid., F. Pedley to Sifton, March 24, 1904, pp. 26–28.

27. At Ottawa. the office hours were from 9:30 a.m. to 4:00 p.m., with one and a quarter hours for lunch. Nevertheless, J. D. McLean was complaining about all the correspondence imposed on the office by the centralization, with a reduced staff; he claimed that they actually had to write some 75 to 100 letters a day, and this with a staff of over 40 (mostly clerks) at headquarters. LAC, DIA Records, vol. 1122, pp. 332–33, McLean to Smart, December 1, 1898; vol. 1125, p. 549, McLean to Miss Yielding, July 25, 1902.

28. *Manitoba Free Press*, December 29, 1896.

29. On the question in general, see J.W. Chalmers, *Education Behind the Buckskin Curtain: A History of Native Education in Canada* (Edmonton: author, 1974); H.J. Vallery, "A History of Indian Education in Canada" (MA thesis, Queen's University, 1942); Kathryn Kozak, "Education and the Blackfoot, 1870–1900" (MA thesis, University of Alberta, 1971); Jacqueline Gresko, "White 'Rites' and Indian 'Rites': Indian Education and Native Responses in the West, 1870–1910," in A.W. Rasporich (ed.), *Western Canada, Past and Present* (Calgary: McClelland and Stewart, 1975), 163–81.

30. LAC, DIA Records, vol. 3674, file 11422, "Report on Industrial Schools for Indians and Half-Breeds," Ottawa, March 14, 1879; C.B. Koester, "Nicholas Flood Davin: A Biography" (PhD dissertation, University of Alberta, 1971), 77–78.

31. LAC, DIA Records, vol. 3920, file 116751-B, Martin Benson to the Deputy Superintendent General, June 23, 1903.

32. "My present impression," he told one of his Liberal colleagues in 1897, "is that there will be no substantial increases in these items [Indian education] in the next four years." LAC, Sifton Papers, vol. 264, pp. 258–60, Sifton to Rev. A. Sutherland, General Secretary, Methodist Church, January 10, 1898; vol. 220, pp. 777–78, Sifton to J.G. Rutherford, MP, June 4, 1897. See also vol. 224, p. 435, Sifton to Rev. G. M. Grant, January 14, 1898.

33. *Debates*, 1899, cols. 5725-6, June 22, 1899.

34. Ibid., 1897, col. 4076, June 14, 1897.

35. Ibid., 1904, cols. 6946–56, July 18, 1904; see also 1903, cols. 7260–61, July 23, 1903.

36. Salaries ranged from $200 to $300; many teachers were not even required to have a teaching certificate.

37. Ibid., 1899, cols. 7480–99, esp. 7483–86, July 14, 1899. With the hope that greater economy and better results might be achieved, there was a proposal made in the department that a hierarchy of schools be established. Children were then expected to attend school between the ages of 6 and 16. All children, under this plan, would begin in day schools, though there was no upper age limit. The more promising and healthy students would attend boarding school between the ages of 8 and 14, and the best of these would be selected for industrial schools. LAC, DIA Records, vol. 1121, pp. 511-3, J.D. McLean to A.E. Forget, March 8, 1898; pp. 692–99, Memorandum, J.D. McLean, July 20, 1897; vol. 1121, pp. 689–91, J.A. Smart to Rev. A. J. Vining, May 30, 1898.

Sifton also opposed "transferring girls from the boarding [to the industrial] schools. In their case the domestic work in which they can assist at the schools in the later years of their pupilship is the best sort of industrial training that they can obtain." Sifton Papers, vol. 265, pp. 403–05, Sifton to Bishop Legal, March 22, 1901.

38. *Debates*, 1904, cols. 6946–56, July 18, 1904. A case in point occurred in 1903-1904 when the Oblate fathers were given permission to acquire the land and buildings of the St. Boniface Industrial School, in return for which they were to build and help support three new boarding schools, in addition to a fourth which was already nearing completion. While the Industrial School could not teach agriculture adequately, it would be taught to the boys at each boarding school, while the girls would be trained "to do house work." LAC, DIA Records, vol. 3920, file 116751-B, passim., esp. Order in Council, January 8, 1904.

39. *Sessional Papers*, 1897, #14, pp. 416–17; 1906, #27, pt. ii, pp. 54–55.

40. LAC, Sifton Papers, vol. 265, pp. 403–05, Sifton to Bishop Legal, March 22, 1901. He wrote, "I would infer from your Lordship's letter that we would in some way have to make good to the Indians what they lose in service through the absence of their boys and what they would get as marriage gifts from prospective sons in law if the girls were at home and eligible for marriage from their twelfth year. Action in that direction would come pretty close to a system of purchase of Indian children, and, it strikes me, would be more open to objection than even the compulsory method." It should be added that years earlier the department had begun the practise of giving the children in Manitoba and Territorial schools a noon-day meal as an inducement to attend, and this practise continued; see J.W. Chalmers, *Education Behind the Buckskin Curtain*, 162–63; LAC, DIA Records, vol. 1120, pp. 692-9, Memorandum, J.D. McLean, July 20, 1897.

41. *Debates*, 1902, cols. 3043–46, April 18, 1902.

42. Several times proposals for increased pay for teachers were made within the department. In 1887 the Deputy Superintendent General, L. Vankoughnet, proposed such action to Prime Minister Macdonald, but it was ignored. In 1891 another proposal was buried, as was a proposal from an Indian Agent and backed by the Indian Commissioner in 1903. This latter suggestion apparently never reached the ministerial level. Only once, and then put obliquely and unsympathetically, does the idea seem to have reached Sifton's desk. Not until about 1912 or 1913 was there a substantial increase in salaries over levels of the 1880s, but they were still too low to compete very effectively for good teachers. LAC, DIA Records, vol. 3965, file 1500000-8; vol. 1120, pp. 692–99, Memorandum, J.D. McLean, July 20, 1897.

43. Ibid., vol. 3920, file 116751-A, Benson to the Deputy Superintendent General, June 23, 1903. Concerning similar sentiments about educational expenditure among the Yukon Indians, see vol. 3962, file 147654-1, vol. 2, esp. F.T. Congdon to F. Pedley, April 1903; and John Ross to Congdon, July 6, 1903.

44. Sifton did make two small concessions in extending departmental obligations, expending up to $5,000 for education among Yukon Indians, an area ignored by the government prior to the gold rush; and permitting halfbreed children residing on Indian reserves to attend the Indian schools. Ibid.; and vol. 3931, file 117377-1C, D. Laird to J.D. McLean, August 27, 1900.

45. See Sifton's speech of November 17, 1902 to the General Assembly of the Methodist Church (Toronto *Globe*, November 18, 1902). Although he was not speaking about Indian education, the points made are applicable.

46. LAC, DIA Records, vol. 3635, file 6567, Pedley to Sifton, March 24, 1904, p. 4.

47. LAC, Sifton Papers, vol. 238, pp. 635–36, Sifton to Rev. S. D. Chown, August 29, 1900.

48. LAC, DIA Records, vol. 1119, pp. 625–28, H. Reed to Sifton, December 26, 1896; vol. 1120, pp. 36-7, Reed to Sifton, January 26, 1897.

49. Ibid., and pp. 734–37, Sifton to Governor General in Council, December 30, 1896; Sifton Papers, vol. 68, file "Minto, Lord 1899," passim.; Lord Minto Papers, vol. 10, pp. 3–5, Minto to Sifton, May 1, 1899, and reply, pp. 6–8, May I1, 1899; pp. 9–10, Minto to Sifton, May 15, 1899.

50. LAC, DIA Records, vol. 1121, Sifton to Governor General in Council, September 11, 1897; see also vol. 1125, p. 164, same, September 4, 1901 (concerning Chief Paul of White Whale Lake), and p. 379, same, March 11, 1902 (concerning Chief Piapot of the Qu'Appelle Agency).

51. Ibid., vol. 3877, file 91839-1, H. Reed to A.E. Forget, July 9, 1896. For another example, see S. Raby, "Indian Treaty No. 5 and The Pas Agency, Saskatchewan N.W.T.," *Saskatchewan History* 25 (1972): 108–09.

52. LAC, Sifton Papers, vol. 106, 83483–92, McKenna to Sifton, December 10, 1901.

53. *Debates*, 1902, cols. 3054-6, April 18, 1902; 1903, cols. 6422-4, July 10, 1903; 1904, cols. 6942–45, 6954–57, July 18, 1904. There was also encouragement for Indians to work with white farmers where "they learn much more than they would on the reserves," particularly "manners, morals, customs and ideas of earning a living in a civilized way." (DIA Records, vol. 3920, file 116751-IA, Martin Benson to Deputy Superintendent General, June 23, 1903, p. 6.) Sifton, however, never went as far as suggested by J.D. McLean, who believed that "it might be advisable … in the case of graduates of Industrial Schools to provide for their ipso facto enfranchisement, and give them locations on their reserves as enfranchised Indians." (Ibid., vol. 1120, pp. 692–99, Memorandum, McLean, July 20, 1897.)

54. LAC, Sifton Papers, vol. 201, 159135, Sifton to Laurier, November 19, 1914; DIA

	1897–98	1902–03	Increase
Cattle	15,767	21,291	5,524
Cleared and natural pasturage (acres)	1,917,019	2,279,922	362,903
Cultivated and made pasturage (acres)	16,703	32,557	15,854
Crops (staples) in bushels	128,447	288,695	160,248
Increase in value of clearing, cultivating, buildings, agricultural products, etc.	$51,006.00	$140,678.00	$89,672.00
Increase in value Live Stock & Poultry, Implements, real property, General & Household effects, Real & Personal Property, Incomes	$6,339,600.67	$11,636,976.90	$5,297,376.23

Records, vol. 3635, file 6567, Pedley to Sifton, March 24, 1904. The figures supplied by Frank Pedley appear at the bottom of page 208.

55. On the history of the issue, see F.E. LaViolette, *The Struggle for Survival: Indian Cultures and the Protestant Ethic in British Columbia* (Toronto: University of Toronto Press, 1973); Robin Fisher, *Contact and Conflict: Indian–European Relations in British Columbia. 1774–1890* (Vancouver: University of British Columbia Press, 1977).

56. LAC, DIA Records, vol. 1121, pp. 399–400, Sifton to Governor General in Council, January 18, 1898.

57. See ibid., vol. 3825, files 60511-1 and 2, passim.

58. LAC, Sir Wilfrid Laurier Papers, vol. 248, 69214–20, Minto to Laurier, January 16, 1903; 69232–38, same, January 17, 1903. Minto claimed that "there is a want in many cases of human sympathy between the white administrator and the Indian," and suggested that "somewhat narrow religious sentiments have not conduced to a sympathetic understanding of the Indian races."

59. LAC, Minto Papers, vol. 6, 30-6, F. Pedley to Laurier, January 30, 1903 (quoting Graham).

60. Minto's sympathy with the Indians reveals considerable innocence about the importance of the dance in Indian life; he saw it simply as a continuing pleasant tradition, in the same way that the Scots wore kilts and played highland games. (LAC, Laurier Papers, vol. 252, 70325-9, Minto to Laurier, February 17, 1903.) Perhaps important was the comment of Comptroller F. White of the North-West Mounted Police that "the objection to Indian dances has changed from the atrocities practiced by the Indians, to the evil influences of the whites and Half breeds who attend the dances and corrupt the poor Indian." (Minto Papers, vol. 29, 38, White to Minto, May 25, 1903.)

61. *Debates*, 1898, cols. 5661–62, 6960–65, May 17, 1898.

62. LAC, DIA Records, vol. 1125, pp. 550–51, McLean to Deputy Superintendent General, July 25, 1902.

63. After firing one Indian Agent for drunkenness, Sifton commented, "I can see no use whatever in endeavouring to elevate the moral tone of the Indian race and sending drunken officials to carry on the work." LAC, Sifton Papers, vol. 243, p. 528, Sifton to Rev. John McDougall, May 14, 1901.

64. LAC, DIA Records, vol. 1124, pp. 507–08, McLean to J. Girard, MP, March 2, 1901.

65. LAC, Sifton Papers, vol. 264, pp. 172–73, Sifton to Rev. J.W. Lawrence, December 10, 1897.

66. LAC, DIA Records, vol. 1121, pp. 511–53, J.D. McLean to A.E. Forget, March 8, 1898. A very useful survey is G. Graham-Cumming, "Health of the Original Canadians, 1867–1967," *Medical Services Journal, Canada* 23 (February 1967): 115–66. This article serves to update the basic study by C.R. Maundrell, "Indian Health, 1867–1940" (MA thesis, Queen's University, 1941).

67. LAC, Sifton Papers, vol. 102, 80470-3, G.A. Kennedy, MD, to Sifton, January 14, 1901. This is substantially confirmed by G. Graham-Cumming, "Health of the Original Canadians," 134. Among the Crees the mortality rate had been as high as 137 per 1,000. Most of this was caused by tuberculosis. By 1929 the tuberculosis death rate had fallen to 8 per 1,000, still 20 times the national average; by 1967 it was less than 10 per 100,000, but still five times the national average.

68. One exception was A.S. Kendall, MP for Cape Breton, who angrily termed the low level of expenditure "simply criminal," and commented that the $3,000 estimate for medical attendance in New Brunswick "would not provide them [the Indians] with coffins in the spring of the year." *Debates*, 1902, cols. 3051, 3053, April 18, 1902.

69. Ibid., col. 3041, April 18, 1902; LAC, Sifton Papers, vol. 265, pp. 423–24, Sifton to Rev. John Fraser, March 29, 1901. It should be pointed out that most doctors only supplemented their incomes by being available as required by the Indians, and did not live on reserves.

70. *Debates*, 1902, col. 3040, April 18, 1902.

71. Ibid., 1903, col. 6329, July 9, 1903. A fairly long debate on aspects of the question is ibid., cols. 6326–52, 6408–09, July 9 and 10, 1903.

72. Ibid., 1904, cols. 6960–64, July 18, 1904; *Sessional Papers*, 1906, #27, pp. xx, 271–78; M. Zaslow, *The Opening of the Canadian North, 1870–1914* (Toronto: McClelland and Stewart, 1971), 227–29; G. Graham-Cumming, "Health of the Original Canadians," 124–25.

73. LAC, DIA Records, vol. 3635, file 6567, Pedley to Sifton, March 24, 1904. Pedley's figures were as follows:

			Decrease
	1890–91	12,155	
Indians on the ration list	1896–97	8,853	3,302
	1902–03	5,928	2,925
	1890–91	1,745,300 lbs.	
Flour	1896–97	1,286,100 lbs.	459,200
	1902–03	991,050 lbs.	295,050
	1890–91	2,029,697 lbs.	
Beef	1896–97	1,409,783 lbs.	619,914
	1902–03	1,206,715 lbs.	203,068
	1890–91	245,742 lbs.	
Bacon	1896–97	149,266 lbs.	96,476
	1902–03	135,887 lbs.	13,379

74. Ibid., D. C. Scott to Pedley, March 3, 1904.

75. Ibid., vol. 119, pp. 616–18, Hayter Reed to Sifton, December 23, 1896. According to the Act, "Indian Lands" included any reserve, or portion of a reserve, surrendered to the Crown, generally to be sold or used for the benefit of the Indians. It also stated, "The expression `Reserve' means any tract or tracts of land set aside by Treaty or otherwise for the use or benefit of or granted to a particular Band of Indians, of which the legal title is in the Crown, and which remains a portion of the said Reserve and includes all the trees, wood, timber, soil, stones, minerals, metals and other valuables thereon or therein." See also ibid., vol. 3875, file 90, 880-2, L. Vankoughnet to T.M. Daly, June 28, 1893.

76. See Stewart Raby, "Indian Land Surrenders in Southern Saskatchewan," *The Canadian Geographer* 17 (1973) 36–52. A case in point is the attitude of Frank Oliver before and after the events of 1885; see W. S. Waddell, "The Honorable Frank Oliver" (MA thesis, University of Alberta, 1950), 58–62, 107–08, 133 n. 101.

77. LAC, Sifton Papers, vol. 264, pp. 87–88, Sifton to Oliver, August 5, 1897. It should be noted that when Sifton went to Ottawa in 1896 he apparently assumed that Indian lands could readily be appropriated by departmental order. It was only after his officials pointed out the difficulties to him, and the Department of Justice ruled in favour of the Indians, that Sifton took the line of adhering to the law. This did not, of course, prevent him from trying to persuade the Indians to agree to certain surrenders, in which respect

he was somewhat more aggressive than his Conservative predecessors. I am grateful for these comments to Dr. John Tobias of Red Deer College, who also generously permitted me to examine some of the work he has done for the Federation of Saskatchewan Indians.

78. *Debates*, 1904, cols. 6952-3, July 18, 1904; see also 1903, cols. 6410-5, July 10, 1903.

79. LAC, Sifton Papers, loc. cit.; DIA Records, vol. 1125, pp. 124–29, J.D. McLean to Sifton, August 13, 1901. On the concept "of the reserve as a thing to be handed down inviolate and in trust," see S. Raby, "Indian Land Surrenders," 46.

80. Ibid., pp. 42, 44; LAC, DIA Records, vol. 4015, file 273023, vol. 1, passim.; and see T.D. Regehr, *The Canadian Northern Railway: Pioneer Road of the Northern Prairies 1895–1918* (Toronto: Macmillan, 1976), 172–74.

81. LAC, DIA Records, vol. 3730, file 26306-1.

82. Ibid., vol. 3571, file 130-18.

83. Ibid., vol. 3571, file 130-19. This experience probably contributed to later Blood intransigence on land sales from the reserve; see ibid., vol. 1547, Deputy Superintendent General to W.J. Hyde, August 9, 1911.

84. The quotation is from Premier J.H. Turner in a letter to J.A.J. McKenna, September 22, 1897, in ibid., vol. 3688, file 13886-2.

85. The extensive files on this issue are in ibid., vols. 3688–90, files 13886-1 to 13886-4; see also *Debates*, 1899, cols. 5703–09, June 22, 1899.

86. S. Raby, "Indian Land Surrenders," passim.

87. Ibid., 49–50; and Raby, "Indian Treaty No. 5," 111–12.

88. See Canada, *Indian Treaties and Surrenders*, 3 vols. (Ottawa, 1891 and 1912/Toronto: Coles, 1971 reprint).

89. *Debates*, 1909–10, p. 784, December 1, 1909. The money accrued from sales was $2,156,020. In addition some 1020 islands were sold, including 242 islets in Georgian Bay judged to be almost valueless; the sales of all islands realized $74,353.

90. See the comments of R.L. Borden and G.E. Foster in ibid., 1906, pp. 719–20, March 27, 1906; also pp. 948–49, 951.

91. The only change was an amendment in 1898 permitting Justices of the Peace to certify the validity of land surrenders. There seems to have been no serious thought given to introducing the contemporary American allotment system, intended to speed assimilation. See S. Raby, "Indian Land Surrenders," 37.

92. LAC, DIA Records, vol. 3848, file 75235-1, McKenna to Sifton, April 17, 1898.

93. LAC, Minto Papers, letterbook (mfm), vol. IV, p. 300, Minto to Lt. Col. F. White, February 23, 1904.

8.   The Indian Pass System in the Canadian West, 1882–1935

F. Laurie Barron

In the winter of 1987, Prime Minister Brian Mulroney attempted to bolster his sagging political fortunes in Canada by speaking out against apartheid in South Africa. On the surface it seemed that he had chosen a "safe" political issue, given that for months on end the news media had been bombarding the western world with electrifying accounts of the brutal racist policies fundamental to South African society. But much to the embarrassment of the prime minister, during a press conference on the occasion of his visit to the Vatican, he was challenged on his right to condemn South Africa when Natives in his own country had been so badly mistreated. Although Mr. Mulroney was quick to deny that blacks under apartheid could be compared with Natives in Canada, the accusation had a ring of truth for those familiar with Canadian history, especially with the treatment of Indians in the prairie west.

The aptness of the analogy with South Africa stems from the nature of government policy following the signing of treaties with the Indians in the 1870s.[1] It was a policy which, in its most characteristic form, can be traced to the assimilationist schemes devised for Indian reserves in Upper Canada after 1828. It was generally assumed that the pre-industrial culture of Indians was anachronistic and that, for practical and humanitarian reasons, Indians should be "civilized," "Christianized," and schooled in the art of agriculture. In effect, they were to be culturally remade in the image of the white rural farmer. The restructuring, it was understood, would require considerable training in the ways of white society. Until this was accomplished, the Indian was to be a ward of the state, bearing a special relationship to the government—that of a protected dependent without full citizenship rights. The training itself was to take place on Indian reserves, separated from white society, in theory to prevent the Indian from absorbing the worst features of civilization, especially the use of alcohol. The entire regime was fundamentally racist, but the aspect which particularly conjured up images of apartheid was the Indian pass system, applied in selected areas of the prairie west. Essentially, the pass system was a segregationist scheme which, without any legislative basis, required Indians to remain on their reserves unless they had a pass, duly signed by the Indian agent or farm instructor and specifying the purpose and duration of their absence. It is also relevant to note that in 1902 a commission from South Africa visited western Canada to study the pass system as a method of social control.

In recent years, the pass system has attracted increasing attention by those interested in federal Indian policy, but its treatment by scholars has not been comprehensive. In 1986 Donald Purich published *Our Land: Native Rights in Canada*, containing two and a half pages on the pass system.[2] The book was written without the benefit of endnotes and the discussion of passes is based largely on the work of Sarah Carter who a year earlier had published a two-page article on the subject, again without endnotes.[3] Likewise in 1986 John Jennings wrote an article on the North-West Mounted Police which devotes three pages to the topic,[4] and passing references to the system can be found in the work of John Tobias,[5] Brian Titley,[6] and others. Among the earliest treatments of the topic is a seven-page collection of documentary material, compiled in 1974 by B. Bennett for the Treaties and Historical Research Centre.[7]

Collectively, existing sources do not paint a very complete picture of the Indian pass system and in some cases they are plagued by misinformation and questionable interpretations. This is true especially of the material concerning the genesis of the system, the extent to which it was enforced, and the duration of its existence. Was the pass system a response to Indian participation in the North-West Rebellion, or did it have earlier antecedents? Did its existence mean a rigorous segregation of Indian society? Did the system survive into the 1930s, as is commonly assumed? These are questions which have both historic importance and contemporary relevance. They also demand a more comprehensive treatment than can be found in present accounts of Indian society.

According to Sarah Carter, the origins of the pass system can be traced to May 6, 1885 when Major General Middleton, camping near Fish Creek during the Rebellion campaign, dispatched a letter to Edgar Dewdney, the Indian commissioner and lieutenant governor of the North-West Territories. In it, he asked whether it would be "advisable to issue [a] proclamation warning breeds and Indians to return to their reserves and that all found away will be treated as rebels."[8] It was this letter, says Carter, which set in motion the process that led to the system of Indian passes.[9] John Jennings, however, disagrees. He argues that "Apartheid came to the Canadian West in 1882" in response to the concerns expressed by Indian Affairs and the police about Canadian Indians passing back and forth over the international border and "The Rebellion merely made the policy [of repression] more blatant."[10] He points out that it was in 1882 that an order in council was introduced to discourage such border crossings and he insists that "Here was the rather innocuous beginnings of a policy that later, in its full development … ran counter to the treaty promises of no restrictions on Indian movement.[11] He also notes that in 1884, predating the Middleton letter, Police Commissioner Irvine alluded to a potential pass system in his annual report, in response to the suggestion of Lawrence Vankoughnet, the deputy superintendent general of Indian Affairs, that such a system would prevent Indians from camping indiscriminately near white settlements.[12]

While Jennings is undoubtedly correct in noting that the discussion of the pass system precedes the 1885 insurrection, his treatment of the actual implementation of a pass system soon after the suppression of the Rebellion is flawed in two important respects. First, he tends to emphasize the role of Lawrence Vankoughnet, leaving the impression that the pass system was born in the upper reaches of the administration. He argues, for instance, that the policy of limiting Indian movement was contained in an 1885 memorandum penned by Vankoughnet, and addressed to Sir John A. Macdonald, the prime minister and superintendent general of Indian Affairs.[13] What he fails to mention, however, is that the content of the Vankoughnet memorandum was actually an edited version of an earlier communication written by Hayter Reed, only recently elevated to assistant Indian commissioner from the position of Indian agent at Battleford. In the summer of 1885, following the Rebellion, Reed had drafted a lengthy memorandum "relative to the future management of Indians" and forwarded it to Edgar Dewdney. It contained some fifteen recommendations, and in substance was a blueprint for the total suppression of Indian society. Especially pertinent for our purposes is recommendation seven:

> No rebel Indians should be allowed off the Reserves without a pass signed by an I.D. official. The dangers of complications with white men will thus be lessened, & by preserving a knowledge of individual movements any inclination to petty depredations may be checked, by the facility of apprehending those who commit such offences.[14]

Dewdney's views on each of the recommendations were penned in the margins of the document. In reference to the pass system, the commissioner not only endorsed Reed's proposal, but even suggested that "It might be thought well another year to legislate in that direction."[15] The Reed memorandum, including the comments by Dewdney, was transmitted to Vankoughnet. He in turn forwarded the document, along with an edited version of the original, to the superintendent general—the document referred to by Jennings. Macdonald responded by writing comments in the left-hand margin of the edited copy. For the most part, these comments consisted of one-word and sometimes single-phrase endorsements of each of the recommendations. But they also included two substantive references, one of which was to the issuing of passes:

> Mr. Dewdney remarks that the pass system could be generally introduced safely. If so it is in the highest degree desirable. As to disloyal bands this should be carried out as the consequence of their disloyalty. The system should be introduced in the loyal bands as well & the advantage of the changes pressed upon them. But no punishment for breaking bounds can be inflicted & in case of resistance on the grounds of Treaty rights should not be insisted on.[16]

What this correspondence indicates is that, from its inception in 1885, the pass system was closely associated with Hayter Reed. Certainly Vankoughnet and others at the ministerial level had been aware for some time of the notion of a pass system, but the official decision to implement such a scheme stemmed directly from Reed's initiative.

Second, in focussing on the role of Lawrence Vankoughnet, Jennings has failed to appreciate that the pass system was created, not by a ministerial decision, but by a local initiative once more associated with the person and career of Hayter Reed. Reed's views had been shaped by his personal experience in Indian Affairs, combined with a certain stereotypical understanding of Indian people. As an Indian agent stationed at Battleford in 1881, Reed had seen his "fondest hopes … frustrated" by what he described as the Indians' "inherent, restless disposition."[17] His annual reports were laden with his concerns over Indians leaving the reserves on the slightest pretext: rumours that the buffalo had returned[18]; reports that "soldiers had landed at Prince Albert in order to take all the Indians prisoners, and abuse their wives and daughters"[19]; unnecessary visits to town[20]; and Thirst Dances "which attracted those from all parts to witness acts of endurance and to hear recounted deeds of valour committed by those now more advanced in years, which, of course, acted upon the young braves as a dime novel of a thrilling nature would upon the susceptible youth of our own race."[21] For Reed, these

Hayter Reed, QC, Montreal, 1894 (Saskatchewan Archives Board/R-B3453, Courtesy of the McCord Museum of Canadian History, McGill University/11-106454).

were acts of civil disobedience which effectively destroyed his best efforts to turn Indians into productive farmers. He cited one example of a reserve from which there had been a mass exodus during hunting season, leaving only four men and a few women fit to work the fields, "the remainder being either blind, old and infirmed, invalids or children."[22] Reed's response was to do all within his power to curb Indian mobility—including the payment of annuities on home reserves only, and the withholding of rations from those who made a habit of being off the reserve—but it is quite evident from his reports that his efforts failed.[23] In light of this experience there can be little doubt that he came to see the pass system as an invaluable instrument of control, fundamental to the very success of the entire civilization program.

Likewise, as assistant Indian commissioner, Reed would have been sensitive to the kind of potential military threat which Indian mobility represented. He was not at Battleford in 1885 when the so-called siege of the older portion of the town took place, but the Indian takeover of Fort Pitt, not to mention the murder of a farm instructor and a rancher in the Battleford area as well as nine others at Frog Lake, undoubtedly left a lingering impression. He also would have been sympathetic to General Middleton's request for a proclamation confining Indians to their reserves. In the end, the commissioner's office, believing there was no legal basis for confining Indians to their reserves, limited itself to issuing a notice advising Indians that it would be in their best interests to stay at home during the hostilities.[24] The notice remained in effect for only six weeks largely because it was introduced only during the latter stages of the Rebellion. It seems likely, nevertheless, that the very notion of pressuring Indians to stay on the reserve through an informal but widely applied policy was an idea that was not lost on Hayter Reed.

In point of fact, Reed was personally responsible for the actual implementation of the pass system in 1885, and evidence suggests that he did so prior to receiving the official blessing of either Vankoughnet or Macdonald. Only two days after Vankoughnet had forwarded Reed's memorandum on the future management of Indians to the prime minister, but clearly before Macdonald had endorsed the recommendations, Reed informed the Indian commissioner that he had already implemented a pass system, its illegality notwithstanding:

> I am adopting the system of keeping the Indians on their respective Reserves and not allowing any [to] leave them without passes - I know this is hardly supportable by any legal enactment but we must do many things which can only be supported by common sense and by what may be for the general good. I get the police to send out daily and send any Indians without passes back to their reserves.[25]

This is the first indication of the actual existence of a pass system, one whose authority rested not on ministerial approval or even law, but on expediency. As it turned out, both Vankoughnet and Macdonald warmly approved Reed's recommendation for such a system, but this should not blur the fact that approval was *post facto* and that the real architect of the Indian pass system as it came into being in 1885 was Hayter Reed.

That the pass system was a violation of what had been promised in the treaties and that it lacked legal justification seemed not to be matters of concern to those who administered the scheme. There was, nevertheless, an attempt to rationalize the existence of the system. Foremost was the explanation that certain Indian groups, because of their disloyalty during the Rebellion, had forfeited their treaty rights and should have their mobility limited.[26] To drive this point home, in 1886 Hayter Reed sent out books of passes to his agents accompanied by instructions that Indians who had been implicated in the Rebellion should be clearly so identified on the front of the passes for the information of the police and others.[27] Vankoughnet also argued to his own satisfaction that, although hunting Indians might have a right to travel where they wished as long as they did not encroach on private property, they did not have the right to frequent villages and towns because incorporated places could be considered property owned by municipalities.[28] But the most pervasive argument was that, whatever rights the Indian might have in theory, the enforcement of the pass system was justified in the higher interest of the civilization program and hence of the Indians' own well being. It was precisely this argument to which Reed had alluded at the time of introducing passes and it was one that would obtain as long as they remained in existence. As Reed explained, "it seems better to keep them [Indians] together for the purpose of training them for mergence

with the whites, than to disperse them unprotected among communities
where they could not hold their own, and would speedily be downtrodden
and debauched."[29] Such arguments, of course, were entirely self-serving and
meant to justify an otherwise untenable encroachment on Indian rights.

This rationalization very much served the interest of government and its
hope for European immigration to the Canadian west. As Sarah Carter has
pointed out,

> In 1885, immigration to the prairies was at a virtual stand-
> still. The Indians and Metis had dealt a crippling blow to
> Macdonald's vision of a densely populated West. The
> National Policy could wither and die unless large numbers
> of settlers were attracted to the West to develop its agricul-
> tural potential and create a staple for export.[30]

In effect, the pass system as an instrument of confinement would go a long
way in dispelling lingering fears of an Indian uprising and in reassuring
prospective settlers of a peaceful and prosperous existence. Equally important, the pass system served the purposes of those in the Department of
Indian Affairs whose *raison d'être* was to oversee the experiment in social
engineering. Often reflecting the racist perceptions of the Victorian age, and
sometimes animated by humanitarian and Christian principles, these men
not unnaturally endorsed the pass system as a logical and necessary means
to achieve their goals. And in the decade following the Rebellion, their
determination was all the more steeled by a series of problems which the
pass system was meant to solve.

One such problem was the determination of Indians to confirm and
renew their Indianness by persistently resorting to traditional practices and
even by incorporating new rituals into their ceremonies. The Sun Dance in
particular was a concern to officials because it took Indians away from agriculture during a season that was crucial to farming. Even more disturbing,
it entailed ideological rituals which served to protect and reinforce the
Indian social system, as well as integrate the youth into Indian society, much
to the detriment of the assimilation program administered in day and residential schools.[31] The Indians' mobility also made them susceptible to troublesome outside religious forces. This was true of the so-called "messianic
craze" or Ghost Dance which in the early 1890s made its way from the
United States into Saskatchewan. Unlike its American counterpart, the
Canadian Ghost Dance was non-militant but intensely Indian in content and
hence remained a covert form of spirituality. Although it embraced a
Christian social morality as a means to salvation, that salvation itself promised an afterlife of traditional Indian culture and fellowship. Not unlike the

Sun Dance, it was essentially an assertion of Indianness in opposition to forced acculturation.[32] A similar concern was expressed about the Mormon religion which Indian Affairs perceived as an alien influence with a potential to foment trouble, among other things because of its sanction of polygamy—the very practice officials had been attempting to stamp out among the Plains Indians.[33] Equally troublesome were certain forms of millenarianism. In 1904, the southern portions of Saskatchewan were set ablaze by rumours that the end of the world was at hand. As it turned out, the inspiration behind the rumour was "a deaf, dumb and half demented Indian boy" from Gordon's Reserve who was promising "that the end of the world for white people was coming, that only the real Indians living in teepees would be spared, and would then have all the world to themselves, and lots of buffalo to hunt..."[34] The incident typified a number of religious movements, in part embracing Christian precepts, but promising a revival of Indian tradition and control. For that reason, it was deemed dangerous.

The evils associated with towns and villages were another problem the pass system was meant to address. In the first instance, these were sometimes centres of disease, with the result that sickness was often transmitted to the reserves with devastating consequences. But more than that, they were seen as sources of immorality—dens of iniquity where Indians wasted their time in pool halls and pestered the local residents for handouts in order to engage in alcoholic binges. It was believed that the urban lower classes were adept at teaching Indians the vices associated with city life and that "degradation [was] sure to follow any close relationship with white people in the early stages of [Indian] training."[35] Of particular concern, often more imagined than real, was the belief that Indian families camped near towns in order to prostitute their women. In 1886, for example, a policeman in Battleford levelled a complaint against farm instructors who were too free in issuing passes, a practice he insisted catered to immorality:

> I beg to state that in my opinion the granting of passes to Indians, especially Indian women, is abused, not by the Agents but by some of the farm instructors. Women are granted passes ostensibly to come into town and work or sell berries. This is in nine cases out of ten only an excuse for prostitution. I have been obliged in several occasions to send back to their Reserves women who had unexpired passes in their possession.[36]

In another case, this time in 1899, the Indian agent at Hobbema received a report that some of his agency women were serving as prostitutes in Red Deer, but upon investigation by the North-West Mounted Police, it was determined that the agent had been misinformed.[37] Nevertheless, it was commonly assumed that Indianness equated with immorality and that towns catered to the baser instincts of Native society.

This was all the more problematic given the fact that residential schools were located in major centres and that parents insisted on visiting their children during term. Such visits often had an unsettling influence on the children and sometimes resulted in the parent removing his child without permission. To curb this situation, and at the same time limit Indian access to the perceived evils of urban life, Indian agents were instructed not to allow Indians off the reserve for the purpose of visiting industrial schools, unless they had a pass showing the time and purpose of their absence and specifying the name of each individual in the group covered by it.[38] They were also instructed to limit such passes to one every three months, although additional passes might be issued in the event that a school child became ill.[39]

Alcohol abuse was deemed a problem in its own right. For the missionaries who ran the schools and churches, the use of alcohol by Indians was seen as a sign of moral turpitude and a major impediment to the conversion process through which the civilization of the Indian was to be achieved. For others, alcohol abuse was a social problem, one which destroyed Indian pride and dignity and preordained a society mired in poverty and destitution. From the beginning, the enforcement of prohibition in the North-West Territories had been systematically sabotaged, first by a permissive permit system allowing non-Indians to import alcohol for personal consumption, and then by the introduction of a license system for the sale of beer. Both measures, despite the fact that the Indian Act prohibited Indians from drinking alcohol, had the effect of illicitly increasing the flow of alcohol to the various bands, and this was compounded again in 1892 when the Territorial Assembly instituted a liquor licensing system for non-Indians.[40] For one thing, the licensing system greatly reduced the cost of bootleg alcohol, and as one observer pointed out, "At present it was a very poor Half-breed or Indian who at intervals more or less extended does not find himself in the possession of 50¢ or 25¢ to buy a large or small bottle of whiskey."[41] In addition to home brew, which was variously bootlegged or made covertly on the reserve, alcohol substitutes were readily available, sometimes with tragic results. In 1906, six Indians from Beardy's Reserve in the Duck Lake Agency obtained two bottles of cologne, known as Florida Water, and consumed them as a beverage, not knowing that the content was 98% methyl alcohol. All six died of wood alcohol poisoning.[42] Then too, because Metis and non-status Indians did not fall under the prohibition provisions of the Indian Act, they not infrequently were able to act as intermediaries in obtaining alcohol for Indians, charging a small fee for their trouble.[43] It was also nearly impossible to scrutinize the activities of those who sold liquor illicitly because, under the new liquor ordinance establishing the licensing system, the police lacked the right to search merchant wagons travelling through the territory.[44] The net result of all these factors was that the liquor provisions of the Indian Act were almost unenforceable, especially once the Indian was allowed off the reserve.

A problem of a different sort had to do with the perception, most vociferously articulated in southern Alberta during the 1890s, that Indians allowed to roam the ranges at will were guilty of butchering cattle. Not untypical of the mood of angry cattlemen was an article that appeared in a Calgary newspaper in 1891. It was a diatribe against the Department of Indian Affairs for giving passes to Indians ostensibly for the purpose of hunting, in order to reduce the outlay of rations to needy Indians, when the only surviving game was cattle.[45] While it applauded the goal of making Indians self-sufficient, it insisted that the practice of indiscriminately issuing hunting passes served the interests of Indian Affairs personnel rather than those of the Indians or of the cattlemen:

> The whole aim and object of an Indian Agent's existence is to shew [sic] a clean ration sheet. … By granting passes for the purpose of "hunting" he gratifies his wander loving charges and soothes the departmental mind with a small "total drawing rations." Whether there is anything to hunt or not is a minor matter. The ration sheet at all events is "clean."[46]

The point of the article was a demand that the pass system be tightened up, confining Indians to their reserves in order to protect the property of cattlemen. Hayter Reed was convinced that the losses were owing to factors other than Indians and even that many of the complaints were based on self-interest, not the least of which was an attempt to increase beef rations on reserves in order to enhance the profits of cattlemen.[47] Such disclaimers notwithstanding, the issue was a thorny one for Indian Affairs because the cattle interests represented a powerful lobby, associated with important ranchers like the Honourable W.F. Cochrane who was well connected in Ottawa. For that reason, there can be little doubt that the matter was handled with care and that efforts to restrain the movement of southern bands were redoubled.

In addition to these domestic concerns, the problem of border crossings continued to haunt Indian Affairs in ways which reaffirmed the importance of the pass system. Singularly important was the terrifying spectre of Canadian Indians making common cause with their American counterparts in a general uprising. Domestic upheaval was bad enough, but given the violent nature of white–Indian relations in the United States, the very suggestion of an international Indian movement was often the excuse for panic. In 1891, it was reported that two Indian runners from the United States had held council with the Bloods in order to solicit aid for an anticipated uprising on the American side of the border. Seemingly, the Bloods were advised to sell their horses and lay in a stock of ammunition and arrows. Were the uprising successful, there would be a joint meeting near Fort Walsh as a prelude to a general massacre on the Canadian side.[48] What made the report startling was that it came on the heels of a general alert by the police following reports that the Sioux south of the Manitoba border were holding a War dance and threatening settlers.[49] In the end, neither the Sioux nor the Bloods proved troublesome, but in the minds of officials the two events very much underscored the need for effective control over Indian movement along the "medicine line" separating the two countries.

Also important in the international context was the issue of customs and quarantine regulations. The ability of Indians to cross the border freely invited the suspicion that the real purposes of visits to the United States were horse stealing and other illicit activities. In addition, the unregulated importation of horses and other animals offered the possibility that livestock diseases could be transmitted across the border. The solution to these evils was contained in a circular letter issued by the Indian commissioner in 1903 and addressed to Indian agents in both Manitoba and the North-West Territories.[50] It was now stipulated that, when granting a pass allowing Indians off the reserve for the purpose of visiting the United States, the agent would be required to include on the back of the pass an exact description of the horses, including brands, that the individual would be taking with him. The implication was that Indians crossing the border without such a pass would be required to pay duty on any horses they attempted to bring into Canada upon re-entry.[51] Moreover, it was stated that, at the time of issuing such passes, agents would be required to notify Indians that on leaving Canada they must report "outwardly" and receive a "let pass" at a regular port of entry, and that on reentry they must report "inwardly" and pay duty on any horses or articles required by customs' regulations.[52] This latter provision was meant to facilitate the collection of duties and monitor Indian activity, and it also had the effect of bolstering veterinary inspection at the border crossings.

Thus, to the same extent that the pass system was born of expediency, it remained in existence long after the Rebellion era because it was perceived by administrators as a necessary weapon in the war against those forces which perpetuated an "uncivilized" Indian society.

As it turned out, the pass system proved to be a less than effective way of restricting Indian movement. The problem was that, lacking legislative sanction, the pass system could not be enforced in law. To get around this, Indian Affairs simply assumed an air of authority and attempted to enforce the system by other means within its power. In some cases, rations and other "privileges" were withheld from those who refused to comply with pass regulations, but the most effective approach was to have the police arrest those found off the reserve without passes and, where possible, prosecute them either for trespass under the Indian Act or for vagrancy under the criminal code.[53] The whole system, however, rested on very shaky grounds and ultimately was undermined by two fundamental factors.

In the first place, Indians themselves refused to tolerate the system and were often aggressive in demanding their rights. In the years immediately after the Rebellion, it was widely reported that Indians were complying with the pass system, but it is equally evident that large numbers simply slipped away from the reserve without obtaining a pass.[54] And by the 1890s, it was a matter of comment in official correspondence that Indians were either subverting the system or overtly ignoring it. In 1896, for example, the police commissioner received a report from Calgary that a patrol had required a group of Sarcee to leave the town but that in defiance they had returned.[55] In the same report there was also mention of a constable who had ordered a group of Indians back to their reserve, but they refused to obey and under the circumstances all he could do was report the matter.[56] As the commissioner was later forced to admit, "Every day the Indian is becoming more enlightened as to the position in which he stands, regarding the laws concerning himself, and it is very generally known amongst the Indians that the Police have not the power to arrest or in fact take any action whatever should they [the Indians] not feel disposed to return to their Reserves when ordered to do so."[57] Perhaps nowhere was the defiance more manifest than in the Indian attitude toward the right to attend Sun Dances. In 1900, it was reported that Indians near Fort MacLeod were "keen on having a Sun Dance [sic] and it is quite clear to me that they mean to have one."[58] Two years later, the Indian agent refused to grant a pass to some Indians from One Arrow Reserve for the purpose of attending a dance in Montana, "but they went just the same."[59] All of this suggests that the Indian was anything but quiet and passive in his response to a system which denied his human and treaty rights. It also repudiates the notion by John Jennings that Indians "put up" with the system,[60] and that the system itself "guaranteed peace ... and that Indians would remain corralled on reserves."[61]

The second factor was that the North-West Mounted Police increasingly had misgivings about enforcing illegal regulations to the detriment of their credibility in the Indian community. In 1884, Commissioner Irvine had expressed reservations about the idea of a pass system because it "would be tantamount to a breach of confidence with the Indians,"[62] but once the system came into being the immediate response of the police was to cooperate. Indicative was a communication in 1888 from the assistant Indian commissioner to the commissioner of police, noting that a number of Indians were camped near Battleford much to the annoyance of local residents, and asking the commissioner to instruct his officers there to enforce the pass system.[63] In response, orders were immediately telegraphed to the officer commanding at Battleford: "Indians without passes must be kept out of Battleford. Arrest all those without passes, and after due warning, if they do not leave neighborhood of town try them as vagrants."[64]

According to one writer, this kind of cooperation became characteristic, so much so that by the late 1880s police qualms about the pass system, at least at the official level, had evaporated.[65] Such a conclusion, however, is not consistent with the correspondence. It is quite clear that by 1890 the police were withdrawing their endorsement of the pass system because they feared that its illegal enforcement would jeopardize the Indians' respect for the law. In 1891, the commanding officer in the Macleod District expressed his concerns about confining Indians to their reserves:

> I doubt the possibility of keeping the Indians at home by such coercive measures as stopping their rations or refusing a pass, they will go in spite of all their Agent can do. ... There is an order throughout the district to turn back any Indians without a pass but a difficulty arises in the fact that few of our men can speak sufficient Blackfoot to make themselves understood and the Indians when it suits their purpose can be very obtuse: they are aware too that we have no legal right to turn them back.[66]

The implications of such a situation were hinted at in a second report, this time by officer R.B. Deane, stationed in Lethbridge:

> As to sending back to the Reserve, Indians who came here without a pass, I do so on every possible occasion, but seeing that the Police have no right to do anything of the kind, it behoves one to be very careful so as not to have to take "back-water."[67]

Among other things, the prospect of an Indian backlash prompted Commissioner Herchmer to seek legal advice and in 1892 he was assured in no uncertain terms, both by some circuit court judges and government law officers, that the pass system was illegal.[68] By the following year, opinion was so strongly against the enforcement of the pass system that in May 1893 the police commissioner issued a general circular ending the practice of sending Indians back to their reserves without legal justification.[69] Three years later, the whole issue was raised once more when, in response to an influx of troublesome Cree from Montana, the Indian Department petitioned the police to keep the newcomers on their reserves. In evaluating the request, the officer commanding in Regina was absolutely adamant that, in responding to the wishes of the department, the police operate strictly within the law. As he explained,

> Should an illegal arrest be attempted and resistance offered there would be no protection to us. Such a result would be disastrous to our prestige with the Indians.[70]

Somewhat later, a final comment on the matter was contained in a letter from the police commissioner to the North-West Mounted Police comptroller:

> The moral suasion power that the policeman exercised in the past, will not always accomplish the desired result today and I am of the opinion that until the law is changed in this respect, it is not advisable to issue an order which we have not the power to enforce.[71]

The change in attitude, both by Indians and policemen, did not end the pass system, but it did alter it in a most fundamental way. By the 1890s, there was mounting tension between the Indian Department and the police,[72] and generally, people like Hayter Reed found themselves on the defensive in justifying the use of passes. Reed himself, having replaced Dewdney as Indian commissioner in 1888 and Vankoughnet as deputy superintendent in 1893, very much reflected the changing perceptions of Indian rights and the application of the law. This was underscored in a remarkable letter which Reed sent to the minister of the interior in 1893. He began by saying that, all things considered, the department had been successful in keeping Indians at home. He then admitted by inference that the old pass system, as it had originally been conceived, was no longer feasible and he concluded with a statement that spoke to a far more limited purpose for the pass system:

> Nomadic by nature they [Indians] would roam when the fit was in them, even if by doing so they left abundance behind them, and an army of soldiers or police could not prevent their slipping away.

> It was especially stipulated by them when they entered
> Treaty that they should not be tied down to their
> Reservations, and although I have often taken the responsi-
> bility of employing police to send them home, the greatest
> caution has to be exercised, for were they to offer resistance
> and conflict ensue, they have the law on their side. Under
> these circumstances Agents must often against their own
> wishes issue Passes to Indians who they know will leave in
> any case, and so preserve an appearance at least of control,
> and a knowledge of their movements.[73]

This was, in fact, an admission that the pass system as an instrument of compulsory confinement was dead. What Reed was saying was that, where possible, the department would continue to assume an air of authority in
requiring passes for those who wished to leave the reserve, but that passes
would be freely issued as a monitoring device to keep track of Indian activity. This, of course, was a far cry from the original purpose of the passes and
had three important implications.

First, it meant that Indians were given much freer rein to travel as they
pleased, especially when engaged in economic activities such as hunting
and wage labour. But their freedom also extended to a range of other activities which, under earlier circumstances, would have been banned. A telling
commentary is the fact that by the turn of the century passes were being
issued for virtually every purpose imaginable and often for extended periods of time. In one instance, a group of northern Cree visiting the Blackfoot
during Sun Dance season was given a pass for no less than 75 days—taking
up the entire summer.[74] Fairs, picnics, sports days, local stampedes, and a
range of off-reserve labour activities catered to a general mobility which
increased through the early decades of the 20th century. As the Battleford
Indian agent reported in 1926,

> The Indians of the Agency are ... visiting all over the coun-
> try and large numbers were at Duck Lake for the Annual
> Catholic Prayer week, the visiting seems to be worse than
> usual this summer and Indians have been passing through
> here heading for Alberta reserves and Indians from there
> are passing to [the] east almost every day.[75]

Second, in abandoning the illegal aspects of the pass system, Indian
Affairs turned to the legislative process in order to deal more effectively
with specific problems. This was true especially of the Sun Dance. In that
respect, the department occasionally found it convenient to invoke the

provisions of an 1884 amendment to the Indian Act banning "give-away" ceremonies, originally intended to stamp out the potlatch in British Columbia.[76] In 1895, an amendment to the Indian Act proscribed all ceremonies involving "wounding or mutilation," an obvious reference to what Sun Dancers referred to as "making braves," and in 1906 (with slight changes in 1914) the Indian Act was again amended to place a general ban on dancing of every description.[77] Evidence suggests that these initiatives were not entirely successful and that, as in other attempts to coerce Indians, band members responded with resistance and threats of violence. Representative was an incident that occurred on Poor Man's Reserve in 1902: apparently, the local Indian agent had a group of Indians arrested and tried for dancing illegally. The offenders were given a suspended sentence, under pain of six months of hard labour should they dance again. They were so incensed that immediately after the trial they cornered the agent and one of them apparently threatened his life. Clearly intimidated, the agent on the following day showed up at the reserve and conceded that the Indians could dance all they wanted, the only stipulations being that they not engage in give-aways and that the farm instructor be present.[78] This was only one of many indications that even legally backed coercion was not always effective in manipulating Indian society.

The third implication is that, in adopting a more limited purpose for the pass system, Indian Affairs guaranteed that the system would survive into the 20th century. According to one source, passes were used in the Battleford area until at least 1918 and in some areas until the mid-1930s,[79] a time frame generally endorsed by other writers.[80] For the most part, this conclusion is based on the existence of two pass stubs issued in Battleford during World War I and on the oral testimony of two Indian Affairs officials who recalled the use of passes in Alberta during the Depression.[81] What is not known is the extent to which the pass system was used during its final stages. It may be assumed that, where warranted and tolerated by Indians, passes were used to the benefit of agency personnel and undoubtedly invested with all the authority that the Department of Indian Affairs could muster; however, given the enduring nature of Indian opposition and the legal limitations placed on passes, it seems unlikely that the system was applied generally or that it survived as anything other than a pale shadow of its original self. The issue is also confounded by a certain semantic confusion. A careful reading of the Battleford Indian Agency papers suggests that by the 1920s Indian agents sometimes indiscriminately referred, not to "passes," but to "permits" allowing the Indians to leave the reserve.[82] The latter term actually had nothing to do with attempts to monitor Indian movement, and more appropriately applied to provisions in the Indian Act prohibiting Indians from selling reserve produce to non-Indians unless they first obtained a permit to do so from the Indian agent. The confusion is reinforced by the fact that there was a connection between passes and permits in that the need for a pass was sometimes contingent upon the Indian getting a permit as a means to financing his activities off the reserve.[83] The confusion of the terms also extended into the Indian community, as suggested by a recent interview of an elder from the James Smith band in Saskatchewan. He vividly recalled that the pass system on his reserve had been terminated by Indian Affairs in the 1930s because of a particular incident. What happened was that an Indian visiting the James Smith band had used his pass as a kind of credit card, charged against Indian Affairs, to finance repairs on his car in order to return home; when others attempted the same thing, Indian Affairs intervened to end the practice.[84] Yet when the elder elaborated on the incident, it became quite clear that he was not describing a pass, but rather a permit, which of course held promise of cash payment once the individual's produce had been sold. What all of this suggests is that, in light of the limited information available, it is not possible to make a conclusive statement about the pass system in its dying moments, apart from the fact that the system, already emaciated, simply passed out of existence unnoticed and without fanfare.

In the final analysis, it must be conceded that the pass system, especially as it was originally conceived, very much justified the accusation levelled against Prime Minister Mulroney. While direct parallels between South Africa and Canada may be imperfect, the fact remains that Canadian attempts to culturally assimilate the Indian were riddled with racist assumptions about the inferiority of Indians and the need to control and segregate them as a people. Hayter Reed and others had no qualms whatsoever in completely disregarding the human and civil rights of those who wished to leave the reserves. And there is every indication that, had they been able to fashion a pass system entirely to their liking, one solidly backed by the might of the police, they would have created a system of control over Indians analogous in some respects to that for blacks in South Africa. By the same token, however, the similarities between apartheid and the segregation of Canadian Indians should not be overstated. In practice, the pass system unfolded in a way which made it only a weak reflection of what transpired in South Africa. The fact is that the legal rights of Indians could not be overridden by administrative expediency, no matter how legitimate the rationalizations seemed. Nor was the political and constitutional climate in Canada conducive to any attempt to give legislative authorization to the pass system. From beginning to end, it evolved as a form of local administrative tyranny, applied selectively, but never enjoying the coercive power and public legitimization conferred by official state sanction. For that reason, it proved to be a rather imperfect instrument of racial oppression.

Notes

This article first appeared in *Prairie Forum* 13, no. 1 (1988): 25–42.

1. See F.L. Barron, "A Summary of Federal Indian Policy in the Canadian West, 1867–1984," *Native Studies Review* 1, no. 1 (Winter 1984): 28–39.
2. Donald Purich, *Our Land: Native Rights in Canada* (Toronto: James Lorimer and Company, 1986), 129–32.
3. Sarah Carter, "Controlling Indian Movement: The Pass System," *NeWest Review* (May 1985): 8–9.
4. John Jennings, "The North West Mounted Police and Indian Policy After the 1885 Rebellion," in F. Laurie Barron and James B. Waldram (eds.), *1885 and After: Native Society in Transition* (Regina: Canadian Plains Research Center, 1986), 228–30.
5. John Tobias, "Indian Reserves in Western Canada: Indian Homelands or Devices for Assimilation," in D.A. Muise (ed.), *Approaches to Native History in Canada: Papers of a Conference Held at the National Museum of Man, October 1975* (Ottawa: National Museum of Man, 1977).
6. Brian Titley, "Hayter Reed and Indian Administration in the West" (paper presented at the Western Canada Studies Conference, University of Alberta, November 1985), 12–13.
7. B. Bennett, "Study of Passes for Indians to Leave their Reserves." Prepared for the Treaties and Historical Research Centre (October 1974).
8. Sarah Carter, "Controlling Indian Movement," 8.
9. Ibid.
10. John Jennings, "The North West Mounted Police and Indian Policy," 228.
11. Ibid.
12. Ibid., 228–29.
13. Ibid., 229.
14. Library and Archives Canada (hereafter LAC), RG 10, Vol. 3710, file 19, 550-3. Hayter Reed to Edgar Dewdney, July 20, 1885.
15. Ibid., August 14, 1885.
16. Ibid., Lawrence Vankoughnet to John A. Macdonald, August 14, 1885.
17. Dominion of Canada. *Sessional Papers*, Annual Report of the Department of Indian Affairs for the Year Ending December 31, 1881 (Ottawa: Queen's Printer), 75.
18. Ibid., 82.
19. Ibid., xvi.
20. Ibid., 82.
21. Ibid.
22. Ibid., 77.
23. Ibid., xvii, 75–76, 81.
24. B. Bennett, "Study of Passes," 3.
25. LAC, Dewdney Papers, North-West Rebellion, MG 27, 2076-87. Hayter Reed to Edgar Dewdney, August 16, 1885. The reference to daily patrols presupposes that the pass system as Reed describes it had been in place for some time, probably even before Vankoughnet had received the Reed memorandum via Dewdney.

26. See Macdonald's remarks referenced in note 16.

27. B. Bennett, "Study of Passes," 4.

28. John Jennings, "The North West Mounted Police and Indian Policy," 229–30.

29. Cited in Sarah Carter, "Controlling Indian Movement," 9.

30. Ibid.

31. Jacqueline Gresko, "White 'Rites' and Indian 'Rites': Indian Education and Native Responses in the West, 1870–1910," in A.W. Rasporich (ed.), *Western Canada Past and Present* (Calgary: McClelland and Stewart West Ltd., 1975), 173–78.

32. Alice B. Kehoe, "The Ghost Dance Religion in Saskatchewan, Canada," *Plains Anthropologist* 13, no. 42, part 1 (1968): 302.

33. LAC, RG 18, Vol. 1220, No. 245. Superintendent Steele to North West Mounted Police (NWMP) commissioner, January 17, 1892.

34. LAC, RG 18, Vol. 1540, file 69, 1904. J.H. Bossange to officer commanding Regina District, August 28, 1904.

35. Cited in Sarah Carter, "Controlling Indian Movement," 9.

36. LAC, RG 10, Vol. 1043, file 100, 1886. S.B. Steele to NWMP commissioner, July 1, 1886.

37. LAC, RG 18, Vol. 1354, file 76, part 3, 1896. Sergeant S.J. Dunning to officer commanding Fort Saskatchewan and District, April 14, 1896.

38. B. Bennett, "Study of Passess," 6.

39. Ibid., 7.

40. See D.M. McLeod, "Liquor Control in the North-West Territories: The Permit System, 1870–91," *Saskatchewan History* 16, no. 3 (Autumn 1963): 81–89.

41. LAC, RG 18, Vol. 1256, No. 359, 1892. Inspector A. Ross Cuthbert to NWMP commissioner, August 16, 1892.

42. LAC, RG 18, Vol. 1571, file 49, part 3, 1906. NWMP commissioner to deputy attorney general, Province of Saskatchewan, September 18, 1906.

43. LAC, RG 18, Vol. 1256, No. 359, 1892. Inspector A. Ross Cuthbert to NWMP commissioner, August 16, 1892.

44. LAC, RG 18, Vol. 1280, file 279, 1893. Inspector Moodie to officer commanding C Division, Battleford, March 15, 1893.

45. LAC, Hayter Reed Papers, MG 29 E106, Vol. 12, file George Davidson, 1891. Unidentified newspaper.

46. Ibid.

47. Ibid., Vol. 14, file T.W. Day. Hayter Reed to the minister of the interior, January 6, 1893.

48. LAC, RG 18, Vol. 1200, No. 245. Sergeant Magnus Begg to NWMP commissioner, January 12, 1891.

49. See series of reports in LAC, RG 18, Vol. 1220, No. 245.

50. LAC, RG 18, Vol. 1523, file 69, 1903. Circular letter by Indian Commissioner D. Laird, August 7, 1903.

51. Ibid.

52. Ibid.

53. LAC, RG 18, Vol. 1100, Nos. 134–35. Assistant Indian commissioner to NWMP commissioner, September 20, 1888.

54. Ibid. Edgar Dewdney to L.W. Herchmer, June 14, 1888; and L.W. Herchmer to officer commanding Maple Creek, August 9, 1888.

55. LAC, RG 18, Vol 1354, file 76, part 3, 1896. Inspector Howe to officer commanding E Division, May 22, 1896.

56. Ibid.

57. LAC, RG 18, Vol. 1456, file 76, 1901. NWMP commissioner to NWMP comptroller, August 27, 1901.

58. Ibid., 1900. (Weekly) report of Superintendent Duane, Fort MacLeod, June 13, 1900.

59. Ibid., 1902. Corporal Denis to officer commanding F Division, Prince Albert, August 8, 1902.

60. John Jennings, "The North West Mounted Police and Indian Policy," 230.

61. Ibid., 232.

62. Cited in ibid., 229.

63. LAC, RG 18, Vol. 1100, Nos. 134–35. Assistant Indian commissioner to NWMP commissioner, September 20, 1888.

64. Ibid., L.W. Herchmer to officer commanding Battleford.

65. John Jennings, "The North West Mounted Police and Indian Policy," 230.

66. Cited in B. Bennett, "Study of Passes," 4.

67. LAC, Hayter Reed Papers, MG 29 E106, Vol. 12, file R. Burton, 1891. Sergeant R. Burton Deane to NWMP commissioner, February 12, 1891.

68. Sarah Carter, "Controlling Indian Movement," 9.

69. The 1893 furor over the issue is discussed in NWMP commissioner to NWMP comptroller, LAC, RG 18, Vol. 1456, file 76, 1901. See also Sarah Carter, "Controlling Indian Movement," 9.

70. LAC, RG 18, Vol. 1354, file 76, part 3, 1896. Officer commanding Regina to NWMP commissioner, July 8, 1896.

71. LAC, RG 18, Vol. 1456, file 76, 1900. NWMP commissioner to NWMP comptroller, August 27, 1900.

72. See Hayter Reed's angry response to criticism of Indian Affairs by the NWMP commissioner; Hayter Reed letter (no heading), March 14, 1890, LAC, Hayter Reed Papers, MG 29 E106, Vol. 14. See also the accusation by Fred White, the NWMP comptroller, that "Indian dept. Officials are so jealous of our Police communicating with Indians," in LAC, RG 18, Vol. 1496, file 76, 1902. Fred White to Major A.B. Perry, August 1, 1902.

73. LAC, Hayter Reed Papers, MG 29, E106, Vol. 14, file T.W. Day. Hayter Reed to minister of the Interior.

74. LAC, RG 18, Vol. 1456, file 76, 1900. (Weekly) report of Staff Sergeant A.F. Brooke, Gleichen, June 16, 1900.

75. Battleford Indian Agent, Monthly Report for July 1926, Glenbow-Alberta Institute (hereafter GAI), Battleford Indian Agency Papers, Monthly Reports, 1926.

76. See reference to "give-aways" in the 1902 incident on Poor Man's Reserve, cited in note 78.

77. F.L. Barron, "A Summary of Federal Indian Policy," 31. The text of the 1906 amendment may be found in B. Bennett, "Study of Passes," 2. See reference to prosecutions under the 1914 amendment in Battleford Indian Agent, Monthly Report for July 1915, GAI, Battleford Indian Agency Papers, Monthly Reports, 1915.

78. The 1902 incident is described in the Crime Report of Constable N.M. Fyffe, January 27, 1904, in LAC, RG 18, Vol. 1540, file 69, 1904.

79. B. Bennett, "Study of Passes," 6.

80. Sarah Carter, "Controlling Indian Movement," 9.

81. B. Bennett, "Study of Passes," 6–7.

82. References to the use of the word "permit" for "pass" are found in Indian Agent S.

Macdonald, Monthly Reports for June 1920 and August 1921, GAI, Battleford Indian Agency Papers, Monthly Reports, 1920 and 1921.

83. The Indian agent at Battleford made the point that most Indians engaged in haying to sell the product in order to keep themselves in funds for fairs, but that farm instructors had been ordered to refuse permits of sale until the Indians had put up enough hay for their own use. See Battleford Indian Agent, Monthly Report for July 1922, GAI, Battleford Indian Agency Papers, Monthly Reports, 1922.

84. Respondent A, interviewed on James Smith Reserve as part of a Native Studies 404.6 course project, University of Saskatchewan, March 1987.

9.   Demonstrating Success: The File Hills Farm Colony

Sarah Carter

"Canada's Prosperous Red Men" was the title of a 1925 article in the New York *Literary Digest*.[1] It was noted that the aboriginal people of Canada, under "wise leadership and intelligent encouragement," made important contributions to the nation's chief industry of agriculture. Most of the item was devoted to the southeastern Saskatchewan File Hills farm colony for ex-pupils of residential schools. The colony was singled out as a fine example of the policies of the Canadian government. The scheme, credited with wonderful results, was briefly described. A portion of a reserve was surveyed into 80-acre lots for the colonists who were each loaned $125 to buy housing material, a yoke of oxen, harness and a plough. From humble beginnings in 1901 when three colonists enlisted, by 1915 the community had grown to 36 farmers and their families and they had over 3,000 acres under cultivation. Readers of the *Digest* were told that the contribution of the colonists to the World War I effort was particularly noteworthy. Per capita it was higher than that of any white community in the province; with but one exception, every able-bodied man enlisted for overseas service.

The File Hills colonists were accustomed to such attention. The colony was featured in numerous journal and newspaper articles as an example of the sound administration of Canada's Department of Indian Affairs which resulted in a happy, contented, even prosperous people. During the war years the colony was used to illustrate the intense patriotism that these "wards" exhibited in return for the kind treatment they received. A 1924 history of Saskatchewan devoted several pages to the colony, "the solution of the Indian problem," and its founder William Morris Graham, who "thoroughly deserved" his recent promotion to Indian commissioner.[2] Here were Native farmers with "big barns, bank accounts and automobiles." The two churches, hospital and farms on the colony "would do credit to white men." Commissioner Graham was quoted as saying that the Natives "instead of being a leech on the country, as might be expected … are an asset to it."

Walter Dieter delivering a welcoming address to Governor General Earl Grey (seated in back of car), File Hills colony, 1906 (Courtesy of the Glenbow Archives/NA-3454-13).

The greatest pride however was taken in the "international" attention the colony received. As part of his 1914 eight-week study of the methods and policies of Native administration in Canada, Frederick Abbott, secretary of the American Board of Indian Commissioners, toured the File Hills colony. His 1915 publication, which was highly complimentary of the "simplicity, comprehensiveness, elasticity and efficiency" of Canadian Native policy, presented the File Hills colony as the best illustration of the Canadian system.[3] Abbott's findings were boasted of for many years in the Canadian press. In a 1921 item in the *Manitoba Free Press* it was proclaimed that the File Hills colony had become "famous over the whole continent of America and has drawn visitors from officialdom at Washington to find out 'how it is done'."[4] Many other dignitaries, including royalty, toured through the colony. Earl Grey, governor general of Canada took a special interest and visited on several occasions, as did his successor, the duke of Connaught.

Readers of the articles and newspaper reports of distinguished visitors to the colony might well be excused for imagining that all reserve residents in western Canada were exceedingly comfortable, if not prosperous, with homes, outbuildings and equipment comparable to those of the surrounding settlers. This was certainly the impression that the Department of Indian Affairs, and especially Graham, the mastermind of the colony, wished to convey. The colony was created with a view to the needs of the non-Native visitor. It was never intended to be a model farm for other aboriginal people.

Tours for them were not arranged, nor were they encouraged to visit individually. The colony did not mark the inauguration of a more widespread scheme aimed at the improvement of living conditions on all reserves. Most prairie reserves were pockets of rural poverty. The poorly fed and poorly clad residents lived in log shacks in winter, canvas tents in summer, and attempted to farm with increasingly out-of-date and out-of-commission equipment. The colony addressed the need, long felt by government officials, to have a "showpiece" reserve which could advertise Canada's sound administration. Through vigorous promotion of the colony the impression was left that this was representative of the work of the department.

The Department of Indian Affairs had always shown concern for public image, particularly in the wake of criticism of its activities following the resistance of 1885. Annual reports from Indian agents and inspectors of agencies were frequently "altered by the excise of paragraphs which it is considered inadvisable to print," before they were sent to the publisher.[5] (One example was the excise of a report of a northern Manitoba agent who found children in a so-called school on one reserve squatting on the ground, huddled in a small canvas tent blackened with smoke.[6]) The department took pride especially in its sterling record in comparison to American policy, and this theme was often emphasized in the partisan press. American crimes against Natives were catalogued, and contrasted with the more just and honourable methods of Canada. The department was congratulated for the "fairness, good faith and liberal consideration which our country has always displayed towards the aboriginal population."[7] A very special effort to exhibit the work of the department was made at the Chicago World's Fair in 1893. Young people from Manitoba and the North-West were taken to Chicago to demonstrate their skills at a variety of trades and household duties, while alongside them were displayed remnants of the "warpath" days, including, according to one reporter "horrid, bloody scalps."[8] A Montreal correspondent wrote that the exhibit "portrayed to all visitors the splendid treatment and intelligent supervision and provision of the Canadian Government for these wards of the country ... it is an 'object' lesson indeed for other nations."[9]

Those who had an opportunity to view actual conditions on western Canadian reserves seldom boasted about Canada's treatment of aboriginal people. A missionary in the Touchwood Hills reported in 1893 that the exhibit at the World's Fair and the annual reports of the department reminded him of "the drawing classes at school just before show or inspection day, at the end of a term. They do not convey a fair idea of the general state of the Indian, and are only a fancy picture of the situation."[10] While the department successfully created a favourable impression of its work through newspaper reports and distant exhibitions, the question of where to send dignitaries such as the governor general when they actually visited the west in order to emerge with the same impression, had long posed a problem. Certain reserves were considered much more "advanced" than others, but prairie conditions were unpredictable from day to day, and visiting dignitaries could be left gazing at wastelands of shrivelled up stalks dried out by hot winds or at barren fields flattened by hail. For an 1895 visit of the governor general the agent at one of the "advanced" reserves was instructed to send word immediately "if by any means you do not desire him to visit you, owing to failure of crops or otherwise."[11] Other considerations had to be taken into account. Where reserve residents keenly felt certain grievances they were likely to place these before distinguished guests, particularly if they were given advance warning of the visit. Some of these problems were sidestepped for the 1901 visit of the duke and duchess of Cornwall and York as the department carefully staged a "demonstration" at Shaganappi Point near Calgary, not on any reserve. Such displays however, involving the movement and provisioning of people, were expensive and regarded as disruptive to farm work.

The establishment of the File Hills colony solved the problem of where to take dignitaries. With its churches and cottage hospital, neatly whitewashed homes surrounded by vegetable and flower gardens, and tree-lined roads, the community presented a most pleasing appearance of pastoral charm, even if crops should happen to fail. This was at a time when it was difficult to find any "advanced" reserves. Government policies of the 1890s prevented reserve farmers from using the technology required to be successful on the prairies, and brought agriculture to a standstill on many reserves.[12] A change in government in 1896 did not brighten prospects for reserve residents. The new Liberal administration slashed the budget for Indian Affairs, dismissing many employees including farm instructors and lowering the salaries of those who remained.[13] This administration showed no commitment to the advancement of agriculture on reserves. This was made vividly clear in a preoccupation with reserve land surrender, which ran counter to efforts to create a stable agricultural economy on reserves. The rationale for the encouragement of land surrenders was that Natives held land out of all proportion to their needs, that they did not effectively use this land, and that it should be placed in the hands of more capable owners.

In western Canada land surrenders were enthusiastically pursued by Graham. He handled the negotiations for the surrender of large tracts of land from the Pasqua, Muscowpetung, Cowessess and Kahkewistahaw bands between 1906 and 1909, reserves in the same district as File Hills. At the same time as he urged bands to sell their agricultural land, Graham was heralded as the person who had done more than any other to promote farming among aboriginal people. "To him," it was boasted in a 1921 *Free Press* article, "belongs the very proud distinction of being the first man to solve the problem of making the Indian take kindly and successfully to farming."[14] Graham was an extremely astute promoter, conveying the impression through the colony that a great deal was being done to assist reserve farmers. The colony was a carefully orchestrated showpiece for the public, and a means of enhancing Graham's own reputation and opportunity for advancement.

The File Hills colony also demonstrated the wisdom of the government's new goals for the education of aboriginal people. The Liberal administration was skeptical of the large sums spent on education unless "the certainty of some practical results could justify the large expense."[15] There was concern that children were being educated "above the possibilities of their station" and that a "distaste for what is certain to be their environment in life" was being created.[16] Deputy superintendent general of Indian Affairs James Smart wrote in 1901 that in the western provinces especially "it may well be that the graduates are for the present doing the greatest amount of good in the direction of elevating their race, by returning to live on their reserves, and … it would appear that for the large majority there is no alternative."[17] In Smart's opinion experience had shown that graduates returned "to the communities of their own race" and "to all intents and purposes remain Indians, with all their deepest interests, affections and ambitions centred in their reserves." Indian Commissioner David Laird reported in 1903 that as agriculture and stock raising were likely to be the pursuits of ex-pupils, only those skills that would prove useful in connection with farm work were to be taught to the boys, and for the girls the emphasis was to be upon practical housewifery, so that as farmers' wives they could become "useful helpmates."[18]

This approach to the education of "backward races" was evident elsewhere in the English-speaking world at this time. Curriculums of "low expectations and practical lessons" predominated. The thinking was that Native people should be taught only those subjects that would directly apply to their daily experience. Instead of giving these people unrealistic ambitions, they should be educated to return to their own rural communities where they could be the "leaven" of civilization. The File Hills colony demonstrated to the public that the place for ex-pupils was indeed back on the reserves which they could help mould into thriving communities. The department's duty was to guard against "retrogression," the tendency of ex-pupils to return to a traditional lifestyle once they graduated, and for this reason it was announced in 1901 that experiments were being undertaken "in the direction of the establishment of little colonies of these graduates on their reserves, in the hope that they will not only retain for themselves the benefits received at the schools but exert a beneficial influence upon their own people."[19]

Graham's colony scheme began modestly and without fanfare in 1901, and for several years the "school-boy colony" was referred to as an "experiment." In February 1901, Graham wrote to the superintendent general of Indian Affairs asking for a share of the funds provided for the assistance of ex-pupils and a month later, $1,500 of the $2,000 set aside in the estimates that year were made available to him.[20] Graham proposed that the southeastern portion of the Peepeekisis reserve in the File Hills be subdivided into 80-acre lots, and the survey of 96 of these was completed in 1902. The File Hills appears to have been chosen, not because of its agricultural suitability and potential, but because this was Graham's scheme, and he had been the Indian agent for these reserves since 1896.

The four File Hills reserves were surveyed in a grid-like fashion in the fall of 1880 for the bands of Little Black Bear, Star Blanket, Okanese, and Peepeekisis, which were predominantly Cree. It was soon recognized from the point of view of agriculture that the File Hills was a poor choice. Surveyor J.C. Nelson visited these reserves in 1884 and found that well over half the land was dotted with swamps, ponds and lakes, poplar bluffs and clumps of willow.[21] This was the western slope. In the centre of the reserves, at the height of the hills, were heavy woods. Prairie land suitable for farming was found only along the eastern slope. (See Figure 1.) Agent Allan MacDonald lamented in 1883 that the reserves were so cut up by lakes and marshes that large fields could not be made.[22] The File Hills reserves also suffered in the late 19th century as they were well back of the settlements that hugged the Canadian Pacific Railway, and were thus remote from any markets for labour or produce. A further disadvantage suffered by these bands was that, after the resistance of 1885, the government regarded them as "disloyal." Their annuities were withheld, and they were ordered to surrender their arms, which limited their abilities to hunt what game there was. The Indian commissioner at Regina, Hayter Reed, formulated a plan to break up the agency altogether, and distribute the people on other reserves in order to put an end to what was regarded as their "fractious" behaviour.[23] Other reasons he cited for this move were "the disadvantages of the district for the cultivation of grain, the dearth of game, and the absence of a market

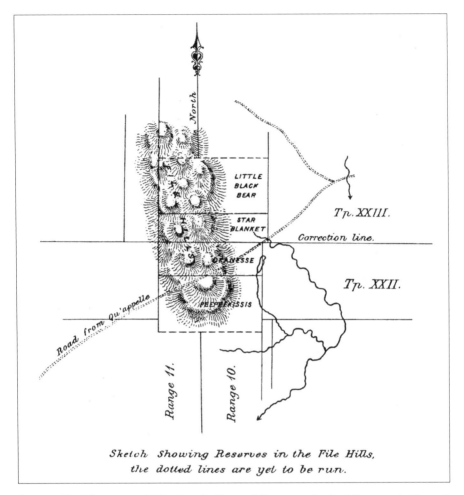

Figure 1. File Hills reserves, 1881. Canada. House of Commons. *Sessional Papers*, vol. 15, no. 6 (1881).

for the industries of the Indians, and of opportunity for them to get freight-ing or other work." The scheme was never implemented even though Ottawa officials concurred with Reed's view.

Matters were not quite as dismal for the File Hills people by 1900. They sold cattle, hay and seneca root, and were gradually increasing their acreage under cultivation. The establishment of a railway branch line in 1905, which ran along the southeast boundary of the Peepeekesis reserve made this a more attractive situation as there was a ready market for grain and stock, which was formerly hauled to Indian Head, a round trip of 80 miles.

Graham and his superiors in Ottawa initially hoped that any possible obstructions to the colony plan could be removed by inducing the four bands to amalgamate, and to congregate on one, or perhaps two, of the reserves.[24] Altogether the population of the four reserves was then 234. Graham thought the bands would "readily give their consent," but this never proved to be the case, even though the effort was made over a number of years. In 1906 Graham reported that he did everything he could think of to bring about an agreement but the Star Blanket and Little Black Bear bands would not consent.[25] Amalgamation and "abandonment" of the Peepeekisis reserve would have allowed Graham a free hand in administering the colony; without this, he had to consult with the band. Admission to the colony, for example, had to be made through a vote of the Peepeekisis band which included all the male voting members, but in the beginning there appears to have been little difficulty getting applicants admitted. Colonists became members of the Peepeekisis band, were allowed a share in the land and other privileges of the band, and gave up membership in their band of origin.

The young colonists were all from other bands; some were from other File Hills reserves but others were from farther afield, such as St. Peter's reserve in Manitoba. It is likely that candidates were not selected from the Peepeekisis band itself as the philosophy was that colonists had to be separated from their family and associates. The colonists soon began to outnumber the original Peepeekisis band members who came to be referred to as the "old guard." They lived on the unsubdivided portion of the reserve, raised cattle and sold hay, wood, and pickets but grew little grain. The presence of the colony left them little opportunity to expand their industries, or to ever consider farming. After the second subdivision survey for the colony in 1906 the original band members were left with less than one-quarter of their reserve, and the portion left to them was the least suitable to agriculture. Their housing and clothing was not of the same standard as the colonists but in their appearance they served a useful function for department propaganda purposes by way of contrast as visitors could clearly appreciate what was being done for the rising generation.

In selecting the colonists, Graham worked closely with the principals of boarding and industrial schools, especially Father Joseph Hugonard of the Qu'Appelle Industrial school at Lebret, and Katherine Gillespie of the File Hills Presbyterian Boarding School which adjoined the Okanese reserve. Gillespie was appointed principal in 1902, the year after the colony was established, and she maintained an avid interest even after 1908 when she left missionary work to marry W.R. Motherwell, a local farmer and Liberal politician. Motherwell became minister of Agriculture in the first

Saskatchewan government (1905–18) and later federal minister of Agriculture (1921–30). As his wife visited the colony regularly so did the minister of Agriculture, often giving lectures on farming and this connection with government may account for some of the public attention the colony received over the years.

Educators and government officials were concerned with what was called "retrogression," the tendency of ex-pupils to "revert" to a traditional lifestyle once they returned to their reserves, or to go "back to the blanket." Some attributed the difficulties of ex-pupils to the chasm between student and parent created by the long period of separation. Most authorities however believed that the progress of ex-pupils was retarded not by the chasm between parents and children but by the "proximity to, and influence of, family connections of the old type who oppose submission to the new order of things."[26] It was part of the "official mind" of the department of Indian Affairs to routinely blame aboriginal people for obstinately clinging to tradition, and for refusing to modify, modernize or improve their lifestyle.

There was recognition however that ex-pupils did not have the means to start farming for themselves, and the department began a program of assisting select graduates who showed an inclination to begin farming on their reserves. Aid in the way of oxen, wagons, harness, seed and materials for home building were loaned to the male ex-pupils, their value to be repaid within four years.[27] Females were given a small sum with which to purchase "useful" articles such as sewing machines or furniture, particularly if they were married to another graduate. As a powerful incentive to return to their reserves immediately, assistance was only offered for two years from their date of discharge.[28] Indian agents were instructed in 1914 to "carefully select the most favourable location for ex-pupils, and [they] should also consider the advisability of forming them into separate colonies or settlements removed to some extent from the older Indians."[29] Lengthy lists were drawn up, recommending some ex-pupils as clean, industrious and worthy of assistance, and describing others as simply "no good."[30] There appear to have been no concerted efforts on other reserves however to establish colonies on the scale of that at File Hills. Elsewhere government officials were disappointed, even with some ex-pupils who were given assistance. The authorities generally agreed with Reverend W. McWhinney of the Crowstand Boarding School who believed that the problem lay with the proximity to the older "lodge" Natives. "It is not pleasant," he wrote, "to see our best and most hopeful boys shipwrecked by these derelicts."[31]

The separation of the "lodge" people from the school people was the method pursued at File Hills, extending the process begun in the educational

File Hills colony band, pre-1914 (Courtesy of the Glenbow Archives/NA3454-36).

institutions. In its discipline and daily supervision the colony was also very much like the schools. "Hardly a day passes," Graham wrote in 1911, "that some officer of the department does not visit them, and if there had been success, it has been the result of this close and constant supervision."[32] As Indian agent, Graham already enjoyed considerable authority. Agents were responsible for enforcing the Indian Act and were justices of the peace under that act. Graham was vigilant in enforcing the act, and the other rigid rules and regulations that governed the colony. Women, for example, were not allowed to visit frequently with each other as they were to be attending to their duties at home, and the use of Native languages was strictly forbidden.[33] Church personnel helped oversee the activities of the colonists. Sermons imparted correct values and attitudes such as industry, self-discipline, and punctuality. Leisure time was controlled as well. Traditional popular recreations or ceremonies, even fiddle dances, were prohibited and were replaced with a brass band, a sewing circle, and lecture groups. The colony had a fine brass band that entertained not only on the colony but in the schoolhouses and towns of the surrounding settlements. Two of the musicians were "natural comedians" who never failed to "bring down the house."[34] In the winter months there were literary evenings and a Farmers' Institute which sponsored visiting lecturers. Baseball was the acceptable summer recreation, as was the annual File Hills agricultural exhibition.

A high premium was placed upon the creation of Christian family

Judging oxen at an agricultural fair in the File Hills colony in 1907 (Courtesy of the Glenbow Archives/NA-3454-25).

homes. One of the steadfast rules of the colony was that no couples were allowed to live together unless "lawfully married by the laws of the country or their respective churches."[35] When a new colonist had his house built he was encouraged to marry. It was explained that this was because "the bachelors with no home ties soon became restless and discouraged."[36] Only graduates of residential schools were regarded as suitable candidates for marriage. Graham explained that these women were the key to making respected and prosperous citizens out of their husbands, and it was also their responsibility to use the skills they learned at school to see their children were brought up in a "civilized way."[37]

The File Hills colony appears to have been unique during its time, but it bears striking resemblances to the model Christian Tsimshian village of Metlakatla established in 1862 by Methodist missionary William Duncan.[38] The residents of this village appeared to its many distinguished visitors to have completely adopted the religious and social values of Victorian England. They wore European-style clothing, attended church, worked at a variety of industries, and observed a set of strict and specific guidelines governing behaviour. They had neat white houses, gardens and picket fences. The Metlakatla system was similarly all-embracing, involving leisure hours that were devoted to brass bands, games such as football, and to the library and museum. This settlement also owed much to the authority and ambition of one man. This "utopia" had broken down by 1887. One of the legacies of the system was a highly politicized people who pressured for recognition of their aboriginal rights and refused to recognize the authority of the Indian agent.[39]

A similar kind of model settlement called Greenwood Village was situated near the Tuskegee Institute in Alabama. This "Model Negro Village," a residential counterpart of the institute, was intended to demonstrate "that blacks could live in the clean, orderly, middle-class way."[40] The colony at File Hills also bore some resemblances to the settlements advocated by individuals and charitable organizations as a means of improving and reforming the needy, the urban working class, and a wide variety of groups such as criminals.[41] The Salvation Army, for example, created farm colonies which aimed at uplifting and reclaiming the thieves, drunkards and other "lost souls" of the city, and making honest, pious, thrifty citizens of them. In "social settlements" such as two in Gary, Indiana in the early 20th century, Europeans, Mexicans and Afro-Americans were weaned away from their cultures and indoctrinated with American customs and values.[42]

A wide variety of rural community experiments were undertaken in the Canadian west in the settlement era from 1885 to 1910.[43] Invariably called colonies, these ranged from the "sacred to secular, from aristocratic and arcadian to democratic and futuristic, from ethnic to nationalist, and from conservative to communistic."[44] Some, like the colony at Wapella sponsored by the Jewish Colonization Association, were, like File Hills, intended to demonstrate that a certain people had a capacity for farming. But the File Hills colony differed from most of these experiments as the primary motive for them was to preserve minorities persecuted elsewhere, to defend religious beliefs and customs. File Hills was established to indoctrinate a group of people to majoritarian values. In many ways they had less freedom to manoeuvre than other prairie colonists. If they withdrew or "migrated," as a few did in the early days, they had few alternatives open to them since they had given up membership in their band of origin, and as status Indians they were not eligible to take up homesteads.

The 18-year-old pioneers of the File Hills colony in 1901 were Fred Dieter, Ben Stonechild, Marius Peekutch, Remi Crow and William Bird. Peekutch and Crow soon deserted, and Bird died of tuberculosis in 1903; Dieter and Stonechild became model colonists for others to follow. Dieter, a grandson of Chief Okanese, attended the Regina Industrial School. Graham liked to boast that this boy was taken from "a home which is today one of the worst hovels on the reserve and where his people were purely Indian in all their habits and do no farming."[45] Dieter had a five-room home with a basement cellar, and in 1911 he had built, on contract, one of the finest barns in the district. He kept cows, pigs and hens, had four "magnificent Canadian horses" and a full complement of farm machinery. Dieter had a hired hand, a non-Native, whom he paid $30 per month. For many years in a row Dieter won a bronze "challenge" shield, donated by Earl Grey in 1907 to "the boys" of the colony. It was to go to the farmer with the best wheat crop and serve as an incentive to all members. Dieter's wife, Marybelle Cote, a grandaughter of Chief Gabriel Cote, was the first bride in the colony. She had also attended the Regina Industrial School.

Among the other names cited in Graham's annual reports as the most successful farmers were John Thomas, Frank Dumont, John Bellegard, Mark Ward and Joseph Ironquill. Ironquill joined the colony in 1905, at the late age of 24. Graham boasted in 1914 that Ironquill's fields were a "magnificent sight," and his buildings "splendid."[46] He had an enormous barn with the name of his farmstead "Lakeview Farm" lettered on the front. Ironquill shipped grain by the carload, and in 1914 had 10 head of heavy horses, 20 head of cattle, as well as pigs and poultry. He managed his farm by employing a non-Native and his wife year-round, paying them $500. Ironquill's clothes were "made-to-order" and he used printed stationary for his business correspondence.[47] In 1917–18 he attended the Manitoba Agricultural College to make a special study of traction engines and their management, and he became expert with motor engines, doing all his own repairs.

Not even Graham had anticipated that colony farmers would have such large operations. He initially thought that 80 acres would be adequate, and had not settled the original settlers on alternate lots. By 1907 nearly every member occupied from 160 to 240 acres. The result was that some of the farmers had a patchwork of eighty acre lots. Ben Stonechild, for example, had one lot interrupted to the south by P. Jackson's, then the agent's, before his next lot could be reached.[48] This meant more road allowances than in ordinary townships, as well as the awkward moving about of men and machinery. By 1906 Graham alerted Ottawa that all the "good farming plots" in the colony were taken up, and that an extension of the survey was required.[49] He felt this had to be done with some haste as he could not "now keep the Indians from plowing fields just outside of the Colony," nor could he "insist on men remaining in their Colony and farming inferior lands when there is better just outside the Colony that they have an equal right to." Graham required the extended survey, which was granted, to maintain his control over the expansion of the colonists, and to permit new applicants. The fact that the "old guard" was to have access to less and even more inferior land does not appear to have concerned officials. (See Figure 2.)

While the colony gave every outward appearance of conformity, the ideal of a model Christian settlement, there is evidence that the colonists

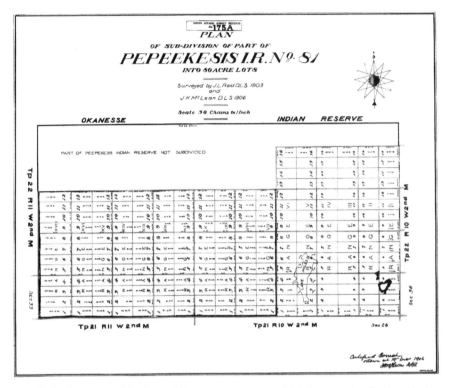

Figure 2. By 1906 most of the Peepeekisis reserve was surveyed into 80-acre plots for the colonists. LAC, National Map Collection No. 0023712.

were not prepared to give up their cultural heritage. Traditional ceremonies and rituals were carried on, despite injunctions against them. These included feasts and funerals, as well as illicit "fiddle dances."[50] There were persistent efforts to hold traditional dances at File Hills, although Graham and his staff attempted to break these up. An 1895 amendment to the Indian Act intended to undermine dancing and other types of ceremonial behaviour was vigorously applied in the prairie region by Graham. In February 1902 the North-West Mounted Police were alerted to the situation at File Hills as the principal of the school there had learned that "the Indians ... were going to attack and destroy the school, in revenge for the Agent having pulled down a building used as a dance house."[51] The assistant commissioner of the police explained that the Indian agent (Graham) had "made many radical changes in the management of the Reserves, some of which, I believe the Indians resent." The attack on the school did not take place but efforts to hold traditional dances continued, and these efforts were not confined to the "old guard." Joseph Ironquill headed a 1910 movement to "start dancing on the colony."[52] In 1914 Graham again complained that he was experiencing difficulty with "an element who are determined to revive dancing which has been a thing of the past for the last 12 years."[53] While he was away in Winnipeg the residents gathered for a dance which was successfully dispersed with the assistance of the clerk and farm instructor. Graham blamed the movement this time on Chief Star Blanket, who had always been "more or less a serious drawback to progess," but was certain that dancing would not be confined to the old Natives if it was allowed to begin. A year later Graham complained that the File Hills Natives wished to go to other agencies to attend dances, and asked that these be stopped altogether, as they had a "demoralizing" effect on the graduates.

Colonists could not simply be ousted if Graham found their behaviour unsuitable. They were expected to assist the agent to "further the interests of the Department," but when they did not yield to this authority they could not simply be ejected from the colony.[54] Privately for example, Graham was concerned about Ironquill and believed that "a serious mistake was made the day this man was admitted to the Colony, and if there is any way by which he could be removed it would mean a great deal for the future harmony and progress of the Colony."[55]

It was Ironquill who also led the 1911 opposition to Graham's desire to admit 50 new colonists and change the method of admitting them. Graham encountered "quite a lot of opposition," particularly from colony members to the entry of new colonists.[56] He found a "tendency on the part of these young Indians who have been doing well, not to listen so readily to advice as they did when they were in poorer circumstances." The colonists were likely taking into consideration the expansion of their own operations as well as the needs of their children. Graham however wished to continue to be at the helm of an ongoing program for ex-pupils. He proposed that the balance of the Peepeekisis reserve be surveyed and that each of the 150 resident members be given a cash settlement of $20 "on the understanding that the Department will have the right, without reference to the Band, to admit, say sixty male graduates."[57] (Graham was well-known for his use of ready cash as an incentive to Indian bands, and he always insisted that the department provide him with money at the time he presented documents for approval.) This money would gradually be repaid by the persons who joined the colony under this agreement. Graham wanted the new people to be settled as quickly as possible, perhaps anticipating the growth of opposition again, and proposed that funds be made available to "grub stake" them while they were breaking land and building homes. In the past beginners had to provide themselves with provisions. In order to avoid future and further defiance of his wishes the new colonists were "to clearly understand when they are admitted, that they must carry out the instructions of the Officers in charge."

The law clerk in Ottawa drafted an agreement which was sent to the band for approval along with a cheque so that distribution could be made immediately. The agreement gave the superintendent general the right to locate future graduates on whatever quantity of land. To Graham's surprise the band voted against the agreement. Ironquill was blamed for this, because he resented authority according to the agent. It was reported to Graham that Ironquill "went to the elders of the original band, who were in favour of the deal at one time and influenced them to oppose the agreement by making false statements."[58] About a month later however, the agreement was submitted to the band again, and the necessary approval was given. It is unclear just what strategies Graham used to overcome opposition, but his persistence was rewarded and he was pleased to report that now "one of the greatest obstacles in starting up graduates has been removed."[59] By 1915 there were nine new admissions to the colony under the new agreement.

Among other evidence that colonists were not prepared to bow to authority was their campaign to have a day school in the settlement rather than send their children to residential schools, but once again they were unsuccessful. This had long been a grievance of reserve parents, but their opinions were seldom taken into consideration. Graham supported the colonists in this, perhaps to maintain good relations and silence opposition but also because a modern day school would make the settlement appear even more like the off-reserve communities he was always comparing it to. The children could carry their lunches to school "as white farmers' children do."[60] He wrote however that "of course I am counting on the Department insisting that Industrial and Boarding schools shall not draft children from this Colony." For a time Ottawa officials agreed that the school should be built, and that the other educational institutions would not be allowed to recruit pupils. The secretary of the department, J.D. McLean explained that as these Natives were "well advanced in civilization, the Department does not think it politic to separate children from their parents by lengthy periods of residence in boarding or industrial schools but on the contrary wishes to keep the home ties intact."[61]

Father Hugonard, who was alarmed at not being able to recruit for the Qu'Appelle school, and at the prospect of Catholic children attending a secular school, was told that the department thought it well to meet the wishes of the colonists, and that the children could be trained at home in household work and agriculture," as is the case with the children of white people." Hugonard quickly alerted Archbishop Adelard in St. Boniface who warned that public discussion, as well as the knowledge and consent of Parliament was required for this departure in practice, as a secular school system could not simply be inaugurated by the department. Restrictions upon recruiting children at File Hills were hastily withdrawn. It appears that the colony did not get a day school until 1949, despite repeated requests from the residents.

The public heard nothing of what went on behind the scenes at the colony as Graham presented only those aspects that reflected well on himself and his work. In his annual reports several themes were continually emphasized. One was that the colony would compare favourably with any other community. "I have lived in this country all my life," Graham wrote in 1907, "and can say without hesitation that, to my mind, no white community has made such a showing as these young people have. The style of farming here is not surpassed in any of the farming districts in the country."[62] He stressed that Native languages were not used, that colonists attended church regularly, and that there were seldom infractions of the Indian Act. The housing on the colony was the most tangible evidence of the success of the program. All were one and a half stories so that sleeping quarters were separate from the living quarters. In the early years the homes were all made of logs which were plastered and whitewashed, but after 1910 more frame structures were built. That the "old ways" had been left behind was also visible in the interiors of these homes which were comfortably furnished with carpets or linoleum, wallpaper, pictures on the walls, sideboards, chairs, sewing machines, clocks, and lace curtains. The annual report of the department for 1904 showed a photograph of three people at the table in Ben Stonechild's house, with tablecloth, tea service, crystal, a pump organ, clock and calender all in view. (Most homes on reserves at this time were one room, with rough planks for flooring, mud fireplaces rather than stoves and no furniture, not even bedsteads.) It was boasted that the women of the colony maintained their homes systematically, "the result of the training they have received at school… If one would visit this colony on a Monday, one would see clothes hanging out to dry at almost every house. If one should go on Saturday, one would find them scrubbing."[63]

Graham claimed that the colonists raised larger and healthier families, and that there was "less sickness in this colony than there is among other Indians on the reserve, which fact is attributable, no doubt, to the manner in which their food is prepared and to the generally improved conditions under which they are living."[64] Eight of the male colonists however died of tuberculosis before 1911, as did 13 children. The chief medical officer, P.H.

Women of the File Hills colony attending a fair in 1907 (Courtesy of the Glenbow Archives/NA-3454-33).

Bryce, concluded in 1911 that the men "were almost certainly infected before entering the colony."[65] Several came from File Hills school which had a particularly high rate of death. At the end of its first 16 years of operation 75 percent of all pupils who had been at the school were dead.[66] The colony death rate however was not high when compared with the situation on other reserves. In his 1922 pamphlet, "The Story of a National Crime," Bryce used the colony as his example of how under normal conditions of housing and sanitation, Native reserve populations could have a low mortality rate.[67] Bryce did not put File Hills statistics to their usual purpose—to show how healthy and prosperous reserve residents were—but used them as a means of highlighting the very different and dismal living conditions of most other aboriginal people of the west. The colonists enjoyed improved health care after 1911 when the department built an attractive "cottage hospital," situated in the centre of the reserve. A trained nurse was placed in charge, and a doctor visited upon request. The hospital demonstrated that the young graduates put their faith in "modern medicine" rather than in the powers of the medicine man. This too was an amenity enjoyed by few other reserve residents. There was a hospital on the Blackfoot reserve, for example, but it was run by the Roman Catholic church, not by the government.

The File Hills colonists distinguished themselves during World War I, and at this time they received their most extensive press coverage. A brief item in a 1915 issue of *Saturday Night*, "The Fire [sic] Hills Indians Do Their Bit," was typical of the attention they received.[68] The work of these people, "an example to many of paler complexion," illustrated the enthusiasm the

Indian Commissioner William Morris Graham with Aboriginal soldiers, their parents and friends from the File Hills colony, 1915 (Courtesy of the Saskatchewan Archives Board/R-B582).

Native people of Canada had for the cause of Great Britain. Even those who had within recent memory "rebelled" against the Crown were now showing their loyalty and commitment, as "among the younger men who contributed to the Patriotic Fund, were two sons and a nephew of Gabriel Dumont, a lieutenant of Louis Riel in the Rebellion of 1885." The contributions of the farmers to the Patriotic Fund, and of the women to the Red Cross Society were detailed, and it was noted that in the surrounding towns the File Hills brass band gave concerts to raise money for the Belgian Relief Fund. It was pointed out that the older "pagan" people were every bit as enthusiastic as the modern farming colonists. *Saturday Night* included the story of an "aged medicine man, Kee wist [who] brought to Mr. Graham a dollar one day, saying, 'It's for those poor, poor people, far across the big water, who suffer so terribly from the war'."

The File Hills people were also featured in a 1916 issue of *The Courier* on "How Dark Men Help the Empire," which was accompanied by a photograph with the caption: "Sepoys, once enemies of England in the East, now in the trenches at Kut."[69] Readers were told that Canadian Natives were also defending the empire. Twenty-four men from the colony enlisted, out of a total adult male population of 38, and several others wished to go but were found to be medically unfit. After rendering assistance at recruitment meetings in the province most of the brass band enlisted. Bandmaster Alex Brass was awarded the Military Cross for conspicuous gallantry in action. In 1917 Graham claimed that "no white community in Saskatchewan ... has given more on an average than these Indians," and after the war it was widely circulated that "the Indians of the File Hills Reserve ... contributed more per capita than any other community in Canada when due allowance is made for their station in life."[70]

With such a high rate of enlistment the war years were difficult for those who remained on the colony. Graham's correspondence for these years was full of complaints that he and his staff shouldered massive added responsibilities. They had to look after the accounts of a large number of women and children, and there were many farms which had to be kept under active operation.[71] It was impossible to place these farms in the hands of tenants because of the shortage of labour. When Graham's 1917 request to have an extra clerk at the agency was turned down he threatened to resign but his dispute with his superiors was resolved by the next year when he was appointed Indian commissioner, moved to Regina, given a greatly increased salary and placed in charge of a "greater production" scheme, which aimed at increasing the amount of reserve land under cultivation.

World War I was the golden age of the colony, at least as far as the public attention it gained. The community was still mentioned in articles of the 1920s such as "Canada's Prosperous Red Men," but even in this the statistics quoted were from 10 years earlier. The colony's major promoter was in Regina, dealing with the affairs of many other agencies, and only visited File Hills once a year. From his distant desk Graham was frustrated by what he knew of the affairs of the colony. His targets were the agent and farm instructors whom he never found up to standard. By 1924 Graham had made up his mind to fire farm instructor Charles Wills because the agency "had not made the progress I expected," and because Wills did not "go round enough amongst the boys."[72] (No matter how aged the colonists got they were often referred to by officials as "the boys.") Wills was given three more months and warned that he was to pursue an energetic policy.

Graham's wrath then descended upon Indian agent F.L. Deacon who was "suspended" for two weeks in November of 1924 for deliberately ignoring instructions. According to the commissioner the cattle herd had decreased by 100 since 1920, and farming operations had increased by only 372 acres in four years.[73] This agency, Graham informed Deacon, had more employees than many others with a much larger population. (Although Graham himself had always claimed that agencies should not be graded according to the number of people supervised, and that where there were more farming Natives the office work load was much heavier.) By August 1926 Graham had turned once again on Wills who was fired for being "much too easy going to properly handle Indians."[74] "The land on the colony," Graham wrote, "is in a deplorable state, and drastic steps are going to be taken to clear the situation up." Wills had apparently not carried out instructions with regard to wild oats and many of the fields were infested with the weed. Shortly after this, agent Deacon resigned because of ill health, and was replaced by George Dodds.

It is not certain which agent author and colonist Eleanor Brass referred to when she wrote that one of Graham's successors "had very dictatorial methods and administered in a negative way. As a result many couples became discouraged and left the colony. Some rented their farms to white farmers and thus avoided having any business with the Indian agent."[75] She and her husband got along well with Deacon so this was likely Dodds, who "came in with the idea that he was either going to make a success of the reserve or break us all. He was a real dictator. It seems as though I was always fighting with him." The Brasses, a young couple, eventually left the reserve altogether. Even some of the original colonists left their farms, especially during the 1930s. Alex Brass, for example, found work off the reserve as a carpenter. Like other reserves during the Depression, the File Hills reserves were short of equipment, horses, seed, feed, houses, and food, and hundreds of acres once under cultivation were idle.[76]

One legacy of the colony was that the Peepeekisis reserve had an unusually high population.[77] Because of this, there was little "vacant" or "unused" land that officials might regard as available for surrender. During the Depression however, when many fields were abandoned, there was pressure placed on the band to lease land to outsiders. It is ironic that in one case pressure to lease was put to bear by the colonists' old friend, W.R. Motherwell, who wanted some land for his farm manager.[78] Band members were very much opposed to the lease of any land as they had to first "surrender" it, and there was concern that "if they surrender they will not get the land back again."[79] In order to make them change their minds, they were refused whatever assistance they were receiving from the department. As always, surrenders or leases of land were regarded by officials as of great benefit to reserve residents. Inspector of Agencies Thomas Robertson explained the reasons for withholding assistance from the band. "The Band can, by leasing some of this land, do a great deal to expedite improvements for themselves and children, and if they do so we will give them all further assistance possible, but I wish to make it clear that we are not wasting money by attempting to help those who will not do anything to help themselves."[80] Not surprisingly, the band eventually consented to a five-year lease although the lease was never renewed.

By 1930, in the annual reports of the Department of Indian Affairs, any special reference to the colony as distinct from the File Hills agency had disappeared, but the settlement was still referred to as a colony as late as 1950 when the File Hills Indian Colony Day School was opened. During the 1950s however, another set of events led to the dispersal of many of the people. In the spring of 1952 some members of the Peepeekisis band protested the status of the original colonists and their descendants, involving over 400 people.[81] An amendment to the Indian Act provided that if ten members of a band protested the rights of any person living on a reserve, a hearing could be held to determine if that person rightfully belonged to the band. Several Saskatchewan bands precipitated action against band members but the Peepeekisis case was unique as it involved not just one or two individuals; much of the population of the reserve was threatened with eviction. If the protests had been allowed membership in the band would have been reduced from 500 to 75 or less. At stake was a loss of status and privileges, a loss of the right to farm or to live on the reserve. The action might be called the "revenge of the old guard" as the protesters were descendants of the original band, they lived on the subdivided portion of the reserve and did not farm.[82] In 1954 a federal commission held a four-day hearing into the charges at Lorlie but reserved a decision. The controversy was not resolved until 1956 when Judge J.H. McFadden of the District Court of Melville, held an eight-day hearing and in December made his decision which preserved the status of the colonists.

During the years that the case remained in limbo the colonists became discouraged as they faced the possibility of leaving their reserve and home. Many had been resident at File Hills for over 50 years and others had been born there and knew no other home. Among the members protested were six widows, nearly all elderly, who would have found it difficult to adjust to new surroundings. Noel J. Finay, a colony farmer and wounded veteran of World War II told the press in September 1956 that "this matter has been prolonged too long and has affected our people economically and morally."[83] Ida Drake of the Women's Missionary Society wrote that "after the first hearing many of our people lost heart and felt that there was no use in cultivating their land or improving their homes for someone else's benefit. Many left their homes altogether and took work off the reserve where possible.

Band funds were also tied up due to the uncertainty of membership status, so that no help towards improvements, etc. could be obtained. During these years much of the land has become infested with weeds.[84]

For a time however, especially during the first two decades of the 20th century, the File Hills colony achieved a standard of living unparalleled on other prairie reserves. What factors account for this? Graham believed that this was due to the policy of the separation of the elders from the young graduates, and to the constant supervision of the colonists. He also once wrote that any success was due to the fact that the operations of the colonists had increased beyond the point where all proceeds were required to pay for such things as twine, threshing, and repairs.[85] When anthropologist David Mandelbaum visited the File Hills in 1934 the agent and clerk gave him the impression that the colony had received large infusions of money during Graham's time. Mandlebaum wrote in his notebook that

> this Agency is the old stamping ground of Graham who was Indian Commissioner for many years. As a result it has better grounds and more buildings than most Agencies … Graham got the idea that if only he could get the young fellows off by themselves, away from the influence of the older people, they would become "good Indians." And so he picked out the land in the Pipikisis [*sic*] Reserve and went through the schools, picking out the likely boys and getting them into the Pipikisis [*sic*] band. Few of the boys were full-bloods. The Colony looked good on paper because a great deal of money was pored [*sic*] into it. But actually there were only three or four good farmers among all the graduates of the schools on the land. When money was not put in at as great a rate, the whole business sagged badly.[86]

Voices of the Plains Cree author and Anglican priest Edward Ahenakew wrote that the key to the functioning of the colony was that the young people accepted the authority of one man, as they had learned to do in school. The colonists

> are under the guidance of an official who has more authority than most, and he is an able man whose authority these young people accept in the way to which they become accustomed in boarding school… I do not think that if he were asked to do the same thing again, that he would be willing. That colony is a tribute to his own ability and to his

strong desire to improve the Indian, but I do not believe that
it is a natural development.[87]

Eleanor Brass, who was born and raised on the colony, wrote that the achievements at File Hills "may be attributed to the initiative of the colonists, who were allowed to conduct their own affairs," combined with the constant encouragement of missionaries and officials. She referred to "by-laws" that the colonists made themselves.[88]

It is unlikely that the agricultural accomplishments of the colony could be attributed to the separation of the elders from the younger school graduates. Officials customarily blamed the state of reserve agriculture on the supposed stubborn resistance of aboriginal people to change, and they overlooked economic, and environmental factors, as well as the role of government policy. Although Graham regularly credited himself with introducing the aboriginal people of the West to agriculture, he arrived on the scene two decades after the beginning of reserve agriculture. Many Plains chiefs and prominent spokesmen of the 1870s, former buffalo hunters, led the way in this respect including Mistawasis, Ahtahkakoop, Kahkewistahaw, Day Star, Pasqua, Poundmaker, and Louis O'Soup. There was no widespread opposition to agriculture, indeed at the treaty negotiations and subsequent assemblies it was aboriginal people who insisted that they should be allowed the means to farm in return for their land. That there was very little to show for these efforts after twenty years was due to a wide variety of factors, including in some cases poor land, limited oxen and implements, seed shortages, restricted access to markets, and setbacks due to drought, frost, hail and prairie fire.[89] Government policies, particularly those of the 1890s, placed obstacles in the way of agricultural expansion. Many had very little choice but to pursue whatever other options were available including the sale of wood, hay, and seneca root, but this was not because of opposition to agriculture.

On the File Hills colony there was concern to create conditions that would allow for the establishment of agriculture, beginning with the initial loan. While loans were offered to select ex-pupils on other reserves, they were not available to any person wishing to begin farming; nor were they eligible to apply for bank loans. Spokesmen made it clear that this was a great grievance of reserve residents. Many were induced to surrender large tracts of their land in the early 20th century largely because they were promised funds to outfit those wishing to begin farming. By 1913 however, the department declared it would no longer make loans to farmers from the land surrender money it held in trust, unless in the form of short-term loans to be repaid from the sale of the crops harvested.[90] If the crops did not cover expenses "farming may be considered a failure and it would be unwise to continue it." There was little concern about whether farming succeeded or not.

The issue of threshing machinery allows comparison between the situation at File Hills and on other reserves. By 1911 the colonists owned, in common, two steam threshing outfits; the department did not purchase these but the farmers were allowed to go into debt with implement dealers. On other reserves the farmers were not allowed to enter into such arrangements. Agents were told that this should not be encouraged, that they would be burdened with collecting debts, and that if one reserve was allowed to make such a purchase it would only lead to others making similar requests.[91] The equipment on reserves, particularly threshing machinery, became increasingly out-of-date and out-of-commission, and was rarely replaced. Agent H. Nichol of the Muscowpetung agency near the File Hills complained in 1913 that there was not an operable threshing outfit in his agency, and he outlined the many reasons why it was impossible for the Natives to pay for one themselves.[92] The department would not allow the farmers to purchase machinery out of capital funds derived from land already surrendered, and the only solution the agent could see was to surrender more land in order to raise the funds. The want of threshing machinery became a chronic problem throughout the prairie reserves. In 1922, for example, it was reported that the Battleford agency, which had a large acreage under cultivation, was greatly handicapped for the want of proper threshing outfits.[93] The son of a farm instructor on one western reserve recalled how difficult it was for Native farmers as they "were fifty years behind the times in their machinery."[94] His father "had an awful time trying to get the Indian agent to buy even one mower for twenty-seven farmers. You can imagine how much hay was harvested with one mower."

The File Hills colony farmers were allowed to purchase the machinery necessary to their enterprise while other reserve farmers were not. It was not so much that money was "poured in" to the colony but that there was concern to create conditions that would allow farmers to enjoy some success. As Graham himself recognized, the colonists got beyond the point of seeing their entire proceeds going to pay their debts, and this allowed them to acquire amenities unheard of on other reserves. Because of their relative prosperity, the colonists were perhaps able to demand a greater say in the management of their own affairs, as Eleanor Brass wrote. Certainly Graham was concerned about the tendency of those who were doing well not to "listen so readily to advice." In his annual published reports Graham claimed to encourage this independence. He wrote in 1911 that particular attention is paid to the matter of giving those Indians who are able to conduct their own affairs, a chance to do so, as I consider this most essential. We have a few among those who first entered the colony who have a comparatively free hand in conducting their own business. Several of these Indians have private bank accounts, which show a credit balance the year round, and against this they draw cheques from time to time.[95]

Graham may simply have been making the best of a situation that presented itself to him, as it seems unlikely that he would have encouraged such independence.

Without doubt some credit for the agricultural achievements of the colony must go to its energetic founder and promoter. Graham's constant supervision of the colonists and the dedication he demanded of his staff must have had its drawbacks, but may also have been of assistance. It is unfortunate that the same energy was not applied to other prairie reserves where farming floundered. Graham was interested in the success of farming only on the colony. Elsewhere Graham sought to alienate Native reserve lands, an initiative that most certainly worked against the best interests of reserve farming.

Notes
This article first appeared in *Prairie Forum* 16, no. 2 (1991): 157–84.

1. *The Literary Digest* (New York), March 7, 1925.

2. John Hawkes, *The Story of Saskatchewan and its People* (Regina: The S.J. Clarke Publishing Co., 1924), 104. William M. Graham was born in Ontario in 1867 and came west with his family in the 1870s. His father James Graham was Indian superintendent for the Manitoba district. He began work with Indian Affairs in 1884, first as a clerk in the Birtle and Moose Mountain agencies. File Hills was the first agency Graham was placed in charge of, in 1896, and he remained resident there for 21 years, although he was appointed inspector of agencies in 1904. Graham was promoted to Indian Commissioner in 1918 when he left File Hills for Regina, and retired in 1932. See E. Brian Titley, "W.M. Graham: Indian Agent Extraordinaire," *Prairie Forum* 8, no. 1 (1983): 25–41; E. Brian Titley, *A Narrow Vision: Duncan Campbell Scott and the Administration of Indian Affairs in Canada* (Vancouver: University of British Columbia Press, 1986), chapter 10, "The Ambitions of Commissioner Graham," 184–99.

3. Frederick H. Abbott, *The Administration of Indian Affairs in Canada* (Washington: 1915), 51.

4. *Manitoba Free Press*, January 1, 1921.

5. Library and Archives Canada (hereafter LAC), Records relating to Indian Affairs, RG 10, vol. 3784, file 41/61, Robert Sinclair to Edgar Dewdney, July 27, 1887.

6. Ibid., Angus Mckay's report, October 4, 1885.

7. *The Empire* (Toronto), January 19, 1891. See also *The Winnipeg Tribune*, December 23, 1890 and *The Week* (Toronto), December 13, 1890.

8. *The Mail* (Toronto), September 15, 1893.

9. *The Gazette* (Montreal), September 19, 1893.

10. *Leader-Post* (Regina), July 6, 1893, and *The Mail*, July 11, 1893.

11. LAC, RG 10, Deputy Superintendent General Letterbooks, vol. 1117, p. 319, Hayter Reed to Amédée Forget, July 20, 1895.

12. Sarah Carter, "Two Acres and a Cow: 'Peasant' Farming for the Indians of the Northwest, 1889–1897," *Canadian Historical Review* 70, no. 1 (1989): 27–52.

13. D.J. Hall, "Clifford Sifton and Canadian Indian Administration, 1896–1905," *Prairie Forum* 2, no. 2 (1977): 129.

14. *Winnipeg Free Press*, January 1, 1921.

15. Canada. House of Commons (hereafter CHC), *Sessional Papers*, Annual Report of the Department of Indian Affairs for 1901, xxix.

16. Jean Barman, "Separate and Unequal: Indian and White Girls at All Hallows School, 1884–1920," in *Indian Education in Canada*, vol. 1, *The Legacy* (Vancouver: University of British Columbia Press, 1986), 120.

17. CHC, *Sessional Papers*, vol. 36, no. 27 (1901), xxix.

18. Ibid., vol. 38, no. 27, (1903), 238–39.

19. Frederick E. Hoxie, *A Final Promise: The Campaign to Assimilate the Indians, 1880–1920* (Cambridge: Cambridge University Press, 1989), 196. See also Kenneth James King, *Pan-Africanism and Education: A Study of Race Philanthropy and Education in the Southern States of America and East Africa* (Oxford: Clarendon Press,1971).

20. LAC, RG 10, vol. 7768, file 27111-2, W.M. Graham to the superintendent general of Indian Affairs, February 4, 1901.

21. Ibid., vol. 3703, file 17,728, J.C. Nelson to Dewdney, December 31, 1884.

22. CHC, *Sessional Papers*, vol. 17, no. 4, (1883), 72.

23. LAC, Hayter Reed Papers, vol. 21, large letterbook, no. 94, Hayter Reed to L. Vankoughnet, November 1889.

24. LAC, RG 10, vol. 7768, file 27111-2, David Laird to the secretary, superintendent general of Indian Affairs, September 30, 1902.

25. Ibid., Graham to Laird, March 31, 1906.

26. CHC, *Sessional Papers*, vol. 45, no. 27 (1911), 347.

27. LAC, RG 10, vol. 1392, circular letter, D.C. Scott, March 12, 1914.

28. Ibid.

29. Ibid.

30. Glenbow-Alberta Institute (GAI), Blood Indian Agency Correspondence, File 97, W.J. Dilworth to D.C. Scott, 1914.

31. LAC, RG 10, vol. 4072, file 431,636, Rev. W. McWhinney to the assistant deputy and secretary, February 26, 1913.

32. CHC, *Sessional Papers*, vol. 46, no. 27 (1911), 520.

33. Eleanor Brass, *I Walk in Two Worlds* (Calgary: Glenbow Museum, 1987), 11.

34. W.W. Gibson, "Indians at Work for the War," *East and West: A Paper for Young Canadians* (Toronto), April 14, 1917.

35. Eleanor Brass, "The File Hills Ex-Pupil Colony," *Saskatchewan History* 6, no. 2 (1953): 67.

36. Alice W. Tye, "Indian Farmers at File Hills Colony," *Nor'West Farmer*, September 5, 1912: p. 1169.

37. CHC, *Sessional Papers*, vol. 42, no. 27 (1907), 158–59.

38. Jean Friesen (Usher), *William Duncan of Metlakatla: A Victorian Missionary in British Columbia* (Ottawa: National Museums of Canada, 1974).

39. Ibid., 127.

40. Louis R. Harlan, *Booker T. Washington: The Wizard of Tuskegee, 1901–1915* (New York: Oxford University Press, 1983), 169–70.

41. Clark C. Spence, *The Salvation Army Farm Colonies* (Tucson: University of Arizona Press, 1985).

42. Raymond A. Mohl and Neil Betten, "Paternalism and Pluralism: Immigrants and Social Welfare in Gary, Indiana, 1906–1940," *American Studies* 15, no. 1 (1974).

43. A.W. Rasporich, "Utopia, Sect and Millenium in Western Canada, 1870–1940," *Prairie Forum* 12, no. 2 (1987): 217–43.

44. Ibid., 222.

45. CHC, *Sessional Papers*, vol. 42, no. 27 (1907), 157.

46. Ibid., vol. 50, NO. 27 (1914), 229.

47. *Winnipeg Free Press*, March 1918, clipping in LAC, RG 10, vol. 7768, file 27111-2.

48. See the map in LAC, RG 10, vol. 6300, file 641-1, part 1.

49. LAC, RG 10, vol. 7768, file 27111-2, Graham to J. McLean, March 9, 1906. The strip Graham recommended was three miles wide and extended to the west boundary of the reserve. It contained 120 lots of 80 acres and 12 of about 120 acres. This left 6,500 acres of the reserve unsubdivided.

50. Brass, *I Walk in Two Worlds*, 13.

51. LAC, RG 10, vol. 6307, file 653-1, pt. 1, J.H. McIllree to comptroller, February 4, 1902.

52. Ibid., vol. 7768, file 27111-2, Graham to J. McLean, June 17, 1911.

53. Ibid., vol. 1394, Graham to McLean, July 31, 1914.

54. Ibid., vol. 7768, file 27111-2, Graham to McLean, June 17, 1911.

55. Ibid.

56. Ibid., Graham to the secretary, Department of Indian Affairs, October 18, 1910.

57. Ibid.

58. Ibid., July 24, 1911.

59. Ibid., Graham to McLean, August 23, 1911.

60. Ibid., vol. 6300, file 641-1, pt. 1, Graham to Scott, September 28, 1909.

61. Ibid., McLean, March 17, 1909.

62. CHC, *Sessional Papers*, vol. 42, no. 27 (1907), 156.

63. Ibid., vol. 46, no. 27 (1912), 520.

64. Ibid., vol. 42, no. 27 (1907), 159.

65. Ibid., vol. 45, no. 27 (1911), 285.

66. P.H. Bryce, *The Story of a National Crime: Being an Appeal Justice to the Indians of Canada* (Ottawa: James Hope and Sons Ltd., 1922), 4.

67. Ibid., 10–11.

68. *Saturday Night* (Toronto), April 17, 1915.

69. *The Courier*, March 25, 1916, in LAC, RG 10, vol. 11198, scrapbook no. 1, 1884-35.

70. LAC, RG 10, vol. 1394, Graham to Scott, January 15, 1917, and Hawkes, *Story of Saskatchewan*, 103.

71. Ibid., vol. 4070, file 427,063-A, Graham to Scott, August 12, 1917.

72. Ibid., vol. 9131, file 306-4, Chas. Will to Graham, May 14, 1924 and Graham to F.L. Deacon, April 24, 1924.

73. Ibid., Graham to Deacon, November 3, 1924.

74. Ibid., September 24, 1926.

75. Brass, *I Walk in Two Worlds*, 19.

76. LAC, RG 10, vol. 9135, file 306-6, T. Robertson to G. Dodds, March 7, 1938.

77. According to the 1929 census there were 239 colonists as well as 45 others on the Peepeekisis reserve. On the other File Hills reserves the population was much lower: Star Blanket - 58, Little Black Bear - 40, Okanese - 31. By 1947 the population on the Peepeekisis reserve had increased to 390.

78. LAC, RG 10, vol. 9135, file 306-6, G. Dodds to Thos. Robertson, February 28, 1938.

79. Ibid., Robertson to the secretary, Department of Mines and Resources, Indian Affairs Branch, January 18, 1939.

80. Ibid., Robertson to Dodds, March 7, 1938.

81. Saskatchewan Archives Board (SAB), annual reports of the Women's Missionary Society of the Presbyterian and United churches, 1887–1956, typescript, 84–85.

82. *Leader-Post* (Regina), June 9, 1954.

83. Ibid., September 17, 1956.

84. SAB, Women's Missionary Society reports, 85.

85. LAC, RG 10, vol. 1390, Graham's annual report, February 4, 1914.

86. Canadian Plains Research Center, Dr. David Mandelbaum Fieldnotes, File Hills 1.

87. Edward Ahenakew, *Voices of the Plains Cree* (Toronto: McClelland and Stewart, 1973), 133.

88. Brass, "File Hills Ex-Pupil Colony," 66.

89. Sarah Carter, *Lost Harvests: Prairie Indian Reserve Farmers and Government Policy* (Montreal: McGill-Queen's University Press, 1990).

90. LAC, RG 10, vol. 7596, file 10116-11, pt. 1, McLean to H.A. Gunn, May 17, 1915.

91. GAI, Battleford agency correspondence, box 5, file 24, W.J. Chisholm to Indian agent, May 22, 1902.

92. LAC, RG 10, vol. 1993, H. Nichol to McLean, September 20, 1913.

93. GAI, Battleford agency correspondence, box 1, file 2, S.L. McDonald to Graham, October 6, 1922.

94. Ibid., Hart Cantelon interview.

95. CHC, *Sessional Papers*, vol. 46, no. 27 (1911), 521.

Patterns of Settlement

10.   Governmental Coercion in the Settlement of Ukrainian Immigrants in Western Canada

John C. Lehr

One of the most intriguing questions concerning the settlement of Ukrainians in Western Canada in the period 1892–1914 is the nature of the relationship between the immigrant and the Canadian Department of the Interior. Most of the Ukrainian immigrants who entered Canada with the intention of seeking homestead lands in the West were leaderless and penurious. Many of them settled on lands now regarded as marginal for agricultural settlement, and rejected or bypassed by settlers of other nationalities. In consequence it has often been assumed that the Canadian government actively discriminated against Ukrainians forcing them to accept agriculturally inferior homesteads on the margins of settlement.

In left-wing Ukrainian-Canadian historiography it has been popular to claim that the settlement of the West was arranged in Napoleonic style. Ukrainian immigrants were allegedly "hurled at the country by the trainload" where the government "allotted" them the worst lands:

> not the clear prairies nor the rolling foothills, but rather the tough, heavily wooded rock strewn, bog infested quarter sections on the northern half of Canada's western parklands.[1]

This claim, which still enjoys popularity in left-wing scholarship, was first voiced in 1898 when the Winnipeg *Nor'Wester* attempted to generate political capital out of an incident in which Ukrainian settlers were treated most unfairly by the government which tried to force them to settle where they did not wish to.[2] Many were later confirmed in their beliefs by the remarks of Sir Clifford Sifton, made in defence of his Slavic immigration policy. Sifton, extolling the virtues of the Ukrainian pioneer, noted that they would settle rough lands rejected by others and would be successful in bringing them into production.[3]

Both Anglo-Canadian and Ukrainian-Canadian authors have alleged government discrimination as well. In 1931, C.H. Young termed the settlement of Ukrainians in the West "a fiasco," and blamed the government for their settlement of submarginal land.[4] In 1947, Vera Lysenko reiterated this theme. She claimed Ukrainian settlement was administered in an authoritarian fashion: "Those in charge of immigration and settlement—hurled the [Ukrainian] settlers at the land without plan or thought for the future."[5] Petro Krawchuk also supports the thesis that settlement of marginal lands was forced upon the Ukrainians by Canadian government officials who "were quite brutal in their dealings with European immigrants, especially so with those [Ukrainians] from Galicia and Bukowina."[6] More recently popular works by Myrna Kostash and Helen Potrebenko imply government indifference to the fate of the Ukrainian settlers, if not an outright determination to exploit them by deliberately placing them on the poorest lands open to settlement.[7] According to Potrebenko:

> The first wave immigrants (1892–1914) were usually easy to handle because they didn't speak English and many were illiterate even in their own language. Immigration agents simply told them where the "good" lands were, pointed them in the direction they were to go and never thought about them again. When a new area was opened to settlement, immigration agents took a group of people there, and then their friends had to follow.[8]

Left-wing Ukrainian-Canadian historiography thus holds the government to be directly answerable for the Ukrainians' occupation of large tracts of agriculturally marginal land. Historians and historical geographers writing from other philosophical standpoints have ascribed Ukrainian settlement on marginal territory to a variety of other causes: ignorance of alternative opportunities; lack of better lands open to settlement; erroneous evaluation of land capability; and an overwhelming determination to secure timber on their homestead land.

The role of the government in the immigration and settlement of Ukrainians in the Canadian West has been examined by Vladimir Kaye; some of the interactions of the government, the immigrants and the press, by John Lehr and Wayne Moodie, but the claims of left-wing historiography that coercion was a significant causal factor of the geography of Ukrainian settlement have not yet been seriously examined.[9] This paper addresses this question of coercion as a factor in the process of Ukrainian settlement in the West. It attempts to explain the often complex but usually consistent relationship between the officials of the Department of the Interior and the newly-arrived Ukrainian immigrant, and seeks also to assess the degree to which the Ukrainians' occupation of submarginal land may be attributed to discrimination by the Crown.

Ukrainian Settlement

Although Ukrainian immigrants had settled in Western Canada as early as 1891, it was not until 1895 that they came to government notice. The numbers entering Canada were few and since they all came from the Austrian administered province of Galicia (Halychyna) they were referred to as Austrians and assumed *ipso facto* to be ethnically German. The mass immigration of Ukrainians to Canada began in 1896 after the circulation of Dr. Josef Oleskow's two immigration pamphlets, *Pro Vilni Zemli* and *O Emigratsii*, throughout the Western Ukraine, but it was some time before Ukrainians began to arrive in the West *en masse* (Figure 1).[10]

Until 1896 all Ukrainians entering the Canadian West looking for free homestead land settled at Star, near Josephburg, about 40 miles northeast of Edmonton, because of the presence of a small settlement of Volksdeutsche from Galicia there. Later arrivals settled in the area because of the growing presence of a familiar social and linguistic milieu, kinship ties and because they were attracted to the physical environment of the aspen parkland belt.

Since they originated from the wooded lands of the Carpathian foothills of Galicia, almost all the Ukrainian immigrants shunned the open prairies

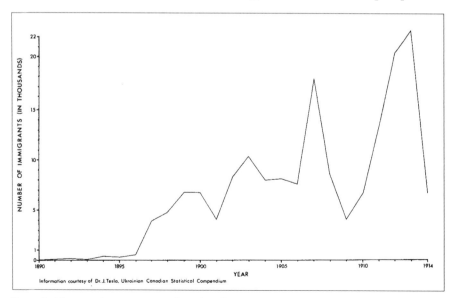

Figure 1. Ukrainian Immigration into Canada, 1891–1914.

and sought the economic and, perhaps, the psychological security of the parkland belt. Costs of settlement were far lower in the parkland than on the open prairie and, for the Ukrainian settlers, few of whom had much capital, the lure of a guaranteed supply of timber, so vital for fuel, fencing, and building, was very strong indeed.[11]

The Canadian government first took an active role in settling Ukrainian settlers in the West in 1896. Until 1900 the Department of the Interior maintained a loose liaison with Dr. Oleskow, of L'viv, who organized and dispatched groups of immigrants from Galicia. Canadian officials attempted to place these groups in Western Canada so as to accommodate both their and Oleskow's preferences for specific locations.[12] During 1896 new settlements of Ukrainians were established in Manitoba, at Cook's Creek (East Selkirk), Stuartburn, and Dauphin, the last two in accordance with the suggestions of Oleskow himself.[13] The immigrants were all well satisfied with the locations, a cause of some satisfaction among the Crown officials charged with the successful placement of immigrants.

At this time the Department of the Interior had no legal authority to require immigrants of any nationality to homestead in any specific location. All immigrants were free to settle wherever they wished on Crown land provided that land had not been set aside as a government timber berth, railway land grant, or Indian Reserve. The small staff of immigration workers scattered throughout the West functioned as advisors and administrators whose duty it was to oversee the orderly occupation of homestead lands and to ensure that settlers were placed so as to reduce agricultural failures and subsequent abandonment of land. No legal authority ever backed their efforts; they achieved their goals through persuasion, by accommodating the wishes of the immigrants and, on occasion, illegally, by deception and application of force.

The mass immigration of Ukrainians began in earnest in 1897. The staff of the immigration branch in the West soon found themselves overwhelmed by their numbers and it became impossible for them to handle incoming Ukrainians on a personal basis. Commissioner of Immigration William F. McCreary, stationed in Winnipeg, found it increasingly difficult to balance the political concerns of his superiors in Ottawa against the wishes of the majority of newly arrived settlers who wanted to join their kinfolk and compatriots already established in the West. While problems of language exacerbated the situation, political controversy surrounding the immigration and settlement of Ukrainians placed the most serious burden on McCreary's shoulders.[14]

The Politics of Settlement

By 1897 the immigration of Ukrainians into Canada had become a political-ly contentious issue. The Liberal administration defended Clifford Sifton's policy of seeking Slavic immigrants but the Conservative opposition and its press attacked the Liberal policy and Slav immigrants with xenophobic fervour.[15] Ukrainians were dismissed as "riff-raff … foreign scum," undesir-able material for building their vision of a British northwest in Canada. Conservative newspapers such as the *Nor'Wester* demanded that the Slavs be segregated from the British and northern Europeans when settled in the West. At the same time they railed against the settlement of any foreigners *en bloc*, arguing that the formation of large ethnically homogeneous settle-ments would constitute a potentially fatal attack upon the Britannic nature of the West, and would cast the future of the Dominion into doubt. This political controversy surrounding the settlement of Ukrainians heightened the need for the government to settle newly arrived immigrants as quickly as possible and to place them in a variety of widely scattered settlements so to prevent the growth of massive block settlements.

Immigration Commissioner McCreary despaired of creating several new centres of Ukrainian settlement across the West without any legal authority to force immigrants into specific locations.[16] Despite the government's refusal to grant him this authority, he and his staff eventually established a scattering of Ukrainian settlements across the parkland belt (Figure 2).

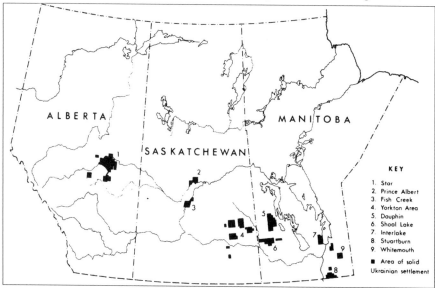

Figure 2. Ukrainian settlements in Western Canada, 1905 (Source: Library and Archives Canada/ Record Group 76).

This was not achieved painlessly. Chain migration encouraged the for-mation of ethnically homogeneous settlements so Crown agents soon became aware of the difficulties of deflecting incoming Ukrainians away from established settlements, where they had relatives, into empty areas newly opened for settlement. There is no documentary evidence that the Department of the Interior ever resorted to draconian measures to achieve their ends. However, in 1897 the Conservative press alleged that Ukrainian settlers were "placed" in the West by being forcibly ejected at random at each station along the railway line between Winnipeg and Yorkton.[17] This unsubstantiated report was strongly denied and labelled as "malicious mis-representation, false-hood and slander," by the Liberal, and generally more responsible press. It was, in fact, probably founded on rumour and hearsay and rebroadcast to generate political capital for the Conservative Party.[18]

Most such sensational allegations had little foundation in fact, but there is no doubt that Crown Agents occasionally employed coercion to attain their aims. What is in question is the frequency with which it was employed, and the extent to which it was a factor in determining the geography of Ukrainian settlement.

Since Crown agents strove to attain the *successful agricultural* settlement of immigrants, it would have been illogical for them to force immigrants to locate in poor areas where the chance of agricultural failure was high. Indeed, immigration agents generally showed a commendable interest in the welfare of those they helped to settle. Their concern was both paternal-istic and personal.[19] They worried about those who ignored their advice and settled in areas with little potential, and often attempted to persuade them to relocate on to better land.

Illustrative of this was the serious view that Crown agents took of the activities of local land speculators among incoming settlers. In the late 1890s speculators were urging newly arrived Ukrainians to purchase 40-acre lots near to the city of Winnipeg. Officials of the Department of the Interior regarded this small acreage as impractical for farming. To prevent the Ukrainians from buying such lots, they ran colonist cars carrying Ukrainains straight through Winnipeg with windows and doors locked—a fairly effec-tive strategy—but one which caused some resentment.[20] Similarly, the Crown attempted to remove immigrants from unpromising locations. For example, a small group of Ukrainians who had settled at Hun's Valley, Manitoba, on sub-marginal agricultural land, were pressured to relocate. They refused and were left to their fate.[21]

Crown agents displayed a similar concern to prevent incoming Ukrainians from settling on sub-marginal land in the Stuartburn area of

Manitoba. This area was initially settled in 1896 as Ukrainians chose land on the eastern margins of the Red River Valley. At first the land homesteaded was of reasonable quality and well suited for the type of stock-rearing operation which the immigrants intended to establish. As settlement progressed subsequent arrivals found the better lands to the west of the settlement nucleus already claimed and so settled on empty lands to the east. Unfortunately the quality of the land decreased dramatically as they moved eastwards. In their determination to settle adjacent to relatives and friends immigrants paid little heed to quality of land.[22]

By the turn of the century it was clear to many observers that immigrants moving into the Stuartburn and Gimli districts were condemning themselves to unnecessary hardship. Alternative sites for settlement were still in abundant supply in Saskatchewan, Alberta, and parts of Manitoba where other Ukrainians were already established. Kyrilo (Cyril) Genik, one of the leaders of Dr. Oleskow's first parties dispatched to Canada in 1896, employed by the government as an official interpreter and *de facto* colonization officer, frequently met incoming immigrant trains at Winnipeg and used all the arguments he could muster to induce arrivals to avoid Stuartburn and Gimli and to go instead to more promising destinations further west.[23] His pleas were often in vain. Immigrants continued to stream into the swamps and marshes of the "Manitoba Badlands," where they reached their homesteads often only after wading through miles of swampy land.[24] Stefan Yendyk, a pioneer of the notorious Kreuzburg (Frazerwood) district of Manitoba's Interlake district recalled the attempts of the local immigration agent Philip Harvey to dissuade his family group from settling in the Interlake area:

> Then they came to our group—it was really a close family group—and asked: "Where do you good people want to go?" And the reply was "Gimli."
>
> "So you want to go to Gimli!? Why do you want to go to Gimli? There is no future there: neither you nor your children will eat bread from that soil. That is poor land, wet and mosquito infested," Harvey told them.
>
> Mrs. Michael Humeny said: "We want to go because my husband's brother is there."
>
> My mother said: "My sister is there."
>
> Others started to tell him that they wanted to go to Gimli because there was plenty of wood. He listened for a while and then said: "Sure my father is there; my brother is there;

my devil, 'chort', is there. All right go! You will break your
necks there. If you go where these other people are going
[Yorkton and Sifton] you will eat bread."

Yes, people should have listened to his advice.[25]

The Conservative *Winnipeg Telegram* later claimed that the Minister of the
Interior callously placed the Ukrainians on such lands without regard for
their welfare and:

> left them to bear as best they could the trials and sufferings
> incident to the attempted settlement of districts that could
> only be reached by walking through five or six miles of
> water. Women have shared with men these sufferings,
> deliberately imposed on them by the Minister...[26]

This was patently untrue, but there were a few instances of immigrants
being pressured to settle in specific locations. This usually occurred when
officials of the Department of the Interior were attempting to create new
nodes of Ukrainian settlement and in the process had to break the chain of
migration and overcome the immigrants' reluctance to settle away from
already established friends and kinfolk.

Coercion

In 1897 a rapid inflow of poor immigrants resulted in the first incident in
which Ukrainian immigrants were forced to settle in a specific location. The
Immigration Sheds at Winnipeg had become packed with immigrants and
their families, most of them destitute Bukovynians, who showed little inclination to either work or select land.[27] The problem showed little sign of abat-
ing and McCreary reported to the Deputy Minister in Ottawa that he anticipated trouble when 539 others would arrive.[28] This precipitated a crisis, for
those already in the Immigration Hall, who having overstayed their time,
were required to move out to make room for the newcomers. McCreary
offered two alternatives: either to proceed on their own to wherever they
wished to settle, or to be settled near Yorkton, Saskatchewan, in an area of
good farmland. Both alternatives were refused. McCreary reported that:

> A more ignorant, obstinate, unmanageable class, one could
> not imagine, I have placed all sorts of plans before them, but
> they give but one answer—"We want to get land in Cook's
> Creek or go [back] to Austria, or we won't leave Winnipeg."
> There is no doubt about it, a certain amount of force has got
> to be used with this class, as they will not listen to reason,
> and the more you do for them the more they expect.[29]

These immigrants were forcibly removed from the Immigration Hall and

Immigrant sheds, Winnipeg, Manitoba, late 1800s (Courtesy of the Archives of Manitoba/N13803).

placed on a train for Yorkton, where they formed the nucleus of a new colony in that district. The immigrants, having failed to act on their own initiative, were deprived of any freedom of choice when events forced the government to take firm and arbitrary action.

From the reports submitted by William McCreary to James A. Smart, the Deputy Minister of the Department of the Interior, it appears that immigrants undecided as to their destination were assigned to areas on the basis of: (1) availability of surveyed lands in the various districts then being settled by Ukrainians; (2) the numbers in each area still in the process of selecting land and (3) the availability of space in the Immigration Sheds throughout the West at the time of colonist train arrivals. Arrangements for settlement were made as far East as was possible, with the Government Agents and Interpreters attempting to sort out immigrants into groups on the basis of their declared destination. Those undecided as to destination were directed to various areas in response to the above criteria and according to their province of origin in the Western Ukraine. McCreary stated that "if they were Galicians from Bukowina [*sic*] I would send them either to Stuartburn or Yorkton; were they Galicians from Galicia proper, I would probably send them to Edmonton."[30]

Little trouble was experienced in settling immigrants in this somewhat arbitrary fashion, for in most instances they were placed in locations which suited their preferences in regards to land type. As McCreary made clear, immigrants were generally placed with others of similar cultural and religious background. Nevertheless, most Ukrainians were understandably reluctant to be directed to settle new areas where none of their compatriots were established. It was during the Department of the Interior's clumsy attempts to establish new settlements by directing immigrants into new areas that confrontation between government and immigrants took place.

The growing number of arrivals in 1898 placed an increasing strain on the system of distribution and settlement administered by McCreary. Attempts to convince settlers to voluntarily settle new areas were fruitless. All wished to go where the others had gone, a Ukrainian trait well remarked by Department officials.[31] Confrontation was not inevitable as Department officials attempted to attain their goals in as non-abrasive a fashion as possible. But this could not always be done.

In April 1898, rail communications between Winnipeg and Edmonton were temporarily cut at Saskatoon. This compounded a complicated and difficult situation which had arisen over the settlement of a group of Ukrainians who wished to go to Edmonton to join friends, but who had no money to pay their fare. The Canadian Pacific Railway Agent was reluctant to offer free transportation as these immigrants had been brought in by the Northern Pacific line. An offer to settle them at Pleasant Home, Manitoba, was refused even when they were threatened with ejection from the Immigration Hall.[32] Eventually the CPR agreed, somewhat reluctantly, to transport these settlers to Edmonton free of charge, but was then unable to do so as it had no engine on the north side of the Saskatchewan River at Saskatoon. In an attempt to break this impasse, Ottawa telegraphed McCreary ordering their settlement "in Townships forty, forty-one, and forty-two, Ranges twenty-seven and twenty-eight West [of] Second,"[33] that is, on the accessible south side of the Saskatchewan in the unsettled Fish Creek district as close to water as possible.[34] McCreary, in acknowledgement, declared his intention of locating as many as possible at Fish Creek and Batoche.[35] This could probably have been done, albeit with some difficulty, had not the same instructions been applied to another trainload of Ukrainian immigrants from the boat "Bulgaria" which arrived in Winnipeg at the same time.

Unfortunately for McCreary, the Immigration Officers accompanying the "Bulgaria" passengers had done their work en route too well, and most of the immigrants were decided on locating in the Edmonton district. Akerlindh, the senior government officer accompanying the colonist train, complained that had their instructions been received earlier, before striking out for more westerly parts:

> we could easily have induced them to go there, [Fish Creek
> or Batoche] but we only received this communication after

they had made up their minds to go to certain parts, and it
would have been very difficult to get them to change their
decision, in fact impossible, and would in my humble opinion look a little odd, after we had given them the best possible advice and information before as to the most suitable
parts, and as I have said above a large number have friends
and relatives in the Edmonton district and were bound for
there and would go nowhere else.[36]

The first attempt at settling the Fish Creek area was thus never really
pressed. It was obvious that to do so would invite confrontation. Of this
group of immigrants, about 700 were eventually directed to Edmonton, 125
to Dauphin and others to Pleasant Home, Yorkton and Stuartburn.[37]
Nevertheless, measures to develop the Fish Creek area were implemented
and it was resolved that future parties would be located there.

Colonization Agent Speers was entrusted with the delicate task of
endeavouring to locate "several families at least of the next large party at
that point."[38] Shortly thereafter a large consignment of Ukrainian immigrants arrived in Winnipeg, much to the dismay of Commissioner
McCreary, who was ill and unable to get about. Overworked, and at the
limit of his patience, McCreary disposed of his problem by dispatching all
53 families (about 300–350 people) to Saskatoon under the control of Speers,
who was instructed to settle them all at Fish Creek. Unaware of this, the
immigrants were led to believe that they were bound for settlement at either
Edmonton or Dauphin.[39]

The reason for the deception, explained McCreary, was that:

It is simply an impossibility, by persuasion, to get a number
of these people to go to a new colony, no matter how
favoured, and some ruse has to be played, or lock them in
the cars as I did last year with those going to Yorkton.[40]

As was bound to happen, the immigrants protested bitterly and broke into
open revolt when they learned of their intended destination. They demanded to be taken to Edmonton or Dauphin, where many claimed to have relatives and friends.[41] Seventy-five of the Ukrainians refused to submit to
government direction or to consider location at Fish Creek. These began to
walk back to Regina. Their major complaint was the treeless environment
and the absence of established Ukrainian settlers.[42] Speers grew desperate
and requested the North-West Mounted Police to turn them back, by force
of arms if necessary, but his request was refused.[43] The intensity of the
Ukrainians' reaction took Speers by surprise. Although he may have

anticipated some argument it is evident that he had little idea that a major confrontation would be precipitated:

> Almost distracted with these people, rebellious, act fiendish, will not leave cars, about seventy-five struck off walking [to] Regina, perfectly uncontrollable. Nothing but pandemonium since leaving Regina. Have exhausted all legitimate tactics with no avail. Policeman here assisting situation—eclipses anything hitherto known. Edmonton, Dauphin or die. Will not even go [to] inspect country, have offered liberal inducements, threatened to kill interpreter. Under existing circumstances strongly recommend their return Edmonton and few Dauphin and get another consignment people special train leaving this afternoon. Could take them Regina. Answer immediately am simply baffled and defeated—quietest and only method will be their return. Waiting reply. Mostly have money and will pay fare. They are wicked.[44]

In a further attempt to placate them and effect their settlement, the Ukrainians were told that recent information from Edmonton and Dauphin indicated that all homesteads in those areas were taken up.[45] To sweeten the pill somewhat the Government Agents also offered to transport the immigrants to their selected homesteads on an individual basis at no charge, with provision of three sacks of flour and five bushels of potatoes for each family.[46]

McCreary was determined not to give in to the immigrants. He felt that a new colony must be established. To back down would perhaps jeopardize the future creation of any new "colonies."[47] He felt, moreover, that the Ukrainians were fabricating claims to have relatives in Edmonton and Dauphin merely as a pretext to join their compatriots in those areas.[48] This was inimical to the government's interests. The immigrants involved were equally determined to exercise their will, and all but a few joined those walking to Regina, determined and, it was claimed, armed.[49] At this juncture McCreary, unwilling to risk an armed confrontation, simply washed his hands of responsibility for their welfare, holding that those walking south "must suffer for their indiscretions,"[50] although ultimately he relented and the dissidents were transported to Edmonton and Dauphin.

Not all was in vain, however, for Crown Agents did succeed in establishing a nucleus for the new settlement with twelve families who were satisfied with the Fish Creek location.[51] This gave considerable satisfaction to those

involved. Having established a nucleus of Ukrainian settlement they anticipated little trouble in locating further immigrants there.[52]

The difficulties encountered in establishing new settlements can scarcely
be overemphasized. Contrary to common supposition, the Ukrainian immigrant was not disposed to go anywhere unless it suited his convenience.
This Commissioner McCreary knew well:

> They are apparently an obstreperous, obstinate, rebellious
> lot. I am just about sick of these people. They are worse than
> cattle to handle. You cannot get them, by persuasion or
> argument, to go to a new colony except by force. They all
> want to go where the others have gone … unless you could
> see them, you could not understand the disposition of this
> class.[53]

It is significant, moreover, that these characteristics enumerated by
McCreary were manifested only when the government sought to channel
Ukrainian settlers into new areas. Difficulties were then experienced regardless of the agricultural quality of the area involved. This suggests that social
factors were paramount in the immigrants' evaluation of any area for settlement. Paradoxically, the government experienced little trouble in settling
some of the worst sub-marginal agricultural areas in the West, for example,
the Kreuzberg area of the Manitoba Interlake, yet they encountered determined resistance to the settlement of far more promising areas, even of areas
which approximated the type of environment being eagerly settled in other
established areas of Ukrainian settlement. A convincing argument in support of this contention is that the number of instances of conflict, even of
mild difficulty in settling incoming Ukrainians, practically ceased after 1899.
Once a number of settlement nuclei had been established the task of the government was greatly eased. Occasion for confrontation diminished as
incoming settlers gravitated to areas where they had relatives and friends.
The interaction between government and immigrant then declined, though
it did not cease.

The lessening of friction between immigrant and government may be
partially explained by the development of a more efficient system of handling immigrants. After 1899 immigrants were routinely sorted as to their
destination at Halifax or Montreal, or while *en route* to Winnipeg. They could
then be shipped directly to their destination, without stop-over in Winnipeg.
This overcame indecision, prevented the more credulous from being influenced by land speculators, and got the settler onto the land without delay.
Yet no matter how efficient the organization of the Department of the

Interior, problems were inevitable when attempts were made to direct Ukrainians into new areas for settlement, given their attitude towards settlement away from friends and kin.

Conclusion

The Department of the Interior was obliged to use force to create a relatively small number of new nuclei of Ukrainian settlements. Once these were established other Ukrainian immigrants could be channelled into them with ease, for most were then eager to locate alongside their compatriots and kin. Thus, although force was used to settle some immigrants, as at Fish Creek, it affected only the first few families placed in the new area. Other immigrants subsequently located in that locality of their own free will, which suggests that the reluctance of the first settlers to accept land in the area was founded largely upon their fear of settlement without the benefits of the security of an already established nucleus of settlers of their own nationality. At Fish Creek the type of land may also have been a factor invoking resistance, but it is difficult to ascertain the degree to which it precipitated the confrontation. It is quite probable that even the independently minded Hutsuls from Bukovyna who led the "Fish Creek rebellion" might have been persuaded to have settled in the area had there been Ukrainians already established there.

Governmental coercion was seldom backed by physical force. Agents of the Department of the Interior attempted to persuade immigrants to go to certain locations by offering inducements of financial aid or provision of supplies. If that failed to win compliance they threatened to leave the immigrants to their own devices; to withdraw government interpreters, deny free transportation and let the immigrants fare as best they could in the face of government indifference to their fate.

Physical violence was repudiated by the government. In 1897, a Jewish interpreter used a whip upon Ukrainian immigrants seeking land near Saltcoats, Saskatchewan. Thomas McNutt, the agent overseeing their settlement, was outraged:

> Even big strong men cringed before him and took the lash meekly, although he was a miserable little runt that a good big lad could handle. I cautioned him not to use that whip any more but he said that was the only way to manage them. I found him striking the women. I kicked him off the platform, and wired Winnipeg to get him recalled or I was through with the whole business. He left on the next train and we saw no more of him.[54]

This white-washed, thatched roofed and decorated house near Buchanan, Saskatchewan, photographed circa 1920, was typical of a traditional Ukrainian housing style that dotted the prairie landscape for several years (Courtesy of the Saskatchewan Archives Board/R-A6577-1).

Such incidents were clearly atypical. When Ukrainian immigrants were subject to coercion in settlement it was initiated by a local or regional official and was not at the behest of Ottawa. Department correspondence dealing with Ukrainian settlement contains no indication that the government ever contemplated the use of force in order to effect any clearly thought-out strategy in the settlement of Ukrainians in the Canadian West.

The Ukrainians' occupation of much sub-marginal territory was not a result of being forced to settle in areas to which they objected on environmental grounds. When coercion was applied it was to prevent the growth of large block settlements which were seen as a potential political danger by the ruling Anglo-Canadian elite. Immigrants were channelled only within the bounds of the parkland belt of the West where they preferred to settle. There is no documented case of coercion applied in a deliberate attempt to prevent Ukrainians from obtaining high quality land or to direct them on to inferior land. On the contrary, the Department of the Interior showed concern over the determination of some Ukrainians to settle on marginal lands so as to obtain a supply of timber or to secure the benefits of settlement alongside friends and relatives.[55] Rather than seek an explanation of the Ukrainians' occupation of extensive tracts of marginal land in the myth of governmental discrimination it should be sought elsewhere, in the strong links which bound Ukrainian peasant farmers together and caused them to want to go "where the others have gone."

Notes

This article first appeared in *Prairie Forum* 8, no. 2 (1983): 179–94.

1. William Harasym, "Ukrainian Values in the Canadian Identity," *Proceedings of Special Convention of United Ukrainian Canadians* (Winnipeg: Association of United Ukrainian Canadians, 1966), 67.

2. *Nor'Wester* (Winnipeg), 23 May 23, 1898.

3. Clifford Sifton, "The Immigrants Canada Wants," *Macleans Magazine* (April 1, 1922): 16, 13–35; also *Winnipeg Free Press*, February 26, 1923. Similar statements were made by officials of the Department of the Interior during Sifton's tenure as Minister. See, Canada, Parliament, *Sessional Papers*, "Annual Report of the Department of the Interior for 1897," 172.

4. Charles H. Young, *The Ukrainian Canadians* (Toronto: Thomas Nelson and Sons, 1931), 57. Young's statement has been quoted without comment by others who certainly do not approach the subject from a left-wing standpoint, but seem to accept his interpretation. See M.H. Marunchak, *The Ukrainian Canadians: A History* (Winnipeg: Ukrainian Free Academy of Sciences, 1970), 87.

5. Vera Lysenko, *Men in Sheepskin Coats* (Toronto: Ryerson Press, 1947), 33.

6. Petro Krawchuk, *The Ukrainians in Winnipeg's First Century*, trans. Mary Skrypnyk (Toronto: Kobzar Publishing Company, 1974), 13. See also Petro Krawchuk, *Na Novyj Zemli* [*In the New Land*] (Toronto: Tovarystva Ob'yednanykh Ukrains'kykh Kanadtsiv, 1958), 82–85.

7. Myrna Kostash, *All of Baba's Children* (Edmonton: Hurtig, 1977), 28; and Helen Potrebenko, *No Streets of Gold* (Vancouver, New Star Books, 1977), 38. Both Kostash and Potrebenko were mostly concerned with the social history of Ukrainian society after settlement at a time when active exploitation did take place. This paper confines itself to the active phase of placement in the land. It does not dispute the interpretations of Kostash or Potrebenko as applied to events in the post-settlement era.

8. Potrebenko, *No Streets*, 38–39.

9. Vladimir J. Kaye, *Early Ukrainian Settlements in Canada 1895–1900* (Toronto: University of Toronto Press for the Ukrainian Canadian Research Foundation, 1964); John C. Lehr, "The Government and the Immigrant: Perspectives on Ukrainian Block Settlement in the Canadian West," *Canadian Ethnic Studies* 9, no. 2 (1977): 42–52; and John C. Lehr and D. Wayne Moodie, "The Polemics of Pioneer Settlement: Ukrainian Immigration and the Winnipeg Press," *Canadian Ethnic Studies* 12, no. 2 (1980): 88–101.

10. For an account of Oleskow's role in Canadian immigration work see, Kaye, *Ukrainian Settlements*.

11. For a consideration of factors bearing upon the choice of location by Ukrainian settlers see John C. Lehr, "The Rural Settlement Behaviour of Ukrainian Pioneers in Western Canada 1891–1914," in Brenton M. Barr (ed.), *Western Canadian Research in Geography: The Lethbridge Papers*, BC Geographical Series, No. 21 (Vancouver: Tantalus Research, 1975), 51–66.

12. Library and Archives Canada (hereafter LAC), RG 76, Vol. 110, File 21103, pts. 1 and 2. Correspondence between Dr. Josef Oleskow, L'viv, and the Department of the Interior, Ottawa, 1895–1900.

13. Kaye, *Ukrainian Settlements*, pp. 135–63.

14. See, Lehr, "The Government and the Immigrant," 42–52.

15. Lehr and Moodie, "The Polemics of Pioneer Settlement," 88–101.

16. LAC, RG 76, Vol. 144, File 34214, pt. 2. William F. McCreary, Winnipeg, to James A. Smart, Ottawa, May 26, 1898.

17. *Winnipeg Telegram*, September 11, 1897.

18. *The Argus*, Stonewall, Manitoba, September 16, 1897.

19. In 1897, for example, Crown officials used their own funds to purchase bread and milk for destitute immigrants *en route* to Winnipeg. LAC, RG 76, Vol. 144, File 34214, pt. 1 (37224). Alfred Akerlindh to L.M. Fortier, Ottawa, May 8, 1897. This would seem to contradict Potrebenko's sweeping statement that Ukrainian immigrants, after arriving in Canada "were cheated by immigration agents ... and other parasites." Potrebenko, *No Streets*, 24.

20. LAC, RG 76, Vol. 144, File 34214, pt. 1. Correspondence between W.F. McCreary, Winnipeg, and James A. Smart, Ottawa, May–July 1897.

21. Ibid., File 34212, pt. 2.

22. John C. Lehr, "The Process and Pattern of Ukrainian Rural Settlement in Western Canada, 1891–1914" (PhD dissertation, University of Manitoba, 1978), 249–99.

23. Harry Piniuta (trans. and ed.), Land of Pain, Land of Promise: First Person Accounts by Ukrainian Pioneers 1891–1914 (Saskatoon: Western Producer Prairie Books, 1978), 85, 99–103; and Peter Humeniuk, *Hardships and Progress of Ukrainian Pioneers, Memoirs from Stuartburn Colony and Other Points* (Steinbach: Derksen Printers, n.d. [1979?]), 43–47.

24. Wasyl Mihaychuk, "Mihaychuk Family Tree" (typewritten manuscript, n.d.), 23; Michael Ewanchuk, *Spruce Swamp and Stone* (Winnipeg: The Author, 1977), 20, relates similar events taking place in the Gimli area of the Manitoba Interlake region settled by Ukrainians.

25. Michael Ewanchuk, *Pioneer Profiles, Ukrainian Settlers in Manitoba* (Winnipeg: The Author, 1981), 128–29.

26. *Winnipeg Telegram*, April 1, 1911.

27. LAC, RG 76, Vol. 144, File 34214 pt. 1 (37582). W.F. McCreary, Winnipeg, to James A. Smart, Ottawa, May 15, 1897. Nestor Dmytriw, the Ukrainian Uniate priest who worked as an immigration officer and interpreter for the Department of the Interior in 1897 gave an evaluation of the problems facing McCreary in *Kanadiyska Rus* [Canadian Ruthenia]. He substantiates McCreary's claims that some immigrants were reluctant to leave the Immigration Hall to seek land or to accept work in the city. Dmytriw's articles originally appeared in the Ukrainian newspaper *Svoboda* in 1898 but translations of some of his articles may be found in Piniuta, *Land of Pain*, 37–51.

28. McCreary to Smart, May 15, 1897, *op. cit.*

29. LAC, RG 76, Vol. 144, File 34214, pt. 1 (37807). W.F. McCreary, Winnipeg to James A. Smart, Ottawa, May 20, 1897.

30. Ibid. (39127). W.F. McCreary, Winnipeg, to the Secretary, Department of the Interior, June 18, 1897.

31. Ibid., pt. 2. Lyndwode Pereira, Ottawa, to J.A. Kirk, Halifax, May 26, 1898.

32. Ibid. (58012). Alex Moffet, Winnipeg, to James A. Smart, Ottawa, April 25, 1898.

33. Ibid. (58085). Frank Pedley, Ottawa, Telegram to W.F. McCreary, Winnipeg, April 27, 1898.

34. Ibid.

35. Ibid. (58120). W.F. McCreary, Winnipeg, Telegram to Frank Pedley, Ottawa, April 27, 1898.

36. Ibid. (58416). Alfred Akerlindh, Winnipeg, to Frank Pedley, Ottawa, May 3, 1898.

37. Ibid. (58850). W.F. McCreary, Winnipeg, to Frank Pedley, Ottawa, May 4, 1898.

38. Ibid.

39. Ibid. (59570). W.F. McCreary, Winnipeg, to James A. Smart, Ottawa, May 18, 1898.

40. Ibid.

41. LAC, RG 76, Vol. 144, File 34214, pt. 2 (59672). C.W. Speers, Saskatoon, Telegram to W.F. McCreary, Winnipeg, May 20, 1898.

42. William A. Czumer, *Recollections About the Life of the First Ukrainian Settlers in Canada* (Edmonton: Canadian Institute of Ukrainian Studies, 1981), 37–39.

43. LAC, RG 76, Vol. 144, File 34214, pt. 2 (59672). L.M. Herchmer, NWMP, Regina, to W.F. McCreary, Winnipeg, May 20, 1898.

44. Ibid. C.W. Speers, Saskatoon, Telegram to W.F. McCreary, Winnipeg, May 19, 1898.

45. Ibid. W.F. McCreary, Winnipeg, Telegram to C.W. Speers, Saskatoon, May 19, 1898.

46. Ibid.

47. Ibid. W.F. McCreary, Winnipeg, Telegram to C.W. Speers, Saskatoon, May 20, 1898.

48. Ibid.

49. Ibid. C.W. Speers, Saskatoon, Telegram to W.F. McCreary, Winnipeg, May 19, 1898.

50. Ibid. W.F. McCreary, Winnipeg, Telegram to C.W. Speers, Saskatoon, May 20, 1898.

51. Ibid. (59942). W.F. McCreary, Winnipeg, to James A. Smart, Ottawa, May 25, 1898.

52. Ibid. (60179). C.W. Speers, Winnipeg, to W.F. McCreary, Winnipeg, May 30, 1898.

53. Ibid. (59672). W.F. McCreary, Winnipeg, to James A. Smart, Ottawa, May 20, 1898

54. John Hawkes, *Saskatchewan and its People*, Vol. 2 (Chicago-Regina: The S.J. Clarke Publishing Co., 1924), 731.

55. LAC, RG 76, Vol. 144, File 34214, pt. 1. William F. McCreary, Winnipeg, to James A. Smart, Ottawa, May 14, 1897.

11.　Con Artist or Noble Immigration Agent? Count Esterhazy's Hungarian Colonization Effort, 1885–1902

Jason F. Kovacs

> Hungarian settlers were strongly influenced by a man who claimed to be of Hungarian royalty, Count Esterhaz [*sic*]. He was a fascinating man, a romantic figure, but he wasn't a count or even an Esterhaz. In fact he was more a con artist. An immigration agent by trade, he lured immigrants to settle the American and Canadian frontiers for a fee ... Esterhaz promised free farms, unbelievable yields from crops, and wealth for any man who could work. What he didn't mention was isolation, winters where the temperatures often reached forty below, and a heavy growth of trees that covered the good farming soil.[1]

The story of Count Paul O. d'Esterhazy's life is dynamic, and the above quote reflects the more recent presentation of Esterhazy as a "con artist" rather than as a "noble immigration agent." Certainly, most descendants of the original Hungarian pioneers who settled in the "Count's Colony," Esterhaz-Kaposvar (1886),[2] do not share this view of Esterhazy, many remembering him instead as a philanthropic, even heroic, figure. Nonetheless, a polarity in interpretations has long characterized Esterhazy's memory. As M.L. Kovacs has noted,

> Esterhazy's person has attracted numerous eulogists and vilifiers alike. He has been presented as a "scion" of one of the best known and richest aristocratic families of Hungary, and as a selfless warmhearted humanitarian. On the other hand, he has been censured an impostor apt to take advantage of everyone, who only assumed his name illegally for devious purposes.[3]

Figure 1. Johannes Packh, a.k.a Count Paul Oscar d'Esterhazy (1831–1912) (Courtesy of the Saskatchewan Archives Board/Pamphlet file: *Almanac of the Hungarian Golden Jubilee of Kaposvar-Esterhazy, 1886–1936*, p. 13).

These negative interpretations may be attributed to several factors: Esterhazy's disputed claim of aristocratic origins; his inflated expectations of the North-West in his 1902 immigration pamphlet; and the extreme hardships that his first groups of settlers encountered, hardships which are still remembered by their descendants.

The earliest attempt to assess Esterhazy's brief, but influential, role in initiating the first wave of Hungarian immigration to the Canadian Prairies was undertaken by A.A. Marchbin (1934). He credited Esterhazy with attempting to ameliorate the "hopeless life" of his exploited compatriots in the mining towns of Pennsylvania. Marchbin further attributed Esterhazy's brief colonization experiment with the government's subsequent extension of colonization efforts using the Austro-Hungarian immigration source.[4] A generation later, G.V. Dojcsák researched Count Esterhazy's putative aristocratic lineage and attempted to discern the origins of the "mysterious Count Esterhazy" (see Figure 1).[5] But it was M.L. Kovacs who produced the first in-depth study of the "Count's" role in attracting Hungarian immigrants to the Prairies by examining Esterhazy's immigration pamphlet, *The Hungarian Colony of Esterhaz, Assiniboia, North-West Territories* (1902).[6] Nevertheless, as Kovacs's work was primarily based on the historical context of Esterhazy's pamphlet, and while Dojcsák's work was confined primarily to the biography of Esterhazy, there is a need for a more detailed analysis of the pioneering years of the Esterhaz settlement (see Figure 2).[7] Accordingly, this paper will examine the formative period of Saskatchewan's first Hungarian colony, with the purpose of highlighting the complexities that underlay

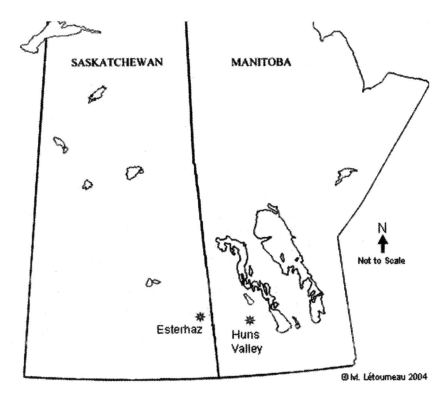

Figure 2. Location of the Esterhaz and Huns Valley Colonies.

colonization efforts. Although primarily concerned with Esterhazy's involvement with the Esterhaz colony, this paper will also address the less well known early history of his first Canadian Prairie settlement (1885), Huns Valley (Polonia), Manitoba.

Beginnings: "Land well fitted for Hungarian settlement"

On May 12, 1885, the governor-general's secretary, Henry Streatfield, acknowledged the receipt of a letter from Count Esterhazy that proposed a settlement scheme in the Canadian West.[8] It would involve Esterhazy's Hungarian brethren, in both the United States and Hungary itself, who the 'Count' proposed to settle in large numbers in the North-West Territories. Apart from farming, Esterhazy's Hungarian settlers would serve the Dominion as members of a local military force in the event of a feared Russian invasion. While eminently unrealistic from the modern perspective, a threat of war between the British Empire and Imperial Russia over their spheres of influence in Afghanistan was of great concern at the time.[9] While his proposed military settlement scheme was rejected, Esterhazy was notified of the possibility of settling Hungarian families onto "an immense tract of excellent land" in the North-West. Streatfield wrote,

> It Seems to His Excellency that if you are aware of the existence of a large number of Hungarian families who might be willing to effect a settlement in the Dominion You could not do better than place yourself in communication with the Department of Agriculture which is responsible for such matters with a view to obtaining a suitable location for a Settlement [...] The Dominion Government is anxious to attract to its territories eligible Settlers no matter from what country, and if the persons in whom you are interested have the qualities which you ascribe to them, they would His Excellency has no doubt receive the utmost encouragement.[10]

Esterhazy immediately forwarded to the Department of Agriculture a translated manuscript of a Hungarian circular that he had written, a number of copies of which his assistant, Géza de Döry, had already sent to several Hungarian communities in the United States:

> To my compatriots!

> After years of great exertions, and struggles with no trivial difficulties, I have, at last, succeeded in finding, here, the desired land, where each one of you may have an opportunity of building up a prosperous future, and happy homes, for your families. You are well aware of the fact, that my life's most ardent desire was always,—and it is even so now,—to assist in lifting my people out of the miserable condition of Servility, so peculiar to the hired "cheap" laborer, and despised Coal-miner,—that has been, in most of the cases, your lot,—in the United States; and to place them, where they deserve to be, in the independent, and respected position of Landowners, and farmers, and thus to insure them the rights, and privileges of franchised Citizens. This opportunity is now within your easy reach...

> I am about visiting that extensive tract of land, situated at no great distance, from the Canada Pacific Rail Road in the North West Territories of the Dominion of Canada. The incomparable productiveness of its Soil, and the healthy, and pleasant condition of its Climate, has already made this

part of the country considerably attractive to farmers, Stockraisers and settlers.—It is there the Royal Canadian Government offers, under certain conditions, a *free* homestead of 160 acres each, to every Settler. I shall send full, and satisfactory information, in this connection, to every One, who will address me *immediately*, who has an earnest desire of joining our Hungarian Colonization…[11]

It was anticipated that the offer of 160 acres of free land would be viewed favourably by the large numbers of Hungarians living in the mining towns of Pennsylvania. Esterhazy informed the Department of Agriculture that 1,000 printed copies of the circular would be required for the United States and Hungary, and that he planned to travel to the North-West to select suitable lands for Hungarian colonization.[12] Certainly, 1885 appeared to be a propitious year for Esterhazy's colonization endeavours: the Métis rebellion had been suppressed; the transcontinental railway was nearing completion; and the Canadian government, the Department of Agriculture in particular, appeared almost desperate for new settlers. For them, the prairie was a "graveyard of immigration schemes."[13] Accordingly, the government was quite anxious to support Esterhazy's plans. John Lowe, Secretary of the Department of Agriculture, urged A.M. Burgess, Deputy Minister of the Interior, that,

In view of the great importance of establishing this colonization, it is desired that effect should be given as promptly as possible, to the request of Count d'Esterhazy. A number of two hundred Hungarian families are shortly expected to arrive.[14]

Esterhazy's request was one that would involve a deviation from the Dominion Lands Act in that it entailed the consolidation of both even-numbered and odd-numbered free homestead lands. The latter were normally reserved for railway companies, but Esterhazy's plan argued for a block settlement that would facilitate the perpetuation of traditional Hungarian culture. He was aware that the even-odd division of lots served to disperse immigrants of different nationalities, thereby intensifying socio-cultural change; this strategy was in line with the government's objective of quickening the assimilation of new immigrants into the Anglo-Canadian linguistic and cultural sphere.

Both the Canadian Pacific Railway (CPR) and the Manitoba & North-Western Railway (MNWR) were willing to make the exchange. By promoting the large influx of Hungarians into the underpopulated West, they would derive revenue from the sale of lands, passage fares, and the increased freight traffic generated by effective settlement. Their enthusiasm to secure Esterhazy's Hungarians is apparent in a telegram from a land agent to the Deputy Minister of the Interior, A.M. Burgess: "Most important to encourage Hungarian settlement—large numbers will follow—hope you will arrange [land] exchange asked for—Railway doing everything possible to encourage these people..."[15] Burgess, however, disapproved of Esterhazy's request:

> To put this scheme in operation involves departure in several respects from the existing Land regulations... The system of dividing the public lands into odd and even numbered sections, the odd to be sold or granted in aid of the construction of railways, and the even to be open for homestead and pre-emption entry by actual settlers, was finally decided upon years ago, and the colonization of the North West has since proceeded on that principle without exception... I can conceive of a great many difficulties which might arise out of any change of a radical nature made at the present time.[16]

The commissioner of Dominion Lands at Winnipeg responded to Burgess, strongly urging his re-evaluation of the proposed land exchange.[17] While Burgess did not reconsider, A.F. Eden, the land commissioner for the MNWR would subsequently allow Esterhazy's first colonists to settle on some odd-numbered sections, a move which partly satisfied Esterhazy's initial request and contributed to the Department of the Interior's eventual decision to grant the exchange of even-odd lots.[18]

In late June, Esterhazy reported to the Department of Agriculture on his recent visit to the North-West. At the invitation of the lieutenant-governor of Manitoba and of the North-West Territories, and also of the land officers of the CPR and MNWR, Esterhazy had inspected lands in the Qu'Appelle Valley. Alongside Döry, a trained agronomist, Esterhazy had spent a week examining the soil and other natural resources in the region, and had come to the conclusion that the Qu'Appelle Valley was well suited for the establishment of agricultural colonies. The land inspected lay within the grant of the CPR, and encompassed parts of what would become the Esterhaz colony. It consisted of Township 17 Ranges 1 and 2; Township 18 Ranges 1 and 2; and Townships 19 and 19a, Ranges 1,2,3,4,5, West of the 2nd Principal Meridian. Esterhazy wrote,

> [T]his large tract, consisting chiefly of timbered land, but interspersed with prairies, clothed with natural grasses, and

adapted by soil and climate, with its two lakes (Crooked and Round Lake), and its innumerable ponds, was well fitted, in my estimation, for a Hungarian settlement of mixed farming operations.[19]

Prior to establishing the Esterhaz colony on some of the inspected Township lands, Esterhazy was directed to a highly forested tract of land northeast of the Qu'Appelle Valley in western Manitoba, where his assistant was to settle the first "Hungarian" settlers in the Canadian West.[20]

First Phase, 1885:
"Not all that we would like in the way of successful settlers"

On August 18, 1885, a land inspector in Minnedosa, a small market town in western Manitoba, reported on the arrival of the first contingent of Esterhazy's Hungarians.[21] Led by Döry, approximately 17 families were in the process of locating themselves on homestead lands some 18 miles northeast of the town along the valley of Stony Creek, southwest of the Riding Mountains, in Township 17 Range 16 West 1st Meridian. The colonists were from Hazleton in the eastern mining region of Pennsylvania, and were for the most part Slovaks or Hungarian-Slavonians, as they were then called. Although a second detachment of twelve families immediately joined the colony, a third group of 95 families left too late in the agricultural season to be incorporated into the colony that year. Theodore Zboray, the representative of the Hungarians at Hazleton Pennsylvania, traveled with the latter detachment. He reported that the prospect of acquiring 160 acres of free government land drove them "without fear of the potential consequences" to leave the coal region late in the season.[22] However, their late arrival in Manitoba forced the majority of them to accept work from the CPR and MNWR companies on a number of construction projects at Minnedosa, Manitou, Portage la Prairie, Sewell, Whitewood, and Regina for the duration of the fall and winter months. Moreover, their late arrival resulted in the first major setback in Esterhazy's Hungarian colonization scheme: at least 18 of the 95 families declined to accept the temporary winter employment on the various railway construction projects, and instead had taken shelter in an immigration building in Winnipeg. Their arrival led to some controversy about the character of Esterhazy's Hungarian settlers. One government immigration agent, for example, wrote:

> The Hungarians sent out here by Count Esterhazy, have not, up to date, been all that we would like, in the way of successful settlers … making the Immigration Sheds their head-quarters. […] They are simply resting here, until they

can go to the United States again, where some of them have already gone.[23]

A caretaker in Winnipeg, however, noted how ill-prepared the newly arrived immigrants were for outdoor work. For example, "J. Holok had a thin suit of clothes, a pair of leather boots, a pair of blankets, no mitts, and not one cent; while L. Petro [sic] had a thin coat and pants, no vest or boots, one pair of cloth mitts, a fur cap, one quarter of a blanket, and five dollars."[24] This reflected the indigent conditions that characterized most immigrants from Hungary at the time as well as the general lack of immediate support given by the Canadian immigration officials to the transitory migrant. Soon, a substantial number of potential settlers, including those who accepted work on the railway projects, left Manitoba for the few urban centres in the region or else returned to the United States. This failure to settle a substantial number of prospective settlers onto the demarcated land of western Manitoba, as well as the resultant controversy that took place around what was then termed an "experiment," was a precursor to a similar incident which would take place with Esterhazy's second colonization project.

For a short period, Esterhazy's first "Hungarian" settlement north of Minnedosa was known as the "New Hungary Colony," but it quickly became known as its post office name, "Huns Valley" (see Figure 3).[25] The Huns Valley colonists encountered numerous hardships. Zboray, for instance, had written in a letter to the Canadian government that the area

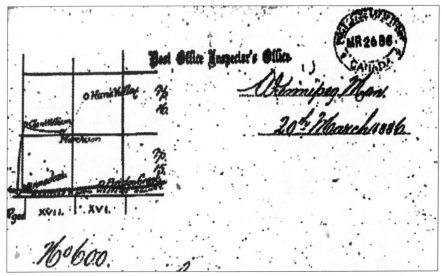

Figure 3. Postal inspection map of the Huns Valley colony, 1886. Source: LAC, RG 3, vol. 52, T-2174, P.O. Inspector, Winnipeg, to The Postmaster General, Ottawa, March 20, 1886.

settled by the first group of "Hungarians" was too thickly wooded, and of a too broken character to answer the purposes of a settlement. He also wrote that the land and the character of the soil at the Huns Valley settlement were not nearly as desirable as in that portion of the Qu'Appelle Valley near Whitewood, the future site of the Esterhaz colony, where apart from superior soils there was a better supply of water, and less brush and underwood. Indeed, upon inspecting the lands previously examined by Esterhazy and Döry, Zboray concluded that the lands of the Qu'Appelle Valley were "as good and desirable as that of the fertile districts of Hungary [and were] well adapted for the purpose of [the] Hungarian Colonization Scheme."[26]

Despite the substantial difference in soil and forest cover between the CPR and MNWR lands, within a year Esterhazy's first colony encompassed a total of 2,000 acres of land. Moreover, the original seventeen families that had taken up homesteads along the valley of Little Stony Creek were reported to have built substantial houses and stables, while a large part of their lands had been partly fenced in and cultivated.[27] Furthermore, a church and school were in the process of being constructed, a village site was being surveyed, and a petition for a post office was approved.[28] The Huns Valley colony was also adequately provided with food supplies: the colony had nine cows, six yoke of oxen, two ponies, and a substantial number of pigs and poultry, while approximately 700 pounds of flour, over 50 pounds of sugar, 10 pounds of tea, and one barrel of salt were stored within the newly constructed houses.[29] Döry provided a favourable report to Esterhazy on the condition of the Huns Valley colony, and commented that the settlers were more content in their new settings than they were in either Pennsylvania or Hungary.[30] Enlarging on this, he later pointed out the large reserve of some 500,000 Hungarian settlers living in the United States who were employed on the railroads and in the iron works, brickyards, cooper shops, and coalmines, many of whom had saved enough money and were thus fit for farming.[31] Esterhazy was able to proceed onto his second colonization project in the Assiniboia District largely on account of both the successful establishment of the Huns Valley colony and the numerical potential of this large immigration source.

Second Phase, Spring 1886:
"Serious trouble may ensue with these people"

The "Hungarian Immigration and Colonization Aid Society" was formed on March 13, 1886.[32] Initiated by Esterhazy and based in Philadelphia, the society was devoted to the promotion of Hungarian emigration to Canada. By the end of April, the society had secured approximately 50 Hungarian

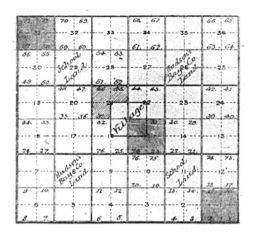

Figure 4. Esterhazy's proposed village site. Source: LAC, RG 7, vol. 141. (Shaded areas indicate the odd numbered sections of land; 1, 15, 21, 31, requested by Esterhazy.)

families in Pennsylvania for the North-West. As the president of the society, Esterhazy addressed the Minister of the Interior with a second request for an even-odd land exchange. In contrast to his earlier successful request for the Huns Valley colony, Esterhazy's newest request entailed the acquisition of an additional odd-numbered section of land on top of an authorized number of three odd sections per township. Esterhazy's request, therefore, would involve the formation of a more compact Hungarian enclave. Indeed, his request included a diagram showing a proposed "village site," and allotment of quarter section homestead lands to consist of 76 families settled together within "easy reach" of their homesteads (see Figure 4).

Owing to the untimely departure of the 50 Hungarian families from Pennsylvania *en route* to the North-West, Esterhazy was not in a position to wait for a reply on his newest request for the formation of a village. As such, the immigration agent was forced to immediately accept the Department of the Interior's original offer with regards to the even-odd land exchange, in hope that his own proposition would be given proper attention. By May 15, several Hungarian families from Ohio had reached Toronto while the large contingent from Pennsylvania was soon to arrive.[33] Although Esterhazy would have to wait for some time before obtaining a response on the proposed land exchange, the agent was promptly notified of a second request regarding financial assistance via Sir George Stephen, the president of the CPR. More specifically, in accordance with the provisions of the Dominion Lands Act, the minister of the Interior was prepared to create a lien in Sir George Stephen's favour upon the homesteads of each Hungarian settler, in return for a grant of capital.[34] The substantial advance of $25,000 would be divided up amongst the settlers in the form of $500 worth of oxen, cows, seeds, wagons, ploughs, and other farming implements while additionally covering the construction of their frame houses by the Canada North-West Land Company (CNWLC).[35]

Upon their arrival at Toronto, the Hungarian families from Pennsylvania

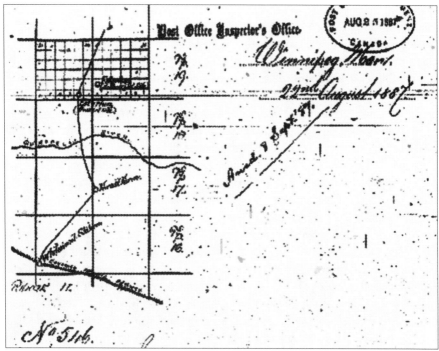

Figure 5. Postal inspection map of the Esterhaz colony, 1887. Source: LAC, RG 3, vol. 55, T-2177. P.O. Inspector, Winnipeg, to The Postmaster General, Ottawa, August 22, 1887.

and Ohio were met by Esterhazy, who accompanied them on their trip west. Unlike the settlers of Huns Valley, the group was for the most part ethnically Hungarian or Magyar. They reached Winnipeg by June 2, 1886. As with his first colonization effort, Esterhazy was able to secure free CPR transportation between Toronto and Winnipeg. Accompanied by approximately 40 families, which represented some 150 people, Esterhazy reached the lands north of the Qu'Appelle Valley, where he founded "Esterhaz" on June 19, in Township 19, Range 1 & 2, 22 miles north of Whitewood (see Figure 5). The settlers started to cultivate the land as soon as they had finished setting up their tents, and a town site in honour of their leader was laid out in the centre of the colony.[36] However, permission for the development of the eponymous village centre was not granted; instead, "Esterhaz" was limited to denoting the Hungarian colony in general.

Less than three months after the Esterhaz colony was established, and following an "urgent request" from Esterhazy, an "Esterhaz" post office was opened in the colony on Section 2, Township 19, Range 2 West of 2nd Principal Meridian. A post office inspector from Winnipeg had earlier described the proposed office as being "situated in a promising section of good country," eight miles south of the nearest office in the English Sumner Colony and 26 miles north of the office at Whitewood.[37] Although the office served only 32 Hungarian families, the postal inspector wrote that the settlement would likely expand rapidly. Indeed, the prompt establishment of the post office was meant to facilitate the correspondence of the settlers with their relatives and friends in Hungary and the United States, and therefore stimulate immigration and the expansion of the settlement.

In September, Esterhazy traveled to Pennsylvania to meet prospective Hungarian settlers at Phoenixville, Manch Chunk, Hazleton, Jeddo, Shamokin, Mount Carmel, and Tamaqua.[38] He also commissioned his own immigration agents in northern Hungary, but the landowning ruling elite were opposed to emigration as it threatened their pool of cheap labour. Consequently, they sought legal barriers towards immigration agents and encouraged anti-emigration propaganda. Although this had little success, it nevertheless posed problems for Esterhazy and he complained about "the well known antagonism by the Austro-Hungarian Government that seems to raise many difficulties and annoyances in the way of this people."[39] The difficulties that faced Esterhazy were not limited to Hungary. Esterhazy also referred to the problems that he had faced in the United States, where he had been subjected to insults by "hostile Irish miners and Liquor dealers."[40] In another letter, he had written of the personal threats to which he had been subjected by the "antagonistic, and anti-Canadian factions" because of the threat emigration posed to cheap labour supplies and local business profits.[41]

Nevertheless, by September Esterhazy had succeeded in selecting 60 men for the Esterhaz colony. Owing to the lateness of the season, and in the absence of instructions from the immigration authorities in Ottawa, Esterhazy advised the party to stay in Pennsylvania until they received "positive instructions." But the impatient Hungarians left the Pennsylvanian stations of Shenandoah, Mount Carmel, and Shamokin on October 1. Prompted by their impulsive decision, Esterhazy was forced to leave Ottawa for Owen Sound, where he met the ill-prepared group. Their fate seemed dismal. Esterhazy had been notified by W.C. Van Horne, the vice-president of the CPR, that the loans furnished by Sir George Stephen only applied to the first 50 Hungarian families of the colony.[42] Esterhazy appealed to John Carling, the Minister of Agriculture, for assistance:

> I have not been idle, in my efforts to obtain from other sources the assistance that is now so much needed, and without which, especially at this season of the year, the greatest suffering must ensue to the immigrants,—but all my efforts have so far, failed me, and the call for help is now

imminent.—Under these circumstances, in order to avert a great calamity to this Colonization Enterprise, I have no alternative but to place this matter before you.[43]

He also warned Carling that the Esterhaz venture was being closely watched by the numerous Hungarian labourers in the United States. Its success, which depended on his garnering of funds on behalf of the newest detachment, would "determine the ultimate Settlement of an immense number in Canada, without the employment of Immigration Agents, and the attendant expense."[44] Esterhazy's written request for $15,000 or $250 per family was, however, in vain: only $500 for transportation and provisions was authorized by the minister for Esterhazy's newest cohort of Hungarians, a measure which in itself only served to encourage the continued westward movement of the group. After learning of their departure for the North-West, Van Horne wrote:

> We were entirely in ignorance of the departure of this party from Pennsylvania until we received d'Esterhazy's dispatch … [I]n my opinion serious trouble may ensue with these people during the coming winter, and that the Company can assume no responsibility in the matter.[45]

Van Horne's opinion was, in part, correct. Esterhazy was soon informed that many of the settlers of Esterhaz were out of both flour and credit, and were thus on the verge of leaving the colony. To make matters worse, a prairie fire had swept through the Esterhaz colony in early October, resulting in the loss of a considerable portion of the colony's hay and timber supply. The prairie fire also slowed the construction of houses and weakened the colony's capability of absorbing the incoming group of Hungarians. By mid-October, only 12 out of 35 frame houses in the course of construction were completed. Consequently, on their arrival at Whitewood on October 21, the Hungarian immigrants (50 men, 5 women, and 7 children) were not allowed to travel north to the colony.

In late October, Esterhazy had signed a contract with the Moore & Hunter Coal and Wood Merchants of Winnipeg, the operators of the Medicine Hat coalmines, as a temporary strategy to tide over the new arrivals.[46] However, it was destined to fail. One week after departing for Cleveland and Phoenixville, Pennsylvania, to meet with 75 families and discuss prospects in the Canadian North-West, Esterhazy received news of the earlier exodus of the Hungarian arrivals from the mine. Refusing to abide by their own contract, the managers of the mine had apparently attempted to take advantage of the immigrants. A letter written by members of the group briefly employed with the coalmine revealed how pointless it was to remain at the mine after Esterhazy's departure:

> [W]e were taken to the coal mines at Medicine Hat, where we were put to work at rates as follows:—Until the mine was cleared of water $1.00 per day, *with* board,—As soon, however, as we had cleared the mine we found that instead of $1.00 per day, with board, we were only paid at the rate of $1.00 per day, deducting from this .75 cents for board, leaving only .25 cents as pay. Even this we could not get from the foreman he alleging that he had paid on our account to Esterhazy $500.00, which that gentleman claimed in payment of our Railway fare from Pennsylvania to the Canadian North West.[47]

The management at the Saskatchewan coalmine also raised food prices for the Hungarian workers who, half-starved, left for the nearby town of Medicine Hat. Ten settlers from the Esterhaz colony had also sought work in the coalmines of Lethbridge, where conditions were similarly distressing: several families were reported to be in destitute conditions and to have taken refuge in a government immigration building in Brandon, Manitoba.[48]

Faced with these developments, W.B. Graham, an agent of the Department of Immigration, commented, "I do not wish to throw cold water on Esterhazy's labours, but I do say, that, so far they have been anything but a success, and have done more harm than good to the cause of immigration."[49] Moreover, in his annual report on the various ethnic settlements of Manitoba and the North-West, Graham had written: "This [Hungarian] immigration, while it has shown features which are highly satisfactory, giving assurances of success, has had some exceptional features of a contrary nature."[50] Further, a lengthy correspondence ensued between the caretakers in Medicine Hat and Brandon and government agents over expenditures on food for the impoverished families. However, Esterhazy was not in a position to travel back to the prairies and remedy the situation. He was too busy reacting to new problems being encountered by the first Hungarian families that were arriving in Canada directly from Europe.

Third Phase, Fall 1886: "The necessity of remaining at home"
In late November, Esterhazy traveled to Montreal to investigate a story that involved the ill-treatment of several newly arrived Hungarian immigrants prior to their crossing of the Atlantic. Soon after his arrival in Montreal, he was informed of the presence of a second group of Hungarian immigrants in impoverished conditions. As with the first group that had come to

Canada earlier on in the month, the second party (four men, three women, and two children) had been swindled out of their meager resources in Hamburg by a steamship agent. The agent had taken all of their money in payment for their passage to Montreal, assuring them that their tickets would be valid for their trip to the North-West. However, the tickets did not take them anywhere beyond the Montreal station. On the very same day, a telegram from Portland, Quebec, was sent to Ottawa: "Two Hungarian women with five children here a week—waiting [for] money from husbands in Count Esterhazy's settlement near Whitewood."[51] As a result of the dismal events in both the Prairie West and across the Atlantic, Esterhazy was prompted to write to Lowe:

> I have addressed to the people of Hungary who are now
> preparing to leave that country ... to urge upon the necessi-
> ty of remaining at home during the winter and await my
> further instruction early next spring [...] those who should
> act contrary to these instructions, shall on their arrival here,
> assume all risks and responsibilities.[52]

Esterhazy had not expected any Hungarian immigrants to arrive until the following spring. The unexpected arrival of the destitute Hungarians, however, led him to believe that the letters he had sent to prospective settlers in northeastern Hungary had been confiscated by local authorities. Esterhazy recognized he had to remedy the problem overseas. In early December, he acquired free passage from Montreal to Liverpool by the Allan Line Steamship to investigate the whereabouts of the money swindlers and to establish with the steamship agents in Hamburg a "proper system of transportation of the Hungarians to the North-West."[53] By late December, Esterhazy had notified the Department of an additional three cases involving 15 potential colonists who were stranded in New York and Philadelphia. In early January, he was approached by one relative in the Esterhaz colony whose brother was put onto a boat to New York and on his arrival charged a considerable amount of money for a train ticket to the Canadian North-West. Unable to muster support from Canada to sort out the problems at Hamburg that had affected at least 40 intending settlers, Esterhazy's patience with the immigration officials of Ottawa had grown thin:

> I am called upon by my people to afford them protection,
> with all the influence and power at my command, against
> all possible calamities incidental to a journey to such a dis-
> tant part of the world; they expect me, as a matter of course,
> to insure them a *direct*, and *safe* transportation from the

Other Side of the Ocean, to the Hungarian Colonies in the NorthWest[...] I cannot divine the reason why the Department, considering the facts given, should insist on treating this important matter with such marked indifference. [T]his unaccountable apathy places me in a piteous predicament, and it shall surely have the effect of Seriously shaking that confidence which my people have heretofore reposed in the Colonization Scheme, more especially if they discover that the sympathy, of the Canadian Government with Our cause in Canada, has no foundation in fact by present appearances.[54]

What Esterhazy was probably unaware of was the fact that conditions in the Huns Valley colony were deteriorating to the point that more settlers were leaving the colony for the immigrant sheds of Brandon and Winnipeg. Indeed, while the demoralized Hungarian immigrants from the coal mine incident were forced to seek shelter in various immigrant sheds, and while those destitute on their arrival in Montreal experienced a similar discouraging introduction to Canada, the settlers of Esterhazy's second colony were not in a much better situation. The settlers of Esterhaz were ill-equipped for what was to be one of the coldest winters in living memory. The severity of the winter of 1886 was magnified by the fact that the newly constructed frame houses provided limited insulation from the cold. Finally, the colonists lacked hay and timber supplies as well as adequate provisions of food and winter clothing. As such, life in the colony became unbearable for the majority of them; they left, and so posed a problem for Esterhazy's future schemes.

Official Reactions, 1887: "The suspension of all operations"
As a result of the exoduses from both coal mine and colony as well as the late arrival of many impoverished Hungarian families in the East, government agencies began to doubt the viability of Esterhazy's Hungarian colonization scheme. The decision was taken to stop the arrival of settlers for the coming spring season of 1887, and Esterhazy's status as a special agent of the government was put under review. As early as mid-February, Esterhazy queried the Department of Agriculture about his future:

The Minister having considered it again advisable to decline to authorize me to take any action, to promote Hungarian Immigration to Canada,—I would beg most respectfully to place before him [...] copies of letters, extracts, reports regarding the two Hungarian Settlements,

"HunsValley" Manitoba, and "Esterhaz," Assa. North West
Territories, both having been established under my directions [...] I would humbly request that, prior to the
Suspension of all its operations, and to its final abandonment, the circumstances leading to this measure, and all the
facts connected with it may be brought to the notice of His
Excellency the Governor General in Council.[55]

The Department failed to provide instructions regarding a large group of
Hungarians in the United States that awaited Esterhazy's definite answer on
permission to emigrate to the North-West. This prompted a second letter to
the Department a month later: "[An] unhappy condition prevails in Ithaca
N.Y., Phoenixville, Penn. and Cleveland, Ohio, where immigration to
Canada is now awaiting, with a degree of impatience, the signal to make
ready for the start."[56] The extent of the failure of Esterhazy's initial colonization scheme, however, was not lost on some government officials. Esterhazy
was not granted permission to continue with his Hungarian colonization
scheme for the spring season, and he temporarily abandoned his Hungarian
colonization efforts. In a letter dated September 14, 1887, Esterhazy
explained his newest effort to overcome his recent failure:

I am now making efforts to correct the errors which were
unwittingly made in the first experiment [...] I am now
employing trustworthy Agents in Bohemia, to invite and
select amongst the well to do farmers... This is a class of
people in every respect superior to the Hungarian
Slavonian Immigrant [...] there [are] no people on the face
of our globe, so thoroughly suited for the North West
Settlements, and with surer promises to make permanent
and successful farmers than these Bohemians. They will not
become a burden to your Government.[57]

Esterhazy assured Burgess that over 100 families were ready to depart
from their homes in Bohemia for the North-West Territories, and enquired
whether the townships held by his colonization enterprise could be reserved
for another 12 months.[58] The Department's response must have been devastating: "The class of settlers [Esterhazy] has been instrumental in bringing
into the country has not been a desirable one and the Commissioner has no
confidence in his scheme for the future."[59] The minister of the Interior subsequently ruled out reviving the reserve lands for the proposed Bohemian
colonization scheme until the Department had "had an opportunity of seeing how the experiment already tried with the Hungarian settlers

operate[d]."[60] Despite an attempt to overcome the lingering controversy surrounding the initial exodus and coal mine scandal —events which were outside of his control—Esterhazy could not strengthen his already tentative position with the government. In the fall of 1887, Count Esterhazy was formally dismissed as special agent for the promotion of Hungarian immigration. Lowe wrote: "[Esterhazy] was very active in promoting Hungarian Immigration ... but he was found to be too sanguine and so made promises which caused subsequent troubles."[61] However, in the very same letter Lowe, who appreciated Esterhazy's work, had also written that there was no reason why Esterhazy "should not have the same colonization advantages in the North West as any others." Further, the vice-president of the CPR wrote to Esterhazy the following year to compliment him for his colonization efforts:

> I know quite well who directed the first Hungarians to the
> North West, and I shall always give you credit for all who
> go there, because none would have gone had you not start-
> ed the movement. I am sorry that the authorities at Ottawa
> have not seen fit to give you a better support in the matter
> ... Perhaps they may yet come to appreciate the importance
> of your work.[62]

It would appear, therefore, that the decision by the minister of Agriculture, the Hon. John Carling, to discontinue Esterhazy's services must have been influenced by Graham's report of December 9, 1886, that the "whole outfit" of Count Esterhazy and his colonization scheme were a fraud. Certainly, Sir George Stephen's loss of some of the principal monies advanced to some of the departed settlers also contributed to Esterhazy's dismissal. Despite his discharge as a salaried agent of the government, Esterhazy regularly inquired into the affairs of his settlements thereafter and continued to encourage Hungarian immigration to the Canadian North-West. Moreover, he would continue to correspond regularly with settlers in both colonies as well as with government officials on developments that unfolded in the settlements. Thus, substantial information on the early history of Esterhaz and to a lesser extent Huns Valley, following his official dismissal, can be readily found in the numerous extant letters written to the "Count."

One such letter, written in 1887 by Döry, describes conditions in the recently depopulated colony: "[A]n opportunity was afforded to me quite recently to visit Esterhaz, where I remained 8 days [...] I availed myself, on that occasion, [to] look around the Colony, and to take observations of all of its good and bad features." According to Döry, 12 of the houses in the colony

Figure 6. Early photograph of a farmstead in the Esterhaz colony, n.d. (probably 1890s). Source: University or Regina Archives, "Kovacs, Martin Papers."

were untenanted, but eight families who had just arrived had "undoubtedly" taken possession of eight of the empty frame structures (see Figure 6).[63] Thus, a clearer picture emerges on the numbers involved in the exodus of 1886–87. A later report written by the postmaster of Esterhaz indicated that only one quarter of the original pioneers brought by Esterhazy remained in the colony the following year, while Esterhazy placed the number of families that left at 24.[64] Conditions in the colony, however, must have significantly improved because the remaining settlers were described by Döry as being "very well pleased with their condition and prospects; they had an ample harvest of excellent crops, especially of roots and vegetables."

Another letter to Esterhazy from Joseph Hendrych, a Czech settler from a Bohemian colony to the southwest of Esterhaz, provides further information on the socio-economic condition of the colony. According to Hendrych, the soils were "excellent" and consisted of black humus with rich sandy subsoil. The year's harvest was not satisfactory, however, owing to the "yet unbroken condition of the virgin soil."[65] More importantly, Hendrych also wrote that although the "climate is very healthy" it is "severe during the winter," and that they had "so far, no reason to complain of our neighbours the Hungarian settlers: it is, however, much desired that an increase of respectable families from our own nationality should soon be brought amongst us, so as to help to infuse more vitality in our colony." However, largely owing to Esterhazy's continued correspondence overseas, the colony of Esterhaz had received approximately twenty more Hungarian families from Hungary itself that year. As such, the Esterhaz colony consisted of some 36 families in 1888, a figure that closely matched the original number that had arrived in the spring of 1886. Esterhazy was therefore in a good position to comment on his successful work to the Department of Agriculture:

> The permanency of the two Hungarian settlements [...] is now a fact beyond peradventure; and the steady and persistent increase of the number of desirable Settlers, by the operation of the Immigration and Colonization scheme, to which I have devoted much time and arduous labor, would seem to hold out the fairest hopes of success, and prosperity of these colonies.[66]

In early February 1889, Rufus Stephenson, a settlement inspector forwarded a highly favourable report on the Esterhaz colony, arguing that the settlement was flourishing and promised to grow in wealth and numbers since some 60 families were expected in the coming spring and summer. Moreover, they would be of a "desirable" class. In order to highlight the encouraging re-growth of the "Hungarian" colony, which was by then composed of both Magyar and Slavic settlers, the inspector imparted an unsympathetic view on those who had left the colony in the 1886–87 exodus:

> [They had] returned to the vicinity of Pittsburg and to the city of New York from whence they came. [They] were not a desirable class, being for the most part rough and uncultivated and in some instances vicious and criminal [and] it is the generally expressed opinion that Canada is better off without them.[67]

On receiving a copy of Stephenson's inspection, Esterhazy immediately wrote the Department of Agriculture to challenge the inspector's claim that a better class of people had replaced those that had left:

> Let me assure you that these people were just as a first rate lot and a very great acquisition to the country [however] during my absence in the East, and by reason of my inability to return to Esterhaz, because of the lack of support received to that effect from your Government, these good people became demoralized, and disgusted and left Esterhaz.[68]

Esterhazy blamed Julius Vass, the postmaster of the colony, who had claimed he had the "entire confidence of the colonists" and was the "real power of the colony." For Esterhazy, the poor situation at Esterhaz during the harsh winter was exacerbated by the "mismanagement" and "rascalities" of Vass, who was appointed government immigration agent and caretaker at Whitewood in early May 1890. He was right: Vass was later prosecuted for embezzling monies belonging to several of the settlers of the Esterhaz colony, and committed suicide that year in a hotel at Wapella.[69]

Official Assessments, 1891–94:
"The desire to improve the condition of his countrymen"

By 1891, circumstances surrounding the Hungarian colonization experiment had markedly improved, and an agent of the Department of Agriculture could report that "there is no class of foreigners who have done better in this country than the Danish and Hungarian settlers."[70] On receiving a copy of the highly favourable letter, Esterhazy offered to direct a large number of Hungarian families from the American North-West to the Canadian Prairies, families which Esterhazy had selected for a proposed colony in the state of Texas. He further emphasized in his letter that he could induce 1,000 families to emigrate from Minnesota and Nebraska to the North-West, and that the settlers would have adequate savings for colonization purposes.[71] Despite a highly encouraging reply by the Department of Agriculture, Esterhazy's settlement scheme never materialized.

Later that year, a joint report on Esterhazy's two colonies provided further evidence of the significant redevelopment of the Esterhaz colony, whose population was now estimated at 350 persons. Commenting on the agricultural progress of the colony, R.S. Park wrote that it was 'simply marvelous.' Aside from listing some of the cash crops that were being cultivated for sale in Whitewood, and noting the fine appearance of the colony's cattle, the inspector also commented on the presence of post offices, schools, and churches there.[72] Indeed, with regards to the Hungarian portion of the increasingly ethnically diverse colony, a log church had been erected that year which immediately replaced the post office as the central focus of the Catholic settlement. According to Park, it was the presence of such institutions in the colony which ensured the prosperity of the settlement.

In May 1893, Esterhazy warned the deputy minister of Agriculture of a threatened collapse of the Esterhaz colony:

> The people of Esterhaz write to me now that the moment for decisive action, on their part, had arrived, and they seem to be in desperate earnest about it,—they emphatically declare to be prepared to abandon the Colony en masse,

and propose to [report] the circumstances that brought
about such collapse [by] means of letters, and newspaper
reports—unless Your Government takes immediate measures to have their intolerable grievances enquired into and
speedily remedied.[73]

The grievances that Esterhazy brought forward on behalf of the settlers
amounted to a series of earlier mistakes which were made by a land agent
who had selected and completed homestead entries for a significant number
of the Hungarian settlers. Owing to the earlier consent given, many settlers
had been residing for years upon lands for which entries could not be legally granted. These settlers had entered the colony soon after the 1886–87 exodus, and had occupied the abandoned homestead lands. For Esterhazy, the
colonists' fear of being potentially removed from their farmsteads amounted to what he called the "insupportable afflictions [which were] visited
[upon] honest and hard working people by the godless management of a
Vampire Land Agency."[74] Increasing dissatisfaction within the colony was
not, however, restricted to the post-1887 settlers. In 1894, Ruttan, assistant
secretary of the Dominion Lands Commission, visited Esterhaz to obtain
information on the internal conditions of the colony. His report placed
greater emphasis on the uneasiness that prevailed amongst the ten remaining pioneer settlers of 1886.[75] According to Ruttan, it was their apprehension
regarding the existence of the original lien that appeared to affect more or
less the entire colony. The settlers claimed that they had not received the
actual value of their loans, for instead of receiving cash they were provided
with oxen and implements for common use. Moreover, while houses could
be built by the settlers with a cash outlay of $25, the original frame structures
which were built by the CNWLC cost between $200 to $300 each.

Ruttan's report highlighted the financial problems faced by the early settlers, which emanated from mistakes made by land agents and government
officials alike. It provides a more realistic picture of the conditions of the
colony. Thus, while accumulated cattle, machinery, and small stock had
"placed the settlers in a fair earning capacity," the farmers found it difficult
to subsist on their year's light crop, which received low prices, as did their
cattle and pigs. Ruttan argued that their inability to afford more livestock
placed the settlers in a very precarious position, especially in the face of the
"not infrequent" crop failure that occurred in nearly all sections of the
prairie lands. He also reported that the chief difficulties included distance to
the nearest market place of Whitewood and, in contrast to Stephenson's
report, the colonists' poor comprehension of English. Ruttan also attempted
to determine what relation Count Esterhazy still had with the Esterhaz

colonists, an objective that no doubt derived from the numerous enquiries that Esterhazy regularly sent the Department. It appeared that Esterhazy was not authorized to represent the Hungarian colony as a whole, but rather was merely acting as a mediator for individuals with grievances towards the Department. Significantly, Ruttan commented on the motives underlying Esterhazy's numerous enquiries into the affairs of the settlers:

> Neither in my interview with these people nor in the information afforded by the papers in our possession is there anything to indicate that Count d'Esterhazy, so far as he has participated in this work, has been actuated by any other motive than the desire to improve the material condition and prospects of his countrymen. Those now in the colony have been in the habit of submitting their difficulties to him, believing that his intercession with the Government will lead to relief that they cannot hope for as a result of direct appeal. They are able to write him in their own language and no doubt this is chiefly why they seek his assistance [...]

> Count d'Esterhazy in so far as his enterprise of settling these people is concerned deserves their thanks and any consideration that our Department may find it possible to extend. I saw this in the firm conviction that however biased and unwarranted the views which he now entertains as to the responsibility for the mistakes from which the colonists suffer his own effort to establish them was prompted solely by a desire for the improvement of the condition of his countrymen; and that in a minor degree he has accomplished this, greatly to their advantage and with benefit also to the section of the Territories in which his countrymen are resident.[76]

Conclusion: Con Artist or Noble Immigration Agent?

Despite an unusually severe winter following the establishment of Esterhazy's second colony in 1886, a winter which resulted in an almost complete abandonment of the colony, the Esterhaz settlement managed to survive and eventually prosper with the subsequent influx of additional Hungarian families. The rapid regrowth of the Hungarian colony was in no small measure a result of Esterhazy's tireless efforts to encourage the settling of the Canadian Prairies even after his status as special agent for Hungarian immigration and colonization was revoked. Moreover, Esterhazy continued

Figure 7. Hungarian silver jubilee honour guard, 1911. Source: Kaposvar Historic Site Society. *Kaposvar: A Count's Colony 1886–1986.*

to act as an intermediary between the Hungarian colonists and government agents well after his departure from the Prairie West. Accordingly, he was well received by the settlers of Esterhaz during his visit to the colony in 1902 for the purpose of compiling his immigration pamphlet. Further, Esterhazy's work was fittingly acknowledged that year in the naming of a newly constructed railway station in the colony's vicinity, the precursor to the establishment of the ethnically diverse village of "Esterhazy" in 1903. More importantly, Esterhazy was later sent an invitation to attend the colony's silver jubilee (1911, see Figure 7). Owing to his failing health, Esterhazy was unable to undertake the long trip from his residence in New York to his toponymic namesake; nevertheless, he promptly responded with a congratulatory letter:

> Upon this solemn occasion I beg God to bless you with His choicest blessings for the meritorious labor you have realized. […] My dear countrymen, may you live in peace and happiness. This is my sincere wish and desire.[77]

Controversy has ensued over the extent to which Esterhazy's colonization enterprises were a success. It appears that Ruttan's assessment of Esterhazy's underlying motive was correct: rather than a charlatan who lured a mass of ex-peasants to the Canadian Prairies for his own devious agenda, Esterhazy may be more accurately understood as a man who earnestly sought to better the socio-economic conditions of his fellow countrymen.[78] Surely, that he may have earned legitimate commissions in doing so, and that he may have not in fact been of aristocratic origins, should not detract from his noble motives and efforts. Count Esterhazy undoubtedly deserves to be remembered not only as the founder of the oldest and richest Hungarian settlement in Saskatchewan,[79] but also as an important catalyst for early Hungarian and Slavic immigration to Canada.

Notes

This article first appeared in *Prairie Forum* 31, no. 1 (2006): 39–60. It is a revised excerpt from my M.A. thesis "Establishing a Place, Constructing an Identity: A Case Study of Place-making in Esterhazy, Saskatchewan" (Department of Geography, Queen's University, 2003). I would like to thank my Master's supervisor, Dr. Brian S. Osborne, for his advice during my thesis research, and his editorial assistance with this paper. I would also like to thank Marcus Létourneau and Robert Huish for their assistance.

1. Video, "Kaposvar: The Faith of Lajos Nagy." Directed by S. Onda (White Pine Pictures, 2000). For a positive interpretation of Count Esterhazy see: *Kaposvar Historic Site Society, Kaposvar: A Count's Colony 1886–1986* (Yorkton: Dowie Quick Print, 1986).

2. The Kaposvar place name became associated with the predominantly Hungarian populated portion of the colony by 1892. Moreover, the Esterhaz place name was largely forgotten after the establishment of the nearby village of Esterhazy (1903). However, for the purpose of this article Esterhaz will be used to denote the Hungarian colony.

3. Martin L. Kovacs [no relation to the author], *Esterhazy and Early Hungarian Immigration to Canada: A Study Based Upon the Esterhazy Immigration Pamphlet* (Regina: Canadian Plains Research Center, 1974), ix.

4. Andrew A. Marchbin, "Early Emigration from Hungary to Canada," *The Slavonic Review* 13 (1934–35): 127–38.

5. G.V. Dojcsák, "The Mysterious Count Esterhazy," *Saskatchewan History* 26 (1973): 63–72. Dojcsák was unable to conclude with certainty whether or not Esterhazy (*né* J.B. Packh) was a legitimate son of the Esterhazy family. Dojcsák also published a book in Hungarian, *Kanadai Esterházy Története* [*The Story of the Canadian Esterhazy*] (Budapest: Magvetö, 1981), which contained his earlier biographic research as well as a short history of Western Canada.

6. Kovacs, *Esterhazy and Early Hungarian Immigration to Canada.*

7. Aside from several works by M.L. Kovacs, shorter research papers pertaining to the Hungarian colony of Esterhaz-Kaposvar include Donald E. Willmott's "Ethnic Solidarity in the Esterhazy area, 1882–1940," in M.L. Kovacs (ed.), *Ethnic Canadians: Culture and Education* (Regina: Canadian Plains Research Center, 1978), 167–76; Ferenc Andai, "Az Észak-Nyugat Kanadai Magyar Telepesek Helyzete a Századfordulón," ["The Status of Hungarian Settlers in Northwestern Canada at the Turn of the Century"] *Történelmi Szemle* 27, no. 3 (1984): 433–44.

8. Library and Archives of Canada (hereafter LAC), RG 17, vol. 525, D-58067, letter from Streatfield, Ottawa, to Esterhazy, New York, May 12, 1885. It is likely that as founder of the "First Hungarian American Colonization Company," Esterhazy had been approached by the CPR and informed of the opportunities in the Canadian North-West prior to his initial colonization proposal.

9. Martin L. Kovacs (ed.), "Settlement, Depression and Alienation: An Episode from Early Prairie History," in *Roots and Realities among Eastern and Central Europeans* (Edmonton: Central and East European Studies Association of Canada, 1983), 138.

10. LAC, RG 17, vol. 525, D-58067, letter from Streatfield to Esterhazy, May 12, 1885.

11. LAC, RG 17, vol. 442, D-48251-80, letter from Esterhazy, Montreal, to J. Lowe, Secretary of the Department of Agriculture, May 30, 1885.

12. Ibid.

13. Kovacs, "Settlement, Depression and Alienation," 138.

14. LAC, RG 15, vol. 348, T-13070, letter from Lowe to Burgess, June 26, 1885.

15. LAC, RG 15, vol. 435, T-13070, letter from F.H. Brydges, Winnipeg, to Burgess, July 10, 1885.

16. LAC, RG 15, vol. 348, T-13070, letter from Burgess to McLelan, July 13, 1885.

17. LAC, RG 15, vol. 420, T-13070, letter from Smith to Burgess, July 30, 1885.

18. LAC, RG 15, vol. 385, T-13070, in letter from Smith to Burgess, August 13, 1885.

19. Sessional Papers (no. 10) A. 1886, "Report on Hungarian Colonization," report from Esterhazy to Minister of Agriculture, June 25, 1885. The railway companies agreed to hold the inspected townships on reserve for a year.

20. Esterhazy's plan was to place approximately 100 families from Pennsylvania under Döry's leadership to settle lands within the grant of the MNWR, while he would lead an equal number of families onto the lands of the CPR.

21. LAC, RG 15, vol. 377, T-13070, letter from N.D. Ennis to T. White, Ottawa, August 18, 1885.

22. LAC, RG 17, vol. 457, D-49848, letter from T. Zboray, Luzerne, U.S.A., to The Government of the Dominion of Canada (Translated by Esterhazy), October 12, 1885.

23. LAC, RG 17, vol. 459, D-50127, letter from Graham to Lowe, November 3, 1885.

24. LAC, RG 17, vol. 469, D-51272, letter from C.F. Herbert, Winnipeg, January 20, 1886.

25. Although Huns Valley was primarily populated by Slavic settlers, the colony had what was later claimed to be the first Hungarian language school in North America (1887–89). See D.G. Berko (ed.), *Amerikai Magyar Népszava: Jubileumi diszalbuma 1899–1909* [*American Hungarian People's Voice Jubilee Album*] (1910), 67.

26. LAC, RG 17, vol. 457, D-49848, letter from Zboray to The Government of the Dominion of Canada, October 12, 1885.

27. Sessional Papers (no. 12) A. 1887, "Report on Hungarian Immigration and Colonization," report from Esterhazy to The Minister of Agriculture, December 31, 1886.

28. LAC, RG 17, vol. 525, D-58067, letter from Eden to Esterhazy, July 14, 1886; RG 3, vol. 53, T-2175, letter from Eden to The Postmaster General, October 21, 1886.

29. LAC, RG 17, vol. 517, D-57001-030, "Hungarian Colony Tp16, R16, West," October 29, 1886; RG 17, vol. 525, D-58067, letter from Döry, Huns Valley, to Esterhazy, New York, January 10, 1887.

30. LAC, RG 17, vol. 525, D-58067, letter from Döry to Esterhazy, January 10, 1887.

31. LAC, RG 17, vol. 545, D-60878, letter from Döry to Eden, July 20, 1887.

32. LAC, RG 17, vol. 481, D-52774, letter from Esterhazy, Philadelphia, to Carling, May 5, 1886. Esterhazy was elected president, Theodore Zboray vice-president and Julius Vass secretary and treasurer of the society.

33. LAC, RG 15, vol. 348, T-13070, telegram from Esterhazy, Toronto, to Burgess, May 15, 1886.

34. LAC, RG 15, vol. 348, T-13070, letter from Burgess to C. Drinkwater, Secretary, C.P.R., Montreal, May 17, 1886.

35. LAC, RG 76, vol. 20, C-4678, "Lengyel Jozsef's account of life in early Esterhaz," July 20, 1902.

36. LAC, RG 17, vol. 505, D-55534, letter from Esterhazy to Carling, October 1, 1886; RG 17, vol. 525, D-58067, extract from *Manitoba Free Press*, July 2, 1886. The colony was named after the Eszterháza palace in the vicinity of Fertöd in western Hungary, which was the seat of the Esterházy family.

37. LAC, RG 3, vol. 53, T-2175, letter from P.O. Inspector to The Postmaster General, July 26, 1886.

38. LAC, RG 17, vol. 501, D-55050, letter from Esterhazy, Philadelphia, to Lowe, September 2, 1886.

39. LAC, RG 15, vol. 348, T-13070, letter from Esterhazy, Ottawa, to Burgess, May 8, 1886.

40. Sessional Papers (No. 12) A. 1887, "Report on Hungarian immigration and colonization," report from Esterhazy, Fordham, New York, to Minister of Agriculture, December 31, 1886.

41. LAC, RG 17, vol. 505, D-55534, letter from Esterhazy to Carling, October 1, 1886.

42. LAC, RG 17, vol. 507, D-55775, letter from Van Horne to Esterhazy, September 24, 1886.

43. LAC, RG 17, vol. 505, D-55534, letter from Esterhazy to Carling, October 1, 1886.

44. Ibid.

45. LAC, RG 17, vol. 508, D-55862, letter from Van Horne to Lowe, October 12, 1886.

46. LAC, RG 17, vol. 509, D-56041, letter from Esterhazy to Lowe, October 23, 1886.

47. Letter by J. Szabo and K. Menjhardt in LAC, RG 17, vol. 510, D-56065, letter from Graham, Winnipeg, to H.B. Small, Accountant, Department of Agriculture, October 29, 1886. The management of the Medicine Hat coalmines claimed dissatisfaction with the productivity of the Hungarians in later accounts.

48. The men left the Lethbridge coalmines due to excessive charges for lodging and water. LAC, RG 17, vol. 515, D-56780, letter from Esterhazy to Lowe, December 6, 1886.

49. LAC, RG 17, vol. 517, D-57005, letter from Graham to Lowe, December 9, 1886.

50. Sessional Papers (No. 12) A. 1887, "Annual report of the Winnipeg immigration agent," report from Graham, December 31, 1886.

51. LAC, RG 17, vol. 514, D-56608, letter from L. Stafford to Lowe, November 30, 1886.

52. LAC, RG 17, vol. 515, D-56780, letter from Esterhazy, Ottawa, to Lowe, December 6, 1886.

53. LAC, RG 17, vol. 515, D-56779, letter from Esterhazy to Lowe, December 6, 1886.

54. LAC, RG 17, vol. 520, D-57476-500, letter from Esterhazy, Fordham, to Lowe, January 11, 1887.

55. LAC, RG 17, vol. 525, D-58067, letter from Esterhazy to Lowe, February 14, 1887.

56. LAC, RG 17, vol. 584, D-65881-910, letter from Esterhazy to Lowe, March 14, 1887.

57. LAC, RG 17, vol. 550, D-81571, letter from Esterhazy to Burgess, September 14, 1887.

58. Prior to his enquiry on the township reserves, Esterhazy corresponded with numerous Czech families in Europe and the United States and invited them to settle in the Canadian North-West. While Esterhazy could not obtain a reservation on the townships for his proposed Bohemian colonization scheme, he acquired German and Czech language immigration propaganda from the Department of Agriculture. In 1891, Esterhazy also proposed to translate government immigration pamphlets into both the Hungarian and Slovak languages while in 1897 he sent another proposal to initiate large-scale Slavic immigration. Although he was not encouraged to engage in any of his Slavic immigration propositions, his correspondences with early Czech migrants and his later commissioned immigration pamphlet which was distributed to the ethnically mixed Hungarian-Slovak-Ruthenian territories of northeast Hungary point to the fact that

Esterhazy was also a significant figure with regards to the first stages of Slavic immigration to Canada. LAC, RG 17, vol. 688, D-78800, May 28, 1891; RG 76, vol. 20, C-4678, November 23, 1897.

59. LAC, RG 15, vol. 348, D-90895, letter from Dominion Lands Commission, Winnipeg, to Department of the Interior, September 30, 1887.

60. LAC, RG 17, vol. 557, D-62534, letter from Burgess to Lowe, November 15, 1887.

61. LAC, RG 15, vol. 348, T-90895, letter from Lowe to Burgess, October 3, 1887.

62. LAC, RG 17, vol. 584, D-65881-912, letter from Van Horne, Montreal, to Esterhazy, New York, May 5, 1888.

63. LAC, RG 17, vol. 568, D-63944, letter from Döry, Huns Valley, to Esterhazy, Fordham New York, December 15, 1887.

64. LAC, RG 17, vol. 594, D-67179, letter from J. Vass to Carling, October 9, 1888; RG 17, vol. 584, D-65881-910, letter from Esterhazy, Ottawa, to Lowe, July 16, 1888.

65. LAC, RG 15, vol. 584, D-65881-910, translation in letter from Esterhazy, New York, to Lowe, January 5, 1888.

66. LAC, RG 15, vol. 584, D-65881-910, letter from Esterhazy, Ottawa, to Lowe, July 12, 1888.

67. LAC, RG 15, vol. 348, T-13070, letter from Stephenson to Dewdney, February 20, 1889.

68. LAC, RG 17, vol. 635, D-72091-120, letter from Esterhazy, New York, to Lowe, January 6, 1890.

69. LAC, RG 15, vol. 348, D-90895, letter from Park, Whitewood, to H.H. Smith, Winnipeg, October 28, 1890. For an in-depth look into the "Vass case" see Kovacs "Settlement, Depression and Alienation."

70. LAC, RG 17, vol. 685, D-78379, letter from T. Bennett, Winnipeg, to Lowe, May 2, 1891.

71. LAC, RG 17, vol. 686, D-78511, letter from Esterhazy, New York, to Lowe, May 12, 1891. Esterhazy was employed at the time with the Southern Pacific Railroad Company and was sent to Florida (1892) and Arkansas (1893) where he inspected land for colonization purposes. Although he could not regain his former status as special immigration agent for the Canadian government, Esterhazy continued to encourage Hungarian immigration to the Prairies and intervened on behalf of potential settlers in his correspondences to the Department of Agriculture. For example, on his recommendation in 1892 several Hungarian families were able to travel directly from Europe to Canada at a time when—as a result of an epidemic of cholera in Germany and Southern Europe— steamship companies had confined their bookings to the Scandinavian countries. LAC, RG 76, vol. 20, C-4678, letter from Lowe to Burgess, February 14, 1893.

72. Sessional Papers (No. 7), A. 1892, "Joint report on Hungarian colonies" letters from Dory, Huns Valley, and S. Park, Whitewood, to the Minister of Agriculture, September 7, 1891 and July 30, 1891.

73. LAC, RG 15, vol. 348, T-13070, letter from Esterhazy to Lowe, May 2, 1893.

74. Ibid.

75. LAC, RG 15, vol. 701, letter from Ruttan to Smith, November 5, 1894.

76. Ibid.

77. *Almanac of the Hungarian Golden Jubilee of Kaposvar-Esterhazy, Saskatchewan, Canada, 1886–1936*, 13.

78. Of course this assessment is limited to the Canadian context of Esterhazy's involvement with Hungarian immigrants in North America. Prior to his arrival onto the Canadian scene, Esterhazy had contributed much in material support to the Hungarian and Slovak immigrants in Pennsylvania and was instrumental in organizing a

Hungarian Presbyterian church (1881) and Hungarian language newspaper (1883). For a brief look into Esterhazy's philanthropic activities in Pennsylvania see: Martin L. Kovacs, "From Industries to Farming," *Hungarian Studies Review* 8 (1981): 45–60.

79. Kaposvar (Esterhaz) was noted as the richest Hungarian colony in Canada by 1910 since several of the original pioneers had accumulated $30–40,000. *Amerikai Magyar Népszava*, 79–80.

12. The Religious Ethic and the Spirit of Immigration: The Dutch in Alberta

Howard Palmer and Tamara Palmer

The Dutch experience in Alberta has much in common with that of many other ethnic groups in the province. The Dutch faced the same problems of linguistic and cultural adjustment which confronted all non-English-speaking immigrants. Also reflecting a common pattern, Dutch migration to Alberta came in three waves: the first wave, which established the basic patterns of Dutch-Canadian settlement in Alberta, arrived between the turn of the century and World War I—the boom years of the Laurier administration; —the second, smaller wave of Dutch immigrants came during the 1920s to rural Alberta; the third wave came after the Second World War, primarily in response to the economic opportunities of an urbanizing Alberta. Most other sizeable ethnic groups in the province, Ukrainians, Poles, Germans, Hungarians, Jews and Mennonites, among others, also emerged out of the growth and interaction of these same three waves of immigration. The Dutch are also similar to a number of other groups in that religious institutions formed the focal point of their identity, congealing rural communities in a close network of commercial and social interaction, social activities and mutual aid.

As part of the fabric of Alberta society, the Dutch inevitably faced the same economic challenges confronting all Alberta residents. By examining their history in Alberta, one can see in microcosm many aspects of the province's history, from the challenges of the pioneer era, through the difficult years of the 1920s and 1930s, to the new society which emerged out of the developments during World War II and the growing prosperity and urbanization of the post-war years.

However, despite the commonality of the immigrant experience in Alberta, the Dutch story has in many ways been unique. Notwithstanding their comparatively large size—the Dutch form the fifth largest ethnic group in the province—they have, for most of their history, been inconspicuous; this and the related absence of controversy surrounding them has meant that many Albertans have been largely unaware of the Dutch presence. The Dutch have not been the focal point of prejudice and conflict which scarred the history of Chinese, Japanese, Hutterites, or Ukrainians in the province. The similarity of their culture to the broader Canadian culture, the absence of prejudice against them, their high rate of cultural assimilation and their dispersed settlement pattern have all combined to produce this phenomenon of "invisibility." And, while religion has been extremely important to the Dutch as it has to many other ethnic groups, with the Dutch, religion has had a very different effect on the maintenance of language and folk traditions. The Reformed churches—the main religious institutions among the Dutch—have promoted group cohesiveness, but they have not played a prominent role in sustaining the immigrants' language or traditions. Indeed, in many Reformed churches, maintenance of the Dutch language and traditions is seen as being inimical to the institution's religious mission.

The unique settlement pattern of the Dutch during the pioneer era has created a particularly fascinating case study of the interrelationship between cultural background and physical environment in Alberta's history. Largely by chance, the original pattern of Dutch settlement was one of wide dispersal and the earliest Dutch settlements were located in four different biophysical zones, from the short-grass prairies of south eastern Alberta, through the mixed-grass prairie and aspen parkland to the fringes of the boreal cordilleran forest. In contrast, many other large, overwhelmingly agricultural groups were concentrated in one region: the Mormons and the Hutterites settled exclusively in the mixed-grass prairie of southern Alberta while the Poles, French Canadians and the Ukrainians settled overwhelmingly in the aspen-parkland region.[1]

The evolution of Alberta's rural Dutch farming communities is primarily a history of settlers' attempts to cope with the special problems posed by the biophysical environment of each region of the province, including such diverse challenges as extreme dryness, soil drifting, heavy bush cover and remoteness from transportation. Thus, the pre-World War II history of Alberta's Dutch settlements provides excellent case studies of the ways Albertans discovered, via the arduous route of practical experience, the problems and opportunities of each region of the province. The population shifts in the various rural Dutch communities—their growth, their stagnation or their decline—provide an example of the larger population shifts which were occurring in different regions of the province from its beginnings to the 1950s. (See Table 1.)

Table 1. Major Dutch Settlements in Alberta (1921–1941)			
	Population of Dutch Origin		
	1921	1931	1941
Monarch-Nobleford	251*	447	494
Granum	142**	205	208
Burdett-Foremost	159	106	106
Alderson	160	25	
Strathmore	270***	449	323
Neerlandia	268	378	449
Lacombe		127	282
Iron Springs	16	70	95
Bottrel		98	147
Rockyford		55	86

*Includes I.D. #68, Municipality of Little Bow #98; and towns of Monarch and Nobleford.
**Includes Municipality of Argyle #99, town of Granum
***Includes Municipality #218, Blackfoot and #219 Bow Valley; #248 Grasswold; #249 Keoma.
Source: Census of Canada, 1921, 1931, 1941.

The institutions the Dutch established were nearly identical from one community to the next. But various rural Dutch communities have not had identical histories because they were located in different biophysical regions of the province and consequently were subject to widely varying environmental constraints.

For the student of human geography, there are many other provocative questions related to the spatial aspects of the Dutch presence in Alberta. One must move beyond simply noting how the current presence of Dutch Reformed churches in 24 Alberta communities reflects the impact of Dutch immigrants across the province, to an awareness of the complex significance of religion within the Dutch community of Alberta. For example, three of the four major Reformed denominations in Canada had their Canadian beginnings in rural communities of southern Alberta.

Religion has also affected both the distribution pattern of Dutch immigrants in Alberta and their differing rates of assimilation in various parts of the province. Region and religious affiliation have been closely linked in the Netherlands, which has meant that when immigrants from a particular region in Holland have immigrated to a particular region in Alberta, the process of chain migration has ultimately resulted in a concentration of

Mr. and Mrs. John Kuyten and son Frank, Strathmore, circa 1913–18. The Kuytens emigrated from Holland in 1912, first settling at Strathmore before farming in the Rockyford area from 1912 to 1945 (Courtesy of the Glenbow Archives/NA-3503-9).

people with similar regional and therefore religious origins. Thus the Dutch pattern of regional religious homogeneity has, on a smaller scale, been recreated in Alberta. Since the ideology and structure of particular denominations affect their adherents' reactions to assimilative forces, religious differences have been reflected in differing rates of assimilation from one area of Dutch settlement to another.

But the Dutch community in Alberta is not a microcosm of the Netherlands society; the denominational pattern among Alberta's Dutch differs considerably from that in the Netherlands. The post-World War II immigrants have represented the most religiously conservative elements of Dutch society and are in many ways a "cultural fragment" of the rural Netherlands of the 1950s. The following pages attempt to elucidate these and other aspects of the social, cultural and geographical patterns of people of Dutch origin near Alberta.

Taming the Land: Dutch Pioneers in Alberta

Near the turn of the present century, a number of factors combined to bring the first wave of Dutch immigrants to Alberta. Those who joined this first group came to Canada for economic reasons. The Netherlands was a small country and it could not support its burgeoning population. The Dutch farmer was faced with a combination of dilemmas which forced him to consider leaving his homeland. Industrialization in the Netherlands and competition from other agricultural nations had precipitated a crisis. The restrictive economic policies of other European countries limited Dutch agricultural exports. At the same time, there was increased competition from North America, which led to reduced prices for agricultural products. Agricultural modernization brought labour-saving machinery, which was a mixed blessing since it turned the permanent farmhand into a seasonal worker faced with intermittent unemployment. On the one hand, because of the economic conditions, few farmers were able to expand their holdings and even fewer were able to begin their own. On the other hand, North America was calling out for immigrants, especially experienced farmers. For many young Dutchmen to whom the land meant stability and success, emigration was the only hope for the future.[2]

In the late 19th century, most emigrants from the Netherlands went to the midwestern and western United States; large concentrations developed in Michigan, Iowa, Illinois, North Dakota, South Dakota, Montana and Washington. In several close-knit, predominantly Dutch communities, the Dutch language could be maintained, Calvinist churches could flourish and the rural society of the Netherlands could be recreated. But by the turn of the century, land in most of these communities had been completely taken up. Immigrants from the Netherlands and Dutch-Americans who wanted to stay on the land began to consider Canada as an alternative. Dutch-Americans joined the influx of over one-half million Americans who came to the prairie provices between 1896 and 1914. Thus, many of the first Dutch immigrants in Alberta came not directly from Holland but from communities of their fellow countrymen which had been established earlier in the United States. This pattern was not unique to the Dutch but was also true of the first Hungarians, Slovaks, Danes, Icelanders, Finns, Norwegians, Hutterites, and Lithuanians in Alberta.

An 1884 poster designed to lure Dutch immigrants to Manitoba advertised "buffalo hunting, deer shooting, salmon fishing" and free land (Courtesy of the Archives of Manitoba/N11763).

Canadian officials were anxious to settle the prairies, and the Dutch seemed to be ideal colonists; they were desirable immigrants in the eyes of both immigration officials and the general Canadian public. First, most had farm experience; second, as "Nordic" northern Europeans, they were thought to be of superior "racial stock"; and third, they were predominantly Protestant and were acquainted with democratic institutions, so it was felt that they would fit easily into Canadian life. Given these prevailing stereotypes and assumptions, both the railways and the government sought out Dutch settlers. J.S. Dennis, the "superintendent of irrigation" for the Canadian Pacific Railway wrote that the Dutch were "the very best settlers."[3]

During the years just before and after the turn of the century, free homesteads were available in Canada's prairie provinces so most Dutch immigrants who came to Canada during the pre-World War I immigration boom settled on the prairies. All of the prairie provinces attracted some Dutch settlers; however, they dispersed across each province. While some rural areas, towns and cities ultimately received significant concentrations of Dutch immigrants, these settlements were not localized in any one part of the prairies. This settlement pattern was a major factor in the subsequent rapid assimilation of the prairie Dutch.

Dutch settlers came later to Alberta than to Saskatchewan or Manitoba, but the number of Dutch in Alberta eventually exceeded that in either of the other prairie provinces. The first and largest settlement was in the area of Granum-Nobleford-Monarch, located in southern Alberta's mixed grass prairie region. This settlement was begun in 1904 by people whose religious roots were in the Reformed Church. The second Dutch settlement, which was founded in 1908 by Dutch Catholics, was located near Strathmore (east of Calgary) in the transition area between mixed-grass prairie and aspen parkland. In 1910 further settlements were begun south of Burdett and north of Alderson (midway between Brooks and Medicine Hat), both located in the semi-arid short grass prairie region of southeastern Alberta. Neerlandia, the only exclusively Dutch settlement in the province, was founded in 1912 northeast of Edmonton on the border between the boreal cordilleran forest and the boreal parkland transition forest.

These settlements received only a minority of the immigrants who were coming from Holland in this first major migration to Alberta; Dutch farmers homesteaded in virtually every part of the province. By the end of World War I, all of Alberta's 17 census divisions had at least a few Dutch families. Nevertheless, it was the few rural settlements which had been established predominantly by Dutch immigrants which ultimately had the greatest impact on Alberta. Dutch families who came individually and settled where there were few other immigrants from Holland assimilated quickly; however, those who came to the rural Dutch communities established their own church institutions and, for a time, preserved the Dutch language and some elements of Dutch culture. The rural Dutch communities also served as nuclei for subsequent waves of Dutch immigrants in the 1920s, the 1950s and the 1960s. Thus (as has been true of so many ethnic groups) the location of the first settlements had a strong impact on the group's eventual overall distribution in the province.

Settlements in Southern Alberta

The settlements at Nobleford, Monarch and Granum combined two streams of immigration: one directly from the Netherlands, the other from Dutch-American settlements. Among the Dutch-American settlers from Iowa and Montana who decided to take up homesteads in this area were people who had originally emigrated from Nijverdaal in the province of Overijssel. The first arrivals came in the spring of 1904 and arranged to meet a group of settlers who would be joining them from the Netherlands. Most of the newcomers began homesteading in the Monarch area, which they named Nieuw Nijverdal in remembrance of their home in the Netherlands.[4]

The Dutch who settled at about the same time in the nearby Granum area (then known as Leavings) were concentrated about 10 miles east of the hamlet. Most of the families were from the province of Groningen in northern Holland. They were strict and devout Calvinists and maintained a closeknit, isolated community.[5]

From 1904 until 1919, more Dutch families continued to settle in the same areas of southern Alberta. The first settlers sought to attract other immigrants to the community through writing letters to Dutch-American newspapers as well as through personal contacts. Some of the newcomers came directly from the Netherlands, while others came by way of brief or lengthy stays in Dutch-American settlements at Sioux City, Iowa, Vesper, Wisconsin, and in Montana. By 1921 there were approximately 250 people of Dutch origin in the Nobleford-Monarch area and 140 in Granum. Despite this influx, however, the communities of Nobleford, Monarch and Granum were not exclusively, or even primarily, Dutch; they were also being settled in larger numbers by Americans and eastern Canadians. But the Dutch came to form a sizeable minority in these areas.[6]

The Dutch immigrants faced all of the problems usually encountered by early homesteaders in Alberta, but in addition they had to cope with a language barrier and a lack of experience with prairie farming. With the initial help of settlers who had come by way of Iowa and could therefore speak English and were acquainted with western farming techniques, the first settlers were able to meet many of the early difficulties. But the settlement faced unique problems because of the area's dryness and its extremely high winds.[7]

Religion played an important part in the settlers' lives and they soon turned their attention to establishing churches. In 1905 a congregation of the Christian Reformed Church, the first in Canada, was organized by a minister who had come for that purpose from the Dutch settlement at Manhattan, Montana. In 1909 the other major Reformed denomination at this time, the Reformed Church in America, formed a congregation in Monarch, also the oldest congregation of this church in Canada.

Another Christian Reformed congregation was formed soon after, 80 miles further east near Burdett, to accommodate families who had moved into the rural area between Burdett and Foremost around 1910 as land became more difficult to obtain near Granum and Monarch. This later settlement did not grow to the same size as its parent settlement since the area was drier and could not support as many people.[8]

Another settlement was started in 1910 northeast of Alderson in one of the driest regions of the province. This settlement, known as "New Holland," grew to 160 people by 1921, but by 1925, it had disbanded because of repeated years of crop failures caused by inadequate rainfall.

The Dutch settlers in the Nobleford and Monarch area were more successful than those in the Alderson settlement had been, nevertheless many challenges remained to be overcome. The settlers faced the difficult problem of soil drifting caused by the combination of dryness, high winds, and inappropriate soil cultivation techniques. The harvest of 1914 was such a disaster that the provincial government had to provide the farmers with seed grain so that they could plant a crop the following spring. By 1916, the Dutch farmers were again able to raise a successful crop, but in 1917, soil drifting in the Monarch area had become so severe that clearly a solution had to be found. One of the settlers, Arie Koole, experimented with the idea of alternating strips of crop and summer fallow. The success of his experiment encouraged other farmers to try his method, which proved so effective that by the 1930s strip farming was widely practised throughout southern Alberta. Strip farming would later help limit the severity of soil drifting during the "dust bowl" of the 1930s.[9]

Despite the many challenges which they had faced, by 1920 Monarch and Nobleford were firmly established. As Herman Ganzevoort has stated in his excellent study of early Dutch immigration to Canada:

> The Dutch settlers began to achieve the economic security and independence for which they had worked so hard. Crop returns in the Nobleford area were high and good prices for their products permitted expansion and investment. More land, implements and horses were purchased

and more ground was broken and seeded. The settlers abandoned their shacks to the chickens and built roomier, more comfortable wooden homes. Barns replaced dugouts and the community took on a prosperous look. Home-sickness lessened as the community grew and conditions were bettered. The Dutch slowly began to cut their ties with the Netherlands and accommodate themselves to Canadian society.[10]

Settlements at Strathmore and Neerlandia

Farmers began settling in the CPR's western irrigation block near Strathmore in 1908. The CPR had established a large irrigation block in the area hoping that the intensive cultivation which irrigation made possible would attract a sizeable population, which would in turn provide increased business for the railway. To facilitate this project, the railway hired special agents to attract different ethnic groups in Europe and the United States; among those which they attempted to entice were the Dutch.

Two Dutch immigrants played an important part in founding the settle-ment at Strathmore. George Boer had immigrated to Canada from the Netherlands in the 1890s. In 1908 he was appointed water inspector of the CPR's ready-made farms in Strathmore. Boer's contact with Father Van Aaken, a Dutch-Catholic priest in Helena, Montana, resulted in the latter's being hired by the CPR to tour the Catholic areas of the Netherlands in search of prospective immigrants for the irrigated farms. Van Aaken's major promotional effort appears to have been in Noord Brabant, a predominant-ly Catholic area of the southern Netherlands; this was the home of most of the immigrants who eventually settled at Strathmore. The Dutch Catholics who immigrated to the CPR's western irrigation block in 1908 and 1909 set-tled four miles northeast of Strathmore in a school district that eventually came to be known as Aakenstadt. Father Van Aaken's plans for a church did not materialize, but a school was built and named after him. The Catholic church which was built at Strathmore in 1910 by Father Van Tighem, a Belgian priest, served Dutch, Polish, German and American parishioners.[11]

A variety of factors combined to limit the economic success and growth of the Strathmore settlement. Although Van Aaken recruited almost 100 fam-ilies, most did not remain in the area. Some who came had no previous farm experience. Also, a severe hailstorm in 1908 put the colony in serious jeop-ardy. In addition, the settlers soon realized that homestead land was avail-able for the taking, whereas the CPR was selling its land. Ultimately, both the CPR and Van Aaken became focal points for the frustrations of the Dutch

Strathmore area settler William Damen, circa 1917. Born in Holland in 1895, Damen farmed at Strathmore until the 1950s, then worked as a furniture maker in Calgary (Courtesy of the Glenbow Archives/NA-4005-4).

immigrants and Van Aaken himself eventually left, along with many of the disgruntled settlers.

George Boer, however, continued to promote emigration to Canada in the Netherlands. As a result of his efforts, a few Dutch families came to the Strathmore area in 1912 and even during the war years. But the CPR lands and agents had begun to acquire a bad reputation; the agents were inclined to promise more than the CPR land could deliver. This is not to say, of course, that the settlement was a complete failure. Several Dutch families remained and the children and grandchildren of these original settlers have become prominent and respected farmers. Thus, while the settlement did not meet the high expectations of its organizers, it nevertheless became a sizeable community. At the time of the 1921 census, there were 270 people of Dutch origin in the Strathmore area.[12]

The basic problems of pioneering in the Strathmore area were similar to those encountered by the Dutch settlers in southern Alberta and, like those further south, the Dutch in Strathmore played an important role in pioneering and developing new land. The major social difference between Strathmore and the other settlements in southern Alberta stemmed not from the influence of the land company in the former nor from the problems of soil drifting and aridity in the latter; rather, the differences reflected the Catholic origins of those who settled in Strathmore and the Calvinist origins of those who settled in the other communities.

Repeating the pattern which characterized the Dutch American experience in the nineteenth century, Dutch Catholics in Alberta were more prone to assimilation than the Calvinists; thus the Dutch in the Strathmore settlement generally became involved in community-wide activities earlier than those who had settled further south. Their Catholic affiliations united them with many of their neighbours rather than separating them, as religious affiliation did in the southern settlements. Intermarriage of the Canadian-born of Dutch background with people outside of the Dutch community was more common in Strathmore than in Monarch and Nobleford. In the southern communities, the church maintained an active social life for young people which encouraged them to marry within the Reformed faith; the Dutch Catholics also married within their own faith but this frequently meant that they married Catholics of non-Dutch background.[13]

The Neerlandia settlement 80 miles northwest of Edmonton was no larger prior to the 1930s than those in the Monarch-Nobleford area or the one at Strathmore, but it was exclusively Dutch; as such, it was one of a small handful of all-Dutch farming communities in all of Canada. Like other ethnic settlements situated on the fringe of settlement in north-central Alberta, such as the all-Black farming community at Amber Valley, its isolation preserved its ethnic exclusiveness. Neerlandia was located on the biophysical border between boreal-cordilleran forest, which could be farmed (if with difficulty) and the boreal-parkland transition forest, which was unsuitable for agriculture. The dense covering of trees and bush and the absence of adequate transportation facilities led to the development of a very different type of agriculture than that practised in the southern settlements.

Neerlandia was begun in 1912 by Dutch settlers who had originally come to Edmonton. Many Dutch immigrants who had first come to the city had no intention of remaining there; rather, they hoped to establish themselves as independent farmers. Most of the people belonged to the Christian Reformed faith. Some of them had come to Edmonton via the United States, but others had come directly from the Netherlands. They lived in the districts of Frazer Flats and Parkdale, areas which were largely occupied by working-class immigrants. But the Dutch immigrants did not want to become a working-class proletariat. Consequently, in 1910 a group of Dutch Christian Reformed immigrants organized an immigration society. The organization's purpose, was twofold: first, to attract other Dutch Reformed immigrants to Alberta from the Netherlands and the United States, and second, to explore the possibilities of locating a tract of land where a Dutch Christian Reformed community could be established. The organizers wrote articles for church newspapers in the United States and the Netherlands which extolled Alberta's vast opportunities. Results were almost immediate: in 1911 several Dutch families responded to these advertisements and immigrated to Edmonton. A scouting committee soon obtained a tract of free land which was large enough for at least 100 families. The only deterrent to the chosen site was its dense covering of heavy poplars and brush.[14]

In 1912, 17 men, both married and single, took up homesteads in the district which they had chosen and named Neerlandia after their home country. More Dutch settlers followed in the next three years. By the end of 1915 they had occupied over 40 quarter-sections and by the time of the 1921 census, there were 268 people in the new settlement.[15]

Neerlandia's colonizers had several things in common—their religion, their relative youth and their ignorance of woodscraft, which was so necessary to success on land covered with heavy timber and dotted with swamps, creeks and small ponds. The settlers came from different backgrounds but many were from urban centres. Most were married and had children ranging in age from infants to 12 years. Despite their lack of experience with the type of farming their new land required, they were adaptable and hardworking and most successfully met the challenge of pioneering.

When the settlers first arrived in Neerlandia after a week-long oxcart ride from Edmonton, their first chore was to build log cabins. Once the cabins were ready, the task of clearing and breaking land could begin. To bring five acres under cultivation, the settler had to work hard all summer, grubbing trees and brush then breaking the land with horses and a walking plow.

Transportation was also extremely primitive, since the community was removed from the province's major transportation network. The community had no rail service and at first, the nearest general store was at Mellowdale, 10 miles south. Isolation forced the settlers to become self-sufficient; it was not long before they could depend almost entirely on game and their own gardens for food. Each pioneer had to become his own butcher, veterinarian, blacksmith, shoemaker and carpenter since none of these services were within 20 miles of their settlement.[16]

In order to accumulate capital, the Dutch pioneers, like those in southern Alberta, found it necessary to work outside of their settlement during part of the year. Some travelled annually to Granum to work on the harvests, or took jobs in nearby logging camps which grew up to supply the lumber needs of rapidly growing towns like Barrhead, the area's major commercial centre.

Unlike the situation in southern Alberta, the major cash flow for the Neerlandia settlers was generated by cattle rather than grain. Since Neerlandia was isolated, wheat was difficult to transport. The abundant moisture of the area produced ample hay crops, so the Dutch settlers concentrated on the raising of cattle, hogs and poultry; most of the wheat they grew was fed to the cattle, which could be herded to the nearest railhead.

During these early years, the settlers were busy building up their livestock herds, breaking up more land and improving their homes; neverthe-

Neerlandia Co-operative Association Ltd. store and service station, 1937. A new store was built the following year (Courtesy of the Glenbow Archives/PD-220-9).

less they soon began to establish community institutions. Since the original impetus behind the founding of Neerlandia was a desire to establish a Christian Reformed community, naturally one of the first institutions in the settlement was a Christian Reformed church. Like many of the community's projects, the church, built in 1915, was constructed with cooperative labour. The church united the settlement and boosted the morale of the pioneers. Remembering the church, pioneer Ted Reitsma recalls that:

> Hardship and trials never dampened our sense of humour. Quite the contrary, they tightened the bonds of solidarity and loyalty we felt for one another. This attitude was encouraged by our church. Services were attended. Snow, rain, mud, 40 or 50 below weather would never be a deterrent. When a familiar face was missing, everybody sought the reason and offered any help needed. In the early period of the settlement, this was the only social contact the settlers had. We were all happy to greet our neighbours and actually looked forward to these Sunday meetings as not only did we get to hear what God had to say to us but we were able to listen to all the happenings in the settlement for the past week be it either good or ill.[17]

The church was served by travelling ministers from other parts of Alberta, who kept the members in touch with other Dutch Reformed settlements in the province. Other early important community institutions were a cooperative society and store which have remained successfully in operation to the present.

The new community of Neerlandia experienced its share of problems and setbacks. Isolation made medical assistance very difficult to obtain. One year the community's crops were devoured by a plague of rabbits and of course the long, severe winters were always difficult. But by the 1920s the rigours of pioneer life were beginning to fade and the community continued to grow as a result of the expansion of original families, the establishment of families by the Canadian-born and the arrival of new settlers. Neerlandia would continue to be dominated by people of Dutch origin, not only by the design of the original settlers, but also because it was on the fringe of settlement. The geography of the area prevented expansion, thus discouraging non-Dutch people from settling there.

Table 2. Dutch in Alberta						
	1921	1931	1941	1951	1961	1971
Total Dutch of ethnic origin in Alberta	9,490	13,665	20,429	29,385	55,530	58,570
Mennonites in Alberta giving Dutch as ethnic origin	3,125	2,033	4,818	4,934	5,740	3,905
Source: Census of Canada, 1921–71.						

The first wave of immigrants established the basic settlement pattern for Dutch immigration in Alberta which would continue until the 1960s. The Dutch were a relatively small group; their presence went almost unnoticed in Alberta. Nevertheless in their own way, they were making an important contribution to the agricultural development of the province. By 1921 (see Table 2) Alberta's population included 9,490 people of Dutch origin.[18]

The 1920s Sequel: A Second Wave of Dutch Immigration

World War I brought the first wave of immigration from the Netherlands to an end; however, a few years after the war, interest in migration to Canada revived. Near the end of the war, the Dutch economy worsened and land, especially in the northern provinces of Friesland, Groningen and Drenthe, became increasingly scarce due to overpopulation. So the Dutch were once again being forced to look beyond their homeland for economic opportunity.[19]

Many Dutch people searching for a new home chose Canada. There were several factors prompting this decision. For many, Canada was a second choice forced by immigration restrictions in the United States. However, there were some positive factors attracting immigrants to Canada. Ontario

Dutch immigrants outside the building for Canadian National Railways, Departments of Colonization and Agriculture, Canadian National Land Settlement Association, Edmonton, 1929 (Courtesy of the Glenbow Archives/ND-3-4564).

was in the throes of massive urbanization and industrialization which was leaving rural Ontario with a severe shortage of agricultural workers. In western Canada, particularly in Alberta, there was still some undeveloped farm land as well as need for agricultural workers. In addition, there was official encouragement of potential immigrants from the Canadian government and the major railways, who actively promoted emigration in the Netherlands. Catholic and Calvinist churches in the Netherlands established competing immigration societies and Dutch journalists came to Canada to describe the country for their restless countrymen. This combination of circumstances created a favourable climate for Dutch immigration to Canada during the 1920s.[20]

Immigrants who were part of this second major movement of people from the Netherlands to Canada were more inclined to settle in Ontario than to travel west. However, approximately 1,200 immigrants came directly from the Netherlands to Alberta during the 1920s, and by 1931 they had pushed the number of Dutch-origin people in the province to 13,665. This second wave of immigration did not have as profound an impact on Alberta as the first, but it did lead to the founding of two new settlements with sizeable numbers of people of Dutch origin—Lacombe in the central region and Iron Springs in the south—which would become important nuclei for Dutch immigrants after World War II. During the 1920s Dutch immigrants also moved into rural areas near Rockyford and Stettler in central Alberta.

The existing Dutch settlements in southern Alberta did not benefit to any great extent from this new influx because they faced serious economic problems. The economic slump of the early 1920s, coupled with problems of arid land, restricted farm income to such an extent that the settlements either grew only slowly, or in the cases of Alderson and Burdett actually declined. As mentioned, by 1925, arid conditions had forced the Alderson settlement near Brooks to disband. The Dutch settlement at Burdett did not disappear since dryness was not as severe, but it declined nonetheless. The majority of those people who lived at Alderson moved to predominantly Dutch communities in the State of Washington, although a few relocated to the Crossfield and Bottrel areas in west-central Alberta where moisture was more reliable. There was also a movement of families from the Nobleford-Monarch areas to Dutch settlements in British Columbia, Washington and other parts of the United States, part of a larger return movement of onetime American farmers who had originally come to Alberta prior to 1920.[21]

World War I had been a period of growth for the Dutch communities in Nobleford, Strathmore and Neerlandia; but their development slowed during the 1920s. Each of these communities received a few families from Holland during the decade following the war, but most of their growth came from natural increase rather than immigration.

The Dutch who began farming during the 1920s did not settle on dryland grain farms; rather, most settled either on irrigated farms near Lethbridge in southern Alberta, or on mixed farms near Lacombe in central Alberta where there was adequate rainfall. When the Lethbridge Northern Irrigation Project was completed in the early 1920s, it opened previously unsettled and uncultivated land like the Iron Springs area north of Lethbridge. Dutch settlers were among those attracted to Iron Springs in the late 1920s and many eventually began raising sugar beets, delivering their produce to the sugar factory at Picture Butte which was completed in 1935.[22]

In several areas in the province, the Canadian Pacific Railway (CPR) continued to work closely with religious denominations to promote colonization. The Dutch settlement at Lacombe provides a typical example of this partnership. William Van Ark had been one of the original settlers at Neerlandia. During the 1920s, he was hired by the CPR as a travelling

colonization agent to scout land settlement schemes in Alberta and to promote immigration from the Netherlands. He travelled frequently to the
Netherlands and used a number of techniques to encourage emigration: one
was to wait outside Dutch churches, Bible in hand, greet parishioners as
they left services and tell them glowing stories of wonderful opportunities
available in the promised land of Canada. In promoting immigration, Van
Ark worked closely with the Calvinist immigration society; consequently,
the settlement which was established at Lacombe was composed almost
exclusively of people belonging to the Christian Reformed faith. Working
closely with the Dutch churches ensured Van Ark and other Dutch immigration agents of much of their success:

> If the agent was able to combine certain aspects of religion
> with his recruitment he tended to be even more successful.
> Orthodox protestants and Roman Catholics readily
> responded to those agents who were able to point to their
> concern for spiritual as well as economic necessities. The
> application of a holy gloss over economic longings made
> the decision to leave the Netherlands just that much more
> palatable, but more importantly, it provided a continuity of
> life which helped retain a certain measure of stability in the
> immigrant's disrupted life. Many agents used religion as
> one more tool in their battery of tricks to create the feeling
> of trust which was so necessary in their work.[23]

The Dutch who settled in the Lacombe area were concentrated approximately 10 miles west of the town in the Woodynook school district located
in a boreal-cordilleran forest bio-physical zone. Lying within sight of scenic
Gull Lake, the mixed farming area could support grain, grass, hogs and
dairy cattle, though it was wooded and required clearing. Some families
moved to Woodynook from overcrowded Dutch settlements in other parts
of the province but the majority of new settlers came directly from the
Netherlands. The community evolved through the same stages as earlier
Dutch settlements; however, conditions were less primitive than in the earlier stages of most of the earlier settlements due to better transportation
facilities.

By 1931, there were 127 people of Dutch origin living in the new settle-
ment near Lacombe. Their numbers were further increased during the 1930s
by the arrival of family members from the Dutch settlement at Cramersburg,
Saskatchewan, where severe drought forced people to leave their land.
Thus, by 1941, the settlement had expanded to nearly 300 people.
Woodynook was not as isolated as Neerlandia had been; nevertheless a

similar sense of mutual cooperation and helpfulness developed. The Christian Reformed Church, which was built in 1935, became the focal point for community activities.[24]

Whether they lived in one of the predominantly Dutch communities or not, most Dutch-Canadians in Alberta were farmers. When it came to non-British immigration, Canadian immigration policy was officially "only farmers need apply," and most of the Dutch who came did to the land; the close-knit rural religious communities they established encouraged them to remain there. In 1931, 64% of the Dutch, as compared to 51% of the total Alberta population, were engaged in farming.[25]

Uphill Years: The Impact of Depression and War

During the depression-ridden 1930s, immigration to Canada was limited to the wives and children of immigrants able to support themselves and to people with enough capital to start a business. Consequently, the number of Dutch entering Canada was drastically reduced, to a total of 3,185 for the entire decade. Few of these immigrants came to Alberta, since Alberta was one of the provinces hardest hit by the Great Depression. Those immigrants who had come during the 1920s had to postpone for another 10 years any hope of economic security. Like so many other immigrants who had come in substantial numbers during the 1920s—the Danes, Hungarians, Ukrainians, Czechs, among others—life was simply a struggle to survive, to stay off relief and thereby to avoid being deported.[26]

Even many of the farmers who had come during the first wave of Dutch immigration prior to World War I found that during the "hungry thirties" they had to return to a pioneer lifestyle. As prices for their grain and farm produce plummeted, like most other rural Albertans, they could no longer afford many of the "luxuries" that they had enjoyed during the 1920s, such as bakery bread, ready-made clothing and coal for heating. Many had to convert their automobiles into horse-pulled "Bennett Buggies." Although the Dutch settlers in the Nobleford-Monarch area had developed techniques to help control soil drifting, they were nevertheless sharply affected by the drought; as a result, one group of people from Monarch moved to Bottrel, northwest of Calgary on the edge of the boreal-cordillerean forest zone.[27]

Despite these hardships the Dutch, as a group, were able to survive the Great Depression as well as or better than most other people in the province. Most were farmers and since many had settled either on irrigated land (at Strathmore and Iron Springs) or in the park belt, they were able to achieve a high level of self-sufficiency; they relied on their own farms for meat, milk, butter, eggs and produce and on themselves for mechanical and blacksmithing work. In addition, the close-knit solidarity of the rural Dutch farming communities meant that those who were having serious difficulty were helped by those who were doing slightly better. As with so many ethnic and ethno-religious groups in the province, mutual aid and cooperation was important to their survival during the bleak years of the 1930s.[28]

For Alberta's people of Dutch origin, the 1940s was a transition period marked by assimilation, patriotism and relative prosperity. The war brought many changes to their lives. The relative prosperity engendered by war facilitated the expansion of their farms. The enlistment of some of their men in the armed forces and the movement of others to urban wartime industries necessitated increased farm mechanization. Dutch-Canadians did not have to face the problems of divided loyalties, since their allegiance to Canada and their family and sentimental ties to Holland merged in the war effort. With their large families, Dutch-Canadians contributed many young men to the armed services; some families sent as many as three or four sons to fight for the Allied cause.

By the end of the war, the Dutch community in Alberta was on the verge of being assimilated. There was a sprinkling of close-knit, church-oriented rural groups of Dutch people in the province, but they did not have any compelling reason to maintain the Dutch language or culture. Religion rather than culture or language stood as the only barrier to intermarriage among the Canadian-born generation who were now playing an increasingly important role in community life. The high levels of mobility created by the war led to more intermarriage and assimilation. But just after the war ended and as urbanization threatened to further erode ethnic identity, a large wave of Dutch immigrants began arriving in the province, increasing the number of Dutch in the existing predominantly Dutch rural settlements, establishing new rural concentrations and bringing a strong Dutch-Canadian presence to all of the major urban centres. Partly due to the large post-war influx, the rural to urban ratio among the Dutch in Alberta would drift dramatically toward an urban predominance in a province where urbanization was the most important and overriding social and economic trend in the post-war years.

Sharing the Boom: Post-War Dutch Immigration to Alberta
The impact on Alberta of this third and largest wave of Dutch immigrants can be seen in census statistics. In 1941, prior to the massive post-war influx, the number of Dutch-origin people in the province was 20,429. By 1961, this number had increased to 55,530. The 2,000 Dutch-born who were living in Alberta in 1941 jumped to over 23,000 by 1961 and the proportion of Dutch-

born among those of Dutch origin had, during the same time period, increased from 15% to 47%. Virtually all parts of the province felt the impact of this new wave of Dutch immigration.[29]

A combination of forces prompted the post-war migration from the Netherlands to Canada. Holland's perennial problem of overpopulation became even more acute in the post-war era due to high birth and low infant mortality rates. In addition, the war had devastated the Netherlands' economy. When the Germans left the country, it had been stripped of much movable property. Approximately 4% of the homes had been destroyed along with one-tenth of the agricultural land. Loss of the Dutch East Indies (Indonesia) after the war dealt the economy a further blow. Overcrowding, unemployment and inflation plagued the Netherlands during the immediate postwar years.[30]

As one response to the population problem the Dutch government became actively involved in promoting and facilitating emigration and set as its goal the departure of 10,000 farm families every year. The government used no overt compulsion; however, it did do everything it could to encourage and expedite emigration; it centralized all emigration activities, provided information to emigrants on their chosen country, offered technial training and negotiated agreements with receiving countries. The Dutch government also introduced a system of subsidies for emigrants which provided, on the average, $220 per person for transportation, board allowance and landing money. At first, only rural workers, particularly farmers' sons who were not able to establish themselves on the land, were encouraged to leave. But by 1953 the general principle under which subsidies were granted became "the desirability of promoting the departure of all those capable of emigrating." Approximately 85% of those who left were assisted by the Dutch government, which even acquired three ships and chartered other ships and aircraft to facilitate the flow of people.[31]

While the Dutch government could promote and facilitate emigration, it was ultimately individuals who had to make the agonizing personal decision of whether or not to leave their homeland and where they should go. Because of the friendly relations between the two countries during World War II, emigration sentiment turned very early to Canada. Princess Juliana had lived in Canada during the war and Canadian soldiers had been the principle liberators of the Netherlands. In addition, economic prospects looked promising in Canada's booming and labour-short post-war economy; Canada's appeal was further enhanced by its relative proximity to the Netherlands in comparison with other potential receiving countries such as Australia.[32]

The Van de Meent family, Dutch emigrants to Canada, pictured departing Amsterdam Airport on May 19, 1954. Left to right: Nico Van de Meent, Elizabeth Van de Meent and Jennie Van de Meent. The all-expenses paid flight was sponsored by the Dutch government. The plane landed at Gander, Newfoundland, then Montreal, Quebec. The family then took the train to Edmonton, Alberta, where they settled (Courtesy of the Glenbow Archives/NA-3796-1).

Thus the third wave of immigration from the Netherlands to Canada, like the first two waves, was composed primarily of people who were seeking greater economic opportunity for themselves and their children. A number of other factors provided additional motivation. For example, many Dutch people had a strong desire to escape the endless governmental "red tape" necessitated by attempts to deal with the problem of overpopulation. (Long waiting lists for employment and housing shortages which often meant the postponement of marriages were commonplaces of Dutch life.) Also, the cold war atmosphere of the late 1940s and early 1950s made many fear the advent of another world war. In addition, the severe flooding of 1953 forced a number of people to leave their homes. Still others wanted to leave Holland to escape what they felt was a restrictive social environment.[33]

For its part, Canada was favourably disposed toward the new Dutch immigrants. Immigration officials felt that they were competent farmers and would remain on the land. Also, some of the turn-of-the-century racist views continued to be reflected in the notion that the Dutch were desirable because they were of "Nordic stock." More reasonably, Canadian proponents of Dutch immigration argued that the Dutch would assimilate rapidly because of similarities between Canadian and Dutch society.

In 1947, the Canadian and Dutch governments, acting upon this mutual attraction between the two countries, negotiated an agreement whereby the Canadians would accept progressively larger groups of immigrants. It was decided that the two governments would determine how many people should come and they would then be placed by the Canadian Immigration Department in appropriate areas, depending on housing and job availability.[34]

Although Dutch immigrants went to many different countries in the post-war era, including Australia, New Zealand, South Africa, the United States, Brazil and Argentina, Canada was the destination of the largest number. Of the 250,000 Dutch who emigrated between 1945 and 1956, 42% came to Canada.

The first Dutch farm settlers in the third wave of immigration began arriving in Canada in June of 1947 under the arrangement known as the "Netherlands Farm Families' Movement." Between 1947 and 1955, the farm family movement comprised approximately 80% of the total Dutch immigration to Canada. After 1951, however, immigrants included not only farmers, but also people with business, professional and technical backgrounds.[35]

Post-war immigration dramatically changed the size and nature of the Dutch-Canadian community. By 1961, there were 430,000 people of Dutch origin in this country. Like those who had come to Canada during the 1920s, most of the post-war immigrants chose Ontario as their destination: over 50% went to southern Ontario where many entered truck gardening, mixed farming, dairying and other forms of intensive agriculture. About 20,000 Dutch immigrants, or 15% of the total, came to Alberta. During the 1950s, Dutch immigrants made up the third largest group coming to Alberta, outnumbered only by the British and Germans. The number of people of Dutch origin in Alberta increased by 89% between 1951 and 1961, more than double the growth rate for the Alberta population as a whole for those years, a period of rapid growth in the province.[36]

Beginning Anew: Settlement of Post-War Immigrants

Several features characterized the post-war wave of Dutch immigrants. It was comprised primarily of farmers, workers and lower middle-class people whose average educational attainment was generally limited to Grades 6 to 8. Most came in family groups under the auspices of a church organization and many were sponsored by relatives who had arrived earlier. All had a strong desire to become independent as soon as possible; farm workers wanted to own their own farms and tradesmen wanted to re-enter their trades or establish their own businesses. Another major characteristic of the movement was initial settlement in areas where the Christian Reformed Church had "field men"; the Lethbridge and Lacombe areas also had available niches in their agricultural economies. The Lacombe settlement more than doubled and Dutch-Canadian settlements also began in Rocky Mountain House and Red Deer due to the presence of an active Christian Reformed "field man" in central Alberta, H.J. TenHove.

Another striking characteristic of this third wave of immigrants was that the majority were farmers who were becoming involved in Alberta agriculture just at a time when the industry was undergoing revolutionary changes.

Technological advancements were making it possible for fewer people to farm larger tracts of land, thereby decreasing the province's total number of farms and farmers. However, with their experience in mixed and intensive agriculture, the Dutch farmers were able to make a successful adaptation to the changing situation by establishing mixed farms and initiating more intensive agriculture in the irrigated areas of southern Alberta and in the central park belt. Those in central Alberta specialized in dairying and potato raising, and they made a significant contribution to the development of both types of farming in the region. For the most part, like the previous wave of immigrants during the 1920s, the Dutch did not become involved in dryland and wheat-belt farming; instead they carved out a place for themselves by taking over the farms of those who wanted to move out of agriculture, by then farming the same land more intensively and, in a few cases, by bringing whole new areas under cultivation. By 1971, one out of every 20 farmers in the province would be of Dutch origin and the Dutch would have made a highly important contribution to the development of agriculture in post-war Alberta.[37]

As in earlier waves of Dutch immigration, the churches played key roles in this third wave; in effect, they took charge of the movement, partly for humanitarian reasons and partly because they were concerned with the immigrants' continued church affiliation. In the Netherlands, prospective immigrants registered with the Immigration Society which their respective churches maintained. In Canada, the churches hired field men whose duty it was to find sponsors for the immigrants who would in turn provide employment and housing for one year.[38]

The irrigated farmlands surrounding Lethbridge attracted the largest number of Dutch farmers during the post-war era. This was due primarily to two factors: the first was the presence of Bernard Nieboer, a farmer from Iron Springs who worked as field man for the Christian Reformed Church; the second was the existence of a severe labour shortage on farms in the area which made it possible for Nieboer to place hundreds of families throughout the district. By the late 1940s, many of the Japanese sugar beet workers who had been evacuated from British Columbia during the war had either acquired their own farms, moved to Alberta's urban centres or left for eastern Canada. At a time when demand for sugar was strong and prices were rising, their departure left a great demand for sugar beet workers and Dutch immigrants seemed to provide a perfect solution to the problem. They were experienced farmers in the prime of life, they were hard workers and they had large families, an indispensable requisite for the gruelling task of cultivating sugar beets. Many of the Dutch families who came to the Lethbridge area were exceptionally large since sugar beet farming required intensive labour and large families (occasionally numbering up to 18 or 19 children) were difficult to place elsewhere.[39]

The major areas of settlement in southern Alberta were on irrigated land near Picture Butte, Vauxhall, Iron Springs, Taber and Brooks. Other Dutch immigrants settled on dryland farms in the older communities at Granum and Nobleford and a few went to Bellevue and High River. Many who were settled in scattered areas soon moved to the major Dutch concentrations. In central and northern Alberta, post-war Dutch immigrants settled in and around Rockyford, Sundre, Lacombe, Rocky Mountain House, Red Deer, Neerlandia, Barrhead, Edson, Peers, and Grande Prairie. The arrival of the Dutch immigrants was usually soon embodied in the building of Christian Reformed churches which sprang up across the province in the post-war years.

The three largest cities of the province-Lethbridge, Calgary and Edmonton-also attracted many Dutch immigrants. Some immigrants came directly to the urban centres; others migrated to the cities when they had completed their one-year farm labour contracts. Prior to 1957, most of the post-war immigrants were farmers; after that time, many Dutch tradesmen and small businessmen began to emigrate to Canada. Consequently, the Dutch communities in the cities began to expand with the presence of a new type of Dutch immigrant. Among Alberta's cities, Edmonton attracted the largest number of post-war Dutch: by 1961, there were 6,739 post-war Dutch immigrants in that city compared to 4,621 in Calgary and 848 in Lethbridge. One reason for the concentration in Edmonton was the existence of a small Christian Reformed congregation in Edmonton which served to attract a number of city-bound immigrants and then provided them with help in finding jobs and housing.[40]

Despite the language and adjustment difficulties they initially encountered, the story of the post-war Dutch immigrants was ultimately a chronicle of remarkable success. The average period of time in which a Dutch immigrant acquired a farm was only three years. In a few years, many Dutch farmers were themselves employing other farm workers and becoming known in many parts of the province for their well-kept, clean and colourful homes and their successful farming practices. Similarly, Dutch immigrants to Alberta's cities were soon able to establish themselves in trades and small businesses as well as in technical and professional jobs. It has been a common experience for Dutch tradesmen to become independent businessmen, owning contracting businesses, machine shops or service stations. Dutch immigrants in cities and town across the province, but particularly in the Medicine Hat-Redcliffe area, have also combined agricultural and business skills in the pioneering and development of flourishing greenhouse businesses.

The Dutch who moved to the cities arrived during a period of economic expansion. The construction booms of the 1950s put labourers and skilled tradesmen in great demand and the Dutch were soon able to establish a strong presence in the construction industry. When they first arrived in the cities, most of the Dutch established homes in immigrant and working-class neighbourhoods. For example, in Calgary they concentrated in Bowness, Montgomery and Forest Lawn; in Red Deer most were on the East hill in Hillsboro and in Lethbridge they lived in North Lethbridge. In all of these districts, relaxed city codes allowed the building of relatively quick and cheap accommodation. Since these areas were the main centres of Urban Dutch settlement, the first Christian Reformed churches were built there.[41]

While the socio-economic composition of the Dutch-Canadian communities in all of Alberta's cities was similar, there were some noteworthy class and religious differences. Calgary attracted a more heterogeneous mixture of Dutch immigrants, in terms of religion and class, than either Edmonton or Lethbridge. While the majority of Calgary's Dutch were tradesmen, as in the other urban centres, Calgary also attracted a number of technicians, draftsmen, engineers and geologists who worked in the oil industry. Some had previously worked in Indonesia's oil fields, but left when Indonesia acquired independence. Many were employed by the Dutch-owned Shell Oil Company, though a number worked for other companies. Calgary also attracted a larger number of Catholic and secular immigrants than Edmonton where a Christian Reformed "field man" helped place Reformed immigrants. Lethbridge's Dutch population developed primarily as a spillover from the surrounding rural areas which had attracted Dutch farmers; consequently the Lethbridge community, reflecting the highly religious and sectarian nature of the rural Dutch-Canadian population, came to have the greatest variety of Reformed denominations in the province (comprising four different Reformed denominations). However, these differences among the Dutch communities in Alberta's cities can be seen as minor variations on a theme of hard work, social and political conservatism, strong, close-knit and patriarchal family life, ardent religious belief and minimal effort to maintain the Dutch language and culture.

While the Dutch in the post-war era have remained more rural than the Alberta average, like other Albertans they have increasingly chosen to live in cities. At the time of the 1971 census, 22% of those of Dutch origin were farmers, compared to 15% of all Albertans; but the typical Dutch experience of the post-war years has been urban. The proportion of Dutch living in urban areas grew from 35% in 1951 to 61% in 1961 and 71% in 1971. The number of Dutch people in rural Alberta decreased only slightly in the same time period, but the large growth in their total number was felt primarily in the urban centres. During a period of dramatic off-farm migration throughout the province (including most of the early Dutch settlements) the total number of rural Dutch has remained relatively constant only because of the establishment of several new rural settlements during the 1950s. The urban trend is reflected in census figures which show that the Dutch now comprise between 3% and 5% of the population in each of the province's major cities: in 1971 there were 14,370 people of Dutch origin in Edmonton, 13,790 in Calgary, 2,190 in Lethbridge, 1,420 in Red Deer, 655 in Medicine Hat and 555 in Grande Prairie. Census figures also confirm the major contours of the urban Dutch experience. Their representation among blue collar workers and the self-employed is above the provincial average, while it is below the provincial average in clerical, managerial and professional occupations.[42]

Religion and the Dutch: the Preservation of an Identity

Among the many post-war European immigrants to Alberta, the Dutch were the quickest to give up their language and to minimize non-religious cultural differences. This was generally true, whether the immigrants were Catholic, Reformed (or indeed joined another Protestant denomination), religious or non-religious. However, the Reformed immigrants made strenuous efforts to erect a complete institutional structure based on their church, which is their main expression of cultural identity. They brought with them a Dutch concept of the central role religion should play in life; their attempt to create a Christian society must, they believe, be reflected in all social institutions, including schools, trade unions, political parties and communications media.[43]

The post-war Dutch migration led to a substantial growth in the two Reformed churches which already existed in Alberta, the Reformed Church in America and the Christian Reformed Church, and introduced two new Calvinist sects, the Canadian Reformed and the Netherlands Reformed. These two new churches had stronger sectarian orientations than either of the previously established Reformed churches. The emphasis in Canada's immigration policy on Dutch farmers and farm hands and the control exercised by the churches in the immigration movement itself led to a re-creation in Canada of Dutch sectarian struggles and to the selective migration to Canada of some of the most religious and conservative elements in Dutch society. In Canada, the rural and church-oriented nature of the immigration movement also led to a shift in the relative proportion of various religious denominations from its configuration in Holland; thus, the Christian Reformed Church, which had been in a minority position in Holland, emerged as by far the largest and strongest of the Reformed churches in Canada and in Alberta. The Christian Reformed Church made up only 10% of the population in Holland, but in the early years of Dutch migration to Canada (1948–52) 41% of the Dutch immigrants belonged to it. With 36 congregations in 24 communities and over 13,000 members, the Christian Reformed Church is the largest and most influential denomination among Alberta's Dutch.[44]

The concern with the need to carry their message to the larger Canadian public has played an important role in the relative absence of efforts in Alberta in the post-war years to maintain the Dutch language and folk culture. Sociological studies show the Dutch in Canada to be the ethnic group with the least language maintenance, and the least desire to maintain their language and culture.[45] Dutch language and culture were seen as impediments to complete social and economic acceptance into Canadian society, including the acceptance of the Reformed churches as something more than Dutch "ethnic" churches. While there are other reasons for the relative absence of efforts to maintain Dutch folk-traditions and language, the religious orientation of the majority of the new immigrants is an important cause. While many other immigrant groups—Romanians, Ukrainians, Hungarians, Poles, Greeks, Italians, Portuguese, Serbs, among others—see religion and ethnicity as inseparable and mutually reinforcing, many Dutch immigrants view the two as being in conflict. For Christian Reformed leaders traces of "Dutchness" delay the acceptance of Reformed churches as fully Canadian churches and impede their ability to have an impact on Canadian society as a whole.

Paradoxically, however, religion has proven to be a significantly stronger force for group cohesion than ethnic identity. The deeply held religious convictions of many Dutch immigrants has prompted them to retain a viable and cohesive group identity, with a wide range of interlocking institutions and activities and minimal intermarriage outside the group, while simultaneously denying or minimizing their ethnic affiliation. Meanwhile, many other ethnocultural groups, whose leadership has been bent on retaining a strong group identity and has, to that end, articulated philosophies and programs of ethnic survival, have been much less successful than the Reformed Dutch in nurturing the continued existence of their group as an unmistakably distinct cultural entity.

Conclusion

Alberta's Dutch-origin population is now diverse, scattered and split along religious lines. It includes people who represent a wide range of lifestyles, from the urban, cosmopolitan and secular to the rural, conservative and sectarian. No longer do farm and church circumscribe the life of most Dutch-Canadians in Alberta.

The social and economic climate of Alberta has been, in many respects, tailor-made for conservative Dutch immigrants. The values of each have been mutually complementary. Most of the newcomers from the Netherlands have been staunch believers in the free enterprise system and have united with the majority of Albertans in their support for first the Social Credit and then the Conservative party. Also, the traditional views of Reformed immigrants with regard to social issues and family life have been in harmony with the consensus in a province long renowned for its "Bible belt" conservatism. The similarity between the beliefs of Reformed people and the dominant values in Alberta has facilitated their adjustment.

Each of the three waves of Dutch immigrants has contributed substantially to Alberta and to the Dutch communities of the province. In contrast with groups like the Ukrainians, Hungarians, Estonians and Romanians, where there have been substantial differences in occupation, education, social background and political beliefs between the three different waves of immigration, often resulting in strain and conflict, there have been relatively few differences among the various waves of Dutch immigration. The socio-cultural and religous backgrounds of people in each wave have been similar, thus greatly minimizing time-of-arrival conflict within the Dutch community. The first wave of immigrants may have been more oriented to the United States than later arrivals, since many of them had lived there before coming to Canada and consequently had developed links with the Dutch-American settlements; but in general, social and religious patterns have been similar for Dutch people coming to Alberta throughout the present century.

The early pioneer communities eased the adjustment of later immigrants by helping them find jobs and housing, giving them essential knowledge about Canadian life and providing them with established churches where they could worship and socialize in a familiar setting. During the post-World War II period, the early settlements at Nobleford-Monarch, Neerlandia and Lacombe acted as magnets for Dutch immigrants. Certainly many would have come to Alberta during this time whether or not there had been earlier settlements, but their presence increased the numbers of Dutch people who chose Alberta as their destination. The postwar immigrants in turn also had an impact on the rural settlements by reinforcing or reviving the Dutch flavour and invigorating community and church organizations.

In the history of the Dutch in Alberta many themes are found which are repeated in the histories of virtually all ethnic communities in the province. The complex motives for migration; the awareness of opportunities in Canada and in Alberta; the role of the CPR and the federal government in promoting immigration and facilitating the "settlement" process; the struggles of pioneering and attempting to eke out a living in a boom-bust economy; the interaction between different generations and waves of immigrants; the relationship between ethnicity, language and religion; the role of religion in community life; the patterns of relations with other Albertans-all are part of the history of every established ethnocultural group in the province. With the Dutch people as with members of nearly all ethnic groups, their awareness of events encompassed not only their own particular part of the province, but also developments in their homeland, in communities of their fellow countrymen in the United States, in other parts of Canada and throughout the province. Their mental maps of Alberta were shaped by the existence of scattered communities to which they were linked by language, religion or family ties. Neerlandia, Lacombe, Nobleford and Monarch were as much a part of Dutch-Canadians' awareness of Alberta as Cardston, Raymond and Magrath were for Mormons; as Dickson, Dalum and Standard were for Danes; or Eckville, Stettler and Barons were for Estonians.

The Dutch provide a particularly explicit example of the typical interplay of religious and economic motives and institutions in the process of migration and of the way in which both the CPR and the federal government made use of religious sentiments and organization to settle rural Alberta. This symbiotic relationship between government, railways and religious groups was clearly part of the history of many other groups, such as Doukhobors, German Catholics, Hutterites, Jews, Mennonites and Mormons. For all of these groups, their desire for economic and/or religious freedom and opportunity, coupled with federal government and CPR desire to have experienced farmers who would remain on the land, were consolidated in schemes for settling the Canadian west. With the Dutch, as with other groups, the government and railways made use of religious communication networks to promote immigration, operating on the assumption that close-knit religious communities would attract more immigrants and had good potential for economic success.

Although many of the Dutch immigrants who came to Alberta were undoubtedly individually devout, once they arrived organized religion often assumed even more significance in their lives. The importance of religion and the church was heightened by frontier isolation, which ensured that the church would become the centre for social activities and the main outlet for cultural identity. The church's centrality was further enhanced by the methods of the CPR and the government, which selectively attracted some of the most devout of the Dutch emigrants and placed them in a framework of overlapping religious and secular structures.

Subtle differences in the geography of religion among the Dutch in Alberta can only be explained by looking at the historical development of the group. Three of the four main Reformed denominations in Canada emerged first in southern Alberta since, prior to World War I, the area attracted the first large and stable settlements of Dutch-Canadians. This naturally led to the establishment of the Christian Reformed and Reformed Churches of America. In the post-World War II era, the attraction of the early settlements combined with a labour shortage in the sugar beet industry brought more Dutch people to the area, some of them members of two more conservative sects, the Canadian Reformed and Netherlands Reformed churches. Their notably large families were ideally suited to the labour intensive sugar beet industry.

Throughout the history of the Dutch in Alberta one sees a constant interplay between Dutch cultural characteristics and the Alberta environment. The years before World War II were a time of trial and error in which Dutch farmers gradually became familiar with the limitations and potential of various regions of the province. The post-World War II years have provided a backdrop for the enactment of numerous dramas of immigrant success in which the newcomers find secure niches for themselves in the emerging patterns of agricultural and urban economic development.

Notes
The authors gratefully acknowledge the assistance of Norma Milton, Joanna Matejko and Betty Wulff in conducting interviews. Dr. Herman Ganzevoort of the University of Calgary was also most helpful. Horst Schmid, former Alberta Minister of Culture, provided research funds for the study.

This article first appeared in *Prairie Forum* 7, no. 2 (1982): 237–65.

1. L.D. Cordes and D.J. Pennock, "Biophysical Constraints of the Natural Environment on Settlement," in Brenton M. Barr and Peter Smith (eds.), *Environment and Economy: Essays on the Human Geography of Alberta* (Edmonton: University of Alberta, 1984).
2. Herman Ganzevoort, "Dutch Immigration to Canada, 1892–1940" (PhD dissertation, University of Toronto, 1975), Chapter 1.
3. H. Palmer, "Nativism in Alberta, 1880–1920" (MA thesis, University of Alberta, 1971), Chapter 2.
4. Nobleford Monarch History Book Club, *Sons of Wind and Soil* (Calgary: Nobleford

Monarch History Book Club, 1976), 233; "Recollections, Mrs. John Hofman, Sr. (née Gertie Veldhuis)" (1970), p. 1 (in possession of Herman Ganzevoort).

5. Unpublished manuscript of Ted Reitsman on history of Dutch in Alberta in possession of authors, p. 1; Granum History Committee, *Leavings by Trail, Granum by Rail* (Granum, 1977), 258, 475, 415.

6. *Sons of Wind and Soil*, 75; Census of Canada, 1921.

7. Ganzevoort, "Dutch Immigration to Canada, 1892–1940," 169–73; *Sons of Wind and Soil*, 233, 383, 359–60, 380, 225, 204, 309, 393, 329, 386.

8. Ganzevoort, "Dutch Immigration to Canada, 1892–1940," 173–74, *Sons of Wind and Soil*, 70, 73–76; *Leavings by Trail, Granum by Rail*, 409; *Shortgrass Country*, 302, 317–18, 391–94, 452–53.

9. *Sons of Wind and Soil*, 70–75, 254; A.E. Palmer, *When the Winds Came* (Lethbridge: the author, 1972), 13.

10. Ganzevoort, "Dutch Immigration to Canada, 1892–1940," 176.

11. J.B. Hedges, *Building the Canadian West* (New York: The MacMillan Company, 1939), 167, 209–10, 284–85; Ganzevoort, "Dutch Immigration to Canada, 1892–1940," 122–24, 179; History Committee, Nightingale Community Association, *The English Colony: Nightingale and District*, 64, 196, 197, and passim; *Edmonton Bulletin*, September 12, 1907; *Calgary Daily News*, March 23, 1909.

12. Dutch families remaining in the area included the Bartelens, Lauweryssens, Pals, Van Wenzels, Willms, Kiemays, Vergouwens, Damens, Voermans, Ver Weires, Den Boers and Kiemenys. At the time of the 1921 census, there were 270 people of Dutch origin in the Strathmore area. *The English Colony*; Census of Canada, 1921.

13. Generalizations based on analysis of *The English Colony*, passim, and interviews Tony Bartelen, August, September, 1979, Lyalta, Alberta.

14. Ted Reitsma, "Neerlandia," 2 (unpublished manuscript in possession of authors); Ganzevoort, "Dutch Immigration to Canada, 1892–1940," 185–88; Barrhead and District Historical Society, *Trails Northwest: A History of the District of Barrhead, Alberta* (Barrhead: Barrhead and District Historical Society, 1967), Chapter 25; *Edmonton Bulletin*, April 4, 1911.

15. Reitsma, "Neerlandia"; Census of Canada, 1921.

16. Reitsma, "Neerlandia"; Ganzevoort, "Dutch Immigration to Canada, 1892–1940"; *Trails Northwest*.

17. Public Archives of Alberta, Oral History Tapes, 73, 81, interview with Ted Reitsma, February 17, 1973; Ted Reitsma, "The Struggles of a Dutch Immigrant," 25 (unpublished manuscript in possession of authors). Reitsma subsequently played an important role in the community of Neerlandia. *Trails Northwest*, 276; Ganzevoort, "Dutch Immigration to Canada, 1892–1940," 187.

18. This number included 3,125 Mennonites of "Dutch" origin. Mennonites in Alberta form a distinctive ethno-religious group and their "Dutch" origins have no real social meaning. Mennonites came to Alberta from Ontario, the US, Manitoba and Russia, and had not lived in Holland for several hundred years. Not all Mennonites registered with the census takers as Dutch; some gave "German" and "Russian" as their ethnic origin.

19. Ganzevoort, "Dutch Immigration to Canada, 1892–1940," Chapter 6.

20. Ibid.

21. Ibid.; *Sons of the Soil*, passim.

22. Coyote Flats Historical Society, *Coyote Flats: Historical Review 1905–1965* (Lethbridge: Southern Printing Company Limited, 1967), 238–41.

23. Ganzevoort, "Dutch Immigration to Canada, 1892–1940," 137.

24. Among the early families in the settlement were the Ten Hoves, Nienhuis, Weeninks, Bruinsmas, Brouwers, Bajemas, Prins, Martens, Hoeves, Siebengas, Tymstras, Salomons, Miendersmas, and Wierengas. Lacombe Rural History Club, *Wagon Trails to Hard Top: History of Lacombe and Area* (Calgary: Lacombe Rural History Club, 1972) pp. 621–64; interview, Frank Prins, Lacombe, September, 1979.

25. Census of Canada, 1931.

26. Ganzevoort, "Dutch Immigration to Canada, 1892–1940," Chapter 7; interview, Mr. A. Noy, July 26, 1979; Rockyford, Alberta.

27. *Big Hill Country: Cochrane and Area* (Calgary: Cochrane and Area Historical Society, 1977), 429, 562–63.

28. Reitsma, "Neerlandia," and "Struggles of a Dutch Immigrant."

29. Census of Canada, 1941, 1961.

30. William Petersen, *Planned Migration: The Social Determinants of the Dutch-Canadian Movement* (Berkeley: University of California, 1955), Chapter 5; Antony Sas, "Dutch Migration to and Settlement in Canada: 1945 to 1955" (PhD dissertation, Clark University, 1957), Chapter 1.

31. Sas, "Dutch Migration," 5–7.

32. Ibid., 9.

33. Peterson, *Planned Migration*, Chapter 6; Sas, "Dutch Migration," 112; interview, Ria Van Holten, Calgary, September 1979; K. Ishwaran, *Family, Kinship and Community: A Study of Dutch Canadians, A Developmental Approach* (Toronto: McGraw-Hill Ryerson Limited, 1977), 37.

34. Sas, "Dutch Migration."

35. Ibid., 37–44.

36. Ibid., 67; Census of Canada, 1951, 1961; Canada Immigration Division, Dept. of Manpower and Immigration Annual Statistics, 1956–69.

37. Sas. "Dutch Migration," 56; interview, Bernard Nieboer, Lethbridge, summer, 1967; interviews, Lacombe, Red Deer, September, 1979. Census of Canada, 1971; tabulations by authors from 1% sample.

38. Sas, "Dutch Migration," 19–21.

39. Niebor interview.

40. Census of Canada, 1961; interview, Simon Bennik, Calgary, September 1979.

41. Interviews, Red Deer, September 1979; *Atlas of Alberta* (Edmonton: University of Alberta Press, in association with University of Toronto Press, c. 1969), 60, 61.

42. Census of Canada, 1951, 1961, 1971. Figures on 1971 occupations from special tabulations, 1% sample.

43. For a good discussion of the religious organizational basis of Dutch society see Ishwaran, *Family, Kinship and Community*, Chapter 2.

44. Petersen, *Planned Migration*, Chapter 9; church membership figure calculated from *Yearbook* (Grand Rapids: Christian Reformed Church, 1979), 10-13.

45. Census of Canada, 1971, "Official Language and Language Most Often Spoken at Home," 28, 23, 24; Ken O'Bryan et al., *Non-Official Languages: A Study in Canadian Multiculturalism* (Ottawa: Minister Responsible for Multiculturalism, c. 1976), 74–155, 192; Maria Goossens, "Degree of Bilingualism among Dutch Immigrants in Calgary," in Regna Darnell (ed.), *Canadian Languages in the Social Context* (Edmonton: Linguistic Research Inc., 1973).

13. American-Resident Migration to Western Canada at the Turn of the 20th Century

Randy Widdis

Relatively few Canadian and American scholars have considered the importance of migration in linking people and communities on both sides of the border. The actual or perceived ease with which Americans and Canadians, particularly those of Anglo-Celtic origin, assimilated into each other's society and the significant difficulty in examining migration across the border given the absence of passenger lists and imprecise census data are the reasons most often given for the neglect demonstrated towards this topic. Yet sources do exist which allow us to reconstruct and analyse this international movement. Whereas work presented elsewhere by the author[1] investigates the causes, patterns and consequences of Anglo-Canadian emigration to the United States, this article examines American-resident (i.e., American-born, Canadian-born, and European-born) migration to western Canada at the turn of the 20th century, noting the origins, distribution, dimensions and causes of this movement, and offering a brief examination of the settlement experiences of these groups in the rural municipality of Estevan.

The Context of Migration
The Broad Picture
Although the first Homestead Act pertaining to western Canada was passed in 1872, the region failed to attract the thousands of Europeans and North Americans moving westward. Between 1870 and 1896, adjacent American lands were filling up while the Canadian Prairies remained largely empty. Kenneth Norrie argues that development of the region before 1879 was constrained by the lack of rail connections to export points.[2] This barrier was removed with the completion of the Canadian Pacific Railway in 1885 and the extension of its subsidiary, the Soo Line, and others to the Canadian

border at various points. Yet high wheat prices in the early 1880s touched off the "Dakota Boom" and western Canada continued to be ignored. Development of the region had to await the settlement of lands to the south and the end of the depression in world wheat prices which lasted until 1896.[3] Canadians constituted a major portion of this settlement with over 120,000 migrating to the American prairies between 1870 and 1890.[4]

The flow of movement shifted northwards after 1896 as the Canadian government capitalized on economic distress experienced by American farmers. Karel Bicha identifies those expulsive forces at work in North Dakota agriculture during this time, but the factors he discusses can be applied to the American prairie region in general.[5] They include significant increases in land prices, marked increases in tenancy and mortgaging rates, and unfavourable climatic conditions. Land in the Red River valley which had sold for $5 to $10 an acre in the mid-1890s increased to $20 to $40 an acre by 1900. The rate of tenancy for North Dakota quadrupled between 1890 and 1920 and by 1910 more than half the owner-operated farms in the state were mortgaged. The period 1900 to 1906 saw an abnormal rainfall with excessive precipitation in both spring and summer during four of these years, delaying planting and harvesting, coupled with drought in 1900 and 1903.[6]

American farmers hungry for cheap land looked northward to Canada, where free homestead land was available upon payment of a $10 registration fee,[7] and where land was selling for as little as $2 an acre in Saskatchewan.[8] Canadian officials, under the directorship of Clifford Sifton, minister of the Interior, exploited this demand for cheap land and instituted a program of land promotion advertising the Canadian Prairies as the "Last Best West."[9] Canadian land agents travelled throughout the western United States in search of potential settlers and organized Free Land Clubs. The government organized a massive publicity campaign in the United States as well as in Europe, providing guided tours for newspaper editors and farm groups and advertising in American magazines and newspapers. The Canadians were well rewarded for their efforts. For example, Paul Sharp notes that over 2,000 replies from the United States arrived weekly in response to the 1919 advertisements placed in American newspapers by the Canadian Land Owners Association of Regina.[10]

In many ways this movement across the border can be seen simply as an extension of the agrarian frontier into a region where "the American farmer found the same system of township sections, quarter sections, homesteads, education reserves, and railway grants ... that he had known in the States."[11] This Turnerian portrait, however, is too simple a picture of settlement in western Canada, a process that has only recently received detailed inspection at the micro-scale.[12] This was, in many ways, an international migration, composed of European- and Canadian-born as well as native-born Americans. Bicha, in fact, argues that a large percentage of the estimated 120,000 North Dakotans moving to western Canada between 1898 and 1914 were ex-Canadians and their children.[13] He suggests that Canadian officials made a conscious effort to attract their former compatriots by concentrating their attention in areas where former Canadians were numerous, and the difficulty of their task was lessened by the fact that many of the ex-Canadians were a "border people" who were easily persuaded to return to the Dominion. These Canadian repatriots came principally from Pembina, Cavalier, Walsh, and Grand Forks Counties, the Canadian-born population of which varied from 14.5% (Grand Forks) to 38.2% (Pembina).[14]

A Closer View

While many Americans and returning Canadians did come to the West as clients of various land companies, the majority operated independently, making decisions as to where to settle entirely on their own. It is this individual nature of the migration process that makes the examination of American and Canadian settlement of western Canada so difficult. The range of documentation is much greater for ethno-religious bloc and land company sponsored settlement than individual North American settlement. However, records do exist which permit one to reconstruct the migration patterns of these groups during the pioneering period of settlement.

Border Crossing Record Sample

The two major border crossing points for Americans and returning Canadians entering the Prairies were at Emerson, Manitoba and North Portal, Saskatchewan, with the CN, Soo Line, and Burlington Northern railways meeting at the former and the Soo Line crossing the latter in 1894 and joining the CPR main line near Moose Jaw. A brief empirical analysis of migrants crossing at North Portal between December 1, 1909 and January 1, 1911, the former date marking the start of the collection of the border crossing records, allows us to compare and contrast the characteristics of the various nativity groups involved in this movement from the United States to Canada.

During this 13-month period, 7,353 migrants were admitted into Canada by the immigration inspectors at North Portal and of this number 414, or 5.6% were Canadian-born heads of families or individuals above the age of 17. Returning Canadians ranked third behind American-born (67.9%) and Norwegian-born (9.6%). The Canadian-born were a varied lot. Most entries stated Canada as place of birth but there is good reason to believe, based on the information collected by those inspectors who asked for province of birth and data on last place of residence for Canadians coming from Canada, that the majority were born in Ontario. Almost 88% of the group had acquired American citizenship and over 50% of those retaining their Canadian citizenship last resided in the United States.

North Dakota was by far the most common place of origin among returning Canadians (46.8%), followed by Minnesota (9.4%), Ontario (referring to people from this province who chose to travel to Saskatchewan through the United States) (8.9%), Michigan (6.8%), Iowa (4.9%), Wisconsin (4.7%), Illinois (4.2%), South Dakota (3.7%), Montana (1.6%), and Kansas (1.4%). The migration field funnelling into western Canada via North Portal was significantly wide, demonstrating the pulling force of this new agricultural frontier. The availability of train transportation reduced the importance of distance as a factor in migration, yet it was largely a movement within the transborder region of the Great Plains. North Dakota was the major place of origin for Saskatchewan- and Alberta-bound migrants (and the lone Manitoba migrant) while considerable numbers to both provinces came from the midwestern region of the United States and the province of Ontario. Considerable numbers of Ontarians continued the tradition of travelling through the United States to western Canada despite the presence of the CPR. Ontario was the place of origin for most British Columbia-bound migrants.

Saskatchewan (48.2%) and Alberta (47.8%) were by far the preferred destinations, reflecting the fact that the migration was composed mainly of farmers attracted to the cheap land available in these new provinces. While the vast majority listed their occupation as farming (78.1%), many were of such a young age that it is reasonable to believe that they were farm labourers prior to their move. This reflects the fact that the vast majority of migrants from the United States came from nearby states and regions where agriculture dominated the local economies.

The majority of migrants were males, supporting one of Ernest Ravenstein's basic principles that males dominate long-distance migration (Table 1).[15] Over 74% of the female migrants indicated that they were travelling to join their husbands in their new homes. This explains in part the large percentage of males who travelled alone, suggesting that many went ahead with their stock and equipment and started the homestead before sending for their families. Canadian-born trailed all other groups in terms of acquiring American citizenship except for French-born whose small number (N=3) virtually excludes them from any meaningful comparison. Canadians proved among the most disinclined among immigrant groups to give up their citizenship although in this case, the requirement of American citizenship in order to obtain homestead land in the United States played a major role in such high percentages of naturalization.

According to Ravenstein, migration is dominated by the young. The average age of the returning Canadian-born migrant was 37.5 years which might lead us to believe that this migration was atypical. Indeed, Canadians (49.1%) ranked next to the English-born (52.0%) among nativity groups numbering over 100 in percentage of migrants over the age of 34 and first (16.2%) among these same groups in percentage of migrants over 49. American-born comprised the youngest migration group. Over 71% of native-born Americans were under the age of 35 as compared to only 50.9% of the Canadian-born. Migration is a contextual process and the fact that almost 50% of the migrants were over the age of 34 reflects the strong lure of free homestead land in western Canada, a force so powerful that it prompted many at later stages of the life cycle to pull up roots. For many Canadians, movement to western Canada represented a later or even last stage in their mobility life cycle, while this movement was for many Americans the first step in this same cycle. Perhaps this also supports to some extent the claim made by Bicha, that ex-Canadians were a "border people," easily persuaded, particularly in light of conditions in North Dakota and elsewhere, to return to Canada. While the average age of the Canadian-born return migrant was 37.5 years, the standard deviation value of 14.1 indicates that there was considerable variance of ages around this mean.

Western Canada appealed to young and old Canadian-born and American-resident alike, but capital certainly facilitated the migrant's adaptation. The average amount carried by the Canadian-born was $4,058, a considerable sum given the availability of homesteads and cheap lands, but necessary to cover the costs of farm making. The considerable deviation around this mean indicates that while some had very large amounts of capital which they may have used in speculative ventures, others had very little money and probably had to work as labourers before they could afford to start a farm of their own. Yet the profile of the average returning Canadian does not match the typical American immigrant, defined by Bicha as a tenant possessing between $800 and $1,400.[16] Whether or not such a discrepancy existed is doubtful given Bicha's questionable analysis.[17] Again among nativity groups numbering over 100, Canadian-born ranked highest in terms of cash on hand with 32.9% reporting they had more than $2,500 on their person. They were followed by the Germans (26.7%), the Norwegians (24.1%), the English (22.0%), the Russians (19.1%), and the Americans (17.4%). Wealth closely correlated with age and life cycle.

Table 1. Characteristics of Migrants by Nativity Crossing the Border at North Portal between December 1, 1909 and January 1, 1911

Place of Birth	Sex						Age											
	Male		Female		Unknown		<20		20–34		35–49		50–64		>65		Unknown	
	#	%	#	%	#	%	#	%	#	%	#	%	#	%	#	%	#	%
USA	4002	80.1	972	19.5	23	0.5	431	8.7	2986	59.8	1072	21.5	316	6.3	43	0.9	149	3.0
Canada	336	81.2	77	18.6	1	0.2	15	3.6	193	46.7	136	32.9	57	13.8	10	2.4	3	0.7
England	44	88.0	6	12.0	0	0	2	4.0	22	44.0	19	38.0	6	12.0	1	2.0	0	0
Scotland	19	76.0	6	24.0	0	0	1	4.0	14	56.0	6	24.0	2	8.0	2	8.0	0	0
Ireland	31	81.6	7	18.4	0	0	0	0	15	39.5	7	18.4	12	31.6	4	10.5	0	0
Germany	296	80.0	73	19.7	1	0.3	11	3.0	178	48.1	139	37.6	33	8.9	7	1.9	2	0.5
Russia	244	86.2	39	13.8	0	0	13	4.6	156	55.1	77	27.2	32	11.3	5	1.8	0	0
Austria	32	84.2	6	15.8	0	0	4	10.5	25	65.8	9	23.7	0	0	0	0	0	0
Hungary	0	0	3	100.0	0	0	0	0	1	33.3	1	33.3	0	0	1	33.3	0	0
France	3	60.0	2	40.0	0	0	0	0	2	40.0	1	20.0	0	0	0	0	2	40.0
Poland	591	83.6	114	16.1	2	0.3	22	3.1	391	55.3	200	28.3	88	12.5	5	0.7	1	0.1
Other	350	86.9	53	13.2	0	0	16	4.0	224	55.6	110	27.3	49	12.2	4	1.0	0	0
Unknown	7	35.0	10	50.0	3	15.0	0	0	1	5.0	0	0	1	5.0	1	5.0	17	85.0
Totals	5955	81.0	1368	18.6	30	0.4	515	7.0	4208	57.2	1777	24.2	596	8.1	83	1.1	174	2.4

Place of Birth	Occupation														Joining Husband		Joining Relatives		Other	
	Farmer		Labourer		Carpenter		Machinist		Merchant		Doctor		Other							
	#	%	#	%	#	%	#	%	#	%	#	%	#	%	#	%	#	%	#	%
USA	3715	74.3	180	3.6	5	0.1	5	0.1	10	0.2	1	0.02	88	1.8	169	3.4	800	16.0	24	0.5
Canada	324	78.2	11	2.7	2	0.5	0	0	2	0.5	0	0	8	1.9	13	3.1	53	12.8	1	0.3
England	43	86.0	1	2.0	0	0	0	0	0	0	0	0	1	2.0	1	2.0	4	8.0	0	0
Scotland	20	80.0	0	0	0	0	0	0	0	0	0	0	0	0	1	4.0	3	12.0	1	4.0
Ireland	31	81.6	1	2.6	0	0	0	0	0	0	0	0	0	0	1	2.6	3	7.9	2	5.3
Germany	287	77.6	10	2.7	0	0	0	0	0	0	0	0	4	1.1	5	1.4	63	17.0	1	0.3
Russia	238	84.1	0	0	0	0	0	0	0	0	0	0	1	0.4	6	2.1	38	13.4	0	0
Austria	27	71.1	0	0	0	0	0	0	0	0	0	0	0	0	5	13.2	5	13.2	1	2.6
Hungary	0	0	0	0	0	0	0	0	0	0	0	0	0	0	2	66.7	1	33.3	0	0
France	2	40.0	1	20.0	0	0	0	0	0	0	0	0	0	0	0	0	0	0	2	40.0
Poland	579	81.9	10	1.4	2	0.3	0	0	0	0	0	0	9	1.3	13	1.8	92	13.0	2	0.3
Other	332	82.4	15	3.7	0	0	0	0	0	0	0	0	4	1.0	4	1.0	46	11.4	2	0.5
Unknown	10	50.0	0	0	0	0	0	0	0	0	0	0	1	5.0	1	5.0	1	5.0	7	35.0
Totals	5608	76.3	229	3.1	9	0.1	5	0.1	12	0.2	1	0.01	116	1.6	221	3.0	1109	15.1	43	0.6

Table 1 (continued)

Place of Birth	Citizenship								People in Party												
	American		Canadian		Other		Unknown		Alone		With Spouse		With Spouse and Children		With Children Only		With Non-Nuclear Relatives		With Single Siblings	
	#	%	#	%	#	%	#	%	#	%	#	%	#	%	#	%	#	%	#	%
USA	4991	99.9	2	0.04	0	0	4	0.1	3792	75.9	171	3.4	267	5.3	641	12.8	3	0.1	123	2.5
Canada	364	87.9	50	12.1	0	0	0	0	303	73.2	17	4.1	24	5.8	59	14.3	1	0.2	10	2.4
England	44	88.0	0	0	6	12.0	0	0	42	84.0	0	0	4	8.0	4	8.0	0	0	0	0
Scotland	23	92.0	0	0	2	8.0	0	0	21	84.0	0	0	1	4.0	3	12.0	0	0	0	0
Ireland	37	97.4	0	0	1	2.6	0	0	30	79	3	7.9	1	2.6	4	10.5	0	0	0	0
Germany	365	98.7	0	0	5	1.4	0	0	223	60.3	19	5.1	60	16.2	61	16.5	0	0	7	1.9
Russia	274	96.8	0	0	9	3.2	0	0	179	63.3	9	3.2	49	17.3	43	15.2	0	0	3	1.1
Austria	35	92.1	0	0	3	7.9	0	0	33	86.8	2	5.3	0	0	3	7.9	0	0	0	0
Hungary	1	33.3	0	0	2	66.7	0	0	2	66.7	0	0	0	0	1	33.3	0	0	0	0
France	5	100	0	0	0	0	0	0	4	80.0	0	0	0	0	1	20.0	0	0	0	0
Poland	686	97.0	0	0	21	3.0	0	0	556	78.6	18	2.6	36	5.1	85	12.0	0	0	12	1.7
Other	390	96.8	0	0	13	3.2	0	0	321	79.7	10	2.5	13	3.2	48	11.9	0	0	11	2.7
Unknown	17	85.0	0	0	0	0	3	15.0	12	60.0	1	5.0	3	15.0	4	20.0	0	0	0	0
Totals	7232	98.4	52	0.7	62	0.8	7	0.1	5518	75.0	250	3.4	458	6.2	957	13.0	4	0.1	166	2.3

Place of Birth	Cash on Hand													
	<200		200–599		600–1199		1200–2499		2500–4999		>5000		Unknown	
	#	%	#	%	#	%	#	%	#	%	#	%	#	%
USA	1727	34.6	704	14.1	396	7.9	383	7.7	426	8.5	444	8.9	917	18.4
Canada	103	24.9	59	14.3	34	8.2	38	9.2	48	11.6	88	21.3	44	10.6
England	18	36.0	13	26.0	4	8.0	3	6.0	6	12.0	5	10.0	1	2.0
Scotland	2	8.0	4	16.0	4	16.0	6	24.0	4	16.0	3	12.0	2	8.0
Ireland	4	10.5	2	5.3	3	7.9	5	13.2	7	18.4	13	34.2	4	10.5
Germany	93	25.1	57	15.4	38	10.3	29	7.8	49	13	50	13.5	54	14.6
Russia	79	27.9	56	19.8	31	11.0	20	7.1	34	12.0	20	7.1	43	15.2
Austria	20	52.6	5	13.2	3	7.9	0	0	3	7.9	2	5.3	5	13.2
Hungary	1	33.3	0	0	0	0	0	0	1	33.3	0	0	1	33.3
France	2	40.0	0	0	0	0	0	0	0	0	0	0	3	60.0
Poland	218	30.8	130	18.4	43	6.1	70	9.9	94	13.3	76	10.8	76	10.8
Other	123	30.5	67	16.6	36	8.9	42	10.4	42	10.4	51	12.7	42	10.4
Unknown	1	5.0	0	0	0	0	1	5.0	0	0	1	5.0	17	85.0
Totals	2391	32.5	1097	14.9	592	8.1	597	8.1	714	9.7	753	10.2	1209	16.4

Source: Canadian Border Crossing Records

Canadian-born from North Dakota dominated the migration to areas surrounding small rural communities in Saskatchewan and Alberta including Maple Creek, Gull Lake, Mortlach, Herbert and Morse in the former and Taber and Seven Persons in the latter (Table 2). The larger centres such as Regina, Moose Jaw, Swift Current, Medicine Hat, Calgary, Edmonton, and Vancouver experienced wider migration fields, supporting another of Ravenstein's principles. Places of disembarkation for Saskatchewan-bound Canadian-born migrants are shown in Map 1. What is most striking about this map is the linearity of the destination pattern. The majority of the places of disembarkation were along the main CPR line and the Soo line.

Access to rail transportation and the market was obviously a major factor

Table 2. Twenty Most Common Destinations by Ten Most Common Places of Origin										
Destinations	Place of Origin (State/Province) (%)									
	North Dakota	Minnesota	Ontario	Michigan	Iowa	Wisconsin	Illinois	South Dakota	Montana	Kansas
Calgary	43.2	18.9	11.6	2.1	6.3	3.2	11.6	3.2	0	0
Moose Jaw	31.0	18.9	17.6	14.9	2.7	5.4	2.7	2.7	2.7	1.4
Swift Current	63.3	0	8.3	8.3	5.0	5.0	0	5.0	0	5.0
Lethbridge	40.0	20.0	0	10.0	5.0	7.5	5.0	12.5	0	0
Maple Creek	87.5	0	0	0	6.3	0	3.1	0	0	3.1
Gull Lake	75.0	0	9.4	3.1	3.1	3.1	6.3	0	0	0
Edmonton	40.7	11.1	11.1	11.1	3.7	0	7.4	7.4	7.4	0
Medicine Hat	52.0	8.0	12.0	4.0	8.0	8.0	0	0	0	8.0
Vancouver	0	42.9	9.5	23.8	0	9.5	14.3	0	0	0
Regina	57.9	5.3	5.3	15.8	0	0	10.5	0	5.3	0
Mortlach	76.5	17.6	0	0	0	5.9	0	0	0	0
Estevan	46.7	6.7	33.3	6.7	6.7	0	0	0	0	0
Weyburn	57.1	0	28.6	14.3	0	0	0	0	0	0
Bassano	50.0	7.1	21.4	0	0	7.1	14.3	0	0	0
Castor	41.7	16.7	0	0	25.0	8.3	0	0	8.3	0
Taber	91.7	0	0	0	8.3	0	0	0	0	0
Herbert	90.0	10.0	0	0	0	0	0	0	0	0
Morse	90.0	0	0	0	0	0	0	0	10.0	0
Seven Persons	80.0	0	10.0	0	0	0	0	10.0	0	0
Stettler	71.4	0	0	0	14.3	0	14.3	0	0	0

Note: italicized destinations are in Saskatchewan. Source: Canadian Border Crossing Records.

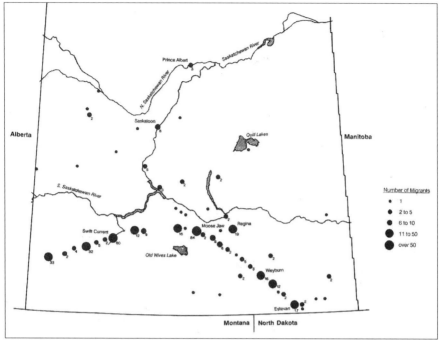

Map 1. Places of disembarkation for Saskatchewan-bound migrants.

in the decision-making process. But of course this assumes that the migrants located at or near the destination points listed in the border crossing records. Because the destinations given to immigration officers were simply the places migrants planned to disembark, the border crossing records are of little use in tracing the migration experiences of American-born and returning Canadian-born. Linking the border crossing destinations with other sources to trace exact location would be a horrendous task. Also, the lack of geographical specificity in terms of pre-migration locations makes backward tracing virtually impossible.

Local Histories Samples
A more useful source for reconstructing migration patterns is the local history. John Hudson has used county histories and information from the North Dakota Historical Data Project to map migration to North Dakota during the 19th century.[18] While the regional patterns derived from these histories are illuminating, the limitations are significant, as John Hudson himself admits. Most county histories were paid for by those whose biographical sketches were included, thus introducing a socioeconomic bias to the sample; and many of these sketches omit mention of places of intermediate residence,

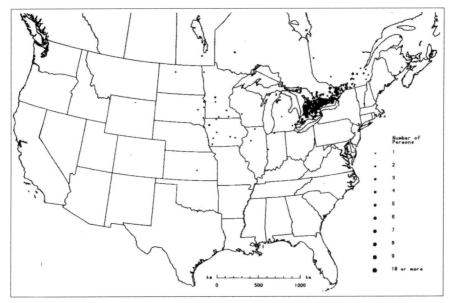

Map 2. Birthplaces in Canada and the United States of the seven rural municipalities sample.

thus making a full understanding of the migration process unachievable. The local histories housed in the Regina Public Library are less problematic than the histories used by Hudson for his work.[19]

Birthplaces and last places of residence were mapped for all (N=1265) migrants born in Canada and the United States before 1900 and settling before 1920 in seven rural municipalities (RMs) chosen for study.[20] Over 54% of the migrants were born in Ontario and they comprised over 91% of the entire Canadian-born group (Map 2). Just less than half of this group had foreign-born parents, with Irish, Scottish, and English ancestry predominating. Next in line, but considerably less significant in terms of size, were migrants born in England, followed by Scotland, Quebec, Ireland, Germany, Russia, Sweden, Norway, Northern Ireland, Iowa and Minnesota. Ontario-born migrants settling in these seven RMs came from all over the province, with the greatest percentage coming from Bruce and Grey counties, a major source region for Hudson's Ontario-born migrants in North Dakota. Rapid population growth in these counties between 1850 and 1880 created an unfavourable population/land ratio, making these counties "likely source areas for subsequent frontiers."[21] The St. Lawrence valley and eastern townships of Quebec comprised a secondary Canadian source region, but the majority of Quebecois who left these areas moved to New England. Only 6.2% of the sample migrants were born in the United States.

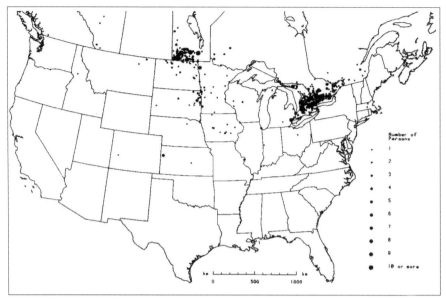

Map 3. Last places of residence in Canada and the United States of the seven rural municipalities sample.

More important, perhaps, for many migrants was last place of residence before settling because it was in this place that strong kin and kith relations shaping their future migration experiences in western Canada may have developed. Over 30% of the migrants moved more than once before settling in Saskatchewan but for the sake of simplicity only the last places of residence are mapped (Map 3), This map includes the last North American places of residence for European-born. Many Ontarians moved directly from their rural Ontario homes to Saskatchewan although there was some internal movement in the province, primarily to urban centres, among the young and to newer agricultural regions among those born earlier in the century. A considerable number had also moved to Manitoba before settling in Saskatchewan. While Ontario continued to be most important as a source region (46.7%), Manitoba in particular (19.3%), Minnesota, North Dakota, and South Dakota formed important secondary source regions. Many of the Scandinavian, German and other eastern European groups settling in Saskatchewan previously resided in Manitoba, the Dakotas, Minnesota and other states in the midwest region. Many of the English-, Scottish-, and Irish-born last resided in Ontario, Manitoba and the upper midwest.

For many American-resident migrants, western Canada represented another stage in their migration histories; for some, it would be their final move. By contrast, the prairie provinces for many eastern Canadians, primarily from Ontario, represented the first region to which they migrated, although considerable numbers did take up residence elsewhere in Ontario and Manitoba before moving further west.

Migrant Experiences in the Rural Municipality of Estevan

A cursory but useful insight into the experiences of Canadian (internal and return) and American migrants in the rural municipality of Estevan (RM #5) is revealed in the local history[22] and homestead records. The city of Estevan is situated approximately 17 kilometres north of the international border, 115 kilometres west of the Manitoba boundary and 215 kilometres southeast of Regina. Although agriculture would become the economic activity around which the region would develop, it was the coal resource which first attracted white settlers to this area.

Well before the community was founded, a number of individuals expressed interest in developing the lignite coal reserves in the area. The deposits at Roche Percée were first mined in 1880 by a group of Winnipegers who loaded the coal on barges which travelled down Short Creek to the Souris River and moved east to the Assiniboine River and on to Winnipeg.[23] During the next few years, more settlers, many originally from Ontario, moved west from the Manitoba border along the so-called "Coal-fields Trail," the anticipated rail route for the Manitoba South-Western Colonization Railway. This company received its charter in 1879 and the following year was granted permission to extend its service from Manitoba to the Souris coalfield. Many farmers in the Roche Percée vicinity operated their own coal mines, waiting eagerly for the arrival of the railway. Yet this line, which subsequently was purchased by the CPR, was not completed until 1892 (Map 4).[24]

It was in that year that Estevan was founded. The major players in the establishment of the community were involved in the Dominion Coal Company who opened a mine on the west side of town. They envisioned the development of an industrial centre based on the coal reserves, but their dreams were quickly shattered as the market for lignite remained very limited.[25] The development of the coal industry around Estevan was retarded because the sub-bituminous coal shipped from Alberta and the United States was favoured by the railways and settlers over the lower grade local coal. Development was also restricted because the bulk of coal-burning equipment was adapted only for higher ranking coals than lignite.[26]

The closing of the Dominion mine and a combination of drought and poor markets slowed development in the early 1890s, but growth was again stimulated with the completion of the Soo Line in 1894. Estevan benefited as

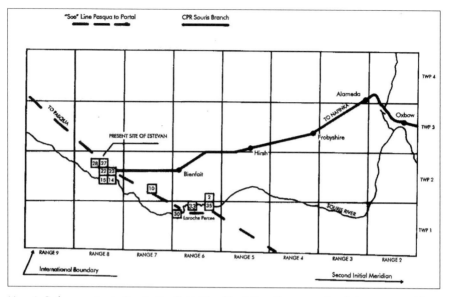

Map 4. Railway routes to Souris Coalfield. The "Soo" Line (Pasqua to Portal) is represented by a broken line (---), the CPR Souris Branch is represented by a solid line (—). Source: Corporate Archives, Canadian National Railway.

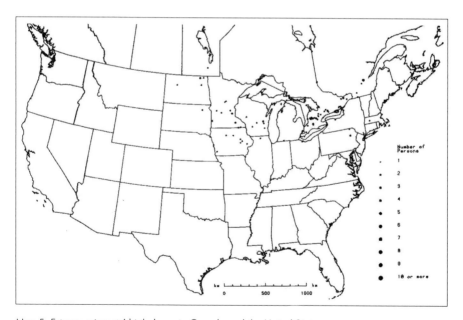

Map 5. Estevan migrants' birthplaces in Canada and the United States.

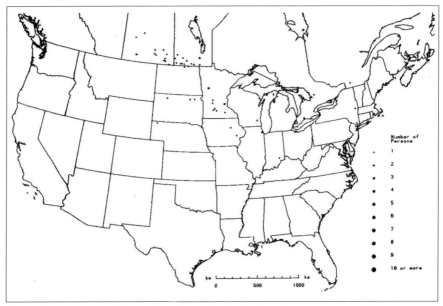

Map 6. Estevan migrants' intermediary places, North American born.

the junction site for the Soo and Souris branch lines. The capital generated by the railways stimulated business and the coal industry. Good growing seasons and the end of the global depression encouraged agriculture in the region and Estevan profited as the major service centre for the expanding hinterland. The clay soil of the area provided the raw material for the development of the town's brick industry.[27] Free homesteads, agricultural prosperity, and the accessibility afforded by the railways attracted immigrants, particularly Americans and returning Canadians, coming from North Dakota, Minnesota, Nebraska and Iowa (Maps 5 and 6). The region also drew migrants from eastern Canada, Manitoba, and other parts of Saskatchewan as well (Map 7). Estevan became incorporated as a village in 1899 and by 1901, practically all of the land within 12 to 16 kilometres of the railway had been taken. In 1904, the Dominion Lands agent reported all desirable homesteads had been taken up within 40 kilometres of any railway in the district. Land prices increased as settlers poured into the area but that did not deter farmers from purchasing land in order to augment their farming operations. By 1903, half of the homesteaders in southeastern Assiniboia had purchased an adjoining quarter section of railway land.[28]

The local history, *A Tale That Is Told*, provides information on 54 Canadian-born (34 from Ontario, 11 returning from the United States, and 9 coming from provinces other than Ontario) and 51 American-born settling

Map 7. Estevan migrants' last places of residence before settling in RM #5.

in the rural municipality of Estevan.[29] Over 47% of the latter group were farmers prior to their move, while almost 10% were labourers, and another 10% came as children. The occupations of 17% are unknown, while the remainder filled a wide diversity of positions including grain buyer, store owner, mill worker, drayman, railroad engineer, grocer, housewife, and livery business owner. As shown, most of these migrants last resided in North Dakota, Minnesota, and Iowa. That many of this group moved to Saskatchewan to enter into agriculture is evident in the fact that 75% of American-born in Estevan listed farming as their primary occupation. Three operated stores in town, two ran waterwell drilling businesses, and others occupied a variety of positions including drayman, carpenter, grain buyer, coal miner, fireman, and machinist. One of this group owned a coal mine, one operated a dray business, and one owned a livery business. A total of 42% homesteaded, 27.5% purchased their land, 5.5% rented, and 25% did not enter farming; 76% of this group remained in RM #5 for the rest of their lives, but we must realize that the local histories are biased towards those who persist over time. Almost 44% of the American-born resided in the RM for over 40 years, 33% lived there between 21 and 40 years, 13% stayed for a duration of 10 to 20 years, and 2% stayed between six and 10 years. The persistence duration of 9% of this group is unknown. Of the 24% who did not remain in Estevan, 11% moved elsewhere in Saskatchewan, 9% moved to British Columbia, and almost 4% (N=2) returned to the United States.

Although the local histories are very useful in capturing the patterns of return and internal Canadian migration and American emigration to western Canada, with few exceptions they say little about the settlement experiences of these groups. Fortunately, some of the accounts provide the reader with greater insight into the reasons for migration. For example, 27-year-old John M. Denton of Emerson, Iowa left that community in 1909 and settled in the Corinne area about 30 kilometres south of Regina. A year later, he and his family moved a short distance to Lang, where he homesteaded. In 1919, John and his family sold their farm and moved back to Emerson. Yet, as the local history recounts, "they found everything changed to what they had been used to and they decided to return to Canada." The following year they came to Estevan where John was employed by Prairie Nurseries in the spring and summer and worked on a threshing crew in the fall. He later worked as a drayman and in winter hauled coal. During the war, John was employed by the CNR and afterwards worked a rented farm with his son. After 37 years in Estevan, John died in 1957 at the age of 69.[30]

Born in Andover, South Dakota, 28-year-old Frank Durick came to Estevan in 1904. Prior to this move, he taught school in Pierpont, South Dakota and homesteaded near Columbus, North Dakota, a few miles south of the Canadian border. He followed his brother Michael and some of his neighbours across the line and homesteaded in the Forest Glen school district (SE¼-20-1-7 W2). Frank managed to acquire five more quarters of land before he passed away in 1950. The local history includes notes from his son, William, which give us insight into the nature of cross-border relations during this period:

> Who living along the border had not smuggled at some time? The amount of traffic of goods across the border depended on the price differences in the U.S. and Canada. Woolen goods were usually cheaper in Canada for the Americans. While the return on farm products was usually greater in the States. As people on both sides were neighbours and attended one's dances and parties the exchange of foreign goods was common. Horses and wagons did not carry licence plates and so even grain and livestock sometimes crossed the border.[31]

Despite the problems associated with the homestead records, they are useful for examining the characteristics of many of the original settlers in the

Table 3. Location of Homesteaders by Township and Nativity, Estevan RM #5

Nativity	Twp1-R7			Twp2-R7			Twp3-R7			Twp1-R8			Twp2-R8		
	No.	Row %	Col. %	No.	Row %	Col. %	No.	Row %	Col. %	No.	Row %	Col. %	No.	Row %	Col. %
Scandinavian	17	27.9	28.3	4	6.6	6.9	3	4.9	5.4	11	18	20	2	3.3	4.9
British	1	5.6	1.7	6	33.3	10.3	1	5.6	1.8	1	5.6	1.8	0	0	0
Other European	1	3.4	1.7	1	3.4	1.7	1	3.4	1.8	1	3.4	1.8	3	10.3	7.3
American	31	19.0	51.7	18	11.0	31.0	8	4.9	14.3	25	15.3	45.5	5	3.1	12.2
Internal Canadian	8	4.4	13.3	24	13.2	41.4	42	23.1	75.0	16	8.8	29.1	31	17	75.6
Returning Canadian	2	13.3	3.3	5	33.3	8.6	1	6.7	1.8	1	6.7	1.8	0	0	0
Totals	60	12.8	100	58	12.4	100	56	12.0	100	55	11.8	100	41	8.8	100

Nativity	Twp3-R8			Twp1-R9			Twp2-R9			Twp3-R9			Totals		
	No.	Row %	Col. %	No.	Row %	Col. %	No.	Row %	Col. %	No.	Row %	Col. %	No.	Row %	Col. %
Scandinavian	3	4.9	7.0	9	14.8	15.5	3	4.9	7.7	9	14.8	15.5	61	100	13
British	2	11.1	4.7	2	11.1	3.4	4	22.2	10.3	1	5.6	1.7	18	100	3.8
Other European	8	27.6	18.6	6	20.7	10.3	1	3.4	2.6	7	24	12.1	29	100	6.2
American	11	6.7	25.6	22	13.5	37.9	20	12.3	51.3	23	14.1	39.7	163	100	34.8
Internal Canadian	16	8.8	37.2	19	10.4	32.8	11	6	28.2	15	8	25.9	182	100	38.9
Returning Canadian	3	20.0	7.0	0	0	0	0	0	0	3	20	5.2	15	100	3.2
Totals	43	9.2	100	58	12.4	100	39	8	100	58	12	100	468	100	—

Source: Homestead Records.

study area.[32] The homesteaders who patented land in RM #5 arrived primarily after the construction of the Soo Line. Of those 23 entering their homestead before 1894, 21 were Canadians, all moving within Canada and most born in Ontario (Map 7). One homesteader was born in the United States and the other was Scandinavian-born, although a resident of the United States. Most of these early homesteads were located adjacent or close to the proposed Souris Branch leading eastward into Manitoba. Only two settlers homesteaded between 1895 and 1899, although several others purchased land adjacent to the Soo and Souris rail lines. Unfortunately few of the records include data on birthplace and, if applicable, previous places of residence, thus making it difficult to say much about the nature of migration among the different national origin groups.

The greatest influx of homesteaders (75.4%) patenting their property arrived during the 1900–04 period. Over 50% of all the homesteaders were not the original settlers on their quarter sections; in fact, many were not even the second pioneer listed in the records. But all those previous settlers abandoned the homestead for various reasons. Over 86% of the "Other European"-born homesteaders (N=29) came during this period, followed by 83.3% of the British (N=18), 80.3% of the Scandinavians (N=61), 80% of the returning Canadian-born (N=15), 78.5% of the American-born (N=163), and 68.1% of the internal Canadian-born migrants (N=182). Many of the European-born migrants had previously resided in the United States. This rapid influx of settlers infiltrated all parts of the rural municipality. The number of British and returning Canadians is too few to warrant attention while the "Other European" category consists of a large number of nativity groups with similar small numbers. American-born were distributed widely throughout the rural municipality although almost 48% located in the first townships of ranges 7, 8 and 9 close to the border (Table 3). Almost 32% of the American-born had Swedish and Norwegian last names and so a significant degree of this migration can be viewed at the same time as second-generation Scandinavian as well as first-generation American. Scandinavians were even more concentrated in these border townships with 27.9% in Township 1, Range 7; 18% in Township 1, Range 8; and 14.8% in Township 1, Range 9. In contrast, Canadian-born were oriented more towards the north of the rural municipality with 40.1% homesteading in the third range of townships, 36.2% in the second tier, and 23.6% in the border townships.

The reasons for this geographic distribution of homesteaders involve many factors, some of which remain hidden from objective analysis. The fact that most homesteaders among all nativity groups filed for entry during the 1900–1904 period indicates that date of settlement is not an important factor explaining this pattern. Except for the wooded slopes along the Souris, the region consisted of prairie grasses and so vegetative cover would seem not to be an important factor in location. Estevan lies in the dark brown soil region. North of the Souris River, medium-textured loam soils on glacial till modified by underlying shales dominate. Light-textured fine sandy soils on glacial lake alluvial deposits comprise most of the first townships of Ranges 7 and 8 in the southeast corner of the RM. Half of the first township of Range 9 consists of medium to heavy clay loams on glacial till moderated by underlying shales. These Trossach soils are less capable of supporting wheat cultivation than the other soils of the RM, but they are by no means unworkable. In most areas the topography is gently undulating to nearly level and most land is well drained, although there are a number of "burn out" pits, low knolls, and poorly drained flats and sloughs.[33] Given the degree of uniformity, soil quality and topography would also seem to have played an insignificant role in location. Relations among these groups were generally harmonious and so they had little reason to avoid each other. Much of the land adjacent to the railways was homesteaded and purchased prior to the homesteader boom and so the influence of the railway would seem to be minimal in explaining the relative concentrations of the Scandinavians and Americans along the border and the Canadians north of the town of Estevan.

Such geographic patterns may be explained by chain and cluster migration among kin and neighbours, although the poor recording of prior residences (less than 10% listed specific last place of residence) and sporadic designation of kinship affiliation in the records themselves make such an assertion difficult to prove. Almost 24% of the American-born homesteaders shared the same last name with one or more of their fellow Americans. Twenty-eight quarter sections were occupied by American-born located adjacent to quarter sections held by American-born with the same last name, and six American-born homesteaders with Scandinavian surnames located adjacent to Scandinavian-born settlers with the same last name, suggesting that a number of Scandinavians and Americans arrived with parents and children who filed in close proximity to one another. Almost 60% of those homestead records listing last place of origin for American-born and Scandinavian-born migrants include communities just across the border in North Dakota such as Bowbells, Bottineau County, and Kenmare. Of the 11 internal Canadian migrants for whom the homestead records list last place of residence, five came from somewhere else in the prairie region. Just over 19% of the internal Canadian-born homesteaders shared the same surname with one or more of their group, suggesting that a significant number of this group came to Estevan with other members of their families. Thirty-six quarter sections were occupied by Canadians located adjacent to quarter sections inhabited by people with the same last name, indicating that internal Canadian migrants also followed or accompanied relatives to Saskatchewan. This largely explains the clustering of this group in the northern part of the rural municipality. By contrast, only two among the returning Canadians shared the same surname.

The overwhelming majority of the homesteaders were male (Table 4). Of the returning Canadians, 75% were married, reflecting the fact that this group was generally older, although ranking second in average age to those born in Britain. Internal Canadian migrants were generally younger than other homesteaders, indicating perhaps that for many of this group, the move to Estevan represented the first and, what many hoped would be, the

Table 4. Estevan RM #5 Homesteader Characteristics by Nativity Group[1]

Nativity	Sex				% Married	# of children of married homesteaders		age at entry (known)		age at patent (known)	
	Males		Females								
	#	%	#	%		ave.	s.d.	ave.	s.d.	ave.	s.d.
Canadian (internal)	178	97.8	4	2.2	54.8	4.4	2.5	31.6	10.5	36.2	10.7
Canadian (return)[3]	15	100	0	0	75.0	3.0	2.8	38.3	11.8	41.5	12.6
American	161	98.8	2	1.2	56.9	3.1	2.6	35.1	13.9	38.6	14.2
British[4]	18	100	0	0	57.1	2.3	1.0	41.8	13.4	45.6	12.8
Scandinavian[5]	58	95.1	3	4.9	49.2	2.4	1.4	35.4	13.7	39.3	23.3

Nativity	$ value of all known improvements at statement[2]		# of cattle at statement		# of horses at statement		# of acres broken at statement		# of acres cropped at statement		average # of years before entry and patent issue
	ave.	range	ave.	s.d.	ave.	s.d.	ave.	range	ave.	range	
Canadian (internal)	868.55	10–1400	4.7	12.6	3.6	6.2	46.0	0–160	38.1	0–160	4.8
Canadian (return)[3]	349.33	80–700	3.1	4.2	3.1	1.9	62.2	25–110	51.5	18–80	3.5
American	350.08	20–2060	4	6.8	3.6	3.7	61.2	0–160	49.8	0–160	3.5
British[4]	485.83	0–1950	6.9	9.5	3.4	3.2	50.8	16–110	35.9	16–70	3.7
Scandinavian[5]	279.15	0–1150	3.6	5.5	2.5	2.9	57.6	0–145	48.8	0–145	4.3

1. not including other Europeans; 2. houses, farm buildings, fences, wells, etc.; 3. never relinquished citizenship (N=4), reacquired Canadian citizenship (N=8); 4. English-born - 11, Irish-born - 5, Welsh-born - 1, Scottish-born - 1, migrating from the United States - 7; 5. Norwegian/Swedish - 45.9% emigrated to Saskatchewan from the United States.
Source: Homestead Records.

last significant stage in their migration histories. In contrast, many of the European-born were experienced in long-distance migration, having come to America before emigrating to Estevan. The fact that Canadian-born home-steaders had the largest families indicates that many of them were still in the child-rearing stage, while many in the other groups had already experienced the departure of their older children prior to their move to western Canada. Yet over 50% of the Scandinavian-born and almost half of the internal Canadian migrants, American-born, and British-born were single. For the most part, unmarried homesteaders were younger than average.

Returning Canadians ranked first in terms of acreage broken and acreage cropped, followed closely by American-born, and then by Scandinavian-born, British-born, and (internal) Canadian-born. Yet while the latter group registered lowest in terms of acreage cleared and cropped, they ranked well above the rest in terms of mean value of all known improvements at the time of their patent. In addition, they rate first (tied with American-born) in average number of horses and second to the British in average number of cattle.

Thus, Canadians present a bit of a puzzle because one would expect the youngest families with the largest number of children and the lowest clearing rates to be among the poorest. Concrete reasons for this apparent anomaly cannot be discerned from the evidence at hand but two possible explanations are offered. Canadians on average took longer to file for patent than other groups and so it is conceivable that some used this extra time to build farm buildings, wells and fences. This might explain the higher average value for improvements and the lower average clearance and cropping rates.

The other possible explanation rests with the other homesteader groups. For a number of reasons, many of these individuals may have come to Canada with less capital in hand. Those who came directly from Europe may have spent a lot of their savings in getting to Estevan. Most European- and American-born came from north-central states such as North Dakota where adverse climatic conditions and rapidly increasing land prices in the late 1890s reduced farm income and made it more difficult for parents to provide for children. It is also possible that some of these groups from the United States had incurred expenses upon transferring land and/or capital to family members not accompanying them to Canada. Again, the nature of the data source means that any explanations offered are only conjectures.

The homestead records present several difficulties in the study of migration and settlement, yet they remain the richest source of information about these subjects in the context of western Canada. I decided to link these records with the landholder information present in the Cummins Rural Directory Maps in order to trace persistence over time. The Cummins Map Company of Winnipeg, founded by Oliver F. Coumins (who later changed his name to Cummins), was a private business producing directory maps for commercial use. Originally located in Regina, this company began producing land owner maps in 1917 based on local assessment rolls for the three prairie provinces. Although no one is certain about the rationale behind their selection of rural areas to be mapped, the primary market for the maps seems to have been residents of the regions shown, suggesting the Cummins mapped relatively heavily settled areas and avoided the sparsely populated southwestern part of Saskatchewan. The success of Cummins's 1917 series prompted them to expand their efforts into Ontario and Prince Edward Island and to create maps for 1918, 1920, 1926, and 1930, after which the Depression felled the company. The original map series for 1917, 1920, 1922, 1926, and 1930 are available in the Saskatchewan Archives in Regina with a microfilm copy of the 1918 series.

I first consulted the Land Location Index to determine the file numbers

Table 5. Persistence among Homesteaders Receiving Patents before 1917 by National Origin, Estevan RM #5

Nativity	1917 (%)	1920 (%)	1922 (%)	1926 (%)
American	38.8	26.4	24.9	18.4
British	54.5	27.3	27.3	13.3
Canadian (internal)	41.5	32.8	27.9	20.8
Canadian (return)	20	13.3	13.3	0
Other European	33.3	25	20.8	12.5
Scandinavian	57.9	42.1	39.5	26.3

Sources: Cummins Rural Directory Maps, 1917, 1920, 1922, 1926; Homestead Records.

for each homestead. I examined each homestead file and then traced each homesteader through the 1917, 1920, 1922, and 1926 Cummins maps (the 1930 map is not available). Table 5 clearly illustrates the notable transiency that characterized the homesteading period, even among those who stayed long enough to prove up their land. Scandinavian-born and internal Canadian migrants displayed a greater propensity to remain in situ although there was considerable turnover among all groups, even when accounting for disappearance from the Cummins maps because of death. According to Michael Comm and Paul Voisey, those settlers who had a "supplementary occupation" were considered to have greater economic stability, which, in turn, resulted in greater persistence.[34] For this study, "supplementary occupation" was taken to mean any additional seasonal work undertaken when absent from the homestead for three to four months a year during the proving-up period. A majority of the homesteaders worked off their homestead during their proving-up period (68.6% of the Canadians, 57.1% of the returning Canadians, 50.7% of the Americans, 50% of the "Other European" group, 46.2% of the Scandinavians, and 33.3% of the British). Most worked in the vicinity, either in the coal mines of Bienfait, Roche Percée, or Coalfield, or as farm labourers for relatives or others. Yet homesteaders engaging in such activity were not more likely to persist than those who had always resided on their homestead land. Relative uniformity in terms of age profiles and land quality would seem to indicate that these factors did not play a significant role in determining persistence among the various nativity groups, but much remains hidden behind the statistics presented in Table 5.

Conclusion

The majority of American residents, including native-, Canadian-, and European-born, migrating from the United States to Saskatchewan at the turn of the 20th century were part of an international movement to what was hailed as the last remaining agricultural frontier in North America. It is very clear that economic opportunity and the presence of kin and kith were influential factors in their decisions to move north of the 49th parallel.

People followed family and friends and economic opportunity, and in this regard the border was not much of an impediment. The arrival of railways and the opening of new frontiers spurred longer distance migration within North America and movement over time became more frequent and more urban-oriented. Yet migration for most remained short distance, even though the cumulative span of migration increased. The Canadian Prairies, however, attracted migrants from both near and far, and the availability of free homestead land meant that this region would be settled by those primarily, but not solely, interested in farming.

Besides attracting American residents, the settlement boom in western Canada at the turn of the century also drew large numbers of people from the eastern part of Canada, particularly from Ontario. This in effect changed the very nature of internal migration in the country, for while such movement was previously short distance, rural-urban in orientation, and often proceeded in stages, after the opening up of the West, it became long distance, rural in direction, and was frequently direct in character. Many did, however, move in stages, migrating to Manitoba and other parts of the Prairies before taking up their land in Saskatchewan, the focus of this analysis.

It is difficult to say anything meaningful about the migrant experience because of the lack of informative sources. The profile that does emerge from the border crossing records and the Estevan case study reveals that returning Canadians were generally an older group. Many had already passed through a number of life cycle and migration stages; they differed greatly in cash and value of property both upon migration and during the proving-up period (the border crossing study showed Canadians to be among the wealthiest of nativity groups crossing at North Portal, while the Estevan study showed returning Canadians to have lower improvement values than other groups with the exception of the Scandinavians); and they were no more likely than other groups to persist in place. By contrast, the border crossing study showed Americans to be among the youngest and, consequently, the poorest of nativity groups crossing at North Portal, contrary to the typical American-born immigrant as portrayed in the literature and the aggregate statistics. Again, it is risky to make any conclusions based on the limited size of the Estevan sample, but it is important to note that at least in this part of the Prairies all groups displayed high rates of transiency. For many, including those who had already made a number of moves, Estevan and other parts of the Prairies would represent just another temporary stage in their migration history.

While the data sources and strategies employed provide insight into the nature and pattern of Canadian and American migration to the Canadian Prairies, they fail to reveal much about the settlement experiences of these groups. Such a detailed analysis awaits the release of the 1911 and 1921 manuscript censuses, which will make possible the tracing of persisters over time, and an intensive examination of assessment and property records, which will allow the researcher to understand better the circumstances and strategies of those who chose to move on. Only then will we be able to appreciate social and geographical mobility, agricultural production, property behaviour, family structure, and social class in this new frontier.

Notes

This article first appeared in *Prairie Forum* 22, no. 2 (1997): 237–62.

1. See for example: "With Scarcely A Ripple: English Canadians in Northern New York at the Beginning of the Twentieth Century," *Journal of Historical Geography* 13, no. 2 (1987): 169–92; "'We Breathe the Same Air': Eastern Ontario Migration to Watertown, New York in the Late Nineteenth Century," *New York History* 68, no. 3 (1987): 261–80; "Tracing Eastern Ontario Emigrants to New York State, 1880–1910, " *Ontario History* 81, no. 3 (1988): 201–33; "Scale and Context: Approaches to the Study of Canadian Migration Patterns in the Nineteenth Century," *Social Science History* 12, no. 3 (1988): 269–303.

2. K.H. Norrie, "The Rate of Settlement of the Canadian Prairies, 1870–1911," *Journal of Economic History* 35 (1975): 426.

3. Ibid., 427.

4. Ibid., 410.

5. K. Bicha, "The North Dakota Farmer and the Canadian West, 1896–1914," *North Dakota History* 29 (1962): 297–98.

6. Ibid.

7. J.H. Archer, *Saskatchewan: A History* (Saskatoon: Western Producer Prairie Books, 1980), 56.

8. Bicha, "The North Dakota Farmer," 297.

9. P.F. Sharp, "When Our West Moved North," *American Historical Review* 55 (1949): 289.

10. Ibid.

11. Ibid., 288.

12. For example, see: M. Lewry, "The Invisible Partner: The Influence of the Financial Sponsor on the Development of Three Nineteenth Century Hebridean Colonies in Western Canada," in A.H. Paul and R.W. Widdis (eds.), *The Moose Mountain Papers*, Regina Geographical Studies Series, No. 5 (Regina: Department of Geography, University of Regina, 1988), 1–23; P. Voisey, *Vulcan: The Making of a Prairie Community* (Toronto: University of Toronto Press, 1988); S. Boyd, "Prairie-Bound: A Geographical Investigation of German, Scandinavian and Canadian-Born Settlement in Southern Saskatchewan, 1896–1930" (MA thesis, University of Regina, 1989).

13. Bicha, "The North Dakota Farmer, " 299.

14. Ibid., 199–300.

15. E.G. Ravenstein, "Census of the British Isles, 1871"; "Birthplaces and Migration," *Geographical Magazine* 3 (1876):173–77, 201–06, 229–33; "The Laws of Migration," *Journal of the Royal Statistical Society* 48 (1885): 214–301.

16. K. Bicha, *The American Farmer and the Canadian West, 1896–1914* (Lawrence: Coronado Press, 1968).

17. A number of scholars including Norrie criticize Bicha for making generalizations unsubstantiated by the data available.

18. John Hudson, "Migration to an American Frontier," *Annals of the Association of American Geographers* 66 (1976): 242–65.

19. For greater discussion of the use of this source, see my article: "Saskatchewan Bound: Migration to a New Canadian Frontier," *Great Plains Quarterly* 12, no. 4 (1992): 254–68.

20. The rural municipality local histories indude: Key West RM #70, *Prairie Grass to Golden Grain*; Mayfield RM #91, *Across Border and Valley*; Cymri RM #36, *Plowshares to Pumpjacks*; Foam Lake RM #276, *They Came From Many Lands*; Caledonia RM #99, *From Prairie Plow to Now*; Mervin RM #499, *Turtleford Treasures*; Pittville RM #169, *Hazlet and Its Heritage*.

21. Hudson, "Migration to an American Frontier," 245.

22. *A Tale That is Told: Estevan 1890–1980* (Estevan: Estevan Book Committee, 1981).

23. *Estevan Mercury*, December 26, 1912: 21.

24. Myrl Leyton-Brown, "The History of Estevan During the Territorial Period" (MA thesis, University of Regina, 1982), 36, 49.

25. *Estevan Mercury*, December 26, 1912: 8–9.

26. Michael Freedman, "A Geographical Analysis of the Estevan Coalfield, 1880–1966" (MA thesis, University of Saskatchewan, 1968), 36.

27. *Estevan Mercury;* December 26, 1912: 9.

28. Leyton-Brown, "The History of Estevan," 58.

29. *A Tale That Is Told.*

30. Ibid., 706.

31. Ibid., 740.

32. For further discussion of this source, see: Widdis, "Saskatchewan-Bound."

33. This background comes from: J. Mitchell, H. Moss and J. Clayton, *Soil Survey of Southern Saskatchewan*, Soil Survey Report No. 12 (Saskatoon: University of Saskatchewan, 1962), 87–90.

34. Michael Conzen, *Frontier Farming in an Urban Shadow* (Madison: University of Wisconsin Press, 1971); Voisey, *Vulcan*.

14. Welsh Americans in Rural Alberta: Origin and Development of the Wood River Welsh Settlement Area

Wayne K.D. Davies

Introduction

The prairie provinces may seem an unlikely place to find the Welsh, a people used to intimate and varied landscapes of green hills, valleys and cloudy skies: a land markedly different from the Prairies—vast, flat or rolling grasslands, overpowered by the omnipresent blue sky and a long, numbing winter, bordered by the trackless lakes and forests of the Canadian Shield and the towering Rockies. Although there are only a few studies of the Welsh contribution to Canada (Bennett 1986; Davies 1986), it is known that people of Welsh origin were among the early European explorers and pioneers in the area that became the prairie provinces, from Button's discovery of the west coast of Hudson Bay in 1612–13, to the work of The Reverend David Thomas Jones, a missionary in the Red River Settlement of Manitoba (Davies 1991). However, the Welsh did not make a major contribution to the massive migration that peopled the area from the end of the 19th century. By 1921, when the peak of immigration had passed, only 0.70% of the Prairies' population was recorded as being of Welsh ethnic origin, compared with 28.48% of English origin, 15.63% Scottish and 11.47% Irish (DC 1921). This relative anonymity was intensified by the fact that most of the Welsh immigrants scattered throughout the countryside, or settled in the bigger towns. However, two Welsh rural concentrations can be recognized. One is the area around Bangor (Saskatchewan), settled in 1902 by migrants from the Welsh colony in Patagonia (Johnson 1962; Thomas 1971). The other significant rural settlement associated with people of Welsh origin—Welsh Americans rather than Patagonians—is in the Wood River region, near Ponoka (Alberta), which is the subject of this study.

The Prairie Context

The massive boom in immigration to the Prairies began in 1896 with the election of a vigorous Liberal administration that saw the rapid settlement of the Prairies as part of a new national priority. It resulted in the rapid growth of the population of the prairie provinces: from 219,000 in 1891, to 414,000 in 1901, 1.33 million in 1911 and 1.96 million in 1921. In 1896, net migration to Canada had sunk to only 17,000 people, but after vigorous promotional campaigns, immigration peaked at 402,000 migrants in 1912–13, most of whom went to the western provinces. But during this peak year of immigration, only 2,019 people were recorded as coming from Wales, less than a fiftieth of the number of English migrants in 1912–13, a fifteenth of the Scottish and two-fifths of the Irish migrants (DI 1914) in the year. Since similar low values were found in other years, this trend means that the Welsh contribution to the prairie population was very small. By 1916 the prairie census recorded only 11,124 people of Welsh ethnic origin: 4,614 in Alberta (0.93% of the provincial total), 3,446 in Saskatchewan (0.53%) and 2,706 in Manitoba (0.48%). Superficially, this small contribution from Wales seems puzzling, given the historic attraction of Canada to the Scottish and Irish, the other Celtic peoples of the British Isles. Only a small part of the explanation can be attributed to the smaller population of Wales. In 1911 the Welsh population of almost 2.5 million was 42% and 45% of the Irish and Scottish populations respectively, and approximately half lived in and around the south Wales coalfield—at most 55 miles long by 25 miles wide—which, incidentally, contained almost as many people as the 1.3 million people spread across the 900-mile width of the three prairie provinces. Obviously the population discrepancies between the Celtic countries cannot explain the massive differences in the relative proportions of their migrants to Canada. Instead, the differences can be attributed to three factors. Many job prospects in Wales, in its early 20th century booming industrial areas, were closer to home for the rural surplus, which could be absorbed within the country (Thomas 1972). In addition, the United States exerted a greater attraction than Canada because of its greater size, employment opportunities and milder climate. Moreover, the presence of many Welsh migrant areas in the United States also eased the newcomer's transition to a new land, whilst its republican government appealed to those who disliked English imperialism. Finally, migrants from Wales were almost certainly under-enumerated; immigration officials often recorded people from Wales as English in the records, especially if they left from the docks at Liverpool. This does not mean that we should question the fact that the numbers were low, relative to the other people from the British Isles, merely that the absolute size recorded in the census, and especially the immigration statistics, were underestimates of immigrants from Wales.

The small numbers of migrants from Wales were probably disappointing to immigration officials since the Canadian government had targeted Wales as a likely source for migrants (Davies 1999a). One major effort aimed at Wales was through the Crow's Nest Pass railway work scheme of 1897, although it has been shown the project was not succesful and was steeped in controversy (Jenkins 1986; Davies 1999b). If the scheme had succeeded in its objective of bringing in a thousand Welsh labourers, a core area of Welsh settlement might have been established in the future province of Alberta, subsequently attracting many other migrants from Wales. However, the failure of the scheme may have had another consequence: the recognition that Wales and the rest of the British Isles would never produce enough people to settle the Prairies. This may well have helped convince immigration officials to allow the immigration of thousands of Eastern Europeans to the Prairies, forever changing the ethnic mix of the region (Lehr and Davies 1993). Indeed, by 1921, 421,000 (21.56%) of the prairie population of 1.96 million were of Germanic and Slavic ethnic origin, although those with British and Irish origins still constituted the majority—55.58% of the total. But the new Liberal immigration initiative did not only focus on Europe. Strenuous efforts were made to encourage emigration from the United States, leading to a massive influx of Americans in search of new lands and opportunities. There were less than 5,000 American-born settlers on the Prairies in 1891 according to Canadian census sources (DC 1891, 1921). By 1901 the figure had reached 40,000, then boomed to 217,000 by 1911, reaching 374,000 in 1921—19% of the prairie population—although many Americans were of British origin. Among the Americans who settled in the West were a small group of Welsh Americans.

The Entry of the Welsh Americans

The northward migration of settlers from the United States was helped by the active promotion of opportunities in the Prairies and by the drought conditions in the American Midwest during the mid-1890s. Yet such "push" factors seem less important than the "pull" factors. In the first place the Canadian Prairies seemed to be a bargain to many in the United States. By selling their farm in the south they could obtain free, or certainly much cheaper, land in Canada. Secondly, the United States frontier was effectively closed by this date, so the problem of where a farmer could secure a future for his sons became a real one—especially for the bigger families. Third, the parkland environment north of Red Deer—a rolling, well-watered area with mixed trees and grass—was far more attractive to those of Western European origin than the arid short grass prairies of the American Midwest or southern Alberta. The obvious difficulties caused by the shorter growing season in Canada had been reduced by the introduction of faster growing crops in the 1890s. The resultant northern flood of Americans gave a distinctive character to the settlement of the western prairie provinces, so that by 1916 there were 198,000 immigrants in the Prairies who had been born in the United States, compared to 282,000 born in the British Isles. Not all of these were Americans of long heritage. Many were European and Canadian immigrants to the United States, or first or second generation descendants. Among this often polyglot group were families of Welsh origin. Some had spent time in the United States after emigrating from Wales; others were first generation Americans of Welsh parents. A group of these settled in several townships east of Ponoka, in the Wood River area, twenty-five to thirty miles southwest of the provisional location planned by the Winnipeg Commissioner of Immigration for Welsh labourers associated with the 1897 Welsh Crow's Nest Pass labourer scheme (Davies 1999b). This led to the creation of the distinctive Welsh settlement area at Wood River, although there was also a scatter of other Welsh settlers in and around Ponoka itself.

The Wood River settlement in Alberta is some six miles east of Ponoka and 60 miles southeast of Edmonton, mainly in the central part of Townships 42 and 43, Ranges 23 and 24, west of the 4th Meridian. Most Welsh settlers had fulfilled the three-year residency and land-breaking requirement of the Canadian homestead regulations to obtain title to a 160-acre allotment (Tyman 1972) or had purchased the standard CPR quarter section (160 acres) parcels in the first few years of the 20th century—at $3 an acre in this region.

Most of the area that became the Welsh rural settlement area (see Figure 1) consists of a rolling or undulating plain southeast of the Bobtail Indian Reserve, with the highest point at the small hill now known as Jenkins Hill (Section 32, Township 42 Range 23)—named after the pioneering Welsh family in the area. In the northeast of the zone that was occupied by the Welsh, the land is flatter, with a gentle slope to the flat valley floor occupied by the slow and meandering Battle River which empties into Battle Lake.

The first detailed maps of the area, surveyed between 1873 and 1893 and published by the federal government in 1897, contain not only the topographic comments of the original surveyors but also the vegetation and soil characteristics. The land is composed of good to fair loamy soil over a subsoil of glacial sands and gravels. The topography is the typical product of glacial deposition. Scattered through the area are small hollows left by the

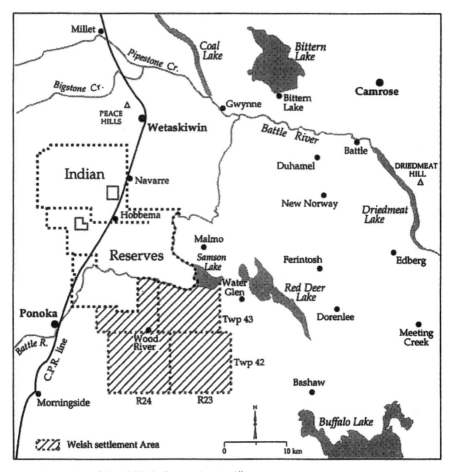

Figure 1. Location of the Welsh Settlement Area in Alberta.

retreating ice, occupied by marshes, sloughs or small lakes. Occasional deeper trenches are found, gouged out by the northwest to southeast trending spillways that had drained the glacial lakes to the west—lakes created by the retreat of the Continental and Rocky Mountain ice sheets. Two large marshes are found in the area: one lies to the north of the Battle River valley; the other, to the west of the Wood River settlement, occupies a half-mile-wide belt in the southern part of Township 43 Range 25. In the early days of settlement the latter marsh provided a barrier to easy communication with the nearest service centre, Ponoka, a town located on the Edmonton-Calgary railway line which was constructed in 1893. The original vegetation of the region was mixed grassland and woods, the latter mainly 20- to 30-foot high stands of popular and willow, but with some patches of spruce and birch

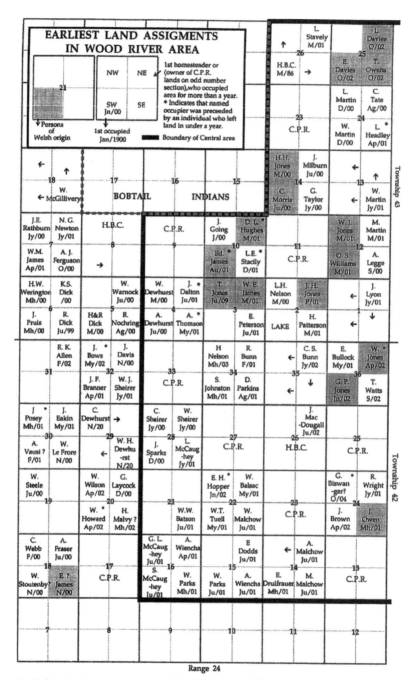

Figure 2a. Earliest land assignments in the Wood River Area—West.

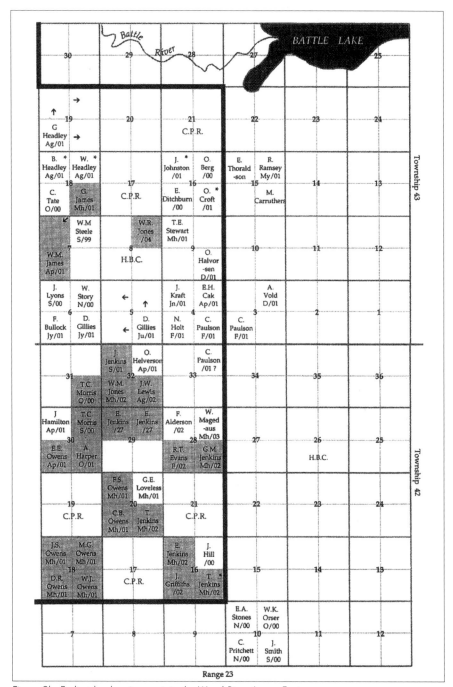

Figure 2b. Earliest land assignments in the Wood River Area—East.

and many areas of dead timber. There is little doubt that the land clearance posed many problems for the first settlers before mechanical devices were used. However, the presence of water and small trees—useful for fuel and occasionally for lumber—were major points of attraction to settlers from drier lands.

A small pioneering group of people of Welsh heritage established themselves in the Wood River region in the first five years of the 20th century (MGM 1974; PP 1973; Hughes and Jones 1981). The vanguard of Welsh settlers arrived in the area in 1900 and 1901, mainly from Nebraska: Caradoc Morris (1900), Hugh H. Jones (1901), Edward James (1901), O.S. Williams (1901), Jesse Owen (1901), J.H. Jones (1901), and the first minister David L. Hughes (1901) , although the latter two moved back to the Unites States by 1906. The names and locations of all the pioneering settlers who had arrived by 1902, compiled from homestead records and CPR land sales, are shown in Figure 2, with a detailed listing by year in Appendix A. Figure 2 shows that this first group of Welsh American pioneers was distributed over a loose cluster across four of the townships south of the Bobtail Indian Reserve.

The next four years saw the addition of a few more individuals of Welsh origin who had lived for some years in the United States and had bought land from the initial settlers: Owen G. Davies in 1905; Hugh F. Davies and Lamark G. Hughes and his parents, Mr. and Mrs. John J. Hughes, in 1906; whilst 1905 saw the arrival of Thomas Jeffreys from Pembrokeshire. He was not the first person in Wood River who came directly from Wales; Jeffreys had been preceded by Mrs. Levi Davies, who emigrated to marry her Cardiganshire-born husband in July 1904, which illustrates the way that Welsh Americans had kept their Welsh links. This area fulfilled the promise that the 1897 Crow's Nest scheme failed to achieve—a western Canadian farming area dominated by the Welsh. However, the area was very small in size: by 1906 there were only 25 family units of definite Welsh origin established on 40 quarter-sections of land. This was rather more than a township of 36 units, but not as concentrated and certainly smaller than the three townships that McCreary, the Winnipeg Commissioner of Immigration, seems to have planned for the Welsh in 1897 as part of the Crow's Nest Pass work scheme (Davies 1999b).

Figure 2 shows that the area was not exclusively Welsh. Indeed, it was one of the earliest American settlers who gave the area a name, as part of the naming of rural areas associated with the development of postal services: Fred Bullock named it after his former residence, Wood River, west of Grande Island in the Platte River valley of Nebraska (Hughes and Jones 1980: 1). Some quarter sections passed through several hands before the land

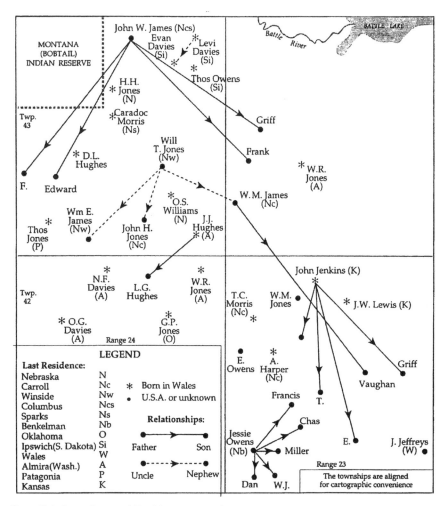

Figure 3. Linkages between Wood River pioneers by 1906.

was officially registered as being occupied and subsequently owned by one person. So the names listed in Figure 2 are the individuals who were shown to be in possession for at least a year. Approximately 10% of the total number of quarter sections in the area subsequently linked to the Welsh were occupied by people who left after a few months; these quarter sections are identified by an asterisk.

Almost half of this group who had arrived by 1905 came from Nebraska, mainly from farms near the small towns of Carroll and Winside, with other family groups from Columbus, Sparks and Benkelman in the same state (Figure 3). The balance of the others came from South Dakota (Ipswich),

Kansas (Arvonia), Minnesota (Lake Crystal), and Oklahoma. Many of the settlers had lived in several American communities, so a complex family migration history is present, although the majority seem to have owned land in their previous American location. The limited number of Welsh surnames and the inevitable duplication of names sometimes made identification difficult. For example, there were four people named Hugh Jones in the Wood River area just before World War I; in this case different individuals can be distinguished by their middle initials—an Americanization in itself—or by a nickname based either on their birthplace or the place where they had lived. It must be emphasized that the information shown in Figure 3 has been processed on the basis of male origins only. This has produced only a small gender bias because in practically all the cases the males were the landowners, although it must be acknowledged that far more information was available on male birthplaces and former residences. In general, therefore, the map of previous origins confirms that the migration that created the initial Welsh concentration was part of the movement of settlers into the Prairies from the United States—even though some of these were of Welsh origin, or were born in Wales and had spent many years south of the border.

Figure 3 shows that some settlers occupied more than a quarter section and that family networks were very important in the settlement process: father-son links dominate, but uncle-nephew and cousin linkages occur, with family members finding land in relatively close proximity. There were three large families with sons of eligible age to obtain their own land. Jesse Owen and his five sons in the south were probably from Benkleman in southwestern Nebraska and arrived in 1901. John J. James, the former county farm manager from Columbus (eastern Nebraska) had been born of Welsh parents in New York State in 1840. He came with four sons in 1903, although another son, Edward, had preceded the family move to the area in 1901. John Jenkins was born in Tredegar in 1853 and his parents had emigrated to the United States (Pennsylvania) in 1869. Subsequently he held land in a Welsh community in Kansas, and came to Wood River with his four adult sons in 1902. However, Figure 3 shows that the largest concentration of this initial group of settlers came from the Carroll-Winside area of Nebraska. So it is certain that these people knew one another and that their connections were reinforced by family linkages. For example, William T. Jones had two uncles, William M. and William E. James, although the two were only related by marriage. Four of the other settlers with known last residences were from the Carroll area: Andrew Harper, Caradoc Morris, T.C. Morris and J.H. Jones. The Levi Davies, Thomas Owen and Evan Davies group had all lived in Ipswich, South Dakota, and may have all been from

Llandewi Brefi, near Tregaron, in Cardiganshire. The John J. Hughes and Hugh F. Davies families had all lived in Altimira, Washington, as had Owen G. Davies, whilst the two Davies were from Cemmaes Road and nearby Machynlleth (Merionethshire) respectively. So the Nebraska, South Dakota and Washington source areas provided at least three major social network associations based on previous location; these must be added to the family linkage explanation which produced this loose clustering of individuals of Welsh origin. This means that the process of government inspired assignment of land in adjacent lots—the pattern found in the Welsh settlement of the London township of Ontario in the 1820s and in the case of the Patagonian Welsh in 1902 at Bangor, Saskatchewan (Thomas 1971)—was not followed here.

The actual pattern of land settlement also provides supporting evidence for the conclusion that the area was settled by an informal process among relatives and people known to one another. Once the core was established other migrants of Welsh origin filled up the area, purchasing land from people who had left, thereby reinforcing the concentration of the Welsh. Figure 3 shows that practically all the Welsh in the central area of this zone were from the Carroll or Winside region of Nebraska, with the Welsh from other parts of the United States displaying a peripheral distribution around them. This suggests that the initial Welsh settlers came to the region within a few weeks of one another, enabling them to register for land within close proximity. Yet Figure 2 shows that within this area there were many individuals who were not of Welsh origin—settlers who were simply attracted to the area and filed their claims at the same time as the advance guard of the Welsh. Hence the Wood River region was far from being a completely concentrated zone of Welsh settlement. Members of other nationalities can be found between and around the Welsh settlers, with a large group of Norwegians to the east, around the settlement of New Norway. In addition, it is worth noting that some other small areas of Welsh settlers were found immediately south and to the southeast of the town of Ponoka, although these minor concentrations did not last for more than a few decades; most of the other Welsh who migrated to rural Alberta scattered throughout the region.

Table 1 shows the family and age characteristics of the settlers in the Wood River area. It is clear that the majority of the first phase of pioneers were married, with an average of over three children, but in the second phase there was an approximate balance in the proportions of married and single people. However, the age structure was much younger since many immigrated from Wales without spending time in the United States and

Table 1. Characteristics of the Welsh Settlers in Wood River, Alberta

a) Family Characteristics

Dates	Married	Single	Unknown	Children	Adult Children	Total Population*
1900–06	14	8	(3)	32	14	85
1907–18	15	16	(10)	31	6	93

b) Ages of the Heads of Families

Dates	Under 29 Years	30–39	40–49	50–59	Over 60 Years	Unknown
1900–06	4	7	7	0	2	(5)
1907–18	13	16	4	0	0	(10)

* Assuming the unknowns were single.
Source: Calculated from family records. Ages of adult females were rarely available.

several found partners amongst the daughters of the original migrants. The known total of 178 residents in Table 1 needs to be adjusted to take into account the loss of a few of the early settlers—mainly through migration to other areas—as well as the birth of additional children and the presence of farm labourers who are not recorded because they were often temporary visitors and did not own land. In total, therefore, the Welsh population was only around 200 by the end of World War I.

It is difficult to be precise about extent of "Welshness" about the Wood River settlers because the family histories are not all available. However, homestead records and family biographies found in local histories make it possible to build up a general picture of the origins of the settlers. Table 2 identifies the last residence of the settlers who came to the Wood River area.

Table 2 identifies the last permanent residence of the settlers, which confirms the dominance of family units coming from the United States. Only those who had spent at least a year in the United States are placed in this category. In the second phase of migration the same pattern is found; but almost a third of the family units had come directly from Wales and over a sixth had spent time in other parts of Canada—mainly Alberta—typically in

Table 2. Places of Last Residence of Wood River Families: Percentage Distribution

Area of Last Residence	1900–06	1907–18
Wales	4	30
United States	89	50
Patagonia	—	2.5
Canada	4	18
Totals (actual numbers)	100% (25)	100% (40)

Table 3. Birthplaces of the Wood River Migrants: Percentage Disbribution

Source Areas	1900–06 (%)	1907–18 (%)
1. Wales		
Anglesey	8	17
Caernarvonshire	8	31
Denbighshire	4	11
Merionethshire	16	8
Montgomeryshire	4	11
Pembrokeshire	4	8
Cardiganshire	16	3
Monmouthshire	4	—
Other Wales	—	8
2. Unknown	32	—
3. United States	4	3
Totals (Actual)	100 (25)	100 (40)

Source: Calculated from family records.

drier areas where the family had not been successful in their pioneering. The distribution of birthplaces is shown in Table 3. Although birthplaces are not known for a third of the initial pioneering family units, it is probable that many were born in Wales, for the phrase "Welsh nationality" keeps occurring in the homestead records, and their obvious attachment to the Welsh way of life is clear from comments in the family histories (MGM 1974; Hughes and Jones 1981). Of the known birthplaces the majority are in the Welsh-speaking heartland of north and west Wales, running from Anglesey, Caernarvonshire and Merionethshire to North Cardiganshire. This pattern of Welsh origins is in great contrast to the Welsh labourer scheme of the Crow's Nest Pass railway, which attracted people mainly from industrial south Wales—despite its goal of attracting farm labourers. Indeed, only one person among the earliest Wood River pioneers, William Rees Jones, seems to have worked on the 1897 Crow's Nest scheme. Like Griffith P. Jones, he was born in Pennal, Merionethshire, an area near Machynileth, that was the original home of several of the other Wood River settlers, such as Hugh F. Davies and Owen G. Davies. After his railway work Jones went to Altamira (Washington), where he met his future wife, and then migrated to Wood River in 1904.

The early Welsh settlers did not have an easy time during their first few years on their quarter sections. The land was still either raw prairie grass-

Table 4. Progress in Land Breaking: Selected Examples

Location	Names (Age) Family	Dates	Land				
			Broken	In Crop	Cattle	Horses	Hogs
T43R24/16NW	Hugh H. Jones (46) + wife & children	1902 1903 1904	4.0 6.0 9.0	2.0 3.0 10.0	— 2 3	2 2 3	— — —
T43R24/10N3	David L. Hughes (?) + wife & children	1901 1902 1903	10.0 11.0 16.0	5.0 20.0 37.0	— — —	— — —	— — —
T42R23/10SW	R.C. Jones (46) Single	1903 1904 1905 1906 1907 1908	— — 6.5 10.0 8.0 9.5	— — 6.5 16.5 16.5 24.0	14 14 12 15 22 22	4 4 6 6 6 6	— — — — — —
T43R24/12SW	Owen Williams (47) Single	1901 1902 1903	3.0 4.0 1.0	3.0 7.0 8.0	36 45 54	2 2 2	— — 2
T42R23/18NW	Jesse Owen (67) + wife and daughter at home Sons (Dan, W.J. and Miller)	1901 1902 1903	25.0 10.0 —	5.0 25.0 35.0	2 3 5	3 4 2	4 4 12
T42R23/18SW	Dan R. Owen (30) Single	1901 1902 1903	5.0 10.0 —	3.0 5.0 —	— — —	3 3 3	— — —
T42R23/18SE	W.J. Owen (40) Single	1901 1902 1903	10.0 25.0 —	— 10.0 35.0	— — —	3 3 —	— — —
T42R23/18NE	Miller J. Owen (21) Single	1901 1902 1903	13.0 2.0 7.0	— 12.0 13.0	? ? ?	? ? ?	? ? ?
T42R23/20SW	Charles B. Owen (20) Single	1901 1902	9.5 8.0	— 9.0	— —	1 1	2 3
T42R24/24NW	Joseph Owen (30) Single	1901 1902 1903	5.5 10.0 —	— 15.5 15.5	— — —	3 2 2	1 1 1

Source: Calculated from homestead records.

land with deep roots, or occupied by small woods and brush. Riven with sloughs and small lakes whose muddy edges added to the difficulty of farming they were the source from which clouds of biting mosquitoes arose to challenge attempts to conquer the land during the summer months. There were no roads: only paths through a wilderness that stubbornly resisted attempts to convert the land into productive farms. Table 4 shows the painful progress of some of the earliest homesteaders in breaking the land. Most were fortunate to clear and crop five to eight acres a year.

In this arduous conquest of a virgin land the value of teenage or young adult children was obvious. These advantages explain the attraction of this new land to the three large families mentioned above—Jesse Owen, John

Jenkins and John W. James—all of whom had several adult sons. Progress in breaking the tough, deep sod of the grassland and clearing the land of the 20- to 30-foot high trees, brush and old stumps, was often slow as Table 4 shows. Before mechanization only horses were available to assist the settlers in breaking the land. One of the striking features of the age distribution of the setttlers was that many of the settlers were middle-aged or even older— Jesse Owen was aged 67—at first sight a major handicap since the brute strength of the young was often needed to clear the land. But in retrospect it seems clear that the middle-aged possessed many advantages over young adults. First, they were likely to have more capital—from the sale of their farms and stock in the United States—to invest in stock, equipment, seed and, perhaps, to buy extra land from the CPR land allocation, the odd-numbered sections throughout the townships that were given to the company to help them construct the transcontinental railway. Second, the older settlers often had adult children. Not only could they claim land for themselves, as did the Owen family (Figure 3), but they also provided an unpaid workforce in the difficult early days of land clearance. In addition, many of the sons found work on other farms, or on the railway and mines in the winter—all of which jobs further supplemented the family income. Indeed, the ability to generate additional monies during the slack winter months in particular was often a crucial factor in the survival of many farm families in these pioneering days. Yet progress was universally slow. Table 4 also shows that after two years on the land it was typical to find that only between five and 25 acres out of the 160-acre quarter section that was homesteaded were cropped. The number of farm animals was also low. Most of the farms had only two or three horses, essential for transportation and for help in clearing and ploughing the land. Table 4 also shows that only R.C. Jones and Owen Williams had anything resembling herds of cattle, with 54 and 22 respectively by the time they received title to the land in 1903 and 1908. The Owen family were the only immigrants to keep a large number of pigs; their acculturation to America is shown by their use of the term "hogs" on the homestead forms.

The unresolved question about the Wood River settlement is why this particular area became the focus of a Welsh concentration. In the absence of clear evidence from the family records of the founding members of the groups, one can only speculate on the precise sequence of events. The most important fact was that this general area was one of the regions being promoted by government agents at the turn of the century, since the lands along the Calgary-Edmonton line had been settled some years earlier. Along this general route, it is likely that the area north of Red Deer would seem to be more attractive to settlers from the Midwest, since the parkland vegetation and abundance of water bodies helped resolve the fear of drought. A more specific location was identified by the comments of the influential Winnipeg Commissioner of Immigration, who had suggested the area east of Wetaskiwin as the place in which to encourage Welsh settlement (Davies 1999b). This probably remained in the minds of local agents and advance delegates from the United States, whilst the publicity of the Crow's Nest Pass work and settlement scheme meant the same general area would have been known to the Welsh in the American Midwest, through their continued contacts with Wales and the news provided in the Welsh monthly newspaper for Americans, *Yr Drych*. Yet all these points are hypothetical and only suggest how the general location was chosen. The choice of the specific area was a result of the small number of individuals of Welsh origin who arrived at a similar time and who established their specific land claims in close proximity. It was the linkages between these Welsh Americans who had made the decision to move to Canada during the few years in which land in this area was available that provide the most important reason for the initial focus of settlement. Most migrations of a group of people involve some respected leader, the person who had the initial idea to move, or who possessed the persuasive power to encourage people to move to a particular place. The individual may not necessarily be a formal leader of an organized colonization but may simply be a person that others would follow, or look up to. It is probable that the man who ministered to the Welsh in the Carroll area of Nebraska occupied such a role, namely Rev. D.L. Hughes. He was one of the first to establish his own farm in Wood River, although he did not stay long, leaving in 1906. John W. Lewis—previously of Kansas but born in Wales at Deiniolen, Caernarvonshire—was another who fulfilled such a role. He was a part time land agent and a contributor to *Yr Drych*. In both of these functions he may have helped profile the area as a zone of Welsh settlement, in Wales and among Welsh emigrants to the United States. Nevertheless, it must be stressed that the process that led to the formation of a small core of Welsh setttlers in Wood River was not a carefully organized formal colonization; rather, it was the result of a number of individuals of Welsh origin making their own decisions, influenced by their friends and neighbours, and guided by the local land agents and the availability of land.

Subsequent Development of the Wood River Settlement

Figure 4 shows the names of the occupiers of land in the area in 1918, when a detailed land occupance map of Alberta was compiled by the Cummins Map Company. It is clear that the total land area that is occupied by the

Table 5. Shifts in the Occupation of Land in Wood River, 1905–1918

Quarter Sections With	1905 to 1918 (% of Unknown)	Composition by 1918		
		Welsh	Others	Unknown
Same Occupiers in 1905 as 1918	45 (34.1%)	16	29	—
Changed	87 (65.9%)	54	24	9
Unknown*	74	34	32	8
Totals (% of Unknown)	206**	104 (55.0%)	85 (14.0%)	17
1902 Composition: (% of Known)		36 (28.1%)	92 (71.9%)	78 —

*Mainly CPR (odd-numbered) sections where land sales could not be traced.
**The 206 quarter sections in the central area of Townships 42 and 43, Ranges 23 and 24.

Source: Calculated by author from Homestead Records, 1918 Cummins Rural Directory Map, and from CPR Sales Records.

Welsh has expanded and forms a much more concentrated zone. Detailed comparison of the names on the individual quarter sections shown in Figures 2 and 4 reveals that there was a great change in the locations of the land occupied by individual families. The details of the land occupance shown in Figure 4 can be summarized in part by Table 5, which shows the shifts in the land occupation in the area between 1905 and 1918, dates when the location of the occupiers of land are known from the homestead and CPR sales records and the Cummins land occupation map.

It is often forgotten that in the early days of land settlement there was a great deal of instability in the land occupance. Figure 4 has already shown that 10% of the initial settlers on a quarter section never completed the requirements so the land reverted back to the government and was reassigned to others. Others left after a few years. In addition, the amount of movement to other pieces of land in the vicinity by earliest settlers is often underestimated. Indeed Table 5 shows that only 34% of the first occupiers of the land in the 1900–02 period were still on the same piece of land by 1918. Obviously this means that two-thirds of the first occupiers had moved in the intervening 16 years. This change shows the degree of instability in the initial settlement of the area. These proportions are based on the two-thirds of the quarter sections in the survey area of the four townships that are known from homestead and CPR sales records. Most of the missing cases were originally CPR lands for which the individual sales records could not be located in the archival sources.

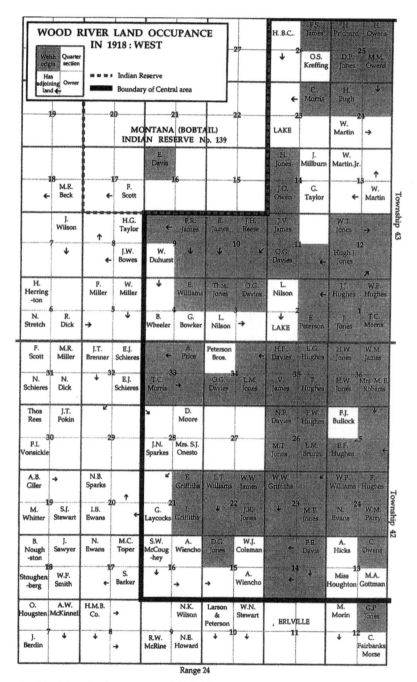

Figure 4a. Wood River land occupance in 1918—West.

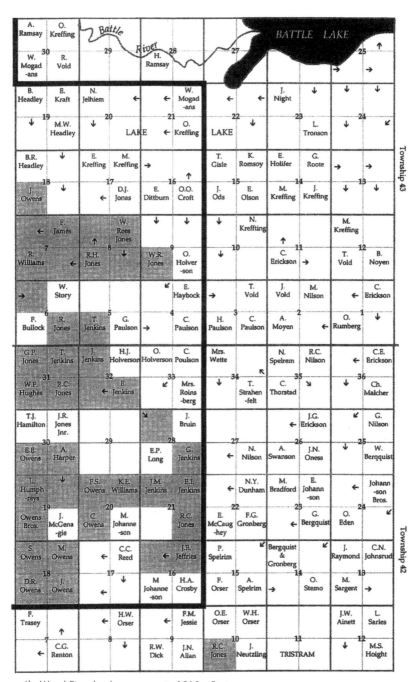

Figure 4b. Wood River land occupance in 1918—East.

Table 5 also enables another generalization to be made about the way in which the area became a concentration of Welsh settlement. In the area for which the first occupier is known, only 28% of the original quarter sections were settled by people of definite Welsh origin. By 1918 the figure had risen to 55%—this is rather an underestimate of the extent of concentration by that date since Figure 2 shows that most of the northeastern area was occupied by people of other ethnic origins. What is also apparent is that the largest number of changes in the survey area between 1912 and 1918 involve the Welsh. This means that the creation of such a concentration of settlers of Welsh origin does not come simply from the occupance phase in which those of Welsh origin bought land that was initially occupied by others. The result of this process was to expand the core area of the Welsh and increase its concentration, as shown in Figure 4, where those areas occupied by farmers of Welsh origin are highlighted.

Another characteristic of the development of the Wood River area is the changing pattern of origins of the migrants in the phase of development from 1906 to 1918. Table 4 has shown that the proportion of migrants whose previous residence was in the United States among the migrants who came between 1907 and 1918 had dropped to a half. Almost a third of the second-phase migrants came directly from Wales, with another sixth who were born in Wales but who had spent a few years in Canada—many in farms in the drier areas of southern Alberta. The early emphasis upon the Anglesey-Caernarvon area as a major source area of migrants is much clearer, for these historic counties account for almost half of the total. So there seems little doubt that many of the people in Wood River traced their origins back to a limited number of settlements in these parts of Wales, in addition to the linkages forged in their phase of American residence. Hence the typical chain migration from some original source areas in the homeland, one so frequently found in studies of migration, seems to be present here. However, it is complicated by the fact that many of the migrants spent time in several parts of the United States—frequently in areas that had concentrations of Welsh—forging additional linkages of friendship and family. This was followed by a re-migration, usually with children, to the final destination in Wood River. Figure 5 shows the process in diagrammatic form, illustrating the way that several areas in the United States represent secondary source areas for the Wood River migrants. Places of historic Welsh concentration, such as Granville (New York) or Lake Crystal (Minnesota) play a part in the secondary flow, suggesting that it took some time for the Wood River Welsh area to be known. This may also explain why almost a third of the 1907–18 migration stream came directly from Wales, many from areas with family linkages

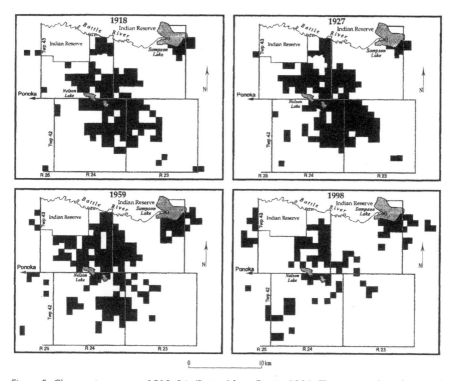

Figure 5. Changes in patterns: 1918–84. (Revised from Davies 1986. These maps show the actual, offset alignment of the townships due to the decreasing width of each successive northerly lines of latitude on which the layout is based. The maps have been adjusted in the other figures for carto-graphic convenience.)

to the original pioneers. By the middle of the first decade of the 20th century the "Welshness" of the Wood River area was known in Wales, which attracted new migrants, adding to the incipient cultural distinction of the area that was being reinforced through the development of schools and churches.

Figure 6 shows that by 1927 the Welsh area of Wood River, as measured by the land units occupied by those of Welsh family origin, remained in approximately the same pattern, with some increase in the degree of concentration. Since the land was all occupied and relatively few new settlers came to the region after World War I, the change cannot be due to major new migration streams; rather it is a function of the fact that an increasing number of the Welsh farmers had increased the size of their holdings, buying up other quarter sections as they became available. Table 6 shows that by 1918 over a third of the farms were larger than a quarter section, compared to only 6.7% in 1906.

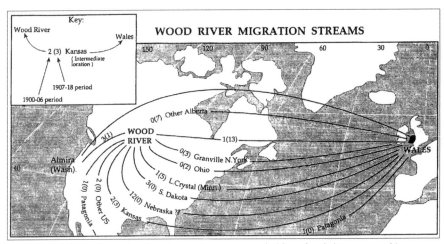

Figure 6. The Wood River migration streams (source: compiled from family history records).

From the peak in 1918 there has been a steady decline in the numbers of farm units occupied by those of Welsh origin. Some migration from Wales certainly continued up to the 1930s, but with members of the original families leaving the area and moving to towns the overall population did not grow. With the deaths of the original pioneers, retirement and sale of land, intermarriage of the children and land consolidation in the period, it is not surprising to find the area occupied by those descended from the Welsh to have shrunk to fifty farm units from almost double that number in 1906. In the first phase of land occupance practically all the farmers occupied a single quarter section. By 1927 only 59% were at this size, whilst by 1959 over half their holdings were larger than a quarter section, a proportion that has remained constant to 1998. However, many of the holdings are now held by one or more family members, producing a complicated pattern of ownership. Many of these land units may be held by parents who have retired, shared among family members or with siblings who have other jobs, but in practice are often farmed as a unit. This means that the size of the effective farm units is certainly understated in Table 6. In practice the area has experienced the prairie trend of increased size of farm units and mechanization of farming, by which farmers often need at least a section of land to be economically viable. The increasing size of farms meant that 1959 was the peak of areal coverage as measured by the number of quarter sections still held by people of Welsh origin, because the decreasing number of units was counteracted by their increasing size.

In spatial terms Figure 5 shows that the growth of the Welsh population from the original pioneers had produced a reasonably solid core area in the

Table 6. Changing Sizes of Farms: The Welsh Land Holdings in Wood River

Dates	Percentage of Farm Ownership Units with Farmers of Welsh Heritage							Total Units of Ownership
	Quarter Section Size Categories*							
	Total	¼	½	¾	1	1¼	>1½	
1906	43	92.5	6.7	—	—	—	—	40
1918	135	66.7	25.8	3.2	4.3	—	—	93
1927	102	59.4	29.7	6.3	3.1	—	1.6	64
1959	146	48.0	26.7	14.7	8.0	1.3	1.3	75
1998	102	48.0	22.0	14.0	12.0	2.0	2.0	50

*Note that by 1998 many holdings were jointly owned by one or more family members in various combinations, or by companies, so the size of the effective or functioning farm unit is underestimated.

Source: Calculated by author.

middle of the four townships of the Wood River area (Twp 42 and 43, Range 23 and 24), one that had expanded marginally and had become even more consolidated by 1918. But by 1959 there was a decrease in the Welsh heritage occupance of the two southern townships (Twp 42, Range 23 and 24) with the sale of land to people with different ethnic origins. By 1998 Figure 6 shows that the old Welsh core area had been reduced in size and was far more diffuse, although the east and southeast part of Township 43, Range 24 and of Twp 43, Range 24 was still dominated by descendants of various Pugh, Davies and Jones families, and two side roads trending north from Highway 53 still bear the names Jones Road and Owens Road in testimony to the Welsh heritage. Elsewhere, an outlier of the Welsh area has spread around Sampson Lake, mainly due to the expansion of the Pritchard family. This originated with Hugh Pritchard's purchase of part of the Phillips ranch in 1931; Hugh, a brother-in-law of one of the early pioneers, R.H. Jones, only arrived in Canada from north Wales in 1914, married Annie Evans, Humphrey Evans's sister, and raised seven children. Elsewhere, there are still small concentrations of other Welsh descendants, such as the Jenkins family in the northwest corner of Twp 42, Range 23, and members of the Griffiths and Owen families in particular scattered in the southwest corner of Twp 24, Range 24. Nevertheless, these scattered outliers only reinforce the general conclusion of the breakdown of the once-dominant Welsh core, producing a much smaller and more diffuse settlement area associated with those of Welsh heritage in the Wood River area.

Cultural Distinctiveness and Decline

The migration of a people with a similar cultural background, together with their settlement in close proximity, is usually enough to create the first stage of a distinctive cultural region. Its consolidation and enlargement require recognition of the region among compatriots and their desire and ability to migrate to this area. But its perpetuation through time as a distinctive culture region requires the maintenance and reinforcement of its cultural characteristics, through the development of separate organizations—schools, churches and community facilities—by which the people maintain their distinctiveness. There is always a built-in momentum for cultural continuity in ethnic settlement areas for a generation or two. But as the original pioneers die, and their children or grandchildren succumb to the acculturating pressures of the host society, the degree of cultural separation is likely to be drastically reduced. Exceptions occur in those cases where there are new migration streams, or the group has strong cultural and religious ties and keeps itself separate, or where there is involuntary segregation due to economic and ethnic prejudice.

In the case of the Welsh in the Wood River area, there have been few factors that have kept them apart from the host society for very long. Economically they have been part of the mainstream of settlers, seeking prosperity on their farms or in local businesses. So the perpetuation of their distinctiveness for more than a few generations was always unlikely—especially in the face of the emerging Canadian identity and new communication devices that increased the degree of contact to places beyond their immediate vicinity. In the case of the Welsh community of Wood River, the process of acculturation increased from the late 1920s and can be related to five major sets of factors—size and migration, changes in Wales, schooling, churches, and organizations—all of which led to a decrease in the use of Welsh and other distinctive cultural practices. This assimilation parallels the case of many Welsh communities in other lands (Ellis 1972; Jones 1952; Jones 1986).

The small size of the Welsh enclave in the sea of new migrants to rural Alberta must be considered a key factor among the reasons why they have not been able to maintain their cultural distinctiveness through time. The number of families of Welsh origin was so small that their survival as a distinctive group was always problematical. Once the land was settled there were few opportunities for new migration streams from Wales to enlarge the size of the Welsh core population and to reinvigorate its cultural heritage. Moreover the process of land consolidation and the problems caused by the economic depression of the 1930s further reduced opportunities in the area.

In the context of commercial activity the rural nature of the region can be seen by the fact that the Wood River area had only one small post office and store, initially on the Bullock property in 1903. For over thirty years this was run by the Thomas Hughes family after their arrival from Glan Conway in North Wales in 1907. Thomas Hughes and his wife died in 1940 and 1942 respectively. The store closed soon after, the victim of the same pressures that were present throughout the Prairies—decreasing rural population and easier access to larger stores in nearby towns. Although the post office remained in the home of John R. Jones for a few years it also succumbed to the centralization processes based on the larger towns. The problem was intensified by the development of all-weather roads, especially Highway 53 between Ponoka and Bashaw in the early 1950s. This meant that the trip to Ponoka took 15 minutes, instead of the best part of a day at the turn of the century, when the path was only a trail and muskeg or fallen trees were ever-present hazards. In any case the locational scatter of the Welsh community meant that the Wood River store was not necessarily the most central location for all, one that would help reinforce neighbourly contacts—a situation that also applied to the churches. It was often easier to obtain needed goods or mail from some other service centre. The local town of Ponoka did act as the main supply centre for the Welsh settlement area. Several Welsh immigrants established businesses there, and many of the Wood River farmers retired to the town. However, Ponoka performed the same function for many other nationalities; so it was never dominated by those of Welsh extraction, unlike some other towns in Alberta with high ethnic concentrations. If anything, the cultural mixture in Ponoka helped increase the degree of cultural integration of the Welsh. Moreover, it is important to emphasize its relatively small size. Ponoka contained only 712 people in 1921 and 2,574 in 1951, although like most district centres in Alberta it has grown in the post-war period and reached 5,861 in 1991. So the opportunities even in this centre were quite limited and could not support new migration waves from Wales.

Even if there had been the opportunity for greater emigration from Wales it is dubious whether any mid- or late-20th-century migration stream would have reinvigorated the Welsh community as it has done with many other ethnic groups in Canada. The increasing modernization and anglicanization of Wales during this century has meant that the turn-of-the-century distinctiveness of the Welsh migrants has been largely lost. The collapse in chapel membership and the continued decline in the use of Welsh as an everyday language has ensured that most people in Wales have been acculturated to English culture, or rather to an international culture based on this language.

Certainly there has been a stabilization in the decline of the Welsh language in the last two decades, even an increase in some areas, as well as a revival of interest in Welsh traditions (Pryce 1986); but most recent migrants from Wales have few cultural symbols or practices to ensure their distinctiveness beyond a generation. Moreover, it is dubious whether many of those whose first language and culture are Welsh would migrate to a rural area of western Canada. They would lose the ability to operate in their culture, and relatively few would find new economic opportunities by way of compensation. Certainly the major advantage of the past—the attraction of free land—is not present now; most opportunities lie in the cities.

The third major force that has aided cultural assimilation in the area has been the school system. At first the establishment of local schools provided a means whereby families of similar background reinforced their identity. However, the use of English as a means of instruction and the presence of non-Welsh families in some of the sections in the "Welsh area" meant that schools were also the medium of acculturation—unless, as with the Hutterites, special permission was sought to use another language for at least part of the day. The opportunity for integration among the Welsh community was also reduced by the fact that they were scattered among several school districts, a product of the difficulty of daily travel and the numbers of children. This meant that there was often more than one single-roomed school in each of the four townships that were settled by the Welsh. In Township 43, Range 24, on the border of sections 2 and 3, the Magic School District was organized in 1902, with Eastside developing to the west. In Township 42, Range 24 the Concord District was also created in 1902, with the school in Section 10. The Climax and Asker School Districts were founded in Township 43, Range 23, in 1902 and 1896 respectively, with schools in Sections 19 and 14, although it must be emphasized that the latter area was one in which many Norwegians settled. Finally, the Eureka and Calumet districts were created in Township 42, Range 23, in Sections 30 and 25 respectively, during 1902 and 1905, with Ellice in the southeast corner in 1907. The creation of so many districts meant that the developing Welsh community did not form a cohesive whole, for there were children of many other nationalities in the various schools. As the Welsh area consolidated, the Magic, Climax and Eureka districts did have a high percentage of their students from parents of Welsh extraction. But Welsh was never a formal part of the curriculum; the children never had the chance to hone any skills they may have learned at home. The result was that English was rapidly confirmed as the predominant language. Thirty years after the first migrants had entered the area Welsh was only spoken occasionally. The consolidation

of most of the small, single-roomed schools into large age-segregated buildings after World War II hastened the process of assimilation. In 1949 the
Mecca Glen school was built to the east of the Wood River area along the
new Highway 53. This building replaced most of the schools named previously, but also included the schools of Water Glen (formerly Fair) District—
in the middle of a belt of Swedish settlers—as well as the Schultz District.
Although a great deal of interaction between various ethnic groups had
already taken place in the area, there seems little doubt that the consolidation of these small school districts substantially increased the mixing of the
population. These changes took place against the background of land holdings consolidation and the rapid decline of the birth rate in recent years,
both of which have reduced the size of the overall population of Welsh background in the region.

It is generally accepted that the survival of the Welsh language was a
product of the Protestant revolution, the translation of the Bible into Welsh
and its use among the people (Pryce 1986; Davies 1993). The people of Wales
took to religion with alacrity from the 18th century onwards, but the frag-
mentation of the Protestants into a number of separate denominations
meant that chapels of many different persuasions vied with one another and
doctrinal disputes and personal antagonisms frequently led to a great deal
of intercommunity bitterness. Many Welsh migrants to other lands kept
their faith and church organizations, including Sunday Schools, and these
were vital in maintaining language and community for many years in North
America. The first 20 years of the Wood River region was no exception. Two
churches catering to Welsh families were established and provided a focus
for community life.

In 1902 the small group of pioneering Welsh families began the process of
organizing their religious beliefs by holding their first religious service in the
barn of William James. This was followed by church services in the home of
Fred Bullock—although these were probably in English—and then in the
Magic school, where Welsh was often the medium in the afternoons, and
English in the evenings. By July 1905 some of the pioneers had registered
their own chapel, The Welsh Calvinistic Methodist Church of Magic—the last
word a rather incongruous and contradictory title until one remembers that
it was the name of the local school district! By 1916 the congregation had built
a new and substantial church with wooden spire, a building that still stands,
although a substantial renovation took place in 1967, one that included a full
basement and additional space (Jones 1976). Many of the early pioneers of
the district are buried in the adjoining churchyard, which was given a new
gate in 1970. The new church was renamed in 1916, taking the more

traditional title of Zion (*Seion* in Welsh), a name derived from biblical sources—and one that was given to many chapels in Wales, as well as used extensively by the Mormons in Salt Lake City. However, in architectural style the church has no resonance with Welsh traditions. It looks more like the Lutheran churches scattered over the Prairies and probably reflects the fact that the builders adopted much of the style of their Norwegian neighbours.

Although the first church members chose to become Welsh Calvinistic Methodist—a very popular denomination among Welsh-speaking congregations in Wales—Zion later joined the Welsh Presbyterian Church of the United States, although its subsequent connections with the Blue Earth Presbytery Church of the United States were severed in the 1930s (Hughes and Jones 1981). In 1939 the members voted to join the United Church of Canada, itself an amalgam of the Methodist, Presbyterian and Congregational churches. At first there was a considerable Welsh language presence in its activities, although it is clear that the English language services attracted people of other backgrounds. But by 1930 the church had become virtually English only, as many of the early pioneers had died and knowledge of Welsh among the new generation had declined—an evolution paralleled elsewhere (Ellis 1972; Jones 1986). The community was fortunate to have Thomas E. Jeffreys among its members. Arrived from Wales in 1905, Jeffreys seems to have had some biblical training in Wales; he soon answered the call of his God and went to the Welsh Bible College in Lake Crystal, Minnesota, returning as a minister to Wood River in 1909. Apart from the years 1921-1924, when Jeffreys went to the Welsh church in Calgary, he ministered to the Zion church until 1936, despite the handicap of being virtually deaf.

A second church, the Wood River Welsh Church, located east of Zion Church, on the other side of the township line that became Highway 53, was built in 1914 on land donated by John J. Hughes. A local history observed that it attracted a large number of Welsh pioneers from many denominational backgrounds, whether Methodists, Baptists, Anglican and Congregational, and that they "blended well together" (Hughes and Jones 1981, 68). This church soon established an association with the Presbyterian Church of Canada. Like Zion it seems to have had regular Welsh services up to 1929. Its first regular minister was J.J. Samuels, who had graduated from Presbyterian College in Carmarthen, although he commuted to Ponoka where he was also the resident minister at the Presbyterian church. After the end of World War I several Welsh American ministers followed, each on two-year ministries—William Davies of Chicago and then J.M. Hughes of Seattle, who first occupied the house built for the minister and his family in 1921. The Rev. O.J. Davies held office from 1923 to 1927. He was followed by

P.O. Pierce from the Bangor, Saskatchewan Welsh settlement. But by 1930 the services were being conducted by ministers from the Ponoka United Church, initially T.R. Davies and then George Young from 1936–40. From 1946 a new arrangement was formalized, that of sharing a minister with the Baptist Church in nearby Concord (Jones 1976). Since Zion Church had joined the United Church, the attempt at separation implies that some of the existing Wood River Church congregation still had some continued doctrinal disputes with members of Zion Church. Neither the arrangement nor the church lasted for long. Unlike the postwar revival of Zion Church, the Wood River congregation became too small to function in the late 1940s, and in 1953 the building was dismantled and sold to a Bashaw group. Although Zion was left as the only local church, few of the former Wood River members joined it, preferring to worship in one of the Ponoka churches.

Initially, both churches had large congregations and were focal points for the Welsh families, each with their choirs, ladies aid societies and cultural activities. There is little doubt that the churches maintained a Welsh cultural presence and were the main reason why the distinctiveness of the Welsh community was perpetuated for so many years. Although both churches seem to have given up regular Welsh services by the late 1920s, occasional Welsh services continued into the 1930s. Cultural events such as an annual *eisteddfod* appealed to both congregations. For example, in the spring of 1933 the Zion minister wrote to a friend in Wales describing the preparations for another *eisteddfod*, observing that he needed to produce 50 typed programs, perhaps a sign of the number of families who were likely to participate (Jeffreys, May 1933). However the decline in the use of Welsh can be seen in the comment: "I only speak Welsh on Sundays as my closest neighbours are English" (Jeffreys, March 1932). He also claimed that he had never heard his young nephew, Iolo, speak Welsh—although he had lived with him since the death of his brother John. During the next year Jeffreys admitted his sermon in Welsh was the first he had given in six months, further evidence of the decline in the use of Welsh in the area (Jeffreys, October 1933).

Unfortunately, there is little documentary information available to provide definitive evidence on the social and religious divisions that led to the development of two different Welsh churches in such a small area. One source (Hughes and Jones 1981) described the separation in the following innocuous way:

> as the district increased in population a need was felt for larger facilities, so that in 1914 the Wood River Welsh Church was built and affiliated with the Presbyterian Church in Canada (67).

There seems little doubt that the increase in the Welsh population in its early days did create a need for more church space. But any review of the development of two churches in such proximity provides another example of the presence of a fatal flaw that existed within many Welsh communities: doctrinal differences that encouraged individuals of a similar cultural background to worship in separate groups. In the early days the services were probably broad enough to appeal to all the small band of early pioneers, but the creation of the first church at Magic as Welsh Calvinistic Methodist created dissention among people of other denominations. For example, Andrew Harper, one of the early pioneers, was a member of the Ponoka Baptists but soon played a prominent role in the creation of the Wood River Welsh Church in 1914. This congregation joined the Canadian assembly of Presbyterians—in contrast to the Magic, later Zion, church which joined the Welsh Presbyterian organization in the United States.

It has proved difficult to find conclusive evidence of the reasons why the early pioneers established two separate churches. Unlike more hierarchical religions such as Catholicism, the leaders of the local congregations played a vital part in accounting for the decisions to have separate churches. The division between the two groups was not simply a matter of individual religious beliefs. It may have been linked in part to the dominance of one form of worship over another in the communities from which the pioneers came—although the link cannot be established with precision. The Wood River members seem to have had more varied backgrounds, both from their origins in Wales and residence in the United States; but at least one of the source areas, Almira in Washington, had been the residence of prominent members of both churches. There is also a suspicion that one of the historic divisions in Wales was also partially responsible for the difference in the church membership, for more of the Wood River Church leaders pioneers seem to have been from south Wales and mid-Wales. Again the division is far from absolute, for families with origins in the Dovey Valley in Wales were in both of the Wood River churches.

These differences may have explained the initial separation in two churches, but it is difficult to understand the continued separation through time. There is little doubt that there was a core in both churches that remained opposed to one another. The geographical location of the farms of the leading members of both churches also provides a partial clue to the differences. Most of the leading members of Zion Church were residents of the Magic district in the southeast of Township 43 and Range 24, overlapping into Eastside and to the northern fringe of Township 42, Range 24. In contrast the Wood River Church seemed to have a wider spread into the Climax and Eureka districts. However, this locational difference was never complete for the Zion minister, Jeffreys, lived in the southeast of Eureka. Nevertheless, it hints at the influence of many of the Carroll group of pioneers and their preference for an American organization, perhaps a product of their familiarity with the organization during their years in the United States. Again the relationship is only partial, because the Harper family had been in Carroll prior to migrating to Wood River. Personal antipathy between individuals was often another reason for the splits in chapels, for there was no outside authority to resolve the differences. But another reason may be involved. It is clear that the presence of two churches provided some social advantages for many in the region. After all, there were more roles to share out—especially in the leadership of choirs—always a prize for those who wished to exercise a major role in the cultural life of the area.

This division within the Welsh community must not be exaggerated: both congregations took part in the local *eisteddfodau* and *cymanfoedd*, so the separation was never complete. However, it does seem significant that many of the original pioneers were also separated at death. Most of the Wood River Church pioneers were buried in the Forest Home cemetery in Ponoka, not in the local Zion churchyard, although the fact that many members of both churches retired to Ponoka, attended churches there and are buried in the local cemetery must be taken into account. In addition, it seems clear that by 1921 the two churches were showing signs of cooperation, or at least running in parallel, because they often shared ministers. Important clues to the relationships between the churches are provided in a set of letters that The Rev. Jeffreys of Zion wrote to an old friend in Wales, The Rev. Bodfan Anwyl, a distinguished man of letters who had taken over the editorship of Spurrell's well-known *Dictionary of Welsh* and who was subsequently employed in the National Library of Wales from 1919 to 1935.

Jeffreys seemed to have been prominent in negotiating some alliance between the two churches when he left the area in 1921, although it did not last. In one of his very first letters to Anwyl he commented:

> When I left this place after spending 18 years here I succeeded in persuading my old church to unite with another here under the same ministry. The experiment is not a very great success and this spring they dissolved the partnership...
> (Jeffreys, August 1926)

Jeffreys had returned to Wood River in 1924, in large part because he claimed that he was tired of the constant arguments and disputes among his Calgary congregation which made his work difficult. Again it is difficult to know how much of this was due to religious differences. It seems clear that Jeffreys had little time for splitting the doctrinal hairs:

> I do not care what anybody thinks of my sermons, if I am to teach the young folks that to be good men and women is a thing worth striving for. I was never much of a theologian. I am less so now… (Jeffreys, March 1927)

Later on in the same letter he praised the merits of being a Presbyterian, implying the chapel had a greater flexibility in approach. Without an analysis of the local church records or informative local diaries it is difficult to be sure of the reasons why the two churches drifted apart again in the mid-1920s. It cannot be only due to rivalry between the ministers at the time, for Jeffreys's letters suggest he was very friendly with the other minister present in 1926, namely The Rev. O.J. Davies, who conducted services in the area from 1923 to the spring 1927. In 1926 Jeffreys refers to his enjoyment in "sitting under" the ministry of O.J. Davies, noting his dignified approach. Later he is more specific:

> he is as fine a man as ever I have met. We co-operate like two brothers and have a great time together. He is an able fellow too but deficient in cheek so will never get very far. (Jeffreys, November 1926)

This cooperation between the two Welsh ministers is in contrast to a predecessor "who resented the friendly relations between his church and mine" (Jeffreys Nov. 1926). Later he complained about a Wood River Welsh Church minister—not named, but probably Rev. Samuel:

> He thought it was in the nature of things that there ought to be antagonism between me and the members of his church and when he found out that his people spoke in most friendly fashion of me he wasn't satisfied and was called to task by one of them. He even refused to co-operate with me in trying to level the differences between the two churches. I lost my enthusiasm for him. (Jeffreys, January 1927)

Although the new separation of the two churches in 1926 was important in pointing to some continuing intracommunity differences, it is difficult to determine a deep-seated religious schism based on religion alone. The Rev. O.J. Davies moved to South Dakota in 1927, which distressed Jeffreys, who complained that "he will be left without another Welsh minister within a radius of several hundred miles" (Jeffreys, March 1927). There are no informative comments in his letters on the subsequent two-year ministry of P.O. Pierce at the Wood River Welsh Church between 1928–30. Afterwards the Wood River Church was again served by ministers from Ponoka, but this time belonging to the United Church, since the Presbyterians had been absorbed within this new grouping. After his retirement in 1936 Jeffreys continued to work on his farm. He sold it in 1940 and lived in Ponoka for five years, finally moving to Victoria, dying at the age of 89 in 1967; but was reburied in Zion churchyard after his wife died. This was a fitting gesture for a man who had devoted his life to a community that seems to have held him in the highest esteem, despite his severe handicap, for Jeffreys admits in his letters he could hardly hear anything—perhaps a useful handicap if there were argumentative factions within the Welsh community! Yet Zion did not lose its way completely when Jeffreys retired. He was followed by ministers from the United Church in 1936 who preached at Zion on alternate Sundays, foreshadowing the Zion congregation's formal decision to join that assembly in 1939. There was a real revival in interest in Zion Church in 1945 when it became the Zion Mission Field, served by student ministers. Under Doug Lapp, a thriving Sunday school seems to have been re-established, one that was still attracting large numbers into the early 1960s as the photographic history of the church indicates (Jones 1976). These developments led to a substantial upgrading and renovation of the church in 1967. The Wood River church seemed unable to match this postwar revival and closed within a decade of the war. Yet even in the case of Zion the last few decades have proved difficult. The financial difficulties of operating a single church, decreasing interest in religion in a declining rural population, fewer Welsh associations as the generations changed and other people moved into the area, led to changes in organizational structure. Zion entered into a more formal linkage with other churches in 1965 when it became part of a rural circuit of two other rural churches. In 1977 came a formal association with the Ponoka United Church, with services conducted by the Ponoka incumbent. Attendance at Zion Church has shrunk to a handful of the older people, a reflection of the decreasing role that religion plays in modern life, as well as the effect of smaller families and rural depopulation.

The two churches were essential organizations in the perpetuation of the Welsh heritage in the area, for the two congregations came together in the various cultural festivals, even though the language was rarely used after 1930. However, there does seem to have been some antipathy between some members of the rival organizations. Such schisms among the Protestants were not the prerogative of the Welsh. By World War I there many other denominations within a township of Wood River, each with churches that usually catered to the particular ethnic group that had settled the area: a Norwegian Lutheran congregation at Asker, Svea Swedish Lutheran north of Battle Lake, a Swedish Baptist at Fair (renamed Water Glen), St. Peter's Evangelical Lutheran, Kreutz (Cross) Evangelical Lutheran and St. Michael's Catholic Mission near Schultz, as well as a Primitive Methodist congregation at Ellice. Nevertheless, the split of the Welsh church community in such a small population did hinder the development of a common sense of identity, although individuals such as Jeffreys worked to keep the channels of communication open between the various groups.

Community interaction among the Welsh pioneers and their neighbours was also found in a number of other local organizations. Singing was never far from a Welsh community's soul and the choirs—both male and female—from this region were famous for miles around, making a substantial contribution to the cultural life of this part of the province. Choirs based at Zion Church were directed for decades by an early pioneer, Owen G. Davies (1875–1958), winning ladies choirs' awards in the Wood River Festival in the 1930s (Hughes and Jones 1981). They were still thriving under Goronwy Davies—a son of Hugh F. Davies—and his wife Elinor, into the 1960s. This couple took an active role in the music festivals in the new Mecca Glen facility during the postwar period. Sports organizations were also popular amongst the young, and soccer teams were founded in the Magic, Eureka, Eastside and Water Glen districts at the end of the first decade of the century, although the Magic and Eureka teams amalgamated in 1923. Rugby, the game which has captured the hearts of so many Welsh, was a relative latecomer in Wales, especially in the rural areas from which many of the original pioneers came; so it is not surprising that there are no real signs of interest in rugby in this area. The local interest in soccer led to the merger of some of the smaller teams into a Wood River team, providing another example of how the Wood River community was emerging out of the smaller school districts into which the area, and the Welsh settlers, had been split. However, the 1930s economic depression, followed by a war which took so many of the young off to fight and by a decrease in the number of children per family, seems to have assisted in the decrease of interest in the game. By 1950 organized soccer seems to have died out in the area, perhaps a function of the growth in the popularity of the Canadian variation of American football promoted in the high schools.

Another source of cultural cohesion among the settlers in the area was provided by the building of Wood River Community Hall in 1919, mainly with volunteer labour, on land donated by Lamark Hughes. This provided the focal point for many lectures, community events and dances when larger facilities than the schools or churches were needed—such as the local *eisteddfod*, a traditional Welsh concert that involves competition between participating choirs, soloists and poets. In 1949 the Wood River Hall had to be moved to make way for the construction of Highway 53 along the boundary of Townships 42 and 43. The date of its construction as an all-weather road shows that the creation of good communications in the area was late. In its new location near Nelson Lake it enjoyed several renovations, but with the creation of better facilities in the new school at Mecca Glen the old hall could no longer compete. It saw the last community festival in 1957. However, the Wood River name still survives in an annual competition for local choirs in the Mecca Glen Hall, although the wider area served by the school ensures that the original "Welshness" of the festival has long been limited. In another context there are few signs of the Welsh presence in the naming of landscape features, apart from Jenkins Hill, the small Davies Lake and the very minor Jones road, all named after local farmers.

Yet one Welsh tradition still survives in the region, although not in Wood River itself. Each August since 1943 a Cymanfa Ganu is held in Ponoka; this is a singing festival based mainly on hymns. Although such festivals were a frequent event in the early days in Wood River, the Ponoka organization was the initiative of some Welsh airmen posted to the Penhold air force base in World War II. They seem to have been mainly responsible for reviving the old Wood River musical tradition and, together with local Welsh church members, helped to relocate it in the local service centre where it is still an annual event. Together with the annual banquet on St. David's Day hosted by the Ponoka Welsh Society, it has kept some Welsh traditions in this part of Alberta alive. It is a pity that its existence is not well known in Wales, and that it cannot be reinforced by formal contact with Welsh cultural organizations, leading to visits of mutual benefit to both areas.

Conclusions

The failure and controversy surrounding the ambitious Crow's Nest Pass railway work and settlement scheme of 1897, designed to bring 1,000 Welsh labourers to the Prairies, may have discouraged potential Welsh immigrants (Davies 1999a). However, the dream of some people to establish a Welsh settlement area in the region did not die; it was fulfilled by a group who had spent many years in the United States. This group, drawn from several origins, but principally from northwest and central Wales, created the only major concentration of Welsh in rural Alberta. Their settlement added to the range of cultural differentiation in the province, even though their impact in numerical terms was much smaller than that of many other groups (Palmer and Palmer 1985). The creation of the distinctive Welsh settlement area in Wood River was a complex process. It was created by a several groups of people of Welsh origin who knew one another because of family and neigh-bourly ties forged in the American Midwest and who registered land claims almost simultaneously on quarter sections in close proximity. The initial core was never exclusively Welsh, but as people moved between sections in the early days of farming and new Welsh migrants were attracted to the area, the area's cultural distinctiveness was increased.

The cultural perpetuation of the community was handicapped by sever-al factors. Essentially the Welsh area of Wood River was too small, too rural and was founded too late to survive for more than a few generations as a distinctive cultural entity—especially given the blows of the Depression and World War II. Depopulation and the increasing dominance of towns, as well as the accelerating secularization of life, meant that even the chapels—for so long the cultural lifeline of the Welsh—declined. Obviously, the compulsory use of English in the schools also hastened the decay of the language. There was no economic basis in such a rural area to attract any new and large-scale emigration from Wales—a migration that may have reinvigorated the Welsh heritage of the area. Even if there had been, the anglicization of life in Wales for most of this century has meant that few of the cultural differences of the Welsh that were found at the turn of the century would have been brought along. After all, much of the distinctiveness of the Welsh at that time, apart from language, was based on a chapel culture that was itself in decay in Wales by the 1950s. Nevertheless, the Welsh heritage is still a factor in the Ponoka area. Many have pride in such a background and still maintain per-sonal links with families in Wales. Unfortunately, there are no real monu-ments or markers, except on Jenkins Hill, to remind the people of Alberta or Wales of this Welsh contribution to the settlement of the Prairies.

Note
This article first appeared in *Prairie Forum* 24, no. 2 (1999): 219–49.
Many people have helped in the completion of this study. Goronwy and Iorweth Davies—part of the first generation of Welsh in Wood River-and their wives Elinor and Laura-described their own recollections of early life in the area and left no doubt in my mind that "warm welcomes" are not found only in the "Welsh valleys." The availability of the local family records in the various centennial publications of small towns and country areas in the Prairies provided an invaluable source material. Special thanks must go to the late Mrs. L. Harries of Cilgerran for assistance in translations and to Eleanor Aubrey of Porth (Rhondda) who translated the letters of The Rev. Jeffreys held in the National Library of Wales. Alberta Historical Resources Foundation assisted with a grant to defray some trav-el and accommodation costs associated with this research. The University of Calgary, especially the Humanities Institute and the Geography Department, also provided me with needed facilities. Marta Styk did her usual splendid cartographic work just before her well-earned retirement. To all I give my thanks.

References

a) Official Sources and Archival Material

ACC (House of Commons, Agriculture and Colonization Committee). Annual Reports. Sessional Papers of The Parliament of Canada, Ottawa.

CPR. Canadian Pacific Railway: Land Sales Records. M.S. in Glenbow Institute, Calgary.

DC. Dominion Census of Canada. 1891–1941: Tables on Population and Ethnic Composition. Dominion Printers, Ottawa.

DI (Dept. of Interior). Annual Reports of Immigration Department. Sessional Papers of The Parliament of Canada. Ottawa.

Jeffreys. The original letters of The Rev. Thomas Jeffreys to the Rev. Bodfan Anwyl are found in the National Library of Wales, Aberystwyth. Copies of the letters in Welsh were translated by Eleanor Aubrey (Ynyshir, Rhondda) and have been deposited at the Alberta Provincial Museum, Edmonton.

RG. Archival Material in National Library, Ottawa. Information on The Welsh can be found in the Ethnic files in which the RG (Record Group) is followed by Subsection Numbers e.g. RG25 Al-Vol. 11. Microfilm versions of this some of this material are identified by microfilm numbers after the RG number e.g. G10425, Vol. 490, 756658, in which the last number identifies the specific document.

Published Sources

Bennett, Carol. 1985. *In Search of The Red Dragon: The Welsh in Canada*. Renfrew, ON: Juniper Books.

Belyea, Barbara. 1994. *The Columbia Journals of David Thompson*. Kingston: McGill-Queen's University Press.

Berton, Pierre. 1984. *The Promised Land: Settling the West, 1891–1914*. Toronto: McClelland and Stewart.

Chamberlain, M.E. (ed.). 1986. *The Welsh in Canada*. Swansea: University of Wales Canadian Studies Group, History Dept. University of Wales, Swansea.

C.N.P. 1979. *Crows Nest and Its People*. Blairmore, AB: Crows Nest Pass Historical Society.

Cousins, W.J. 1981. *A History of the Crow's Nest Pass*. Edmonton: University of Alberta, MA thesis, 1952. Republished by Historic Trails Society of Alberta.

Davies, John. 1993. *A History of Wales*. London: Penguin.

Davies. W.K.D. 1986. "The Welsh in Canada: A Geographical Overview." Pp. 1–45 in M.E. Chamberlain (ed.), *The Welsh in Canada*.

——. 1991. "A Welsh Missionary at Canada's Red River Settlement, 1823–38," *The National Library of Wales Journal* 27: 217–44.

——. 1999a. "Falling on Deaf Ears? Canadian Promotion and Welsh Emigration to the Prairies," *Welsh History Review*.

——. 1999b. "Send A Thousand Welsh Labourers! Welsh Emigration and the Crow's Nest Pass Scheme," *Welsh History Review*.

Dunae, P.A. 1986. *Ranchers Legacy*. Edmonton: University of Alberta Press.

Ellis, D.M. 1972. "The Assimilation of the Welsh in Central New York," *Welsh History Review* 6: 424–50.

Evans, Betty. 1983. *The Welsh Heritage in Calgary*. Calgary: Calgary Welsh Society.

Grover, R. 1962. *David Thompson's Narrative: 1784–1812*. Toronto: The Champlain Society.

Hughes, Kelt and Griff Jones. 1981. *From Wales to Wood River*. Ponoka: Ponoka Herald.

Jenkins, Gwyn. 1986. "W.L. Griffith and the Welsh Emigration to Canada, 1897–1906." Pp. 81–93 in M.E. Chamberlain (ed.) *The Welsh in Canada*.

Johnson, Gilbert. 1962. "The Patagonia Welsh," *Saskatchewan History* 15: 90–94.

Jones, Emrys. 1986. "The Welsh in Nineteenth Century London." Human Geography From Wales, W.K.D. Davies (ed.). *Cambria* 12, no. 1: 149–69.

——. 1952. "Some Aspects of Change in An American-Welsh Community," *Transactions of the Cymmrodorion Society*: 15–41.

Jones, W.G. 1976. *History of Zion Church*. Wood River/Ponoka, AB: Ponoka Herald.

Lehr, J. and W.K.D. Davies. 1993. "Canada's Ethnic Diversity." Pp. 131–57 in W.K.D. Davies (ed.), *Canadian Transformations: Perspectives on a Changing Human Geography*. Swansea: Canadian Studies in Wales Group, History Dept., University of Wales, Swansea.

MGM. 1974. *Mecca Glen Memories*. Ponoka, AB: Mecca Glen Historical Society.

Palmer, H. and T. Palmer. 1985. *Peoples of Alberta*. Saskatoon: Western Producer Prairie Books.

PP. 1973. *Ponoka Panorama*. Ponoka, AB: Ponoka and District Historical Society.

Pryce, W.T.R. 1986. "The British Census and the Welsh Language." Human Geography from Wales, W.K.D. Davies (ed.). *Cambria* 13, no. 1: 79–100.

Taylor, C. 1982. "Paddy's Run: A Welsh Community in Ohio," *Welsh History Review* 11: 302–16.

Thomas, Brinley. 1972. *Migration and Urban Development: A Reappraisal of British and America Long Cycles*. London: Methuen.

Thomas, L.H. 1971. " From the Pampas to the Prairies," *Saskatchewan History* 24, no. 1: 1–12.

Tyman, J.L. 1972. *By Section, Township and Range*. Brandon: Assiniboine Historical Society.

Tyrrell, J.B. 1916. *David Thompson's Narrative of His Explorations*. Toronto: The Champlain Society (republished, New York: Greenwood, 1960).

	Appendix A		
	Pioneering Welsh Families in Wood River: By Year of Migration to Area, 1900–1918		
Date	Head (Wife) and adult sons	Birthplace (Old Counties) Last Residence	Last Residence
1900	Caradoc Morris (Emma)	N.K.	Sparks, NE
1901	John H. Jones	N.K.	Carroll, NE
1901	Hugh H. Jones (Flora 1903)	Anglesey	NE
1901	D.L. Hughes (nk)	Wales?	NE?
1901	Owen Williams	Anglesey	NE
1901	William T. Jones (nk)	Wales?	Winside, NE
1901	William E. James	Wales?	Carroll, NE
1901	William M. James (Lydia)	N.K.	Carroll, NE
1901	Thomas C. Morris (Ann)	Aber, Caern.	Carroll, NE
1901	Andrew Harper (Anne)	Cardigan	Carroll, NE
1901	John W. Lewis (nk)	Deiniolen, Caern.	Arvonia, KS
1901	John Jenkins (Mary) & 4 sons	Tredegar, Mon.	KS
1902	Griffith P. Jones (m Carrie 1902)	Pennal, Merion.	Iowa/OK
1902	Jessie Owens (nk) & 5 sons	N.K	Benkelman, NE
1902	Levi Davies (nk. m 1904)	Llandewi Brefi, Card.	Ipswich, SD
1902	Evan Davies (Elizabeth)	Llandewi Brefi, Card.	Ipswich, SD
1902	Thomas Owens (Mary)	Wales (as above?)	Ipswich, SD
1903	John W. James (Margaret) & 5 sons	New York State	Columbus, NE
1904	William R. Jones (Jane Ellen)	Pennal, Merion.	Almira, WA
1904	Richard C. Jones	Carno, Mont.	L.Crystal, MN
1905	T.E Jeffreys (Mary, 1933)	Pembroke, Pembs.	Wales
1906	Owen G. Davies (Mary, 1913)	Machynlleth, Mont.	USA
1906	Hugh F. Davies (Anne, 1907)	Cemmaes Road, Mont.	Almira, WA
1906	Lamark G. Hughes	N.K	Almira, WA
1906	John J. Hughes (Jane)	Wales?	Almira, WA
1907	Thomas Hughes	Glan Conway, Denb.	Wales
1907	Robert Williams (Mary)	Lanfairfechan, Caern.	Wales
1908	Jack Lewis (Florence, 1921)	Deiniolen, Caern.	Wales
1908	Hugh T. Jones	Chwilog, Caern.	Granville, NY
1908	Thomas Jones	Eglwys Fach, Denb.	Patagonia
1909	Hugh D. Jones	Trevor, Caern.	Wales
1909	Will Parry (see Parry below)	Bryngwran, Angl.	L. Crystal, MN
1909	William F. Hughes (Margaret)	Llangefni, Angl.	L. Crystal, MN
1909	John Williams (Jane)	Wales	Wisconsin, AB
1909	John O. Jones (nk)	Merion.	Granville, NY

	Appendix A, continued		
Date	Head (Wife) and adult sons	Birthplace (Old Counties)	Last Residence
1910	(Mary Parry & 2 sons: Dick, Harry)	Bryngwran, Angl.	Wales
1910	John R. Jones	Glyn Ceriog, Denb.	BC
1910	William W. Griffiths	Harlech, Merion.	USA
1910	John O. Owen	Bontddu, Merion.	Iowa, CA
1910	Owen Humphreys	Bryngwyn, Angl.	Wales
1910	Hugh W. Jones	Festiniog, Merion.	Granville, NY
1910	John Griffiths	Wales	KS
1910	Sam R. Davies (Mary)	Cardigan	S.AB
1910	Emrys Williams	Carno, Mont.	Wales
1911	William R. Roberts (Mary)	Racine, Wiscon.USA.	Magrath, S. AB
1911	William Thos. Edwards	Wales	Iowa
1912	Hugh M. Pugh (Stella 1915)	Pennal, Merion.	ND & SK
1912	Richard L. Reese (Anne)	Llanbrynmair, Mont.	Ohio & Edmonton
1912	William George	Cilgerran, Pembs.	Wales
1912	William Williams (Hawen)	Llanbrynmair, Mont.	Wales
1912	William M. Williams	Chwilog, Caern.	Wales
1912	Robert H. Jones (Laura 1910)	Clynnog, Caern.	Vermont & Idaho
1913	Humprey Evans (Alice 1921)	Caern.?	Wales
1913	Evan Lloyd	Newtown, Mont.	Wales
1913	Henry Whitticase	Newtown, Mont.	Wales
1913	Bill Harper (Mabel 1929)	Cardigan, Cards.	Wales
1913	David S. Jones	Pembs.	Wales
1913	Hugh Evans (Jenny 1920)	Denbigh.	Lake Crystal & Idaho
1914	John Jones	Arthog, Merion.	Wales
1914	William Williams (Susan)	Dolgellau, Merton.	Edmonton
1914	Hugh Pritchard	Caern.?	Wales
1914	Ira Edwards	N.K	Kansas & Edmonton
1915	William J. Evans (Doris 1915)	Denbigh	Idaho
1917	Owen T. Jones (nk)	Capel Coch , Angl.	L. Crystal, MN
1918	Lewis Humphreys (Catherine)	Llanbrynmair, Mont.	Edmonton
1918	Wm. Robert Jones (nk)	Llanddeiniolen, Caern	Almira, WA
1918	Hugh Roberts	Pentrefelin, Angl.	Emporia, KS

(Compiled from: Homestead records; Hughes and Jones, 1981; P.P. 1973; M.M. 1974)
Notes. The pioneers are listed by family head, but the wife's name is listed in brackets if known, otherwise it is shown by the following symbol: nk. The date of marriage is only listed if it took place after arrival in Wood River. N.K.: information on origin is not known. Question marks are also used if there is some doubt about the reliability of information, such as birthplace.
Some of these pioneers returned to the United States or Wales after a few years, or upon retirement, so the names do not necessarily appear on the maps of land occupance. Adult sons who accompanied parents and held land in their own right are not listed separately.

15. Immigration and Return Migration of German Nationals, Saskatchewan, 1919 to 1939

Grant W. Grams

Prior to World War I German immigrants were viewed as well-behaved contributing members of Canadian society. But during the war Germans were termed "enemy aliens" and their previous image became tarnished; after World War I German immigration to Canada was barred. By April 1923 immigration legislation was altered allowing German agriculturalists and their families to enter the country. In January 1927 all restrictions against Germans were lifted. Due to the Great Depression restrictive immigration legislation was enacted in August 1930 and in March 1931. After World War I Germany's emigration authority had tried to keep their citizens at home; emigration abroad was seen as threatening the whole country. If emigration was to occur the German government believed that South American countries offered the best possibility for German nationals to retain their culture, for German language schools and closed German settlements favoured South America. Emigration could strengthen existing German settlements in the world; such communities could act as a potential export market abroad. It was hoped German nationals could serve the Fatherland in a trading and economic capacity. Canada was not a recommended destination due to the danger of assimilation and the loss of German labour, but by 1920 Germany's emigration authority noticed that Saskatchewan appeared to have the strongest and most cohesive German community in Canada. It was noted that most German speakers were from Eastern Europe, not from Germany. Authorities emphasized that emigrants had to endure harsh economic conditions, discrimination, cold winters, low wages and unbearable isolation; therefore only farmers could consider migrating to Canada.[1] In Germany it was hoped that some individuals would return to Germany if Germany's economy improved. In this way the emigrant was hopefully not lost but could help in Germany's revival. During the Nazi era the resurgence of the German economy, and recession in Canada made Saskatchewan a fertile area for possible return migration.[2] This essay will examine the migration of German nationals to Saskatchewan between 1919 and 1939. Immigration statistics will also be used to show the numerical fluctuations in the province. Ethnic Germans and German settlements will be referred to periodically, but these topics will not be the focus of this article. Saskatchewan appeared to offer German speakers the possibility of retaining their German culture; in retrospect, this phenomenon did not occur.

During the early period between the wars immigration was encouraged. Many believed Canada's prosperity was linked to expanding agriculture and increasing the population. Newcomers were encouraged to settle in western Canada. This attempt appears to have achieved some success; e.g. between 1921 and 1931 the population increased from 8,787,949 to 10,376,786, a growth of 1,588,837 or 18.1%.[3] The increase in population was slower between 1931 and 1941 largely due to restrictions in immigration due to the recession. By 1941 the population rose to 11,506,655 representing an increase of 1,129,869 or 9.8%. Statistics from the 1941 census reveal an apparent emigration of 241,567 individuals from Canada, although Saskatchewan saw a slight increase in population between 1931 and 1936. Overall, between 1931 and 1941 Saskatchewan showed a migration of 157,545, which was compensated by a natural increase in population of 131,752, resulting in a decline in population of 25,793 or 2.8%. Most of this population loss

Table 1. German Nationals in the Prairie Provinces, 1911–1941					
1911	Population	Ethnic Germans		Born in Germany	
Saskatchewan	492,432	68,628	13.94%	8,300	1.1%
Manitoba	461,394	34,530	7.48%	4,294	.70%
Alberta	374,295	36,862	9.85%	6,102	1.04%
1921					
Saskatchewan	757,510	70,500	9.31%	6,409	1.3%
Manitoba	610,118	25,900	4.25%	2,227	.48%
Alberta	588,454	28,800	4.94%	4,606	1.23%
1931					
Saskatchewan	921,785	138,499	15.02%	9,832	1.07%
Manitoba	700,139	57,312	8.19%	3,561	.51%
Alberta	731,605	63,410	8.67%	8,121	1.12%
1941					
Saskatchewan	895,992	130,258	14.54%	6,310	.70%
Manitoba	729,744	41,479	5.68%	2,285	.31%
Alberta	796,169	77,721	9.76%	5,867	.74%

involved inter-provincial migration, although some was due to emigration, either to the United States or to Europe. The number of German speakers in Canada fluctuated accordingly—403,417 in 1911, 294,635 in 1921, 473,544 in 1931 and 464,682 in 1941. The number of German nationals also went through similar upheavals—39,577 in 1911, 25,266 in 1921, 39,163 in 1931, and 28,479 in 1941. In the Prairie Provinces these figures are broken down in Table 1.[4]

From 1911 to 1921 the population of Saskatchewan increased by 265,078 or 35%. In contrast, the number of German nationals in Saskatchewan decreased by 1,891 or 23%. This fall was due to some claiming other citizenship in an attempt to avoid negative connotations associated with Germany. Only in Saskatchewan and Alberta was the percentage of German nationals over 1% of the provincial population. Table 2 displays statistics indicating time of entry. The largest number of German citizens entered the Prairie Provinces between 1921 and 1930, e.g. Saskatchewan 44%, Manitoba 46%, Alberta 49%.[5]

Table 2. Time of Entry of German Nationals to the Prairie Provinces, 1921–30								
Province	Total	No Info.	To 1911	1911–20	1921–30	1931–35	1936–39	1940–41
Manitoba	2,285	5	708	344	1,061	83	68	16
Saskatchewan	6,310	8	2,094	1,139	2,791	201	72	5
Alberta	5,867	12	1,514	1,125	2,880	274	58	4

Part of the lure of Saskatchewan for all German speakers were the German communities and inroads already established within the province. These included German-language newspapers, and German settlements and organizations. Saskatchewan was viewed as a place where German nationals would retain their culture and support Germany when its economic situation improved. Although Saskatchewan appeared to have many advantages to German speakers, some found reasons to complain or leave the province. Georg Wimmer emigrated in the summer of 1924 from southern Germany to Saskatchewan but returned home after one year, citing cold weather and poor treatment. Wimmer was settled through Verein Deutsch Canadier Katholiken (Society of German-Canadian Catholics–VDCK) on a Saskatchewan farm; although he found the food and accommodations satisfactory, he was unhappy that he was forced to sign a work contract in English. He had expected to receive much higher wages for his agricultural work, and he cited immigration literature in Germany which falsely portrayed Canada. Another German, Milian Schmitt, complained about the observations and publications of Erich Koch, a former member of the German parliament that travelled in Canada in the fall of 1926. Upon his

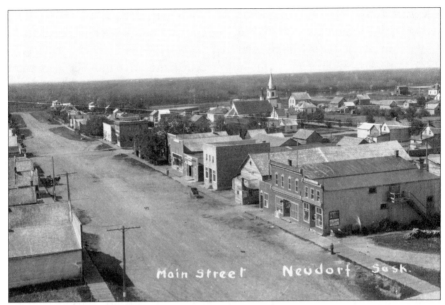

Neudorf, Saskatchewan, circa 1927. Settlement of the district began between 1890 and 1900 with the arrival of Russian and Galician German Lutherans. The name Neudorf—German for "new village"—dates to the establishment of the Neudorf Post Office on July 1, 1895. The name was chosen by Ludwig Wendel Sr. (1842–1909), the first postmaster, after his home town of Neudorf in Galicia, crown land of the Austro-Hungarian monarchy until 1918. With the coming of the railway in 1904, Wendel later donated the land upon which the village now sits on the condition that the name Neudorf be adopted for that of the community. In 1906 the population of Neudorf was 159; by 1921 it had grown to 500. The community's numbers fell during the 1930s to 420 by 1941; during the post-War years, however, the village rebounded (Courtesy of Murray J. Hanowski, Neudorf).

return to Germany Koch wrote newspapers articles advocating German emigration to Canada; he believed assimilation was not a threat to Germans and good economic opportunities were available to all newcomers.[6] Like Wimmer, Schmitt lamented about publications in Germany describing the working conditions and opportunities for immigrants in western Canada. Schmitt worked on a farm near Melville, Saskatchewan; he felt Koch's optimistic portrayal of Canada motivated thousands of his fellow Germans to emigrate, causing them untold suffering and regret. Schmitt felt that he was treated unfairly, suffering from exploitation, low wages and poor working conditions on a Saskatchewan farm.[7]

Similar to Koch, other Germans wanted to see the lands of immigration first hand and experience the challenges of living abroad. Saskatchewan came under increased scrutiny. German emigration occurred partially through religious emigration offices in Germany that had forged connections in Canada. One example was the Sankt Raphaels Verein (Saint

Raphaels Society–SRV), Hamburg. It aided German Catholics in emigration to Canada. The SRV also wanted to find lands of immigration that were compatible for German nationals, and they had an alliance with the VDCK.[8] After German immigration was allowed in 1923 the VDCK noted "within a few years the number of German colonists will increase considerably especially in Saskatchewan."[9] Max Größer and Georg Timpe made observations of Canada on behalf of the SRV. Größer travelled from May to June 1924 in Canada, but little is known of his observations in Saskatchewan. Timpe travelled in Canada and the United States between November 1926 and February 1927; in Saskatchewan he noted St. Peter's and St. Joseph's Colony. Both met with his approval, as he believed the colonies would help immigrants avoid assimilation. Timpe also supported a limited immigration of German nationals to Canada although he continually reminded potential German emigrants that Canadian winters were cruel.[10]

The SRV's Lutheran counterpart in Germany was the Hamburg Auswanderermission (Hamburg Emigration Mission–HAM) which had established an affiliation with the Lutheran Immigration Board (LIB), a German-Canadian Lutheran immigration society. Like the SRV, HAM also sought lands of immigration that were compatible for German nationals to reside. In 1924 Dr. Pastor Friedrich Caspar Gleiss, European LIB representative and a Lutheran minister, travelled in Canada for six weeks assessing the country as an emigration destination. Baron Eduard von Stackleberg, an expert agriculturalist, accompanied Gleiss. In Saskatchewan the two men visited Rosthern, Lake Lenore, St. Benedict, Hanley, Yellow Grass, Markinch, Lipton, Neudorf, and Grenfell. Some of the 50 locations in St. Peter's Colony were also visited, the most notable being: Muenster, Humboldt, Carmel, Bruno, Cudworth, St. Benedict, St. Leo, Leofeld, Fulda, Marysburg, Lake Lenore, Annaheim, Englefeld, Watson, Willmont, Dana, Peterson, St. Scholastica, St. Oswald, St. Martin's and Naicam. Stackelberg was particularly enthralled with the St. Peter's Colony. The two men visited it on September 10, 1924 and saw a wonderful example of a large, closed, successful German Catholic settlement. Stackelberg noted that it contained a seminary for ministers, hospital, schools and churches. The colony was so successful that it attracted a Lutheran congregation on the edge of the settlement. The Lutherans had a German-speaking pastor serving about 40 families. All these elements helped bind the community of 10,000 German speakers together while supporting their common German language and heritage. Stackleberg described the soil as being fertile, the farms large. Many of the original settlers were German-Americans and came to the area in 1904. Some were practically penniless, but 20 years later had become prosperous possessing goods, property and cash. Stackleberg cautioned that the first winter was long, hard and lonely, but one became accustomed to the new climate. The settlement had other pluses including the support of the *Deutsch-katholischen Volksverein* (German Catholic People's Society–DKVV). This society was founded in 1909 to promote Catholic and German interests while cultivating good relations with the provincial Liberal Party. Stackelberg noted that their goals appeared to be successful as relations with the provincial Liberals were good. Stackelberg observed that in all matters of education and minority questions the *Deutsch-Kanadischer Verband von Saskatchewan* (German-Canadian Association from Saskatchewan–DKS) and the Catholic Church cooperated together with the German-speaking Lutherans and Mennonites. The DKS strove to protect the German language and culture throughout Saskatchewan.[11] Both Gleiss and Stackleberg supported a small-scale selective immigration to Canada for German nationals, partially based on their positive assessment of Saskatchewan.

Hermann Wagner, Gleiss' successor, made observations of Canada and the United States between May 5 and August 21, 1928. In Canada Wagner was especially interested in visiting the two main provinces of German

The executive of the Regina chapter of the *Deutsch-Kanadischer Verband von Saskatchewan*, post-1928 (Courtesy of the Saskatchewan Archives Board/R-B11258).

emigration, Saskatchewan and Alberta. On June 11 Wagner was in Saskatchewan. There he visited Langenburg, Yorkton, Melfort, Neudorf, Lipton, Regina, Wapella, Saskatoon, Rosthern, Prince Albert, St. Walburg, North Battleford, Lashburn, Lloydminister and St. Joseph's Colony. St. Joseph's Colony consisted of Leipzig, Carmelheim, Handel, Revenue, Tramping Lake, Broadacres, Denzil, St. Johannes, Grosswerder, Primate, St. Peter's, St. Donatus, Macklin, Kerrobert, St. Franziskus, Holy Rosary/ Rosenkranz, Salvador, Scott and Wilkie. Some communities in St. Peter's colony were also visited, but it can only be stated with certainty that Wagner visited Muenster and Humboldt. Wagner repeated Stackelberg and Gleiss' favourable appraisal of German Catholic colonies in Saskatchewan. He also believed Regina and Rosthern deserved honourable mention as pillars of the German communities. Wagner noted conditions in western Canada were favourable for German emigrants.[12] In March 1930, of the 1,326 families resident in St. Joseph's Colony 1,186 or 89% were German speaking.[13] According to Lehmann, German Catholic immigrants "were deliberately directed to Saskatchewan." Lehmann placed the number of German nationals at both St. Peter's and St. Joseph's colonies at 10%.[14] According to Guth and her study of Denzil, a settlement in St. Joseph's Colony, 9% were German nationals.[15]

One settlement proposal in Saskatchewan stemmed from Dr. Justus Schmidel. Before the war Schmidel had emigrated from Germany to the United States, studied medicine and practised as a medical doctor in British Columbia. When the war began he was interned, and in 1920 deported to Germany: after World War I the Canadian government deported hundreds of German nationals who were residents in Canada. It was widely believed that deportation would provide work for returning World War I veterans and other loyal Canadians. Deportation procedures made no distinction between prisoners of war (POW), German internees, and those guilty of immigration-related offences. The Canadian Department of Immigration and Colonization ignored and violated immigration law and procedures to deport Germans as POWs; deportation was open to interpretation and was abused to deport individuals depending on their current situation and nationality.[16] Why Schmidel was deported is open to speculation. In Germany he found employment with the International News Service and worked for the Canadian National Railway (CNR). Schmidel promoted a CNR film entitled "Canada: seine Bodenschatz und landwirtschaftlichen Möglichkeiten" (Canada: Its Mineral Resources and Agricultural Possibilities). According to Germany's emigration authorities the film encouraged German emigration, and did not accurately portray conditions in Canada. The film depicted a young German man arriving in Winnipeg, Manitoba in the depths of a Canadian winter. He was able to find work immediately. He quickly learned local farming techniques and was able to buy his own farm. German emigration authorities found the film to be inaccurate for several reasons: it portrayed a poor German emigrant arriving in Canada, then going from success to success before ending as a prosperous large landowner. It was also believed the government of Canada was behind the film. Schmidel gave public lectures, which were intended to entice those individuals debating emigration; he acknowledged that some in Germany exaggerated possibilities in Canada, but he distanced himself from such claims and people. The chances of becoming rich were small, but a comfortable life through agricultural labour was there.

In the summer of 1926 Schmidel travelled via the CNR to Canada searching for suitable land for a German settlement. St. Walburg, Saskatchewan was chosen as an appropriate location. The intention was to have a German-speaking community in order to preserve and protect their common German culture. Schmidel picked St. Walburg because it already contained Canadian-born, American-born and Russian-born German speakers, as well as German nationals. These German speakers that resided in the area would contribute to the success of the community. St. Walburg already had a German library and church. Schmidel wanted Germans that could perform physical labour and had ten thousand marks. Land could be bought for $10 to $15 an acre; debts incurred through land acquisition were to be paid over 33 years at 7% interest. In June 1927 Schmidel arrived aboard the ship Bremen, accompanied by 21 Germans. Those with larger amounts of money bought farms close to St. Walburg, complete with buildings and livestock, while others with smaller amounts took over homesteads eight kilometres away. The Germans that travelled with Schmidel testified to the quality of the land and his helpfulness. All believed more German settlers could only help the colony grow and prosper. Schmidel hoped for an endorsement from the Auswärtiges Amt (German Foreign Office–AA) officials in Canada, but they refused. Dr. Ludwig Kempff, German ambassador in Montreal from 1920–37, believed the majority of German immigrants could not succeed if they came to Canada and immediately bought land and set themselves up as independent farmers: they needed Canadian farming experiences before starting out on their own. Dr. Max Lorenz (November 1926–April 1929) at the German Consulate (GC) in Winnipeg, Manitoba did not support the settlement scheme, yet he did concede that the area chosen was appropriate because the recent German emigrants had the support of the ethnic Germans resident in the area. He also viewed the quality of the land as good;

but Kempff remained skeptical of the settlement. Schmidel tried to ensure the colony's survival, and returned to Germany in October 1927.[17] According to Eckhardt Kastendieck, a German national who had been living in the area since 1925, Schmidel was helpful and good-natured, but was not the honest, upright individual he portrayed while in Saskatchewan. He explained that

> one day he found out that my wife who had been a regis-
> tered nurse had brought a little medical cabinet with some
> drugs from Germany. He looked all over[;] after he was
> through some of the medicines containing morphine were
> missing. We paid closer attention to the whole thing and
> found out that he was a morphinist[,] too. Beides being a
> gen[ius] he had other habits too.[18]

Near St. Walburg another group of German nationals came to reside. In 1929 a group of 20 families from Germany agreed to settle together at Loon Lake, Saskatchewan, 48 kilometres from St. Walburg. Most were from the state of Thuringia, but some members of this group were from Holstein, Mecklenberg and Westphalia. There were eight farmers, one typesetter, one shoemaker, one tailor, two cabinet-makers, one bank employee, one sailor, two engineers, one painter, one health spa director and one vegetable deal-er. Nazi ideology was able to make inroads with this group in the 1930s: they became known as the Loon River Nazis.[19]

Although most in Canada encouraged attempts to increase the popula-tion, some wanted Germans excluded or a selected immigration to occur. A few believed that elements in Germany were interested in rural areas of Saskatchewan for the exclusive settlement of German nationals.[20] These facts encouraged the formation of the Royal Commission for Immigration and Settlement (RCIS). Additional information on the workings of German immi-gration can be gleaned from this investigation, which held 40 sittings and heard from over 400 representatives of farm, labour, church, government and patriotic organizations, as well as individuals on immigration and related matters between January 4 and September 10, 1930. The results of the RCIS called for a controlled immigration that safeguarded the entrance of British immigrants with checks and control measures.[21] Several members of the German Canadian community gave their testimony. Reverend Christian Kierdorf, manager of VDCK, testified that his organization aided the settle-ment of German-speaking Roman Catholics within German Catholic areas in Canada. The society had many contacts in the west, especially Saskatchewan. These German speakers were largely from Poland, Russia, Romania, Hungary and Germany. Kierdorf stated that he received hundreds of letters from Europe asking for his help in immigrating to Canada. According to Kierdorf the VDCK's work was widely known in Europe amongst charitable organizations and church members; Canadian immigration requirements had to be followed, as well as being a member of the Catholic Church. Kierdorf estimated that 50% of the immigrants that came to Canada via the VDCK were settled permanently; others migrated to other locations or had relatives elsewhere and simply moved on. Between 1924 and 1930 the VDCK settled roughly 5,000 men—with families a total of 10,000 to 12,000 ethnic Germans; approximately 50% resided in Saskatchewan. Some single women were also aided in coming to Canada, working as domestics. Kierdorf estimated that in 1929 the VDCK helped 100–150 German-speaking domestics enter the country. The domestics settled throughout western Canada, but it is not known how many remained in Saskatchewan.[22]

The LIB was established in 1923 for reasons similar to the VDCK. The LIB

St. Martin's (Billimun) Roman Catholic Church, built 1926. In 1909 representatives of a group of German-speaking colonists from the Russian Crimea selected the area 8 miles northwest of the present village of Mankota, Saskatchewan as their future home. In 1910 the first contingent of settlers arrived, and by the mid-1920s over 80 families had relocated to the settlement from their homeland in Europe. The first church was erected in 1914 on land donated by Valentine Deringer. A second and larger place of worship was built in 1926. It was destroyed by fire the following year but, undaunted, the residents of the district constructed the church pictured here within a year. It was blessed by Archbishop Mathieu of Regina in July 1927 and has become, over the years, the most prominent landmark in the district. In March 1983 St. Martin's ceased to function as an active church and was designated an historic site the same year (Courtesy of David McLennan/University of Regina).

aided German-speaking Lutherans from Poland, Russia, Germany, Czechoslovakia, Austria, Bukowina, Galicia, Latvia, Estonia and Hungary. The LIB aided roughly 16,000 German-speaking Lutherans to emigrate from Europe. H.W. Harms, president of the LIB, western branch, explained that in the years 1927–29 the LIB settled 7,141 German-speaking Lutherans in western Canada. After its inception the LIB settled a total of 10,573 in western Canada with 3,080 German speakers residing in Saskatchewan. At the time of his testimony in January 1930, Harms estimated that 75% were still resident in Canada. Approximately 80% had been farmers in Europe, or those that had lost everything in the war and wanted a new start in life. Harms estimated that 10% to 15% of the immigrants were from Germany; from this figure he noted that the majority were from northern Germany.[23]

German immigration to Canada was not only complicated by World War I, but also by the varied countries where German citizens were born. As can be seen below (Table 3), the majority of German nationals were born in Germany, but 1,021—nearly one-fifth—were born outside of Germany while holding German citizenship. The fact that parts of Saskatchewan contained many Germans speakers, and the number of foreigners in the province was approaching 50% in the 1920s and 1930s caused some to be concerned, but this fact also encouraged some German speakers to settle in the province. Table 3 shows the breakdown of the country of birth and gender of all German nationals living in Saskatchewan and still possessing German citizenship in 1931.[24]

Table 3. Country of Birth and Gender of German Nationals in Saskatchewan, 1931											
	Austria	Czecho-Slovakia	Germany	Hungary	Yugo-slavia	Poland	Romania	Russia	USA	Other	Total
Total	84	20	4,370	17	15	172	51	390	218	54	5,391
Male	57	12	3,130	9	7	98	27	217	97	31	3,685
Female	27	8	1,240	8	8	74	24	173	121	23	1,706

The *Verein für das Deutschtum im Ausland* (Society for Germans Abroad–VDA), an important German cultural organization between the two World Wars, noticed that ethnic Germans preferred to settle in Saskatchewan through the support of religious immigration organizations. These decisions were influenced by those in Germany, which firmly believed that German speakers had built solid German communities in parts of Saskatchewan.[25] VDA also claimed that Regina was the centre of ethnic German communities due to spiritual and secular organizations having their administrative headquarters there.[26] Some VDA contributors were cautiously optimistic that Saskatchewan offered the possibility for cultural and linguistic retention. Wilhelm Dibelius, professor of English at Berlin University and VDA observer, noted that too many children of German-speaking immigrants spoke English. Yet he believed a language struggle between immigrants and English speakers would occur in Saskatchewan. In 1928 Dibelius noted that foreigners made up 47% of Saskatchewan's population, as against 43% in Manitoba and 40% in Alberta. He believed that it was because of this mixed population that the German culture might succeed in Saskatchewan.[27] Canadian statistician Hurd also noted the precarious situation for Canadian authorities in Saskatchewan. He wrote: "in Alberta almost half of the population is now of non-British extraction and in Manitoba and Saskatchewan more than half—indeed in Saskatchewan, considerably more than half." He added that "Saskatchewan had over twice as many foreign as British-born, and just under two thirds of the former were of European birth."[28] In certain parts of Saskatchewan it was possible to have German religious language instruction; however, this was limited to half an hour a day, provided the local clergy was proficient in German. The question was one of assimilation and language retention of immigrants. Dibelius believed that Germans might be able to control their own destiny by voting as a block in provincial elections and forging strong relations with other ethnic groups. Dibelius' protégé, Heinz Lehmann, also believed that Saskatchewan offered German speakers the best place in Canada for ethnic retention. He also noted that religious instruction played a role: in St. Joseph's Colony 46 nuns taught German religious lessons to their pupils. Lehmann, like Dibelius, knew it was a question of assimilation and language preservation: schools were a powerful weapon of ethnic absorption into the English-speaking world. Lehmann theorized that World War I had given the WASP majority the opportunity to encourage a policy of assimilation. This factor, combined with the fear of being engulfed by a non-English population, spurred the governments of western Canada to the assimilation of immigrants.[29]

Another important German cultural organization, the *Deutsche Ausland Institut* (German Foreign Institute–DAI), also thought highly of Saskatchewan and its closed German Catholic settlements. DAI believed St. Peter's and St. Joseph's Colonies would stop the assimilation process. The DAI also credited the DKS as uniting all German speakers in the province, regardless of religion or land of birth, to act together for common goals. It was believed that the DKS could lobby the provincial government for change and strengthen the German culture. The DAI also viewed the Liberal Party as a friend of all German speakers: the provincial Liberal Party was praised for their impartiality, honesty and good relations to its foreign-born population.[30] Lehmann also contended that the Saskatchewan Liberal election victories between the wars were partially due to the German vote.[31]

Another keen observer of Saskatchewan and its German citizens living within its borders was the AA. By 1925 the AA considered Canada to be one of the lands of immigration that was appropriate for German nationals. This estimation was partially due to Kempff and his appraisal of the conditions of German speakers in Saskatchewan. Part of his duties was to visit German communities and review the conditions German emigrants encountered in Canada.[32] Kempff discouraged German nationals from settling in areas where he believed they would be quickly assimilated, e.g. Ontario. Employment in eastern Canada demanded a good knowledge of English, which threatened German customs and language. Western Canada was conducive to retaining the German culture and heritage because an agricultural lifestyle did not demand the use of English, and block settlements appeared possible. The GC believed that the German culture and language could be best preserved when German speakers lived together in closed settlements, which were available in Saskatchewan. In addition Kempff feared that Canadian industries, which employed Germans with trades, could produce finished goods that would compete with German goods. As German emigration to Canada increased after World War I, Kempff observed that the main destination for all ethnic Germans was Saskatchewan. The GC noted also that Saskatchewan was the preferred destination for German-speaking immigrants, e.g. in 1926 Saskatchewan attracted 5,023 ethnic German emigrants while Manitoba attracted 4,103 and Alberta 786. Canadian statistics reveal that 10,943 ethnic Germans emigrated to Canada in 1926. According to Kempff's numbers, it appears that 90.58% settled in western Canada, with 45.9% settling in Saskatchewan. Kempff observed that ethnic German Protestants showed a tendency to settle in Alberta, Manitoba and Ontario while German Catholics migrated to Saskatchewan. This was partially due to closed settlements such as St. Joseph's and St. Peter's Colonies.[33] Mr. and Mrs. Joe Hinz confirmed Kempff's observation: they reported that German speakers moved to the area to be near other ethnic Germans of the Catholic faith. Hinz stated that most people came for religious and cultural reasons. In the colonies German-speaking priests encouraged the use of the German language and German traditions. German nationals also espoused this sentiment. Many German speakers thought by living in these colonies they were supporting the German culture in Saskatchewan and ensuring that the settlement would retain the German language and traditions long after their death. They noted that "there were definitely people that thought by coming to this colony, they were German branded and would be a German

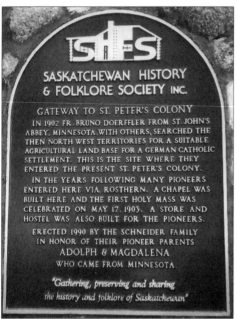

SASKATCHEWAN HISTORY
& FOLKLORE SOCIETY INC.

GATEWAY TO ST. PETER'S COLONY
IN 1902 FR. BRUNO DOERFFLER FROM ST. JOHN'S
ABBEY, MINNESOTA, WITH OTHERS, SEARCHED THE
THEN NORTH WEST TERRITORIES FOR A SUITABLE
AGRICULTURAL LAND BASE FOR A GERMAN CATHOLIC
SETTLEMENT. THIS IS THE SITE WHERE THEY
ENTERED THE PRESENT ST. PETER'S COLONY.
IN THE YEARS FOLLOWING MANY PIONEERS
ENTERED HERE VIA ROSTHERN. A CHAPEL WAS
BUILT HERE AND THE FIRST HOLY MASS WAS
CELEBRATED ON MAY 17, 1903. A STORE AND
HOSTEL WAS ALSO BUILT FOR THE PIONEERS.
ERECTED 1990 BY THE SCHNEIDER FAMILY
IN HONOR OF THEIR PIONEER PARENTS
ADOLPH & MAGDALENA
WHO CAME FROM MINNESOTA.

*Gathering, preserving and sharing
the history and folklore of Saskatchewan*

This plaque on the southeast edge of Cudworth, Saskatchewan commemorates the founding of St. Peter's Colony in 1902 (Courtesy of David McLennan/ University of Regina).

colony that would still exist today."[34] Anderson also stated that some residents of St. Peter's Colony had emigrated from Europe to Saskatchewan via the USA.[35]

In April 1927 Lorenz wrote the AA emphasizing that Saskatchewan was compatible for German nationals retaining the German language and culture. He believed that it would be in Germany's interest to direct German immigration to Saskatchewan whenever possible. It appeared that the AA heeded this advice: a little over three months later, the AA told Germany's emigration authorities that those Germans who had already made up their minds to emigrate to Canada but did not have a concrete destination in mind, should be encouraged to settle in Saskatchewan. Representatives of the AA and members of the German government made the same assessment: Saskatchewan offered the best possibilities for cultural and language retention of Germans in Canada. Lorenz was convinced that Saskatchewan German speakers were the strongest politically in Canada. It was believed cultural efforts would be enhanced through ethnic German politicians such as J.M. Uhrich. The 1925 provincial elections saw three ethnic Germans elected—Dr. J.M. Uhrich, H.M. Therres and Anton Huck. Of these three men Uhrich was the most influential. He had served in the provincial cabinet of 1922 and in 1923 received the portfolio of Department of Public Health; in 1926 he also received the portfolio of Public Works.[36] Lorenz reported that Saskatchewan's German speakers had the best economical and political position in Canada. He maintained that the political influence of Saskatchewan's ethnic Germans was much greater than the number of politicians elected. Lorenz concurred with Kempff that the best possibility was a rural existence where German speakers and their children had little contact with the English language and culture; industrial areas and large cities were English-speaking domains averse to retaining the German culture. Lorenz believed Manitoba and Alberta had a lot of mineral wealth; he expected both provinces to increase in industrialization and population, causing Germans to lose out culturally. German elements were not strong enough to have a large political impact due to being scattered throughout the province and divided among their different religions and areas of origin. In Manitoba, the size and influence of Winnipeg was also a concern as city life was dangerous to the retention of the German language and culture. Land in Manitoba, in comparison to other areas of western Canada, was expensive although tracts of land were available but had to be cleared of trees. Land in Alberta was also seen to be expensive, with stretches of dry land unsuitable for agricultural use. Both the provinces were destined to undergo industrialization and large-scale immigration, making German speakers within each province a smaller part of the total population.

Saskatchewan was seen as the most favourable destination of German emigrants due to its lack of industrialisation and economic diversification. This was based on the fact that the present mineral production of the province was small, with no large-scale projects or developments being planned. Land was cheap and mostly free of bush. German emigrants were largely farmers and would not be forced to learn English for employment opportunities. Lorenz believed Saskatchewan offered the best opportunities for closed settlements that would enhance the work of the German-Canadian immigration aid organisations while strengthening existing German settlements and serving Germany's interests. He suggested that German nationals be strategically dispersed throughout ethnic German settlements to serve both as a physical and cultural link to Germany. Some in Germany and Canada incorrectly believed Germans in Saskatchewan had more control than was actually the case. The concentration of German speakers was already occurring through the work of the religious immigration boards, the network of family and friends, railway, immigration and shipping agents. The impact of German nationals had already been observed within the German clubs and societies in western Canada. German nationals could serve as cultural leaders within German areas and cultural ambassadors outside. Lorenz believed the present level of German nationals coming to Canada was large enough to cover the cultural needs of Canada's German speakers. He wanted all Germans after arrival to work as farm hands, for one to two years in order to learn Canadian farming techniques. Lorenz noted the provincial Liberal Party took German concerns on minority education seriously. The GC believed the DKS acted on behalf of Saskatchewan's ethnic Germans and were successful in putting pressure on the provincial Liberal Party.[37] Lorenz's successor in Winnipeg was Dr. Kurt

Martin, serving from April 1929 to August 1930. Martin also made observations concerning the province's German speakers. One development that caught his eye was the influence of the DKS. Martin attended meetings of the DKS in March 1930 and believed this organization had potential to place pressure on the provincial government. The DKS lobbied the provincial government for freedom of religion and language. Martin advocated that more German speakers become politically active and promote minority rights and education. He estimated the DKS's strength at 200 to 300 members.[38] The GC observed that settlement in Saskatchewan meant that German emigrants remained farmers and did not come into competition with German industries or export markets, which was compatible with the revival of the German economy.[39]

Subsequent AA personnel in Canada were not concerned with immigration owing to the Great Depression nearly ending German immigration to Canada. During the Nazi era German legislation was passed in an attempt to keep German labour at home, thus making emigration nearly impossible. But the AA remained a strong supporter of the German culture in western Canada. Heinrich Seelheim served as German Consul in Winnipeg from August 1930 to October 1937. Like the other AA representatives that came before him, Seelheim took the opportunity to get to know German speakers in western Canada. During the 1930s he travelled through western Canada explaining the new Germany and Nazi ideology. He was a true convert to the Nazi cause as well as an anti-Semite. Wilhelm Rodde served as German Consul in Winnipeg from October 1937 to the outbreak of World War II. Rodde was a fanatical believer in Hitler and more violently anti-Semitic than his predecessor; he undertook essentially the same administrative and cultural tasks as Seelheim. AA representatives abroad always had to produce travel documents etc. for their own nationals and, if they were in dire straits, aid them in their return to Germany. Concern for AA officials in Canada during the Nazi era shifted from immigration to the return migration of German nationals.[40]

From 1933 to 1935 the Nazi government did not encourage German citizens residing abroad to return. Although those that returned would be helped by Germany's welfare organizations, finding suitable residence and work was often difficult.[41] With the Nazi party solidifying their grip on power in Germany affiliated organizations were founded in Canada. On January 1, 1934 the *Deutscher Bund* (German Alliance) Canada was founded. Although there were local groups throughout much of Canada the *Bund*'s strength was in western Canada. The largest provincial membership was in Saskatchewan. This was due to its large number of recent immigrants and their high percentage amongst the total population. Saskatchewan also had, at one time or another, more than 40 *Bund* groups for a total of between 800 and 1,000 *Bund* members. Recent German immigrants often found it hard to adjust to Canadian society and its economy. Even after becoming Canadian citizens they clung to positive stories from Germany and the new leadership provided by Hitler. By 1935 the Nazis had transformed Germany with new programs and new opportunities, thus displaying a positive new image to those that had emigrated earlier. Germany began to look very attractive to those languishing from the effects of the recession overseas. By late 1936 the official German policy regarding return migration became flexible.[42] The fact that relatives and German officials encouraged Germans to return only caused the movement to swell; a reduction of transportation costs for citizens of Germany by German shipping lines facilitated this migration of peoples. By 1938 Germany's insatiable desire for labour dictated that healthy Nazis could receive support in their bid to return to the Reich. At the same time in Canada there was a distrust of Nazis by most Canadians, which only served to further isolate some German nationals in Canada. Rodde noted that the anti-German press in Canada, plus the depression, combined to encourage Germans of western Canada to return to the Reich. Germany wanted all levels of workers in the Reich. Rodde became active in encouraging German speakers in western Canada to migrate to Germany through assurances of employment and improvements at home. Due to the depression Saskatchewan became fertile recruiting grounds for return migration.[43]

Rodde was good friends with Ernst Wilhelm Bohle, director of the Nazi's Ausland Organization (Foreign Organization–AO). The AO was part of the Nazi Party; it was responsible for all German nationals abroad. The AO wanted all German nationals abroad to have an ideology that was compatible with Nazi beliefs and actions. The AO also controlled the *Rückwandereramt* (Return Migration Office–RWA), which was responsible for administering and controlling the return of German nationals from abroad.[44] The *Volksdeutsche Mittelstelle* (Ethnic German Arbitration Bureau–VoMi) cared for ethnic Germans and former German nationals who had become citizens of other countries and wanted to be re-naturalized. It organized a bureau entitled *Übersee Abteilung* (Oversea Section), that wanted to come to Germany.[45] Both the AO and VoMi guided German speakers to Germany with the help and advice of the German Consulates abroad. Both administrations worked similarly in getting German speakers accommodation and work in Germany.[46] The AA was in charge of examining potential returnees to insure they would be an asset to Germany. Certain segments of the German community abroad were to be denied re-entry into

Germany, such as Jews, Communists, and spies. The German consuls usually did the actual interviews. The ideal repatriated German would be politically loyal to the Nazi Party while being an economic asset due to their
trade. In Canada the GC in Winnipeg was responsible for interviewing and
screening the potential Rückwanderer in western Canada, while the
embassy-consulate in Montreal was responsible for those in eastern Canada.
In early 1939 Rodde wrote the AA that his office was flooded with inquiries
about return migration. These came from both German nationals and ethnic
Germans from the Prairie Provinces, with the majority coming from
Saskatchewan. This was due to bad harvests, the anti-German press in
Canada and the lure of *Grossdeutschland* (Greater Germany) after the unification of Austria and the Sudetenland with the Fatherland. Most of those
who wanted to return were farmers. Rodde reported that 500 German
speakers migrated to Germany from western Canada.[47] The American
Consulate General in Winnipeg noted that between July 1938 and July 1939
hundreds of German speakers went to Germany from the Prairie Provinces;
all were able-bodied workers with families, who had been persuaded to
return to Germany by offers of security and employment by Rodde.[48]

German statistics for return migration of German nationals prior to
World War II are not complete, but in 1938 over 200 German nationals
returned from Canada. In 1939 the number was roughly 450; it is not known
how many were from Saskatchewan.[49] Paul Otto was an impoverished
German immigrant suffering from the Great Depression in Saskatchewan;
he was deported prior to World War II. Statistically he may have been considered a return migrant by the Nazi administration.[50] Another possible candidate was Ernst Poppelbaum; he farmed near Punnichy, Saskatchewan. He
was suffering due to the recession in Canada; in contrast Germany offered
him a job and a future. He, like other German speakers in Saskatchewan,
wanted to return to Germany in the quest of a better life.[51] The most well-
known and documented case of German speakers returning to Germany is
the story of the Loon River Nazis. Schilling, the leader of the Loon River
Germans, was a fervent Nazi and an advocate of the *Bund*. He enthusiastically recruited more German speakers to join the Nazi organization. William
Bundschuh stated that Schilling persuaded him to join by explaining the
benefits of receiving German literature and assistance, plus he would
receive financial aid from Germany if he encountered any monetary hardships. Already in 1935 other Germans from the area had given up on
Saskatchewan, thinking that Nazi Germany offered better opportunities
than the Canadian prairies.[52]

Some members of the Loon River Nazis had written AA representatives

Sudeten-German refugees were temporarily housed in this "boxcar village" at St. Walburg in 1939. Vocally opposed to Adolph Hitler, they came to Saskatchewan having fled Czechoslovakia for their lives. Ironically, a number who moved on to settle in the Loon River area, roughly 60 km north of St. Walburg, occupied lands vacated by earlier German settlers—the "Loon River Nazis"—who had returned to Germany supportive of Hitler and the Nazi regime (Courtesy of the Saskatchewan Archives Board R-A27615-5).

in Canada in early 1939 to receive information and help for their impending return to Nazi Germany. After spending 10 years in the Saskatchewan bush, being taxed to their physical limits, some members of the group agreed to end their misery and return to the New Germany. Schilling was commended for his work on behalf of Nazi Germany, most notably his personal attempts to forge a connection between Germany and the local Germans. For the Nazi German newspaper in Canada, *Die Deutsche Zeitung für Kanada* (The German Gazette for Canada–DZ), these return migrants served as proof of the better opportunities of Nazi Germany compared to the melting pot of Saskatchewan. The DZ highlighted the discrimination these individuals felt in Canada, which encouraged them to return to Nazi Germany, a country where they would be treated fairly, a land where an honest day's work resulted in full pay and contentment.[53]

The Loon River Nazis were a group of 18 Germans and their families that left Saskatchewan by bus for New York in mid-July 1939. They departed on the German ship *Bremen* on July 25, 1939. From the Schilling group of roughly 50 people, at least 19 were *Bund* members. This group consisted of both German nationals and Canadian citizens, as some had become citizens while residing in Canada. In theory they were German citizens and could obtain any services offered by the German administration such as the AO. Unfortunately they suffered, as many return migrants did, from their years away from the Reich. One of their reasons for their departure was the labour shortage in Germany. Nearly one month before the outbreak of the war the Loon River Nazis were in Germany. These individuals were assigned to labour in the Fritz Saubel works in Weimar making war materials. What they desired, as many return migrants wanted, was a position where their experiences abroad would be taken into consideration and appreciated. Their years of challenges together against Mother Nature, they rationalized, could be put to use in eastern Prussia as farmers. Prussia needed agricultural workers but, due to most Germans avoiding farm work, Polish labourers were often used. German officials wanted to strengthen the German culture in this area, fearing the influence of Polish immigrant workers. In Germany the wishes of the Loon River Nazis were ignored. They were told that they could best serve the Reich as factory workers; their farming knowledge could be put to usage after the war. Little is known about their existence in the Reich, but Goetz wrote that because some of them became Canadian citizens they were treated as foreigners, not as returning German citizens. This made finding decent employment in Germany very difficult. The Loon River Nazis are one example of German nationals who immigrated prior to the Great Depression, were discontented with their existence in Saskatchewan, and returned to Germany on the eve of World War II.[54]

Although Saskatchewan was believed to offer Germans cultural retention in Canada, this proved to be untrue. The geographical isolation of German farmers in this Prairie province did not offer them a better future than other Canadian provinces. Today there are no noticeable effects of the German language and culture in everyday life in Saskatchewan. German nationals and other German speakers became part of the English-speaking majority despite their cultural hopes and appraisals of Saskatchewan. The terms cultural mosaic or multiculturalism were not part of Canadian vocabulary between the wars. Despite the cultural effort of German communities, churches, societies and individuals, their efforts were largely without long-term effect.[55]

Notes

This article first appeared in *Prairie Forum* 33, no. 1 (2008): 39–64.

1. Werner Bausenhart, German Immigration and Assimilation in Ontario 1783–1918 (Toronto: Legas Press, 1989), 90–93; Kurt G. Tischler, "The Efforts of the Germans in

Saskatchewan to Retain Their Language Before 1914," *German-Canadian Yearbook* 6 (Toronto: Historical Society of Mecklenburg Upper Canada, 1981), 58–61; Grant Grams, *German Emigration to Canada and the Support of its Deutschtum during the Weimar Republic—The Role of the Deutsches Ausland Institut, Verein für das Deutschtum im Ausland and German-Canadian Organisations* (Frankfurt am Main: Peter Lang Publishers, 2001), 14–22, 72–75; Jonathan F. Wagner: *Troubles in Paradise: Letters to and from German Immigrants in Canada, 1925–1939* (St. Katharinen: Scripta Mercaturae Verlag, 1998), 8; Jonathan Wagner, "The Deutscher Bund in Saskatchewan," *Saskatchewan History* 31, no. 2 (Spring 1978): 48; Jonathan Wagner, *Brothers Beyond the Sea* (Waterloo: Wilfrid Laurier Press, 1981), 13; Manfred Grisebach, "Auswanderung als Verlust und Gewinn unseres Volkes," in Dr. Hermann Rudiger (ed.), *DAI im Neuen Reich* (Stuttgart: Ausland und Heimat Verlag Aktiengesellschaft, 1935), 89–92.

2. Bundesarchiv Berlin (hereafter BAB) R901/30023: Deutsche Kolonial Gesellschaft to RMI, Berlin February 21, 1919; Politisches Archiv des Auswärtiges Amtes (hereafter PAAA) 67396 Rückwanderung Kanada: Wilhelm Rodde GC to Volksdeutsch Mittelstelle, Winnipeg February 13, 1939; BAB NS9/65 Nathrath Rückwandereramt an alle Zweigestellen des RWA, February 7, 1939.

3. Library and Archives Canada (hereafter LAC) C10432 File 902168 Part 4: Population and Immigration following the War, Scott Superintendent of Immigration; LAC C10432 Part 1, Vol. 610: Calder to Colonel Smith, May 13, 1919; Canada, *Eighth Census of Canada 1941*, Vol. 1 (Ottawa: Edmond Cloutier, 1946), 14; M.C. Maclean, *An Analysis of the Stages in the Growth of Population in Canada* (Ottawa: Dominion Statistics, n.d.), 42.

4. Canada, *Origin, Birthplace, Nationality, and Language of Canadian People (1921 Census)* (Ottawa: F.A. Acland Printer, 1929), 103; Canada, *Special Report on the Foreign Born Population* (Ottawa: Government Printing Bureau, 1915), 14; *Canada Yearbook 1933* (Ottawa: Dominion Bureau of Statistics, 1933), 120–21; LAC, RG31, Vol. 1417, Memorandum to Mr. Coats; Canada, *Eighth Census of Canada 1941*, Vol. 4, (Ottawa: Edmond Cloutier, 1946), 2–3; Canada, *Census of the Prairie Provinces*, Vol. 1, *1946* (Ottawa: Edmond Cloutier, 1949), 35, 247, 489. M.C. Urquhart (ed.), *Historical Statistics of Canada* (Toronto: Macmillan Company of Canada, 1965), 18; Canada, *Eighth Census of Canada, 1941*, Vol. 1: 14–26, 86–89; Maclean, *Analysis*, 42; LAC, RG25, Series 855-E, Vol. 1964, File 855 E Part 1, Robertson [Memorandum] Fascist Propaganda and the Naturalization Act, March 14, 1939. Canada, *Origin, Birthplace, Nationality, and Language of Canadian People*, 103.

5. Canada, *Eighth Census of Canada, 1941*, Vol. 4: 701–03.

6. Grant W. Grams, "Sankt Raphaels Verein and German-Catholic Emigration to Canada," *The Catholic Historical Review* (2005): 92; Grams, *German Emigration to Canada*, 241–71; Grant W. Grams, "Wilhelm Dibelius and His Influence on German-Canadian Studies," *The German-American Yearbook* (2004): 131–32; Wagner, *Troubles in Paradise*, 11–15, 175.

7. BAB R1501/1794, Milian Schmitt to [GC], August 14, 1927.

8. Grams, "Sankt Raphaels Verein and German-Catholic Emigration to Canada," 89.

9. St. Mary's Province Archives, Saskatoon, P. Max Kassiepe to [Kierdorf], August 7, 1923.

10. Georg Timpe, *Durch USA und Kanada von See-und Landfahrten* (Hamburg: Anton Lettenbauer Druck und Verlag, 1929), 62–74, 161–80; Grams, "Sankt Raphaels Verein and German-Catholic Emigration to Canada," 92–93.

11. Paul Rohrbach, *Das Deutschtum über See* (Karlruhe: Wilhelm Schille und Co. Karlruhe, 1931), 138–42; Eduard Stackelberg, *Reisebrief aus Kanada, in Der Auslandsdeutsche* (Stuttgart: Das Deutsche Auslandsinstitutverlag, 1924), 611–12, 707–09, 741–44; Heinz Lehmann and G. Bassler, *The German Canadians, 1750–1937: Immigration, Settlement and Culture* (St. John's, NF: Jesperson Press, 1986), 267.

12. Bundesarchiv Koblenz (hereafter BAK) R57-474-20 Nr.28/764: Bericht über meine Studienreise nach Kanada und den Vereinigten Staaten von Nord-Amerika von 5 Mai bis 21 Aug. 1928 (Wagner-Hamburg); Hermann Wagner, *Von Küste zu Küste* (Hamburg: Verlag der Ev. luth. Auswanderermission, 1929), 110–15.

13. W. Schulte, *St. Joseph's Kolonie* (Regina: Western Printers Association Ltd. , 1930), 125.

14. Lehmann and Bassler, *The German Canadians*, 204–12, 266.

15. Gwendolyn Guth, "Rural Reichsdeutsch in Saskatchewan's St. Joseph's Colony, 1926–1949" (unpublished, 2004), 6.

16. BAB R1501/1797: GC to AA, Lorenz, July 27 1927; BAB R1501/1794: RA to RMI, Hintrager February 3, 1927; BAB R1501/1794: Hintrager RA to RMI November 1, 1926; Jonathan Wagner, *A History of Migration from Germany to Canada, 1850–1939* (Vancouver: University of British Columbia Press, 2006), 188; BAB R1501/1794: Deputy Minister of DIC to Kempff GGC, January 8, 1927; LAC, C10432, File 902168, Part 1, Vol. 610, DIC to Mr. Featherstone, August 12, 1919; LAC, RG25 A-2, Vol. 203, File I43-70 to I43-99, Under Secretary of State to Colonial Office, October 10, 1919; LAC, RG25 A-2, Vol. 203, File I43-70 to I43-99, [British] Foreign Office to Robertson, October 18, 1919; B. Roberts, *Whence They Came: Deportation from Canada 1900–1935* (Ottawa: University of Ottawa Press, 1988), 66–70.

17. BAB R1501/1794, K. Specht to Schmidel, July 27, 1927; BAB R1501/1794, Schmidel to Lorenz GGC, August 2, 1927; BAB R1501/1794, Lorenz GC to AA, August 8, 1927; BAB R1501/1797, Schmidel to GGC Montreal, July 27, 1927; BAB R1501/1480, RMI to AA February 19, 1927; BAB R1501/1794: Vortrag über Kanada von Justus Schmidel; BAB R1501/1797, Lorenz GC to AA, July 27 1927; BAB R1501/1794, Hintrager RA to RMI, February 3, 1927; BAB R1501/1794, Hintrager RA to RMI, November 1, 1926; BAB R1501/1795: Kempff GGC to AA Montreal October 3, 1927; BAB R1501/1797: Lorenz GC to AA, July 27, 1927; BAB R1501/1794, Kempff GGC to AA, Montreal, August 3, 1927; Grams, *German Emigration to Canada*, 25.

18. Saskatchean Archives Board (hereafter SAB), C81, Eckhart Kastendieck interview by D'Arcy Hande, August 8–9, 1977.

19. Jonathan F. Wagner, "Heim Ins Reich: The Story of the Loon River Nazis," *Saskatchewan History* 29, no. 2 (1976): 41–46. The Loon River Nazis will be discussed later in this work.

20. BAB R1501/1794, Future of Canada–Protest against Alien Immigration, in *The Times* (London), June 9, 1927; LAC, RG76, Vol. 108, File 18428: *The Journal*, January 22, 1928.

21. David E. Smith: Prairie Liberalism: *The Liberal Party in Saskatchewan 1905–1971* (Toronto: University of Toronto Press, 1975), 141–43; T.J.D. Powell, "Northern Settlement 1929–1935," in Michiel Horn (ed.), *The Depression in Canada: Response to Economic Crisis* (Toronto: Copp Clark Pitmann Ltd., 1988), 53.

22. SAB, R249, Vol. 44, Kierdorf Testimony to RCIS, Winnipeg, May 6, 1930.

23. SAB, SA4, Vol. 2, H.W. Harms Testimony to RCIS, Saskatoon, January 31, 1930.

24. LAC, RG31, Vol. 1417, Memorandum to Mr. Coats.

25. VDA Pressemitteilungen Ende Jan. 1930, Die Lage der Kanada-Deutschen, Nr. 408, Berlin; Hugo Grothe, *Kleines Handwörterbuch des Grenz- und Ausland-Deutschtum* (Berlin: R. Oldenbourg Verlag, 1932), 175.

26. Heinz Lehmann, *Das Deutschtum in Westkanada* (Berlin: Junker und Dünnhaupt, 1939), 220.

27. PAAA R60032 Abt.VIa Deutschtum im Ausland Band1 Nr.1: Bericht, Dibelius: 21–23.

28. W.B. Hurd, *Ethnic Origin and Nativity of the Canadian People* (Ottawa: King's Printer Ottawa, 1941), 41–51.

29. Heinz Lehmann, "Kanada," in Carl Petersen et al. (eds.) *Handwörterbuch des Grenz- und Auslanddeutschtums, Band III* (Breslau: Ferdinand Hirt, 1938), 272; Heinz Lehmann, "Der Kampff um die deutsche Schule in Westkanada," in Hermann Ullmann (ed.), *Deutsche Arbeit* (n.p.: 1936), 72–74; Lehmann, *Das Deutschtum in Westkanada*, 349.

30. Alan Anderson, *German Settlements in Saskatchewan* (Saskatoon: Saskatchewan German Council, 1990), 12–13; Fritz Wertheimer, *Von deutschen Parteien und Parteiführern im Ausland Berlin* (Stuttgart: Zentral-Verlag, 1927), 33; Fritz Wertheimer, *Von deutschen Parteien und Parteiführern im Ausland Berlin* (Stuttgart: Zentral-Verlag, 1930), 21–22; *Der Auslandsdeutsche* (Stuttgart: Verlag das Deutsche Ausland Institut, 1923), 516–17; *Der Auslandsdeutsche* (1926), 695; *Der Auslandsdeutsche* (1930), 647–49, 826–27.

31. Lehmann, *Handwörterbuch*, 272; Lehmann, Der Kampff um die deutsche Schule in Westkanada," 72–74; Lehmann, *Das Deutschtum in Westkanada*, 349.

32. BAB R1501/1792, Heilbron AA to RMI, Reichsarbeitsministerium, Reichswirtschaftsministerium, Reichsministerium für Ernährung und Landwirtschaft, Preussische Ministerium für Handel und Gewerbe und RA, March 9, 1925.

33. BAB R1501/1794, Lorenz GC to AA, Winnipeg, April 20, 1927; PAAA R77347 Abt. III Deutschtum in Kanada, Politik 25, Kempff GGC to AA, January 28, 1928; BAB R1501/1792, Heilbron AA VI to RMI, March 25, 1925; BAB R1501/1793, Kempff GGC to AA, November 23, 1925; PAAA R60032 Abt.VIa Deutschtum im Ausland Band1 Nr.1: Lorenz GC to AA, August 10, 1927; PAAA R77347 Abt. III Deutschtum in Kanada, Politik 25: Kempff GGC to AA, January 7, 1928.

34. SAB, A210, Mr./Mrs. Joe Hinz interviewed by George Hoffmann, July 11, 1973.

35. Anderson, *German Settlements in Saskatchewan*, 12–13.

36. BAB R1501/1794, Lorenz GC to AA Winnipeg, April 20, 1927; Anderson, *German Settlements in Saskatchewan*, 328; *Der Auslandsdeutsche* (1930), 826–27; Lehmann, "Der Kampff um die deutsche Schule in Westkanada," 26, 72–73; BAB R1501/1794: AA to RA July 31, 1927; PAAA Deutsches Konsulat Winnipeg Wa Deutsche Einwanderung Allgemeines: Lorenz GC to AA, April 20, 1927; Tischler, *Efforts of the Germans in Saskatchewan*, 136–37; *Der Auslandsdeutsche* (1926), 127; PAAA R60032 Abt.VIa Deutschtum im Ausland Band 1 Nr.1: Lorenz GC to AA, Winnipeg, November 28, 1927.

37. BAB R1501/1794, Lorenz GC to AA Winnipeg, April 20, 1927; PAAA R60032 Abt.VIa Deutschtum im Ausland Band1 Nr.1: Lorenz GC to AA Abt. VI, August 10, 1927; PAAA R77347 Deutschtum in Kanada: Lorenz GC to AA, August 30, 1927.

38. *Der Auslandsdeutsche* (1930), 124–25, 199; PAAA R60032 Deutschtum im Ausland (Canada), Martin GC to AA, March 30, 1930; PAAA R60032 Abt. VIa Deutschtum im Ausland Band 1 Nr. 1: Martin GC to AA, March 20, 1930.

39. PAAA R127498 Allgemeine Wanderungsfragen: Aufzeichnung über Allgemeine Auswanderungspolitik (Lenkung der Auswanderung) Dr. Martin, Berlin, February 23, 1931.

40. Wagner, "Heim Ins Reich: The Story of the Loon River Nazis," 27–28, 37–41; Wagner, *Brothers Beyond the Sea*, 41–43; Martin Robin, Shades of Right (Toronto: University of Toronto Press, 1992), 256–58; PAAA Heinrich Seelheim Personalakte Nr. 804g Band 1: Seelheim GC to AA, November 29, 1930; LAC, RG30, Vol. 5624, File 3, Western Manager CNR to A.G. Sinclair Department of Colonisation, June 16, 1932.

41. BAB R43II/137b: Göring, Der preußische Ministerpräsident Geheime Staatspolizei to RMI, Berlin, January 14, 1934; National Archive Record Administration (hereafter NARA) RG59 File 862.012/77: J.P. Chamberlain Columbia University to John Farr Simmons Department of State, March 7, 1935; NS–Volkswohlfahrt der Auslandsorganisation der NSDAP Rundschreiben Nr. 6, Grüßner, Berlin, April 1, 1935, in

Mitteilungsblatt der AO der NSDAP, p. 7; Mitteilungsblatt der Auslands Organisation der NSDAP, Ruberg Hamburg, June 14, 1935, Folge 19 Nr.14/35.

42. Robin, *Shades of Right*, 246; Wagner, *Brothers Beyond the Sea*, 243, 270–71; SAB, Kastendieck interview; Robert H. Keyserlingk, "Allies or Subversives? The Canadians Government's Ambivalent Attitude towards German-Canadians in the Second World War," in Panayi Panikos (ed.), *Minorities in Wartime National and Racial Groupings in Europe, North America, and Australia During the Two World Wars* (Oxford: Berg Publishers, 1993), 249–55.

43. PAAA Winnipeg Nr. 16 Ku6 DAF: DAF AO [Kanada] to DAF Berlin, July 10, 1939; PAAA R67396 Kult E Rückwanderung Kanada: Eckner GGC Montreal to AA, July 13, 1939; Wagner, "Heim Ins Reich: The Story of the Loon River Nazis," 41–49; PAAA 67396 Rückwanderung Kanada: Rodde GC to Volksdeutsch Mittelstelle, February 13, 1939.

44. Rückwandereramt, in Mitteilungsblatt der AO der NSDAP 1937, Berlin, November 15, 1937, Andersen, Folge 53, Nr. 320/37, p. 6; Belehrung der Rückwanderer, in Mitteilungsblatt der AO der NSDAP 1939, Folge 7, Nr. 29/39, Blatt 1, p. 21; Bohle, E.W.: Das Deutschtum–geschlossen hinter Adolf Hitler, in Wir Deutsche in der Welt, Herausgegeben von dem Verband Deutscher Vereine im Ausland e.V. NS Schriftums 1936, Kommissionverlag Verlaganstalt Otto Stollberg GmbH Berlin, pp. 15–16; Bohle, Ernst Wilhelm: Das Auslandsdeutschtum, in Dr. H.H. Lammers and Hans Pfundtner (eds.) Grundlagen, Aufbau und Wirtschaftsordnung des nationalsozialitischen Staates, Industrieverlag Spaeth und Linde, Band 1, Gruppe 2, Beitrag 22, 1938; Wagner, *Brothers Beyond the Sea*, 41–43.

45. NARA, Archive II, United States Department of State, Reports on Interrogation of German Prisoners-of-War, made by members of the Department of State, Special Interrogation Mission (September 1945– September 1946), headed by DeWitt C. Poole: I Reel M 679 RG 59 Nr. 84; BAB R43II/1409: Der Leiter der Volksdeutschen Mittelstelle to Reichsminister Dr. Lammers, Berlin, August 1, 1939; Valdis O. Lumans, *Himmler's Auxiliaries, The Volksdeutsche Mittelstelle and the German National Minorities of Europe, 1933–1945* (Greensboro: University of North Carolina, 1993), 129–30.

46. PAAA Winnipeg 17 Ku6: Grothe NSDAP Rückwandereramt: NSDAP to Rodde, Berlin, August 6, 1938; H. Brakelmann, "Freud und Leid bei unseren Ruckwanderer," in *Zwischen Heimat und Fremde*, 32 Jahrgang Berlin 1939, pp. 5–6; Bernhard F. Koch, *Abenteuer Kanada. Erlebnosbericht eines deutschen Jungen* (Berlin: Grenze und Ausland Verlag, 1943), 141–56; "Deutsche Volksgruppen aus dem Osten kehren Heim ins Reich," in *Der Deutsche Auswanderer*, 37 Jahrgang Jan. Feb. 1941 Heft 1 Berlin, pp. 4–5; NARA T81 Roll 141 Nr. 017866–017871: Ratsherr Götz Stuttgart–Gedanken zur planmässigen Rückfuhrung Reichsdeutscher und Volksdeutscher ins Reich, May 16, 1939.

47. PAAA Winnipeg 17 Ku6: Grothe NSDAP Rückwandereramt: NSDAP to Rodde, Berlin, August 6, 1938; PAAA R127500 Kult E Rückwander USA 1937/40: Jerosch NSDAP Amt VI to AA, August 22, 1938; NARA 85 File 56056/49, United States vs Paul Knauer No. 8676, October Term 1944, April Session 1945, May 29, 1945: Documents on German Foreign Policy 1918–1945 Series D (1937–1945) Vol. IV From Neurath to Ribbentrop (October 1938–March 1939): Director of the Cultural Policy Department, Stieve, Berlin, December 19, 1938, Document 513, pp. 657–59. PAAA R67396 Kult E Rückwanderung Kanada: Rodde GC Winnipeg to GGC Ottawa, February 2, 1939.

48. NARA, RG 59, Department of State 1930–1939 File 862.20242/20, George Gregg Fuller, American Consulate General Winnipeg to Secretary of State Washington, July 19, 1939.

49. PAAA R67303 Kult E Band 19, Nr. 11 Auswanderungsstastistik: Übersicht über die Rückwanderung im Jahre 1938; PAAA R127499 Kult E 7b Rückwanderung: Übersicht über die Rückwanderung im Jahre 1939.

50. G.S. Mount, *Canada's Enemies: Spies and Spying in the Peaceable Kingdom* (Toronto: Dundurn Press, 1993), 65.

51. PAAA R67445 Kult E Rückwanderer Außereuropa: Schrebler Reichsminster für Ernährung und Landwirtschaft to AA, April 5, 1939.

52. LAC, RG13, C1, Vol. 966, File B, Bundschuh, William—Objection heard at Calgary, January 22, 1940; LAC, RG117, Vol. 1880, File 2010, Province of Saskatchewan to Alois N. Schneider, February 27, 1940.

53. LAC, K173 [Bundes Archiv Koblenz], R57, DAI No. 1102, File Kanada Goetz, Reise durch Nord-Mittel und Südamerika, 1936–1937, Kanada Correspondence, Reports, Articles, 27-8-18-10, 1936: Strölin [DAI] to Hugo Schilling, February 4, 1937; PAAA Winnipeg Nr. 16 Ku16 NSDAP Kanada: Krüger NSDAP Kulturamt to Landkreis Kanada, Aug. 1, 1939; Karl Götz, *Brüder über dem Meer* (Stuttgart: J. Engelhorns Nachf., 1938), 88, 130–43, 150–51; PAAA R67448 Kult E Rückwanderer, Werner Queck to AA, February 25, 1939; Abschied von Canada, in Deutsche Zeitung für Kanada, July 26, 1939, pp. 5, 8; "Wieder eine Rueckwanderergruppe," *Deutsche Zeitung für Kanada* (August 9, 1939), 5.

54. LAC, RG76, C4689, RCMP to D[irector] of C[rime] I[nvestigation], July 31, 1939; NARA RG59 Department of State 1930–1939 File 842.00 PR/158, Daniel Roper Legation United States of America to Secretary of State, Ottawa, August 2, 1939; Wagner, "Heim Ins Reich: The Story of the Loon River Nazis," 41–49; NARA T81, Roll 143, Nr. 018101919-20: [Karl Götz] to Richard Beye, April 4, 1941.

55. Robert S. Graham, "The Anglicization of German Family Names in Western Canada," *American Speech* 30 (1965): 260–64; Robert S. Graham, "The Transition from German to English in the German Settlements of Saskatchewan," *Journal of the Canadian Linguistic Association* 3, no. 1 (March 1957): 9–13; A. Becker, "The Germans in Western Canada, A Vanishing People," *Canadian Catholic Historical Association* 42 (1976): 29–49.

Ethnic Relations and
Identity in the New West

16. Instilling British Values in the Prairie Provinces

David Smith

Of the three great streams of immigration into the Canadian West—the American, the continental European and the British—only the last has failed to attract significant academic attention.[1] Three practical considerations partly account for this oversight: the sheer size of the group, the mobility of its members and the dispersed pattern of their settlement.[2] Except in rare instances land reserves were not set aside for the British, and Clifford Sifton's unhappy experience with the Barr Colonists at Lloydminster confirmed his opposition to new reserves for any group.[3] Thus the case-study approach, often used with profit to examine the non-British in their isolated colonies, was less suitable for investigating the British who, except for exotic hybrids like the Patagonian Welsh, were widely scattered over the prairies.

Another impediment to research was the long established view that British settlers were reinforcements for the dominant Anglo-Saxon culture. This was the interpretation of the imperialists before World War I who wanted "to keep Canada British" and of the xenophobes afterwards who predicted "race ruin" if "foreign" immigration went unchecked.[4] The ethnic stereotypes these views once reflected are well known, but the more lasting influence of the British settlers on Canadian thought and attitudes remains largely unexplored. Today, the equation of "British" with "English Canadian" is no longer directly made, and at official levels it is rejected. Nevertheless, the exclusive categories derived from theories of deux nations and "two founding races" or from policies of bilingualism and biculturalism have helped keep alive both the distinction between the British and other immigrants and the identification of the former with English Canada.[5]

It was always an exaggeration to say that "if you scratch an English Canadian, you'll find he is British"; but how much of an exaggeration? To what degree were British immigrants able to transport their values and beliefs intact and then transmit them to others? To what extent did the harsh

A group of Londoners examine a window display advertising farms in the prairie provinces. Advertising was a key to attracting British immigrants to the prairies and various methods were used. In this photograph, taken circa 1912, onlookers are viewing a working model of a grain elevator in the window of the Canadian Government's Emigration Offices in London, England (Courtesy of the Saskatchewan Archives Board/R-A259).

pioneer experience moderate or even obliterate past attitudes and practices? What impact, for instance, did existing Canadian national feeling have on imported values? The adjustment made by other nationalities has been recounted in the new literature spawned by recent interest in multiculturalism, but the accommodation which British settlers had to make to their new environment has gone largely unstudied. This was because, in the words of one student of immigration, the "easier acculturation" of the British into Canadian society was "assumed," or because "the situation [was] so defined that the behavior of the British immigrant [became] the norm of successful assimilation."[6]

Without more study there can be no confident answers to these questions. In the meantime, the British "inheritance" must be treated with caution if it is not to become a selective explanation for chosen features of the Canadian political system. The strength of the collectivist thought and practice manifest in the Co-operative Commonwealth Federation (CCF), and visible in certain policies of the older parties, has been attributed in part to the influence of British ideas carried by British immigrants. For example, the first three leaders of the CCF in Saskatchewan were British-born. Yet the relationship, while apparent, remains unexplained.

The difficulties encountered early in the century by the two projects reviewed in this article, whose ultimate objective was to reinforce British values, suggest that even a "charter" group like the British enjoyed few advantages when it came to settlement. Success or failure had little to do with patriotism and everything to do with the environment and economy of western Canada. The virtues of race and Empire, the cornerstones of British values to the passionate minority who proclaimed them, were never widely endorsed. Even in the election of 1929 in Saskatchewan, when the Ku Klux Klan and the Conservative and Progressive parties made loyalty a central issue in the campaign, the subject became enmeshed with the much older and very Canadian question of separate schools.

In the history of western Canada, the Church of England's special Fund, established in 1910, and the Empire Settlement Act of 1922 were unique experiments because of the powerful private and public institutions involved, the major financial commitments received and the reserves of goodwill enjoyed by each. No group of American or continental European immigrants ever had such an array of support. Yet both undertakings were remarkably ineffective. The intangible objective of instilling British values was a rhetorical goal whose realization could never be tested by empirical means. Regardless of what privileges he might enjoy because of his origins (and the English, as opposed to the Scots and Irish, possessed relatively few because of their reputation as poor farmers), the British settler started afresh along with all immigrants, most of whom had little knowledge of the rest of Canada.

The Western Canada Fund of the Church of England

The Anglican Church's far-flung missionary work in the 19th century made it a prominent institution in the Canadian North-West. However, it was ill-equipped to deal with the rapid growth of the prairie provinces and especially the large "foreign" population which appeared before the First World War. To the Church leaders the new conditions represented a "crisis" that required a special response; a sense of urgency pervaded their creation of the "Archbishops' Western Canada Fund."[7] Invoking the Church's "special responsibilities in regard to the British Empire," the Archbishops of Canterbury and York appealed for "money and men" as well as "interest and prayer" for the Church in that new region of Canada "linked with England by the bonds of history and institutions, of language and affections." While the call for help made no mention of British immigration, beyond the need for more clergy, the subject was of continual interest to the hierarchy of the Church; through the Anglican Church's own agencies, a host of associated charitable organizations, and most directly through the parish clergy, its leaders exercised a strong influence over the exodus of people, by no means all of whom were Anglicans, from the British Isles.

Because the Church of England was a state church, opportunities existed for its clergy to involve themselves with the work of Canadian immigration officers at every level, beginning with the search for eligible immigrants. In a letter to Ottawa, a London-based official of the Immigration Branch described the problems which this could present:

> Our Officer was very kindly entertained at luncheon by the Vicar of the parish, and was instructed by him and his wife as to the style of address they wished given to the village people and children and our lecturer was specially informed that he was not to discuss the advantages of Canada as far as the young women were concerned, because there was already a great lack of domestic servants in that vicinity; but they were quite willing he should talk to the young men as the Vicar and his wife had no objection to their emigrating, there being no further house accommodation in the village, and it was not the intention of those who controlled and owned the village to have an increase in the number of inhabitants, or to put up additional accommodation.[8]

Canadian society, especially in the prairie provinces, recognized no similar privileges on behalf of the Church of England in Canada. Yet the bond of mutual feeling conferred advantages in the selection of immigrants which modified if not undermined Clifford Sifton's explicit and unsentimental resolve to take only agriculturalists, without regard to nationality: "The men who are directing the Canadian Immigration propaganda on both sides of the Atlantic," said the Commissioner of Immigration at Winnipeg, "are of British blood and several of them are British-born. Naturally they prefer British stock."[9] But despite such evidence of sympathy, the Anglican Church faced special difficulties in reconciling the demands of new pioneer communities, the existing federal system, and the imperial obligations that arose from its position as the established Church in the mother country. In any conflict of obligations, the Empire had always to come first and for the Church, as for the British government, the interests of the Empire were defined from the vantage point of the British Isles.

The pace of development, if that is the right word for towns that grew up sometimes in a matter of days, fostered local attitudes which one British visitor likened to the "Greek feeling of civicism."[10] But the Anglican Church shared in the experience of community building less often than the Presbyterian and Methodist Churches because its people were fewer and more isolated. Hence the building of churches was more difficult and the erection of Sunday Schools and other parochial organizations often impossible. The Church of England therefore suffered two crucial disabilities: few converts were made, and those who were members found themselves exposed to the pervasive influence of the non-conformists, either by direct proselytization or indirectly through community pressure. For instance, the selection of "the school teacher was frequently determined by the local [non-conformists'] need of an organist or Sunday School superintendent."[11]

Parish contact with the thousands of new settlers pouring into the region proved impossible. The Archbishops' Fund thus directed its efforts toward establishing missions at Regina in Saskatchewan and at Edmonton and Cardston in Alberta. In organization and objective there were imperial precedents for this response. The Regina mission grew out of the work of Reverend Douglas Ellison among railway construction crews, which duplicated his earlier experience in South Africa. The Edmonton and Cardston missions were patterned after the Bush Brotherhood plan used in Australia, which sent teams of clergy and laymen to the isolated settlers. Despite their pedigree and the missionaries' commitment, the experiments on the prairies proved of limited success. The initial advantage of the railway mission in reaching new arrivals out to earn money before taking up homesteads disappeared once they had moved onto the land, and the clergy in Alberta discovered that they could not maintain their obligations to Anglican settlers through visits made infrequent by distance and the vagaries of weather. To these reasons must be added the influence of World War I, which took the lives of some of the English missionaries, while the disruption attending it discouraged others from returning to Canada.

The ecumenical spirit encouraged by limited facilities and shared pioneer experiences made church union in a number of prairie communities a fact long before the creation of the United Church of Canada in 1925. But nowhere did this union embrace the Church of England, whose organization, interests and very name struck even some Anglicans as "strangely unsympathetic" to its surroundings.[12] If the Church appeared "too English" to some, to others it seemed very Canadian, and the difference in perspective was not explained solely by the side of the Atlantic on which one stood. Anglican leaders in Canada could be as exercised as their British brothers by the great issues of the day in England: disestablishment of the Church in Wales, the parliamentary crises of 1910 and 1911 and, inevitably, Ireland. Yet on other matters, such as ritual, western Canadians could prove so traditional that they often frustrated efforts by British leaders to recruit all but high-church clergy for the prairie provinces. Having to rely on an external source for clergy underlined the Church's "Englishness," while at the same time

Anglican clergy on the trail to the next homesteader's farm, circa 1912. Attracting enough clergy to meet the needs of the settler was not always easy—the distances were great, and clergy had to combine the life of a pioneer with their work within the church (Courtesy of the Saskatchewan Archives Board/R-A25865).

financial support from the mother church emphasized its dependence on what one priest called "the pennies of maid-servants in England."[13]

The contrast with the Presbyterians and Methodists was particularly striking. The 1911 Census revealed that the Presbyterians were by far the largest denomination in the prairie provinces. In Saskatchewan and Alberta the Church of England also lagged behind the Roman Catholic and Methodist Churches in numbers of adherents; even in Manitoba, where it came second, there were fewer than half as many Anglicans as Presbyterians. The Presbyterian Church was "the most `Canadian' body" not only because of its size but because it had succeeded in creating an organization that accommodated better than any other religious group the regional divisions and sympathies of Canada.[14] Canadian-trained and usually Canadian-born ministers moved about the country as called, but maintained contact with Canadian colleagues and debated Canadian issues in annual asemblies long before air travel made such regular meetings commonplace in other contexts. In this forum and through the office of its Superintendent of Western Missions, the national Presbyterian church was made aware of the needs of the West, which included not only those of the embryonic congregations across the prairies but also of the thousands of non-British immigrants. At the same time that the Church of England was establishing missions to reach Anglicans, the Presbyterians (and Methodists too) were busy working among the Ruthenians.[15]

The Archbishops' Fund, rather than infusing a national Anglican response to the problems of the West, inspired regional jealousies. Maritime Anglicans, already unhappy about the westward "movement of both men and money," now complained that they were being ignored by the Church's leaders in England.[16] When it was decided to spend some of the Fund on the education of Canadian clergy, both the Archbishop of Canterbury and Trinity College, Toronto, agreed that Trinity College was the best place to spend it rather than at colleges in the West "which from the necessity of case are only struggling into life." Displaying an impressive command of regional rhetoric, the Archbishop of Rupert's Land assumed the role of western advocate and rejected such centralist assumptions.[17]

Mindful of its imperial obligations, especially in an area of Canada marked by ambiguous sentiment toward the British Empire among immigrants from the United States and continental Europe, the Church of England identified itself with projects for which there was scant evidence of popular support. The Edmonton mission gave its blessing to a move by Alberta Anglicans to establish "higher class" schools than the government institutions which accepted "all classes and all sexes." The argument in favour of a British "public school" on the prairies was that it would produce "the type of man needed ... to share in the development of the Empire."[18] At the university level, Trinity College, Toronto, pledged itself ready to provide the strong leaders that the West and the empire required to bolster Anglo-Saxon convictions before the threatening multitude of "foreigners." Few westerners disagreed that education was the vehicle for instilling values, but even fewer demonstrated enthusiasm for a proposal which would see the growth of private religiously based schools. That was a fractious and familiar subject in provinces whose "schools question" was still a fresh memory. The goal of the minority in this instance guaranteed that it would remain such.

Even with an established institution like the Church of England behind it, the Archbishops' Fund could never be counted more than a modest venture. It was a one-sided effort with initiative, money and personnel coming from Great Britain, and for that reason the Fund had always to compete with the many other demands upon the Church's resources.

The Empire Settlement Act

By way of contrast, the Empire Settlement Act of 1922, the second experiment at building "the Empire on sure and lasting lines," brought together both public and private bodies with superior finances and organization in the Dominions as well as the United Kingdom.[19] The origins of the Act can be traced to early discussions on trade and immigration at the Imperial Conferences of 1907 and 1911, to the adverse effects of the war on British prestige and power, and to the encouraging experience of imperial co-operation in wartime. With the return of peace, British authorities saw directed immigration to the Dominions as one way of creating a stronger Empire. As with the Anglican experiment, the initiative again rested with those in Great Britain to make the new scheme a success. The British Government secured the necessary legislation, designated a formal body in the Colonial Office (the Oversea Settlement Committee) to take administrative charge, and allocated 3 million pounds a year to underwrite its activities. The money was to

Second class passengers and baggage on board the S.S. *Empress* of Britain, no date (Courtesy of the Saskatchewan Archives Board R-A12676).

be spent on a 50/50 basis, with those governments or private bodies who agreed to participate providing the other half, for the purpose of assisting the passage of immigrants, and helping them settle on the land or training those without agricultural skills before they took over their farms.

The Canadian government chose to make a very limited commitment, following instead the route of administrative regulation and frugal expenditure. Although reticence was to be expected from the government of Mackenzie King, whose quest for dominion autonomy was frequently fed by a suspicion of British motives, even limited acquiescence by Ottawa in the scheme marked a shift from pre-war attitudes which had originated with Clifford Sifton.

Sifton had resolutely opposed assisted immigration (not to be confused with the payment of bonuses to booking agents, a practice which he had accepted as necessary if Canada was to compete with other countries for immigrants). He believed that "once a man is taken hold of by the government and treated as a ward he seems to acquire the sentiments of a pauper, and forever after will not stand on his own feet."[20] His inflexibility stemmed from fear that assisted passage would open the door to urban immigrants and, even worse, to unemployed labour. Federal politicians had reason to avoid the opposition such immigrants would raise from Canadian labourers, but Sifton's stubbornness was more than the result of political calculation. He believed that Canada's wealth rested in her natural resources on the prairies, and that to develop these she required large numbers of capable immigrants. These, he felt, would be found mainly among American and continental European farmers; hence his disregard for the English workmen.

But after World War I and to some degree because of the jingoism inspired by it, the emphasis of debate turned from economics to sociology and particularly to the effects of "foreign" immigration on Canada's social cohesion. The King government proved more sensitive to criticism than its predecessors, not least because it depended for support in the House of Commons on Progressives who disagreed with the old "cosmopolitan" policy. But even in Saskatchewan where the Liberals dominated the legislature and courted the non-English vote, the premier, Charles Dunning, grew equivocal on the subject: first favouring British immigration, then discouraging "slackers" from the Old Country, while claiming to recognise the contributions made by the non-British and all the time condemning racial prejudice.

The Canadian government's subdued response to the objectives of the Empire Settlement Act disappointed the authorities in London, the more so because they believed that support among Canadians for strong British immigration was widespread, the need for Empire building acute, and the resources in England available. The Oversea Settlement Committee was itself subject to pressure from British groups like the Salvation Army, whose indefatigable Commissioner, D.C. Lamb, saw "the continuing foreign domination of the far West [if] not exactly a menace … cause for grave concern."[21]

Those charged with administering the Act formed their opinion of Canadian attitudes from contact with senior officials in the federal Department of Immigration and Colonization. And throughout the 1920s the impression received was that the Liberal government was one of the few places in Canada where anglophiles did not dominate opinion. The Department's deputy minister, who described himself as "one of those intensely interested in . . . stemming the flow of undesirables from Central Europe," assured them that there was "increasing evidence of the development of sound public opinion on the question," while another officer urged the Oversea Settlement Commitee to pursue "a vigorous settlement policy" to combat the dangers perceived from separatists in Quebec and from "the large infusion of alien blood in the West" which had left the British population of southern Alberta and Saskatchewan outnumbered.[22] Even so prominent an official as the Canadian advisory officer to the League of Nations at Geneva, Dr. Walter Riddell, corroborated this interpretation. After advising the Committee to work through Canadian interest groups to bring pressure on the provincial and federal governments, he counselled patience: "with the change of government in Canada which seems imminent the situation should change."[23]

But when the change did come in 1930, economics had once again asserted its dominance, with dismal consequences for any immigration project. In the meantime, however, a series of agreements under the umbrella legislation of 1922 did bring several thousand British settlers to the prairies. Some agreements were concluded that affected other provinces as well, as when fishermen were brought from the western isles of Scotland to the west coast of Canada and single men and women to Ontario, but the bulk of immigration was directed to the prairies.

Among the schemes were several to prepare British workmen to become grain farmers. The Canadian Cottages Agreement of 1924 committed the British government to erect homes on operating farms in the West where immigrants might reside temporarily while gaining experience (at the Canadian government's expense) as farm labourers. Another, the Hoadley experiment, named after its instigator, the Minister of Agriculture of Alberta, George Hoadley, brought over 100 poor-law and grammar-school boys to be trained in western Canadian farming methods. The boys were also regarded by the planners as the progenitors (with British girls to be sent out as nurses

Women from England and Ireland who came to Canada in 1920 to work as domestics (Courtesy of the Saskatchewan Archives Board/R-B2604-1).

or domestics, depending on their background) of new British families in Canada.

The railways, which had played a major role in the settlement of the prairies before the war, took only a small part under the Empire Settlement Act. This poor performance was due to a combination of late entry by the Canadian Pacific Railway and bad organization on the part of the government railways, whose immigration activities in the 1920s seem not to have been communicated even to the Department of Immigration and Colonization.[24]

By far the largest project was the "3,000 Families Scheme," under which the Canadian government provided established farms through its Soldier Settlement Board to British settlers, and the United Kingdom government provided cash advances of up to 300 pounds per settler for the purchase of stock and equipment. Distinctive in the history of western Canadian immigration for the amount of government assistance offered, the scheme was also unique for the degree of community interest aroused. Settlers arriving in small groups, often only a single family, were welcomed by delegations composed of local farm, government and church leaders and ushered to farms made ready for occupancy. The Land Settlement Branch of the Department of Immigration and Colonization administered details of the program, from organizing the local receptions through to reporting on the settlers' adjustment. And from 1925 until the end of the decade the Branch believed, and reported, that the scheme had demonstrated "how much more advisable it is for us to seek colonists among [British] people rather than from among continental European types."[25]

But the combination of close supervision and personal interest, as well as the availability of established farms in settled areas, rendered the scheme a singular and, as it turned out, short-lived achievement. The experience of these British settlers bore little resemblance to that of other westerners. Arguably no farmer could have been prepared for the terrible conditions to come, but the preselected settlers, favourites of imperial, federal, provincial and local governments, were doubly vulnerable to hardship because they had never encountered it in any form on the prairies. As well, their brief residence in the West, their isolated situation (as compared to that of the many central Europeans who had settled in identifiable communities) and the characteristics they shared with Canadians of British origin in different regions of the country gave them an option to move which was rarely available to other immigrants. The toll grew after 1929 as drought and depression devastated the southern portions of the three provinces where most of the families had recently been placed. The three thousand were reduced by two-thirds. Some (11%) returned to Great Britain, while the rest moved out of the region and in most instances out of farming.[26]

Even before the exodus, a body as favourably disposed to British immigration as Saskatchewan's Royal Commission on Immigration and Settlement had commented critically on the reverse onus implicit in the scheme: "If our hopes are to be realized and a larger proportion of British-born are to come … it will be because they sail from Britain imbued with the necessary willingness to accept conditions of life as they are here, rather than because we have re-adjusted those conditions."[27] This was an understated and unexpected vindication of Clifford Sifton's fear of the British labourer-turned-farmer. Obviously there was a limit to what government might do for the settler. For Sifton the limit was considerably lower than for those who argued that it was "best to be British," but for both it ultimately came to the truth, as Sifton had once remarked, that no one but the settler could hold the plough.

Conclusion

British immigrants themselves recognized the problems facing them on the prairies. Except for those brought under the auspices of the Empire Settlement Act, few others came during the decade. However, federal restrictions on entry to all but domestics, farmers and the close relatives of those already in Canada forced many thousands to disguise their intentions: "The number of Britishers giving the prairies as their destination were less than half as great as the number destined to Ontario and Quebec [but] the British-born population of the prairies increased by only 3000 during 1921–31 … while that of the central region [increased] by 83,000."[28]

This disappearance of British immigration to the prairies helps to explain the strident debate which mounted toward the end of the decade. The British settlers apart, the period was one of obvious growth and change. This contrast produced in some of those of British stock a sense of threatened decline and excessive fear. J.T.M. Anderson—director of education for New Canadians of Saskatchewan between 1918 and 1922, author of a book on the same subject and later Premier in the province's Co-operative Government between 1929 and 1934—was well known because for a decade and a half he had preached on the dark theme of "existing evils." It was to be expected that he and the Oversea Settlement Committee should make contact, for Anderson was active in multifarious bodies with a single patriotic aim. In this instance only the name was new: The Fellowship of the Maple Leaf for the supply of British Teachers for Western Canada. The Fellowship in turn was the offspring of the prairies' greatest apostle of Anglo-Saxondom, the Reverend George Exton Lloyd. Lloyd's labours in the field and through the Anglican Church predated even the Archbishops' Fund (for which he could take some credit in helping sponsor) and had had a conspicuous beginning with the Barr Colony and the founding of Lloydminster.[29]

That many of the same people were active in the Fund before the war, and after it in work carried out under the Empire Settlement Act suggests not only continuity but aging. The sense of mission might never waver, but the elect who possessed it were older and relatively fewer. The majority of the British settlers were a heterogeneous lot devoid of any singleness of purpose except a desire to break and cultivate their own land. With the notable exception of the French in the West (and to the lasting detriment of official bilingualism in the region) all immigrants accepted English as the necessary medium of communication. But such pragmatic use of the language is not to be equated with the easy transmission of British values.

The failure of both the Archbishops' Fund and the Empire Settlement Act to achieve their objectives reveals the wisdom of one observer who commented, without fully appreciating the significance of his insight, that "the West is nothing less than a 'new nation'."[30] By 1930 it had become clear that this "nation" was to have no unifying set of either British or French values. Whether it was or is yet a multi-cultural society depends on the interpretation given that ambiguous term. What is certain is that Anderson and his British Canadianizers would be disappointed, and possibly shocked, that the debate as to the nature of the West goes on—they would have said it should have been British.

On the basis of this study it is apparent that attempts to transmit values and institutions met with only limited success where they did not remain open to the social, geographic and economic influences present in the new land. Theories of religion and of settlement had little impact on the actual behaviour of people. Robert England, that prolific chronicler of prairie settlement, was no doubt correct when he observed, some decades after the great migration, that "every immigrant settler in Canada carried a memory of past culture" and that in this respect the newcomer was like "an amputee [who] sometimes feels the phantom pain of a missing limb."[31] The important question for students of western Canadian history is what the settlers, including the vast numbers of immigrants from the British Isles, put in place of their lost culture.

Notes

This article first appeared in *Prairie Forum* 6, no. 2 (1981): 129–42.

1. On American immigration the most comprehensive works are R.H. Coats and M.C. McLean, *The American-Born in Canada: A Statistical Interpretation* (Toronto: Ryerson, 1943) and Marcus Lee Hansen, *The Mingling of the Canadian and American Peoples*, vol. 1 (Toronto: Ryerson, 1940). There is no single work on European immigration that may be cited but for a comparison of the rich material available on the Ukrainians, for example, and the spare corpus on British settlers not devoted to Upper Canada or the arrival of the *Hector*, see respective entries in Andrew Gregorovich, *Canadian Ethnic Groups Bibliography* (Toronto: Department of the Provincial Secretary and Citizenship of Ontario, 1972), 180–87 and 179–89. See, also, Scottish entries, 164–72.

2. Coats and McLean, *The American-Born in Canada*, 15, cite the inflow of British-born population to the prairie provinces between 1901 and 1911 as 190,666. In his study of *The British Immigrant: His Social and Economic Adjustment in Canada* (Toronto: Oxford University Press, 1935), Lloyd G. Reynolds cites the following census figures of the British-born population in the prairie provinces: 50,440 (1901), 242,519 (1911) and 308,430 (1921), Table 3a, p. 298.

3. Library and Archives of Canada (hereafter LAC), Sifton Papers, Letterbooks, vol. 255/809–10, Sifton to Colonel S. Hughes, February 11, 1904. In this same letter Sifton admitted that the policy of group settlements may have been "misguided" but was necessary "in the early days of the immigration movement when we were forced to do anything and everything to get people."

4. For a judicious appraisal of the Canadian imperialists, see Carl Berger, *The Sense of Power: Studies in the Ideas of Canadian Imperialism, 1867–1914* (Toronto: University of Toronto Press, 1970), esp. Chapter 5. The spectrum of anti-foreign sentiment from restrained to vituperative may be found in Saskatchewan, Royal Commission on Immigration and Settlement, Records of Proceedings, 1930.

5. Mary Vipond, "Canadian National Consciousness and the Formation of the United Church of Canada," *United Church Archives Bulletin* 24 (1975): 9.

6. William Petersen, *Planned Migration: The Social Determinants of the Dutch-Canadian Movement*, vol. 2 (Berkeley: University of California Press, 1955), 130.

7. Lambeth Palace Library, Papers of R.T. Davidson, Archbishop of Canterbury, 1903–1928, Special Subjects: Canada No. 1 1903, 1909–10 (hereafter LPP, Davidson Papers, Box I), "The Archbishops' Western Canada Fund: An Appeal of the Archbishops to the Church and People of England," February 26, 1910. All quotations in the paragraph are from this document. Two articles on aspects of the Fund's work, both by Rev. David J. Carter, may be found in *Journal of the Canadian Church Historical Society* 10, no. 4 (December 1968): 202–16 and *Alberta Historical Review* 16, no. 1 (Winter 1968): 10–17.

8. Saskatchewan Archives Board (hereafter SAB), Canada, Immigration Branch Records, Reel 2.548. J. Obed Smith, Assistant Superintendent of Immigration to W.D. Scott, Superintendent of Immigration, November 19, 1910. The connection between clergymen and migration had been recognized in 1894 by Sir Charles Tupper when, as High Commissioner for Canada, he had had prepared for distribution a pamphlet entitled "The Advantages of Canada for Emigrants." Composed of papers by three Anglican clergymen, it was directed, said one of them, "to the better middle class ... to whom the conditions of English commercial life are a source of perplexity" and for whose children Canada might provide an answer. Immigration Branch Records, Reel 2.606.

9. LPP, Davidson Papers, Box 1, Bruce Walker to Rev. D. Ellison, August 6, 1909. The Department also provided the Archbishop of Rupert's Land with "full lists of the names and destinations of all Anglican Families and Individuals as they [land] in Quebec." Archbishop of Ottawa to Davidson. Ibid., July 4, 1910.

10. LPP, Davidson Papers, Box 1, B.K. Cunningham to Rev. J.V. Macmillan (secretary to the Archbishop of Canterbury), July 28, 1911. Boosterism and its detrimental effect on the Anglicans' expansion is discussed by Rt. Rev. Bishop Ingham and Rev. Clement Burrows, *Sketches in Western Canada* (London: Hodges and Stoughton, 1913).

11. LPP, Davidson Papers, Box 1, Rev. D. Ellison to Davidson, December 20, 1909, p. 6. Ellison's 32-page letter explains the Church's problems, its strengths and weaknesses and the need for immediate action.

12. LPP, Davidson Papers, Box 1, B.K. Cunningham to Rev. J.V. Macmillan, July 28, 1911. Unlike United Church leaders but like Roman Catholic spokesmen, the Anglicans did not look upon "denominationalism [as] a waste," Vipond, "Canadian Historical Consciousness," 5. See as well George Thomas Daly, *Catholic Problems in Western Canada* (Toronto: Macmillan, 1921), 83.

13. LPP, Davidson Papers, 1913 (B. 17), typescript of unsigned letter to *The Canadian Churchman*, February 20, 1913. For a description of a service by an Oxford-trained priest in "the attic of an implement shed," see J.F.B. Livesay, *The Making of a Canadian* (Toronto: Ryerson, 1947), 68.

14. E.B. Mitchell, *In Western Canada Before the War: A Study of Communities* (London: John Murray, 1915), 83.

15. Presbyterian missions to the foreign immigrants began early in the 29th century. See John S. Moir, *Enduring Witness: A History of the Presbyterian Church in Canada* (n.p., Bryant Press, 1975). See also Marilyn Barber, "Nationalism, Nativism and the Social Gospel: The Protestant Church Response to Foreign Immigrants in Western Canada, 1897–1914," in Richard Allen (ed.), *The Social Gospel in Canada* (No. 9, National Museum of Man, Mercury Series, Ottawa, 1975) and W.G. Smith, *A Study of Canadian Immigration* (Toronto: Ryerson, 1920), 39.

16. LPP, Davidson Papers, 1910 (c. 2), Archbishop of Nova Scotia to Davidson August 1, 1910.

17. LPP, Davidson Papers, Box 1, correspondence between Davidson and the Archbishop of Rupert's Land, October 10–November 3, 1910.
18. LPP Davidson Papers, Special Subjects: Canada No. 3, 1913–15, copy of prospectus for the Western Canada School Company Ltd., dated January 20, 1913.
19. Public Record Office, London, England, (hereafter PRO), CO 721/19, Memorandum "The Soldier Settlement Board of Canada, re: Agricultural Training Centres for Ex-Imperials in Canada" (May 18, 1920). The two most complete accounts of the origins and operation of the Empire Settlement Act are: John Thomas Culliton, *National Problems of Canada: Assisted Emigration and Land Settlement with Special Reference to Western Canada* (no. 9, McGill University Economic Studies 1928), and G.F. Plant, *Oversea Settlement: Migration from the United Kingdom to the Dominions* (London: Oxford University Press, 1951). G.F. Plant was secretary to the Oversea Settlement Committee (OSC).
20. LAC, Sifton Papers, Letterbooks, vol. 230/787–89, Sifton to W.W. Buchanan, February 11, 1899. Sifton's disparaging view of the British worker was substantiated by a British Parliamentary Committee with which he had an indirect connection: "Agricultural Settlement in the British Colonies" (Tennyson Committee), Cds. 2978 and 2979 (1906).
21. PRO, CO721/81, Lamb to W. Banks Amery, December 15, 1923.
22. PRO, CO721/43, J. Black to T.C. Macnaghton (Chairman, OSC), May 23, 1922 and C0721/ 16 "confidential" memorandum by Macnaghton re: visit of Jean S. Robson, liaison officer between Department of Canadian Council of Immigration of Women for Household Service, March 10, 1920.
23. PRO, CO721/118, memorandum re: "Interview with Dr. Riddell, September 1925," by Gladys Potts, OSC member representing Society for the Oversea Settlement of British Women, September 16, 1925.
24. PRO CO721/92, J. Bruce Walker, Director of European Emigration for Canada, to E.T. Crutchley (OSC), March 7, 1927. According to Plant, the Canadian National Railways scheme "dealt with only seven families" of whom four "withdrew before 1936," *Oversea Settlement*, 110.
25. PRO, C0721/106, John Barnett, Superintendent, Land Settlement Branch to Macnaghton (OSC), April 6, 1925. For more on the "3,000 Families Scheme," see Culliton, *National Problems of Canada*, Chapter 5.
26. Plant, *Oversea Settlement*, pp. 106–08.
27. Saskatchewan, Royal Commission, *Report*, 23.
28. Reynolds, *The British Immigrant*, 74, footnote 2. The phenomenon of "drift" is alluded to in C.A. Dawson, "Canada as a Country of Immigration," in *Proceedings of the Ninth Annual Meeting of Canadian Agricultural Economics Society* (Saskatoon, June 1937), 67.
29. Lloyd's intemperate criticism of non-British immigrants in the 1920s has attracted ridicule a half-century later. It will be unfortunate if he is remembered only for his irritating opinions while his good works and boundless enthusiasm for the West are forgotten. See, for brief accounts of his activity, C. W. Vernon, *The Old Church in the New Dominions: The Story of the Anglican Church in Canada* (London: Society for Propagation of Christian Knowledge, 1929), 200–01, and W.F. Payton, *An Historical Sketch of the Diocese of Saskatchewan of the Anglican Church of Canada* (Prince Albert, Saskatchewan, 1973), passim.
30. LPP, Davidson Papers, Box I, Bishop of Qu'Appelle to Davidson, in 9 pp. manuscript compiled from answers to questions submitted to western Canadian bishops, February 1910 (italics in original).
31. Robert England, "Ethnic Settlers in Western Canada: Reminiscences of a Pioneer," *Canadian Ethnic Studies* 8, no. 2 (1976): 19.

17. Who Were They Really? Reflections on East European Immigrants to Manitoba Before 1914

Fred Stambrook and Stella Hryniuk

This chapter concerns itself with the Jews, Poles and Ukrainians who came to Manitoba (and to other parts of the prairies) in the 1880s and especially in the period 1890 to 1914. It poses four main questions: Where did they come from? What sort of people were they? How did they interact in their East European homelands? How did they interact in rural Manitoba? As it is well-known that immigrants bring with them not only their brute strength but also their personal talents and their communal cultural baggage, our enquiry may cast fresh light on the experience of these peoples in their new Canadian homeland.

The answers to the questions we pose have in the past often been taken for granted. A fuller enquiry may establish that the accepted picture is correct only in part. Mainstream Canadian historians, concerned primarily with nation-building and the development of political institutions, have not considered such issues. Canadian ethnic historians for the most part and for various reasons have until recently focussed their attention on institution-building within their particular communities and on recording the achievements of outstanding individuals of their groups—an approach generally labelled as filio-pietistic.[1]

First, let us provide some context. The peopling of the prairies by immigrants from East Central Europe, and thus the story behind their emigration from their ancestral homelands, is part of the general history of emigration from Europe to the Americas. Some 55 million Europeans emigrated overseas between 1821 and 1924, three-fifths of them to the United States.[2] Nevertheless, each of our ethno-cultural groups has regarded its experience as unique to itself. Obviously there are particular features in each emigration, especially in that of the Jews. But "trans-oceanic migration was only one aspect of a bewilderingly complex pattern"[3] of European peoples

Immigrants at an employment agency, likely in Winnipeg, circa 1910 (Courtesy of the Archives of Manitoba/N11598).

moving from the overpopulated rural regions to cities within Europe and to cities and open lands in the New World. "Emigration," says Frank Thistlethwaite, "was in fact intimately connected with the quickening of communications, markets, commerce and capital which ... was the first phase of the establishment of a modern economy."[4]

Such features came fairly late to East-Central Europe, which prior to 1914 in general had not yet developed the industrial base that could absorb the large numbers of people who were prepared to travel in search of jobs (a preparedness that denoted an unprecedented increase in mobility). To quote Thistlethwaite again, "all the evidence goes to show that Europeans in general emigrated in large numbers while there were no opportunities in the home country and ceased to do so when opportunities once again existed."[5]

The three peoples who are the subjects of this article were quite late participants in the general migration pattern, though Ukrainians and especially Poles were already in the habit of seeking seasonal work outside their home regions, and Jews in the Austrian Empire were migrating in quite large numbers from the northern province (Land) of Galicia to Vienna. The great majority of those who came to the Prairies before 1905–07 clearly came to stay (unlike many of the immigrants to the USA, of whom about one-third returned to their ancestral homelands).[6] Often, of course, family members did not all come at once; fathers and brothers were sometimes the forerunners, who saved or borrowed money to bring over other family kin. After around 1905 migration patterns changed somewhat, as more single men came to western Canada, and many of these, other than Jews, probably with the intention of saving money and returning to their homelands.[7]

But where were these homelands? And what sort of people were these settlers from East-Central Europe? Ethnic authors, and mainstream Canadian historians in following them, have provided facile answers. The Jews were "Russian Jews." The Ukrainians were peasants from the eastern part of Galicia and from Bukovina, two provinces in the north-east of the Austrian Empire. As for the Polish settlers of Manitoba, no one after 1945 really seemed to know where they came from, though it was thought that most of them came from Galicia.

Let us deal first with the geographical aspect. The picture is clearest for the Ukrainians. The overwhelming majority of Ukrainian settlers on the prairies did come from Eastern Galicia and Bukovina. Some, however, were from other parts of Ukraine, from Carpatho-Rus (under Hungarian dominance) and from Dnieper Ukraine, i.e. from the Russian Empire, perhaps after an intervening period in Galicia[8] or in the United States. Their "cultural baggage," coloured by the systematic suppression of their language in the Russian Empire, differed considerably from the experiences of Galician and Bukovinian Ukrainians, who in the freer atmosphere of constitutional Austria were developing their political, cultural and economic institutions.[9]

Polish Canadian authors believed but did not really know that most of the Polish settlers of Manitoba and the prairies before 1914 came from Galicia, and that perhaps most of these came from Eastern Galicia. This has now been confirmed, despite all the difficulties of differentiating Poles and Ukrainians in the data, by the Polish historical demographer A. Pilch, who adds that "Colonists who settled on farms in Canada ... seldom returned."[10] A number of their interactions with other ethno-cultural groups can be better understood because in Eastern Galicia ethnically Polish peasants lived in close contact with both Ukrainian and Jewish villagers.

As for Jewish migrants to Manitoba, the descriptor "Russian Jews" has been deeply etched into historical writings. Even if true, it is such a broad generalization as to be almost meaningless. Certainly most "Russian" Jews shared to some extent at least in the *shtetl* (small town) culture of the traditional Pale of Settlement during what has been termed the "golden period in the history of the Jewish soul."[11] But they were not homogeneous, in part because of the vast territorial expanse of the Russian Empire. Conditions differed: for example, some Jews lived outside the Pale[12]; others came from Bessarabia, where Jews were legally allowed to own land; some lived in the countryside, quite far removed from any *shtetl*[13]; and some were involved in the industrial workers' movements in Vilna or Minsk, or lived in abject poverty in Odessa.[14] In any case there would be a wide range of experiences, depending on the size of the *shtetl*, its proximity to a major industrial city, and so on. Many Jews did not come from any part of Russia at all, but from Romania,[15] where there were also pogroms and poverty, as well as from Galicia and even England.[16] Other Jews, though from parts of the Pale, spent years in England, South Africa, or the United States before coming to the prairies[17]; their experiences and outlooks were obviously different from those of the men and women who came directly from Russia.[18]

What sort of people were these immigrants? The accepted version for all three groups is that they were desperately poor. Many of them certainly were so by the time they arrived, weary and bedraggled, at the CPR station in Winnipeg.[19] Their very appearance lent support to the venomous racist comments that were to be a feature of part of Winnipeg's Anglo-Canadian press right up to World War I: the main target were the Ruthenians, as Ukrainians were then termed, but also all Galicians.[20] Immigrants never look their best immediately upon arrival after weeks of travel over land and sea, especially if their baggage has gone to Buenos Aires by mistake[21]: if they gave the appearance of great impoverishment, this was sometimes a misleading impression, though nonetheless true in many cases.

The general migration literature suggests that it is not the very poorest of a society who emigrate, but rather those with some initiative and imagination.[22] The Polish Canadian historian Victor Turek seemed to deny this possibility,[23] but appeared to base his opinion on unverified generalities. Certainly in the cases of Ukrainians and Jews it is clear that most of the migrants to Manitoba and the prairies did not belong to the poorest strata of their respective societies.

Regrettably, it is not possible at this remove in time to obtain quantifiable data about the socio-economic standing and modest affluence or poverty of individual immigrants of a hundred years ago. Not even their possessions upon arrival in Winnipeg were a sure indication of their financial means in the old country, for money had to be expended for fares and subsistence over several weeks, as well as, often, on bribes for frontier officials.[24] What follows on this issue is perforce fragmentary and anecdotal.

Least evidence seems to be available for the Polish immigrants. Turek referred to them as being "from the poor classes of small landowners or landless peasants," "the poorest people," "a peasant of sub-marginal type."[25]

These characterizations seem unwarranted; we allow ourselves some spec-ulations about the reasons behind them later. For the Jews and Ukrainians there is such evidence, some of it from interviews with surviving pioneers or their immediate descendants: it is, of course, open to one of two objec-tions: either that family members wanted to draw a contrast between pover-ty in the old country and success in the new one, or that it was a matter of pride to downplay poverty and exaggerate family status in the ancestral homeland. We tend to be sceptical of unifactorial explanations, so we offer evidence here which suggests a more nuanced type of immigration.

For the Jewish settlers in Manitoba, one can cite the following, among many others: Isaac Adleman's parents arrived with "a lot of English money" and could afford to buy a farm at La Broquerie along with 40 head of cattle and horses. Jack Markson's father was "well-to-do" in Lithuania. Faige Mindess (whose husband came in 1913) had a "nice home" and 60 fruit trees in Russian Poland. Rose Moscovitch's father was a merchant in Romania, with a comfortable three-room house, and could afford to have Rose private-ly tutored in Romanian and German. John Pullan's father was "well-to-do in Russia."[26] Sam Soloway's father had done well in Russia and had a few hun-dred dollars saved when he came to Canada in 1912. Ann Springman and her husband were "quite comfortable" in England.[27] Nellie (Nacha) Moskowitz's family in Jassy, Romania, were "business people of very com-fortable means" who could send her to school in Bucharest. Beryl Pearlman's grandfather, an overseer on an estate, was able to have Hebrew teachers live in his home to tutor his children (the family were the only Jews in the village). The Friedguts lived in "comparative ease" in Russia, with a housemaid and nursemaids. Pauline Shack's parents "owned land but they couldn't keep it under their own names," so they paid another person to be the owner of record, and they had lots of cattle also.[28]

As for the Ukrainians, we have some reports of children of pioneers in the Stuartburn and Ethelbert areas. "We were not poor. My father owned his own eight to ten morgs of land … and didn't have to work for others"; "father had four morgs of ploughland and two horses and worked for himself, not for the pan [lord/large landowner]"; "My mother had land … and owned a little store … [My parents] didn't have to work anywhere else for earnings"; "My father and uncle worked only on their own land, and even had to hire others to work for them"; "We had sixteen morgs and the finest agricultural build-ings."[29] These pioneers were clearly not the impoverished and down-trodden peasants of the literature, a fact that was well recognized at the time by, for instance, the radical Galician Ukrainian author Vasyl Stefanyk, who described the peasant emigrants to Canada in 1899 as moderately wealthy, owners of land, and free of debt.[30] The first group of settlers organized by the pioneering advocate of Ukrainian emigration to Canada, Dr. Oleskow, had on average $302 per household on arrival in Quebec City in 1896.[31] There are records of other early Ukrainian settlers, some of whom arrived with little or no capital but others with sums of between $400 and $700, and one with $1000.[32] As Michael Ewanchuk has noted, Ukrainian settlers "were not exactly destitute," though Orest Martynowych is probably correct in thinking that as the years went by and as the "pull" factor strengthened, more poor peasants (and young single men without much money) joined the immigration to Canada.[33]

"Peasants": what image does that word conjure up? In the English language (and to some extent in other European languages) there is a pejorative connotation to the word. It appears to denote a subsistence agricultural smallholder of low culture, superstitious, with smelly clothes, barefoot, dirty, living in a hovel,[34] cultivating his land with primitive implements. This sort of image probably has its appeal to urban intellectuals. It is not, in fact, an image that applies to Eastern Galician agriculturalists in the late 19th century, at the time of their emigration to Canada.

These people, whether Ukrainians or Poles, were indeed agrarian smallholders. Information on good agricultural practice was being disseminated in the villages through the medium of enlightenment societies, whether Ukrainian or Polish, and their newspapers, by Agricultural Circles (Kolka rolnicze) and their publication in both languages, as well as by the Galician Agricultural Association. Under these influences, peasant agriculture became more intensive, crop yields improved, and new cash crops were introduced. Critics of Galician peasant agriculture took notice only of the decreasing size of peasant holdings, and not of what the smallholders— regardless of size of holding—did with them. They completely failed to see that animal husbandry had assumed an ever more important role in the peasants' lives and incomes: by the turn of the century it was contributing more to the peasant's cash income than field crops.[35] As one letter to a newspaper noted,

> Our grandfathers had twenty or more morgs but didn't get as much from it as the grandsons now get from four or six morgs. From one morg of field they got two wagons of bad hay, today we get 10–15 wagons of clover. Our grandfathers did not have buildings for cattle, now the grandsons build "German-style" barns, that have ladders and good doors and are whitewashed inside and out.[36]

Eastern Galician peasants, Ukrainian and Polish alike, were becoming more literate, more aware of the outside world, more self-confident.[37] It was their expanded horizons and rising expectations which enabled them to envisage a better future for their children in Canada and stimulated them to emigrate.[38]

Galician "peasants," then, were not ignorant simpletons but hard-working and often progressive agriculturalists. And, like peasants practically anywhere in Europe, they were more than that: some were also labourers on the estates of large landowners; some migrated seasonally to Prussia and Saxony; and others were carters and wagoners, rural postmen, blacksmiths, coopers, cartwrights, carpenters, cantors, harness makers, tailors, shoemakers, basket-weavers, potters, masons, well-diggers, quarry and forestry workers, and so on.[39] Many peasants were versatile—which stood them in good stead when they came to Canada—and it is not always clear whether their main occupation was in one of their artisan capacities or in agriculture on their own land.[40]

Just as the picture of the sturdy Ukrainian peasant in his sheepskin coat is etched in the Canadian folk memory, so is the depiction of the Jewish pedlar with his hand cart or perhaps a one-horse wagon.[41] It is only fairly recently that it has come to be realized that "Economic status in their new home was not necessarily congruent with how these families lived in the countries of Eastern Europe."[42] In fact, there were tens of thousands of Jews in the Russian Empire who derived their living from the soil: as of 1900, Jews there owned more than five and a half million acres of land, though many Jews were labourers rather than owners or lessees.[43] But the great majority were artisans, traders, and towards the turn of the century, industrial workers.[44]

Jewish industrial workers, although they came to develop their own political orientations, clearly had experiences, including interactions with Polish, Belarus or Russian urban workers, that differed from those of Jewish artisans and traders. Artisans followed occupations such as tailor, cobbler, wheelwright, woodcarver, boatman, goldsmith, etc.[45] There is a difficulty in determining the scale of some of the upper-end artisan occupations—was a goldsmith someone striving to make ends meet in a small *shtetl* or an affluent merchant? And what of family members in Romania or the Russian Empire, described as lumber merchants and landowners, buyers and sellers of grain, honey, wool, etc., or storekeepers?[46] Is a grain or cattle dealer, or a dealer in raw furs,[47] a poor itinerant trader or a person of some status and affluence? In some of the cases cited here, the latter would appear to be true.

If trading and storekeeping, as well as artisanship, dominate the traditional picture of Jews in Eastern Europe, they were nevertheless also found in other occupations, besides the agricultural which has already been mentioned. One immigrant's mother had had bookkeeping training in Russia; Edith Nemy's mother had a business in Ekaterinoslav, Ukraine, making corsets and surgical foundations[48]; Ben Victor's father was a Russian army surgeon; and Polly Firman was a nurse in Russia.[49] As we get into the 20th century—and so it was also with the Ukrainian immigrants—there was a greater sprinkling of professionals among the settlers. One had studied civil engineering in Russia[50]; another was a Hebrew teacher from Galicia who had written books and who strongly believed that only through working the land would Jewish people gain respect.[51] Several had received all or portions of their medical education in Romania or Russia; B.J. Ginsburg is described as coming to Canada at age 18, in 1912, with considerable education and as having already authored a number of short stories which had been published in the Russian press.[52]

It is clear that a large proportion of the male migrants of each of the three groups had served in the armies of their respective countries.[53] A desire to avoid conscription was often among the reasons given by some men or their descendants for the decision to emigrate[54]: this is no doubt true of some, but in other cases it may be conjectured that compulsory military service was accepted, willingly or not, as the norm, and that, around the turn of the century, it was not the traumatic experience that North American historians, for whom conscription is alien, would have us believe. Some either enjoyed or benefitted from their military service: Abe Padolsky's father learned to be a tailor while serving in the Russian army; and George Evasiuk liked to impress the girls in his village with his Austro-Hungarian army uniform.[55]

In the 20th century there are more recorded instances of Jews and Ukrainians leaving their original homelands and coming to Manitoba for essentially political reasons. Pavlo Krat, who came from an affluent background, was a revolutionary socialist in the Russian Empire.[56] Hryniuk's grandfather left the Chortkiv region of Eastern Galicia to escape retribution for having diverted Ukrainian votes to the Jewish candidate in the *Reichsrat* election of 1912, thereby assisting in the defeat of the Polish conservative candidate.[57] Bertha Plotkin's two brothers were members of a Jewish defence group in Belarus who felt it necessary to flee in 1904. A member of the Pullan family was in the Bund and distributed illegal literature; fearing discovery, he came to Canada in 1910. Ben Victor's firm socialist views as a teenager made Russia unsafe for him. Sam Yaffe ran away in 1906, with the Tsarist police on his heels.[58] On the other hand, the attribution of nationalist political reasons, among others, for the emigration of Poles from Galicia, allegedly ruled by an "alien" power, is spurious: Polish peasants in Galicia were oppressed by Polish magnates and gentry, not by the Austrians.[59]

Of course there were also young men, and no doubt women too, who came to Manitoba simply because they were adventurous.[60] For women, however, there were more cultural constraints. Aside from the pioneering work of Frances Swyripa on Ukrainian women in Canada, there has as yet been little systematic study of the role of women in the three immigrant communities, let alone of their role in the immigration itself.[61] Yet it is clear that sometimes women functioned as the *de facto* heads of families in the emigration process. Anna Friedgut's mother, for example, packed up her family—four young children, her young brother and two young cousins—and came to Canada in 1906, while her husband was serving in the Russian army.[62] Domenica Paulencui, a widow with three grown children, came from Bukovina in 1899, bringing a steel plate with holes to serve as the top for her future home-made stove, as well as seeds for medicinal herbs, for she functioned as "doctor" to her community. In some other instances it seems clear that the decision to emigrate was a joint one, and not made by the male alone.[63]

Some degree of poverty *and* the desire to satisfy increased expectations, especially "for the sake of the children," were thus the main motives behind emigration. Persecution of Jews in the Russian Empire and in Romania, and pogroms, were additional factors in the Jewish emigration. Although pogroms and persecution were frequently mentioned by Jewish settlers and

Jewish immigrant agriculturalists from Romania on the Canadian prairie in the early 1900s (Courtesy of the Saskatchewan Archives Board/R-B1781).

their offspring as *the* reason for emigration,[64] Dan Stone's argument that emigration of Jews from Russia was a steady stream which experienced further growth for a year or two after each wave of pogroms is quite persuasive.[65] However, the fear of pogroms was ingrained in the Jewish psyche, not only in the Russian Empire and in Romania, but also in nearby Eastern Galicia, where they did not take place.[66]

This brings us to the relationships between the three peoples who are the subject of this article. The received "truth" is that there were deep antagonisms between them. The extent to which this applied to the Eastern Galician and Bukovinian villagers who formed the bulk of the immigrant groups of Ukrainian and Polish ethnicity is, we suggest, highly problematic.

In a very different context, the English historian A.J.P. Taylor has sagely noted that "it is always difficult, if not impossible, to prove a negative."[67] Our aim here is somewhat more modest: we are suggesting that the Polish-Ukrainian antagonism in Galicia, so obvious and at most times so strong, was an antagonism of the political elites and of their immediate followers, and did not extend into village life until shortly before World War I.

The evidence—pro and con—is with one exception fragmentary. Here we concentrate on only one side of the issue. The most obvious point to be made about the relationship between Poles and Ukrainians in Eastern Galician villages is the very frequent intermarriage between members of the two groups. Poles were generally Roman Catholics and Ukrainians Greek Catholics, and there was a very sensible arrangement in respect of children of such mixed marriages: children followed the religion of their same-sex parent. The frequency of such mixed marriages argues for inter-group social activities, even though some villages had fairly distinct Ukrainian and Polish sections.[68]

Apart from this single but very significant element of intermarriage, other specific instances may be cited: The Polish populist newspaper *Przyjaciel ludu* was read by some Ukrainian villagers too.[69] In the 1880s, the reading club in the small market town of Strusiv subscribed to both the Ukrainian and the Polish language press.[70] There is negative evidence also. A recent article on Polish patriotic celebrations among peasants in Galicia could cite no involvement of Polish villagers in Eastern Galicia except for a few villages around Lviv.[71] Turek decried the fact that those Polish settlers in Manitoba who came from Eastern Galicia "did not possess a developed national spirit and sense of national identity." Indeed, Polish peasants in Galicia as a whole recognized that they owed many of their freedoms to Austrian constitutionalism; they respected Austria and fought bravely for their emperor and for Austria during World War I.[72]

So, of course, did Galicia's and Bukovina's Ukrainians, whose political leadership at the very outset of the war called on the Ukrainian people of Austria to staunchly defend their homeland and the Austrian state against the Russian bear[73]—which they did: for instance, the 41st Infantry Regiment, composed almost entirely of Ukrainians and Romanians from Bukovina, fought valiantly till October 1918.[74] As for Ukrainian villagers' views on Poles, a distinction must be drawn between how they regarded the predominantly Polish large landowners[75] and how they regarded and interacted with Polish villagers.

In some villages 20–30% of the population was Polish. The frequent intermarriages have already been noted. Villagers might go to different churches, but the adults might afterwards compare the different sermons they had heard.[76] Village solidarity would also manifest itself against outsiders, as in a letter to the newspaper *Batkivshchyna* in 1885, where the Ukrainian correspondent compared the long-established Polish people of his village, whose "houses are clean" and who "speak Ukrainian now," to the low standards of hygiene of "Mazurs" (i.e. Poles) recently recruited by a large landowner. As one informant, born in 1904, has put it, "in our two villages, relations were harmonious" until just before World War I, when "the big boys with feathers in their hats [i.e. members of the Polish Sokol] started agitating."[77]

As for relationships of Ukrainians and Poles with Jews in the Eastern Galician countryside, there was of course anti-Semitism, though—as already noted—no pogroms. The question really is: how significant was anti-semitism in the villages from which the Ukrainian and Polish settlers came? The noted Ukrainian scholar and author Ivan Franco thought it was "silent, latent in peasant huts. Folk proverbs and tales breathe antisemitic spirit."[78] It is quite possible that in Eastern Galicia, as in nearby Hungary, virulent anti-semitism was more an urban than a rural phenomenon. Certainly sections of both the Polish and Ukrainian press tried to whip up anti-Jewish feeling in the countryside,[79] featuring examples of usury, the alleged promotion of drunkenness by Jewish tavern-keepers and the assumed profiteering of Jewish merchants, as well as promoting the concept of non-Jewish shops.[80]

Though their children might go to the same schools, Jews certainly lived separate social lives in the small towns and villages of Eastern Galicia. Contacts, except on rare occasions, were commercial ones. Nevertheless, villagers were accustomed to having Jews in their midst—"in" but not "of" the village. Within fairly well defined bounds, village Jews lived at peace with their Christian neighbours; and Ukrainian peasants perhaps even preferred Jewish estate owners to Polish nobles. There was resentment if Jews were seen as dominating the commune council, or by the 1890s among Ukrainians conscious of their nationality if Jews opposed the establishment of village reading halls.[81] But there could be accommodation also, as in the prosperous market town of Khorostkiv, at Uhniv, and no doubt elsewhere. In Khorostkiv the town council consisted of twelve each of Jews, Poles and Ukrainians (though only the latter two could be elected as Mayor). In the town of Uhniv, in the northern part of Eastern Galicia, relations between Ukrainians and Jews in Austrian times (i.e. pre-1918) were described as good.[82] And although villagers might be envious of the Jews' possession of cash, many realized that the Jews were perhaps poorer than they were themselves. The concept of village solidarity could come into play here also: "our Jews" were all right, and could be commended for their helpfulness.[83] The picture, in other words, was more nuanced than is generally thought.

These attitudes towards one another were significant in Manitoba too. Anti-semitism is practically absent from the recorded experiences of Jewish storekeepers in the central Manitoba countryside.[84] Ukrainians and Poles deliberately settled and lived alongside one another, and with Jewish storekeepers, with no more problems than any other neighbours—in the Interlake, in the Beausejour region, on the southern slopes of Riding Mountain, and so on. The settlement of Zbaraz, 100 kilometres from Teulon, for instance, was founded by Poles and Ukrainians; the people were said to have spoken Ukrainian, but read and wrote in Polish. There are, in the Interlake, cemeteries with both Polish and Ukrainian names, and the two peoples might attend the same church services, as at Lac du Bonnet: the Poles, like the Ukrainians, were often without priests.[85] Ukrainians in Manitoba, as in the homeland, sometimes went unwillingly to Roman Catholic services, as they feared Latinizing influences and longed for priests of their own.[86] There was cooperation between the two ethnic groups in establishing school districts in Manitoba, and one school board in the early 20th century kept its minutes in its own mixture of English, Polish and Ukrainian.[87]

Manitoban school inspectors were surprised and impressed by the efforts which many Ukrainian (and Polish) settlers made prior to World War I to provide educational opportunities for their children. Outside Winnipeg itself, Ukrainians and Poles utilized the 1897 amendment to the Manitoba Public Schools Act to establish over 100 bilingual school districts.[88] In doing so, three features of the recent Eastern Galician experience came into play: the strong emphasis on elementary education and the building of schools; the experience of self-administration, under central supervision, of local school districts; and the principle and practice of bilingual education.[89] Experience in local government generally also helped Ukrainian and Polish

A Polish "peasant" woman and Polish children in a kindergarten class at the All People's Mission in Winnipeg's North End, 1910 (Courtesy of the Archives of Manitoba/N7928).

immigrants to set up their own municipalities, and to participate in local government and politics at quite an early date. Jews too had such experience in Eastern Galicia and in Bukovina, while by the 20th century some of those from the Russian Empire had been exposed to enlightenment ideas and drawn into political and labour union activities.[90] The notion propagated by James Jackson, that these immigrants had to be taught the democratic process,[91] is thus quite erroneous.

All three peoples, being accustomed to communal living, were dismayed to discover that the Dominion Lands Act prevented the formation of concentrated village clusters. All three displayed a deep attachment to their respective religions and their rituals, and all three longed for appropriate religious care. This was easiest for the Jews to provide, at least in Winnipeg,[92] and most difficult for the Greek Catholic Ukrainians, for the Vatican had forbidden married priests, customary in the homeland, to function in Canada. There were a great number of pleas to the Church authorities in Lviv for priests and church books.[93] As soon as possible each of the three groups established its own institutions, modelled on those in the homelands, including its own newspapers.[94] However, just as in the homeland, there were signs of increased secularization within each group. Among Ukrainians and Poles (concurrently with their knowledge that they—or at least their children—had to learn in English and become Canadian),[95] this secular trend mingled of course with anti-clericalism, radicalism, and a gradually heightening sense of nationalism or at least ethnicity. Ukrainian radicals established the short-lived Seraphim Church in Manitoba, and a little later, under Presbyterian auspices, the Independent Greek Church. Later still their feeling that the growing Greek Catholic Church in Canada was too authoritarian and insufficiently nationalist helped to create the split that led to the formation of Canada's Ukrainian Greek Orthodox Church.[96] Some Poles too rejected the leadership which the clergy of Winnipeg's Holy Ghost Roman Catholic Parish attempted to exercise over the immigrant group, and invited the breakaway Polish National Catholic Church (formed in 1904 in the United States) to extend its activities to Canada.[97] On the other hand, Jews who had imbibed Socialist ideas in Europe gravitated to the labour movement.

The real problems between Poles, Ukrainians and Jews in the rural homeland date from the period of the Polish Republic, 1918–39: they must not be improperly juxtaposed into the first period of immigration, pre-1914, when relations between the three groups appear to have been generally quite good.[98] Perhaps they were to some extent united by their common antagonists: the cold and the Anglo-Canadian establishment (which *inter alia* generally refused credits to members of all three groups).

The three groups often organized in such a way that they lived alongside their "old country" neighbours; and in Winnipeg's North End they shared space with other immigrants too. The co-existence of Ukrainians and Poles, harkening back to Galicia, was of particular importance to the Poles, the smaller of these two groups—indeed, they have been described as a "Polish minority within the Ukrainian minority."[99] Certainly the two communities were close, both in the countryside and, perhaps to a lesser extent, in Winnipeg; and the homeland practice of intermarriage between Ukrainians and Poles continued in Manitoba. The Jewish merchant who could speak or at least understand Polish and Ukrainian and who knew the needs of his customers and tried to satisfy them was appreciated both in rural and urban areas.[100] Louis Rosenberg may have exaggerated only a little when he wrote that during the pioneer period "The Jewish storekeeper ... was adviser, letterwriter, translator and friend" who extended credit to farmers.[101]

Our final reflections concern the reasons for the misunderstandings and misinterpretations of the past of each of our three peoples. It appears to us, first of all, that each group has looked at its experiences in isolation, or at most in the ways in which it interacted with the Anglo-Canadian establishment. Second, each group's authors have brought their own nationalist and/or political perspectives to bear on their tasks. Stambrook has speculated that Jewish Canadian authors were for a long time uninterested in their European past, and in what this might mean for their Canadian experience, because their recollections were so bitter ("Why take into their new life the memory of pogroms by night and existence in the ghetto ?"[102]). Or it might be that the second generation was embarrassed by the cultural baggage of the first, and that Reform Judaism sent a strong message to leave behind the trappings of Orthodoxy, and to look forward and never backward.[103]

Polish Canadian writers have been nationalists. Turek had a dearth of evidence about the background of Polish immigrants to Manitoba, and thus relied heavily on American studies for his general interpretation. Basically, with little or no direct evidence, he regarded the pre-1914 Polish immigrants to Manitoba as impoverished emigrants, ignorant, and from the very poorest stratum of society. Turek believed that the lack of economic development of the Polish territories was due to policies of the occupying powers, Galicia being the least developed: "Nothing else but the difficult economic conditions forced these immigrants out of their native land," but in any case most of the pre-1914 Polish immigrants did not intend to stay.[104] We have here a typically nationalist position: the migrants were longing to return home to their native land (though it is clear that most of the Polish settlers in Manitoba had come to stay). In some other respects, however, Turek was too good a historian for his nationalism to sit easily: he recognized that there was no political oppression of Poles in Galicia, that the population had benefitted under Austria, and that much of the poverty he discerned was the fault of what he called the "narrow-minded and egoistic landed classes"— though he could not quite bring himself to call these the Polish nobility and gentry.[105]

As for the gloom and doom interpretations of Galician and Bukovinian Ukrainian history, we suggest a number of reasons for these. Some Ukrainian Canadian writers have simply liked the contrast between the alleged terrible poverty in West Ukraine and the progress that Ukrainians have made in Canada. Other, generally more scholarly, authors are the intellectual heirs of the late 19th-century radicals who so bitterly and with cause criticized the socio-economic inequities of their contemporary Eastern Galicia; they tend to look at what Ukrainians there did not have, instead of what they had and did. Further, they have not been free of the influence of Soviet and Polish Marxist writers who were concerned, and constrained, to find nothing good to say about "Austro-Hungarian imperialism." Finally, and regrettably, historians tend to repeat one another, or at least their preferred sources: Ukrainian Canadian historians seem to like to portray

Galician Ukrainians as drunkards, citing a study which is highly questionable and whose results support the gloom and doom theory they love to perpetuate—that they drank to excess to drown their misery is the obvious refrain.[106]

Ukrainian and Polish Canadian historians also like to quote the Polish Galician industrialist Stepan Szczepanowski, who in 1888 published a book whose title translates as "Galicia's Misery." It was a clarion call to the Polish aristocracy, much ignored, but made memorable by Szczepanowski's assertion, without evidence, that 50,000 Galicians died each year of hunger and starvation.[107] Possibly this held true for the early 1870s, when epidemic disease was also rampant, but thereafter it is fiction not fact. Yet it is this fiction which is repeated over and over again—a good stick with which to beat capitalist landlord agriculture and "inefficient" peasant agriculture alike, with foreign imperialist power structures thrown in as well.

In conclusion, let us recognize that the past is not as it has been made to appear: it is much more varied than traditional Canadian writing has perceived. Our three peoples were hard-working and often versatile immigrants who brought with them their traditional cultures and value systems. But they also brought with them a forward-looking attitude and what has been called a "geographic empathy"—the ability to imagine themselves doing well in another geographic region. They were not the poorest of the poor of their homelands, but rather people of some standing, initiative and imagination, with a variety of talents. For many of them it was in their first years in Canada, not in Europe, that they experienced real poverty and hardship. And in Manitoba, whether in the countryside or along Winnipeg's Selkirk Avenue, their interactions with one another were for the overwhelming part harmonious. It is time to review the pre-1914 period in the light of the evidence on these immigrants.

Notes

This article first appeared in *Prairie Forum* 25, no. 2 (2000): 215–32.

1. For a succint overview see G. Friesen and R. Loewen, "Romanticism, Pluralism, Postmodernism: The Ethnic Historiography of Prairie Canada," in H. Braun, W. Klooss (eds.), *Postmodernization? A Comparative View of Canada and Europe* (Kiel, Germany: n.p., 1995), 49–64. Volume 2 of *Manitoba 125: A History* (Winnipeg: Great Plains Publications, 1994), though intended for a general audience, in fact treats the immigration and settlement experiences of East-Central Europeans more comprehensively than do the standard histories of Manitoba: W.L. Morton, *Manitoba, A History* (Toronto: University of Toronto Press, 1967) and J.A. Jackson, *The Centennial History of Manitoba* (Toronto: McClelland and Stewart Ltd., 1970). The "blight of ethnic parochialism" was also obvious in the United States, see T.L. Smith, "New Approaches to the History of Immigration in Twentieth Century America," *American Historical Review* 71: 1265. Orest Martynowych, *Ukrainians in Canada: The Formative Period, 1891–1924* (Edmonton:

Canadian Institute of Ukrainian Studies Press, 1991), is an exception among Canadian historians of an ethnic group.

2. F. Thistlethwaite, "Migration from Europe Overseas in the Nineteenth and Twentieth Centuries," *XIe Congres International des Sciences Historiques, Rapports,* vol. 5 (Uppsala: n.p., 1960), 35. By no means all of the immigrants to the USA or Argentina stayed there; it has been estimated that the "repatriation rate" for the USA may have been as high as 30% and for Argentina 53%; cited in ibid., 39.

3. Ibid., 42.

4. Ibid., 52.

5. Ibid., loc. cit. For the "ordinariness" of migration—no matter how special for any one individual or family—see also, in brief, Dirk Hoerder, *People on the Move: Migration, Acculturation, and Ethnic Interaction in Europe and North America* (Providence, RI: German Historical Institute, 1993), esp. 5–23.

6. Ibid., 5. Polish Canadian historians, however, maintain the opposite, but their evidence is drawn from the United States and is not persuasive for the Canadian prairies—see footnotes 10 and 25 below.

7. Victor Turek and other Polish-Canadian authors have maintained that returning home with money was always the motive of the majority of Poles, but Turek cited American studies which do not appear to apply to Poles on the Canadian prairies: V. Turek, *The Polish-Language Press in Canada: Its History and a Bibliographical List* (Toronto: Polish Research Institute in Canada, 1962), 46; H. Radecki with B. Heydenkorn, *A Member of a Distinguished Family: The Polish Group in Canada* (Toronto: McClelland and Stewart, 1976), 4 and 28 (though there is some ambivalence on this point on p. 28).

8. For example, Paul Crath (Pavlo Krat), a political refugee from Tsarist Ukraine, spent 1906–07 in Eastern Galicia before coming to Winnipeg; Martynowich, *Ukrainians in Canada*, 255.

9. Ivan L. Rudnytsky and Peter L. Rudnytsky, *Essays in Modern Ukrainian History* (Harvard: Harvard Ukrainian Research Institute, 1988), 23 and 335–45; O. Subtelny, *Ukraine: A History* (Toronto: University of Toronto Press, 1990), 323–34; S.M. Hryniuk, *Peasants with Promise: Ukrainians in Southeastern Galicia, 1880–1900* (Edmonton: n.p., 1991), passim, esp. 90–107 and 194–215.

10. V. Turek, *Poles in Manitoba* (Toronto: Polish Research Institute in Canada, 1967), 32–33, also 11; Radecki, *A Member*, 26. R.K. Kogler, *The Polish Community in Canada* (Toronto: Canadian Polish Research Institute, 1976), 2–3, states, more correctly we believe, that Polish immigrants to Canada in the period 1850–1890 were from Prussia/Germany and after 1876 also from the Russian Empire. However, these immigrations were mostly to Eastern Canada. B. Heydenkorn, "The Social Structure of Canadian 'Polonia'," in T.W. Krychowski (ed.), *Polish Canadians: Profile and Image* (Toronto: n.p., 1969), 39, gives a more nuanced picture of the post-1890 immigration. He identified the Rzeszow county of West Galicia as the source of many of the migrants, as well as Russian Poland and some parts of Eastern Galicia. A. Pilch, "Migration of the Galician Populace at the Turn of the Nineteenth and Twentieth Centuries," in C. Bobinska and A. Pilch (eds.), *Employment-seeking Emigration of the Poles World-wide XIX and XX C.* (Cracow: n.p., 1975), 77–101, especially 90. That there were some from Prussia is clear, see for example, Turek, *The Polish-Language Press*, 99, for early Polish Catholic priests in Winnipeg, who often spoke better German than Polish, and J. Samulski, *Pamietnik emigranta polskiego w Kanadzie* (Warsaw: n.p., 1978).

11. Quoted from A.J. Herschel by G. Tulchinsky, "The Contours of Canadian Jewish History," in R.J. Brym et al. (eds.), *The Jews in Canada* (Toronto: Oxford University Press,

1993), 16; see also H. Gutkin, *Journey into Our Heritage: The Story of the Jewish People in the Canadian West* (Toronto: Lester & Orphen Dennys, 1980), 15–26.

12. Archives of the Jewish Heritage Centre of Western Canada, Winnipeg (hereafter AJHC), MG 6, F 23 "Sybil Heft Family Tree." This and other files marked * consist of term exercises in the University of Manitoba course "Jewish History IV," completed in October 1951.

13. T. Cashman, *Abraham Cristall: The Story of a Simple Man* (Edmonton: privately printed, 1963), 10; M.R. Marrus, *Samuel Bronfman: The Life and Times of Seagram's Mr. Sam* (Hanover: University Press of New England, 1991), 23; AJHC, MG 6, F 27, Beryl Pearlman*.

14. E. Mendelsohn, "Jews and Christian Workers in the Russian Pale of Settlement," *Jewish Social Studies* 30, esp. 244–50; H.M., "Das Judische Elend in Odessa," in A. Nossig (ed.), *Judische Statistik* (Berlin: n.p., 1903), 287–92; see also S.J. Zipperstein, "Russian Maskilim and the City," in D. Berger (ed.), *The Legacy of Jewish Migration: 1881 and Its Impact* (New York: n.p., 1983), 31–48.

15. In 1899, more than 2,200 Romanian Jews arrived in Canada, B.G. Sack, *History of the Jews in Canada*, vol. I (Montreal: Canadian Jewish Congress, 1945), 244. See also F.G. Stambrook, "Early Jewish Immigration to the Prairies: Some Problems and Some Agendas," *Jewish Life and Times* 4: 85–87.

16. Joe Freed's mother was from Galicia, as were Moses Margulies and Oscar Feuer (AJHC, transcripts of tapes 358, 205 and 189), and Maxwell Cohen's grandfather (H. Gutkin with M. Gutkin, *The Worst of Times, The Best of Times: Growing up in Winnipeg's North End* (Markham, ON: n.p., 1987) Isaac Adleman came from England (AJHC, tape 183); Ann Springman, though born in Lithuania, lived for 20 years in England, where her husband had a fish and chips shop, before coming to Canada (AJHC, tape 215); the Goldstein family (AJHC, MG 6, F 92), though coming to Winnipeg from Britain in 1879, also had Eastern European roots.

17. Joe Freed's father (AJHC, tape 358); see also the background of some of the people of the Edenbridge, SK, settlement, in S. Belkin, *Through Narrow Gates: A Review of Jewish Immigration, Colonization and Immigrant Aid Work in Canada (1840–1940)* (Montreal: Canadian Jewish Congress and the Jewish Colonization Association, 1966), 79–80.

18. *Jewish Life and Times*, vol. 6, p. 4; this volume, edited by R.R. Rostecki, is entitled "Personal Recollections: The Jewish Pioneer Past on the Prairies."

19. Would-be emigrants often had to bribe customs and police officials, or employ locals to smuggle them over the frontiers; such services could deplete a migrant's capital: see Central State Historical Archives, Lviv (TsDIAL), Fond 146, opys 4, sprava 2448, for an April 1888 report that the customs police at Oswiecim knew of a railway stationmaster in Grybow who sold ship tickets; another report of the spring of 1888 from the frontier police at Brody and Pidvolochysk on illegal migration of Russian Jews and German colonists through Galicia; a report of September 25, 1889, from Pidvolochysk about locals helping emigrants from Russia to come into Austria on foot, thereby evading frontier posts; a report from the Cracow police chief of August 28, 1890, on local people helping Romanian Jews and Mennonites from Russia to cross illegally into Germany, etc. See also O. Negrych, *Toil and Triumph* (Winnipeg: privately published, 1981), 22–27.

20. J. Petryshyn, *Peasants in the Promised Land: Canada and the Ukrainians, 1891–1914* (Toronto: Lorimer, 1985), 94–101; see also L. Wawrow, "Nativism in English Canada," in B. Heydenkorn (ed.), *From Prairies to Cities: Papers on the Poles in Canada at the VIII World Congress of Sociology* (Toronto: Canadian-Polish Congress, Canadian-Polish Research Institute, 1975), 78–90.

21. Ministry of Agriculture, *Annual Report 1892* (Sessional Papers No. 7), 105.

22. See, for example, B.P. Murdzek, *Emigration in Polish Social and Political Thought* (New York: East European Monographs, 1977), and H.S. Nelli, *From Immigrants to Ethnics: The Italian Americans* (New York: Oxford University Press, 1983). For a Ukrainian couple who are described as ambitious, enterprising, and unwilling to wait for their inheritances in Galicia, see N. Evasiuk, *George & Anna* (Chicago: the author, 1981), 36–37.

23. Turek, *Poles*, 2, 25, 27 ("Canada has attracted the poorest people"), 35.

24. See footnote 19 above; see also *Jewish Life and Times*, vol. 6, pp. 3–4.

25. Turek, *Poles*, 2, 27 and 35; see also Kogler, *Polish Community*, 3.

26. AJHC, tapes 183, 414, 245, 201, and 74.

27. AJHC, tapes 224 and 215.

28. AJHC, MG 6 F 90, "Moscovitch family"; MG 6 F 27 (*); MG 6 F 16 "Anna Friedgut"; *Jewish Life and Times*, vol. 6, p. 2.

29. Interviews by Hryniuk in June and July 1979 with Mr. Horobec, Stuartburn, Mrs. Seniuk, Ethelbert, Mrs. Sokolyk, Dominion City, and Mrs. Rekunyk, Stuartburn; V. Havrych, *Moia Kanada i ia: spohady i rozpovidi pro ukrainskykh pioneriv u Kanadi* (Edmonton: n.p., 1974), 18. One *morg* is approximately 0.575 hectares.

30. *Hromadskyi holos* (Lviv), May 1, 1899.

31. Martynowych, *Ukrainians in Canada*, 79.

32. See W.J. Kaye, *Early Ukrainian Settlements in Canada, 1895–1900* (Toronto: University of Toronto Press, 1964), 304–05 and 350–52; M. Ewanchuk, *Spruce, Swamp and Stone: A History of the Pioneer Ukrainian Settlements in the Gimli Area* (Winnipeg: the author, 1977), 24; Martynowych, *Ukrainians in Canada*, 79–80.

33. Martynowych, *Ukrainians in Canada*, 80, see also Ewanchuk, *Spruce, Swamp and Stone*, 24 and 25. Elsewhere, Martynowych has greatly exaggerated the amount of capital Ukrainian peasant immigrants needed to start farming in c. 1900: O.T. Martynowych, *The Ukrainian Bloc Settlement in East Central Alberta, 1890–1930: A History* (Edmonton: Alberta Culture, 1985), 124; see Kaye, *Early Ukrainian Settlements*, 350–57 for the success of Ukrainian farmers with less and sometimes much less capital than Martynowych regards as essential.

34. On Ukrainian village houses and farmsteads in Eastern Galicia see S. Hryniuk and J. Picknicki, *The Land They Left Behind: Canada's Ukrainians in the Homeland* (Winnipeg: Watson & Dwyer, 1995), 8–16; W.T.R. Preston, "Report of Inspector of Agencies in Europe," Canada, *Sessional Papers*, vol. 10, p. 17; Havrych, *Moia Kanada*, 18; F. Vovk, *Studii z ukrainskoi etnohrafii ta antropolohii* (Prague: n.p., 1916), 104–06 and 114. The houses were usually of two rooms, thatched, sturdy and whitewashed, but generally with earthen floors, in a fenced-off yard.

35. For a summary see Hryniuk, *Peasants with Promise*, esp. 125–30. Among Ukrainians, Greek Catholic village clergy played a significant role in improving agricultural practice. See also S.M. Hryniuk, "Peasant Agriculture in East Galicia in the Late Nineteenth Century," *Slavonic and East European Review* 63, no. 2, and W. Pruski, *Hodowla zwierat gospordarskich w Galicji w latach 1772–1918*, 2 vols. (Wroclaw: n.p., 1975). F. Bujak, a noted Polish Galician scholar, commented that peasants were deriving a greater income from animal husbandry than from grain; F. Bujak, *Galicya*, vol. I (Lviv: n.p., 1908), 313.

36. *Batkivshchyna* (Lviv), March 8, 1889.

37. For Ukrainian peasants in particular see Stella Hryniuk, "Sifton's Pets," in L. Luciuk and S. Hryniuk (eds.), *Canada's Ukrainians: Negotiating an Identity* (Toronto: University of Toronto Press, 1991), 3–16 and 391–97. While more work needs to be done on Polish villagers in Eastern Galicia, there is no real reason to think that their development differed greatly from that of their Ukrainian neighbours.

38. V. Stefanyk, in the article cited in footnote 30 above, noted that the fairly affluent peasants who were leaving gave as their motive for emigrating that it was "for the good of the children." On rising expectations see also the interviews cited in footnote 29 above, and Hryniuk's interview with Mrs. L. Salamandyk, June 19, 1979, Mr. J. Storoschuk, June 20, 1979, and Mrs. K. Chubaty, July 9, 1979.

39. Hryniuk, *Peasants with Promise*, 25; Hryniuk and Picknicki, *The Land They Left Behind*, 36–45. Young Jacob Smerechanski was a blacksmith; although about to inherit land, he decided to come to Canada; O. Negrych, *Toil and Triumph: The Life and Times of Anton and Yevdokia Smerechanski* (Winnipeg: n.p., 1981), 13–14. In the years 1907–12, an average of 75,000 Ukrainian seasonal workers went to Germany each year; Rudnytsky, *Essays*, 336–37.

40. It was, and has continued to be, a serious grievance of social critics of conditions in Galicia that peasant smallholders were, for the most part, not engaged full-time in agriculture. While in Eastern Galicia it was a mark of pride not to have to work for the pan, there is no indication in the literature that peasants found it demeaning to have a secondary occupation. It was the traditional way of earning extra income—just as it is for peasant smallholders in Germany today.

41. A.A. Chiel, *The Jews in Manitoba: A Social History* (Toronto: University of Toronto Press, 1961), 16–17.

42. V. Rachlis, "Biographical Note," in C. Harvey, *Chief Justice Samuel Freedman: A Great Canadian Judge* (Winnipeg: Law Society of Manitoba, 1983), 1; Stambrook, "Early Jewish Immigration," 87.

43. S. Ettinger, in H.H. Ben-Sasson (ed.), *A History of the Jewish People* (Cambridge, MA: n.p., 1976), 865; S.W. Baron, *The Russian Jew Under Tsars and Soviets* (New York: Schocken Books, 1976), 75–80. See also AJHC, Jack Markson, Tape 414: "father [in Lithuania] was well-to-do. He owned land and grew grain," he was also a grain dealer and raised cattle and horses; Tevel Finkelstein's father leased farmlands and timberlands in Volhynia, Ukraine: AJHC, MG 6 F 26 (*); also *Jewish Life and Times*, vol. 6, p. 2.

44. H.M. Sacher, *The Course of Modern Jewish History* (New York: Dell Publishing Co., Inc., 1958), 188 and 245; Ben-Sasson (ed.), *A History*, 861; Mendelsohn, "Jews and Christian Workers," passim.

45. AJHC, Tapes 183, 243 and 267; MG 6 F 28 (*), "The Fields"; *Jewish Life and Times*, vol. 6, p. 3; Gutkin, *The Worst of Times*, 224.

46. AJHC, Rose Moscovitch, Tape 201; Sam Soloway, Tape 224: Mr. Soloway's father had "a few hundred dollars" on arrival in Canada, so he was clearly not of the desperately poor stratum in Russia.

47. AJHC, Sidney Gitterman, Tape 349.

48. AJHC, Archie Micay, Tape 324; Edith Nemy, Tape 258.

49. H. Medovy, "The Early Jewish Physicians in Manitoba," *Historical & Scientific Society of Manitoba Transactions* 3, no. 29: 32; AJHC, Polly Firman, Tape 199.

50. "… but a Jew could not get a job": AJHC, Ida Paul, tape 250, talking about her brother. Louis Zuken, not a professional but a pottery worker in Horodnize, Ukraine, was unemployed after leading an unsuccessful strike; he arrived in Winnipeg in 1912: G. Tulchinsky, *Taking Root: The Origins of the Canadian Jewish Community* (Toronto: Lester, 1992, 1997), 176.

51. AJHC, Oscar Feuer (speaking of his father), Tape 189. The father had sent his eldest son to agricultural school in Austria to get experience. On the Jewish "Back-to-the land" movement see also S.E. Rosenberg, *The Jewish Community in Canada*, vol. 1 (Toronto: McClelland and Stewart, 1970), 76.

52. Medovy, "Early Jewish Physicians," 28, 30 and 34.

53. In the 1890s the proportion of Jews in the Russian army was greater than the proportion of Jews in the population of the Russian empire: B. Goldberg, "Zur Statistik der Judischen Bevolkerung in Russland laut der Volkszahlung von 1897," in Nossig (ed.), *Judische Statistik*, 261–62. In Austria-Hungary the reverse was true: I. Deak, *Beyond Nationalism: A Social and Political History of the Habsburg Officer Corps, 1848–1918* (New York: Oxford University Press, 1990, 1992), 174.

54. AJHC, Rose Moscovitch, Tape 201 (about her uncle); Turek, *Poles in Manitoba*, 35 (reference to lengthy compulsory military service); Negrych, *Toil and Triumph*, 15–16; Marrus, *Samuel Bronfman*, 21; *Jewish Life and Times*, vol. 6, p. 1.

55. AJHS, Abe Podolsky, Tape 267; Evasiuk, *George & Anna*, 52.

56. See footnote 8 above.

57. But the Poles were still waiting for him when he returned from Canada in 1919: interviews with Mr. W. Michalchyshyn, Winnipeg, most recently on September 4, 1995, and with Mr. E. Michaels, Portage la Prairie, most recently on September 9, 1995.

58. AJHC, Bertha Plotkin, Tape 244; AJHC, John Pullan, Tape 74; Medovy, "Early Jewish Physicians," 32; Gutkin, *Worst of Times*, 54.

59. Turek, *The Polish-Language Press*, 46. Galicia enjoyed almost total autonomy within the Austrian empire after c. 1868. The Polish nobility and gentry, by electoral manipulations and the use of economic and political power, in effect ran Galicia to suit their own purposes.

60. For instance, a Soltzman came to Winnipeg c. 1880 and worked for the Hudson's Bay Company, rather than join his father's prosperous fur business in Russia: AJHC, MG 6, F 25 (*).

61. F. Swyripa, *Wedded to the Cause: Ukrainian-Canadian Women and Ethnic Identity 1891–1991* (Toronto: University of Toronto Press, 1993); see also L. Singer, "'God Could Not be Everywhere—So He Made Mothers': The Unrecognized Contributions of Early Jewish Women Pioneers 1880–1920," in F. Stambrook (ed.), *A Sharing of Diversities* (Regina: Canadian Plains Research Center, 1999), 101–12. A. Kojder, "Women and the Polish Alliance of Canada," in B. Heydenkorn (ed.), *A Community in Transition: The Polish Group in Canada* (Toronto: Canadian Polish Research Institute, 1985), 119–204, deals mainly with the Toronto scene from the 1920s onwards.

62. AJHC, MG 6, F 16, Anna Friedgut. Bertha Plotkin came with her mother (a widow) and sister in 1905, but her two brothers were already here; AJHC, Bertha Plotkin, Tape 244.

63. *Banner County: A History of Russell and District 1879–1967* (Russell, MB: n.p., n.d.) 172–73; Evasiuk, *George & Anna*, 38.

64. AJHC, Sam Soloway, Tape 224; Molly Medovy, Tape 206; Noel Ginsberg, Tape 359; etc. See also the typescript memoirs of Mendel Peikoff, who was quite well off in Tsarist Russia, in AJHC, 12, file 31.

65. D. Stone, "Poverty, Not Persecution: The Main Cause of Jewish Immigration Before World War I," unpublished paper presented at the Jewish-Mennonite-Ukrainian Conference, University of Manitoba, August 1995. See also L. Dinnerstein, "The East European Jewish Migration," in L. Dinnerstein and F. Jaher (eds.), *Uncertain Americans* (New York: n.p., 1977), 217.

66. Pogroms were attempted in Polish Western Galicia in the 1890s, but prevented by the Austrian authorities; see Piotr Wrobel, "The Jews of Galicia," *Austrian History Yearbook* 25: 131. In 1898 an attempted pogrom in Tarnow was foiled, to the indignation of Viennese anti-Semites, by the Austro-Hungarian cavalry. In "Ukrainian-Jewish Antagonism in the Galician Countryside during the Late Nineteenth Century," in P.J.

Potichnyj and H. Aster (eds.), *Ukrainian-Jewish Relations in Historical Perspective* (Edmonton: Canadian Institute of Ukrainian Studies Press, 1988), J.P. Himka argues that Ukrainian-Jewish conflict in Eastern Galicia was economic and political in nature, with little religious prejudice, and that this was a crucial difference. See also footnotes 78 and 80 below.

67. A.J.P. Taylor, *War by Timetable: How the First World War Began* (London: Macdonald & Co, 1969), 105.

68. One Polish authority has noted that in the period 1896–1909 one quarter of Polish men and women in Eastern Galicia chose Ukrainian marriage partners: cited in Turek, *Poles in Manitoba*, 281, fn. 6. See also Hryniuk, *Peasants with Promise*, 5. On intermarriage and Polish participation in Ukrainian church observances see also *Uhniv ta uhnivshchyna* (New York: n.p., 1960 [Ukrainian Archive, vol. 16]), 366–67.

69. "… my heart was stirred at how eductional a paper it was for villagers, farmers, poor people"; letter from a Ukrainian villager to *Przyjaciel ludu* of 1891, as cited in K. Dunin-Wasowicz, *Czasopismiennictwo ludowe w Galicji* (Wroclaw: n.p., 1952), 150.

70. Hryniuk, *Peasants with Promise*, 100.

71. K. Stauter-Halsted, "Patriotic Celebrations in Austrian Poland: The Kosciuszko Centennial and the Formation of Peasant Nationalism," *Austrian History Yearbook* 25: 79–95.

72. Turek, *Poles in Manitoba*, 11; H. Radecki, *Ethnic Organizational Dynamics: The Polish Group in Canada* (Waterloo, ON: Wilfrid Laurier University Press, 1979), 43; T. Kulak, "Miedzy austriacka lojalnoscia a polska narodowoscia," in W. Bonusiak and J. Buszko (eds.), *Galicja i jej dziedzictwo, vol.I, Historia i polityka* (Rzeszow: n.p., 1994), 57–67; see especially the quotation on p. 67.

73. For a grandmother from Bukovina who recalled "the benevolent reign of Franz Joseph" see L. Gulutsan, *Tell Us More, Nanyo: Family History of Dmytro Gulutzan* (duplicated typescript, n.p., 1981), 7; see also J-P. Himka, "The Snows of Yesteryear," *Cross Currents: A Yearbook of Central European Cultures* 10. For the Ukrainian declaration of 1914 see Subtelny, *History*, 340.

74. R.G. Plaschka, "Die revolutionare Herausforderung im Endkampf der Donaumonarchie," in R.G. Plaschka and K. Mack (eds.), *Die Auflosung des Habsburgerreiches* (Munich: n.p., 1970), 23.

75. S. Hryniuk, "Polish Lords and Ukrainian Peasants: Conflict, Deference and Accommodation in the Late Nineteenth Century," *Austrian History Yearbook* 24: 119–132.

76. Hryniuk interview with Mr. E. Michaels, September 9, 1995.

77. *Batkivshchyna*, January 9, 1885; Hryniuk's interviews with Mr. E. Michaels, most recently on September 9, 1995.

78. Quoted from one of Franco's book reviews in A. Wilcher, "Ivan Franko and Theodor Herzl," *Harvard Ukrainian Studies* 6: 241.

79. Wrobel, "The Jews of Galicia," 131 and 132; Himka, "Ukrainian-Jewish Antagonism," 111–149. The evidence for Himka's thoughtful study comes principally from the mid-1880s, from the Ukrainian language newspaper *Batkivshchyna*, whose editors, as he notes (pp. 112–113), were pursuing a deliberately anti-Jewish policy and probably censoring items from the villages that were favourable to Jews. For Hungary see W.O. McCagg, "Jews and Peasants in Interwar Hungary," *Austrian History Yearbook* 21: 60.

80. See also Hryniuk, *Peasants with Promise*, 5.

81. Hryniuk's conversations with her grandmother, Mrs. K. Michalchyshyn, at various times in the 1970s; Himka "Ukrainian-Jewish Antagonism," 119 and 131. Reading halls or clubs, where local people could read journals or listen to them being read aloud, were

established in many East Galician villages and small towns, especially from the 1890s onwards. Some of them acquired modest libraries; many of them featured dramatic presentations, singing, and other social activities. Ukrainian reading halls also held patriotic manifestations. There were also Polish and Jewish reading halls: Hryniuk, *Peasants with Promise*, 95–107 and 198–99.

82. *Istorychno-memuarnyi zbirnyk Chortivskoi okruhy* (New York: n.p., 1974 [Ukrainskyi arkhiv, vol. 26]), 377; *Uhniv ta uhnivshchyna*, 319 and 370–371.

83. See, for example, ibid., p. 321; also Himka "Ukrainian-Jewish Antagonism," 113 and 119–20, and Evasiuk, *George & Anna*, 41–42, including the footnote on p. 41.

84. The one instance that we have found to date relates to anti-Semitism in an Anglo-Canadian village near Neepawa. The shopkeeper and his family found it expedient to move to Holland, Manitoba, where they prospered; *Jewish Life and Times* 6: 35–36.

85. *Zbarazhchyna*, vol. 1 (New York, 1980 [Ukrainian Archive, vol. 30]), 700 and 703; A. and J. Matejko, "Polish Peasants in the Canadian Prairies," in Heydenkorn (ed.), *From Prairies to Cities*, 18–22; E.M. Hubicz, *Father Joe: A Manitoban Missionary: A Biographical Account of the Life of Father Ladislaus Joseph Krelociszewski* (London: Veritas Foundation Publication Centre, [1958]), 28–29 and 35; idem, *Polish Churches in Manitoba* (London, 1960); Radecki, *Ethnic Organizational Dynamics*, 45 and 48–50.

86. For Ukrainian Greek Catholics in Manitoba see S. Hryniuk, "Pioneer Bishop, Pioneer Times: Nykyta Budka in Canada," CCHA, *Historical Papers, 1988*, 21–40; Martynowych, *Ukrainians in Canada*, 182–206. Ukrainian Orthodox settlers from Bukovina were deliberately left exposed to Russification in Canada by the Romanian-dominated Greek Oriental Church of Bukovina, ibid., 189.

87. S.M. Hryniuk and N.G. McDonald, "The Schooling Experience of Ukrainians in Manitoba, 1896–1916," in N.M. Sheehan et al. (eds.), *Schools in the West: Essays in Canadian Educational History* (Calgary: Detselig Enterprises, 1986), 162.

88. Ibid., 163. Ukrainian/English schools easily predominated: there were two Polish/English bilingual schools, and five in which Polish, Ukrainian and English were used; H. Radecki, "How relevant are Polish part-time schools?" in B. Heydenkorn (ed.), *Past and Present: Selected Topics on the Polish Group in Canada* (Toronto: n.p., 1974), 62–63.

89. Ibid., passim; Hryniuk, *Peasants with Promise*, 65–76. The Immigration Agent in Dauphin estimated in 1900 that "fully 35 per cent of male adult Galicians can read and write in their own language [i.e. Ukrainian], and many of these can also read and write Polish"; nearly all children who had attended school in Galicia could read and write— quoted in Hryniuk and McDonald, "Schooling," 157.

90. Ibid, 162; on local government in Galicia see Hryniuk, *Peasants with Promise*, 9–19 and 197–99. Tulchinsky has noted ("The Contours," p. 5) that Jews coming to North America displayed "a hybrid mixture of deeply pious, rigid orthodoxy ... and a complex melange of philosophies such as Marxism, socialism, anarchism, Zionism, bundism, and other ideals, especially among the young who had been exposed to the intellectual world outside of the Pale of Settlement."

91. Jackson, *Centennial History*, 160.

92. Though some Jewish families deliberately moved from Winnipeg to a Jewish farming settlement in order to be able to observe the Jewish Sabbath, see for example, AJHC, Ann Levi Baker interview, Tape 213.

93. See the sources cited in footnote 86, also the Sheptytsky papers in TsDIAL (Lviv), Fond 408, opys 1, sprava 680, e.g. letter from Fork River, Manitoba, January 2, 1902, from Ethelbert, March 9, 1902.

94. For the Polish group see in particular Turek, *Poles in Manitoba*, 159–217, and Radecki,

Ethnic Organizational Dynamics, 45–52. For the Ukrainians see M.H. Marunchak, *The Ukrainian Canadians: A History* (Winnipeg: Ukrainian Academy of Arts and Sciences in Canada, 1982), 107–11, 162–67, 240 and 261–72. For the Jews see Chiel, *The Jews in Manitoba*, 72–107, 111–17, and 131–38.

95. The concept of multiple loyalties must have been too strange for nativist Anglo-Canadians, but retaining their language and culture while developing loyalty to Canada was an obvious and sensible survival strategy for Ukrainian immigrants, as no doubt for other migrants. What, one wonders, would Empire loyalists have made of the Ukrainian Canadian choir which in 1995 sang "O Canada" at the annual Dauphin festival in the Ukrainian language? For attention to schooling and to the learning of English see Hryniuk and McDonald, "Schooling Experience," passim, and B. Heydenkorn, "*Gazeta katolicka*—The First Polish Language Weekly" in B. Heydenkorn (ed.), *Heritage and the Future* (Toronto: n.p., 1988), 214.

96. Martynowych, *Ukrainians in Canada*, 189–93 and 214–20; P. Yusyk, *The Ukrainian Greek Orthodox Church of Canada, 1918–1951* (Ottawa: n.p., 1981), 79–96.

97. Turek, *Polish-Language Press*, 66–67 and 99; Heydenkorn, *Gazeta katolicka*, 209. The Polish National Catholic Church attracted some adherents because it used Polish in place of Latin in the mass.

98. An exception is to be found in Winnipeg municipal politics, when Ukrainians and Jews were pitted against each other: H. Trachtenberg, "Unfriendly Competitors: Jews, Ukrainians, and Municipal Politics in Winnipeg's Ward 5, 1911–1914," in Stambrook (ed.), *A Sharing of Diversities*, 135–156. For good inter-ethnic relations see *Jewish Life and Times* 6: 33–37.

99. Radecki, *Ethnic Organizational Dynamics*, 33; Turek, *Poles in Manitoba*, 52.

100. Turek, *Poles in Manitoba*, 109 and 153–54; Radecki, *Ethnic Organizational Dynamics*, 33; Matejko, "Polish Peasants," 23–24; Chiel, *Jews in Manitoba*, 58; Rosenberg, *Jewish Community*, I, 120.

101. L. Rosenberg, *Canada's Jews: A Social and Economic Study of the Jews in Canada* (Montreal: Bureau of Social and Economic Research, Canadian Jewish Congress, 1939), 183–84. On the Peikoff family of merchants in Rossburn, who were there from 1909 till 1950, see Rossburn History Club, *On the Sunny Slopes of the Riding Mountains: A History of Rossburn and District*, vol. 1 (Rossburn: n.p., 1984), 21 and 324–26. Fred Malaniuk left his family "with hardly any food" when he set off to find work, "but as he went through Rossburn he stopped to see Mr. Peikoff who had a store. He arranged to send back to us a hundred pounds of flour and some salt," ibid., 109. No doubt Malaniuk was not the only Ukrainian settler who made such an arrangement with Mendel Peikoff. According to one of his sons, "Peikoff's general store was the town's meeting place," S.S. Peikoff, *Yesterday's Doctor: An Autobiography* (Winnipeg: Prairie Publishing Company, 1980), 19—the description is probably of the early 1920s. A much appreciated Jewish merchant in Oakburn, active after World War I, has had a park named after him in the town.

102. Cashman, *Abraham Cristall*, 13.

103. Stambrook, "Early Jewish Immigration," 84, also E. Paris, *Jews: An Account of Their Experience in Canada* (Toronto: Macmillan, 1980), 274 and 11.

104. Turek, *Poles in Manitoba*, 2, 25, 27, 31 and 35; the quotation is from p. 33. On the allegedly non-permanent character of the migration see Turek, *The Polish-Language Press*, 46.

105. Turek, *Poles in Manitoba*, 25 and 42.

106. There is no evidence that Ukrainians in Galicia had a greater problem with alcohol than any other European peoples: S. Hryniuk, "The Peasant and Alcohol in Eastern

Galicia in the Late Nineteenth Century: A Note," *Journal of Ukrainian Studies* 11: 75–85; for an interpretation that relies on dubious 1876 data and assumptions, and treats these as valid for the remainder of the pre-1914 period, see Martynowych, *Ukrainians in Canada*, 6.

107. S. Szczepanowski, *Nedza Galicyi w cyfrach i program energicznego rozoju gospodarstwa krajowego* (Lviv: n.p., 1888), esp. 55–57.

18. Plain Racism: The Reaction Against Oklahoma Black Immigration to the Canadian Plains

R. Bruce Shepard

Previous examinations of popular attitudes towards immigrants to western Canada have been dominated by the concept of "nativism."[1] One of the leading proponents of this theory has defined nativism as, "opposition to an internal minority on the grounds that it posed a threat to Canadian national life."[2] The concept fuses prejudice and nationalism to explain why western Canadians reacted negatively to a wide variety of immigrants during the settlement period. Nativism is thus a general theory, and has proven to be useful in gaining an understanding of the general negative reaction to many immigrant groups.

Its strength as a general theory is also nativism's major weakness as a tool for understanding the reactions to particular groups. Proponents of nativism offer a hierarchy of acceptability to explain such differences, but this is insufficient because it does not explain where such attitudes originated, how they were transmitted, or why the level of antagonism varied from group to group. The purpose of this article is to draw attention to these problems by focussing upon the exceptional response to Black Oklahomans who migrated to the Canadian Plains before World War I. This article is also a call for the application of other theories to the Canadian Plains' experience in order to gain new perspectives on the reactions to immigration.[3]

Nativism does not deal adequately with the existing prejudices brought to the Canadian Plains by the majority groups. Settlers from Britain, the United States, and eastern Canada had well-developed views on Blacks long before they stepped down from the immigrant cars. Nor does nativism help to explain how such prejudice was reinforced, and transmitted throughout the developing society. In the case of the Black Oklahomans, prairie newspapers were an important source of stereotyping before the Blacks arrived, as well as of negative opinion when they appeared at the border. Finally, nativism does little to explain the variety of responses to immigrants. The reaction to the Black Oklahomans was qualitatively different from that directed at other groups. The intensity of the emotion generated was out of all proportion to the relatively small number of Blacks who came north.[4]

The white, English-speaking peoples of the North Atlantic have a long history of racism directed at Blacks. The origins of this prejudice are buried in the periods preceeding the first British contacts with Africa. These first contacts were not positive and, unfortunately, served as the basis for the development of a number of stereotypes, many of which are still in circulation.[5]

The Victorian era was a particularly negative one for the development of race relations. The worldwide expansion of the British Empire, made possible by technological superiority, served to confirm British views of their own racial supremacy. For example, when a band of Jamaican peasants rioted in 1865, the venerable London *Times* argued that,

> It seems impossible to eradicate the original savageness of the African blood. As long as the black man has a strong white Government and numerous white population to control him he is capable of living as a respectable member of society… But wherever he attains to a certain degree of independence there is the fear that he will resume the barbarous life and the fierce habits of his African ancestors.[6]

Such attitudes were part of the milieu of Victorian Britain, and were brought to the Canadian Plains by British immigrants. These opinions fused with the virulent racism which emanated from south of the forty-ninth parallel, and was brought north by white American immigrants. The United States has a long history of racism, which need not be chronicled here. It is sufficient to note that white Americans disliked Blacks, and during the late nineteenth century went to considerable lengths to segregate them. Indeed, some American immigrants saw the Canadian Plains as an escape from contact with Blacks.[7]

Eastern Canadian immigrants to the Canadian Plains were not free from the taint of racism. While Canada's admission of escaped slaves prior to the American Civil War is often touted as an example of racial tolerance, the lives of the Blacks once in Canada were in fact far from ideal. Blacks were subjected to economic and social discrimination in eastern Canada, imposed by a racially conscious society. At one time, both Ontario and Nova Scotia legislated racially separate schools.[8]

The extent of eastern Canadian prejudice towards Blacks can be gauged from the fact that objections to Black settlement on the plains were being raised in the east even before western Canadians voiced their disapproval of the idea. As early as 1899 the Immigration Branch of the federal Department of the Interior was replying negatively to the suggestion that Blacks be allowed to settle on the Canadian Plains. The Branch informed its agent in Kansas City that "it is not desired that any negro immigrants should arrive in Western Canada ... or that such immigration should be promoted by our agents." When a Black man from Shawnee, Oklahoma Territory contacted Canadian authorities in 1902 on behalf of a group of Blacks, he was informed by L.M. Fortier, Secretary of the Department, that, "the Canadian Government is not particularly desirous of encouraging the immigration of negroes."[9]

In spite of such official disapproval, a few Black settlers did find their way northward, apparently lured by Canadian government advertisements in their local newspapers. The Laurier government had undertaken an extensive advertising campaign in the American mid-West trying to attract farmers. These advertisements found their way into Black newspapers in the Oklahoma and Indian Territories. They appeared in Black newspapers such as the Boley *Beacon*, the Clearview *Patriarch*, and the influential Muskogee *Cimeter*. The Black Boley *Progress* carried one item on March 16, 1905 stating that the Canadian Plains were warmer than Texas, and carried numerous other advertisements in subsequent years.[10]

These Canadian advertisements attracted a number of Black farmers. Several Black families located near Maidstone, in what would become the province of Saskatchewan, in the spring of 1905. They were joined by at least one other Black family in the autumn of 1906.[11] This trickle did not attract much attention, however, nor did it generate comment in Canada. The reaction to Black immigration did not begin until events in Oklahoma began forcing more Blacks to look for a haven outside of the state.

The Oklahoma and Indian Territories became the state of Oklahoma in 1907, and the white controlled government immediately set about segregating Blacks along the lines established by the older southern states. In 1907 a "Jim Crow" segregation law was passed, and in 1910 Blacks were disfranchised. Racial violence accompanied these legislative moves, and while many Black Oklahomans resisted, others began making plans to leave the state.[12]

A spurt of Black migration followed each of the Oklahoma segregation developments. A Black family moved to Wildwood, Alberta, from Oklahoma in 1908. Twenty Black families from the state followed in short order. Several families added to the growing Black population in the Maidstone, Saskatchewan, area that same year. In 1910 a Black family, including 10 children, arrived in Maidstone from Tabor, Oklahoma.[13]

White actors in Blackface at Sheho, Saskatchewan, 1923 or 1924. Members of a "minstrel show," the actors performed comedy routines, songs, and dances stereotyping Black culture (Photograph obtained from Emil Sebulsky, courtesy of Helen Wunder, Sheho area).

Oklahoma's segregation policies were a major factor in Jeff Edwards's decision to move to the Amber Valley area of Alberta, just east of Athabasca. The Blacks who went north to eastern Canada were fleeing slavery, he said, "We in Amber Valley are here because we fled something almost as hard to bear—'Jim Crowism'." Edwards left Oklahoma in 1910 and on the train to Canada met another Black man, Henry Sneed, who was also heading north. Sneed later returned to Oklahoma to begin organizing a larger party of Black emigrants.

Sneed returned to Clearview, Oklahoma, in August 1910. He had no trouble attracting prospects due to Oklahoma's racial policies. Meetings were held in various parts of the south, and in 1911 emigrants from Oklahoma, as well as Kansas and Texas, gathered in Weleetka, Oklahoma, to begin their trek. The first group consisted of 194 men, women and children, and no less than 9 carloads of horses and farm implements. Another group of 200 began gathering in the same town soon after the first band departed, but waited to hear if the first party was admitted before setting out.[14]

The Sneed party was stopped at Emerson, Manitoba, while a rigorous medical examination was carried out. Fearing that an attempt would be made to keep them out, one Oklahoma newspaper reported, the leaders of the group had appealed to Washington, and the United States Consul at Ottawa was directed to determine whether Black Americans, as a class, could be excluded under Canadian law. It was decided that no Canadian regulation specifically relating to Black immigration existed, so the group was allowed to enter. Still, prospective Black emigrants had to be uneasy, especially when the Guthrie *Oklahoma Guide* reprinted the Kansas City *Journal's* notation that, "The exodus has been bitterly opposed by a large per cent [*sic*] of the white population of the Canadian provinces."[15] That they were not wanted on the Canadian Plains would become increasingly clear to Black Oklahomans in the months ahead as Canada served notice that it intended to keep the northern plains white.

The Canadian reaction to the Black immigrants was plain racism. The dominant groups who settled on the Canadian Plains had well-developed views of Blacks. This prejudice was confirmed, and transmitted throughout the developing society, by the racist portrayal of Blacks in prairie newspapers. Blacks were the butt of jokes and cartoons which regularly appeared in western journals. Blacks were also negatively pictured in numerous advertisements. Minstrel shows were very popular at the time, and were frequently advertised.[16]

Far more serious were the sensationalist reports of exceptional contemporary stories involving Blacks. For example, in the spring of 1910 the Edmonton *Capital* gave prominent coverage to the murder confession of a local Black man. James Chapman had gone to the Mounted Police and admitted to having helped a white woman poison her husband in Stillwater, Oklahoma, over a year earlier. Chapman and the woman had then fled to Alberta. While there was no connection between this story and the arrival of the Black immigrants, it is significant that this news item appeared in the same issue of the *Capital* as an item announcing the Edmonton Board of Trade's decision to try to stop Black immigration. Given its portrayal of the two events, it is also not surprising that less than a week later the same Edmonton journal would editorialize that,

> The Board of Trade has done well to call attention to the amount of negro immigration which is taking place into this district. It has already attained such proportions as to discourage white settlers from going into certain sections. The immigration department has no excuse for encouraging it at all ... we prefer to have the southern race problem left behind. The task of assimilating all the white people who enter our borders is quite a heavy enough one without the color proposition being added.[17]

By the spring of 1910, the Edmonton Board of Trade felt that it was time for action on the question of Black immigration. At its monthly meeting on April 12, the Board unanimously passed a resolution calling the federal government's attention to the "marked increase" in Black immigration to the Canadian Plains. The Board said that it felt that the foundations for a "negro problem" were being laid. In the Board's opinion the Blacks were a "most undesirable element," and it urged the authorities to take immediate action to stop more from entering the country.[18]

Canadian immigration authorities were in fact already concerned with the developing Black influx, and were trying to stop it. At first they tried to stop immigration literature from reaching Blacks in Oklahoma. When this proved haphazard, immigration officials tried using vigorous medical examinations at the border as a deterrent. This latter manoeuvre proved to be without value when healthy Black men, women, and children presented themselves for admission. Henry Sneed's group shattered the medical examination idea late in March 1911 and this, plus their numbers, attracted considerable publicity. This publicity in turn provoked comment, and revealed the deep feelings on the Canadian Plains on the subject of Black immigration.

When their Great Northern train arrived in Emerson, Manitoba, Henry Sneed's group immediately attracted attention. The local newspaper, the Emerson *Journal*, reported the arrival of "men, women and pickaninnies," and then commented that the town had been decorated with "coons" ever since. They had money, farm implements, and livestock, it continued, and were generally of a "good appearance." Yet Blacks were not the most desirable class of settlers, in its opinion, although it would be difficult to reject them once they had come this far. The *Journal* then prophetically suggested that it would be better to stop the migration at its source. This is precisely what the Canadian government eventually did.[19]

The Sneed party's arrival and entry, once their medical examinations were completed, was noted across the Canadian Plains, and there was immediate comment. On the day the party arrived in Winnipeg, a Brandon woman, who signed herself "An Englishwoman Who Had Lived in Oklahoma," contacted the editor of the *Manitoba Free Press* with her concerns. She began by regretting the invasion of "thousands" of Oklahoma Blacks into Canada. Since she was concerned with the welfare of the country, and had no great interest in Oklahoma's, she was sorry that Canada was being saddled with people that the southern states did not want. It was Canada's misfortune, if not the country's own fault, that it had not yet passed a law barring Blacks. Since liberty was not to be confused with license, she continued, one would only enjoy true freedom by being restrained. Yet everyone learned by sad experience, only usually too late. Those who had never lived in Black-inhabited areas and had only been in contact with "well-disposed" Blacks, would find the disgust felt towards them unintelligible, she said. Those who did know their habits, however, could only see Blacks as "undesirable"—they could never be colonists or settlers. In concluding, she argued that, "As negroes flourish in a hot country and do as little work as possible, it is hoped that Jack Frost will accomplish what the authorities apparently cannot."[20]

No doubt because of the interest stirred, when the Sneed party reached Winnipeg the local *Manitoba Free Press* was at the station with a reporter. In his article, the reporter noted that not one of the 194 Black homeseekers had been rejected at the border, and indicated that, "a good deal of speculation is rife as to the outcome of the new movement." He then gave a brief history of how the group came to Canada.

The reporter then turned his attention to the question of assimilation, after conceding that it was generally recognized that the best settlers were those who could easily be incorporated into the population. It was argued with some truth, he said, that the Blacks must forever be unto themselves, and were therefore not the best class of settlers. Yet as the regulations then stood, "there is absolutely no means by which the better class of negro farmer may be rejected."[21]

A "member of the much maligned and hated race," Samuel H. Gibson, contacted the *Free Press* after this article appeared to thank the paper for its "fair, candid, and impartial statement." He wanted to thank them, he said, because as far as he was aware they were the first western Canadian newspaper to get all of the facts and to express an "unbiased opinion." He continued by asserting that, "Much has been said and written on the matter (Black immigration); but, for the most part, I opine, it has emanated from persons whose minds are warped by blind prejudice, and who, therefore, are incompetent to sit in judgement on any question of which impartiality is the principal element."[22]

Like its Winnipeg counterpart, the Edmonton *Journal* had a reporter waiting at the station when the Sneed group arrived, indicating once again the importance attached to their appearance. At five o'clock in the morning everyone on the train was very, very tired. Yet even then their spirits were not dampened, and one member of the party managed to have fun with the reporter. Alighting from the train, one Black man announced to the newspaper man that he was so tired that he felt like he was turning yellow. The reporter said he, "reeled, staggered, and leaning against the station building felt a little faint at coming on such a supposed revelation." He said he had heard the expression "yellow coon" used in jest, but never thought he would come across such a type. Approaching the Black jester, the journalist was able to see under the station's lights that in fact the Black man had not changed colour, and he was able to inform the Oklahoman that, "such an affliction had not overtaken him."[23]

Mr. R. Jennings, editor and managing director of the *Journal*, noted that the Black immigration was causing considerable uneasiness. He did not find this at all surprising, and in his words, "Whether well-founded or not, we have to face the fact that a great deal of prejudice exists against the coloured man and that his presence in large numbers creates problems from which we naturally shrink." Yet if the Blacks met the existing immigration requirements it seemed impossible to deny them entry, in Jennings's opinion. Given these circumstances one could but wish them well in their new homes, and hope that they conducted themselves so that the ill-will directed at them was dissipated. They could become useful if they followed Booker Washington's idea of salvation through hard work. There would be plenty of that where they were going, he concluded, and if they were able to turn their wild land into productive farms they could prove more desirable citizens, "than any of those who are now speaking so contemptuously of them and are loafing about the city streets."[24]

Not all Albertans, however, were willing to be quite so liberal. In a front page news item the Calgary *Herald* informed its readers of the large Black party's arrival in the provincial capital. They were a much talked about group, it noted wryly, "Heralded throughout their entire journey by more widespread publicity than they would have received had they been the latest thing in a minstrel show." The men were all strong and sturdy, and the immigration hall was full of "tumbling pickaninnies" which promised another successful generation.

In the same issue, J.H. Woods, editor and managing director of the *Herald*, concluded that the Black immigration was the first fruits of reciprocity with the United States. The "colour question" was soon going to agitate the public, and he found Frank Oliver's approach to the question "tepid." It seemed as if the Minister of the Interior was allowing the colony to establish itself, and that he somehow hoped to sweep them back southward. Teddy Roosevelt's question of what to do with the Blacks was being answered, Woods said, by sending them to Alberta. "Reciprocity," he concluded, "means that Canada is anxious to take all that America does not want."[25]

The public was already agitated. On March 31, 1911, F.T. Fisher of the Edmonton Board of Trade had penned a seven-page letter to Frank Oliver. Fisher noted that the subject of Black immigration had been broached a year before, but that the influx had grown considerably. It was time for "drastic action" since there was evidence that "bitter race prejudice" would develop in the areas the Blacks were settling. There was no room for argument, and the contention that the Blacks were good people and farmers was irrelevant. One only had to look to the United States to see what would happen if too many Blacks came north. He had white settlers in his office, he said, the very best sort of settler, who would not go to where the Blacks had located. In concluding, Fisher argued that serious trouble was brewing. In his words,

> White settlers in the homestead districts are becoming alarmed and exasperated and are prepared to go to almost any length. People in the towns and cities ... are beginning to realize the imperative necessity of effective action; and it only needs a slight effort to start up an agitation which would be joined in by practically every white man in the country. There is every indication that unless effective action is taken, such an agitation will be put in motion in the near future.[26]

Oliver did not need Fisher's warning for he was receiving other evidence of the white mood on the Canadian Plains. The Secretary of Edmonton's Municipal Chapter of the IODE, Mrs. A. Knight, forwarded a petition against Black immigration from her organization to Oliver. She informed him that they had held an emergency meeting on March 27 to discuss the question of Black immigration, and they were against it. As if to echo Fisher's assertion of possible trouble in areas where the Blacks were locating, A.I. Sawley, Secretary of the Athabasca Landing Board of Trade, wrote to Oliver that, "When it was learned around town that these negroes were coming out there was great indignation, and many threatened violence, threatened to meet them on the trail out of town, and drive them back." Sawley also said that as there already were Blacks in the area, and only a few whites had as yet located there, there was a danger of it becoming all Black. He suggested that as a remedy the new Black arrivals be segregated with a group that had already located near Lobstick Lake.[27]

For the time being Sneed's group was unperturbed by the controversy they were creating, as they joined one of their preachers in celebrating their apparent good fortune. The Black minister gathered a group of 75 together in one of the outsheds of the Edmonton immigration hall, and sitting on wooden stumps and boxes they heard him say that God had made Canada a free country, but that it was up to them to make the best of it. The reporter covering the event was impressed by the fact that the preacher never mentioned or referred to the United States, and the journalist took this to mean that the group was very impressed with what they had seen on the northern side of the international boundary.[28] Their apparent satisfaction was to be short-lived, however, when an unfortunate accusation was made which further aroused anti-Black prejudice on the Canadian Plains, and initially reflected upon the entire group, and any future Black settlers.

Shortly after six o'clock on April 4, 1911, 15-year-old Hazel Huff was found by a neighbour lying unconscious on the kitchen floor of her Edmonton home. She had a handkerchief securely tied over her eyes and had apparently been drugged with chloroform. The neighbour immediately contacted a doctor and the police. When the girl regained consciousness she told the police that she had answered a knock at the door, and was grabbed by a Black man who tried to drug her. She fought him but was overpowered, she said, and did not remember anything after that point.

When her parents returned home they searched the house and found that a diamond ring and some money were missing. According to one report, the father became so enraged that he took his daughter and went searching for the assailant armed with a revolver. The police believed two Black men were involved, although they only arrested one by the name of J.F. Witsue. He was charged with robbery two days later, but the police refused to elaborate when pestered by reporters.[29]

The news of the supposed attack spread as quickly as the proverbial prairie fire, but managed to pick up a few embellishments on the way. In addition, several newspapers immediately linked the Black settlers with the incident. The Calgary *Albertan* assured its readers that no criminal assault other than the administering of the drug had taken place, and in a later editorial argued that, "The assault made by a colored man upon a little girl in Edmonton should open the eyes of the authorities in Ottawa as to what may be expected regularly if Canada is to open the door to all the colored people of the republic and not bar their way from open entry here." The Edmonton *Journal* apparently deserted its former moderate stance, since it reprinted this comment verbatim and with no rejoinder. The Calgary *Herald* argued that the attempts to colonize Blacks north of Edmonton had to be carefully examined. The drugging of the girl in Edmonton could be taken as an indication of what could happen in Alberta as a result of American Blacks being allowed to settle in Canada.[30]

On Saturday, April 8, the Lethbridge *Daily News* published an editorial entitled "The Black Peril." It noted that the assault upon the Edmonton girl had come very soon after the arrival of the large party from Oklahoma, and argued that this was a warning to the authorities of what to expect if Blacks were allowed to enter the country. Canada did not need a "negro problem." The Blacks who were in the country had to be kept away from homesteads, it continued, for in the more isolated areas, where the women were often left alone, there would be an ever present horror. "Keep the black demon out of Canada," was its stand.

This was too much for a local Black farmer, L.D. Brower, and he contacted the Lethbridge *Daily Herald* to reply. After noting the *News*'s comments, Brower attacked its argument. He asked what that paper thought of the immorality of slavery, and whether it knew that Black men had defended white women during the American Civil War? The source of the *News*'s prejudice was its jealousy at the progress the Blacks had made since 1865, and thus it would deny Blacks the right to freely enter Canada. The Edmonton story was probably a fake, and while waiting for the truth he would farm his land and the Blacks further north would tackle the wilderness. The *News*, in the meantime, could continue to supply its form of "intellectual food," but, he said, "I submit to the judgement of the fair minded Canadian citizen, which of us is best improving his God-given talents."[31]

The Saskatoon *Phoenix* announced the incident to its readers in a front page item with a large headline: "A Negro Atrocity—White Girl Flogged and Assaulted by Late Arrivals at Edmonton." It said that the first Black atrocity since the large party arrived from the United States 10 days before had been reported. The Regina *Morning Leader* carried substantially the same item on its front page, which prompted a comment from the Edmonton *Daily Bulletin*. Perhaps because of its close association with Frank Oliver, the *Bulletin* had remained strangely silent on the question of Black immigration in general, and on the Sneed group in particular. The Regina report aroused the editor, John Howey, to state that,

> Bad news not only travels fast, but like a snowball on the down grade, the further it goes the bigger it grows. This particular item picked up a second negro and a flogging between Edmonton and Regina. It can hardly have been less than a murder and a lynching when it reached Toronto, and a free-for-all race war by the time it got to New York.[32]

Even when it was determined that the Black man charged had no connection with the settlers, feelings against the group in Edmonton remained high. Furthermore, the feeling was growing stronger, and in one journalist's opinion another such incident would push the "rowdy element" to the lynching point. Even the saner members of the community believed that the Black influx had to be stopped. J.H. Woods of the Calgary *Herald* editorialized that the "negro problem" was the most serious then facing the United States. Edmonton had the sympathy and support of the whole west in protesting the Black immigration, and it was hard to understand Frank Oliver's apathy to the situation.[33]

These reports would indicate that the age-old sexual mythology surrounding the Black man was being reinforced in many white western Canadian minds. Indeed, when Fritz Freidrichs of Mewassin, Alberta, contacted the Immigration Branch on April 12 to voice his disapproval of Black immigration, his major concern was that, "These negroes have misused young girls and women and killed them." This was tragic, but the full dimensions of the tragedy were not revealed until nine days after the supposed assault when the girl confessed to having fabricated the whole story.

According to the Edmonton *Journal*, the young girl "had not been attacked and overcome by a big, Black, burly nigger who was intent on robbing the house, as was first believed." The girl had lost the diamond ring involved, and fearing punishment, had made up the tale. She became frightened with the commotion caused and, when a man was charged, decided to confess. Interestingly, the Edmonton Chief of Police had known the truth for several days, but had sworn the family to secrecy. No explanation was given for this action.[34]

The girl's story had an impact, before she confessed, and cannot be divorced from the agitation against Black immigration which continued to grow. On the night of April 7, Mr. C.E. Simmonds of Leduc addressed a "representative gathering" at the Conservative Party club rooms in Edmonton. After discussing and deprecating the Liberal's reciprocity policy, he turned his attention to the subject of immigration. Just as British Columbia did not want to be called "Yellow British Columbia," Simmonds said, he did not want his province to be labelled "Black Alberta." It was time immigration reflected personal rights; they all had a right to choose whom they wished to live near. He did not want Alberta to be Black, he repeated, or even Black in spots, and he believed that the province would not stand for a Black invasion. "I can only see one way out of this difficulty," he concluded, "and this is to put the present government out of power and bring in one who will listen to our pleas... Way down in Ottawa they do not think of the matter as seriously as we do, and therefore the interest is lacking."[35]

The Edmonton Board of Trade was determined that Ottawa would listen, and it launched a vigorous petition campaign. After giving a brief account of early Black immigration into Alberta, the Board's petition argued that these people were but the advance guard of several more hundreds, and that their arrival would be disastrous. It continued,

> We cannot admit as any factor the argument that these people may be good farmers or good citizens. It is a matter of common knowledge that it has been proved in the United States that negroes and whites cannot live in proximity

without the occurrence of revolting lawlessness, and the development of bitter race hatred... We are anxious that such a problem should not be introduced into this fair land at present enjoying a reputation for freedom from such lawlessness as has developed in all sections of the United States where there is any considerable negro element. There is no reason to believe that we have here a higher order of civilization, or that the introduction of a negro problem here would have different results.

It was then urged that immediate steps be taken to stop any more Blacks from settling on the Canadian Plains.[36]

The Edmonton Board set up a special committee to oversee the distribution of the petition throughout the city. Copies were placed in several banks and hotels downtown and in the Board of Trade Office, and plans were made to canvass door-to-door. The committee was perhaps spurred by a newspaper report originating in Vancouver that a Colonel Tom J. Harris of Sapulpa, Oklahoma, was planning to bring more Blacks into Canada. The Kentucky-born "Colonel" was quoted as saying he would bring five thousand "niggahs" north before the summer ended. Members of the Edmonton City Council may also have seen the item, for when a letter from F.T. Fisher of the Board of Trade was read at a council meeting on April 25 it was immediately acted upon. Only one alderman, Mr. McKinley, voted against endorsing the Board of Trade's action.[37]

Local Blacks did not tamely submit to the Board of Trade's efforts, and tried to nullify the effectiveness of the petition campaign. The tactic used was to have several Blacks follow a canvasser, interrupt any conversation he might have trying to get signatures, and try to dissuade anyone from signing. Secretary Fisher of the Board of Trade deprecated these efforts arguing that the Blacks did not "appreciate the spirit" in which the petitioning was being done. The local Blacks should recognize that the idea of excluding Blacks was merely an attempt to prevent the recurrence of the situation in the United States, and that their own position would be vastly more intolerable with a larger Black community. "Those negroes who have been here some time," Fisher said, "have had a square deal and been treated as whites, but if you would get a few thousand more in, conditions would be much changed. They would then be treated as they were in the south." He also claimed that nearly everyone approached was signing and, while his 95% success rate is questionable, over 3,400 Edmontonians eventually did sign.[38]

The Edmonton Board of Trade also had considerable success when it contacted other such groups across the prairies, and by the end of May 1911 the

Robert and Ester Crump, Edmonton, Alberta, circa 1920. The Crumps migrated to Alberta from Oklahoma in 1911 or 1912. They were first in Calgary, then Edmonton, before finally settling at Breton (then known as Keystone), Alberta. Today, on the fourth Sunday each February, the Breton & District Historical Museum hosts "Black History Day" to commemorate Black settlement in the district in the early 1900s (Courtesy of the Glenbow Archives PA-3439-9).

Strathcona, Morinville, Fort Saskatchewan, and Calgary, Alberta, Boards of Trade had either endorsed or joined the Edmontonians in urging that Black immigration be stopped. They were joined by their counterparts in Yorkton and Saskatoon, Saskatchewan, and Winnipeg, Manitoba. On April 29, Francis C. Clare, Secretary-Treasurer of the Edmonton Chapter of the United Farmers of Alberta, wrote to the Immigration Branch to say that his group was, "in full sympathy with the resolution passed by the Edmonton Board of Trade." On the same day, J.M. Liddell, Secretary-Treasurer of the Pincher Station, Alberta, Chapter of the UFA, also wrote to Ottawa to register his group's disapproval of Black immigration, and to urge that they be excluded permanently. In his words, "we consider negroes undesirable as fellow citizens in this Province." The Edmonton Builders Exchange, an organization of many contractors' groups, sent a separate petition calling Black immigration a "serious menace." A.I. Sawley of the Athabasca Landing Board of Trade again wrote to Frank Oliver stating, "Canada is the last country open to the white race. Are we going to preserve it for the white race, or are we going to permit the Blacks free use of large portions of it?"[39]

In Saskatoon, the local Board of Trade's endorsement of the Edmonton position brought praise from the Saskatoon *Phoenix*. The action may seem to have been rather harsh, the journal argued, but it was convinced that it was in the best interests of both Canada and the Blacks. The two races could never have anything in common and, while the coming of a few might be all right, hundreds would be a far more serious matter. Several days later "Fair Play" contacted the newspaper to challenge its argument, and having lived in a Black town this writer felt qualified to speak on the subject. He argued that the Blacks could be as good citizens as whites, and included some statistics from a federal Department of Justice Report on prison inmate populations to prove his contention.

Unfortunately for "Fair Play," the data he cited was open to a challenge, as *Phoenix* noted two days later when an editorial appeared answering his letter. The statistics proved the opposite, the paper said, since they showed Blacks to have a proportionately higher inmate population than whites. *Phoenix* then went on to argue that the "problem of the negroe [*sic*]" on the North American continent was America's, and had no place in Canada. The agitation against the Black man's entrance was due to the large numbers of Americans living in Western Canada, for, "there is no inherent unfriendliness towards the black man in this country."[40]

The assertion that the anti-Black feelings being expressed on the prairies were from white American settlers was not new, but it did not go unchallenged. When Estelle Coffee of Neilburg, Saskatchewan, contacted the Edmonton *Journal* at the height of the Black immigration controversy she asked why "the people of this country accept the negro as their equal socially and object to them as neighbors?" Obviously a former American, this woman attempted to poke a hole in the inflated Canadian claims of racial tolerance, and tried to get them to accept some responsibility for the agitation then underway. She found it hard to understand why the people of the north who believed, preached, and practiced social equality, objected to Black settlers. It would be easy to understand why a white Southerner would object to living with Blacks; "We do not accept them as our equals at any time or in any way." She wanted to know if it was right to keep Blacks from settling in Canada when everyone seemed so anxious for them to have every advantage. If Southerners could live with thousands of Blacks, she concluded, surely Canadians could tolerate a few hundred.[41]

While western Anglo-Canadians displayed a degree of hypocrisy on the race question, this by no means indicates that other Canadians were somehow free from the taint of racism. Describing Blacks as "that special element, the worst of all," Arthur Fortin, LLB, of St. Evarist Station, Beauce, Quebec, contacted Frank Oliver to assure him that any government action to stop the Black influx would meet with the approval of that part of French Canada. He personally felt that they should try "to prevent or at least control the immigration of Darkies into the Dominion. Just as it does for the Chinies—the Hindoes—and the Japs." After the Winnipeg Board of Trade passed its resolution on the Black immigration question, the German language *Der Nordwesten* of that city, after quoting from the document argued that,

> dass die vielen Faelle von Lynchjustiz im Sueden der
> Staaten, von denen wir fast taeglich lesen, and bei denen es

KEEP THE NEGRO ACROSS THE LINE

THE WINNIPEG BOARD OF TRADE TAKES DECIDED ACTION

Not Good Settlers or Agreeable Neighbors Either

Winnipeg, Man., April 19.—The Winnipeg board of trade this evening passed a strongly worded resolution, which will be forwarded to Ottawa, condemning the admission of negroes into Canada as settlers.

It is set forth in the resolution that these new-comers are not successful farmers nor agreeable neighbors for white settlers. The board also passed a resolution similar to that of the Manufacturers' association on the proposal to amend the railway act to enable the railway commission to suspend railway tariffs or charges on appeals from patrons of the railways against which grievances are held.

Newspaper item concerning a resolution passed by the Winnipeg Board of Trade condemning Black settlement in Canada. From the *Albertan*, April 20, 1910 (Courtesy of the Glenbow Archives/NA-3556-1).

sich fast ausschliesslich um Verbrechen handelt, die von Negern begangen worden sind, wohl jeden, abgesehen von anderen Gruenden, ueberzeugen duerften, wie wenig wuenschenswert ein solcher Zuwachs unserer Bevoelkerung ist.

Es waere zu wuenschen, dass noch andere oeffentliche Koerperschaften von der Art der hiesign Handelskammer sich dem Protest der letzteren anschliessen.[42]

The commentary and agitation against Black immigration could not but come to the attention of Parliament, and the subject was raised several times in the House of Commons. Even before the large Sneed party arrived, Frank Oliver was questioned on his Department's policy regarding Black immigrants. The Minister of the Interior, in a blatant falsehood, assured the House on March 2, 1911 that "there are no instructions issued by the Immigration Branch of my department which will exclude any man on account of his race or colour." The subject was again broached a few weeks later, and Oliver admitted that there was a strong sentiment against the admission of Blacks. He again assured the House that Blacks seeking admittance to Canada would be subject only to existing provisions regarding immigration.

Robert Borden, the Conservative Party Leader and Leader of the Opposition, noted that a great deal depended upon how strictly those regulations were applied, and he thought it would be very unfortunate if anyone were excluded because of their colour. Not all Conservatives were quite so sympathetic to the Blacks, however, and on April 3, William Thoburn, the Conservative member for the Ontario riding of Lanark North, asked Oliver whether the government was prepared to stop the developing Black influx, and whether it would not be preferable, "to preserve for the sons of Canada the lands they propose to give to niggers?" That Black immigration was linked to other "coloured" immigration in many Canadian minds was again revealed in the comments of William H. Sharpe, the Conservative member for the Manitoba riding of Lisgar, who rose on May 1 to state that, like British Columbians, he wanted a "white west" and urged the government to stop the flow of blacks.[43]

Through its previous actions it is clear that the government, like many westerners and several Members of Parliament, did not want Blacks on the Canadian Plains. Action on the problem was difficult, however, since the reciprocity negotiations with the United States had only recently concluded, and remarks by President Taft on the subject had fanned Canadian nationalism. A volatile subject like Black immigration could easily become involved, upsetting an already precarious situation. Indeed, as has already been noted, one Calgary newspaper had linked the two subjects in a very negative fashion.

The American Government was likewise concerned with what was happening, but it too faced a delicate situation. The American Consul-General at Winnipeg, John E. Jones, had already intervened on behalf of one group of Black Oklahomans in the spring of 1911, and later determined that the Commissioner of Immigration for Western Canada had offered the medical inspector a fee for every Black he rejected. Late in April, Jones was in Washington to discuss the issue with Assistant Secretary of State Wilson, and to present a memorandum from Winnipeg Immigration officials saying

Canada might bar Blacks because they could not adapt to the climate and therefore were liable to become public charges. Since the United States had itself banned Asian immigration it had little room to manoeuvre. Given the already strained state of Canadian-American relations, the American State Department did not wish to pursue the matter. In addition, Washington's inability and reluctance to aid Black Americans at home was implied by the influential New York *Times* when it commented on the Oklahoma migration and Canada's reaction to it. In its words,

> it is necessary to consider the facts as well as the opinions, and with a certain sentiment of toleration and humility. It is difficult to take any high view regarding the inhospitality of Canadians, both citizens and officials, toward `nationals' who are fleeing from equal intolerance at home, and ill-treatment at the hands of both neighbors and legislators.[44]

Canada still faced the problem of how to stop the Oklahoma Blacks from coming north. The most expedient answer, as the Winnipeg memorandum indicated, was simply to bar them, and that approach had already been suggested to Oliver. It had also been proposed by the Calgary *Herald*, whose Ottawa correspondent had noted that Section 38, sub-section "c" of the Immigration Act of 1910 gave the government the power, with an order-in-council, to exclude for a period, or permanently, any race deemed unsuitable for the climate. There was a problem with this approach; the distinct possibility that it would deter white Americans from heading north once it was publicized. Indeed, Poynter Standly of the Canadian Pacific Railway Colonization Department in Chicago had written to Oliver on April 28 to complain that newspaper reports citing this argument had already stopped some whites from migrating. This did not stop the Minister of the Interior and on May 31, 1911 he sent a recommendation to the cabinet for an order-in-council barring Blacks from entering Canada for a period of one year.[45]

The federal Cabinet passed the order on August 12, 1911. The order stated, in part,

> For a period of one year from and after the date hereof the landing in Canada shall be and the same is prohibited of any immigrants belonging to the Negro race, which race is deemed unsuitable to the climate and requirements of Canada.[46]

The order was never implemented, however. It was repealed on October 5, 1911 on the pretext that the Minister of the Interior was not present when it had been passed.[47] The fact that the original was passed at all indicates the

CANADA WILL BAR THE NEGRO OUT

Official Notice Given by Dominion to United States Consul

UNFITTED FOR HEALTHY CLIMATE

The Action of Dominion Leading to Conference in Washington

27/4/11 — *Albertan*

Washington, D.C., April 26. — The plans of the Dominion of Canada to adopt restrictions against the entering of their country by American negroes was the subject of a conference today between Assistant Secretary of State Wilson and John E. Jones, consul general of the U. S. at Winnipeg. Mr. Jones presented a memorandum from the Canadian immigration authorities indicating that the American negro may be barred on the ground that he could not become adapted to the rigorous northern climate and consequently might become a public charge. Such action is authorized by the Immigration act of Canada.

Most of the recent negro immigrants to the Dominion have gone from Oklahoma into the Peace River territory. Many more negroes, attracted by the liberal land inducement of Canada, it is reported, are about to start for the northern border.

Newspaper article printed in the *Albertan*, April 27, 1911, regarding the Washington meeting between John E. Jones and Huntington Wilson. The text reads, "The plans of the Dominion of Canada to adopt restrictions against the entering of their country by American negroes was the subject of a conference today between Assistant Secretary of State Wilson and John E. Jones, consul general of the U.S. at Winnipeg. Mr. Jones presented a memorandum from the Canadian immigration authorities indicating that the American negro may be barred on the ground that he could not become adapted to the rigorous northern climate and consequently might become a public charge. Such action is authorized by the Immigration act of Canada.

"Most of the recent negro immigrants to the Dominion have gone from Oklahoma into the Peace River territory. Many more negroes, attracted by the liberal land inducement of Canada, it is reported, are about to start for the northern border" (Courtesy of the Glenbow Archives/NA-3556-3b).

depth of Canadian feeling on the Black immigration issue. This incident also underlines the intensity of the pressure emanating from the Canadian Plains to put a halt to the Black immigration.

The chronology of events involving the order-in-council indicates that it was a "pocket order," to be used if the federal government's scheme to stop the migration at its source proved ineffective. In fact, the plan proved to be successful. At some point in April or May 1911, the federal authorities sent the first of two agents to Oklahoma to try to stem the Black tide. His work was successful, and Canada decided to send a second agent, a Black doctor from Chicago, in June 1911. The Black doctor's efforts proved to be particularly effective, especially when coupled with the negative publicity regarding Canada's reception of their kinsmen which appeared in the Black Oklahoma press.[48]

The reaction to the Black Oklahoma immigration to the Canadian Plains was unique, and is not explained by the theory of nativism. As a general theory nativism has been useful in beginning to understand the general negative response to many immigrant groups. Yet its strength as a general theory is also its weakness as a means of assessing the reactions to particular groups because it does not explain the origins of such attitudes, how they were transmitted, or why the reaction to some groups was stronger than to others.

Nativism does not account for the prejudice brought to the Canadian Plains by immigrants. The dominant groups which had settled in the area had well developed views of Blacks before the Oklahomans arrived. Nor does nativism account for the way in which this prejudice was confirmed, and spread by the prairie press which portrayed Blacks in a racist manner. The coverage of Black immigration in western journals reinforced this prejudice, and insured that when Blacks stepped down from the immigrant cars they were greeted by a virulent racism unlike that experienced by any other group of settlers. The intensity of the emotion generated against the Blacks was out of all proportion to their relatively small numbers. The reaction on the Canadian Plains was also tinged with a sexual dimension not found in the reaction to other groups. In addition, prior to World War I no other group had an order-in-council passed to keep them out; even orientals were allowed to enter provided they paid a head tax. The response to the Blacks was plain racism.

Notes

This article first appeared in *Prairie Forum* 10, no. 2 (1985) 365–82.

1. For example, Howard Palmer (ed.), *Immigration and the Rise of Multiculturalism* (Toronto: Copp Clark, 1975); W. Peter Ward, *White Canada Forever: Popular Attitudes and Public Policy Toward Orientals in British Columbia* (Montreal: McGill-Queen's University Press,

1978); and Howard Palmer, *Patterns of Prejudice: A History of Nativism in Alberta* (Toronto: McClelland and Stewart, 1982).

2. Palmer, *Patterns of Prejudice*, 7. This book also contains the most complete discussion of the nativist theory, as it has been applied to western Canada (see pp. 5–15).

3. There are at least three approaches which need to be tested. Given Canada's less nationalist traditions, a comparative study with the United States is overdue, and is likely to reveal the American bias of the nativist theory. A Marxian analysis would also be useful although, given the left's traditional emphasis on economic factors, there may be problems in explaining the virulence of the reactions to immigrants during a period of prosperity such as the settlement era. Finally, it would be interesting to apply to Canada the theory advanced by Charles Herbert Stember in *Sexual Racism: The Emotional Barrier to an Integrated Society* (New York: Harper and Row, Colophon Books, 1976).

4. It would appear that there were between 1,000 and 1,500 Black immigrants. This estimate is based upon the 1921 Census which showed 1,444 Blacks living in Alberta and Saskatchewan. Canada, *Census of Canada, 1921*, vol. 1, *Population*, 355.

5. An excellent analysis of the pre-contact ideas, and the English encounter with Africa is found in Winthrop D. Jordan, *White Over Black: American Attitudes Toward the Negro 1550–1812* (Baltimore: Penguin Books, 1969), 3–43.

6. *The Times*, November 13, 1865. Two students of British racial thought have both argued that the Jamaican Rebellion had a major effect upon the development of Victorian racial attitudes. See Christine Bolt, *Victorian Attitudes to Race* (London: Routledge and Kegan Paul, 1971), 75–76; and James Walvin, *Black and White: The Negro and English Society 1555–1945* (London: Penguin Press, 1973), 172.

7. The extensive literature on American racial attitudes is too long for citation here. An excellent starting point for an examination of this question is the aforementioned Jordan, *White Over Black*. Of particular interest, because it deals with attitudes in an area which later produced many white American emigrants to the Canadian Plains, is Eugene H. Berwanger, *The Frontier Against Slavery: Western Anti-Negro Prejudice and the Slavery Extension Controversy* (Urbana, Illinois: University of Illinois Press, 1967, 1971).

That some white Americans thought of the Canadian Plains as refuge from contact with blacks was revealed to me in a private conversation with a Saskatchewan homesteader who had come north with his parents after the turn of the century. He claimed his father had said the reason they left Iowa was "to get away from the cyclones and the niggers."

8. The literature on Black Canadians is not extensive, but it is growing. The standard is Robin Winks, *The Blacks in Canada: A History* (New Haven: Yale University Press, 1971). Also see, Frances Henry, *Forgotten Canadians: The Blacks of Nova Scotia* (Don Mills, ON: Longman, 1973); Donald H. Clairmont and Dennis W. Magill, *Africville: The Life and Death of a Canadian Black Community* (Toronto: McClelland and Stewart, 1974); Headly Tulloch, *Black Canadians: A Long Line of Fighters* (Toronto: NC Press, 1975); Crawford Killian, *Go Do Some Great Thing: The Black Pioneers of British Columbia* (Vancouver: Douglas and McIntyre, 1978); and Daniel G. Hill, *The Freedom-Seekers: Blacks in Early Canada* (Agincourt, Ontario: Book Society of Canada, 1981). A particularly useful recent addition to this list is James W. St. G. Walker, *A History of Blacks in Canada: A Study Guide for Teachers and Students* (Ottawa: Minister of State for Multiculturalism, 1980). See Walker, *History of Blacks*, 110 and 114 for the Ontario and Nova Scotia school segregation laws.

9. Library and Archives Canada (LAC), Department of the Interior, Immigration Files, RG 76, vols. 192–193, file 72552, part 1 (microfilm), letter to P.H. Burton from Lynwoode Pereira, May 8, 1899; letter to J.S. Crawford from L. Pereira, 23 January 1899; letter to

Frank Pedley from W.H. Williscraft, August 11, 1902; letter to W.H. Williscraft from L.M. Fortier, August 14, 1902.

10. Harold Troper, *Only Farmers Need Apply: Official Canadian Government Encouragement of Immigration from the United States 1896–1911* (Toronto: Griffen House, 1972) is the best account of Canada's attempt to lure American farmers northward. Troper argues, however, that no advertising was submitted to the Black press (124), and that because of their high illiteracy rate Blacks had no way of becoming informed about Canada (123).

The existence of Canadian advertisements in Black newspapers refutes the first claim. It is possible that Canadian officials were not aware of these advertisements, particularly if they contracted through a press service. As for the claim of Black illiteracy, Blacks in Oklahoma had a rate of only 12.4% by 1920. In any case, it takes only one literate person to read a paper to a group of illiterates, and once word of a movement is started it spreads rapidly.

For examples of Canadian advertisements in Black newspapers see, Boley *Beacon*, February 20, 1908, March 19, 1908; Clearview *Patriarch*, March 2, 1911, May 18, 1911; Muskogee *Cimeter*, January 8, 1909, February 4, 1910, December 2, 1911; Boley *Progress*, March 16, 1905, October 12, 1905, January 18, 1906, March 11, 1909, January 13, 1910. On Black literacy see Lerone Bennett. Jr., *Before the Mayflower: A History of the Negro in America, 1619–1961*, revised ed. (Baltimore: Penguin Books, 1961, 1964), 240; and *Fourteenth Census of the United States Taken in the Year 1920*, 11 vols. (Washington: Government Printing Office, 1922), vol. 3, *Population*, 814.

11. Saskatchewan Archives Board (SAB), Saskatoon, Homestead Files, files no. 974641, 932470, 932469, 86519A.

12. See R. Bruce Shepard, "Black Migration as a Response to Repression: The Background Factors and Migration of Oklahoma Blacks to Western Canada 1905–1912, As a Case Study" (MA thesis, University of Saskatchewan, Saskatoon, 1976), Chapters 2 and 3 for the background to these developments.

13. Glenbow-Alberta Institute, Calgary, Alberta, F.F. Parkinson File, Interview with Tony Payne by F.F. Parkinson, March 1963. SAB, Homestead Files, files no. 2244587, 1658268, 1977533. A number of other Black Maidstone settlers arrived during this "Jim Crow" period, but since they did not list a last place of residence it is difficult to determine if they started their trek in Oklahoma. Given the preponderance of Oklahoma Black settlers, however, the odds are that they too were from that state. See files no. 2134943, 1478445, 1544822.

14. Stewart Grow, "The Blacks of Amber Valley—Negro Pioneering in Northern Alberta," *Canadian Ethnic Studies* 6 (1974): 17–38; Calgary *Albertan*, April 24, 1911; Winnipeg *Manitoba Free Press*, April 27, 1911.

15. Kansas City *Journal*, n.d., reprinted in the Guthrie *Oklahoma Guide*, April 20, 1911.

16. For contemporary examples see, Winnipeg *Tribune*, April 3, 22, 1911; Winnipeg *Manitoba Free Press*, January 8, 1910, March 4, 1911; Regina *Leader*, March 27, 1911, April 8, 1911; Edmonton *Journal*, April 17, 1911, May 10, 1911; Calgary *Herald*, April 1, 1911, April 4, 1911; and the Calgary *Eye Opener*, June 18, 1910, and February 11, 1911.

17. Edmonton *Capital*, April 13, 16, 1910.

18. LAC, Immigration Files, part 1, Unanimous Resolution of the Edmonton Board of Trade passed at the monthly meeting held on April 12, 1910.

19. Shepard, "Black Migration," 95–97; Emerson *Journal*, March 24, 1911.

20. Winnipeg *Tribune*, March 22, 1911; Saskatoon *The Phoenix*, March 23, 24, 1911; Regina *Morning Leader*, March 24, 1911; Lloydminster *Times*, March 30, 1911; Edmonton *Journal*, March 24, 1911; Edmonton *Daily Bulletin*, March 25, 1911; Calgary, *Alberta Herald*, March

24, 25, 1911; Glenbow-Alberta Institute, Calgary, Negroes in Alberta File, newspaper clipping, Calgary *Albertan*, March 24, 1911; Lethbridge, *Alberta Daily Herald*, March 22, 1911; Winnipeg *Manitoba Free Press*, March 27, 1911.

21. Winnipeg *Manitoba Free Press*, March 27, 1911.

22. Ibid., March 31, 1911.

23. Edmonton *Journal*, March 25, 1911.

24. Ibid., March 27, 1911.

25. Calgary *Herald*, March 25, 1911.

26. LAC, Immigration Files, part 3, letter to Frank Oliver from F.T. Fisher, March 31, 1911.

27. Ibid., letter and petition to Frank Oliver from Mrs. A. Knight, March 21, 1911.

28. Edmonton *Journal*, March 30, 1911.

29. Ibid., April 5, 6, 1911. Glenbow-Alberta Institute, Negroes in Alberta File, Calgary *Albertan*, April 5, 1911.

30. Glenbow-Alberta Institute, Negroes in Alberta File, Calgary *Albertan*, April 5, 1911. Calgary *Albertan*, n.d., reprinted in the Edmonton *Journal*, April 8, 1911. Calgary *Herald*, April 5, 1911.

31. Lethbridge *Daily Herald*, April 11, 1911. The *Daily News*'s editorial is contained in Bower's reply to it.

32. Saskatoon *The Phoenix*, April 5, 1911; Regina *Morning Leader*, April 5, 1911; Edmonton *Daily Bulletin*, April 7, 1911.

33. Calgary *Herald*, April 6, 1911.

34. LAC, Immigration Files, part 3, letter to the Immigration Branch from Fritz Freidrichs, April 12, 1911; Edmonton *Daily Bulletin*, April 13, 1911; Edmonton *Journal*, April 13, 1911.

35. Edmonton *Journal*, April 8, 1911.

36. LAC, Immigration Files, part 3, Petition from Residents of Edmonton and Strathcona, April 18, 1911; Edmonton *Journal*, April 19, 1911.

37. Edmonton *Journal*, April 22, 24, 25, 26, 1911.

38. Edmonton *Daily Bulletin*, April 27, 1911. John Edwards, "History of the Colored Colony of Amber Valley," December 21, 1970 (unpublished paper in the author's possession), 3. Troper, *Only Farmers Need Apply*, 138–39. Troper notes that Edmonton's population in 1911 was 24,882.

39. LAC, Immigration Files, parts 3 and 4, Resolutions forwarded to Frank Oliver from the Fort Saskatchewan, April 28, 1911; Morinville, April 29, 1911; Strathcona, May 3, 1911; and Yorkton, May 1, 1911, Boards of Trade; letter to Frank Oliver from Francis C. Clare, April 29, 1911; letter to Frank Oliver from J.M. Liddell, April 29, 1911; petition to Frank Oliver from the Edmonton Builders Exchange, May 4, 1911; letter to Frank Oliver from A.I. Sawley, April 17, 1911. Glenbow-Alberta Institute, Negroes in Alberta File, Calgary *Albertan*, May 20, 1911. Saskatoon *The Phoenix*, April 26, 1911. Winnipeg *Tribune*, April 19, 1911.

40. Saskatoon *The Phoenix*, April 28, 1911, May 6, 8, 1911.

41. Edmonton *Journal*, April 22, 1911.

42. LAC, Immigration Files, part 3, letter to Frank Oliver from Arthur Fortin, April 5, 1911; part 4. newspaper clipping, Winnipeg *Der Nordwesten*, April 26, 1911:
"[W]e would like to add that the numerous instances of lynch law in the southern states, about which we read almost daily and which deal almost exclusively with crimes likely each committed by Negroes, these instances should convince us, apart from other reasons, how undesirable such an increase is to our population. It would be wished that other public corporate bodies like the Board of Trade join in the protest."

43. Canada, House of Commons, *Debates*, 1910–11, 3: cols. 4470–71, March 2, 1911; 4: cols. 5941–48, March 23, 1911; 4: cols. 6523–28, April 3, 1911; 5: cols. 8125–28, May 1, 1911. Ernest J. Chambers (ed.), *The Canadian Parliamentary Guide, 1910* (Ottawa: Mortimer Co. Ltd., 1910), 105–06, 162 and 168. Also see Robin W. Winks, *The Blacks in Canada: A History*, 306–07.

44. Winks, *Blacks in Canada*, 301–11. New York *Times*, April 2, 1911.

45. LAC, Immigration Files, part 3, letter to F. Oliver from Poynter Standly, April 28, 1911; part 4, memo to Frank Oliver from W.D. Scott, March 23, 1911; Order-in-Council Recommendation, to the Governor-General from F. Oliver, May 21, 1911. Calgary *Herald*, April 17, 1911. Canada, *Statutes of Canada*, 9-10 Edward VII, Chapter 27, An Act Respecting Immigration, May 4, 1910, Sec. 38, sub-sec. "c". Also see Troper, *Only Farmers Need Apply*, 140.

46. LAC, Orders-in-Council, RG 2/1, vol. 269, no. 1324, August 12, 1911.

47. Ibid., vol. 772, no. 2378, October 5, 1911.

48. R. Bruce Shepard, "Diplomatic Racism: The Canadian Government and Black Migration from Oklahoma, 1905–1912," *Great Plains Quarterly* 3, no. 1 (Winter 1983): 5–16.

19.   The Irish in Saskatchewan, 1850–1930: A Study of Intergenerational Ethnicity

Michael Cottrell

More than any other European nation, Ireland in the 19th and 20th centuries was characterized by emigration. Between 1800 and 1920 over eight million people departed the country for a variety of destinations including Great Britain, the United States, Canada, Australia, New Zealand and South Africa.[1] This massive out migration gave birth to a populous and far-flung diaspora which by 1900 numbered over 50 million and virtually circled the globe. The timing of this exodus was arguably as significant as its volume, for the fact that large-scale Irish emigration coincided with the opening up of many of these countries to European settlement ensured that the Irish had an enormous influence on their subsequent development. As virtual pioneers of the ethnic experience in many neo-European settler societies, it is therefore not surprising that the Irish have been a source of great fascination for ethnic historians.[2] To date, however, most studies of the Irish diaspora, including its Canadian dimension, have tended to dwell on its most visible elements. Generally this has resulted in a focus on first generation emigrants who arrived at their destination during periods of heavy Irish emigration and who settled in areas where Irish immigrants constituted a significant proportion of the population. Thus, much of what we know about the Irish experience in Canada refers to those who settled in the eastern provinces roughly between 1815 and Confederation.[3] Regarding their children and grandchildren, or Irish emigrants who came later and who settled in other regions of the country, little is known.

The following study of the Irish in Saskatchewan between 1850 and 1930 seeks to expand the temporal and geographic focus of analysis of the Irish diaspora in Canada. Although no mass movement of emigrants from Ireland to the prairie provinces occurred, individual Irish people played key roles in the westward expansion of the Canadian frontier and the transformation of the West into a settled agricultural society in the late-19th and early-20th centuries. Furthermore, because many of the early settlers in Saskatchewan were Canadians of Irish origin, who continued the mixing of Irish traditions into the new prairie society, examining their migration westwards facilitates an analysis of Irish ethnicity in Canada as a dynamic, multigenerational phenomenon. In particular, by focussing on the development of the Orange Order and the Roman Catholic Church in Saskatchewan, two of the most important institutions transported by earlier Irish immigrants to British North America and subsequently brought West by their descendants, this study highlights the continuing influence of Irish immigrant culture on the development of Canadian society well into the 20th century.

Unlike French Canadians and Scots, the Irish showed little interest in the fur trade which shaped the development of the West in the first two centuries after contact. However, in the momentous changes which occurred after 1850 a number of Irish played prominent roles. In 1857 Captain John Palliser, a member of a wealthy Anglo-Irish family from County Waterford, persuaded the Royal Geographic Society to sponsor a scientific expedition through Rupert's Land. Published in 1862, *Palliser's Report* confirmed the findings of contemporaries such as Henry Youle Hind that large parts of the Prairies, especially the Red and Saskatchewan River valleys, were suitable for agricultural settlement. These findings did much to change the prevailing image of the Prairies from that of a frozen wasteland to a potential agricultural Eden, and began a groundswell of enthusiasm for the annexation of the West by the British North American provinces. A vocal proponent of this western expansion was Millington Henry Synge, cousin of the famous Irish playwright, who served as subaltern in the Royal Engineers stationed in Ottawa in the 1850s. Synge was one of the first to propose railway construction as a vehicle for western development, as a mechanism for integrating the Prairies with the eastern provinces, and ultimately as a means of linking all of British North America from the Atlantic to the Pacific under the British flag.[4]

Palliser's and Synge's vision of western colonization became a reality with the purchase of Rupert's Land by the Canadian government in 1869 and the completion of the Canadian Pacific Railway in 1885, a project in which Irish labourers played no small role. The resulting transformation of the northern Prairies into a commercial agricultural society opened up tremendous opportunities for settlers, but also caused enormous dislocation to the aboriginal peoples of the area. After signing treaties with the federal government in the 1870s, the Plains nations were confined to reserves and subjected to an aggressive *civilization* policy which sought to transform them from nomadic hunters to sedentary, Christian agriculturalists. In this process, too, the Irish were directly involved, and the work of Father Constantine Scollen was a significant case in point. Born in Ireland in 1841, Scollen joined the Oblate Order and came to Canada in 1862 to the mission at St. Albert. There he worked with Cree and Blackfoot people, learned the Cree language and assisted the famous missionary Father Lacombe in compiling a Cree grammar and dictionary. Present at the negotiations of Treaties 6 and 7, Scollen used what influence he possessed to persuade the chiefs to sign the treaties and continued to work among the Plains nations until 1885. The missionary priest had a great fascination with traditional cultural practices, and he worked tirelessly to protect Native people from unscrupulous traders and to ensure that the government fulfilled its treaty promises. Ultimately, however, he was committed to the destruction of the culture with which he sympathized, and he may be seen as an agent of the westward march of Euro-Canadian culture and in particular the global expansion of Roman Catholicism which was one of the main spiritual accomplishments of the Irish diaspora.[5]

No discussion of Irish involvement in the opening of the West would be complete without mention of Clifford Sifton. Born in Ontario to an Irish immigrant family from County Tipperary, Sifton moved to Winnipeg in the 1870s and became one of the leading spokesmen for western interests. As minister of the Interior in the Laurier government from 1896 to 1905, Sifton revitalized the somnambulant Immigration Department and launched a massive advertising campaign in Britain, the United States and Europe. Determined to attract settlers who were familiar with the climatic and agricultural conditions encountered on the Prairies, he showed particular interest in those he dubbed the *Sheepskin People* from Central and Eastern Europe. One of the most effective Interior ministers in the history of the department, Sifton deserves much of the credit for the great immigration boom which brought close to a million settlers to the Prairies in the late-19th and early-20th centuries.[6]

Before Sifton assumed control of the Immigration Department, a number of efforts to promote prairie settlement had been made by the federal government. Parcels of land and assisted passage were offered to preferred groups and resulted in bloc settlements of various nationalities. One such scheme envisaged the establishment of an Irish colony in the North-West under the close supervision of the Roman Catholic Church. Proposed by Prime Minister Macdonald as part of a Conservative campaign to win Irish votes in Ontario in the early 1880s, it was also endorsed by the Irish-born bishop of Toronto, John Joseph Lynch.[7] Despite their backing, however, the scheme never materialized, nor did a subsequent proposal by Canadian Pacific Railway president George Stephen to settle 10,000 Irish tenant farmers along the newly constructed railway.[8] These early failures had significant long term consequences for the Irish diaspora. The large flow of emigrants from Ireland in the late-19th and early-20th centuries continued primarily to the United States and Great Britain and only a very small percentage of the approximately 1.5 million people who left Ireland in this period settled in the Canadian West.[9] The arrival of these immigrants and the migration of Irish-born and Irish-origin settlers from eastern Canada to the Prairies was therefore a largely individualistic and unassisted enterprise, in contrast to the collective experience of groups such as the Ukrainians, Hutterites, French Canadians and Scottish crofters.[10] Few large Irish bloc settlements emerged on the Prairies and, at least demographically, the impact of the Irish was far less than it had been in the earlier settlement of eastern Canada.

Table 1. Irish in Saskatchewan, 1901–31

Year	Total Population	Irish Origin	Irish % of Saskatchewan Population	Saskatchewan % of Canadian Irish
1901	91,279	10,644	11.7	1.1
1911	492,432	58,069	11.8	5.4
1921	757,510	84,786	11.2	7.7
1931	921,785	104,096	11.3	8.5

Nevertheless, as the figures in Table 1 indicate, the Irish presence in what became Saskatchewan was both significant and visible. In 1881 people of Irish origin constituted close to half of the small non-Native population of the North-West Territories; and in 1891 there were almost 2,000 Irish-born settlers in the area. Ten years later the total Irish-origin population numbered over 10,500. In 1911, when Saskatchewan was included in the Canadian census as a province for the first time, the Irish were a significant element within the emerging provincial mosaic. Out of a total provincial population of 492,000, just over 58,000, or approximately 12% of the population, claimed Irish origin, and these constituted an extremely diverse cohort. About 10% were born in Ireland, the majority of whom were young single men, predominantly from the northeastern province of Ulster.[11] The bulk of the Irish-origin population, more than 70%, came from eastern Canada, with Ontario being the single greatest source, followed by the Maritimes. The remainder of the Irish-origin population came from the United States. In fact almost one-quarter of the Americans who moved north during the settlement of the Canadian Prairies were either Irish born or of Irish origin.[12]

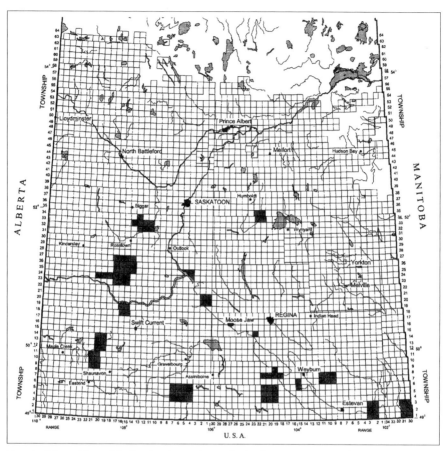

Map 1. Adapted from T.D. Regehr, *Remembering Saskatchewan: A History of Rural Saskatchewan* (Saskatoon: University of Saskatchewan Extension Division, 1979), with permission of the author. Concentrations of Irish settlement are shown in black.

Although Irish settlers were scattered throughout the population, a tendency toward geographic propinquity was apparent in the development of a number of settlements with an Irish component (see Map 1). It is apparent from the map that by 1911 more than 10 distinct Irish concentrations had emerged in different parts of the province; and as with all other nationalities, Irish nostalgia was reflected in their choice of place names. Communities such as Limerick, Roscommon, D'Arcy, McGee, Shamrock, Sinnett, Glasnevin, Kilronan, Mullingar, Clonfert, Lurgan and Erinferry were a testament to the early presence of the Irish in these areas and to their determination to stake their claim to the territory by establishing a continuity between the world that they left, however remotely, and their new homes.[13]

The arrival of these people in Saskatchewan represented another, and in some cases final, stage in the great spread of the Irish diaspora westward across North America in the 19th and 20th centuries. Typical of most early settlers, the Irish who came to Saskatchewan were motivated primarily by the desire to own land. In 1911 more than two-thirds of the Irish-origin population lived in rural Saskatchewan, and the vast majority of these were either homesteaders or were working as farm labourers to accumulate the resources necessary to begin homesteading. For those who came directly from Ireland the availability of 160 acres for $10 under the Homestead Act offered the prospect of more land than could ever be realistically aspired to at home. It also provided an opportunity to escape the bitter sectarianism and oppressive landlord system in Ireland. As Andrew Lowry from County Donegal confided to a reporter from the *Regina Leader* upon his arrival in 1883:

> Between taxes and rack rent there is no living for the farmers now in Ireland [while here] there is a hope and go and eagerness about the people ... no bowing and scraping, no "yer honour sir" ... no landlords to fight and every man stands on the same great platform of a broad equality.[14]

For the many more who came from eastern Canada or the United States, the opening of the Canadian Prairies came at an opportune time for it coincided with the closing of the agricultural frontier in Ontario, the Maritimes and the American Midwest. Typically undertaken as part of an extended family strategy, migration to Saskatchewan held out the prospect of commercial expansion while also maintaining the integrity of the family unit.

The experience of Irish settlers in Saskatchewan was therefore overwhelmingly a homesteading one, but there was nevertheless tremendous diversity within that experience. Some, like the Milligans, a multigenerational family which came from Ontario and homesteaded in Wadena, north of Qu'Appelle in 1881, enjoyed steady success on the original and adjoining homesteads. Because of the sheer size and early arrival of their family, the Milligans became the nucleus of the local community. The original homestead doubled as a trading post, post office, church, and briefly a North-West Mounted Police detachment. The Milligans helped establish the first school and Anglican church, operated a carting business and had the honour of having a local creek and bridge named after them.[15] Others were not so fortunate. Pioneer society was characterized by a high degree of mobility and uncertainty, where success and stability, if achieved at all, frequently came only after numerous attempts and repeated failures. More typical of this was the experience of the Barnes family, who emigrated from Belfast to

A highway sign indicating the location of Shamrock, a small village in southern Saskatchewan (population 20 in 2006). Although Irish settlers in the district were few, their early arrival is reflected in the name of the community (Courtesy of David McLennan/University of Regina).

Toronto in 1882 and homesteaded in the File Hills area in 1892. Their first effort was a complete failure and the family embarked on a mobile quest for paid employment over the next 10 years which took them through Lebret, Indian Head and Regina. In 1907 they homesteaded again in the Rosetown area and this time, with the support of married children on adjoining quarter sections, their enterprise flourished. All three farms were broken and cultivated within five years and as the area filled up with settlers Tom and Agnes Barnes became pillars of their community.[16]

Few of the Irish who came to Saskatchewan were as fortunate as James Andrew McBride, born in County Kerry in 1861. When he was a child his family moved to Iowa City and in the mid-1890s James and his brother-in-law joined the migration north to homestead near Weyburn. His ambitions extended far beyond the quarter section, however, and he shortly established the Weyburn Lumber and Elevator Company with his brother-in-law. McBride then built the Golden West Grain Company, eventually operating 17 elevators in southern Saskatchewan. In 1917 he purchased a seat on the Winnipeg Grain Exchange. In the early 1920s he branched into the retail trade, building 14 grocery stores and three bakeries in the Weyburn area. In the course of creating this empire, McBride became a major shareholder in the Weyburn Security Bank, president of the Weyburn Board of Trade,

James Andrew McBride (1861–1940) (Courtesy of the Saskatchewan Archives Board/R-A20705).

alderman on the Weyburn City Council, and founder of the Weyburn chapter of the Knights of Columbus.[17]

On the other end of the scale was Mike McGinley who came to Regina from Ireland in the early 1900s. A young, single man, he homesteaded in the Saltburn district about 1912 and like many settlers he worked at various labouring jobs to support his farm. The winter of 1920 saw him employed by the Prince Albert Lumber Company, cutting trees near The Pas. He was killed by a falling tree just after Christmas and was buried in an unmarked grave in the Manitoba bush.[18] Different again were the experiences of three young people from Northern Ireland who arrived together in Prince Albert on June 27, 1928. One of them, whose name is not remembered, worked on a farm near Shellbrook for three days and promptly returned to Ireland. The other two, Patrick Grimes and Elizabeth Vauls, one a Catholic and one a Protestant, arrived as sweethearts and married shortly after. A mechanic and avid soccer player, Patrick Grimes was never a day out of work in a succession of garages in Prince Albert. He and his wife lived to see four generations of Grimes, and the couple resided in the same house in Prince Albert until their deaths in the mid-1990s. At least some members of the Grimes family still embrace Ireland as part of their identity.[19]

The Irish who settled in Saskatchewan thus experienced a great variety of fortunes and were to be found in virtually every walk of life. Most were homesteaders, but people of Irish origin were also found in the labouring and servant classes; they were prominent in the hotel and saloon business; many joined the North-West Mounted Police; they were conspicuous among the Christian clergy, the teaching and legal professions, real estate and insurance sales and, later, in the medical professions. Some were extraordinarily successful while others were complete failures. For the majority, great hardships had to be endured before even modest success was achieved.[20] Nevertheless, it is also clear that as a collectivity, people of Irish origin enjoyed a number of significant advantages which made their adjustment to the Prairies easier than for many other groups. Although there are references to the occasional speakers of Irish Gaelic, the vast majority who came from Ireland, and all who came from eastern Canada and the United States, spoke English as their first language. As part of the linguistic mainstream, no barriers thus existed to their immediate participation in the business, social or political spheres when they arrived on the Prairies. Indeed, Irish settlers in Saskatchewan, both Protestant and Catholic, became ardent champions of the primacy of the English language in the new province. Regardless of where they came from, the Irish were also familiar with the British political, legal and educational systems, and the bureaucratic ethos which governed them. When compared with the challenges faced by groups such as the Ukrainians, Russians or Hungarians, who had to learn a new language and familiarize themselves with a completely alien system, it must be said that the Irish experience was far less traumatic.[21] The timing of their arrival was also crucial, for in many areas of Saskatchewan the Irish were among the very first white settlers to establish themselves. These advantages serve to

Early Irish arrivals in what is now Saskatchewan were members of the Lemon family. They migrated from Ireland in the early 1880s and settled south of Fleming, North-West Territories. A wedding party is pictured here at a home built in 1894 for their oldest son John on the occasion of his marriage (Courtesy of the Saskatchewan Archives Board/R-A20448).

Nicholas Flood Davin (1840–1901) (Courtesy of the Saskatchewan Archives Board/R-A6665).

explain one of the striking features of the Irish experience, which was the pioneering role played by the men and women in community formation and the construction of public institutions in the province of Saskatchewan. Whether building schools or churches, organizing school boards or parish structures, or participating in rural and urban politics, the contributions of Irish settlers far exceeded their proportion of the provincial population.

Ireland's most prominent and indeed most controversial contribution to the early public life of Saskatchewan was undoubtedly Nicholas Flood Davin, founding editor of the *Regina Leader* and Conservative member of Parliament for Assiniboia West from 1887 to 1900. A passionate promoter of the interests of his adopted home, Davin frequently found himself at loggerheads with his own party's National Policy, which was unpopular in the West. He was also an advocate of minority education rights and women's suffrage. A respected journalist, writer and poet, he is credited with the first literary work to be written and published in the West. Blessed with eloquence and a quick wit, he was a popular public speaker—a perennial favourite at St. Patrick's Day events across the country—and his reputation as a bon vivant followed him from Toronto to Regina to Ottawa. However, his well-known fondness for alcohol and a long-term public affair with a Regina woman marked him as a man with deep character flaws. In 1900 Davin was defeated by Walter Scott, who would later become the first premier of Saskatchewan. With his political career apparently ended and his dreams of greatness unfulfilled, Davin fell into a severe depression and took his own life in a Winnipeg hotel room in October 1901.

Ironically, one of Davin's most enduring legacies in the West came from an obscure report on the education of aboriginals which he produced as part of a patronage appointment in 1879. Commissioned by the Department of the Interior to formulate policy in this area, the *Davin Report* recommended the establishment of residential and industrial schools which would not only impart academic and technical training but which would also facilitate the assimilation of aboriginal people into Euro-Canadian society by separating children from their parents' culture. This report became the blueprint for the residential school system which is now acknowledged to have inflicted tremendous damage on aboriginal people and their cultures. One wonders whether Davin, had he realized the long-term impact of his recommendations, would have been so cavalier in undertaking the project.

While Davin rose to become a member of the political elite, one who represented the interests of the West on the national stage, countless other Irish individuals made more modest but nevertheless vital contributions to the building of public institutions in the province. The O'Gorman family, who migrated from New Brunswick to the area around Macklin in 1905, were clearly blessed with great organizational and leadership skills. Attachment to the Roman Church was one of the major cultural values which the Catholic Irish brought West, and was obviously a priority for the O'Gormans. Their humble soddy was host to the first Catholic services in the area, usually provided once a month by itinerant priests, and in 1906 Thomas O'Gorman was the driving force behind the creation of St. Mary's parish. He organized the raising of funds, supervised the construction of the first Catholic church and secured a resident priest for the parish. His wife Mary was the founding president of St. Mary's Parish Catholic Benevolent Women's Association, a mutual assistance and charitable organization for Catholic families. The O'Gormans also took the lead in establishing the Bride School, and through their relatives in Ireland, secured the services of a young woman, Harriet Donnelly, as the first teacher in the school.[22]

The O'Gormans' concern with education was also typical of many Irish-origin settlers in Saskatchewan and was perhaps best exemplified by Edward Daniel Feehan. A third-generation Irish Catholic born in Prince Edward Island in 1891, Feehan came west to Regina in 1912 to become a high school principal. After various other administrative positions in Regina, he moved to Saskatoon in 1917 and served as supervising principal of the city's separate schools until 1945, and as superintendent of Catholic education in Saskatoon from 1945 to 1956. Feehan was active in the Knights of Columbus, served on the building committee of St. Mary's Church and hall, and was a founding member of the St. Mary's Credit Union. Among his many public accolades were the King George and Queen Elizabeth medals received in 1935 and 1957, and the naming of E.D. Feehan High School in his honour in 1967.[23]

That the Irish zeal for organizational activity was not monopolized by men is demonstrated by the record of Mrs. R.J. McAuslan. Originally from County Tyrone, the McAuslans came from Ontario in the early 1900s with a number of other Quakers from eastern Canada, Britain and Ireland to establish a Society of Friends colony in the Swarthmore district north of Unity. Mrs. McAuslan clearly had a powerful commitment to community service and the energy to match. Her numerous activities included membership in the Stoughton Church Committee, organist and Sunday School teacher, school trustee, president of the Women's Missionary Society, president of the Swarthmore and later the Saskatchewan Ladies Aid and Homemaker Society, and president of the Swarthmore Women Grain Growers' Association. For her outstanding service to her community which spanned more than 50 years, Mrs. McAuslan received many awards and commendations, including the King George V medal in 1937.[24]

Notable also among people of Irish origin in Saskatchewan was a strong commitment to the trade union movement. This tradition had deep roots in the agrarian secret societies formed to protect peasant rights in Ireland, and these combinations were then brought by Irish immigrants to many parts of the diaspora. An underdog mentality, an aversion to perceived exploitation and a determination to ensure that their rights were respected characterized many Irish emigrants and their descendants. This tradition was admirably upheld by Thomas Molloy, who came to Clark's Crossing with his Irish-born parents from Nova Scotia in the 1880s. Apprenticed to the printing trade in his teens, Molloy worked in the office of the *Regina Leader* and served as western correspondent for the *Montreal Daily Star*. His involvement with the labour movement began as a shop steward at the *Leader* office, and he quickly rose through the ranks to become president of the Regina Typographical Union in 1905. From there he worked to create an umbrella organization for the different unions in the city, and in 1907 he became founding president of the Regina Trades and Labour Council. In 1927 he was appointed Deputy Minister of Labour, holding this position throughout the bleak Depression period. A tough negotiator, Molloy is remembered to have frequently used whiskey as a bargaining strategy. One of the leading figures in the growth of organized labour in Saskatchewan, he was also an active member of the cooperative movement, helping to draft the first provincial credit union legislation in 1936.[25]

Countless other individual stories could be told, but the general pattern is obvious: a great many of the Irish who came to Saskatchewan came early; they were part of the linguistic majority; they were familiar with how the system operated; and most possessed the resources which presaged economic success. Indeed, while individual Irish people distinguished themselves, their collective impact on early prairie society was perhaps even more significant. Like all migrants the Irish brought to the West certain traditions, institutions, social patterns, and ideological orientations which for many had been tempered by one or two generations in North America. Because of the timing of their arrival and relatively privileged position, the Irish were extraordinarily successful in transferring their traditions to the West and mixing them into the rich mosaic of the emerging Saskatchewan society. Striking examples of this process are provided by the fortunes of two peculiarly Irish institutions—the Orange Order and the English-speaking Roman Catholic Church. Both of these had evolved over centuries in Ireland as expressions of the cultures of Irish Protestantism and Irish Catholicism, and when they emigrated, the Irish transported their religious and cultural differences virtually intact. Throughout the diaspora, these institutions encapsulated major parts of the two Irish identities and became vehicles for the inter-generational transmission of these identities in different parts of the world, including Saskatchewan. Indeed, the prominence which these institutions achieved in the province is perhaps the best evidence of the collective impact of the Irish on the early social, religious, political, and ideological development of Saskatchewan.

The Orange Order was born in the charged sectarian climate of Ulster in the late 18th century to defend the interests of Protestant settlers against perceived Catholic aggression. Taking its name and inspiration from King William of Orange, whose victory at the Battle of the Boyne in 1690 secured Protestant ascendancy in England and Ireland, Orange principles involved an uncompromising defence of the British Crown and Protestant hegemony in Ireland, and its most visible manifestation was, and still is, the annual July 12 parades commemorating the Boyne.[26] When Protestants began to leave Ireland in large numbers after the Napoleonic Wars, Orangeism was part of the culture which they transported and recreated in their new homes. The British North American provinces proved to be extremely fertile ground for its expansion, in part because the institution was ideally suited to the conditions and values of that frontier society. Throughout Ontario and the Maritimes, the Orange Lodge became central to the social life of many settler communities, frequently serving as a school, church and town hall and offering one of the few opportunities for socializing. Membership also afforded practical benefits in the form of mutual aid from a network of like-minded individuals which was often vital for survival in a harsh environment. The Orange Order also flourished in Canada because of its religious and ideological compatibility with the Loyalist ethos of the existing English-speaking population. The Order's uncompromising anti-Catholicism struck a chord in a community which viewed the French Canadian population of Quebec with suspicion and hostility, and its hyperloyalism dovetailed with British settlers' attachment to the monarchy. Thus the Orange Order became a powerful political force, especially in Ontario, and could count numerous mayors, members of Parliament and even prime ministers as members. Over time, also, it transcended its early ethnic roots and came to include people of English, Scottish and mainland European origin as well as Irish immigrants and their descendants within its ranks. Between 1860 and 1910 it is estimated that one-third of all adult English-speaking Canadian males belonged to the organization at some point in their lives.[27]

At Confederation, therefore, the Orange Order retained its Irish roots, icons and lexicon, but it had also become an integral part of Canadian society; and from this influential position it sought to articulate a vision of the Canadian future. For Orangemen Canada was British and Protestant, and they rejoiced in the belief that these attributes represented the highest advance of human civilization. They insisted that the rest of Canada be incorporated into this British Protestant community and they offered themselves as unrelenting defenders of that polity against all potential threats, whether from French Canadians, Roman Catholics, immigrants, republicans or others. In a sense the Orange Order was the quintessential Canadian institution because it maintained the solidarity of British Protestant Canadians at the local level, and linked the local communities into a larger constituency which was national, imperial and Protestant.[28] And it is not surprising that as Canadians migrated westwards after Confederation, Orangemen, with their long tradition as *Queen's frontiersmen*, were in the vanguard of that process.

The first Orange Lodge west of Ontario was established in Red River in 1870, and as increasing numbers of settlers arrived the Order experienced rapid growth. Between 1892 and 1908 the Order grew from 16 to 41 lodges in the province with a total membership of 1,424. By the early 1930s, when the Order reached the peak of its popularity, membership had grown to 68,000, belonging to 274 lodges.[29] In its composition the Order appealed primarily to Canadians of Irish and British origin and to immigrants from these areas. Irish-born Orangemen, especially from Ulster, were prominent among the early membership. The first grand master of the Grand Orange Lodge of the North-West Territories in 1892 was A.G. Hamilton from Moosomin, with W.J. Kernaghan from Prince Albert as grand secretary. Born in Counties Tyrone and Londonderry respectively, both spent about 10 years in Ontario before moving West. Kernaghan followed Hamilton as grand master in 1893 and served for two years in that capacity.[30] Lodge appeal was also strong

Orangemen's Day parade in Whitewood, Saskatchewan, July 12, 1912. The Loyal Orange Lodge in Whitewood was in existence as early as 1892, and ceased to function in 1947 (Courtesy of the Whitewood Museum).

among Protestant immigrants from Scandinavia, Germany and Holland. Notably, Protestant immigrants from the United States remained largely aloof from the organization.[31]

As had happened originally in Ireland and then in eastern Canada, the Orange Order in Saskatchewan evolved into a multifaceted institution which offered a variety of services to its members and to the larger society. It was at one and the same time a social and recreational club, a mutual assistance network, an educational and moral improvement society, a social welfare organization, a vehicle for the expression of religious and cultural values, and an ideological and political lobby group. For those who subscribed to its values, membership in the organization made very good sense. New arrivals in the province, whether from eastern Canada, Ireland or elsewhere, were provided access to familiar rituals, human contact, easy entry to the local community, and a wealth of practical assistance which was often the difference between success and failure when attempting to build a new life in Saskatchewan. Orangemen were sworn to support other members and this mutual aid extended to help in securing accommodation and employment, advice on the location and availability of good land, assistance in house construction, loaning tools and equipment, extra hands at harvest time, ensuring that families were assisted in the event of sickness or death, and an extensive life insurance policy for all members. Before the advent of radio and television and the widespread availability of automobiles, the Orange Lodge was vital to the social and recreational life of many communities. Weekly meetings were occasions where members could socialize free from family constraints, and larger activities provided welcome breaks from the isolation and hard work which characterized pioneer society. The high point of the Orange calendar, the *Glorious Twelfth*, became large communal events which brought together members and non-members, young and old, for a public holiday and colourful spectacle which fell conveniently between planting and harvesting.[32]

As well as providing practical assistance and extensive social and recreational opportunities, the Orange Order was dedicated to the moral and intellectual improvement of its membership and, by extension, of the larger society. A "high standard of moral excellence" was one of the prerequisites for acceptance, and members were expected to adhere to an exacting code of behaviour. Specifically, they were required to be "men of humane disposition, kind behaviours and enemies of all unchristian [sic] conduct ... desirous of propagating charity and good will ... with a hatred of cursing and swearing and taking the name of God in vain ... men prudent, temperate, sober and honest."[33] Since the Order appealed to a broad spectrum of the population, obviously not all were of sterling character, but given the amount of time devoted to disciplinary matters in meetings it is clear that most lodges had high standards for admittance and maintained an ongoing monitor on members' behaviour. The Order thus played a vital role in a raw frontier society with a surplus of males. By tempering the excesses of anti-social behaviour, the Orange Order was a positive socializing force in that it promoted values which on many levels enhanced self-restraint, cooperation and societal harmony.[34] One of the most enduring achievements of the Orange Order in Saskatchewan was the Orange Benevolent Home for orphans and young boys at Indian Head. Established in 1917, the orphanage provided refuge for countless thousands of young people in need of a home, and it is still in existence at this time.

In a similar vein, the Order sought to improve its membership through a variety of educational activities centred in the lodges. Religious instruction was obviously a priority, and the chaplain of each lodge was required to provide regular Bible readings and expositions to encourage the faith of members and to keep them abreast of various developments within the Protestant churches. Lodges were also required to maintain a library where books were circulated regularly and which also served as a reading room. In the days before public libraries, especially in rural areas, this was an extremely valuable service since it was often the only access that adults had to reading material. Lodges also attempted to keep members informed of current social developments by sponsoring public lectures on a broad variety of topics by visiting speakers, and the national Orange newspaper, the *Sentinel* provided an Orange perspective on regional, national and international affairs. It was not without some evidence therefore, that Orange leaders could boast that Saskatchewan lodges "produced some of the best informed minds to be found in the province, men in all ways prepared to play a leading role in whatever enterprise or pursuit they should settle on."[35]

As was to be expected given that Ulster was its spiritual birthplace and that there was a large Irish presence in its membership, the Orange Order in Saskatchewan evinced continuing interest in Irish affairs. Speeches delivered by Grand Masters at the annual provincial meetings provided a running commentary on Irish developments and an opportunity to affirm Orange principles. Opposition to Irish Home Rule was an article of faith for Orangemen both in Ireland and throughout the diaspora, and Orangemen in Saskatchewan stood firmly with their brothers on this issue.[36] "Ulster Protestantism was placed in Ireland," according to Grand Master Armstrong in 1916, "as the guardian of liberty and good government against the malignant encroachment of popery upon the lives, the faiths and the freedoms of British citizens," and his predecessor pledged unwavering support for the embattled minority of Ulster:

> Ulster's friends will not desert her in her hour of trial. Loyal hearts in Canada beat in unison with those in the Emerald Isle. Many in Saskatchewan have pledged their assistance and I can assure [you] that the help from the west will be of no mean proportion.[37]

Resistance to Home Rule was a rearguard action however, and in 1921 all of Ireland, with the exception of six counties in Ulster, became independent of the United Kingdom. While Orangemen in Saskatchewan denounced the "handing over of [Ireland] to a papal Parliament," they nevertheless rejoiced that Ulster at least had been saved for the Empire, and their brothers in the six counties were entreated to hold fast:

> If [Ulster] Protestants put their trust in God and follow the battle cry of our leader of old "No Surrender," they will prevail. Right and justice have conquered disloyalty, sedition, treason, arson, theft, murder and Ireland will become a bright and shining jewel in the British diadem of nations.[38]

The situation in Ireland thus assumed a continuing significance for the

Orange Order in Saskatchewan, but of much more immediate importance were local and national issues. As in Ireland and eastern Canada, the Orange Order in Saskatchewan was an exclusively Protestant organization devoted to the promotion of British and Protestant ideals, based on the conviction that these represented "liberty and freedom in the broadest sense."[39] Members were aware that their early arrival in the West and extensive organizational network gave them enormous influence in moulding the new society emerging on the Prairies, and like all charter groups, Orangemen sought to impose their own image on that society. The first Grand Master of the North-West Territories stressed the responsibilities and opportunities which faced the organization in the 1890s when he explained:

> We are engaged in laying the foundation for future genera-
> tions to build upon, may we make them truly Protestant …
> our primary duty is to make loyal British subjects of those
> who are making their homes in our midst and to maintain
> Protestant ascendancy.[40]

Over the next half century the Order remained true to these principles and developed into a powerful political pressure group which served as one of the most passionate champions of a British, Protestant Saskatchewan. In espousing these values, Orangemen responded with a suspicion which occasionally verged on intolerance towards those they perceived as a threat. Not surprisingly, the most prominent challenge was believed to come from Roman Catholics, and Saskatchewan Orangemen were as suspicious of Catholicism as had been their Irish and eastern Canadian forebears. In particular, the Order saw the separate school system as part of a Catholic conspiracy to enhance its own special privileges and to undermine the public school system. Insisting that "one public school for all is sound doctrine on this continent because it inculcates a common morality and guarantees religious freedom," Orangemen were outraged when the Autonomy Bills that established the new province in 1905 contained provisions for publicly funded separate schools in Saskatchewan.[41] And this began a debate over education which developed into one of the most poisonous political issues in Saskatchewan over the next 30 years.[42]

The virulence of this debate stemmed in part from the fact that it had implications which went far beyond merely how children were educated. Since many of the Roman Catholics during the early settlement period were French Canadians, and separate schools allowed for French as a language of instruction, it was easy to view such schools as vehicles for the extension of French linguistic rights in the new province. In the eyes of one Orange spokesman, "Separate Schools were part of an attempt by our French fellow citizens to establish upon this continent a French and Roman Catholic nation."[43] This was anathema to Orangemen and indeed to most contemporary English Canadians, because it directly challenged their own vision of the nation's future. The majority of English-speaking Canadians, including, as will be seen later, those of Irish Catholic origin, espoused the view that English should be the sole language outside of Quebec. Further complicating the school question were its implications for the large number of European immigrants who came to Saskatchewan at the turn of the century. Many of these were also Roman Catholic, and the separate school system provided for instruction in languages other than French or English where student numbers warranted. In the opinion of many English-speaking Canadians, allowing instruction in a "foreign" language greatly hindered the acquisition of English by these immigrants and raised the unsettling prospect of the province becoming a second Tower of Babel, fragmented by a confusion of tongues, with no shared values.[44] Orangemen were quick to point out the consequences of this situation:

> We have the danger of bilingualism or rather polylingualism in our own province—There are schools in this province today where English is treated as a foreign language—As Canadians we desire to see the children of our foreign population develop into good citizens of the Dominion. We cannot hope to make the foreign element absorb the British ideals until they first master the means of communication of those ideals, the English language. The preliminary teaching of which should be acquired in schools.[45]

Separate schools thus became a symbolic battleground for two competing visions of how the province of Saskatchewan, and by extension the country of Canada, should evolve: as a mosaic where many different nationalities, cultures and languages would have equal standing, similar to what we now call multiculturalism; or as an extension of the eastern provinces where all newcomers would be assimilated to English Canadian values and the English language.[46] This approach has come to be known as Anglo-conformity, and while the Orange Order in Saskatchewan was not alone in espousing such homogeneity, it was certainly among its strongest exponents. A particularly uncompromising statement of this philosophy was contained in a speech delivered by the Saskatchewan Grand Master in 1920:

> There is no room for the hyphen in our citizenship ... it is a danger to the country and a hindrance to the building up of

a united and homogeneous people. He that is not with us is against us. We have but room in this country for one flag, one language, one school, one throne, and one Empire. This country is British and we must insist on the residents of this country being British and the only way … this can be accomplished is by educating the children in a non-sectarian national school where the language of use and instruction is English.[47]

In translating these ideals into political reality, however, the Order was frustrated by the Liberal Party's domination of provincial politics from 1905. Faced with this situation Orangemen generally leaned towards the provincial Conservative Party, an identification which became increasingly public in the 1920s. The best evidence of the growing alliance between the Orange Order and the Conservative Party was the meteoric rise within the party of Dr. J.T.M. Anderson, an Orangeman from Saskatoon. Born in Fairbanks, Ontario, to an Irish immigrant family from Ulster, Anderson came to Saskatchewan in 1908. In 1919 he moved to Saskatoon to assume the position of Director of Education for the province of Saskatchewan. In 1920 he joined the Orange Lodge in Saskatoon and became recording secretary in 1924. In the same year he was elected Conservative Member of the Legislative Assembly for Saskatoon, and his talents rapidly propelled him into the upper echelons of the party. He was chosen as leader of the party in late 1924, and although he stepped down from the position briefly in 1926 he continued as House Leader. In March of 1928 he resumed the leadership of the Saskatchewan Conservative Party.[48]

Anderson's entry into provincial politics coincided with the arrival in Saskatchewan of the notorious Ku Klux Klan and the beginning of one of the most turbulent periods in provincial politics. Most commentators agree that the extraordinary, albeit short-lived, popularity of the Klan in Saskatchewan stemmed from its ability to exploit the fears of a segment of the population concerning demographic and social changes occurring in their midst. Postwar immigration and differential birth rates were transforming the ethnic and religious composition of the population, with the result that Protestants of British origin were losing their majority status. The prospect of being swamped by those they termed "foreign born," many of whom were also Roman Catholic, was extremely alarming for the Anglo-Protestant population, posing as it did a very real threat that they would lose control of the province's institutions. As evidence of this they pointed to the education system, for not only was the separate school system thriving, but it also appeared that French and "foreign" Catholics were beginning to exert undue influence within the public schools in some areas. To make matters worse, the Liberal government appeared indifferent to these concerns, leading many to conclude that their own government had been captured by those same hostile elements.[49]

Such heightened passions afforded an ideal climate in which the Klan could thrive, since it successfully combined nativism, anti-Catholicism and Francophobia into one coherent message and provided an outlet for the growing sense of insecurity among segments of the English-speaking population. What is frequently overlooked in discussions of the Klan in Saskatchewan, however, is its connection to the Orange Order. Although Klan rhetoric was far more extreme and intolerant than most public pronouncements of Orange leaders, their positions on immigration, the French language and the influence of the Roman Catholic Church were almost identical. The Orange Order and the Klan also appealed to roughly the same segments of the population and there was considerable overlap in membership. Klan speakers were also frequently invited to address Order functions in the late 1920s, a great favourite being J.J. Maloney, a fiery renegade priest. The remarkable success of the Klan in Saskatchewan can therefore be attributed, at least in part, to the fact that the ground had been prepared in advance by the Orange Order. This was particularly true in the sense that Orange activities and rhetoric over the previous 40 years had predisposed a considerable section of the population to become exercised over the issues of race, religion, language and education.

The Klan's popularity and the heightened interest which it focussed on these contentious issues were astutely exploited by the Conservative Party under Dr. Anderson, and culminated in the election of the first Conservative-led government in Saskatchewan in 1929. As premier of the province from 1929 until 1935, Anderson moved to address the issues which had for long been of concern to Orangemen and which more recently had formed the basis of the Klan's campaign. Acting as his own minister of Education, the premier introduced amendments to the School Act which prohibited the use of religious symbols and the wearing of religious garb in public schools. In the second session of the legislature, this was followed by changes which greatly reduced the use of French as a language of instruction in Saskatchewan schools.[50] In 1930 the Anderson government established a royal commission to study the issue of immigration to the province. One of the most detailed briefs was presented by the Orange Order, and not surprisingly it argued strongly in favour of imposing severe restrictions on non-British immigrants for the foreseeable future.[51] In power until 1935, the Anderson government found itself confronting the Great Depression, which

J.T.M. Anderson (1878–1946) (Courtesy of the Saskatchewan Archives Board/R-A629-1).

brought unprecedented misery to the people of Saskatchewan. The collapse of the farm economy and massive urban unemployment soon distracted attention from the issues of language, race and education which had caused such bitterness in the late 1920s.

The election of the Anderson government in 1929 may be seen as the high point of Orange political influence in Saskatchewan, and it also coincided with the peak of the organization's popularity. Although the Orange Order continued to be a presence in rural Saskatchewan until the 1960s, the years after 1930 witnessed a steady decline in membership.[52] Rural depopulation and the advent of mass media drained its membership base, and as the pioneering generations disappeared the original need for the support which the Order provided ceased to exist. The values which the Order espoused also diminished in appeal after World War II, as notions of diversity and multiculturalism gained favour. Nevertheless, it is clear that the Orange Order had an enormous influence on the development of the province. It played a vital practical role in facilitating the social and cultural adjustment of early Protestant, English-speaking pioneers; and it also provided a medium for interlinking them with their co-religionists from Protestant, northern European countries. The Order also articulated a coherent vision for the future cultural development of the province, and although this vision fell into disfavour in the years after World War II, there is a sense in which the Order was undone by its own success. Though we pay lip service today to the concepts of bilingualism and multiculturalism, the reality is that Saskatchewan is a predominantly English-speaking community with a relatively high degree of cultural homogeneity among its non-aboriginal population. This may be considered the enduring legacy of the Orange Order.

In Saskatchewan, as indeed in all of Canada, the Orange Order embodied a major part of the identity of Irish-origin Protestants. Although certainly not all belonged to or even supported it, the Order nevertheless enumerated a basic cultural identity common among Irish Protestant emigrants and their descendants, and it was a perspective which also resonated with other settlers, especially those from Protestant, northern European countries. In a similar way the Roman Catholic Church embraced a large part of the identity of the remainder of the Irish-origin population, the approximately 35% who were Catholic. Like their Protestant counterparts, the Catholic Irish in Saskatchewan consisted mainly of second- and third-generation descendants of earlier emigrants who came from eastern Canada and the United States, and of a small number who came directly from Ireland.[53] And like the Protestants, the Catholic Irish brought with them to the West a well-developed culture which had originally been forged in Ireland and then tempered by various North American environments.

Catholic culture in Ireland evolved after the 17th century, largely in response to British colonialism. Discriminated against on the basis of their nationality and religion, and excluded from property and power, Irish Catholic identity fused a deeply Anglophobic separatist nationalism and a powerful attachment to the Roman Catholic Church. Over time these two ingredients became virtually synonymous in the homeland, and they were further solidified while being dispersed to the four corners of the world by the massive 19th-century emigration. Catholics who emigrated from Ireland, especially during the Great Famine exodus of the 1840s, encountered a great deal more religious and racial prejudice than did their Protestant counterparts and, initially at least, had more difficulty in adjusting to their new environments. This early dislocation, combined with continued British control over the homeland, contributed to an abiding sense of historical grievance among many Irish Catholic emigrants and their descendants throughout the diaspora.[54] The intergenerational transmission of that identity from Ireland to Ontario and then to Saskatchewan was captured almost in caricature in the reminiscences of one unfortunate English settler:

> I lived on a farm with a family ... Irish, west of [Regina]. A good sized farm. Irish. Not Ulster but southern Irish. God how they hated Englishmen ... . They'd come to Ontario about 60 years ago. Their grandfather had. Both of these were actually born in the bush outside of Toronto but Irish as Paddy's pig. Talk about the Tories and the Corn Laws and the Famine and the English and you never heard such hatred. There I'd sit with them night after night and there was no use me defending the English because at school and prep and Oxford I hadn't ever heard of the Corn Laws. But

> by God I know what they are now. I think the Irish by their
> very nature bring a lot of these things down upon them-
> selves. A treacherous lot.[55]

In Canada, also, the Irish invested enormous energy into the Roman Catholic Church; and throughout the Maritimes, Ontario and subsequently the West, they were largely responsible for creating the English-speaking dimension of this institution. In the process they found spiritual sustenance, a relatively safe vehicle for expressing their community consciousness, and a powerful symbol of their ethno-religious identity.

As in other parts of the diaspora, Irish Catholic emigrants and their descendants in Canada developed a new identity over time which combined aspects of their Old World inheritances with their New World environment. In particular, this evolution was shaped by the ambiguous, double-minority status which they held within Canadian society.[56] Adherence to Catholicism and a lingering Anglophobia made them a religious and cultural minority within a predominantly Protestant, English-speaking community which exalted loyalty to the Crown as one of its chief public virtues. As a result, the Irish remained objects of suspicion and targets of sporadic *No Popery* campaigns, frequently led by their hereditary Orange enemies.[57] As English-speakers, moreover, the Irish were a linguistic and cultural minority within the Canadian Catholic Church which had previously been dominated by French Canadians from Quebec. In the late 19th century, therefore, they were increasingly at loggerheads with their French co-religionists both for control of the church and in formulating the relationship between Canadian Catholicism and the larger non-Catholic Canadian society.

Irish Catholic assimilation in Canada thus occurred in the context of the two solitudes, and the identity which they developed was essentially a compromise or middle ground between the two. Distance and time gradually diminished the bonds with the Old Country, and while many still proclaimed their Irish heritage and enthusiastically supported the Irish Home Rule movement, their Canadian residence and birth, their Catholic affiliation and English language increasingly became the foci of their identity.[58] English-speaking Canadian Catholics became their new term of self-identification, and historians refer to them as Anglo-Celtic Catholics because, although dominated by the Irish, they were also associated with English, Scottish, American and other Canadian Catholics whose first language was or became English. Loyalty to Canada as an independent, English-speaking religiously pluralistic nation within the context of a commonwealth of equal partners, became their ideal definition of Canadian society; and this provided common ground with the two dominant cultural traditions in Canada.

With French Canadians they shared a strong commitment to Catholic rights, especially denominational education, and with British Protestants they shared a belief in the primacy of the English language and the duty of citizens to subscribe to Canadianism. One of the clearest articulations of this new Anglo-Celtic Catholic identity was provided in a speech by Charles Murphy, an Irish Catholic M.P. from Ontario, in 1904:

> We must cultivate a Canadian national sentiment. Let us who are Irish Catholics identify ourselves with Canadianism in all our hearts. In the days when we were discriminated against in the fashion I have … described, it was necessary that we should stand together as Irish Catholics for the better breaking down of the walls of brass. But now that we are on equal footing with the rest of the population it is in our interest and duty, while ever remembering Ireland and doing our best to assuage her griefs and promote her aspirations for Home Rule, to be loyal first, last and all the time to Canada, than which a fairer land and one with a greater or nobler future does not exist on earth.[59]

This, then, was part of the cultural baggage which Catholics of Irish origin brought to Saskatchewan and which shaped their responses to their new home. One of the most striking features of their behaviour in the West was that their first priority, after basic survival, was to practice their religion. In Regina, Saskatoon, Sturgis, Moose Jaw, Lanigan, Sinnett, Young, Prince Albert, Clark's Crossing and elsewhere, the Irish built a parish network from the ground up. Men and women with names like O'Brien, O'Grady, O'Mahoney, O'Leary, McCarthy, Gallagher, Grimes, Leddy, Ryan, Feehan, Quinn, Molloy and Mooney were the pioneers of the English-speaking Catholic Church in Saskatchewan.[60] They opened their homes for the first masses, originally provided infrequently by itinerant clergy. They formed parish committees, raised money, and built churches and parish halls. They staffed the numerous parochial organizations and, most importantly, they devoted their lives as priests and nuns to the far-flung pioneer congregation. Involvement in the church allowed Irish-origin settlers to establish a continuity with their past and to recreate their spiritual community, and the church also played a vital role in facilitating their social and material adjustment to the Prairies.

Like their Protestant counterparts, therefore, religion was the primary focus of individual and collective loyalty for the Catholic Irish in Saskatchewan, and their organizational constructs also emanated from the church. Although various nationalist and ethnic societies were established

St. Patrick's Roman Catholic Church in Herbert, Saskatchewan, built in 1912 and named for the patron saint of Ireland. Although many who settled in the Herbert region were Mennonites, many of St. Patrick's parishioners were of Irish descent. Prior to the construction of the church services were held south of Herbert in what was known as the Donnellyville district, named after the Donnelly family who had settled in the area and who had ancestral roots in County Armagh, Ireland. St. Patrick's Church in Herbert officially closed in 1983 due to a declining number of parishioners and a shortage of priests to officiate. The building was last used for a funeral service for Cecilia Donnelly in August 1989; in 1996 the structure was sold to Patricia Donnelly, of Montreal, formerly of Herbert, to be restored and displayed as a historical site. St. Patrick's Cemetery is still maintained north of the town (Courtesy of David McLennan/University of Regina).

in Saskatchewan, the single most important public organization which people of Irish origin created was the Knights of Columbus. This organization was established in New Haven, Connecticut by an Irish priest in 1882 to foster fraternity among Catholic men and encourage the performance of *charitable, educational and patriotic works*. Introduced to Canada by Irish Canadians in Montreal in 1897, a western district was formed by Irish Canadians in Winnipeg in 1906, and the first Saskatchewan chapter was formed by Irish Canadians in Regina in 1907. In 1923 Saskatchewan Knights established their own state council, and by 1930 there were 22 chapters of the Knights of Columbus organized in the province with a total membership of 14,800.[61] Membership in the Knights offered Catholics many of the same practical benefits which the Orange Order provided its Protestant members. It served as a forum for socializing, a ready-made support network, and an outlet for the talents and ambitions of Catholic laymen.[62] Like the Orange Order it also encouraged service to the larger society, and in the process it accumulated an impressive list of philanthropic achievements. These included the construction of St. Patrick's Orphanage in Prince Albert, fund raising for St. Peter's College in Muenster, Campion College in Regina and St. Thomas More College in Saskatoon, the operation of the Catholic Immigration Welfare Society and the Knights of Columbus Army Huts project during both World Wars. Its female auxiliary, the Catholic Women's League, was also active; and among its most enduring legacies was Rosary Hall in Regina, which provided lodging and work for homeless women, care for troubled girls, assistance to female immigrants, a children's shelter, hospital visitation, and fund raising for various charitable endeavours.[63]

Although dominated initially by Catholics of Irish origin, the Knights of Columbus transcended ethnicity and appealed to Catholics of many different nationalities. English, Scottish, Welsh, Germans, Hungarians, Ukrainians, Poles and Americans all belonged to the organization, and it thus served as an effective forum for ethnic fusion. Membership in the Knights bound together Catholics of Irish and many other nationalities, forging the personal bonds vital to the creation of community cohesion in pioneer society. This was especially evident in marriage patterns, with high rates of intermarriage between the Irish and other Catholic groups represented by the Knights of Columbus. The one exception to this was the frequency with which Irish men married aboriginal women. Notable also was the fact that very few French Canadians belonged to the Knights of Columbus, in part because of the English language orientation of the organization. This was symptomatic of the wider differences between Irish and French Catholics in the West.

The Catholic Church and the Knights of Columbus thus served as vehicles for transmitting Irish Catholic culture to the Prairies and for integrating the Irish-origin Catholics with other settlers. What is clear also is that their early dominance of these institutions and proficiency in the English language allowed the Irish to become spokesmen for non-French Catholics in the province, and they proved themselves to be extremely assertive in protecting and promoting Catholic interests. One early resident of Saskatoon recalled "a small contingent of Irish ancestry ... only one of tranquil and mild opinion! They certainly added to the liveliness of frequent controversy and debate on local religious and political issues."[64] Like their Protestant counterparts, Catholics of Irish origin sought to impose their mould on Saskatchewan society, particularly in the area of education, and they did this in a manner consistent with the behaviour of their co-religionists in other parts of the Irish diaspora. It has been suggested that separate or denominational education systems were among the most important cultural legacies of Irish Catholic emigration. Wherever in the world they settled in numbers Irish Catholics pressed, often at great personal and collective sacrifice, for their own education system publicly funded, but controlled by the church.[65] This was certainly true of those who settled in Saskatchewan, as the single most important political issue they faced in the early years of the province was the controversy over separate schools. As previously mentioned, the Autonomy Bills of 1905 established a dual school system in Saskatchewan, but many non-Catholics resented this imposition. Catholics, including those of Irish origin, were therefore constantly on the defensive to protect their constitutional rights. Since the Orange Order tended to be the most vocal exponent of the extreme Protestant perspective (before the arrival of the Ku Klux Klan), Irish Catholics were faced with their old enemy in a new environment, and the term "Orangeman" became their catchword for all enemies of Catholicism in Saskatchewan.[66]

But while Irish Protestants and Catholics and their descendants relived their ancient sectarian feud in Saskatchewan, the situation on the Prairies was complicated by the presence of new players. As in eastern Canada, the church in the West was originally dominated by French Canadians, and many of the Eastern European immigrants who arrived at the turn of the century were also Roman Catholics. Thus, as well as being confronted with their old Orange enemies, the Irish found themselves a minority within the Saskatchewan Catholic population and were forced to share the Church with others. This relationship, especially with the French, was often uneasy.

Tension between the Irish and the French in the West was an inevitable product of the desire of both groups to control an institution which each saw as peculiarly their own. Although a minority of the Canadian Catholic population, the Irish had already established substantial control of the church hierarchy in the East, and as they moved west they continued to demand the creation of English-speaking parishes and the appointment of English-speaking, preferably Irish-origin, clergy.[67] Language proved to be the most obvious source of contention between the Irish and the French, but this was more a reflection of a deeper conflict. Both groups had fundamentally incompatible visions of the future of the church in Saskatchewan; and these visions were microcosms of the contemporary polarization of views at the national level concerning the nature of the Canadian character and identity and the extent of cultural dualism in Canada. Concerned about the survival of their language and culture as well as their religion, French Canadians envisioned a significant degree of segregation, religious, cultural and linguistic, for Catholics in Saskatchewan. As well as insisting on the right to control their own education system, they were staunch defenders of French and other minority linguistic rights, and they fought hard to maintain their primacy within the church hierarchy in the West. Anglo-Celtic Catholics, on the other hand, led by the vocal and aggressive Irish, were convinced that English would become the dominant language in Canada and that Catholicism could only progress on the Prairies if its adherents adopted that language. Thus, while the Irish insisted on religious and educational segregation, they advocated considerable integration in linguistic, cultural and social areas. They argued that Catholics should assimilate to the Canadian mainstream through the adoption of the English language and Canadian norms, and as English-speakers familiar with British culture, they saw themselves as the ideal group to preside over this process.[68]

The conflict between the French and the Irish in Saskatchewan was therefore nothing less than a "struggle to ensure the domination of one cultural tradition as opposed to another."[69] It juxtaposed two very different visions of the future of the church in the West, one assertive and integrationist, the other defensive and isolationist, and it understandably generated strong passions. From the Irish perspective, the identification of the French language and culture with Catholicism threatened the social acceptance and political rights of all Catholics and provided fodder for anti-Catholic bigotry. They accused the French of being aggressively racialist, of "arrogating to themselves as rights those things which were merely privileges [and of] generating a deep resentment in the hearts of even the fair-minded Protestant people [towards Catholicism]."[70] Ironically, the views of Irish Catholics on cultural dualism and minority linguistic rights closely paralleled those of the Orange Order, and this was not lost on the French. *Les Orangistes* and *les Irlandais* were birds of a feather from the French perspective, both bent on assimilation and Anglicization, and both seen as bitter enemies of French culture. They were, in the words of one French commentator, "anational et contre nature."[71]

The outcome of this struggle between Anglo-Celtic and French Catholics was determined in part by demographic changes within the Catholic population in the province. As Table 2 shows, between 1901 and 1931 the percentage of Catholics who were French declined from over 90% to less than one-third, and French influence waned in accordance. Virtually all episcopal appointments after 1911 went to English-speaking, frequently Irish origin, candidates, and the French were reduced to one bishop and a small core of parishes. Once in control of the church, the Irish also sought to implement their vision of Catholicism in the province; and they were successful in many crucial areas, including postsecondary education.[72] Thus, while

Table 2. Religious Composition of Saskatchewan Population, 1901–31				
Year	Total Population	Catholic	French Catholic	Other Catholic
1901	91,279	27,651	23,251	4,400
1911	492,432	90,092	42,152	47,940
1921	757,510	147,342	46,031	101,311
1931	921,785	233,979	50,700	183,279

French Canadians in Saskatchewan have succeeded in maintaining many aspects of their religion, language and culture, the Catholic Church in the province was destined to develop primarily along the English-speaking, integrationist lines envisaged by the Irish.

In conclusion it may be said that the story of the Irish in Saskatchewan is a varied, fascinating and important one, which weaves together two of the most significant developments in the evolution of this country: the creation of largely white, English-speaking, settler societies on the Prairies between 1850 and 1920, and the intergenerational spread of the Irish diaspora westwards across North America after 1815. The main contention of this study is that these two processes were linked, and that the Irish diaspora was a vital element in the establishment of the province of Saskatchewan. Although it may seem redundant to comment on the migratory proclivities of emigrant groups, the fact nevertheless requires emphasis because of its singular importance. People of Irish origin who settled in Saskatchewan came from a culture with a long tradition of migration in search of social and material advancement, and a tendency to define economic opportunity in terms of land ownership. Since the settlement of the West attracted those who were willing to migrate in order to own land, it is not surprising that the Irish constituted a significant proportion of the early pioneer population. Thus they were active agents in the great historical changes which occurred on the northern Plains at the turn of the century: in particular, the westward expansion of the Canadian political and settlement frontier; the transition from Aboriginal to non-Aboriginal control of resources; and the development of a commercial, agricultural economy.

Like all other settlers, the Irish who came West entered an unfamiliar environment and one of the most inhospitable climates in the world. Some of them were defeated by the challenge, but a great many possessed resources which privileged them in frontier society. Early arrival, white skin, Christian adherence, commercial acumen, proficiency in the English language, familiarity with the British Canadian political, legal and educational traditions, and considerable organizational ability ensured that the Irish adjustment, though often difficult, was not the traumatic and dislocating experience encountered by many other groups. This study has documented the involvement of Irish-origin settlers in the establishment of churches, schools, and hospitals; in building civic, municipal, provincial and federal political structures; and in creating fraternal organizations which were an essential cohesive force in pioneer society. In short, the Irish played an enormous role, especially given their relative numbers, in constructing the public institutions of the province of Saskatchewan.

More significant than the contributions of the many individuals documented here, however, was the collective impact of the Irish in shaping the early development of the province. Irish-origin settlers, both Protestant and Catholic, brought with them well-developed cultures which combined their Old World inheritances with the assimilation and accommodation to North American, primarily eastern Canadian norms, which had taken place over one or two generations of immigration. Revolving primarily around religious affiliation, the most visible institutional manifestations of intergenerational Irish ethnicity in Saskatchewan were the Protestant and Roman Catholic Churches. These churches, and organizations such as the Orange Order and the Knights of Columbus which evolved out of them, served primarily as vehicles for transferring and recreating Irish culture on the Prairies. In this they were typical of the behaviour of Irish immigrants and their descendants in virtually all other parts of the diaspora. In Saskatchewan, as in Ontario, Chicago, New South Wales, Auckland, Glasgow, and other places too numerous to mention, Irish emigrants adjusted to local circumstances, but sought to do so on their own terms. Like all charter groups they attempted to mould Saskatchewan society in their own image. In this process their institutions acted as forums for ethnic fusion which integrated Irish Protestants and Catholics with settlers of other nationalities, and provided a vital force for cohesion in an ethnically diverse pioneer society. However, Irish ethnicity also created great tension with other elements within the pioneer population which did not share their vision of how the province of Saskatchewan should evolve.

People of Irish origin were assertive proponents of Canadianism, and they offered two versions of that ideal which differed in some respects but which also shared several fundamental assumptions. Irish-origin Protestants who settled in Saskatchewan saw Canada as an English-speaking, majority Protestant country, an integral part of the British Empire, with a clear separation of church and state and a high degree of cultural homogeneity along Anglo-Canadian lines. As articulated by the Orange Order, this manifested itself in a powerful commitment to maintain the "imperial connection," the dominance of the English language and the primacy of the public school system as the vehicle for propagating those norms and for assimilating weakening of ties with Britain, suspicious of the Roman Catholic separate school system, and overtly hostile to minority, especially French linguistic rights, or any concession to cultural diversity. The Anglo-Celtic vision of Canada developed by Catholics of Irish origin was less intolerant of heterogeneity, but it nevertheless had much in common with its Protestant counterpart. They too envisaged Canada as a predominantly English-speaking country, but as an autonomous nation within the British commonwealth. They insisted on religious pluralism and the right to denominational education, and the Roman Catholic Separate School system was one of their enduring creations. But Anglo-Celtic Catholics promoted no such separation in the areas of culture or language. Committed to the primacy of the English language and Anglo-Celtic Canadian cultural values, they were generally as intolerant as the Protestants of French and other minority groups' linguistic and cultural rights.

The vision of Canada and the province of Saskatchewan which people of Irish origin articulated was in some senses a narrow one, especially from today's more tolerant perspective. But it was a natural product of their historical experiences and cultural inheritances. Forged in Ireland and transported to Canada by earlier emigrants, these inheritances were modified by the Canadian environment and then brought west by their descendants. Therein lies perhaps the strongest evidence of their impact on the development of the province. For the primary vehicles for implementing their vision and assimilating others to it—the Protestant and Roman Catholic Churches and the organizational infrastructures which emanated from them - were in fact Irish institutions which had over time become integral parts of mainstream Canadian society. It is also a vision of the Prairies which has endured. Despite the waning attachment to the British monarchy and the adoption of bilingualism and multiculturalism as official policy, there is much about the province of Saskatchewan today that can be attributed, at least in part, to the Irish and Irish Canadians. Allegiance to the Canadian federation, the dominance of the English language, the numerical strength of organized Christianity, the Public and Roman Catholic school systems, organized labour, cooperatives and credit unions, the relatively high degree of cultural homogeneity among the non-aboriginal population—and green beer on St. Patrick's Day—these are among the enduring legacies of the Irish in Saskatchewan.

Notes
This article first appeared in *Prairie Forum* 24, no. 2 (1999): 185–210.
1. D. Fitzpatrick, *Irish Emigration, 1801–1921* (Dundalk: Dundalgan Press, 1984), 1.

2. For a sampling of the vast historical literature on Irish immigrants see D.H. Akenson, *The Irish Diaspora: A Primer* (Toronto: P.D. Meaney, 1993).

3. C. Houston and W.J. Smyth, *Irish Emigration and Canadian Settlement: Patterns, Links and Letters* (Toronto: University of Toronto Press, 1990); D. Wilson, *The Irish in Canada* (Toronto: Canadian Historical Society, 1989): R. O'Driscoll and Laura Reynolds (eds.), *The Untold Story: The Irish in Canada* (Toronto: Celtic Arts of Canada, 1988).

4. I. Spry, *The Palliser Expedition: The Dramatic Story of Western Canadian Exploration, 1857–1860* (Saskatoon: Fifth House, 1994); M.H. Synge, *Great Britain: One Empire* (London: n.p., 1852); and R.D. Francis, *Images of the West: Responses to the Canadian Prairies* (Saskatoon: Western Producer Prairie Books, 1989), 82ff.

5. Provincial Archives of Alberta, C. Scollen Papers; W. Hildebrandt, et al., *The True Spirit and Original Intent of Treaty Seven* (Montreal and Kingston: McGill-Queen's University Press, 1996), 58–59.

6. D.J. Hall, "Clifford Sifton: Immigration and Settlement Policy, 1896–1905," in H. Palmer (ed.), *The Settlement of the West* (Calgary: University of Calgary Press, 1977), 605. Other notable Irish boosters of western settlement were John Macoun and N.F. Davin. See W.A. Waiser, "Macoun and the Great North-West" (MA thesis, University of Saskatchewan, 1976).

7. G. Stortz, "Archbishop Lynch and New Ireland: An Unfulfilled Dream for Canada's Northwest," *Catholic Historical Review* 68, no. 4 (1982): 612–24; M.Cottrell, "Irish Catholic Political Leadership in Toronto, 1855–1882: A Study of Ethnic Politics" (PhD dissertation, University of Saskatchewan, 1988), 400–54.

8. *Regina Leader*, March 8, April 26, May 10, 1883.

9. D. Fitzpatrick estimated that Irish emigration to Canada in this period comprised only 1/14th of the total outflow. D. Fitzpatrick, "Irish Emigration in the Later Nineteenth Century," *Irish Historical Studies* 22 (1980): 130–31.

10. For a study of the assisted and collective nature of Scottish crofter settlements see W. Norton, *Help Us to a Better Land: Crofter Colonies in the Prairie West* (Regina: Canadian Plains Research Center, 1994). On Ukrainians see J.C. Lehr, "The Government and the Immigrants: Perspectives on Ukrainian Bloc Settlement in the Canadian West," *Canadian Ethnic Studies* 11, no. 2 (1977): 42–52.

11. D. Fitzpatrick suggests that Irish emigrants to Canada in this period came in roughly equal numbers from the industrialized region around Belfast and the "more backward and agricultural counties" of Donegal, Mayo and Galway. They were more likely to be lower middle class or farmers than those who emigrated to the United States in this period, who typically were from the labouring and servant classes. Fitzpatrick, "Irish Emigration in the Later Nineteenth Century," 130–31.

12. *Census of Canada*, 1881, 1891, 1901, 1911, 1921.

13. E.T. Russell (ed.), *What's in a Name?* (Saskatoon: Western Producer Prairie Books, 1973), 63, 77, 101, 126–27,167,185, 192, 204, 274, 292, 294.

14. *Regina Leader*, May 3, 1883.

15. Foam Lake Historical Society, *They Came From Many Lands: A History of Foam Lake and Area* (Foam Lake: Foam Lake Historical Society, 1985), 650ff.

16. Wilkie Historical Society, *Fifty Years of Progress: A History of Wilkie and District* (Wilkie: n.p.,1967), 218–19.

17. *Columbianism in Saskatchewan, 1907–1982* (Saskatoon: Knights of Columbus State Council, 1982), 197.

18. Swarthmore Home and School Association, *Golden Threads: The History of Swarthmore, 1905–1980* (Swarthmore: n.p., 1984), 287.

19. Patrick Grimes, taped interview, February 11, 1994.

20. Fascinating insights into the difficulties faced by one Irish emigrant with the harsh climate and the often alien nature of the Saskatchewan landscape is provided by the correspondence of Ernest Cochrane. Public Records Office of Northern Ireland, E. Cochrane Papers, T3504/1/7–43.

21. Akenson, *The Irish Diaspora*, 39–40.

22. Macklin Home and School Association, *History of Macklin and Community* (Macklin: n.p., 1955), 6–24.

23. *Columbianism in Saskatchewan*, 234.

24. *Golden Threads: The History of Swarthmore*, 32ff.

25. Interview with Bob Lindsay, Saskatoon, August 1995.

26. H. Senior, *Orangeism in Ireland and Britain, 1775–1836* (London: Routledge and Keegan Paul, 1966).

27. C. Houston and W.J. Smyth, *The Sash Canada Wore: A Historical Geography of the Orange Order in Canada* (Toronto: University of Toronto Press, 1980).

28. Houston and Smyth, *Irish Emigration and Canadian Settlement*, 185.

29. Saskatchewan Archives Board (SAB), Grand Orange Lodge of Saskatchewan. Annual reports 1908 and 1934 (hereafter GOLSK.AR).

30. SAB, Grand Orange Lodge of the Northwest Territories. Annual Reports (hereafter GOLNT.AR), 1892, 1893, 1894, 1895.

31. The Order's strong commitment to the monarchy was generally unpalatable to Americans. See G. Houston and W.J. Smyth, "Transferred Loyalties: The Orange Order in the United States and Ontario," *American Review of Canadian Studies* (1984).

32. For an excellent account of a typical July 12 celebration in the town of Young in 1924 see the *Saskatoon Phoenix*, July 14, 1924.

33. SAB, GOLNT.AR, 1896 and 1904.

34. The Orange Order, for example, was a strong supporter of prohibition and for a period actually banned hotel keepers and other dealers in liquor from membership. SAB, GOLNT.AR, 1898 and 1899.

35. Ibid., 1900.

36. For a general outline of Irish history in this period see F.S.L. Lyons, *Ireland Since the Famine* (Glasgow: Fontana, 1978), esp. 141–471.

37. SAB, GOLSK.AR., 1914–1916.

38. Ibid., 1923.

39. Ibid., 1911.

40. Ibid., 1903.

41. SAB, GOLNT.AR, 1892.

42. The best overview of this issue is K.A. Macleod, "Politics and the French Language," in N. Ward and D. Spafford (eds.), *Politics in Saskatchewan* (Toronto: Longmans, 1968), 124–60.

43. SAB, GOLSK.AR, 1920.

44. M J. Barker, "Canadianization Through the Schools of the Prairie Provinces Before World War I: The Attitudes and Aims of the English-Speaking Majority," in M. Kovacs (ed.), *Ethnic Canadians: Culture and Education* (Regina: Canadian Plains Research Center, 1978) , 281–332. For a contemporary analysis see J.T.M. Anderson, *The Education of the New Canadian: A Treatise on Canada's Greatest Educational Problem* (Toronto: J.C. Dent, 1918).

45. SAB, GOLSK.AR, 1912.

46. H. Palmer, "Reluctant Hosts: Anglo-Canadian Views of Multiculturalism in the Twentieth Century," in R.D. Francis and D.B. Smith (eds.), *Readings in Canadian History: Post-Confederation* (Toronto: Holt, Rinehart and Winston, 1986), 185–201.

47. SAB, GOLSK.AR, 1920.

48. M. Cottrell, "J.T.M. Anderson: Orange Premier of Saskatchewan" (paper presented to the British Association for Canadian Studies, History and Biography Conference, 1991).

49. P. Kyba, "Ballots and Burning Cross: The Election of 1929," in Ward and Spafford, *Politics in Saskatchewan*, 105–23.

50. McLeod, "Politics and the French Language," in Ward and Spafford, *Politics in Saskatchewan*, 147ff; R. Huel, "The Anderson Amendments and the Secularization of Saskatchewan Schools," *GCHA Study Sessions* 44 (1977): 61–76.

51. SAB, GOLSK.AR,1921, pp. 14ff.

52. There are currently eight active lodges in Saskatchewan.

53. For a recent anecdotal study of one such group see J. Coughlin, *The Irish Colony of Saskatchewan* (Scarborough: Lochleven Publishers, 1995).

54. L.J. McCaffrey, "Irish Catholicism and Irish Nationalism: A Study in Cultural Identity," *Church History* 42 (1973): 524–34. See also various articles in M. McGowan and B. Clarke (eds.), *Catholics at the Gathering Place: Historical Essays on the Archdiocese of Toronto, 1841–1991* (Toronto: Canadian Catholic Historical Association, 1993).

55. B. Broadfoot, *The Pioneer Years, 1895–1914* (Toronto: Doubleday, 1976), 153.

56. J.S. Moir, "The Problems of a Double-Minority: Some Reflections on the Development of the English-speaking Catholic Church in Canada in the Nineteenth Century," *Histoire Sociale/Social History* 41 (1971): 54–61.

57. J.R Miller, "Bigotry in the North Atlantic Triangle: Irish, British and American Influences on Canadian Anti-Catholicism, 1850–1900," *Studies in Religion* 16, no. 3 (1987): 289–301.

58. For an excellent analysis of the assimilation of Irish Catholics in Toronto see M. McGowan, "We Are All Canadians: A Social, Religious and Cultural Portrait of Toronto's English-Speaking Roman Catholics, 1890–1920" (PhD dissertation, University of Toronto, 1988).

59. Ibid., 327.

60. M. Cottrell, "John Joseph Leddy and the Battle for the Soul of the Catholic Church in the West," *CCHA Historical Studies* 61 (1995) : 41–51.

61. C. Kaufman, *Faith and Fraternalism: The History of the Knights of Columbus* (New York: Harper and Row, 1982). For an overview of the development of the Knights of Columbus in Saskatchewan see *Columbianism in Saskatchewan, 1907–1982*.

62. J.J. Leddy, from Saskatoon, for example, rose to become supreme director of the Knights of Columbus in North America, chair of the Knights of Columbus Army Hut Project, Trustee on the Saskatoon Separate School Board, and he served on the executive of the provincial Conservative Party. See Cottrell, "J.J. Leddy."

63. *Columbianism in Saskatchewan*, 74.

64. St. Thomas More College Archives, Saskatoon. J.F. Leddy Papers, "Growing Up in Saskatoon."

65. D.H. Akenson, *The Irish Diaspora*, 273.

66. For a humorous account of boyhood conflict between Catholics and Protestants in Saskatoon see J.F Leddy Papers, "Growing Up in Saskatoon."

67. R. Huel, "The Irish-French Conflict in Catholic Episcopal Nominations: The Western Sees and the Struggle for Domination Within the Church," *CCHA Study Sessions* 42 (1975): 51–70.

68. R. Choquette, *Language and Religion: A History of English–French Conflict in Ontario* (Ottawa: University of Ottawa Press, 1975); B. Rainey, "The Fransaskois and the Irish Catholics: An Uneasy Relationship," *Prairie Forum* 24, no. 2 (Fall 1999): 211–17.

69. R. Huel, "Irish-French Conflict," 53.

70. Library and Archives Canada, Charles Murphy Papers. J.J. Leddy to C. Murphy, May 6, 1931.

71. Rainey, "The Fransaskois and the Irish Catholics," 211–17.

72. For an analysis of the struggle between the French and the Irish over post-secondary education in Saskatchewan see M. Cottrell, "J.J. Leddy and the Battle for the Soul of the Catholic Church."

20.   The Geographical Background to Church Union in Canada

John C. Lehr

In 1924 three of the largest nonconformist denominations in Canada, the Presbyterian, Methodist and Congregationalist churches, voted to merge in "organic union" to form the United Church of Canada.[1] Today, three-quarters of a century after their union, the United Church has arguably become the "national" church of Anglophone Canada.[2] In 1991 it claimed a membership of more than three million, about 11% of Canada's population, and it draws its adherents from every province and territory.[3]

Before the Act of Union these three nonconformist churches competed with each other and with the Anglicans, Baptists, and the more fundamentalist evangelical churches, for the allegiance of the Protestant population across the country. Among the non-English "foreign" immigrant population, they competed for converts to the Protestant creed. Nowhere was this competition more intense and more clearly seen than on the frontier of settlement in the western Canadian prairie provinces from the 1890s onwards.

The settlement of western Canada was accompanied by a vigorous national debate about the nature of the society which would emerge on the prairies.[4] Anxious to settle the West, the Canadian government sought immigrants from eastern Canada and the United States. Since few Francophones were attracted to settle on the prairies, the great majority of immigrants to the prairies were Anglophone and Protestant. In terms of immigration, government policies always favored immigrants from mostly Protestant northwestern Europe. In the 1890s the character of immigration into western Canada changed as other nationalities from central and eastern Europe were attracted to the West in increasing numbers. Many of these arrivals were Ukrainians, adherents of the Greek (Russian) Orthodox Church, or were *Uniates*, members of the Eastern Rite Roman Catholic Church. In the eyes of many Canadian Protestants these denominations were strange indeed, and they were reluctant to consider those who professed allegiance to them as true Christians.[5]

The interior of Poplar Grove United (Presbyterian) Church southwest of the town of Broadview, Saskatchewan (Courtesy of David McLennan/ University of Regina).

Almost all hues of the political spectrum in Canada agreed that it was in the national interest that these foreign elements should be inculcated with Canadian values as quickly as possible, and that high priority should be placed on their assimilation into the main-stream of Canadian society in the most expeditious manner possi-ble. Cries for the assimilation of foreigners were mixed with demands that this heathen ele-ment be "Christianized" and freed from the corrupting influ-ence of their clergy, who were generally portrayed as the forces of darkness.[6] For Canadian Protestants, to undertake mission-ary work among the foreigners in Canada was equated with the prosecution of missionary endeavors in distant lands. It was also portrayed as analogous to a military campaign to spread enlightenment and serve vital national interest:

> Reconnoitering parties have done the work, and in the great
> lands of heathenism the demand now is for an army of
> occupation. "Reinforcement! Send us reinforcements!" is
> the urgent call of the missionaries, and not by twos and
> threes, but by scores and hundreds? Heathenism is still
> strongly entrenched, and the position cannot be carried by
> the sudden dash of a "forlorn hope," but only by a vigorous
> and perhaps protracted siege.[7]

The Canadian Protestant Churches

Organic union of the Protestant churches had been suggested in the 1880s, at a time when the Methodists and the Presbyterians were both unifying the diverse branches of their churches into a common stream. This was then interpreted as a call for closer cooperation rather than as a call for a theolog-ical and organizational merging. For the Anglicans, organic union with other Protestant denominations, while attractive in some respects, promised to extinguish the admittedly faint hope of eventual union with the Roman or Greek Churches.[8] The Baptists rejected union because they saw a "fatal impediment" to union with other Christian churches in matters of baptism; citing Romans 6.4 in support of their inflexible position, they rejected paedo-baptism and insisted on retention of full-immersion adult baptism.[9]

To a secular outsider the differences between the Congregationalists, Methodists and Presbyterians lay less in theological doctrine than in their organizational structure and systems of governance.[10] All these noncon-formist churches had their origins in Great Britain. Congregationalism had its roots in the English Puritanism of Tudor times. Presbyterianism and Methodism had their roots in the teachings of John Calvin at the time of the Reformation. There were differences in the churches' positions on predestination as well as some disagreement about the nature and ritual of baptism, but not so great as to be beyond compromise. Similarly, the Congregationalists, Presbyterians and Methodists differed in their systems of governance: as their name implies, the Congregationalists granted the greatest autonomy to the individual congregations; the Presbyterians grant-ed a good deal of autonomy to congregations; whereas the Methodists were more centralized, with a more formal structure of church governance.

In 1921, a few years before the churches achieved organic union, the

Oxbow Methodist Church Choir, 1898 (Courtesy of the Ralph Allen Memorial Museum, Oxbow. Donated by Mrs. Grace Quinn, Oxbow).

Congregationalist Church was the smallest with a population of 30,574, of which 12,762 were active members; the Presbyterian Church had a population of 1,408,812, of which 369,939 were active members; and the Methodists, with a smaller population of 1,158,714, had 407,261 active members, slightly more than the Presbyterians.[11]

"Overlapping" in Western Canada

The Congregationalist, Presbyterian and Methodist churches came into the Canadian West by the migration of their members from Ontario and the British Isles. Their members were mixed together in mostly small, rural, English-speaking communities scattered across the prairies. It was common to find several Protestant churches in a single community of a few hundred people. This "overlapping," as it was termed, meant that congregations were often small. Consequently the financial resources of each church's congregations were stretched to the limit and there was a perpetual problem of raising sufficient funds to pay for the services of a resident clergyman, or even an itinerant preacher serving a circuit of several congregations. In the less established and poorer districts, mission grants from central church authorities were needed to maintain church operations.[12]

It soon became apparent to the churches that maintaining a church and minister wherever even a small congregation was present was inefficient. It posed major financial burdens and created serious staffing problems. Even in the best of times it was difficult to attract young clergy to the small towns on the prairies, where the pay was poor and the sense of isolation deterred many prospective ministers.[13] Church publications and reports alluded to the sense of frustration felt by many clergy who saw little chance of building their congregations without poaching from the congregations of the other Protestant churches. Evangelism among the already Protestant Anglophone congregations seemed redundant, literally preaching to the converted, and carried risks of "fostering sectarianism, which impoverishes rather than enriches community life."[14] Nonconformists had no illusions about the slim possibility of success proselytizing among the Roman Catholic congregations. Furthermore, it was apparent to all but the most inflexible on matters of doctrine that the nonconformist churches shared many doctrinal viewpoints and, indeed, that their religious philosophies were sufficiently close to warrant interdenominational cooperation. Presbyterian minister W.D. Reid wrote that:

> everywhere in Alberta, particularly in the little villages and towns, [are] two churches at least, the Methodist and Presbyterian both struggling for existence; often deep-seated

> quarrels, and jealousies going on between denominations, and both churches drawing heavily on the home mission funds of the respective denominations. I said [to a fellow minister] that "This is a perfect scandal, a disgrace to Christianity, and a misappropriation of the mission funds of the people. [The Churches] must get together."[15]

By the turn of the century, Methodists, Presbyterians, and Congregationalists in some prairie communities, especially in Alberta, had begun to work cooperatively, sharing buildings and, on occasion, clergy and services.

Perhaps the greatest impetus for the development of interdenominational cooperation came from the churches' determination to bring the Protestant creed and Canadian values to the foreign communities then emerging across the Prairies. The Presbyterians took the lead in this work, dispatching its workers to live among the eastern European settlers whose bloc settlements were scattered across the parkland belt from south-central Manitoba to east-central Alberta. Shortly after the turn of the century they established a series of bridgeheads in the Hungarian and Ukrainian colonies across the prairies. Medical and educational missions were established at strategic points adjacent to, or within, the developing foreign colonies. In Manitoba a Medical Mission was established at Sifton in 1900, followed by another at Teulon in 1902, which was "of great service in the relief of suffering and the recovery of the sick, as well as justifying its existence from a missionary point of view."[16] Other medical missions were established at Ethelbert in 1903; at Wakaw in 1903; at Canora, Saskatchewan, in 1914; and at Vegreville, Alberta, in 1908 (Figure 1). Aware of the Ukrainians' difficulty in obtaining priests and of the discontent of the nationalist-leaning, grassroots, Ukrainian intelligentsia, the Presbyterians seized the opportunity to establish the Independent Greek Church as a conduit for evangelical Protestant propaganda and an entry into the Ukrainian-Canadian community. By 1905 it had a following of 25,000, with a further 39,000 allegedly "studying it with a friendly attitude, attending its services with some regularity," but still undecided about their allegiance.[17] Along with medical aid or educational opportunities, these missions offered church services, Sunday schools and Bible study in an attempt to win converts. The Ukrainian-language weekly newspaper *Ranok* [Dawn] was also established and supported by the Presbyterian Church to promote Presbyterianism among the Ukrainian population.

A small medical mission was established at Pakan, Alberta, in 1901 by a Methodist doctor and missionary (Figure 1). Elsewhere the Methodists were slower off the mark: a Committee on Home Work was only established in

Figure 1.

1902, and it was not until 1906 that Methodist Home Mission work was seriously undertaken on the prairies. Medical missions were established at Lamont in 1911, with clinics at Chipman, Radway, and Bellis. The Women's Missionary Society provided residential homes for girls at Wahstao in 1904 and Kolocreeka in 1908.[18] Outside of Alberta, until 1912, activity was confined to work among the "foreign" population of the city of Winnipeg.[19] Until then, in the foreign colonies the Presbyterians had "the whole field to themselves."[20] The smaller Congregational Church confined its mission work to the urban areas and the north, but seemed to favour overseas mission work in Africa and India. The Baptists did not maintain any missions, but by 1917 had three "Russian" missionaries in the West, one in each Prairie province.[21]

Notwithstanding the move toward cooperation and even talk in favour of church union, the Methodists were clearly concerned about Presbyterian

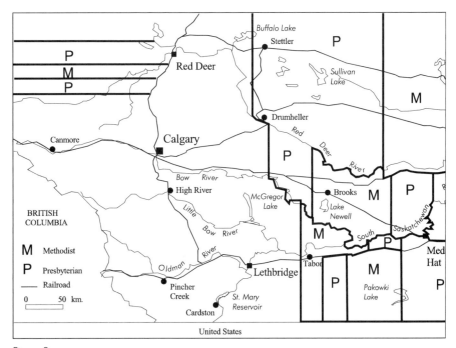

Figure 2.

territorial dominance in the foreign colonies across the prairies. James Woodsworth, Superintendent of Missions for the Methodists, reported that "developments during the present year, in which a clearer understanding with our Presbyterian brethren [concerning] reoccupation of new territory, especially of strategic points, may help us to determine our policy in developing rural missions in foreign colonies."[22] Shortly thereafter, two Missions to serve the foreign population were established, one at Fort William in northwestern Ontario, the other in Winnipeg to serve the surrounding rural area.[23]

As the Methodists prepared to move into the rural mission field in western Canada, ministering to the foreign population, "overlapping" became a crucial issue. In previous years competition between Methodists and Presbyterians merely led to economic inefficiencies and, perhaps, to the erosion of the morale of those caught in such circumstances. In the foreign districts, competition for proselytes among the immigrant populations would be unseemly and risked compromising the message of the Protestant Churches. Evangelical Protestants believed that they were working for a national cause, not only denominational interests; thus, in the West, the quest for the Canadianization and assimilation of foreign-born people transcended sectarian interests. There was concern about the impression that would be given to foreign settlers when confronted by three of four Protestant churches and a fear that they would wonder which was the true *Christian* Church [author's italics].[24] In Alberta, a Central Joint Committee of the Presbyterian, Methodist and Congregationalist Churches drew up a constitution for church cooperation in the mission field. Territory in Alberta (Figure 2) was mapped to create a series of zones assigned to either the Methodists or Presbyterians for pastoral work, so as to eliminate overlapping.[25] Following this, an attempt was made to assign nationalities to each church, that is, for each church to specialize along ethnic lines in its evangelical work. The arrangement proved to be unworkable, probably because of the fragmented geography of ethnic settlement across the prairies.[26] Anxious to avoid inefficient competition, Methodists and Presbyterians increased their efforts to cooperate regionally in their missionary and social work. Demarcating spheres of action on a thematic basis was proposed so that, for example, one church would establish schools for girls, the other schools for boys.[27] Presumably dismissing this as impractical since specialization by the kind of services offered would not eliminate the problem of geographical overlapping, the churches turned instead to geographical solutions, assigning specific areas to each church as their exclusive domain. In the Athabasca Landing area, for example, the Methodists agreed to take all the territory north of Township 62 to Township 70, east of the fifth meridian and west of Range 19. The Presbyterians took the area south of this.[28] Along the Wetaskiwin branch line of the CPR, the Methodists and Presbyterians adjusted their operations so that there were only two cases of overlapping.[29] The territory along the Grand Trunk Pacific Railway from Edmonton west to British Columbia, some 200 miles, was assigned to the Methodists, while the territory along the Canadian Northern was given to the Presbyterians. In other cases on the prairies each church was responsible for alternate towns along a railway line. One writer observed that "newcomers to districts along such railroads who desired to remain Methodist had to be careful about their destinations, while those who wanted to continue Presbyterian had to look well to their predestination."[30] For many individuals a switch of church allegiance was the pragmatic response.

Whereas territorial cooperation was emphasized in Alberta, in Manitoba and Saskatchewan the response to overlapping, in English-speaking districts at least, was the negotiation of "Local Church Unions" which appeared first in Saskatchewan in 1908, and shortly afterwards in Manitoba.[31] In southern Saskatchewan, for example, there were 136 Presbyterian mission fields receiving aid in 1912; in 50 of these fields there was "overlapping"

Methodist Annual Picnic, Craik district, Saskatchewan. The photograph would predate 1921, the year of the union of Methodist and Presbyterian churches in Craik (Courtesy of the Craik Archives and Oral History Society Inc.).

with the Methodist Church. Negotiation eliminated all but nine cases of overlapping by 1920; the rest were eliminated prior to organic union in 1925.[32] In Saskatchewan, as elsewhere across the prairies, local unions of self-supporting mission fields found it difficult to pay both a Methodist and a Presbyterian preacher, so a plan was developed which permitted each church to remain affiliated with its parent denomination. Under so-called "Double Affiliated Union," two congregations in a given center worshiped together with a minister of one denomination, but continued to make contributions to support the missionary activity of their own specific church. These Double Affiliated Unions were assigned to Methodist and Presbyterian ministers for four-year alternating terms.[33]

The outbreak of World War I in 1914 created a manpower crisis for the churches in the West. In 1914 many young clergy of all denominations rushed to enlist in the Canadian or British armies; for the next four years the churches had to compete with the armed forces for personnel. Hundreds of theology students, otherwise destined for service with their church in western Canada, instead saw service with the armed forces.[34] The dearth of new clergy pushed the cause of interdenominational cooperation in the missionary field: in 1914 the churches formally agreed to divide the prairies into geographical spheres of influence. The Presbyterian Church was given the

St. Andrew's United Church at Moffat, Saskatchewan, was built in 1891 replacing a frame structure that had dated to 1884. The church was originally a Presbyterian church, and area Methodists had attended Greenville Methodist Church three miles to the south. By the 1940s, however, the Methodists were attending St. Andrew's on a regular basis (Courtesy of David McLennan/University of Regina).

foreign colonies in the territory served by the Canadian Northern and Grand Trunk Pacific Railways east of Edmonton; the Methodists were given the foreign colonies in the prairie territory served by the Canadian Pacific Railway. The smaller Congregationalist Church had found it difficult to compete with the larger and far better organized Methodist and Presbyterian Churches in the quest for "foreign" adherents and so "hardly ventured into the hinterland at all, except in later years when it accepted a special responsibility for certain Swedish and German settlers [in the West]."[35] In the early 1920s, under a cooperative scheme in preparation for union, the Congregationalists were allocated a "definite area in Saskatchewan."[36] This agreement governed the development of missionary activity from that time forward, until the impetus of cooperation and increasingly frequent local unions of Methodist and Presbyterian congregations culminated in the push for the full organic union of the two churches in 1924.

Conclusion

Forces arguing for union of the Protestant churches in Canada were felt across the nation, but they were felt most keenly in the prairie West. In a new territory, opportunities for cooperation were more numerous and even those otherwise little disposed to contemplate acceptance of the doctrines of rival denominations could see the logic of interdenominational cooperation, if only for economic reasons. A pragmatic frontier response to this was seen in the scores of local unions arranged across the prairies and in the formalization of such cooperative endeavours by local synods. The economic rationale for interdenominational cooperation was especially pertinent in the mission fields among non-English-speaking communities. Here the logic of cooperation was accepted by most, if not all, of those involved, since operations in the foreign colonies were both difficult and expensive. The small Congregationalist Church lacked the means to pursue evangelical work on the prairies and preferred to direct its scarce resources to missionary work overseas.[37] Although better positioned to conduct mission work in western Canada, neither the Methodists nor the Presbyterians had an adequate number of missionaries who were conversant in Ukrainian, and it was difficult to penetrate into the bloc settlements without offering something to attract the population to the missions. Although many Protestants clearly thought otherwise, the Ukrainian community had its own religions with which it identified very closely. Few Ukrainians were attracted to an alien, somewhat bland, straight-laced religion by the simple pull of a new theological interpretation of the Bible; hence it was necessary to attract them by offering the social, educational or medical services lacking in their areas of settlement. Staffing and equipping residential schools, medical clinics, and hospitals was costly; duplication of such services was not in the interest of either church. Furthermore, evangelical work aimed at "Christianizing" and assimilating the foreign population was seen as work of national importance: it demanded synchronization of effort and the presentation of a united Christian and Canadian front.

It is suggested here that the geography of the Prairie West, combined with Protestant zeal to mold this emerging community in its own image, was the catalyst for organic church union. The West, furthermore, was an emerging region with a mixed population where denominational lines were never so rigidly drawn as in the older communities in eastern Canada. In the new prairie communities the influence of American Methodists and Presbyterians, who were generally more flexible on doctrinal matters than were their Canadian-born counterparts, also fostered a pragmatic response to church union.

In 1924, when the three churches voted on whether to undertake full organic union of their churches, the results were revealing.[38] Methodist and Congregationalist congregations across Canada voted overwhelmingly in favor of church union; Presbyterians in the West were overwhelmingly in

Poplar Grove United Church southwest of Broadview, Saskatchewan, built in 1902 for the area's Presbyterians. It replaced an earlier structure; the adjacent cemetery dates to 1887. The church closed in 1970 but is still used for special occasions. It was designated a Municipal Heritage Property in 1987 (Courtesy of David McLennan/University of Regina).

favour; but in Ontario and the Maritime provinces the vote was split. Many congregations there voted not to join the new United Church. These dissenting congregations differed little from those in the West in terms of their social origins and theological convictions; the great difference was that in the prairie West geographic imperatives were a powerful catalyst for church union.

Notes

This article first appeared in *Prairie Forum* 27, no. 2 (2002): 199–208.

1. For a concise political and theological history of church union in western Canada see N. Keith Clifford, "Church Union and Western Canada," in Dennis Butcher et al. (eds.), *Prairie Spirit: Perspectives on the Heritage of the United Church of Canada in the West* (Winnipeg: University of Manitoba Press, 1985), 283–95.

2. Nostik Ahn, "The Changing Church in Society: A Study of the United Church in Canada: The Basis and Origin of Church Union" (M.Theol. thesis, University of Winnipeg, 1972), 93.

3. According to census data, United Church membership, like that of the other major Protestant groups in Canada, has been falling both in absolute and relative terms. In 1981, 9.9 million Protestants constituted 41.2% of the population; in 1991, 9.7 million members represented only 36.6%. United Church membership fell from 15.6% to 11.5% between 1981 amd 1991. See Statistics Canada, "Population by Religion 1981 and 1991

Censuses, Canada," http://www.statcan.ca/english/Pgdb/People/Population/demo32.htm

4. See, John C. Lehr and D. Wayne Moodie, "The Polemics of Pioneer Settlement: Ukrainian Immigration and the Winnipeg Press," *Canadian Ethnic Studies* 12, no. 2 (1980): 88–101.

5. There is a considerable literature dealing with both the strategies of the Protestant churches in their attempts to lure Ukrainian immigrants to the Protestant cause and the Protestant Churches' perceptions of Ukrainians, their religion, and their culture. See, for example, Orest T. Martynowych, "'Canadianizing the Foreigner': Presbyterian Missionaries and Ukrainian Immigrants," in J. Rozumnyj (ed.), *New Soil—Old Roots* (Winnipeg: Ukrainian Free Academy of Sciences, 1983), 33–57; J. Rozumnyj, *Ukrainians in Canada: the Formative Period, 1891–1924* (Edmonton: Canadian Institute of Ukrainian Studies Press, University of Alberta, 1991), 214–36; Vivian Olender, "The Cultural Implications of Protestant Missions," in Manoly R. Lupul (ed.), *Continuity and Change: The Cultural Life of Alberta's First Ukrainians* (Edmonton: Canadian Institute of Ukrainian Studies Press, University of Alberta, 1988), 221–26; Vivian Olender, "The Canadian Methodist Church and the Gospel of Assimilation, 1900–1925," *Journal of Ukrainian Studies* 7, no. 2 (1982): 61–74; George Emery, "Methodist Missions among the Ukrainians," *Alberta Historical Review* 19, no. 2 (1971): 8–19; and Michael Owen, "Keeping Canada God's Country: Presbyterian School-homes for Ruthenian Children," in Denis Butcher et al., (eds.), *Prairie Spirit: Perspectives on the Heritage of the United Church of Canada in the West* (Winnipeg: University of Manitoba Press, 1985), 184–201.

6. Most Protestant clergy held a poor opinion of the Ukrainian churches and decried the influence of their clergy. For an extreme view of one Methodist worker in the West see, Reverend (Captain) Wellington Bridgeman, *Breaking Prairie Sod: The Story of a Pioneer Preacher in the Eighties, With a Discussion of the Burning Question of "Shall the Alien Go?"* (Toronto: Musson Book Company, 1920). This book is a disgraceful, xenophobic, slanderous diatribe against the moral and ethical character of Ukrainian immigrants. Concluding that they were all beyond redemption, Bridgeman advocated the seizure of their property and their mass deportation back to Europe.

7. Methodist Missionary Society, *Annual Report*, 1907–8, p. 1.

8. E. Lloyd Morrow, *Church Union in Canada: Its History, Motives, Doctrine, and Government* (Toronto: Thomas Allen, 1923), 40–47.

9. Ibid., 34–39.

10. For a detailed discussion of the differences between the three Churches see, Morrow, *Church Union in Canada*, 157–213; Thomas Buchanan Kilpatrick, *Our Common Faith* (Toronto: The Ryerson Press, 1928); and Arthur S. Morton, *The Way to Union* (Toronto: William Biggs, 1912).

11. S.D. Chown, *The Story of Church Union in Canada* (Toronto: The Ryerson Press, 1930), 109–10.

12. Peter Strang, *History of Missions in Southern Saskatchewan* (Regina: the author, 1928), 7–8.

13. For a fictional account of the social and economic conditions faced by a minister in a small town on the prairies in the 1930s see Sinclair Ross, *As for Me and My House* (Toronto: McClelland and Stewart Ltd., 1970).

14. Turtle Mountain Survey Committee, *Turtle Mountain District, Manitoba, Including the Municipalities of Whitewater, Morton and Winchester, Report on a Rural survey of the Agricultural, Educational, Social and Religious Life* (Toronto: Department of Social Service and Evangelism of the Presbyterian and Methodist Churches, June–July 1914), 63.

15. Cited in Morrow, *Church Union in Canada*, 101.

16. Turtle Mountain Survey Committee, *Turtle Mountain District, Manitoba*, 63.

17. Minutes of the 23rd Synod of the Presbyterian Church 1905, p. 31. United Church Archives, University of Winnipeg.

18. E.S. Strachan, *The Story of the Years: A History of the Women's Missionary Society of the Methodist Church, Canada, 1906–1916* (Toronto: Women's Missionary Society, Methodist Church, Canada, 1917), 67–87.

19. "Report of the Senior Superintendent of Missions [James Woodsworth] 1910," United Church Archives [UCA] Victoria University, Toronto, Methodist Church of Canada [MCC] Methodist Home Missions [MHM] Fonds, Board of Home Missions, General Correspondence and Reports, Box 1, File 12.

20. "Report of the Central Committee on the Work Among European Foreigners in Canada," UCA, Victoria University, MCC, MHM, typewritten ms. p. 13, Box 4, File 10.

21. "Manitoba Conference, Report of Commission on Work among Non-English Speaking People [1917]," UCA, Victoria University, MCC, MMS, Box 4, File 10, Reports on the work among non-English immigrants.

22. James Woodsworth, "Report of Senior Superintendent of Missions 1912, "UCA, Victoria University, MCC, MMS Box 3 File 6, Nov.–Dec. 1912.

23. UCA, Victoria University, MCC, MHM, Annual Reports 1913–14, Report of J.S. Woodsworth, p. xiii.

24. See, Morrow, *Church Union in Canada*, 49–69.

25. "Report of Arthur Barner, Superintendent of Missions in Southern Alberta on the Matter of Cooperation and Local Union Churches within that Community," UCA Victoria University. MCC , MHM fonds. Box 8 File 17, 1919–25.

26. Ibid.

27. Minutes of the 32 Synod of the Presbyterian Church 1914, p. 15.

28. Murray Wenstob, "The work of the Methodist Church among settlers in Alberta up to 1951, with special reference to the formation of new congregations and work among the Ukrainian people" (B.D. dissertation, University of Alberta, 1959), 54.

29. Annual Report of the Methodist Missionary Society, 1911–1912, p. ix.

30. Edmund H. Oliver, *The Winning of the Frontier* (Toronto: The United Church Publishing House, 1930), 138–39.

31. Wenstob, "The Work of the Methodist Church," 66. Strang identifies the period 1912–20 as the period when local Cooperating Committees dealt with overlapping in Saskatchewan: Strang, *History of Missions in Southern Saskatchewan*, 181.

32. Strang, *History of Missions in Southern Saskatchewan*, 182.

33. Ibid., 184.

34. James Woodsworth to Rev. C.E. Manning, August 2, 1916. UCA Victoria University, MCC, MHM fonds. Box 4 File 9, July–Dec. 1916.

35. Claris E. Wilcox, *Church Union in Canada: Its Causes and Consequences* (New York: Institute of Social and Religious Research, 1933), 45.

36. Ibid.

37. Ibid., 46.

38. Murdo Macpherson and Douglas Campbell, Plate 34, "Religion," in Don Kerr and Deryck Holdsworth (eds.), *The Historical Atlas of Canada 1891–1961*, Vol. 3 (Toronto: University of Toronto Press, 1990).

Index

Saskatchewan: A History, 370
Saskatchewan Ladies Aid and
  Homemaker Society, 518
Saskatchewan River valley
  as suitable for agriculture, 508
Saskatchewan, University of, 76
Saskatchewan Valley Land Company, 91
Saskatoon-Battleford Trail, 84, 86
Saskatoon Board of Trade, 496
Saskatoon *The Phoenix*, 84, 93, 99–101,
  493, 496–97, 504–05
Saskatoon Separate School Board, 541
Saturday Night, 252–53, 262
Saubel, Fritz, 432
Saulteaux Indians, 17
Sawley, A.I., 491, 496, 505
Scandinavians, *see* immigrant groups,
  Scandinavian
Schafer, Charles, 54
Schmid, Horst, 344
Schmidel, Dr. Justus, 419–21
Schmitt, Milian, 415–16
Schnell, Joseph
  Laurier, 53
School Act
  amendments to, 527
  school system, 191, 240, 251, 534, 550
  as civilizing Indians, 194, 196
  compulsory use of English at, 408
  ex-pupils of chosen for agriculture,
    243
  as medium of acculturation, 398–99
  as public, 447, 524, 538
  as separate, 443, 447, 525–26, 534, 538
  see also English language; Indians;
    schools
schools, bilingual
  English/Polish, 479
  Polish/Ukrainian, 468
schools, boarding, 189–90, 207, 242, 250
schools, day, 190, 207, 219, 250–51
schools, industrial, 189–90, 193, 198,
  207, 221, 242, 250, 517
schools, mission, 189
schools, residential, 219, 221, 235, 250,

517
  graduates of as suitable for marriage,
    245
  denigration of aboriginal languages
    in, 5
*Schools in the West: Essays in Canadian
  Educational History*, 479
Schulte, W.
  St. Joseph's Kolonie, 434
Scollen, Father Constantine, 509
Scott, D.C., 186, 205–06, 210, 261–62
Scott, W.D., 455, 506
Scott, Walter, 204, 516
Scots, *see* immigrant groups, Scottish
Security Elevator Company, 49
Security Lumber, 46
Seelheim, Heinrich, 428
Select Committee on Agricultural and
  Colonization (1876), 64
Selwood, H. John, 54
  *Prairie and Northern Perspectives:
    Geographical Essays*, 54
  *Reflections from the Prairies:
    Geographical Essays*, 55, 128
Selwyn, Dr. A.R.C., 63, 70, 77
  expedition of, 63–64
Senior, H.
  *Orangeism in Ireland and Britain,
    1775–1836*, 540
*Sense of Power: Studies in the Ideas of
  Canadian Imperialism, 1867–1914, The*,
  454
Sentinel, 523
Seraphim Church in Manitoba, 470
Serbs, *see* immigrant groups, Serbian
sermons
  as imparting desired values, 244
Settlement of the West, The, 539
settlements, 7, 22, 42, 45, 47, 88, 105, 119,
  162, 246–47
  density of, 95, 167, 170, 188, 203, 369
  failure of, 19, 124
  on former Indian lands, 199–200
  of people with similar cultures, 396
  process of, 30, 36–37
  and promotional literature, 31, 170